D0180351

Termite Hill

TERMITE HILL

TOM WILSON

BANTAM BOOKS
NEW YORK • TORONTO • LONDON • SYDNEY • AUCKLAND

TERMITE HILL
A Bantam Book / August 1992

All rights reserved.
Copyright © 1992 by Tom Wilson.
Library of Congress Catalog Card Number: 92-6307.
No part of this book may be reproduced or transmitted in any
form or by any means, electronic or mechanical, including
photocopying, recording, or by any information storage and
retrieval system, without permission in writing from the publisher.
For information address: Bantam Books.

ISBN 0-553-37033-2

Published simultaneously in the United States and Canada

Bantam Books are published by Bantam Books, a division of Bantam Doubleday
Dell Publishing Group, Inc. Its trademark, consisting of the words "Bantam
Books" and the portrayal of a rooster, is Registered in U.S. Patent and
Trademark Office and in other countries. Marca Registrada. Bantam Books, 666
Fifth Avenue, New York, New York 10103.

PRINTED IN THE UNITED STATES OF AMERICA

0 9 8 7 6 5 4 3 2 1

This work is dedicated to those who grow misty-eyed whenever the "Star Spangled Banner" is played, and to those who would dare to fight to keep the American dream alive.

ACKNOWLEDGMENTS

No writer, even of fictional accounts, can work in a vacuum. For *Termite Hill*, I had the luxury of having the support of two experts, both close friends who were once also comrades in arms.

Today the top graduate at the USAF Electronic Warfare Officer course at Mather AFB, California receives the Colonel Mike Gilroy Award. As a captain, Mike emerged from the Vietnam War as a respected hero. He went on to shape the future of electronic warfare for the Joint Services, Air Force and NATO. During the writing of *Termite Hill*, Mike spent much of his valuable time helping me get my facts straight and encouraging me to continue. Thanks, old buddy, and thanks for reminding me of the old Thai saying about true friendship: "A great number of people will drink with you. Very few will die with you."

Jerry Hoblit has many times proven himself to be a true friend. When I first met him, I thought the ring-knocking West-Pointer was a boisterous fighter jock who loved to fly and fight . . . and win. After flying an eventful tour over North Vietnam with Jerry in 1966/67, I confirmed that first impression. A fighter weapons school graduate and instructor as well as a canny Wild Weasel tactician, he went on to become an astronaut-qualified test pilot, a test squadron commander, and a superb logistician. But his heart never strayed from the guys in the operational fighter squadrons. Jerry spent many hours reviewing *Termite Hill* for technical accuracy.

I would like to toast the United States Air Force, and especially the group within who called themselves the fighter mafia and dedicated their lives and careers to correct the many inequities of leadership, training, and tactical employment. Together they built the finest Air Force in the world, and provided inspiration for this series.

Finally and perhaps most importantly, my late mother taught me to read at the tender age of three and, shortly thereafter, to enjoy literature. If it had not been for her persistence I would not have begun the novel. Without the enduring support of my wife Andrea, who is also my chief critic, listening post, and personal editor, I could never have finished it.

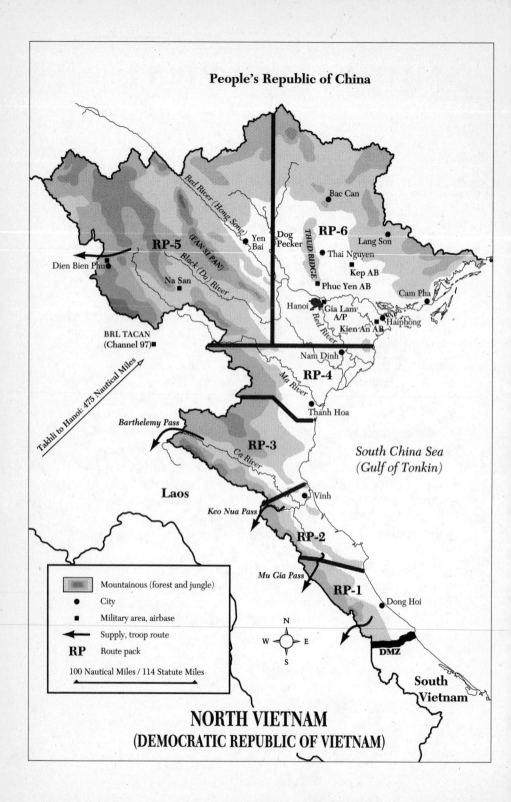

People's Republic of China

RP-6

RP-5

(FAN SI PAN)

Red River (Hong Song)

Black (Da) River

Dien Bien Phu

Na San

Yen Bai

Dog Pecker

THUD RIDGE

Bac Can

Lang Son

Thai Nguyen

Kep AB

Phuc Yen AB

Cam Pha

Hanoi

Gia Lam A/P

Kien An AB

Haiphong

Red River

BRL TACAN (Channel 97)

Nam Dinh

RP-4

Ma River

Takhli to Hanoi: 475 Nautical Miles

Thanh Hoa

Barthelemy Pass

RP-3

Ca River

Laos

South China Sea (Gulf of Tonkin)

Keo Nua Pass

Vinh

RP-2

Mu Gia Pass

RP-1

Dong Hoi

Mountainous (forest and jungle)

City

Military area, airbase

Supply, troop route

RP Route pack

100 Nautical Miles / 114 Statute Miles

N

W E

S

DMZ

South Vietnam

NORTH VIETNAM
(DEMOCRATIC REPUBLIC OF VIETNAM)

BOOK I

Today—Termite Hill, Democratic Republic of Vietnam

Precisely ninety-three miles west of Hanoi, the Da River, which flows southeast to Thanh Hoa, is joined by a small tributary from the southwest. In the "V" of the union is a low mountain, barren and desolate and pocked with deep craters.

American pilots once called it Termite Hill.

Tribesmen travel from the mountainous region near the Ma River in eastern Laos down the ancient, hard-pack trade road into Vietnam and ford the Da near the intersection of the stream and in full view of the mountain. They are taking wild game, betel nuts, scrawny chickens and pigs, and crude baskets to market to trade for rice, salt and ammunition as they have done every few months for centuries. But they are especially wary as they pass by the mountain. Like the local villagers, they call it Dead Mountain. It looks eerie and forlorn. The tribesmen believe it is inhabited by spirits.

Years before, the elders of the short, bandy-legged group remember, the mountain had been tall and proud, thickly forested and lush, loud with the busy sounds of monkeys, birds, and flying insects. Of course, the mountain had been alive then.

When the War of Unification was raging and the Americans flew their airplanes loaded with bombs toward the Great Hong valley, the tribesmen had astutely found another market far to the west, and for several seasons had gone there. They'd heard stories that the mountain had angered the Americans and that they were killing it, but few had believed they could succeed. Few things are so tenacious as the spirits of rocks and mountains.

When the Americans stopped flying overhead, the Ma tribesmen returned to their old route and the closer market towns. They were amazed at what they saw when they looked across the tributary to the mountain. No sign of life. Quiet, except for an occasional stirring of wind across its barren and desolate ground.

Nothing grows there now. During the rainy season the

3

heavy downpours wash great amounts of red soil from the mountain, so much that the Da River changes to the color of blood as it flows past, and every dry season it seems that the mountain has shrunk again. They wonder if someday it will disappear altogether.

The tribesmen were puzzled, so they asked the people at Bac Yen, the farm village nearest the mountain, what had happened.

The villagers were annoyed by the questions of the ignorant tribesmen, but they finally confided that American airplanes had dropped great numbers of bombs and sometimes would even shoot their guns at the mountain. Everyone knew the Americans were crazy, the villagers said. There was no reason to destroy the mountain, but they had.

The Ma tribesmen left, still perplexed and wondering why the Americans had chosen that particular mountain to kill.

CHAPTER ONE

Friday, November 25th, 1966—1417 Local, Route Pack Six, North Vietnam

Tiny Bechler

Twenty-four aircraft were in the strike force: six flights, with four F-105 Thunderchief fighter-bombers in each flight. Each aircraft was loaded with six M-117 750-pound general-purpose bombs. The target was the Yen Bai railroad siding and loading facility, a minor way-station on the railway that snaked northwest out of Hanoi and followed the Red River to China.

During the briefing it had been forecast as a routine mission, and the mission commander had said there shouldn't be much trouble if everyone did their jobs. *A quick in and out strike. Barely poke our noses over the Red River,* he'd said, like he'd known what he was talking about. Tiny was a lieutenant and he'd only been flying combat for three weeks, so he'd believed him. A few of the old head pilots, who'd been at Takhli more than a month, said the target might be more difficult. They joked that Yen Bai was either Ho Chi Minh's home town, where he'd gotten his first piece of tail, or the place he just stored all his extra guns. They said it was defended so well it was ridiculous, considering its minor importance.

Red Dog, the third flight in the procession, entered North Vietnamese airspace at 0717 Greenwich Mean Time, so heavily laden with bombs and fuel that it could maneuver only sluggishly. Tiny was Red Dog two, wingman for the new squadron commander who was even newer to combat than he was. Lieutenant Colonel Lee was entering Route Pack Six, the

5

meanest area of North Vietnam, for the first time. Tiny was
determined to be as helpful as possible.

Jim Lee

Lee craned his neck to ensure his four-ship flight was
properly spaced. Lieutenant Bechler was flying several hundred feet off to the starboard side, turning and weaving in the
jinking maneuver. Farther out off his left wing, the third and
fourth aircraft flew in staggered echelon. Everyone seemed to
be in their proper places.

The flight wove its way through the sky, high above the
green forested mountains. White, billowing clouds towered in
the distance, appearing deceptively serene. Jim disliked sham.
The weather should be angry and threatening, and exhibit the
bleakness of war.

He was flying at 545 knots calibrated airspeed, and
although he had flown faster, he was rushing to a destiny he
would not be fully able to control. With every passing minute
they penetrated ten statute miles deeper into the heart of North
Vietnam. The bombs and bullets were live, the switches were
hot, the enemy would shoot. It was difficult to push the
thoughts back, but he was neither a coward nor a quitter.

Lee was a God-fearing man, a loyal husband, a proud
father of three bright children, and an intense believer in
America. His records showed early promotions to major and
lieutenant colonel. He was a distinguished graduate of the
USAF test pilot course at Edwards, with a formal education
capped by a two-year tour at MIT where he'd completed a
doctorate in physics. He was on NASA's alternate astronaut list
for the Apollo space program, but he had been in that status
since submitting his application the previous year. Instead of
waiting with dwindling hopes for someone to be disqualified
from the primary list, he had volunteered for a combat tour.
Combat experience was a requisite for a successful military
career.

At McConnell AFB, where Lee had been sent to become
combat ready in the F-105D, he'd earned creditable scores on
the gunnery range. He'd flown box-patterns and dive-bombed
practice bomblets onto a bull's-eye etched onto the ground, and
strafed white panels hung between telephone poles. The

tactical targets, barrels stacked up to simulate buildings and junked cars to simulate tanks, appeared more realistic from the air, but he'd learned little about combat flying. The instructors mentioned some in combat maneuvers but he couldn't practice them because they were considered too dangerous for peace-time training.

He'd departed for Southeast Asia in mid-October, his end assignment unspecified. He was to attend jungle survival school in the Philippines, and somewhere en route he'd be issued amendments to his orders showing his final destination.

When he'd finished the survival course, he'd cooled his heels for a week waiting for the amendments. He'd called Hickam Field and learned that his records had been circulated ever higher through the PACAF headquarters hierarchy, and finally had been passed to the ultimate boss. General Roman, commander at Pacific Air Forces Headquarters at Hickam Field, Honolulu, had personally reviewed Jim Lee's records. The loud, foulmouthed four-star, one of the small clique of bomber generals who had run things in the Air Force since its inception, was heir apparent to the Air Force chief of staff. He was a powerful man who got his way.

When the amendments to Lee's orders arrived, telling him to report to Takhli Air Base in central Thailand, they also directed that his Air Force Specialty Code be changed from 1115E to A1115E, meaning he would be sent there as a squadron commander. An accompanying message advised him that the PACAF/CC had shown personal interest in his assign-ment.

The selection had pleased Jim. He was a recently pro-moted lieutenant colonel, so "squadron commander" would look very good on his records.

While he'd been clearing on base, dropping off his hand-carried records and receiving the half-dozen *mandatory briefings,* General Roman had telephoned B. J. Parker, the Takhli wing commander, to tell him that Jim Lee was his choice to take over the newly vacant squadron command job. Jim had learned about the call when he'd reported to the wing commander, and it embarrassed him. He'd explained that he had not requested the squadron commander's job.

"Every now and then the general does something like this to remind us fucking cowboys down here who's boss," Parker had said when he welcomed him aboard. "That's what the general calls fighter pilots," he'd added.

Jim disliked being caught in the middle. He'd told Parker that he may have been away from operational flying for five years, but that he prided himself on being a good pilot. Yet he would gladly serve in whatever capacity Parker wished until he'd proven himself. Parker had assured him he wasn't about to try to reverse Roman's decision. He assigned Jim to command the 357th squadron. He'd have some of the best flight commanders in the wing. Listen to them, he'd said, and in no time at all Lee'd get back into the swing of operational flying.

Lee had left the colonel's office to move into his trailer, then to take charge of *his* fighter squadron. He felt good about the assignment.

During his first week, Jim was given five indoctrination flights over the lightly defended southern panhandle of North Vietnam. On the second one, flying armed reconnaissance near the coastal city of Dong Hoi, he'd noticed flashes of small-arms fire on the ground. He had held his aircraft up high as suggested by the pilot in the accompanying aircraft and had not felt unduly threatened. On his ensuing missions he'd bombed dense forests, which intelligence said hid suspected truck parking areas, with growing confidence.

One morning at a wing staff meeting, the short wing commander had announced to his assembled deputies, staff officers, and squadron commanders: "Colonel Lee's ready to take his turn in the barrel with the rest of us. Welcome aboard, Jim."

It was to be a straightforward mission to the edge of pack six, but he was cautioned that even the easiest of missions there could be rough.

Before noon, Jim Lee had written his wife that he was about to take his first flight into the area of North Vietnam designated "Route Pack Six" by headquarters.

There's a unique kinship, he had penned, *between pilots who have flown across the Red River into pack six. When I return from this afternoon's mission, I'll be one of that group. I've always regarded the camaraderie of fighter pilots as one of the things that makes the trials worthwhile. This is an elite group within another. I'm interested in discovering why they feel this way. It'll also make my job as squadron commander,*

*with men assigned who have advantages of time and experi-
ence with tactical flying, much easier once I'm regarded as a
part of their special group.*

I'll continue this letter tonight and tell you more.

They'd flown over the rugged mountains of northwestern
North Vietnam for ten minutes without incident. According to
Jim Lee's map, not many miles ahead the mountains would
dwindle to wooded foothills, then abruptly end. Beyond would
be the broad valley, shaped and nurtured through the years by
the Red River.

As they passed over a small flatland between two mountain ridges, the radio silence was shattered by an excited voice.
*"Whiskey flight, we've got bogeys at our ten o'clock, heading
west."*

Lee stared out to the left and forward of the flight.
Whiskey flight was only a minute or two in front of Red Dog.
He looked about the skies, saw nothing, keyed his radio, and
spoke carefully to keep his voice calm and steady.

"Red Dog flight, be on the lookout—" His radio transmission was interrupted.

*"This is Whiskey lead. We got two MiG-17's at our nine
o'clock high, coming in fast. We're breakin' left and into 'em,
Whiskeys."*

Lee almost maneuvered, but checked the impulse. He was
leading Red Dog, not Whiskey flight. He stared about the sky,
adrenaline pumping hard.

*"Whiskey three and four, take the starboard MiG! He's
starting to turn."*

"Whiskey three, roger!" The voice strained under the
stresses of g-forces.

Jim Lee looked frantically to his left and right. *"Red
Dogs—"* His transmission was interrupted by another excited
radio call.

*"Whiskey three, this is lead, you still got a visual on your
MiG?"*

Sounds of high-g grunting came over the radio. *"I got him
in sight."*

*"Whiskey two, this is lead. Let's clean 'em up and
engage. The port-side MiG's at our eleven, going left to right."*

"Two is jettisoning."

Again Jim Lee began his radio transmission to the flight,

voice crackling with apprehension. *"Red Dog flight, this is lead. Keep a good lookout and report anything you see."*

"Red Dog!" snapped the previous voice, *"stay off the air unless you see something. Whiskey flight's engaged by MiG's!"*

Lee burned with embarrassment. The rebuke had come from a flight commander assigned to his own squadron. He glanced down at the flight line-up card on his kneepad to note the name—Major Crawford—and resolved to talk to him after they got back on the ground.

Whiskey's chatter continued. *"Whiskeys, let's break it off. The MiG's are still headin' north and we're getting close to the Chinese buffer zone."*

The flight responded.

"Whiskey two, roger."

"Three."

"Four."

Lee wondered if Crawford wasn't a bit MiG-happy. Shouldn't he have used defensive tactics, not immediately gone on the attack? He'd look into it. His nervousness was waning and he was better able to discipline his emotions.

Red Dog flight was over foothills, approaching the valley. The Doppler radar navigation system showed twelve miles to the target. Beyond the foothills, the Red River valley was flat and featureless—a patchwork of rice paddies painted in shades of dull greens, yellows, and browns, interrupted by laceworks of reservoirs and irrigation canals.

The weather was acceptable, with only a few distant clouds marring their visibility. The mission wouldn't be called off. The counter showed nine nautical miles to go. Their ground speed was 550 knots, about nine nautical miles a minute, so time to target was about a minute. His breathing became harsh, the suck and hiss loud in his earphones. *Don't hyperventilate,* he told himself, trying to ration his breathing in the confinement of the oxygen mask.

He could see the wide, muddy river, then the town of Yen Bai. White puffs of flak spattered here and there above the village.

The fighters in front of Red Dog were visible as dark specks in the distance, now soaring upward as they approached the target. The number of white puffs increased, then increased again, growing into a blanket, and he felt it would be impossible to fly through the shrapnel hidden there. New danger! Larger, charcoal-gray blossoms, aimed bursts from the bigger guns, moved about in intelligent patterns, seeking the individual aircraft diving toward the target. The dark bursts were guided by optical systems and precision radars.

As Lee watched, he realized that he might be about to die. Bitter bile rose and soured in his gorge and he had to fight down the puke that threatened. Sounds of his breathing seemed even louder than the roar of the jet engine.

They were close now, and across the river he could see the railroad tracks snaking into and out of the town. He looked intently to his two o'clock, to the edge of the town, and picked out the railroad siding. Smoke and dust obscured the far side of the siding where bombs had landed beyond the target, and another group exploded to the left, wide of the target. The last pilot in the flight announced that his bombs had hung up and wouldn't release. The siding, hardly visible through the heavy white blanket of flak, was undamaged.

Whiskey flight, which should have been next, had dropped its bombs to engage MiG's. It was Red Dog's turn! Lee caught his breath, and the lump in his chest grew until it seemed about to burst.

"THIS IS BIG EYE. BUSTER AT ALPHA GOLF THREE! I REPEAT. THIS IS BIG EYE. BUSTER AT ALPHA GOLF THREE!"

An airborne radar aircraft calling MiG's. He didn't have time to check the location.

Concentrate on the bombing problem, he chided himself, feeling calmer. He estimated the angle to the railroad siding to be twenty degrees. Slightly back and off to his right was the small, flat-topped hill they had been briefed to watch for. They should begin their climb to the perch, in order to properly set up for the dive-bomb attack. Something inside paralyzed him, making him pause again. He gulped a breath to clear his head.

"Red Dog is climbing," he radioed, his voice unsteady.

"Two."

"Three."

"Four."

A hundred yards off his left wing, four flak bursts exploded in a symmetrical pattern. Lee pulled the control stick aft and to the right, then pushed the throttle forward. He held the throttle outboard in the afterburner detent, and the big turbojet engine roared its complaint as he was pulled upward in a steep climb.

Two fireballs streaked past his canopy, others swept upward in great arcs, and he knew the gunners were aiming for him. Four more dark bursts blossomed ahead. Sweat from his forehead stung his eyes as the altimeter rapidly indicated 9,000, then 10,000 feet.

An annoying squeal in the earphones of his helmet confused him. He looked about the cockpit, then settled on the radar warning equipment. A steady, bright-red light read LAUNCH, accompanied by a white light reading SAM.

"Red Dog lead, this is two! We've got SAMs at nine o'clock."

He heard the radio call, but for a moment did not comprehend. He realized then that the words had come from his wingman. He rolled to his left, trying to sight the missiles he'd been told looked like flying telephone poles.

He depressed his radio button, yelling hoarsely, *"I don't see them!"*

"They're at our seven o'clock now, Red Dog lead!" The wingman's voice was emphatic.

He rolled the aircraft over on its back and sharply nosed the big fighter into a steep dive, praying the missiles wouldn't be able to keep up.

Tiny Bechler

At first Tiny stuck like glue to his leader's side as they headed earthward into the maelstrom of flak. They were doing better than 650 knots and approaching 7,500 feet when he made his urgent radio call.

"Red Dog lead, this is two. The missiles passed behind us. We're well clear."

Colonel Lee did not respond.

"Lead, we better pull out!" Tiny Bechler cried as they dove through another thousand feet. A few more seconds and they wouldn't be able to recover! He eased back his throttle.

Again Red Dog lead did not respond, although Tiny saw the aircraft's nose rotate slightly upward. Not enough! The damned fool was going to kill them both!

"Red Dog two is pulling up and left!" Tiny called. He jinked left, pulling on the stick and dragging the throttle to idle,

muttering, "Enough of that shit!" He tried to keep Red Dog lead in sight as his aircraft mushed toward the ground.

He was sinking fast! He slapped at the red jettison button and felt the aircraft grow lighter as the bombs released. Tiny watched with exasperating helplessness as flak puffed about him. He sank through 5,000 feet, continuing to settle toward the hamlet. His leader was below, blocked from vision as the nose of his aircraft continued to rotate upward.

Bechler made one more attempt on the radio, calling, *"Pull out, lead!"* as he passed through 4,000 feet, still sinking. The features of the town became distinct as he fell. Wooded structures and a few concrete buildings lined the narrow, earthen streets of the village. He saw muzzle flashes from small arms; he could even see the antlike humans who fired them. As the thrust of the engine finally began to push the jet into a recovery arc, the ants had grown limbs and tracers from small arms zipped angrily past his canopy.

Tiny cursed while circling back to altitude, periodically rocking his wings and looking hard for his leader's aircraft. He scanned the area of the village on the Red River. Smoke from the intense antiaircraft gunfire mixed with bomb smoke, creating a thick haze about the periphery of the village. He finally saw an aircraft, very low, beyond the town and all alone over the valley. It was no MiG. Unlike American jet engines, theirs were smokeless. This one trailed a wisp of smoke.

"Red Dog lead, this is Red Dog two, turn west! You are going in the wrong direction, Red Dog lead! Turn west!"

Red Dog lead turned sharply and began to climb.

Relieved, Tiny radioed in a calmer voice. *"Red Dog two is at your ten o'clock, lead."*

No response. Was lead's radio damaged?

He glanced inside the cockpit. The radar warning equipment was chattering, showing a couple of tracking AAA radars, but the SAM light was off. He reset his switches for GUNS-AIR, changed his sight, and selected boresight position on his radar in case he encountered MiG's. He double-checked. All switches properly set. He looked out again at Red Dog lead and saw that Lee was still climbing and that the smoke trail was blacker. Somewhere during the dive he'd been hit by the hail of sharpnel. He was burning!

"Red Dog lead, you're trailing smoke!" called Tiny, eyes glued to the Thud as it continued to climb.

Still no response.

Red Dogs three and four had scattered like quail during the SAM launch and the subsequent lack of directions from lead. Tiny snorted at their lack of air discipline, still staring at lead. Then he realized that Lee was setting up for a dive-bomb attack on the target!

The guy was in a burning airplane and he was still going to deliver his bombs? *Jesus!*

Red Dog lead was nosing over into a thirty degree dive attack on the rail siding. Tiny gaped, watching the flak concentrating about the lone Thud like a thick and furious white and gray cloud. Lee was in his dive, nearing release altitude!

He rooted in admiration. *Bite 'em in the ass, Colonel!*

The airplane exploded in an bright fireball. A direct hit had detonated the bombs while they were still on the aircraft.

Tiny felt numbed. Lee had shown he'd had balls. It was Tiny who had deserted his leader.

"Red Dog lead is down in the target area," he called in a leaden voice.

Another flight of F-105's dove at the rail siding. The blankets of flak looked more intense, if that was possible.

"Beaucoup flak down here!" someone yelled over the busy radio frequency. Number three in that flight was hit in the fuselage by shrapnel from a 57mm round, but his wingman checked him over on the way out and declared him flyable.

Someone called a single bogey north of the target. Tiny radioed that he was alone and orbiting north of the target, but he looked about carefully in case they'd seen something he had not. He felt alone and exposed. Hell, he *was* alone and exposed.

After one more good look back toward his leader, Red Dog two turned west and fell in a couple of miles behind another flight on their way out of the target area. "Fucking dumb shits," Tiny muttered into his mask. "Assholes!" talking about no one in particular and everyone in general. And talking about himself especially.

After his intelligence debriefing at the command post, Tiny learned that of the twenty-four aircraft sent out to bomb the siding at Yen Bai, only two had hit the target with their bombs. The twelve bombs from the two successful aircraft had done considerable damage. Captain Lewis's string of bombs had destroyed five boxcars on the siding. His wingman had damaged the loading platforms and the electrical and mechanical switching devices there. Intelligence reported an initial estimate that the yard and siding would be unusuable for some forty-eight hours.

First Lt Tiny Belcher went straight to his hootch and stayed there that night, listening to sad Western music and brooding about the poor flight discipline he'd shown. He resolved that it would never happen again.

Lieutenant Colonel Lee was listed as MIA in the post-mission report to Headquarters, Seventh Air Force in Saigon. Jim Lee's unfinished letter was forwarded to his wife with the rest of his belongings. Col. B. J. Parker, the wing commander, wrote his sympathy to Elaine Lee, and advised her that Lee had been listed as missing in action, but that there was little hope he'd survived.

26/1800L—Takhli RTAFB, Thailand

The 355th Tactical Fighter Wing had seventy-one F-105 Thunderchief aircraft and seventy-nine fighter pilots. These were divided between three fighter squadrons, the 333rd, the 354th, and the 357th. From 1545 hours on November 25, until 1800 hours the next day, the 357th had no squadron commander assigned. It took that long for the wing commander to gain reluctant approval from his headquarters for the candidate of his choice.

Lt Col. Mack MacLendon

At the 355th TFW command post, Mack got the telephone call from the wing commander at 1806 hours; ten minutes later he had his desk cleared out and the contents in boxes. At 1820 he told the on-duty staff that the major would be taking over his duties as OIC of the command post. He got the major to help him by carrying a box, and they left the command post at 1829, walking and carrying their boxes and discussing the major's new duties.

At 1833 they entered the 357th Tactical Fighter Squadron

building. A short-cropped, scowling, cherub-faced lieutenant who was the approximate height and shoulder-breadth of a standard doorway was manning the duty desk. The small room behind the duty desk was six-by-eight with Plexiglas schedules on the wall and a sturdy counter opening into the main room. Two captains and a lieutenant leaned over the counter arguing about the flying schedule.

Mack approached the desk and grunted to the group over the top of the box: "Where's the commander's office?"

The lieutenant waved a hand for him to wait until he was through with his debate.

Mack looked around, then mistakenly entered an office where a tech sergeant, reading glasses drooping on his nose, hunt-and-peck-typed on a report. Mack backed out, then found the adjacent door with the black plastic tag that read COM-MANDER. At the same time one of the captains at the duty desk did a double take and peered closer at his rank.

"Squadron, ten-hut!" the captain bellowed.

"As you were." Mack juggled the box and opened the door wide, held it for the major, then followed him inside. After they'd placed their boxes beside the desk, the major waved a cheery hand and was off to take over his duties as chief of the command post.

The massive lieutenant was at the door, looking distressed. Mack motioned him inside.

"Sir, I didn't know you were . . . uh . . ."

"You the duty officer?"

"Yes, sir. Tonight and tomorrow morning."

"I'm Mack." He held out his hand, and the lieutenant awkwardly shook it.

"Tiny Bechler, sir."

"Got some coffee?"

"I'll brew a fresh pot. How do you take it, sir?"

"Has the last mission aircraft landed?"

"Yes, sir. We don't have any night sorties scheduled."

"Forget the coffee and get me a cold beer." He handed the lieutenant a quarter.

"Yes, *sir!*" He was off.

Mack sat at the no-frills metal desk and surveyed the office. Barren of ornamentation, except for black-framed eight-by-ten photos of President Johnson, Secretary of Defense McNamara, and Secretary of the Air Force Brown lined up from left to right behind him. The colors, an American flag and a blue and silver Air Force standard, were in holders on either side of him. A large 357th Tactical Fighter Squadron plaque and an aerial photo of the base adorned the opposite wall. The squadron emblem was a dragon with a long, forked red tongue. Polite people called them the dragon squadron. Others called them the clit-lickers. The unit had maintained a good reputation in war and peace since being formed some twenty-three years earlier. The window to his left looked out on the flight line and the long rows of camouflage-painted F-105 aircraft parked there. Twenty-four Thunderchiefs were assigned to the 357th, and the squadron tail-flash, the large, white letters painted on the tail, read RU.

On the desktop before him were a calendar and a day-old squadron roster. Mack glanced down the list, lined through *Lt Col Lee, J.F.*, and substituted his own name.

He called out the admin sergeant's name. The serious-looking NCO he'd seen next door hurried in. He introduced himself and told him what he wanted done with the roster—to add the new name at the top and a legend at the bottom in a different type style. He intended to use the original squadron roster to keep score. He'd done the same when he'd assumed previous commands.

As the sergeant hurried off, Mack started putting his belongings away. He was positioning an age-worn, wooden desk plaque, with the name MACK MACLENDON ornately bracketed by carved F-84's, at the front of the desk when he realized someone was looking in.

A captain dressed in a Shade 1505, short-sleeve, khaki-colored Class-B uniform, hovered near the door, peering into the room.

"Help you?" Mack asked pleasantly.

"You're the new squadron commander, sir?"

"Yep. Brand new."

"I'm Captain Maisey, sir. Welcome to the 357th."

"Thank you."

The captain smiled, looking like he wanted to say more.

"Help you?" Mack repeated.

"I spoke with Colonel Lee yesterday morning, and he was going to make me his squadron exec. Keep track of the flying schedule, run admin, things like that."

"Yeah?" Mack put out his pen holder set, a present from his wife.

"I was just wondering if I could do the same for you, sir?"

"You fly Thuds?"

"Yes, sir."

"How long you been here?"

"Two weeks, sir."

"I've got an ops officer, an admin sergeant, and a first shirt assigned, so I won't be needing an exec." A minute later he looked up and saw that the captain was still there.

Captain Maisey swallowed. "I'd be glad to help any other way I can, sir."

There was one in every unit.

Mack continued unpacking. "What's the wing-loading advantage of a Thud over a MiG-21, Captain?"

Maisey looked ill at ease. "I . . . uh . . . I don't know, sir."

"How about the range of a SAM?"

"Thirty miles?"

"What's your crew chief's wife's name?"

The captain thought he had that one, so he promptly barked out his answer. "He's a staff sergeant and I don't fraternize with enlisted men, sir."

"How many nautical miles from Hanoi to the Gulf of Tonkin?"

"I . . . uh . . . ."

"Approximately."

"Seventy-five?"

"You scored zero out of four. The MiG-21 has the wing-loading advantage by a hell of a long shot, a SAM's range is nineteen nautical miles, you ought to know your crew chief better than your brother, and it's fifty-three nautical miles from Hanoi to the coast. As a combat fighter pilot you've already got the most demanding job in the Air Force, so try to learn everything you can about it, then we'll worry about additional duties. Anything else?"

"No, sir."

"That's all."

The captain turned.

"One other thing, Captain Maisey."

"Yes, sir."

"Flying suits are the uniform of the day for my pilots,

fatigues for my admin and maintenance people. Headquarter pukes have to wear Class-A's and Class-B's so we can tell them from the people who count. We only have to wear them to weddings, funerals, and when we get decorated by the headquarter pukes."

Lieutenant Bechler was behind the captain, holding a frosted beer bottle and trying hard not to grin.

"Yes, sir," the captain mumbled, and fled.

"Here's your beer, sir."

"Thanks, Tiny. Now bring me tomorrow's flying schedule."

"Yes, sir."

"Where's your beer?"

"I'm on duty, sir."

"The last airplane's down. Get a beer if you want one, then bring me the schedule."

"Yes, *sir!*"

Mack had finished unpacking the first box and was working on the second when Tiny returned, carrying a beer in one hand and the hand-printed schedule in the other.

"Sergeant Hill will type up the schedule as soon as you've approved it," Tiny said.

"When he's done changing the roster, and you're done getting hold of some people for me, you can both go to dinner. There's no morning combat missions for the squadron, so I won't be finished with the schedule until after the flight commanders' briefing in the morning."

"Flight commanders' briefing?"

"Get hold of the operations officer and tell him I'd like to see him ASAP, then tell the flight commanders we'll meet at oh-six-hundred hours here in my office."

"Yes, sir."

"Thanks, Tiny." He finished unpacking.

Sergeant Hill came in and handed him the roster.

"Thanks, Sergeant." The roster was neatly done.

"Welcome to the squadron, sir."

"It's damned good to be here."

Fifteen minutes later, a grinning, boyish-looking lieutenant colonel pushed his head into the doorway. Johnny T. Polaski, the squadron operations officer. They had been stationed together in Germany, but Mack hadn't seen much of him since he'd gotten to Takhli three weeks before.

"Couldn't believe it when I heard you were taking over, Mack. Congratulations."

"Me, either. Hope I didn't move in your way."

"Not at all. I just made button colonel, and anyway, I'd much rather spend some time learning from a pro before I get my shot at it. Good to have you aboard, sir."

"Grab a beer and let's go over the squadron roster so you can let me know what the hell I've inherited here."

"I just happen to have brought one." Johnny T. took a drink from a fresh Coors bottle, then dragged up a chair and leaned over the desk, trying to read the roster upside down.

Mack surveyed the list.

	357 TFS KEY PERSONNEL ROSTER	As of: 25 Nov 66
Cmdr:	~~Lt Col Lee, J.F.~~ (K)	MacLendon, T.F.
Ops:	Lt Col Polaski, J.T.	
A-Flt:	*Maj Hall, M.S.	
	**Capt Smith, J.A.	
	Capt Huffmeier, C.L.	
	Capt Maisey, K.R.	
	Capt Meyer, J.C.	
	1/Lt Bechler, H.J.	
B-Flt:	*Maj Ralston, M.A.	
	**Capt Lewis, B.L.	
	Capt Clark, C.R.	
	Capt Raymond, T.W.	
	1/Lt Rodriguez, G.M.	
	1/Lt Singleton, T.S.	
C-Flt:	*Maj Crawford, P.T.	
	**Capt Lutz, B.T.	
	Capt Murphy, M.K.	
	Capt Larkins, T.T.	
	1/Lt Mullens, M.W.	
	1/Lt Silva, J.S.	
D-Flt:	*Capt Swendler, O.A.	
	**Capt Takahara, T.	
	Capt Maier, R.L.	
	Capt Spalding, J.J.	
	1/Lt Brown, C.C.	
	1/Lt Capella, R.S.	
WW-Flt:	*Maj Phillips, G.P./Capt Stewart, M.S.	

```
Atch:            Col Parker, B.J. (Wing Cmdr)
                 Maj Foley, M.T. (Wing Weapons Ofcr)

Maint:           2/Lt Shilling, D.D./CMS Roberts, C.A.
1st Sgt:         M/Sgt Silvester, T.S.
Admin:           T/Sgt Hill, P.C.
P.E.:            S/Sgt Perez, S.L.              Notes: 100=Finished Tour
                                                      C=Status Change
Flt Srgn: Maj Roddenbush, D.L.                        W=Wounded
                                                      R=Rescued
'Flight Commander                                     P=POW
**Ass't Flight Commander                              M=MIA
                                                      K=KIA
```

"I know some of the people, but I haven't had the chance to see any of them in combat except Sam Hall, and that was a hundred years ago when we were flying F-84's in Korea."

"Sam's doing a fine job. Probably the best flight commander in the entire wing. He's a damned good leader of men."

"Always was. How are the other flight commanders?"

"Tops. Mike Ralston just came here after upgrading out of F-102's, but he'll be solid once he gets some stick time flying the Thud and a few combat missions behind him. Pete Crawford is a superb pilot and a good leader, and Swede Swendler is nearly as good. A couple weeks back, Swendler was put in for a Silver Star, and Seventh Air Force was so impressed with the write-up they're upgrading it to an Air Force Cross."

"What did he do?"

"He was leading a flight on a strike up near Hanoi, and three out of the four aircraft were shot all to hell by antiaircraft fire, including Swede's bird. He was nursemaiding the group back toward the border when two MiG's jumped them. Swede sent his flock on ahead, then did a hard turn and started to kick ass. Shot down one MiG and damaged the other one."

Mack was impressed. He looked at the list again. "How about the rest of the men?"

"Remember Benny Lewis from Spangdahlem, Germany? Benny has developed into one hell of a stick-and-rudder man. Next best would probably be Mike Murphy, but Jimbo Smith and Toki Takahara are also damned good. You're getting a good bunch of captains, Mack."

Mack rubbed his chin. "I just talked with a guy named

Maisey. I wasn't impressed. I hadn't been here five minutes and he was already brownnosing for a job."

"Ken just got here himself. He's a naval academy grad, so he can't be all bad."

Johnny T. was also an Annapolis graduate, and Canoe-U grads stuck together. He continued. "I don't know what kind of stick he flies, but he's gung ho and trying to take on extra work."

"Let's put that on hold and give him the chance to learn about flying combat, okay?"

"You're the boss."

"I see Glenn Phillips is here."

"He's the best Wild Weasel pilot in the wing. You been here long enough to learn much about the Weasels?"

"A little. Supposed to keep the SAMs off our backs. I've flown ten missions with the other squadrons, and on all but four of them all the Weasel birds were either shot up or broke so we didn't have them along."

"You mean the one good airplane they've got left. The rest were either lost or so heavily damaged we can't put them back together. They've taken heavy losses. Down to one Weasel crew per squadron, with one good Weasel bird so they take turns flying."

Mack was reading the roster. "I see we've got two guys attached to the squadron for flying purposes."

"The wing commander and the wing weapons officer, a guy named Max Foley. Max has a good reputation. Colonel Parker's okay too, as long as you treat him like he's the world's greatest war hero and combat leader."

Mack grinned. "B. J.'s got sound judgment. He made me squadron commander, didn't he?"

"B. J. doesn't like being called B. J."

"I heard." Mack drained the last of his beer and suppressed a belch. It tasted as good as he felt.

"It's no picnic here, Mack, but I believe we're about to get things under control."

"Think so?"

"By themselves, the MiG's aren't bad, and neither are the guns. It's when you mix the two it starts making you nervous. When you add surface-to-air missiles that come up at you like striped-ass apes, it gets damned concerning. But we're getting a handle on things. You keep jinking and moving and the flak won't get you. You keep your eyes out, and your wits about you and you can handle the MiG's. SAMs are tough, but now we've got warning equipment that tells us when they've launched, and if you get a good visual on the SAMs in time, you can dodge them."

"You guys had a bad mission yesterday. What happened?"

"Yesterday should have been an easy counter towards the magic one hundred, but it just went sour. Sometimes it's like that, the easy ones are tough and the tough ones are easy."

Col B. J. Parker stuck his head in the door. "You two all that's here?"

Both men jumped to their feet.

"At ease." Parker spoke into his hand-held radio to tell the command post he'd be at the 357th squadron for a bit, then took a chair and leaned back.

B. J. was a short, plump man, with curly black hair and watery blue eyes. He was driven by ambition, and many who worked for him disliked him, for he was not charismatic and he did not easily generate admiration. But he was known to have a knack for picking the right men for the job, then generally staying out of their hair. The formula worked; they made him look good and he ran an effective wing. Mack felt he could work with him.

"You feel easy with the job, Mack?" the wing commander asked.

"Yes, sir. I was getting a rundown on the men from Colonel Polaski."

"I'll be brief, so you can get on with more important things, but I thought I'd better drop by and give you my standard spiel about what I expect out of my commanders."

Mack had received the briefing when he'd arrived to take over the command post, but B. J. had likely forgotten.

"I don't want you to forget that our purpose is to take as much of the load as possible off our ground forces in South Vietnam. We're not trying to win any kind of unconditional surrenders, like in World War Two. We wanted to do that, we'd nuke the bastards. We've got a limited war, with two primary objectives like we had in Korea.

"First, we're trying to put sufficient pressure on the North Vietnamese so they'll get the hell out of South Vietnam and give democracy a chance there. If nothing else, so long as we're bombing in their mother country, a lot of North Vietnamese have to remain up there to defend it and can't be down south making trouble. Second, we're trying to cut off the flow of supplies they're shipping south. It's damned difficult to conduct an interdiction campaign, considering all the restraints we have to operate under, but I expect you and your men to follow the rules. Understand?"

Mack nodded.

"There aren't many units doing the job. Nothing like the numbers we had in World War Two or even Korea. There's just Takhli and Korat flying F-105's, the guys at Ubon and Da Nang flying F-4's, and the Navy flying A-6's. Here at the 355th, we get more pack six missions than any of the others. Headquarters knows they can rely on us for the toughest missions, and they give them to us. We've got more bombs on target and more MiG kills than anyone else, and let's keep it that way."

"We'll do our part, Colonel."

B. J. Parker started down the home stretch of the briefing. "Mack, I command more than four thousand men. We have a detachment of KC-135 tankers and another of EB-66 aircraft. The Navy, the U.S. merchant marine fleet, Military Airlift Command, and a fleet of trucks carry hundreds of tons of fuel, weapons, and supplies here each week. Our country is paying millions of dollars for the right to maintain this base. All of that is for one reason, and that is so your men can put bombs on the target. I expect you to give them the proper guidance to do that." B. J. then told him he expected him to attend the Monday morning staff meetings, turn in reports and paperwork on time, keep his men in line, and always remember that he was there if Mack needed him.

"I'll remember."

B. J. got to his feet, done with his speech. The men stood also. He radioed the command post to tell them he was en route to his quarters, then excused himself and left.

Johnny T. heard the outer door close and shook his head slowly. "That's the third time I've heard it. I sort of favor the part about the merchant marines and the truck drivers."

"Poor overworked bastards. Let's head over to the officer's club for some dinner."

CHAPTER TWO

Sunday, November 27th—0700 Local, Takhli Royal Thai Air Force Base, Thailand

Benny Lewis

The crudely constructed hootches were lined up behind the officer's club. Hootches for the pilots of the dragon squadron, the rocket squadron, and the pig squadron. Hootches for the EB-66 and KC-135 crews. Hootches for support officers.

They were long, wooden buildings. Inside each the tropical heat and red-brown dust was stirred by noisy fans on stands. Wooden shutters were propped open on the long sides of the hootches, and framed screens were fitted to the doors and windows in vain attempts to keep out assorted flying, crawling, and burrowing jungle insects. Twenty bunks to a hootch. Each two bunks arranged in a neat, eight-by-ten area separated from the next by freestanding metal lockers. Each hootch was guarded at night by a Thai soldier—for theft by the civilians working on base was common—and was kept clean by a hootch-boy. Most of the guards slept soundly at night. Most of the hootch boys were older than the officers who lived there.

The hootches had no running water. Showers and sanitary facilities were contained in other buildings behind them, one for each three hootches. Boardwalks of rough-hewn two-by-sixes ran along the backs of the hootches to the shower buildings. A long boardwalk ran along the front of the hootches, right to the club, where the men ate, drank, and socialized, and left to the flight line, where most of them worked. Networks of ditches ran alongside and underneath the

25

boardwalks and wandered off in odd directions to carry torrents of monsoon rainwater away to canals the Thais called *klongs*.

Captain Benny Lewis ambled in the direction of the club, yawning lazily in the heat. His light complexion had grown a bronzed hue, and his blond hair was bleached by the merciless Thai sun. He had a pleasant, yet alert and confident air, and although he was not tall, was built as solid as a fireplug, with broad shoulders and a thick chest tapering to a narrow waist. He worked to stay in good condition; it also helped with his g-tolerance when he flew.

It had been a sleep-in morning with nothing scheduled, and he felt no remorse for lazing about the hootch until seven. There was plenty of time to eat breakfast, wander through the on-base Thai market, then figure something out for the afternoon. Days off were rare. More often some duty or other was assigned on nonflying days.

It was time to write his weekly letter. It had been a month since his last letter from home, but that was understandable: Bets had the kids to keep her busy. He composed his letter in his head. He mentioned the hot, humid weather, the interesting Thai marketplaces, the inexpensive black star sapphires and gold bracelets, the friendliness of the Thai people, and how it would be nice for them to visit Thailand together when the war was over. He added that he missed her and the kids and to *take special care of yourself*. Finally, he added footnotes for their four-year-old son, things like *you're the man of the family until I get back,* and for their two-year-old daughter, *you're getting to be a big girl—watch out for those kindergarten fighter pilots—Ha! Ha!* His letters were all about the same. He could write one, make a dozen copies, and send them out weekly.

Still, a warm feeling overcame him at the thought of his family.

Max Foley stepped out from the doorway of his trailer into the brilliant light, shading his eyes with both hands. He was a major, and field-grade officers lived in trailers rather than the hootches. Max, a skinny and angular man, fumbled to pull on a pair of wraparound, nonissue sunglasses then perched his blue cunt-cap squarely on his head. Max Foley was known for his quick, analytic mind, but this morning he was less than alert.

Benny high-balled a quick salute and smiled. "Breakfast?"

"Yeah." The sound emerged as a forced croak. Foley's face was so cut up from his morning shave he looked like he'd lost a fight with an angry lawn mower. Benny had been at Takhli longer and was better acclimated. He could drink and socialize until one in the morning, sleep, then get up at four-thirty, brief at four-forty-five, and be sufficiently alert to fly at six-fifteen. He was amazed at the amount of pickling and general abuse a human body could not only endure, but adapt to.

The two were silent as they plodded down the boardwalk, zippers of their flight suits pulled down to mid-chest to capture any slight wisp of breeze, losing the battle as sweat soaked the fabric at their armpits and crotches and ran down their chests and backs.

Benny wore a gray go-to-hell hat, the Aussie bush hat adopted by the fighter jocks in Southeast Asia, low on his forehead to shadow the sunlight. Both sides of the brim were snapped up into position. Captain's bars were pinned onto the front of the hat's crown, and hash marks were carefully penned on its right side to show the numbers of missions he'd flown over North Vietnam. About half were in red ink, reminders of the times he had flown across the Red River into pack six, the most heavily defended area on earth. Intelligence said there were more hostile SAMs, guns, and MiG's there than in any other area of equivalent size—anywhere.

They rounded the corner of the O' Club in time to watch Tiny Bechler park the dragon squadron's crew van near the front door. Tiny crawled out, shoving on the sliding door that squealed in protest as it moved along its rusty track. He shoved again, harder, and the door closed with a crash. "Damn thing's falling apart," he complained. That was Tiny's way. He bitched and put on a mean air that the other pilots generally ignored.

"You treat it like shit," said Benny congenially. "That's why it's falling apart." Max was still wincing in pain from the screeching sound of the door.

Tiny glared, mostly to project his asshole image, but his salute was crisp and proper. Benny and Max returned it, and the three entered the large dining room. A dozen men were eating breakfast, talking, and reading their *Bangkok World* and *Stars & Stripes* newspapers. The Bangkok papers were plump and had colored banners, so it must be Sunday. It was easy to lose track of such things. Tiny Bechler bought one at the counter and they proceeded to a table.

No Hab, the waitress, brought coffee and menus and hovered cheerfully at table-side for their orders. They surveyed the menu selections as if it mattered.

"Orange juice!" croaked Max.

No Hab looked intently at her pad and wrote furiously. She chewed gum and generally did a great imitation of the waitresses she had seen in vintage American movies.

Max smiled through his hangover fog. "And bacon and eggs."

"No hab bacon," she replied.

"Hash," he said.

"No hab hash."

"Ham."

"No hab ham."

"Shit!" Foley exclaimed.

"Hab," she joked.

"Sausage," he tried.

"No hab."

"Fuck," he exclaimed. "What *do* you have?"

No Hab giggled.

"Steak?"

"Chicken flied steak?"

"Yeah," he said in quiet triumph.

"No hab."

"S-O-S?" he tried.

"Hab S-O-S!" She scribbled and smiled, delighted.

The all ordered S-O-S, eggs and fried rice. Benny pulled the comics from Tiny's newspaper and started reading "Blondie."

Tiny lit a Camel and mused. He'd been quieter than usual lately, since the Yen Bai debacle. "You on the afternoon go, Major Foley?"

Foley grimaced. "No. I'm supervisor of flying this afternoon." SOF duty was assigned to field-grade officers, who would maintain a general vigil over the flying operation for the deputy commander for operations and wing commander.

Tiny's Camel torched and sizzled, emitting a sulfuric aroma. He stared at the foul-smelling cigarette with a secretive look that showed he knew something. "You're flying, Captain Lewis."

Benny pried his attention from Dagwood's antics and looked up. "I thought I was off."

"Colonel Mack called all the flight commanders into his office at oh-six-hundred and changed the afternoon schedule around. You're leading Falcon flight on the afternoon go."

"I'll be damned." Benny thought for a moment. "How about Mike Ralston?" Ralston was new to the airplane and was considered somewhat of a ham-fisted pilot, but he was also a senior major, B-Flight commander, and Benny's immediate boss.

"You've replaced him on the schedule. Colonel Mack says rank doesn't make a damn when his people's asses are on the line."

"That *is* different," Benny said. As befit their rank and position, flight commanders normally led in the air as they did on the ground. The change could prove embarrassing.

Like most flying units, Takhli flew in a formation called the fluid four. There were "elements" of two aircraft, with two elements making up each four-ship flight. The flight leader and his wingman were the lead element. Number three was leader of the second element, and four was his wingman. Flight lead always flew in front, with his wingman flying on one side and the second element on the other. That way the leader could concern himself about managing the flight while the rest of the pilots kept a good lookout.

Senior pilots led both elements. The wingmen positions were filled by lower-ranking officers with less experience, such as Tiny Bechler, so they could learn the discipline and gain the experience they'd need to lead in the future.

"What do you think of your new squadron commander?" Max asked. Word had spread quickly.

"We were stationed together in Germany," Benny answered. "Colonel Mack's a good leader with a lot of fighter experience."

Lt Tiny Bechler was not noted for his subservience. He stabbed a forefinger toward Max Foley, who had pinned on major's leaves the month before. "I've been told he flies a good stick and he takes care of his people. Some of the guys weren't pulling their weight, just because they had the rank, and now they're gonna have to. Like Ralston."

Max grimaced with the pain of his hangover. "Major Ralston to you, Tiny. You've gotta learn to show respect."

"Fuck off." Tiny grinned to show he wasn't serious.

Benny regarded Tiny. "Mike Ralston is still learning the F-105 and some of the finer arts of flying and surviving in high-threat areas. Which, I may add, isn't all that easy."

"Amen," echoed Max.

"But Mike knows his limitations. He's not afraid to ask questions and he's not too proud to listen when you tell him something. The ones to watch out for are the guys who think they're better than they are, not the Mike Ralstons."

"Like Colonel Lee?" Tiny asked.

"He was just in over his head," Max said.

Benny drank a gulp of black coffee, paused, then listened. Tiny looked ill at ease as they talked about Jim Lee. No one had chewed his ass about not sticking with Lee through his wild maneuver over the target, but everyone knew he'd shown poor form, including himself.

"I've got to say one thing for Colonel Lee," said Tiny. "That reattack he was trying to make through all that flak was the hairiest thing I've ever seen."

Foley agreed. "Yeah, but not smart. Nobody should fly a thirty degree dive-bomb in a high-threat area. Too shallow and predictable, and you're too low to the ground."

"Maybe. But it took balls. No radio, on fire and burning, and still he was trying to get his bombs on the target." Tiny swallowed and looked away.

"If you'd stayed with him, probably neither one of you'd have come home," Max said.

"Did you guys know Lee had just finished a Ph.D. program?" asked Benny, pulling their attention away from Tiny's transgression.

"I heard," Foley said.

"Bet you didn't know that a message came into personnel about him the day he was shot down? That he'd been accepted for the Apollo program? He was supposed to report to the hospital at Brooks Air Force Base tout suite for his qualification physical."

"You're shitting me." Even Tiny was impressed.

They thought about that for a while. Then Benny and Max started talking about tactics and basics of combat flying. Things like: "A good fighter pilot instinctively knows his position in the airspace relative to the rest of the world. He knows his flight's position, the enemies' position, and he can anticipate the next move that both are going to make." And: "One day you'll have it, another day you won't. You've got to recognize your limitations on a day-to-day basis, know when to press and when to hold back."

Foley was the wing weapons officer and part of his job was to talk about tactics with the other pilots. Benny just liked to talk about flying.

Benny and Max were experienced. Between them, they had 5,000 hours of fighter time, almost 4,000 of which was spent in F-105's. Both had come to Takhli from Nellis Air Force Base, where they'd taught in the fighter weapons instructor's course, the Air Force's graduate school for their top fighter pilots. The other Thud pilots said they were two of the best. Foley was outstanding at air-to-air combat tactics, and was able to think three or four maneuvers ahead of most adversaries. Benny Lewis had velvet hands, and some said he could get more performance out of the F-105 Thud than any man alive.

Tiny judiciously kept quiet and listened to learn a secret or two.

Maj Glenn Phillips approached, his flight suit impeccable, his jungle boots glistening, his newspaper folded neatly under his arm. He smiled to show perfect teeth and a cleft chin.

"Mind if I join your table?"

Max squinted. "Shit, Glenn, don't you sweat?"

Benny motioned at the empty seat. "It's S-O-S this morning."

Max shook his head in disbelief. "You can't not sweat. It's not fucking human to not sweat." He glanced at Benny and Tiny. "I was sweating like a pig when we came in. You guys too. But Glenn isn't sweating."

No Hab approached, scribbled on her pad as Phillips dictated his S-O-S order, then giggled when he propositioned her. Most females giggled a lot when they were around Phillips. Women young and old, from Denmark to North Africa, from Las Vegas to Tokyo, had fallen prey to his good looks and charm.

"No Hab," Phillips said quietly in his rich, pleasant voice, "you have captured my heart. Come to my hootch and I'll show you how to do a snap roll."

Max focused bloody eyes on Phillips. "A snap roll?"

No Hab walked away with a special twist to her hips, glancing back over her shoulder. She had no idea what Phillips was talking about, but it was obvious she wouldn't mind trying whatever it was.

Phillips was a West Point graduate. As a first lieutenant only two years out of pilot training, he'd won second place in the Air Force's Top Gun competition. Shortly after pinning on his captain's railroad tracks, he'd been selected as a Thunderbird demonstration-team pilot. His Thunderbird tour had been cut short when flaws were discovered in the F-105B, but he'd gained the name and the fame. Next, Glenn had finagled his way into the fighter weapons school at Nellis, another sweet deal, and had been assigned to the headquarters in Europe at Weisbaden, Germany. Well liked by the colonels and generals there, he'd made major two years below the zone. Glenn Phillips was slated to wear stars.

Benny got along well with Phillips, who in peacetime had often been regarded by his peers as an egotistical ass. Most of the complaints were sour grapes, for Phillips was a fine officer and a superb pilot. He didn't just crawl into a fighter, he wore it. He put it on, became a part of it, and flew *with* it. As in the biblical sense, he *knew* the F-105, and could coax it to do things others could not. Benny felt that same way when he flew, and he shared a kinship with those who knew the feeling.

At Takhli, Phillips was assigned to fly an especially dangerous mission and that made up for some of his pomposity. Tiny Bechler made little secret of the fact that he disliked Phillips, regardless of what mission he flew, perhaps because Glenn's ego matched his own.

"Any of you guys seen my bear?" Phillips asked.

Benny bunked in the same hootch as Mal Stewart, who was also called Phillips's Bear, but mainly just "the Bear." "He's sleeping. Got in from town this morning and woke up the whole place when he stumbled into a fan and a locker. Once he had everyone awake, he passed out beside his bed. He was still there when I left, curled up on the floor next to his bunk, snoring. I shook him to tell him he ought to get in bed, but I couldn't wake him up." Benny then said, smiling, "You oughta get him under better control."

Max laughed, clutching at his forehead.

"Put him on a leash," Tiny Bechler growled.

Phillips frowned, sadness tugging at his face. "He's got me confused. He goes to sleep in the airplane, snores all the way to the tanker, then wakes up and just wants to kill commies. Mean bastard, with balls that drag the ground."

Phillips's dangerous mission was called Wild Weasel, a new concept in the Air Force. It involved two-seat fighters and backseaters they called "bears."

Max Foley regarded Phillips. "How the hell did the Air Force come up with the Wild Weasel idea, Glenn?"

"You tell him, Benny." Glen nodded toward Maj Les Ries, the Wild Weasel pilot from the 354th squadron sitting at another table. "I want to ask Les if he knows when our replacement airplanes are supposed to arrive. Be right back." Glenn took his coffee and went across the room.

Foley looked at Benny. "That's right. You went through Wild Weasel training too, didn't you?"

"Yeah. It's an interesting story. A completely new concept."

In early 1965, the president had ordered American fighter bombers to attack targets in North Vietnam, hoping to relieve the growing pressure the North Vietnamese were bringing to bear in the south. The gomers had a lot of guns, of all sizes, but the fighter jocks found that they could fly above the guns' effective altitudes, and the few MiG's they had didn't worry them much.

But shortly after the bombing campaign started, Russian surface-to-air missiles and tracking radars were photographed being off-loaded at Haiphong. SAMs had never been used in combat, so they created a great deal of concern. The president's advisers decided the Russians were bluffing and wouldn't really turn the SAMs over to the North Vietnamese. But, they cautioned, if SAM sites were attacked and Russian advisers were harmed, that might provoke them to change their minds. The fighter pilots were told not to interfere while the batteries were being set up.

In June of 1965 the SAMs were launched by the dozens and shot down increasing numbers of Air Force and Navy aircraft. Low altitudes were already untenable due to intense ground fire and antiaircraft artillery. Now the medium and higher altitudes, where the deadly SAMs were most effective, were equally inhospitable. The airspace within fifty miles of Hanoi and Haiphong became a killing ground.

Strike flights had been sent to attack the SAM sites, but with disastrous results. The fighter pilots had difficulty locating the camouflaged sites, and when they thought they'd found them, they encountered flurries of SAMs from blind sides, heavy barrages of flak, and intense small-arms fire. They suffered terrible losses, and the sites they attacked were empty! The real ones were camouflaged and nearly impossible to find.

President Johnson ordered that a solution be found, and the Air Force gave the matter its highest priority. A committee was formed at the Pentagon. A new, highly specialized mission was settled upon, to seek out and destroy the SAM sites. The aircrew would consist of an experienced fighter pilot and an electronic warfare officer, a flying officer trained to fight radar-controlled threats. The aircraft would be a two-seat fighter equipped with electronic homing systems. *Wild Weasel* was the classified code name, and the aircraft, aircrews, as well as the concept, were called by that name.

They'd picked F-100F Super Sabres because they were readily available. After a frantic development effort, the rear cockpits of the aircraft were fitted with miniaturized radar-analysis and homing receivers. The electronic warfare officer would analyze the SAM radar's signal and give the pilot directions so he could locate the SAM site. The first crews were picked and hastily trained, then given a pep talk by Harold Brown, the technically astute secretary of the Air Force, and sent off to fly over North Vietnam to see if the concept worked.

After three months of dangerous trials, heavy losses, and considerable doubts, one of the crews homed in on a North Vietnamese SAM radar and attacked the site with two cannisters of 2.75-inch, high-explosive antitank rockets.

When the surviving Weasel pioneers returned to the states to train replacement crews, they suggested that a faster, tougher aircraft with better range, the F-105F, be outfitted to replace the aging F-100's.

In mid-1966, the Wild Weasels were deployed to both F-105 bases, first to Korat, then to Takhli. Glenn Phillips and his bear had been in the group. They flew the specially equipped F-105F's and used electronic equipment to find SAM batteries, or launched Shrike radar-seeking missiles at them to keep them preoccupied while the other F-105's attacked their targets. Few of the strike pilots envied them. They, too, flew daily into the face of the defenses, but they tried to minimize their exposure. Wild Weasels went out of their way to duel with surface-to-air missiles. That was their job.

Benny Lewis had been trained as a Wild Weasel pilot, in the group following Phillips, but upon arrival at Takhli his backseater had developed chronic airsickness. The backseater had been transferred to EB-66's and seemed happier there. EB-66's were much slower aircraft, well protected from MiG's, and flew at safer distances from the antiaircraft guns and SAMs.

Benny Lewis had become a strike pilot, which he figured was just as well. He preferred single-seat fighters, with no one to hear him belch, mutter to himself, or critique him when he sang corny flying songs.

Phillips returned to their table just as Benny was finishing his monologue and the breakfast group was pondering the improbability of the Bear's sanity. Unlike the backseater Benny had parted ways with, Mal Stewart thrived in the fighter environment and enjoyed the dangerous mission.

Tiny ventured a guess. "Maybe he doesn't understand what the hell's going on."

"Could be," Phillips said, "but he sure knows where every missile is, and he can see MiG's when they're still ten miles out." He regarded the others seriously. "You know what he says when he crawls into the back cockpit and gets strapped in?"

They leaned forward.

"He says, 'Driver, take me to work and wake me when we get there.' "

Everyone smiled, even Tiny Bechler. Phillips was likely stretching the truth, but that was part of being a fighter pilot. They enjoyed talking about "bears," the only group the strike pilots—excepting Tiny Bechler and a few recalcitrant diehards—accepted as their own. After the Takhli Weasels had flown their first few missions out in front of the strike force, the single-seat pilots started calling the backseaters "bears," like the ones found in arcade shooting galleries. When the enemy shot at Wild Weasels they'd just roar, turn around, and attack. The nickname had stuck, and Wild Weasel pilots were often advised to keep their "bears" on their thirty-six-inch chains, that being the distance between the front and back cockpits.

No Hab arrived with their orders.

Tiny Bechler downed his orange juice in a single gulp before regarding Phillips. "You hear what Colonel Mack did this morning?"

"Yeah," Phillips replied, with no further comment. Colonel Mack's new order wouldn't affect Glenn. In the 357th, the Wild Weasels had been attrited from five down to one aircrew and a single aircraft, and Phillips was the flight commander of himself and his backseater.

Phillips and his bear were considered the best and certainly the most aggressive Wild Weasel crew in the wing. Mission commanders sought them to fly on the toughest targets. B. J. Parker, the wing commander, asked their advice on matters concerning enemy defenses, and used them to distribute information to the other Weasels. Even if there had been a full complement of crews, no one would argue with Phillips's position as the 357th squadron's WW-flight commander, and no one would argue that he shouldn't lead the Weasel flights in the air.

"What do you think of Colonel Mack, Glenn?" asked Foley.

Phillips joked. "Pretty impressive for an old guy who never finished college."

Tiny, who had been wolfing his food down, mistook Phillips's pun as a slap against his latest hero. He stopped eating and bristled. "That's a stupid thing to say. What does college have to do with flying fighters and leading people?"

The below-the-zone major with 2,500 flying hours glanced at the first lieutenant bars on Tiny's flight suit and gave a shake of his head. "Just concentrate on your flying and cut out the wise-ass insubordination, Lieutenant. You've still got a lot to learn."

Considering the matter handled, Glenn turned to his reconstituted scrambled eggs, which were splattered with S-O-S and tasted like cardboard.

Tiny Bechler stood, self-conscious and red-faced at the rebuke. He gathered the front sections of his newspaper and stalked, stiff-legged, toward the cashier's cage.

Phillips watched him leave without comment.

"I think Tiny's going to be a good pilot," Benny said.

"Maybe, if he can remember he's just a lieutenant."

"I enjoy flying with the kids we're getting from the

academy," Max said, partly to needle Phillips. "Most of the time they hang right on the wing and don't ask questions."

Tiny Bechler was one of several recently arrived first lieutenants who'd gained their commissions from the fledgling Air Force Academy at Colorado Springs. Vietnam would be the first taste of combat for academy graduates. Previously, a percentage of West Point and Annapolis graduates had taken commissions in the Air Force to provide a backbone of regular officers. Officers like Benny and Foley, who'd gained their commissions through ROTC and flight cadets were proud of the Air Force's own academy, while former Annapolis midshipmen and West Point cadets maintained a wait-and-see attitude, with more than a touch of prejudice for their *senior* academies.

Phillips dabbed his mouth with his napkin, then stared thoughtfully at the doorway through which Tiny had disappeared. "I need a good wingman. I'll try him, see if he learned anything from what happened with Lee."

"He'll be good," Max said, "if he lives through the next few missions."

Phillips mused.

Max leaned forward, elbows on the table. "Were you on the Yen Bai mission, Glenn?"

"Yeah. I was leading the Weasel flight. We were on the defensive the entire time."

"Out of twenty-four Thuds, only two got their bombs on target. That's shitty."

"Only two," Phillips concurred. "Our friend here and his wingman. Wasn't for Benny there wouldn't have been any damage done to the target at all."

Benny grimaced. "I believe it when they say Ho Chi Minh's girlfriend runs a cathouse there. The flak was so thick you could land on it and get out and take a stroll on the stuff."

Phillips said, "We're going to have to make damned sure we stay alert any time we go to pack six, even on the ones we think are going to be easy. The only good thing about it is that it can't get much worse."

27/0900L—Hanoi, Democratic Republic of Vietnam

Lt Col Xuan Nha

Xuan Nha entered at the heels of Colonel Trung, his superior officer, peering about the reception room of the cultural hall, the largest annex of the sprawling Russian Embassy. More than fifty newly arrived Russian advisers were in the room. The colors of their cloth collar tabs and epaulets told their specialties. Red for ground force, blue for air force, black for rockets and artillery. Senior officers from the Vietnamese People's Army, Air Force, and Army of National Defense mingled with their counterparts among the new arrivals.

As happened whenever he was in the presence of Russians, a blanket of suspicion descended over Xuan. He privately called them *Tay,* a derogatory term for Westerners.

Xuan Nha was short, even for an Annamese, but he was broad of shoulder and built powerfully through his back and arms. He had strong facial features with an embarrassing hint of a Caucasian look. His jaw was large and often taut, and his nose was sharply pointed, like that of a sparrow. He had once been plagued with that nickname. His eyes appeared deceptively lazy, giving him a soft and gentle air. He was neither.

Col. Feodor Dimetriev, senior adviser from the Soviet air defense command called PVO Strany, hailed Colonel Trung with a friendly wave. A large, beefy Russian stood at Dimetriev's side, holding a steaming cup of tea and generally looking ill at ease. The collar tabs and epaulets of his tropical uniform showed a single gold star embroidered onto black cloth, announcing him as a major in the missiles and artillery branch. He was the one Xuan studied as they crossed the room.

Colonel Trung smiled graciously as he shook hands with Dimetriev. "Very good to see you, Feodor," he said in Vietnamese, slowly so to be easily understood. Trung was a soldier, but he also knew his diplomacy, a nicety that Xuan preferred to leave to others.

Feodor Dimetriev returned the pleasantry in the same language, then talked about the weather and the unseasonable showers. It was about to rain at that very moment, as it had done every morning recently, even though this should have been the beginning of the dry season. During the small talk Xuan examined the new major. The man had a florid complexion and was overweight. No older than Xuan's thirty-two years, he had a paunch and was growing jowls. His coarse brown hair was cropped closely, as the Russians did when preparing for their tour in Vietnam. Sweat soaked his service uniform and his skin glistened with moisture. He held a hand over his mouth to suppress a belch. He was indeed, decided Xuan Nha, just another Western *Tay* pig. He had expected more, for the man had a glowing reputation.

Colonel Dimetriev introduced his companion. "Major Nicolaj Gregarian arrived last night from Haiphong with our latest group of advisers. He is one of our true experts on guided rocket systems and coordinated defenses, on temporary loan from PVO Strany Headquarters."

"Temporary?" asked Xuan.

"Six months. I requested his services for a longer period, but unfortunately," Dimetriev clapped the major on the back, smiling broadly, "next summer he is scheduled for promotion to lieutenant colonel and to take over the development of a new guided rocket system. Unfortunate for us, but fortunate for Major Gregarian and Mother Russia, right Nicolaj."

Colonel Trung listened politely, but Xuan Nha frowned at the news. He had hoped to work longer with the touted Russian rocket expert. It was difficult to break in a new adviser, to wash away the strict, dogmatic Soviet approach to combat and make room for innovation. Sometimes it was impossible to convince the hardheaded Russians that they must use diverse engagement methods to exploit the slightest vulnerability of the enemy. The war changed monthly, weekly, sometimes daily, for it was a tactical war and that was the way of tactical thinking. Xuan Nha hoped the Russian major could accept such flexibility.

Gregarian was uncomfortable under his scrutiny, and shifted his bulk awkwardly, muttering something incomprehensible. After a moment Xuan Nha realized the Russian was having trouble understanding and putting words into Vietnamese.

"Welcome to Hanoi," Xuan said in passable Russian. "I am *Podpolkovnik* Xuan Nha, and this is my superior officer, *Polkovnik* Trung."

Gregarian eased somewhat. They shook hands.

"I've heard of you," said Gregarian to Xuan Nha in Russian, quite ignoring Trung and Dimetriev. "Please excuse my Vietnamese. They rushed me through the Asian Affairs language course, and I have little aptitude for that sort of thing."

"Ah, but he is a wizard with radars and guided rocket systems," said Dimetriev, also speaking in Russian. *"Mayor* Gregarian will be working with you, *Podpolkovnik* Nha."

Xuan Nha smiled. "We can always use advice from *real* experts." Only Trung realized that Xuan was being facetious. Xuan Nha knew every vacuum tube, resistor, and set screw of the systems under his command. When he'd commanded the 23rd guided rocket battalion he had directed the destruction of fourteen enemy aircraft, a feat unmatched by any man in the world, including this Russian *expert,* Nicolaj Gregarian.

Dimetriev continued. "Unfortunately, others wish to share Nicolaj's valuable time. *General-Mayor* Luc wants him to depart for Yen Bai tomorrow, to help set up the new P-50 radar being transported to the western mountains."

One-star general Luc was commander of the People's Army of National Defense, the branch of the People's Army dedicated to the defense of the Republic, and the man to whom Trung and Xuan Nha owed and provided allegiance. Still, Xuan Nha wished to start working with Major Gregarian immediately. He assuaged his impatience by remembering that the new P-50, the best command and control radar the Soviets had to offer, might help that effort.

"We are lucky the radar was not destroyed." Xuan addressed Gregarian in his direct manner. "Three nights ago the P-50 arrived at Yen Bai along with two new SON-9 artillery engagement radars and twenty-four S-60 guns."

"Ah, yes," said Gregarian. "We were told by *General-Mayor* Luc."

Xuan Nha raised an eyebrow. "Did he tell you the Americans bombed the railroad siding the next afternoon as the P-50 radar was being unloaded."

"Yes, but he said the P-50 was undamaged."

"Only because our men fiercely defended the siding. The fornicating dogs destroyed one of the artillery radars, four guns, and a boxcar loaded with ammunition. Thankfully they missed the P-50 and the second artillery radar."

Nicolaj Gregarian's face came to life. "The P-50 is extremely valuable. It must be moved to safety immediately."

Colonel Dimetriev frowned. "Could American intelligence have found out about the shipment? Why else would they pick that particular rail siding at that particular time?"

Colonel Trung looked embarrassed. "Yesterday we captured an American *kapitan* who had flown on the raid and questioned him at some length. It was luck."

"Perhaps the Cubans could be of assistance there. They had perfected persuasive questioning to a fine art." Dimetriev smiled. "The Cubans hate the Americans with all their Spanish passion and love it when they can get their hands on one."

Xuan Nha spoke, his voice particularly quiet. "I personally interrogated the American pilot. He's telling the truth."

"The Cubans know their American neighbors well, perhaps better than either you or we. They would like to help."

"Not in this particular case," said Xuan with a firm tone. "The American pilot told the truth. I was quite . . . persuasive."

"Ah, I see," said Dimetriev.

Although Castro had recently offered everything from cigars to sugar and combat troops, the North Vietnamese couldn't accept assistance from the Cubans. Their closest ally, the People's Republic of China, scorned the island regime, claiming they were hopelessly revisionist, a dictatorship with few trappings of true Marxism. In turn, Castro made no secret that he vastly preferred Soviet ideology to that of China. Also, the Cuban economy was maintained only through the Soviet policy of paying them much better than world prices for all the sugar they could produce.

The North Vietnamese leadership worked closely with China, for the PRC was their primary source of political support, weapons, and technical aid. But for the past twenty months, following Alexei Kosygin's visit to Hanoi in February of 1965 offering sophisticated antiaircraft defenses, they had been slowly drawn to the Russians. Hanoi played the part of a maiden infatuated with two suitors but unwilling to choose, and received massive attentions from both, for both stood to gain.

Since Peter the Great the Russians had attempted, in spurts and starts, to build a credible navy. The Soviet admiralty had orgasmic dreams about Vietnam's superb warm-water ports. If Ho Chi Minh could indeed create a homogeneous Vietnam under Hanoi's control, the dream could happen. But the North Vietnamese had to win to make it happen, and they had an Achilles' heel. They were vulnerable to air attack. The Soviets had decided the rewards were worth their most Herculean efforts to help them fend off air attacks.

On the other hand, the Chinese didn't want a loose cannon on deck at their back door, as the Vietnamese historically became when freed from Chinese influence. The People's Republic of China wanted a single, communist Vietnam, but they wanted it to remain under their control, so they shipped huge numbers of arms.

As the giants vied for favor, the North Vietnamese were increasingly forced into a balancing act. Trung, a mere colonel, certainly could not appear to favor either over the other, for the North Vietnamese needed help from both.

They needed small arms, MiG-17's, MiG-21's, the superb guided rocket systems, and the radars—as well as technical advisers for all of these—from the Russians. They needed textiles, vast numbers of artillery pieces, rockets, and F-6's, and MiG-19's manufactured in the People's Republic of China. They needed the Chinese to allow rail shipment of Soviet arms through their country, and to keep Soviet flight training schools open in China for their pilots.

"I will take the Cuban suggestion under advisement," Trung said smoothly. "Of course, I will have to pass it on to my superiors, and you know how slowly governments move."

Dimetriev smiled. "There are certain decisions that should be made."

Colonel Trung used his fallback response. "I am but a soldier."

Xuan Nha was impatient with the political overtones. "Could we discuss the defensive systems?"

With a pointed glance, Trung silently relayed displeasure at Xuan's impatience.

Colonel Dimetriev turned to Nicolaj Gregarian. "*Polkovnik* Trung is commander of ground and air defense troops in sector one, encompassing the entire northern part of the country. *Podpolkovnik* Nha is commander of defenses for the Hanoi area."

"Including antiaircraft artillery?" asked Gregarian, traces of derision apparent in his tone. Russian military planners had decided that artillery was ineffective against modern warplanes traveling at supersonic speeds, so Soviet doctrine relegated AAA to a tertiary role behind interceptors and guided rockets. But for the Soviet propensity to add new weapons while keeping the old ones, there would be no such weapons in their inventory. Many of the guns and artillery radars they supplied to the North Vietnamese were remnants from the Great Patriotic War, supplied by the Americans under their generous lend-lease programs.

"Antiaircraft artillery," retorted Xuan Nha, "has been responsible for the majority of our successes. We shoot down three Americans with artillery for every one with rockets or interceptors."

"I read the reports before I left Moscow. You have done well with what you have, but I will help create a network of rockets, interceptors, and artillery that the Americans *absolutely* cannot penetrate."

Those were words Xuan Nha wished to hear. "A wall of steel," he muttered.

"What is the extent of your area of responsibility, *Podpolkovnik* Nha?"

Xuan nodded tersely to Trung and Dimetriev. "With your concurrence, *kamerades,* I will take *Mayor* Gregarian to our headquarters where I can better brief him."

Gregarian looked interested.

"Of course," said Dimetriev, his diplomatic smile glowing. Colonel Trung also nodded, barely hiding his annoyance.

"I'll ensure," said Xuan Nha, "that the *mayor* is returned in time to prepare for his trip tomorrow."

"Do that," growled Trung.

Colonel Trung

As the two departed, Dimetriev reverted to Vietnamese. "He is all business, your Lieutenant Colonel Nha."

"Yes." Trung wished his subordinate had tolerated at least a few more minutes of social duty rather than leave him alone with the other new Russian advisers. Xuan Nha had irritable traits, and to Trung's mind he placed entirely too much trust in the sophisticated rocket defenses. Trung supposed, however, that he must put up with the man's peculiarities if he was to retain his valuable services.

"Xuan Nha is a man of action," he simplified. He did not add that Nha despised bureaucracies, social affairs, and all *Tay,* including Russians, or that he was pleased to see Gregarian only because he might be a key to obtaining more sophisticated equipment. "He served in the Army of Liberation." The Vietnamese term was *Viet Minh.*

Dimetriev turned to friendly chitchat. "I've heard he was a hero in your great victory at Dien Bien Phu?"

"We served together under General Luc there when Luc was only a major. It was General Van Tien Dung himself who called Xuan Nha the 'Tiger of Dien Bien Phu.'"

Colonel Trung took a small, dark breakfast cake from a tray on the table. He had developed a tolerance for heavy Russian food during his two visits to Moscow to demand and cajole additional weapons. He nibbled at the tasteless cake, reflecting.

Success and heroism at the French fortress still harvested rewards. Gen Van Tien Dung had masterminded the plan and logistics for that brilliant victory. Major Luc had been charged with transporting the artillery, unseen, ninety kilometers along roadways and mountain trails. Captain Trung had selected the placement of the artillery pieces.

Sub-lieutenant Xuan Nha had ensured that no one leaked word to the French. Once he lined up a queue of forty women and shot them all, for there was a rumor that one had leaked intelligence to a French soldier. It had been an effective lesson to others.

Then Xuan Nha had tirelessly motivated hordes of men, women, and children to haul the big guns and heavy ammunition up the steep mountainsides overlooking the French fortress. He executed so many slackers that the barrel of his pistol warped with heat. The human oxen had been too terrified to falter in his presence, and he seemed to be everywhere at once. The guns were placed. Then, as the great barrages on the French runways and barracks began, and human waves of Viet Minh threw themselves upon the French Union Forces below, the oxen continued to haul ammunition up impossible hillsides made slippery by the gory juices of those who had been crushed under the awful weight of falling artillery pieces.

More than 2,000 French had died at Dien Bien Phu, and 10,000 more were taken prisoner. The heart was taken out of the French campaign. The great powers had partitioned the country, and the great war for liberation was ended.

General Dung had been honored as the wizard of Dien Bien Phu, and was now charged with planning the intricate military actions of the second great struggle, this one against the Americans and their puppet Army of the Republic of Vietnam. General Luc commanded the VPAND, and was entrusted with the defense of their country. Colonel Trung was charged to defend Hanoi and Haiphong.

And as they had done at Dien Bien Phu, they regarded Xuan Nha as one they could rely on to make their plans succeed. At Dien Bien Phu they needed him, and he had not faltered. Today he was one of few who understood the technical systems they used to defend the country, and again they needed him. They also looked with favor on Xuan Nha's brilliant wife, Li Binh, who sat at the side of powerful party leaders.

Still, Colonel Trung decided he must speak to Xuan about the lack of patience he'd displayed at the Russian Embassy. They were both warriors and could talk together. He was more fearful of Li Binh, who wielded her considerable power with the subtlety of a poised cobra. He would handle the matter judiciously.

Xuan Nha

Xuan led the Russian major to his staff car, an aging Peugeot left by the French, peering up at the darkening skies as a few drops of rain began to sprinkle. Soon the rain would come in torrents. Sgt Van Ng, with his one eye and scarred face, opened the rear door for them. The patch and twisted scar tissue made the sergeant appear mean, perhaps more so to a *Tay*, for Gregarian eyed him warily as he got in. Xuan smiled, inwardly pleased at the Russian's discomfort.

"Back to the headquarters," Xuan directed. Sgt. Van Ng grinned through his mask of scars.

Xuan turned to Gregarian. "How much do you know about our operations, *Mayor*?" he asked in Russian.

"I was briefed that VPAND is much like our PVO Strany, with radars, interceptors, rocket systems, and antiaircraft artillery."

Xuan raised his hand. "The interceptors operate independently. We work together, but the People's Army Air Force is not part of VPAND."

Gregarian sighed. "Pilots are often difficult to work with."

"We are effective, but our operation could be improved."

"I have ideas that may help. First though, we must get the P-50 long-range radar into a safe position. I feel that with the older early-warning radar that is already operating at your Phu– uh . . ."

"The old P-1 radar is at Phuc Yen airfield, twenty kilometers northwest of here. We have an air regiment there, and they use the P-1 only to control interceptors. That was the way your advisers wanted it."

"But how do you coordinate your defenses if there is no central control?"

"Before each air raid certain areas are assigned to inter- ceptors, others to guided rockets and artillery."

"That is archaic. You should tie the old radar and the new P-50 together with communications lines and control *all* the defenses with them," Gregarian said.

Xuan Nha agreed, but he had not been able to convince his superiors. He said nothing.

They rode through the city with its obvious French influences. Wide boulevards prevailed throughout the northern *quartier*.

The rain came suddenly, pelting against the windshield and running down the side windows in sheets. Sgt. Van Ng slowed to a crawl, for visibility was poor. Thunder boomed in the distance, then a loud crash was heard nearer. After a couple of minutes, the rain diminished to a steady downpour and they picked up speed again.

"Very nice," grunted Gregarian, pointing out to the tree-lined streets. "I saw great damage from bombing when we came from Haiphong last night, but I see none here."

Xuan Nha said, "As long as Hanoi is safe, the people know we are invincible. The Americans help by making sure they *don't* bomb Hanoi."

Gregarian looked perplexed.

"America is a colossus of armed power, but its political leaders are timid. They void their bowels when they think of either you Russians or China entering the war. Their fears are our greatest ally."

Gregarian shook his head in disbelief that the Americans were not trying to bomb Hanoi off the face of the earth.

"My wife is in charge of two important departments in the Ministry for External Affairs, and her people labor relentlessly to ensure that world opinion remains sympathetic to our cause. They pass out truth, but do so very carefully."

"To whom does your wife pass her information?"

"Ahh, but those are her secrets. She lives in a different world than we do, but often her efforts are as effective."

Xuan pointed to a large government building they were passing. "One of the colonial administrative buildings the French erected in 1897. They made Hanoi the capital of all of French Indochina when they realized the people of Laos, Cambodia, and our poorer brothers in the south were accustomed to taking their orders from here. For nearly two thousand years we have approved their governments, punished them when they've erred, and received fair payment for our leadership. Outsiders have tried to change that. The Chinese in ancient times, the French after the Japanese occupation, the Americans now, but always we've regained our position of dominance over Southeast Asia."

"History is with you."

"History and the force of arms. We are the warriors, they are the followers."

Gregarian pointed to hundreds of manholes, six feet apart, that lined the center of the street. "What are those?"

"Air raid shelters. Each can protect an occupant from a bomb landing fifty meters away. General Luc has ordered them placed throughout the northern and central *quartiers*."

"In case the Americans change their minds about bombing?"

"And to show that even if the Americans attack, we will survive. Earlier this year the old people and the children were evacuated to the countryside."

"To protect them?"

"Yes. Ho Chi Minh loves old people and young children."

"I thought Hanoi was the safest place in the country?"

"It is."

"Then you've created a fortress with only able-bodied soldiers inside."

Xuan Nha motioned to the left at a huge expanse of

concrete. "Ba Dinh Square, where victory rallies are held, and that large building beyond is Ba Dinh Hall, where our politburo meets.

A few blocks later they approached two large buildings.

"Headquarters for the Vietnamese People's Army," Xuan Nha said. "Our shrines to military bureaucracy."

The driver turned in at the second massive building, drove slowly through a guarded checkpoint, then proceeded to a rear entrance.

"This building was headquarters for the French Union Forces. When we took over in 1954, in many instances we merely changed the words on the offices from French to Vietnamese. Change the names and the uniforms, and all headquarters are quite similar, don't you think?"

They exited the car and hurried to the protection of the overhang of the lobby entrance.

"My offices are on the fourth floor."

"That seems vulnerable to air attack."

"Perhaps that vulnerability reminds us to do a good job of protecting Hanoi. Come, let us go up and meet my staff. Then we'll go to the basement and I will show you the command center from which we control our defenses."

27/1015L—Takhli RTAFB, Thailand

Mike Ralston

Ralston pushed his way through the crowd in the briefing theater, finally taking a seat between Benny Lewis and Sam Hall.

Benny quietly handed him a flight plan card. He and Mike peered up at the flight lineup displayed on the board, which showed Lewis as Kingfish flight leader. Ralston had moved himself to number three, leading the second element.

Mike had only been at Takhli for two weeks, but he'd quietly measured the men in B-Flight and believed he'd made a good choice. "Sorry about interrupting your day off, Benny. Colonel Mack suggested an unofficial policy change for the flight commanders to select our best pilots to lead the pack six missions. Fair or not, that puts you in the barrel. I'm new in the Thud. A couple weeks from now and I'll be giving you flying lessons." The corners of his lips tugged upward. "But right now I'm in the listening mode. I'd be silly to do otherwise."

He nodded at Colonel Mack, who stood talking to Major Foley, the wing weapons officer. "I think it's a wise move on his part. He's going to be good for the squadron."

Benny agreed. "I've known him for a while. He'll do."

"I never developed much confidence in Colonel Lee. It was too bad, what happened to him, but Colonel Mack knows what he's doing and he puts that feeling across."

Ralston filled in his flight lineup card, with the different pilots' names, aircraft assignments, and codewords for the mission, from the information shown on the various Plexiglas boards in front of the room. He clipped the flight plan and the lineup card to a small board he could secure around his leg when he strapped into the airplane.

They listened to a joke Sam Hall was telling. Sam's Southern drawl and tendency to ridicule himself along with the others in the squadron made his humor special. He knew how to turn bleak occasions into bearable ones. Sam was a large man, very black, from rural Alabama, and he cast aspersion upon all things Northern or citified. He openly and equally disliked Communists, Governor George Wallace, and Northern peaceniks. He was also the ranking flight commander in the 357th squadron, flew a fairly good stick, and had more than a thousand hours flying the Thud.

Mal Stewart, the one they called the Bear, pushed through the group at the door and seated himself nearby. Tall, raw-boned, and tough-looking, he was part Oklahoma Indian. He wore sunglasses, which had become a trademark of sorts, both indoors and out, to briefings, and even in the darkness of the officers' club bar. Probably to cover up hangover eyes, Mike thought wryly. Glenn Phillips, seated in the front row, turned to speak with him and the Bear nodded curtly before assuming a slouching position.

Some of the pilots said the Bear slept through the mission briefings; swore that when you were beside him you could hear faint snoring. He slid low in his seat, fingers laced on his chest, and remained immobile as others milled about, joked, or jotted down flight information.

Ralston glanced about the room. "Look at all these people. Why does it seem so damned lonely up there?"

Thirty-three men were jammed into the small theater to

hear the mission briefing. Here they would receive general target and weather information, as well as any special instructions or new restrictions from higher headquarters. Following the mission briefing, they would break up into smaller groups to discuss flight profiles and tactics. At the mission briefing the senior officer, called the mission commander, ran the show. Afterward, at the individual flight briefings, the flight leaders would be in charge.

The aircrews sat, drinking coffee from paper cups as they told jokes and passed on nuggets of expertise. The same ritual accompanied every mission briefing, held before the morning, afternoon, and occasional evening combat missions. They all waited for the *Execution Word,* a code word designating the target for the strike force, to be passed down from higher headquarters.

Flight and target information for the afternoon mission was posted on the backlit panel:

NOVEMBER 27

Takeoff	Time:	1330L/0630Z
	Altimeter:	30.65"
	Temperature:	36C
	Weather:	Clear/Scattered

Pri Tgt	JCS 21:03	
	Yen Vien Rail Siding/ Loading Facility	
	Air Refueling:	Green Anchor
	Tgt Coord:	21 -07'-50"N
		105 -53'-02"E
	Tgt Alt:	225'
	TOT:	2200Z
	Altimeter:	30.11"
	Weather:	Scattered/Broken
	Defenses:	Medium AAA/SAM
	EXECUTION:	DAYBREAK

Alt Tgt 1	Vinh Ferry Facility (Submerged)	
	Air Refueling:	Blue Anchor Ext.
	Tgt Coord:	18 -41'-22"N
		105 -41'-53"E
	Tgt Alt:	S/L
	TOT:	2145Z
	Altimeter:	30.14"
	Weather:	Scattered
	Defenses:	Light AAA
	EXECUTION:	NIGHTFALL

<u>Alt Tgt 2</u> Suspected Truck Parks
      Air Refueling: Blue Anchor Ext.
      Tgt Coord: Area of 18 -19'N
                       104 -55'E
      Tgt Alt: 1,750' to 2,400'
      TOT: 2125Z to 2155Z
      Altimeter: 30.21"
      WX: Clear/Scattered
      Defenses: Small Arms
      Execution Word: NOONTIME

The mission commander was Lt Col Mack MacLendon, who carried the heavy responsibility for executing the mission as directed. Mike Ralston studied him closer, remembering what he'd heard about the man.

A slender man of medium height with a boyish shock of unruly brown hair, Colonel Mack first struck you as average and unprepossessing. You might overlook him in a crowd unless you noticed the hooded eyes that expressed the quiet determination and awareness of a calculating hunter. Eyes that were alive, brown and green and flecked with yellow glints, and that were said to be of exceptional acuity.

From the front of the room Mack's voice was soft and easy. "Gentlemen, before we begin the formal part of the briefing, let's go over some basics."

He pointed at the illuminated board. "As you can see, the defenses vary for today's options. At Yen Vien, there would be SAMs, triple-A, and maybe a few MiG's from Phuc Yen or Kep. At Vinh, there'd be fifty-seven millimeter triple-A and maybe even a SAM or two. At the parrot's beak, we'd see small-arms fire."

He paused and surveyed the room.

"Let's talk about some rules we should use no matter where we go. In the high-threat areas, we take our losses, and some of those can't be avoided. A bigger complaint I've got is that we're taking too many losses in the low-threat areas. We've lost five aircraft in low-threat areas in the past month to small-arms fire. Why?"

He looked out at the fighter jocks, and they listened because he was one of them. "We're pressing too damn close in the face of small-arms and triple-A fire, that's why. Some of you are flying too low, too slow, and too predictable."

A hand rose amid the group.

Colonel Mack said, "Go ahead."

Redhead Mike Murphy, known for flippancy and his way with females on the ground, and his fastidiousness in the air, proceeded carefully, partly to feel out his new commander.

"I think you're right, sir. We have been pressing too close in the low-threat areas. That's because it's damn hard to see most of the targets we're assigned. If we're weathered out of the first two targets and go to the beak today, we're supposed to go after suspected truck parks."

A disgruntled murmur arose from the jocks. They despised "suspected truck park" missions.

"Well, sir," Murphy continued, "it's hard to see anything along the trails in the jungle, and they hide their trucks damned well. You've got to get down among them to see 'em, and when you do you expose yourself. Even when we get a forward air controller, he's usually flying an O-1 Bird Dog and can't get in close because of the small-arms fire. We still have to press in if we're going to get our bombs on the target."

"Are you sure, Mike?" Colonel Mack asked.

Murphy was openly impressed that Mack already knew his name. "Yes, sir."

"Anyone got a solution? I say *a* solution because you never want to be caught with only one tactic for a situation."

Silence.

"Tell you what. I'll give it a shot. Here's rule one."

Colonel Mack pulled a cardboard sign from the table before him, and held it up in front of the group.

DON'T FLY BELOW 4,500 FEET!

"Back in 1945, I flew P-47 Jugs at Normandy. We saw heavy small-arms and triple-A fire over some of the targets there. One of the novelties around the fighter group was a collection of these cards, with some rules that had been learned the hard way from 1914 to that date. I kept a set, to remind me that some things don't change, like the fighter jock's propensity to ignore teachings of the past. I took them to Korea where we were flying F-84's and we used them. Sure as hell, when I got here a couple weeks ago I found a lot of you guys in need of studying this old card.

"What it means, gentlemen, is that small arms and antiaircraft artillery have great difficulty tracking and hitting a fast, maneuvering target flying above the magic altitude of forty-five hundred feet. Inscribe that altitude in your brain, and fly above it at all times. Try to pull out above that altitude when you deliver bombs. Stay up there even when you're just around small-arms fire."

Mike Murphy spoke up again, grumbling. "You can't see the ten-cent targets they hide in the jungle from forty-five hundred feet."

Colonel Mack said, "I'll agree with that. You can't see them, so try to outsmart them. Don't operate a flight of four big, noisy jets down in the muck with them. Stay up high on one side of the target and send one guy in low from the opposite side. Let him pop over them from behind, get his look-see, and get the hell out of there. Bomb the position he calls over the radio, or maybe get him back up with the rest of of the flight to lead the strike in on the target. When they get wise to that one, try something else."

He looked out and met their eyes. Each pilot knew he genuinely gave a shit about their survival.

"No matter if we go to a high- or a low-threat area, some of the rules are the same. Stay above the small-arms fire, keep your speed and energy level up for maneuvering, and keep moving around so you don't make a fat target. Okay, that's the sermon for today."

An intelligence officer named DeWalt, a skinny second lieutenant with glasses and acne, had entered the room and stood near the doorway. He proceeded to the board then and printed the word DAYBREAK in bold letters with yellow chalk. Colonel Mack looked on with interest, then motioned the lieutenant to take his place at the podium.

DeWalt indicated a large-scale map of North Vietnam. His shrill voice and his attempt to speak with gravity conjured an image of a child trying to imitate an adult.

"We have just received confirmation from Seventh Air Force that this afternoon's target is the Yen Vien railroad siding located immediately north and across the river from the Hanoi restricted area."

The murmuring diminished as the impact sank in. Yen Vien had been prebriefed on earlier occasions but authorization to strike the target had never come. It was very close to Hanoi, and would likely be a tough one.

"Defenses in the target area are considered to be of medium intensity, with several fifty-seven millimeter batteries and possibly as many as three active surface-to-air missile sites within range of the target area."

Phillips's Bear stirred from his slouching position, sat upright, and leaned forward. He then removed the military-issue sunglasses and gazed intently at the map. His eyes were indeed red and swollen, Mike noticed.

Holding the black rubber tip of his pointer at a red X several miles northeast of the rail siding, Lieutenant DeWalt continued. "This SAM site, Lead nineteen, is photo-confirmed to be occupied, as is this one"—he moved the tip—"Lead nine."

He shifted the pointer again. "Another site, Lead one, is also believed to be occupied. It's located here, on the northern edge of the Hanoi restricted area."

He held the pointer on the site for a few more seconds, then moved it in a circle about the rail yard. "Several thirty-seven and fifty-seven-millimeter batteries are located about the perimeter of the rail yard, and their fire is coordinated by a Firecan radar, located somewhere in the vicinity, probably within a couple of miles of the target. Reconnaissance photos and intelligence reports about the area are laid out on the tables next door. They're classified, so don't remove them from the room."

The lieutenant paused, reading from a stack of papers for a moment before looking up at the group.

"Explicit instructions are provided from Headquarters, Air Force regarding this target. They are of such importance that Colonel Parker, the wing commander, had to acknowledge their receipt, and must certify that all of you were properly briefed before takeoff."

The lieutenant's voice was rising in pitch.

"The instructions are to be read to all pilots participating in the mission." He coughed nervously, as if the paper was sacred due to its lofty origin. "All due precautions will be taken to ensure that damage is *only* inflicted upon the railroad siding. No—repeat *no*—damages are to be inflicted upon the city of Hanoi or other targets in the area. To ensure this, no aircraft are to overfly any part of the city of Hanoi."

A few angry growls circulated through the group.

Colonel Mack nodded. "Is that all?"

"Yes, sir."

"Thank you, Lieutenant." He turned to the doorway. "Smiley, it's your turn."

The lieutenant left the podium and was replaced by rotund and jovial Capt Smiley Boye, one of the wing weather officers.

Boye spoke energetically, as if discussing an upcoming football game. "The target area is presently obscured, with towering cumulus clouds extending in a storm line from southern China through the length of North and South Vietnam. Tops of the clouds as high as forty-seven thousand feet, with absolutely no breaks in the clouds."

"Shit," groaned a fighter jock.

"Not typical weather for this time of year," Boye said. "We passed the tail end of the summer monsoon season a couple weeks ago, and should be getting more clear weather, but it's not working out that way. Lately it's been like this in the morning, but clearing in the afternoon. This particular storm is expected to begin to dissipate within the hour, and at your projected time over target you should find scattered cloud conditions."

"What probability is there that it'll clear up enough for us to see the target?" Colonel Mack asked.

The weatherman paused. "The forecasters in Saigon say sixty percent."

"Their track record hasn't been too good lately."

Smiley sighed. "As much as I hate to argue with my brethren weather officers, I must agree that the crystal balls in Saigon have been a bit foggy lately. In their defense, it's nearly impossible to accurately forecast changes right now, but they're doing their best, sir."

"No pilot reports?"

"No PIREP's yet. Recce birds from Udorn will be going into the target area in an hour, but the weather is changing so fast I doubt their report will do you much good."

"I hate to take a herd of airplanes in there if we're not going to be able to see either the defenses or the target."

"I understand, sir, but the Seventh Air Force forecasters are the ones with satellite and classified reporting station information. All we've got to work with here is the net A weather station reporting, the same as civilian airports get. The classified station reports, combined with TIROS satellite data, give them a better, more complete picture. We have to leave the forecasting to them whenever we get into critical situations."

"Thank you, Smiley." Colonel Mack returned to the podium. Smiley Boye stopped at the door to take a wistful look at the men in the room, then abruptly hurried out.

MacLendon mused. "Glenn?"

"Yes, sir?" Phillips answered smartly.

"I want your Wild Weasel flight to stay twenty miles out in front today. Take a close look at the weather and let me know just how bad it is before I commit the rest of the force."

Glenn pursed his lips thoughtfully.

"Benny?"

"Yes, sir?" Benny Lewis leaned forward and listened closely.

Colonel Mack was looking at the lineup on the board. "You're flying flak suppression, so you'll be carrying a full load of CBU-24's."

"Roger, sir."

"I want you to approach with minimum exposure and hit them from north to south. Make one pass and haul ass. No screwing around in the target area after you drop, okay?"

"Yes, sir."

"And don't continue south over Hanoi. Break away shortly after release. That way you'll avoid overflying the restricted area."

"Will do, sir."

"I'm leading the first strike flight. Sam, you're second. Remember that damned restriction."

From beside Mike, Maj Sam Hall drawled, "Aww. Would I try to hurt anyone in Hanoi?"

Laughter.

Colonel Mack walked to the map and studied it closely. He touched his finger on a high knoll on Thud Ridge, the mountain crest that had gotten its nickname when the first F-105's had made strikes in the Hanoi area. "I'm going to pop up over the ridge just north of this rise and swing out over the flatland before attacking from the northeast."

Mack looked over to Lewis. "I'll be right on your tail, Benny. Make a radio call when you start your pop-up for the dive-bomb, and again when you roll in. I'll begin my roll-in about fifteen seconds after your second call. Got it?"

"Yes, sir, I'll call on squadron common when we go into the pop and as we roll in." Squadron common frequency was 357.0 megacycles, the same as their squadron number, easy to remember in the excitement of combat.

"Sam, you go into your dive fifteen seconds after me."

"Yes, sir. I'd like to come in from west of the target and pull off to the northeast."

"Okay, Sam."

Sam continued. "Our flight will regroup and make a quick swing by Kep, if you don't mind." MiG-17's were sometimes based at Kep airfield, forty nautical miles northeast of Hanoi.

Colonel Mack thought for a moment. "I dunno. You'd be out of mutual protection. Your fight'd be all alone there, with no one to call on for help."

Sam Hall said, "And no one to watch."

"You know the rules, Sam. You can't shoot MiG's on the ground."

"I know, but we've gotta go where they are if we want to shoot 'em down. I saw two, three MiG's last time we were in that area, just milling around up there like they had nothing better to do."

"Okay, you can fly over there and give them something to worry about, but watch your fuel. Don't engage if you're low on gas, and sure as hell don't let them drag you into China."

"We'll play it safe, sir."

"Jimbo, you're third on the target. I want your flight on the target fifteen seconds after Sam's flight."

"Roger, sir," responded Jimbo Smith. He was a steady and reliable flight leader.

"And finally you, Mike." Colonel Mack was speaking to Mike Murphy, the redheaded captain who hung around with Jimbo Smith and the Bear.

"Start your pop-up fifteen seconds after Jimbo."

"Yes sir."

"Both of you tail-end-Charlies are going to have to contend with a lot of smoke and dust from the bombs of the first flights. Get your pilots to study offsets from major landmarks that aren't likely to become obscured by the smoke, like the Doumer bridge or a turn in the Red River. Just make goddam good and certain you don't overfly the city in the confusion. And if you aren't sure of your position, don't drop."

Mack scanned the room with a sweeping gaze. "I just got this job and I'd like to keep it for a while."

Murmurs of "yes, sir" filled the room.

"Good. Now, EB-66's? Who's the lead aircraft commander?"

A major stood. "Major Rickert, sir."

"Your two aircraft will be orbiting forty-five miles north of the target area, in a racetrack formation, concentrating on jamming the acquisition radar frequencies and calling out SAM launches. That right?"

"Yes, sir."

Mack glanced at a sheet of paper he held. "Says here that F-4's from Ubon Air Base will rendezvous with you at TACAN channel ninety-seven at fourteen-hundred hours local, oh-seven-hundred zulu time." He indicated the EB-66 aircrews in the corner of the room. "You guys help keep the SAMs off our backs, okay?"

He then swung his gaze back to the fighter jocks. "We've got enough operational ECM jamming pods for three of the four strike flights, and for the flak suppression flight. Sorry Jimbo, not enough pods are working to go around. I picked your flight to go without since you're sort of in the midst of the confusion."

"Don't like the damn things anyway," Jimbo Smith said, echoing the sentiment of many others in the room. "I can't see anything on the radar warning scope when the jamming pod's on, and I like to know when a SAM's coming my way."

Colonel Mack turned to Glenn Phillips. "And what about our Wild Weasels?"

Phillips stood slowly and approached the map. "Just as you directed, we'll fly twenty miles out in front of the strike force to check on the weather. I'll make two radio calls to confirm the weather, one when we reach the Red River, here at the dog pecker"—he pointed to a curl in the river that indeed appeared on the map like its namesake—"and the other one here"—he indicated a point north of Hanoi—"after we've crossed over Thud Ridge. The Bear will be monitoring the defenses, so I'll add any heavy SAM activity to our reports."

Phillips's Bear was contemplating the map. Suddenly he stood up, raised a finger, and jabbed at the defenses marked in red on the big map. He spoke in an irritated baritone rumble.

"Those SAM site locations are bullshit. I checked the photos of the Lead nine SAM site they're talking about this morning, and it's two weeks fuckin' old, so we don't know what to expect from there." He shook his head in disgust. "And Lead nineteen SAM site isn't fuckin' occupied, at least it wasn't yesterday afternoon, because we were near there and took a quick look to check out the photos.

"There's an active SAM site over on the west fuckin' side of the ridge that we reported but isn't shown there. You guys can mark it on your maps about ten miles east of the dog pecker."

He changed the direction of his jabbing finger toward the youthful lieutenant intelligence officer, who was increasingly red-faced.

"I told you all that yesterday at the fuckin' intelligence debriefing. You gotta learn to listen, Lieutenant."

DeWalt mumbled something about lack of confirmation, looked to MacLendon for support, then stared miserably at the map with its red markings.

The finger continued its accusation. "And you're also fucked up if you think the defenses are anything like medium around Hanoi. They're heavier than we've ever fuckin' seen. So much radar activity there yesterday we could hardly believe it."

He emphasized his point by angrily pulling on his sunglasses and slouching back down into his chair, eyes and emotions masked.

The pilots were thoughtful. Phillips's volatile bear was normally quiet during the mission briefing. Whenever he did speak up, whether to question tactics or explain intricate details of enemy triple-A or SAM systems, his degree of agitation was measured by the number of misplaced familiar adjectives in his speech. It was apparent the Bear was less than happy with the target intelligence.

Glenn Phillips flashed his confident smile at the assembled pilots and broke the silence. "If the site west of Thud Ridge has his radar turned on, the Bear will line us up with his electronic gear and we'll make a Shrike radar-homing missile attack. Then I'll go into a climb and fire another Shrike at Lead nine, if its indeed there, presenting a very fat, broadside target to another site we think may be immediately north of the rail siding. I plan to present the SAM battery commander with such an obvious target that he would feel derelict in his duty if he did not come on the air and fire at us."

Glenn erased the existing Lead 19 mark from the board, then drew a new red X at a spot not far north of the target. "That look about right?"

The Bear almost imperceptibly nodded.

"Once he's fired his SAMs, we'll dodge them, roll in from the south so we'll remain clear of the restricted area, and bomb the *real* Yen Vien SAM site."

Phillips looked thoughtfully at the pilots who would be flying as numbers two, three, and four in the Wild Weasel flight, then slowly smiled. "You guys try to hang on, because it's going to be a hell of a ride."

Tiny Bechler glared at Phillips's theatrics.

Mike Ralston knew that Phillips had personally gone to MacLendon and asked for Tiny to be his wingman. It was obvious that Tiny didn't like it.

Mack MacLendon was also looking at Tiny, taking it all in without comment. He shifted his gaze and looked quietly about the room. "Any questions?"

The pilots were silent.

"If not, let's break it up and attend our individual flight briefings. Let's have good radio discipline up there for a change. Stay off Navy common unless you have an emergency."

He was referring to the habit attributed to Navy aviators of using 243.0 megacycles, the radio frequency reserved for emergencies, for routine calls.

The room slowly emptied as the pilots made their way toward smaller rooms for the flight briefings.

27/1120L—People's Army HQ, Hanoi, DRV

Xuan Nha

Xuan Nha and Major Gregarian were in the Army of National Defense's command center in the basement of the headquarters building, hovering over a large table with its glass-covered map of the area. Nha explained the current dispositions of the rocket batteries, easily switching between speaking Russian to Gregarian and Vietnamese to his staff.

"The three rocket batteries of Happiness battalion are presently operational at these fixed locations in the northern suburbs of Hanoi." He pointed to three positions marked on the map. "Happiness one, Happiness two, and . . . Happiness three."

Gregarian asked, "Communications between the sites and the headquarters?"

"The Hanoi batteries use telephone lines as well as radio communications, but all the others use only radio and are not secure, so periodically we change their code names. All except one, which I will explain later.

"Truth battalion protects the southern side of the city. There are presently two permanent firing batteries, and another is being added, which will give us six permanent rocket batteries. Those two battalions are responsible only for the protection of Hanoi. Six batteries, with rocket launchers in each battery."

"Very good," Gregarian said, examining Nha's selection of locations.

"Now for our mobile battalions. Each has one mobile P-2 acquisition radar and three firing batteries, and each battery has one tracking radar and six launchers. The batteries of Steel, Cobra, and Dragon battalions deploy to various prepared locations north of Hanoi. Bamboo, Grass, and Gold are deployed south of the city. They are all relocated every eight to twelve days, unless we think a reconnaissance aircraft has photographed their position. Then, of course, they relocate immediately."

Gregarian looked skeptical. "You move them that often?"

"My men can tear down an entire battery and be ready to move within four hours. That includes defueling the rockets, loading rocket cannisters, launchers, the control van, communications truck, and the radar. We move to the next location, never more than two hours away. There we level the tracking radar and launchers, load and fuel the rockets, string communications wire, put up the camouflage nets and check out all systems in six hours."

Nicolaj stared. "You can meet these times?"

Xuan Nha said, "I insist the batteries make their entire move within twelve hours. If they do not, I replace the battery commander. If it is due to poor leadership, I also replace the battalion commander."

Xuan watched as respect grew in Gregarian's expression. The Soviet army's mobile ground forces took much longer.

"We move them at night or in bad weather, so they cannot be seen by reconnaissance aircraft. A mobile battalion moves only one of its batteries at a time, keeping the other two rocket batteries prepared to fire, protecting each other as well as the site that is moving."

Xuan could tell Gregarian was excited. He was giving him information to report to his headquarters, who would disseminate it to the ground forces command. Rapid mobility was key to the Soviet army's war plans for Europe.

"Much different than I expected," muttered Gregarian.

Xuan went on. "I have one more rocket battalion, consisting of only two batteries, which I keep constantly moving to guard critical shipments, to protect troops concentrations preparing to move south, or to defend targets I believe will be attacked. Like the queen in a game of chess, I move Tiger about in bold strokes. Tiger one and Tiger two batteries have preemption authority on all railways and highways. One day I may tell them to set up on the Da River, far to the northwest, the next week they may be twenty kilometers south on the great Hong River, and perhaps three days later at Phuc Yen airfield, twenty kilometers north."

Nicolaj Gregarian tried to digest it all. "You have the two battalions here at Hanoi, six rocket battalions that move short distances every ten days or so, and this Tiger battalion, which is moved about at random."

"Let me explain the importance we place on defense of the Hanoi area. To date you have sent us systems to equip twenty-five battalions. Eleven batteries have either been destroyed in bombings or accidents, or were cannibalized for parts. Twenty-one battalions remain in the People's Army."

"A large number to defend a country of such modest size," said Gregarian.

"Here in my Hanoi area, we have concentrated half of all the defensive weapons in the country. Most of the remainder is used in the Haiphong area, around the ports of Haiphong, Nam Dinh, and Thanh Hoa. Less than one-tenth of our defenses are located elsewhere. In all of Zone Two, the entire southern region, there are only two rocket battalions and ten medium artillery companies, and half of those are located at Vinh. For the remainder, we provide modest numbers of small arms. Mobile small arms and some thirty-seven millimeter pieces are sent to protect troops and supply routes in Laos, Cambodia, and the south."

"Why don't you provide them with guided rockets and heavy artillery?"

"Priorities. Most of all we must protect the Hanoi area. Next we must protect Haiphong and the northern ports. If we lose those, the war effort is jeopardized. If we lose Dong Hoi, or even Vinh, we only lose people. Even if my request is approved and we receive more rocket systems, most would be deployed here in the north."

Gregarian thought about that for a moment. The Russians felt much the same about Moscow as the North Vietnamese did about Hanoi.

"In my area, we now have nine operational P-2 acquisition radars, twenty-six tracking radars and command vans, one hundred and fifty-six launchers, and some twelve hundred rockets in our inventory. For the seven mobile rocket battalions, we have sixty-seven locations, engineered and ready for use, and each month we add more."

"Impressive," said Gregarian. "That is more than we have in the Moscow district."

"Yes, but we are at war. I wish we had twice as many."

Wraith-thin Major Wu approached them and interrupted. In addition to being chief intelligence officer, Wu was also Xuan's political officer, with direct connections to the Lao Dong party headquarters. Xuan was lucky, for Wu was his wife's favorite nephew and his loyalty to her, and Xuan Nha, was unquestioned.

"Colonel Nha, two reconnaissance aircraft have just completed their camera runs," he announced.

Xuan Nha waited.

Wu pointed at the map table. "Two Voodoos came from the west, flying just beneath the overcast. They crossed the Hong River here, south of Yen Bai, proceeded to the mountains north of us, and made their camera runs here, paralleling the Hong River."

Xuan Nha narrowed his eyes, then ran his own finger along the flight path. "Get Major Nguy," he said to Lt Quang Hanh, his communications officer. The baby-faced lieutenant was seldom far from his side.

"I'm here, Colonel," said Nha's calm and competent executive officer from behind them. He crowded in beside the others to stare at the glass-protected map.

"It is to be a big one," said Major Wu, the intelligence chief. "At least fifty fighters from Thailand, coming in two waves from the two Thunder plane bases." He confidently tapped a pencil on the airfield symbol just across the river from them. "I believe they will attack Gia Lam."

"Perhaps," said Major Nguy, who was less quick to make judgments. "Or perhaps it is the Doumer bridge or the rail yard at Yen Vien."

"The weather?" snapped Nha.

Major Nguy referred to a note. "Gia Lam advises the overcast will begin to lift within the hour. Broken clouds by thirteen-hundred. Scattered clouds by fourteen-hundred."

Xuan held his breath for a moment, calculating, then turned to Quang Hanh. "Alert all rocket battalions to expect an attack in that area. After thirteen-hundred they will be authorized to fire rockets freely at all targets within fifty kilometers north, south, and west of Gia Lam."

The lieutenant said, "Yes, sir."

Xuan turned to Major Nguy. "Colonel Trung is still with the Russians, so alert General Luc's office of the probability of attack at that location. Advise the Gia Lam control tower that flight operations are to be suspended after thirteen-hundred. Then coordinate with Lieutenant Colonel Thao Phong's staff that I have authorized indiscriminate firing of rockets west of Gia Lam after thirteen-hundred."

"That will make him unhappy," Nguy said.

"Just tell him." Thao Phong was one of Xuan Nha's few close friends.

Major Nguy hurried away.

Xuan turned to Gregarian, realizing that he had understood little of the conversation. "*Podpolkovnik* Thao Phong is my counterpart at the air regiment at Phuc Yen airfield," Xuan explained in Russian. "He feels our rockets and artillery just make his pilot's lives more dangerous, and that if we'd go away, his MiG's could take care of the Americans."

Nicolaj concurred. "Pilots are like that."

"Before each attack, we allocate some areas to rockets and artillery, and others to his MiG's. We make him nervous. Phong's pilots fly with their identification transponders turned on, so even if his MiG's stray into our area he believes we can easily sort out the radar returns before we shoot. He can't understand that those things take time and we must react quickly."

"Pilots," Gregarian muttered.

A sergeant rushed over and spoke with Major Wu, who caught Xuan Nha's attention. "No enemy activity at the border yet."

Xuan Nha jabbed his finger at the western border with Laos. "The Americans predictably fly the same route when the target is near Hanoi. We have listening posts in Laos and along our border there, and they relay information by radio, from post to post. That way we have half an hour warning before each attack."

"It will be better when we have the P-50 radar set up in the mountains there."

Xuan agreed. "Yes, if we get the communications system you spoke of, but for now we must use the listening posts. I don't expect the Americans to attack before thirteen-hundred. The afternoon attacks from Thailand are often predictable, normally between thirteen- and fifteen-hundred."

Major Nguy returned, a small grin on his face. "Lieutenant Colonel Phong ordered me to advise you that you must be fornicating with deranged monkeys. He wishes to send patrols to the western border, to engage the American fighters long before they attack."

The VPAAF was infamous for ignoring the requests of the VPAND.

"No western patrols! I am acting for Colonel Trung in his absence, and I forbid them. Tell Phong that his mother indeed begged me to fornicate with her, but I did not wish to contract syphilis. Also tell him his pilots must remain east of the target area after thirteen-hundred if they don't want rockets up their tailpipes."

"Yes, comrade Colonel," said Major Nguy, his smile broadening.

Colonel Trung entered the communications center, just arrived from the reception and still in his dress uniform. Xuan gave him a concise briefing.

"Good," Trung said simply, then pulled Major Wu and his own intelligence officer aside for a quick update on the tactical situation.

Xuan watched them, then turned to Gregarian. "Would you like to see the battle firsthand?"

"What?"

"Tiger one is deployed near Bac Ninh, less than fifty

kilometers from here. We can be there before the attacks begin."

"Yes," the Russian finally said. "I'd like that."

The squat Vietnamese had observed Gregarian's face as the man hesitated. *Perhaps a little fear,* he decided, but the man was no coward. Xuan told Major Nguy to act in his place during his absence, then hurried out of the command center, Gregarian puffing at his heels.

27/1220L—Takhli RTAFB, Thailand

Tiny Bechler

Phillips's briefing for Hawk flight was thorough, and he made it clear that he wanted no surprises once they were airborne. Then he looked hard at Tiny, as if he expected a screw-up, which did little to brighten Tiny's already poor disposition. As soon as the briefing ended, Tiny broke away from the others and walked alone toward the squadron personal equipment shop, wearing a scowl. He intended to stick to Phillips's wing like glue. If Phillips crashed, there would be two holes in the ground. He'd show the prima donna West Pointer what flight discipline was all about.

Phillips and the Bear trudged along up ahead, deep in conversation. *Strange about the Bear and his outburst,* Tiny thought. Something told him, however, that he was probably right. Tiny didn't think much of backseaters in fighters, but Mal Stewart had a good reputation with the squadron pilots.

He saw Benny Lewis standing in front of the vending machines outside the personal equipment shop.

"I missed lunch," Lewis said quietly, showing a candy bar. "Couldn't face another chicken fried steak. That's all they've had for the past week." He guzzled Coke and took a bite from the Butterfingers.

Tiny sympathized as he got his own orange soda and candy bar from the machines. "I had the *chicken flied steak* with *flied lice* on the side. It's all beginning to taste the same."

"I understand why Thais eat rice bugs," said Benny. "They can't cook."

Rice bugs were fat beetles the Thais picked up, inspected closely, and then ate with great relish. Sometimes they would simply bite off the rice bug's head and stuff the body into a pocket to save it for later. It was said the female beetles tasted best. Or maybe it was vice versa.

Tiny skinned the wrapper back on his candy bar. "Sounds like you've got a tough one. Flak suppression can get hairy, and this may be a mean mission."

Benny shrugged. "Some are worse than others." He looked closer at Tiny. "You ever fly in a Weasel flight before?"

"No."

"It won't be a cakewalk, having to fly out in front of the strike force like that. Phillips is damned good, but he's got a hell of a job. Toughest part might be trying to stay up when he starts moving around. When he starts to maneuver hard, your best bet is to fall into trail behind him and stay there."

Tiny's eyes smoldered with anger as he thought of Phillips commandeering him. *Fucking prima donna, no good, son of a bitch, bastard.* Tiny's stomach was turning sour; the junk food didn't help. He refused to yield to physical ailment and bit into the candy bar.

His mind switched tracks. "Sometimes I wonder why we put up with this crap."

"What do you mean?"

"Why don't we just ignore the frag orders and go in and win the war? Hit the MiG's on the ground, bomb the shit outta the ships bringing in the supplies, hit the dikes and flood the farms, and take out all the damn trucks lined up in Hanoi. Then maybe even take out Hanoi and Haiphong. How long you think they'd last before they started to cooperate?"

"Not long."

"Then why don't we do it? Ignore the bastards in Washington and just do it?"

Benny eyed him. "George and the boys didn't want it that way."

"George?"

"George Washington. The guys in civvies tell the guys in the flying suits what the hell to do. That's the way it is. Philosophy later, Tiny. Time now to gird the loins for battle."

Tiny took another bite of candy and watched Benny go into the personal equipment shop. He finished the soda and followed, his indigestion and disposition getting worse.

The pilots kept their parachutes stowed on individual racks along with their combat vests, g-suits, and helmets. Tiny

wore a a size XL–T (extra large–tall) in everything made of
cloth, and his eight hat size mandated an extra-large helmet.
He looked over his equipment to ensure it was in order, then
stopped as he saw the vest.

"Sarge!" he roared.

Staff Sgt Sal Perez, NCOIC of the shop, hurried to Tiny's
rack.

"Yes, sir."

"What the hell is this shit?" Tiny held up the new vest
made of mesh fabric. His old one had been made of canvas. He
had specifically told the sergeant that he did not wish to change
to the new material.

"Directive out of Seventh Air Force Headquarters, sir. All
the vests had to be changed to mesh."

Tiny's eyes were narrow and signaled danger. "Where's
my old one?"

"Thrown away, sir," mumbled Perez, "as they directed."

Tiny glared at the sergeant as he tried on the vest. It fit
well. He checked the contents. Two survival radios were
snapped into special pockets stitched into the fabric, as well as
two baby bottles filled with water, a holster for his .38 Special,
Combat Masterpiece–issue revolver, a spare ammunition
pouch, a small survival kit with compass, mirror, and essentials, and a first aid kit.

"It's all there," the sergeant said in his matter-of-fact
tone. Sergeant Perez took pride in his job.

"Assholes," grumbled Tiny. Bureaucracies at headquarters, Perez, why couldn't they leave well enough alone.

He checked that he had his dog tags and that they were
taped so they wouldn't make noise if he found himself on the
ground trying to quietly evade a bunch of gomers. He patted
the right chest pocket of his flying suit to ensure the packet
with his Geneva convention ID card was there. He placed his
wallet, most of his folding money, and his pocket change into
the cubbyhole marked BECHLER. Personal belongings stayed
behind, for they might be useful to the enemy if you were shot
down. Finally he picked his revolver from the pistol rack,
swung out the cylinder, and peered inside.

"Goddammit!" he exploded.

Perez had been waiting for the outburst.

"What's wrong, sir?" he asked patiently.

"There's only five bullets in here. Every damn time I

check my gun out, it's only got five bullets in it. It's a six-shooter and a six-shooter holds six bullets. What if there's six goddam gomers between me and getting rescued? You want me to get fucking captured because I've got only five bullets and there's six gomers?"

"No, sir," said the sergeant. "It's just that there's a regulation that says we load five bullets, with an empty chamber under the firing pin."

"Shit." Tiny pulled a bullet from a pouch in the vest, pushed it into the empty chamber, and snapped the cylinder back into place. Another lieutenant, an Academy classmate who was flying in Benny Lewis's flight, whispered for him to lighten up on Perez.

Tiny glared straight ahead, ignoring him as he continued to prepare for the flight. He zipped on the g-suit and vest, slung the parachute over his shoulders, then carried the helmet to the oxygen stand and gave the mask a thorough pressure check. Finding nothing further to bitch about, he stalked out to the waiting crew van.

The vehicle was stuffed with pilots waiting to be driven to their airplanes. It was hot, and the inside of the van smelled like a football locker room at halftime.

As luck would have it, Glenn Phillips and his bear were in the van and Tiny had to endure a lecture on how Phillips liked to see all the canopies in the flight raised and lowered at precisely the same time. Tiny mumbled his concurrence before escaping when the driver finally stopped at his aircraft.

The sounds and smells of the flight line engulfed him. Acrid smells of kerosene, the basic ingredient of jet fuel, and of hydraulic fluid. Shouts from shirtless, sun-bronzed load crews as they maneuvered bomb racks and missiles under pylons; loud banter between mechanics and crew chiefs; the shrieking of engine start-carts and the roar of jet engines revving in the distance.

As the van drove away, Tiny Bechler was met by the crew chief of his F-105D. They walked around the big fighter, checking its general appearance, the crew chief pointing out the weapons load and the minor maintenance discrepancies noted on the previous mission.

Tiny stopped suddenly and a smile flickered, then grew on his face. He stood back, looking up, and shook his head in wonder.

"Hello, beautiful," he muttered. "I've missed you."

CHAPTER THREE

Sunday, November 27th—1230 Local, Takhli RTAFB, Thailand

Benny Lewis

Benny watched as the last of the heavily laden KC-135 Stratotankers rolled down the runway, rotated, and took off. Thermal waves rising from the hot runway blurred his vision, distorting the big airplane's image as it diminished in the distance.

He watched with interest as the first element of the flight in front of him, Hawk, led by Phillips and his bear and carrying heavy weapons loads, took the active runway. They ran up their engines, then Phillips released his brakes and began rolling. His wingman followed after five seconds of spacing interval. He seemed to rumble down the runway for an eternity. *Oh, you ground-loving whore,* Benny thought. The first aircraft, then the second, rotated their noses skyward and after another long pause began to fly. The next two aircraft were already chasing them down the long runway.

"Kingfish, you're cleared onto the active," radioed the tower operator.

Benny nodded to his wingman, then pushed the canopy lever forward. The four canopies came down in ragged unison. The heat in the cockpit became stifling and would remain so until the engine was revved enough that the airflow cooled things. He pressed the bayonet connector of his oxygen mask into its receptacle at the side of his helmet, tugged at the straps at the sides of the mask to pull it taut, and began breathing a mixture of oxygen and ambient air. He taxied to the left side of the runway, stopped, and watched as his lieutenant wingman

70

rolled into position beside him. He pushed the throttle forward to check the engine at full military power. Oil pressure and engine temperature were normal. Benny pulled his throttle back to idle.

"Kingfish, you are cleared for takeoff."

Benny released his feet from the brakes and smoothly pushed the throttle forward. He was rolling. His wingman would follow in five seconds.

He pushed the throttle outboard, then after a long two-second count, felt the afterburner kick him in the ass. Three seconds later he felt a second boost as water was injected into the engine.

The huge jet emitted a deep-throated roar as he accelerated down the runway; in the heat of the afternoon it seemed he would never reach flying speed. *World's fastest tricycle,* he thought. Finally he felt it, the familiar sensation that told his body that the aircraft had overcome the bonds of weight and gravity and was capable of flight.

Benny rotated the aircraft's needle nose upward, still in afterburner and rolling on the main gear at 190 nautical miles per hour. Finally the main gear became unglued from the runway and he was airborne. He immediately raised the landing gear and flaps, and experienced a rush of excitement as the aircraft continued to accelerate and climb.

He changed to departure control frequency, checked in, and found the controller in a conversational mood.

"Good afternoon, Kingfish. Climb and maintain five thousand feet until three miles from the end of the runway, then turn left to a heading of oh-one-fiver and climb to twelve thousand feet. Contact Brigham on prebriefed frequency."

Benny keyed his mike. *"Kingfish copies."*

"Good hunting, Kingfish."

Benny pulled the throttle to the right, out of burner, to allow the rest of his flight to catch up.

He had started the left turn to fifteen degrees heading, climbing toward the refueling rendezvous point called "Green Anchor." He turned in his seat, first to his right to confirm that his wingman was tucked into position, then to his left, looking back toward the field. Mike Ralston and his wingman were airborne and coming into position too fast. Then he was gratified to see the silver petals of Ralston's speed brakes open at the rear of the big jet engine. After a few seconds Ralston retracted his speed brakes. He had to tap his afterburner once to reach cospeed, then smoothly pulled into position on Benny's left wing.

Using afterburner wasted fuel, but Ralston had joined up aggressively and that was good. Benny looked them over, a mother hen checking her chicks.

"Kingfish, check in," he called, requesting a radio check from each flight member.

"Two!"

"Three!"

"Four!"

The responses were immediately and crisply given. All radios were in working order.

As the flight climbed through 6,000 feet, steady on the correct heading, Benny made his next call. *"Kingfish, after-burners,"* he said slowly, *"now!"* and stroked his own throttle outboard into the A/B position.

The others followed, their afterburners leaving a smoky path. The rate-of-climb needle leaped and they soared upward like great, primeval birds.

Benny waited for a long moment, savoring the headiness of flight. Finally he prepared to change radio frequencies to get directions to their tanker from Brigham, the ground radar site.

"Kingfish, go button four."

"Two!"

"Three!"

"Four!"

He could tell from the chorus of voices that they shared his exhilaration.

He depressed the radio button, waiting for the radio to electronically tune to Brigham's frequency. A tanker, Green 31, was calling on the frequency, advising he was on station. Smooth going thus far.

"Check in, Kingfish," he radioed.

"Two!"

"Three!"

"Four!"

"Green 31, this is Kingfish. We are passing through flight level one-six-zero, and will rendezvous on time. Noses are cold."

He had just advised the tanker that the fighters were at 6,000 feet and climbing, that they would be at the Green

Anchor coordinates on time, and that their MASTER ARM–
WEAPONS switches were in "off" position, which effectively
safed all the weapons. The tanker crews were most concerned
about forward-firing ordnance like rockets, missiles, and the
Gatling gun. An error could be disastrous for the flying gas
station.

The refueling went well, though number four had trouble
steadying down and had to make three attempts before getting
connected for his fuel transfer. They pulled back from the
tanker at the drop-off point on time, with all fighters topped
off. Ralston's refueling went smooth as glass. Mike had been
right: It would not be long before he would be hard to beat.

They were well out over the flatlands of Laos. The Plains
des Jars lay to the right, a barren and brownish-purple high
desert that had served as a major battleground just the year
before. Two of Benny's friends had been shot down there in
Thuds deployed from Japan. One had been captured and
dragged into a village, where he'd been spread-eagled and
hacked into pieces by the Communist Pathet Lao as his friends
flew overhead in full view. The fate of the other pilot was still
unknown.

The tanker made a long, sweeping left turn, back toward
the safety of Thailand. *"Drop a bomb for us, Kingfish,"* the
tanker pilot called.

*"Ah roger, Green Anchor 31. Thanks for the gas. King-
fish, let's go squadron common frequency,"* called Benny.

The flight checked in on 357.0.

Long minutes of idleness passed, the flight maintaining
radio silence as they grew closer to the combat arena. It was a
very private time, time for the brain to adjust to the imminence
of danger, to mull over the details of the mission. Time for
Benny to mutter a short prayer for Bets and the kids. He never
pressed his luck by asking for intervention for himself. He had
chosen his lot. They were the innocents.

Below, the ominous, purple plain turned to green grass-
land and rolling hills. Flat-topped mesas popped up occasionally, green versions of the brown ones Benny remembered in
the American Southwest.

Ten minutes before crossing into North Vietnam, Benny
heard the Bear calling on the radio, announcing that the Weasel
flight was passing over the channel 97 TACAN navigation
station.

"Hawk flight is over the checkpoint."

Channel 97 was located on one of the flattop mesas. The critical outpost was manned by tough Central Intelligence Agency contractors, Laotian tribesmen who were often surrounded by very unfriendly Communist troops. They were resupplied by Air America C-130 airdrops and protected by Air America T-28 aircraft.

Benny monitored his TACAN distance-measuring equipment. They were twenty-three miles behind Hawk flight. *Not bad,* he thought. He nudged his throttle forward until he was flying at 460 knots calibrated airspeed.

Two minutes and thirty-five seconds after Hawk's call, Benny passed over the TACAN station which translated into the twenty nautical mile separation Colonel Mack desired.

"Kingfish is at the checkpoint," he called, his voice low and calm.

Back and to his left he could see another flight of Thuds. Falcon, Colonel Mack's flight. He craned his neck back and could see the other two flights of F-105's.

Falcon, Swift, Crane, and Eagle flights called in rapid succession as they passed over the checkpoint.

"Hello Mister Ho," he muttered. They were in North Vietnamese airspace.

"Green 'em up, Kingfish. Let's go to Guns–Air," Benny called, pushing up his throttle. He'd reminded the pilots in his flight to check the positions of their weapons switches, to select and arm the M-61 Gatling gun, and to prepare the gunsight for possible MiG engagements.

Kingfish flight acknowledged.

Towering cumulus clouds lay to the north and south of their flight path; far ahead they were clumped close together. Poets enjoy the romantic beauty of plump, rounded clouds. Pilots do not, for cumulus clouds spell thunderstorm and can spit out hailstones the size of baseballs. These can either be ingested and cause a jet engine to flame out or simply beat the aircraft to pieces. A cloud in which a mountain is hidden is appropriately called a "hard cloud." Combat pilots do not like clouds because they limit visibility and hide such things as surface-to-air missiles and MiG's.

Benny looked with increasing apprehension at bank after bank of cumulus clouds that lay in their path.

The large, mountainous, sparsely populated area of North

Vietnam that stretched from the Laotian border to the Red River was designated as pack five, which they had to cross to get to the pack six targets. In the westernmost part of pack five lay the village and airport of the infamous Dien Bien Phu. The Thud pilots called it "Dee Bee Pee." Sixty-five miles east-south-east of Dee Bee Pee was Na San, another small town and airfield built by the French.

The F-105's passed six miles south of Na San, and they could see the badly cratered runway, made unusable by earlier bombing raids.

Dense teak forests grew in all directions, covering steep mountainsides. Periodically they flew past karsts—barren, jagged sandstone hills honeycombed with caves. The rugged terrain and dense jungle hosted few visible villages, although they were briefed that tribes inhabited clusters of straw huts there. Tigers and jungle bears roamed the areas over which they flew, cobras and pythons slithered, and monkeys and exotic birds inhabited the trees. Now and then they passed over valleys with cleared farmland, or small plantations with rubber trees planted in neat rows. From one farm, Benny saw muzzle flashes, perhaps from a gutsy farmer who resented the noisy intrusion. *A shotgun?* he wondered. The fighters were passing more than two miles over the farmer's head.

He checked to ensure the radar warning equipment was indeed turned on, since it had thus far been silent.

He searched for Phillips and his Hawk flight on his radar. He finally saw a momentary blip at twenty-two miles, but the radar refused to lock on.

As they grew closer to the Red River, Benny's adrenaline began to pump faster. He methodically focused his eyes at varying distances in the sky around the aircraft, down at the ground, then inside the cockpit for a quick sweep of the tapes and gauges. It was a regimen he practiced, training his eyes to wander in that pattern.

Look for MiG's and friendly aircraft for a mental count of ten, a count of two for ground targets, a count of three for the cockpit. Make each observation count by taking your time. Keep your head moving, eyes slowly sweeping, and don't stare unless there's something to stare at.

In the sky, look for motion and shapes and glints of sunlight off aluminum and canopies. On the ground, observe the terrain and features you are passing over. Look for landmarks, drifting smoke, and oddities. In the cockpit look at the flight instruments by searching for exception, ensuring things are as safe and normal as you want them.

For all three regimes of vision, look for what's wrong, and don't waste time with the things that are right.

Benny's Doppler navigation system showed twenty-four miles to the turn-point at the Red River when Phillips made his radio call.

"Falcon lead, Hawk is at the dog pecker. We have about five-eighths cloud coverage. One big cumulus cloud is just to the south of the turn-point, so cross the Red River five or six miles north of the planned route."

Colonel Mack responded quickly. *"This is Falcon, Hawk. Can you tell anything about the target area weather yet?"*

"Not yet. There's a . . . Hawk flight, we have a valid SAM launch at our three o'clock!"

"I've got a visual on the SAM!" The caller did not identify himself, but his voice trembled with emotion.

Phillips again. *"Hawks, prepare for a SAM break."*

"The SAM is getting close!" The pilot making the call still did not identify himself.

Phillips again, irritation in his voice. *"Okay, Hawks. Ready . . . ready . . . break!"*

The radio was silent for a moment.

Phillips came back on the radio, grunting under the strain of heavy g-forces as he called back to the strike force. *"Gentlemen, there's a SAM site right in the area we predicted, just west of the ridge. You're going to be in his range when you cross the valley and as you approach the ridge. We're going to try to get a missile off at him."* Harsh breathing sounds over the radio. *"Damn! He's turned his radar off. Falcon, watch out for him when you come by."*

"Roger, Hawk lead," said Colonel Mack.

Benny visually checked that his flight was in proper formation as they crossed the Red River five miles north of course.

A chatter erupted on the radar warning equipment. A three-ringer strobe denoted a strong tracking signal from a Firecan, the radar used with antiaircraft artillery.

"Kingfish, expect flak. We've got a tracking Firecan." Benny saw flashes of light a few miles ahead on the ground. *"Keep it moving, Kingfish,"* he called.

His pilots were weaving and turning their fighters in random patterns as they began to cross the pancake-flat valley. Several symmetrical patterns of dark flak bursts erupted around the flight. Patterns of fours and sixes.

"Kingfish, let's turn on our music," said Benny.

The flight responded, advising that their ECM jamming pods were on. A yellow fault light told Benny that his own pod was not working. He would receive no help from that source.

He heard the rattler sound and saw the flickering strobe on the radar warning equipment. It as weak, a one-ringer. *"We've got SAM activity, Kingfish,"* said Benny.

"Eagle flight, the SAM's tracking us. We've got a launch, babes." It was Mike Murphy.

"Eagles, I've got a good visual on two missiles." Again, Murphy's voice. *"Let's wait, babes. Let's wait."* Mike was calm, talking to his flight, making them wait until the missiles were too close to respond to their maneuver.

"Let's take it down, Eagles." Murphy said, his voice rising.

Benny strained, looking back to get a visual sighting on the missiles. He saw two aircraft from Eagle flight diving toward the ground in their evasive maneuvers.

"Keep your energy up, Eagles," called Murphy, telling his flight to keep their throttles pushed forward. *"We're clear of the SAMs, but look out for flak."*

A string of three brilliant orange and black explosions went off harmlessly behind and left of Kingfish flight. The SAMs had missed their targets.

But the flak did not.

"Shit," came a lonesome call over the radio.

"Weeep, weeep, weeep, weeep." The sound told them that a parachute had opened, activating its emergency beeper on the emergency Guard channel.

"Eagle three is down!" called Murphy over the air.

Eagle three was Tommy Larkins, one of the old heads.

Colonel Mack's voice. *"This is Falcon lead. We can't help him here. Mark his position and press on, Eagle."*

"Weeep, weeep, weeep, weeep . . ." The sound of the emergency beacon was shrill and haunting.

"This is Eagle four. I think I see the chute."

"Join back in formation, four," said Murphy.

"Weeep, weeep, weeep, weeep, weeep . . ."

Phillips's radio call was faint, difficult to hear over the sound of the emergency beeper. *"Hawk flight, missiles away."* Benny assumed Phillips was firing at one of the Hanoi SAM sites.

Then, *"Hawk lead, we got a MiG at our seven o'clock, close! Break left!"* Tiny Bechler's voice sounded guttural as he pulled g's.

"Weeep, weeep, weeep, weeep, weeep . . ."

Colonel Mack's voice on the Guard channel. *"Eagle three, this is Falcon lead. If you can read me, turn off your beeper."*

"Weeep, weeep." The beeper shut off. The sudden quiet on the radio was almost as unnerving as the racket had been.

Another SAM radar was swinging its tracking beam through the sky, this one from the target area. The strobe on Benny's equipment went from one to two, then to three rings, pointing toward his eleven o'clock position. The radar receiver chattered like a rattlesnake. The SAM radar was tracking his flight.

"Kingfish, let's be on the lookout for SAMs, eleven o'clock," said Benny, trying hard to keep his voice even.

"This is Kingfish three. I've got a steady SAM launch light."

The SAMs were targeted on Mike Ralston!

In the distance Benny saw a missile, tiny in perspective, tail aglow against the dark. *"I've got a visual on the SAM, Mike. It's at your twelve o'clock."*

"Roger, Kingfish lead. I don't see it." Ralston's voice, while excited, was not panicked. *Good man,* Benny thought.

"Kingfish three, go afterburner and get your energy level up, and turn left about forty-five degrees. Don't break until it gets closer."

"Three."

Benny felt his admiration for Ralston grow as his instructions were quickly followed. *"You'll be pulling sharply up and toward the missiles, Kingfish three."*

A second missile appeared in the distant gloom, then yet another, all with that bead of fire at their tails.

"I still don't see the SAMs, lead," radioed Ralston. *"You call it."*

"Prepare to maneuver, three. You'll be breaking up and to your right in a few seconds," called Benny.

"Roger, Kingfish lead." Ralston rolled his aircraft to the

right, still in afterburner, nose slightly down in a shallow dive to pick up airspeed.

"That's it," whispered Benny. "Build up your energy for the maneuver." He was staring at the SAMs.

One by one the SAMs' booster sections dropped away, still trailing fire. The liquid-fueled sustainer rockets ignited and the three SAMs lurched forward, propelled to incredible speeds in excess of Mach three, all flying in perfectly symmetrical echelon.

They were closing fast on Ralston. It was time!

"Weeep, weeep, weeep, weeep . . ."

"Break now, three!"

"Weeep, weeep, weeep . . ."

An emergency beeper had been turned on at the critical instant, masking Benny's radio call.

Ralston had rolled his aircraft over just a bit more, but he was not maneuvering.

"Weeep, weeep, weeep, weeep . . ."

"Kingfish three, break!" shouted Benny into the mike.

"Weeep, weeep, weeep, weeep . . ."

Mike Ralston either heard him or saw the missiles at the last moment, for the nose of his aircraft started upward, but not nearly in time. The first missile detonated less than a hundred feet from the big fighter. The edge of the explosion scarcely touched the Thud but thousands of fragments showered through the fighter's fuselage.

The aircraft was still flying.

"Weeep, weeep, weeep, weeep . . ." The lonesome beeper continued.

The second missile copied the flight path of the first, but failed to detonate until it was beyond Ralston. The third SAM exploded closer yet to Kingfish three, bright orange momentarily enveloping the aircraft. Again, Benny knew the shards of metal had torn through the aircraft, shredding metal and flesh.

"Weeep, weeep, weeep." The beeper was again turned off. Benny watched Ralston's airplane continue to soar.

"Kingfish three," he called in a leaden tone, knowing Ralston was dead.

Phillips's voice sounded over the radio. *"Falcon lead, this is Hawk. Target area visibility is clear. There are clouds to the north and south, but the target is clear."*

"Roger, Hawk. Did the rest of you get that transmission?"

"Swift flight reads loud and clear," replied Sam Hall.

"Crane lead copies," Jimbo Smith said.

"Eagle reads you," said Mike Murphy.

Benny watched Ralston's aircraft as it began to nose over.

"Kingfish three?" he called once more.

The Thunderchief, containing the body of Maj. Mike Ralston, slowly nosed over and plummeted earthward.

"Kingfish lead, this is Falcon lead. Did you copy Hawk's radio transmission?" It was Colonel Mack's voice.

Benny's voice wavered, *"Repeat for Kingfish."*

"Weather over the target area is acceptable. The mission is go."

Benny blew out a long breath as he watched Kingfish three smash into a knoll at the base of Thud Ridge.

"Roger, sir. Understand it's a go," he finally answered.

Benny's left hand trembled on the throttle. "Fuck!" he muttered.

"What's your position, Kingfish four?" he asked of Ralston's wingman.

"I'm at your nine o'clock and have you in sight."

"Come up on my left, four. We'll start our climb in about twenty seconds."

Benny tried to get the sight of Ralston's Thud out of his mind. *Jesus,* he thought. *The damned airplane just kept flying like nothing was wrong. Like a ghost was flying it.*

He crossed the ridge at the peak he had preselected.

"Kingfish, we're at the offset point." He selected afterburner and started his climb. *"Kingfish lead is going into the pop-up."*

"Two."

"Four."

The three fighters climbed toward their roll-in altitude.

"Kingfish lead is through ten thousand feet," he called.

He could see the rail siding clearly, beyond the foothills and to his right. *"Target is in sight,"* he called. *"I can see fifteen or twenty railcars on the siding."*

"SAMs!" called someone in the flight, for there was suddenly a three-ring rattlesnake signal accompanied by a squeal and a bright LAUNCH light.

He scanned, saw smoke and dust from missile firings, then saw the missiles. *"We've got SAMs at three o'clock, Kingfish,"* Benny called.

"Hawk flight, go to trail formation," Phillips cried out. *"I've got a visual on the site and we're going in for a bomb delivery."*

The SAM boosters were dropping off. The sustainers propelled the missiles sharply forward, toward Benny's Kingfish flight.

Benny clenched his teeth. *"Kingfish is approaching twelve thousand feet. Get ready, Kingfish."*

"Two."

"Four."

Benny rolled his aircraft sharply over and into a forty-five-degree dive-bomb. It was unlikely the SAMs would be able to maneuver with him during the delivery, but he yanked the stick abruptly to the left, then to the right to add to the tracking problem of the SAM operators.

"Kingfish flight's in!" he announced.

Benny searched the ground for muzzle flashes. That proved to be an easy task, for the earth below was winking brightly as the big guns fired at his flight. *"The guns are on all sides of the target, Kingfish. Let's release high for maximum coverage."*

The flak became intense, scores of black bursts flashing and blossoming about the flight. He adjusted his dive angle slightly to concentrate on the area immediately north of the target, the source of the majority of flashes. *"Kingfish lead is taking the north side,"* he called.

He pickled at 8,000 feet, then felt a slight jar as the four CBU-24's were released. The clamshell shapes would spin through the air, then open and spew out hundreds of grenade-like cluster bomblets. He began his pullout.

"Kingfish, let's pull off to the southeast," he told the flight.

"Break it off, Hawks! We've got multiple SAM launches from two sites. We'll be going down and left," Phillips's voice said.

"Falcon is into the dive," said Colonel Mack.

"Falcon lead, they're shooting like hell down there."

"They're supposed to shoot down there," quipped Colonel Mack.

Red streaks rose in crazy sheets, trying to track Benny's Thud.

"Swift is rollin' in," Sam Hall drawled a few seconds later, his voice steady.

Benny was clear of the target, climbing eastward through intense clusters of flak, when his aircraft bucked wildly. He was hit! He checked. No emergency lights, all instruments seemed normal, and he was still climbing. He rolled his aircraft to the right, looking back at the target. Sparkles danced about the north side of the rail yard, his CBUs detonating. More sparkles to the east, then to the west sides of the target as those of his wingmen struck the ground. He rolled and jinked left.

Falcon flight's bombs impacted into the railcars on the side of the railroad siding nearest the loading ramps. The heavy cars were tossed like toys.

"Crane flight is in," called Jimbo Smith.

A Firecan triple-A radar rattled and showed two rings. Benny ignored it, banked, and looked left, then saw a Thud drawing closer. Kingfish four was joining up.

"Eagle flight is rolling in." The voice was Mike Murphy's.

"Swift four is hit!" was followed by a hiss of static.

"Four, dump your bombs and pull out." Sam's Southern drawl became more noticeable in tense situations. He was answered by the loud hiss.

"This is Swift two. I just saw two MiG-17's east of the target area."

"Falcon lead is off to the west," Colonel Mack radioed. *"Swift two, what's the position on the MiG's?"*

Swift two's transmission was garbled due to the g-forces of his pullout.

"Swift lead is off the target to the east," called Sam Hall. *"I got Swift four in sight, and I'll join up with him. You hear that, four?"*

Static answered him. Swift four could receive but not transmit on his radio.

"You hang in there, four. They don't make 'em mean enough to take on both of us."

Smith called, *"Crane lead is off the target to the north."*

Benny worried about the remnants of his own flight. He looked hard, but could only see number four, now flying formation on his left wing.

"Kingfish two, say your position."

"Kingfish two's at your six o'clock, lead. I'm in trail."

"Crane lead is off the target to the north," Jimbo Smith called.

"Kingfish lead, we've got a MiG at our eight o'clock, low!"

Benny jerked his head to his left, and scanned the sky beneath them, and finally saw a MiG-17, wing up and in a slow turn. It was at their nine o'clock, traveling toward their eleven o'clock and Kep airfield. The MiG was less than three miles distant.

"Set up for Guns–Air, Kingfish," He double-checked his own WEAPONS SELECT switch, confirming it was in the proper position. The Gatling gun should be ready and the sight preset. He continued his hard turn to cut off the MiG, and wished to hell he was carrying AIM-9 heat-seeking missiles. Headquarters picked their ordnance loads and often gave air-to-air missiles only to the F-4 units.

"Let's get rid of the tanks, Kingfish." He jettisoned the external fuel tanks hanging beneath his inboard pylons. The aircraft was cleaned up for battle, without drag resistance from fuel tanks or bombs.

"Watch out for the second MiG, Kingfish lead," advised Colonel Mack.

"Eagle lead is off the target. Let's join up over the ridge west of the target, Eagles."

Benny was turning to keep the MiG at his eleven o'clock position. *"Get up on the right wing, Kingfish two. I want a good lookout. Watch our rear quadrant."*

"Roger, lead."

"Kingfish four," Benny called, *"keep a good visual on our three to six o'clock, and don't let the second MiG sneak up from down low."*

"Four!" came the immediate response.

"Kingfish, let's go into burner for a count of five." Benny held his throttle outboard until the afterburner kicked in. After five seconds of boost he pulled the throttle out of the A/B detent, his eyes fixed on the MiG-17. He scanned the sky momentarily, then glued back onto the MiG.

Benny keyed the radio. *"Kingfish two, four? Still with me?"*

"Two."

"Four."

He was closing on an intercept point with the MiG. The

radar refused to show range-to-target, and the MiG was beginning to jink and dive to add to the tracking problem. He judged the distance to be 4,000 feet and slowly closing. He continued on the intercept path.

"Lead, Kingfish four. I've got a visual on the second MiG. He's at four o'clock, coming in."

"Range?" asked Benny, holding his course.

"Five or six thousand feet and closing."

"Keep him in view. Tell me if you see a missile flash."

"I'd like to engage him, lead."

"Negative. Go burner, Kingfish."

He pointed the Thud directly at the MiG's position, then checked that the radar was on and caged at boresight to get accurate range for the attack. He was in burner again and the MiG loomed closer. He got his range readout: 1,200 feet and closing.

His range bar read 800 feet when he depressed the trigger and heard the gun growl. He led a bit at first, then walked the firehose of 20mm rounds down the length of the fuselage. The MiG shed chunks. A flash at the left-wing root of the MiG. A belch of smoke, then fire engulfed the aft fuselage of the silver aircraft. Benny pressed the trigger to a half-detent so the gun camera would capture the kill on film. Closing too fast! He swung up and left, then reversed back to watch.

The MiG pilot bailed out; his chute opened before the silver plane nosed over into its final dive. Benny felt a rush of exultation as he came out of afterburner. He searched the sky for a moment before getting a position on his two wingmen, several hundred feet back on either side.

"You still got the other MiG in sight, Kingfish four?"

"Roger, lead. He dropped back when we went into burner. He's at four o'clock, about two miles out now, turning east."

"You've got the lead, four." Kingfish four, a lieutenant who had never led a flight in peacetime—and certainly never in combat—turned hard to his right. It was Benny's practice to place the pilot with the best visual sighting into the lead during the initial maneuvering. He'd take lead back once they were established on the attack.

Benny's aircraft yawed violently, crabbing sideways through the sky. He fought the stick, kicking and holding in right rudder to ease the yaw. He remembered feeling the jolt over the target. The Thud was tough, and when the gauges had shown nothing amiss, he had thought it inconsequential. In the excitement of the MiG chase he had forgotten about being hit. His airspeed began to slacken, even though the throttle was forward. The other two aircraft were pulling ahead.

"This is Kingfish lead. Four, continue your attack. Two, drop back and check me over. I've got a problem."

Kingfish two throttled back, making a wide S-turn to bleed off airspeed. He finally settled into position off Benny's right wing, then slowly maneuvered around the Thud to examine it for battle damage.

The lieutenant was beneath Benny's fuselage when he made his assessment. *"You've got some pretty hairy damage to your left wing, lead."*

"What the hell do you mean by hairy?" Benny exploded, then calmed himself. *"Be more specific, Kingfish two."*

"There's a hole the size of a basketball completely through the wing, and part of your landing gear's blown away. The landing gear strut has, uh, wedged down through the mess. About four feet of bent metal from the underside of the wing has slipped down around the strut. It's like a speed brake."

"Yeah," Benny said. *"I can feel it in the controls. The airplane's yawing like a bastard."*

"I don't see fluid or anything coming out."

"Good. Now check my fuselage."

After a pause, *"Looks okay."*

"What's your fuel status, two?"

Kingfish two pulled farther away from Benny to total his fuel. *"I've got more than forty-eight hundred pounds, Kingfish lead."*

Benny had 4,200 pounds. He was in far worse shape, however, because of the drag of the metal hanging under the wing. He would continue to use fuel at a high rate, couldn't accelerate, and would be unable to maneuver due to the damaged aileron. His wingman could fly for fifty minutes or so, long enough to reach the tankers. Benny could only guess, but felt he probably had twenty minutes of fuel . . . or less.

He searched the sky ahead and tracked the flight path of Kingfish four, then saw a glint in the distance. The MiG-17 was still well out of range.

"Kingfish four, break off your pursuit. We're Bingo fuel. What's your fuel status?"

"I've got forty-six hundred pounds, Kingfish lead. Request permission for one pass on the MiG."

"Negative. Break it off. We're back at your five o'clock in a right turn. Let's get out of here."

"Roger, lead." Kingfish four sounded discouraged at being deprived of his kill.

Benny set up on a due westerly course, then carefully throttled back to 390 knots to conserve fuel. He held the rudder to the right and continued to fight the control stick. The ailerons would move only in jerks and spasms.

He reviewed his dilemma. Out over the badlands with a badly wounded bird and not enough fuel to make it to a tanker. He would have to bail out, and there was little chance of rescue unless he made it back past the Red River so helicopters would be able to reach him.

How far past the Red?

Forty miles, he quickly decided. Make it back forty miles or more beyond the Red River and find an unpopulated area. *How far was he from the Red?*

He fumbled with the map of his kneeboard, put his finger on the dog pecker, and switched his Doppler navigation system to the coordinates. It read 327 nautical miles. *Damn!* The navigation system was terrible in the best of times and was now grossly in error.

He peered at the map and estimated the Red River crossing to be fifty nautical miles away. That would take him seven or eight minutes.

Kingfish four was joining on his right wing.

"Kingfish lead, Falcon," Colonel Mack radioed. *"Sounds like you've got a problem."*

Benny relaxed a bit at the sound of MacLendon's steady voice. *"My left wing's torn up, Falcon lead, creating a lot of drag. I'm using a lot of fuel."*

"What's your fuel state?" asked Colonel Mack.

"Three thousand pounds and dropping fast."

The radio erupted with sound. *"THIS IS BIG EYE. BUSHMAN AT ALPHA GOLF TWO! I REPEAT. BUSHMAN AT ALPHA GOLF TWO!"*

Big Eye was an EC-121 aircraft with a powerful airborne radar and eavesdropping receivers. Bushman was today's code name for MiG's. Benny checked out the A-G-2 coordinates on his map. The MiG's were flying in the same general area as Kingfish.

"Kingfish, be on the lookout for MiG's," Benny called. *"Keep your eyes open."*

Think positive, he told himself. Better MiG's than SAMs. He knew he couldn't evade a surface-to-air missile with the wounded Thud, but logic told him the North Vietnamese wouldn't likely fly SAMs into the same area as the MiG's. And if MiG's showed up, the two lieutenants would keep them sufficiently occupied for him to get away.

"Kingfish lead, Falcon lead," called Colonel Mack. *"We're setting up for Res-CAP in case you need it. Two flights will continue outbound to refuel, and I'll hold for you with the other two flights at the dog pecker. I've alerted Red Crown to get rescue on the way."*

"Roger, Hawk lead." Benny was starting to fight the controls.

The three F-105's of Kingfish flight crossed Thud Ridge at 11,000 feet. He checked his fuel status and felt alarm. He was down to 2,600 pounds.

"Come on, you bitch." Benny's right leg trembled from the exertion of constantly holding the rudder.

Kingfish two and four were a few hundred feet off each wing, jinking and turning and looking for the MiG's called by Big Eye. Benny computed again and began to feel more confident that he could make it to a safe area before running out of fuel.

As they crossed a stream called the Lo, halfway between Thud Ridge and the Red River, his altitude had dropped to 8,000 feet.

No MiG's so far, and no SAMs.

"Thank you, God," Benny whispered just before his radar warning equipment sounded. A two-ring Firecan, triple-A radar.

Three miles ahead muzzle flashes blinked from twenty or more gun positions placed about a small, man-made knoll, but he was unable to jink or maneuver due to the limited amount of control he had over the aircraft. Scattered groups of flak bursts began to walk across the sky, searching for the flight.

"Keep it moving around, Kingfish," he called for the benefit of the other two aircraft.

His altitude was 7,500 feet. Too low, but it would take too much fuel to climb higher.

They were approaching the Red River when a pattern of flak bursts exploded directly in his path, then just off his left wing. The aircraft lurched and shuddered violently. He fought the stick and rudders to remain upright, but by the time he brought it under control he was down to 6,000 feet.

"*This is Kingfish lead. I just took another hit,*" Benny radioed, his voice shaking slightly.

More flak bursts, concentrating on him now that they had found his altitude and track. He pushed the throttle forward, fighting the controls to remain upright and on course.

"*Kingfish lead, you are trailing smoke.*" He recognized Kingfish four's voice.

As they crossed the Red River, smoke began to trickle into the cockpit. Benny switched to one hundred percent oxygen.

"*Kingfish two has bogeys at our ten o'clock!*"

"*I believe you're looking at us, Kingfish.*" It was Colonel Mack. "*Falcon has you in sight. We'll be joining up.*"

Across the Red River the elevation of the terrain began to rise rapidly. Benny was forced to push in more throttle yet, using precious fuel in an attempt to climb as he approached a ridgeline.

"*Kingfish lead, you're on fire. You've got flames at the rear of your fuselage. It doesn't look too bad yet, but it's growing.*"

"*Kingfish, Falcon is a mile out and closing.*" Colonel Mack paused. "*Get prepared to step out of that thing, Kingfish lead. Don't press it much longer.*"

The smoke was black, roiling about his feet and slowly rising, making it difficult to see the flight instruments.

"*Kingfish lead, see if you can . . .*" The radio went dead. Benny tried to transmit but heard no audio feedback indicating the radio was functioning.

Smoke was thick in the cockpit, stinging his eyes, making vision impossible. Benny reached down with his left hand to the handle at the side of his seat, found it, and sharply rotated it upward. The canopy was blown away, clearing the smoke.

He blinked his eyes rapidly to regain his vision and could see the green of a mountainside in his flight path. He pushed the throttle full forward and pulled on the stick. The dying

F-105 skimmed over the mountain crest just yards above the treetops. Benny held the stick back and remained in full throttle, his eyes on the next mountainside, less than three miles distant.

His feet were hot on the rudder pedals; something was burning brightly down there.

"Hang on, damn you! Hang on a while longer!" he yelled to the airplane, which sluggishly began a slow climb.

The Thud was still climbing when the stick and rudder pedals were suddenly no longer connected to their control surfaces. The aircraft immediately went into a left roll.

The Thud continued to climb in a crazy pattern, the engine still roaring with life. He waited, the fire at his feet more intense, his boots so hot the nylon fabric was scorching. The world revolved as the aircraft continued its slow roll.

Benny waited out one more revolution. Then the big fighter started to pitch over. It was no longer flying when he pulled the ejection lever.

The others watched as Benny Lewis's ejection seat blasted from the F-105 by explosive charges under the seat. Lewis's arms and legs flailed in the airstream. Too often, ejection from the Thunderchief caused a compression fracture of the lower back due to the violence of the ejection explosion. They hoped his back and limbs were okay.

Even before Benny's parachute was fully opened, the burning F-105 began to come apart, falling to the earth in smouldering chunks.

"*Weeep, weeep, weeep . . .*"

They circled, eyes pinned on Lewis, watching intently until they thought they saw him move in the parachute, raise his arms to grip the risers, and pull himself upward.

"*Weeep, weeep.*"

The beeper was shut off. Benny Lewis was alive.

27/1445L—Near Bac Ninh, DRV

Xuan Nha

Tran Van Ngo knew he had done well and that Tiger would receive credit for destroying yet another enemy fighter.

It was his thirteenth in the months since taking command of the battalion. Xuan watched as Tran reached out from the engagement commander's seat, activating the switch to sound the all clear siren. A steady, wailing sound flooded through the van, crowded with both people and electronic equipment.

The van was constructed to accommodate the four personnel required for command van operations: the azimuth and elevation radar operators, the rocket control officer, and the range correlator, who was also engagement commander. Today Xuan Nha, Nicolaj Gregarian, and Lt Quang Hanh were also crowded inside, making the van tight-quartered and hot.

Maj Tran Van Ngo, commander of Tiger battalion, never allowed anyone else into the commander's seat when he was at either of his two firing batteries. Xuan Nha had done the same when he had been commander, yet a twinge of irritation passed over him as he noted the ease with which Tran Van Ngo handled his position.

The 23rd Rocket Battalion was assigned the code name Tiger in honor of the Tiger of Dien Bien Phu. Under Xuan Nha, the 23rd had been the first to shoot down an American aircraft in the war. Xuan wore the Red Star of Gallantry for leading them as they destroyed six aircraft in a single month. He had served as the first commander of Tiger Battalion; it was very special to him.

He longed to return to Tiger and destroy enemy aircraft with this wonderful, complex weapons system. He was the best. Better than Tran Van Ngo, better than Nicolaj Gregarian. Better because he possessed the four secrets of military success: intelligence, persistence, bravery, and ruthlessness. Few military men possessed all four characteristics in that perfect blend. Xuan Nha existed in harmony with his profession as a technical warrior.

His greatest weakness was his penchant for esteem. He gloried in the name Tiger of Dien Bien Phu, and in the respect that glowed from the eyes of superiors and subordinates.

The field phone rattled. Lieutenant Hanh, his baby face gleaming with perspiration, quickly answered, for Xuan Nha was awaiting Major Nguy's report from headquarters.

"It is the report, comrade Colonel."

Xuan took the radio-telephone as the others went outside to escape the unbearable heat. He spoke with Major Nguy for a few minutes before hanging up, face impassive.

He joined the men outside, where they waited in the shade of a sprawling banyan tree. They were impatient to hear how it had gone. Others were gathering: radar and communications technicians, rocket specialists, drivers from the transportation platoon, siting engineers, even the cooks and laborers. They were filthy in their stained field uniforms and smelled of grease, dirt, sweat, smoke, dust, and even rocket fuel. Xuan remembered the odors with nostalgia.

He needed no notes, for his memory was excellent, and he spoke in a low, even voice so the men had to crowd close and listen attentively. "Five, perhaps six aircraft were shot down. Three in the first attack, three in the second."

"Ha!" exclaimed several of the men. A rocket loader laughed exultantly. It was one of the finest days in memory.

"Artillery claims two positive kills and another probable one, seen descending and trailing smoke as it departed to the west. If their reports are accurate, the artillery company at Tuyen Quang shot down two American attackers."

"If!" cried out the exuberant one. There was competition between the artillery and rocket battery troops, who held that the guns could be operated by simpletons.

"One rocket kill in the first attack. Yours here at Tiger one, of course."

A swell of cheers.

"Happiness two battery destroyed an aircraft in the second attack."

Silence. The mobile battalions believed that the men assigned to the permanent sites around Hanoi were soft. They ridiculed their clean barracks, impeccable uniforms, and often-painted and polished systems. The men of the batteries of Tiger battalion were the proudest of them all; but perhaps also the most unkempt.

"Lieutenant Colonel Thao Phong is claiming a kill for his interceptors, but as we all know, fighter pilots lie."

There were laughs and wide grins.

Xuan's voice rose in volume. "But . . ." The men quickly grew silent, for Xuan Nha was sometimes unpredictable with his moods.

He dropped his voice again. "There was severe damage to the Yen Vien rail yards, where more than fifty carloads of weapons and supplies were located."

The boxcars had been waiting their turn to be hauled into

the safety of Hanoi, presently glutted with Chinese and Soviet arms shipments.

The men waited pensively for Colonel Nha's verdict.

"First reports are that seventy artillery men and railroad personnel were killed in the attack. The reports are still arriving at headquarters from Yen Vien, and the final numbers will be much higher.

"And Colonel Phong reports one of his interceptors was lost due to mechanical failure."

Again, there was silence, before Nha said, "Everything considered, it went well."

The smiles returned, followed by a roar of triumph.

"Congratulations, Tiger one!"

Xuan Nha interpreted his news for Gregarian's benefit.

The Russian mused. "Two aircraft killed with rockets?"

"Yes."

"It could have been more."

"That is why I want even more rocket systems."

Maj Tran Van Ngo, who had been congratulating his men, joined them. This was his first chance to meet Gregarian. He had been busy preparing his battalion, Tiger one battery here and Tiger two battery located twenty kilometers northeast, for the air attack when he and Xuan had arrived. Xuan watched as the two shook hands and exchanged greetings. He was proud of his protege. Gregarian, he noticed, frowned at Ngo's smelly uniform. *You'll learn how it is, Russian,* he thought.

When the two were silent, Xuan took Tran Van Ngo's arm in his strong hand. "One more kill and your total will equal mine."

"It was you, comrade Colonel, who entrusted me with your battalion, and who constantly provides the means of success. I am eternally grateful."

Xuan smiled. "Then perhaps I should claim today's kill."

Tran Van Ngo deadpanned. "We would not want others thinking that yours was the hand that trembled on the launch panel, would we, Colonel?"

Xuan snorted in mock disgust. He liked his young, brash major, whom he had named to fill his position. Xuan lit a Salem cigarette, popular at the headquarters because it was the same band that President Ho Chi Minh smoked. He inhaled pleasurably.

Xuan switched to Russian. "So what do you think of Tiger one and our operation, *Mayor* Gregarian?"

"I have much to see before I make final suggestions, *Podpolnikov* Nha, but I noticed that *Mayor* Ngo was hesitant before switching the transmitter into dummy load when the radar-hunter aircraft began its attack."

Gregarian glanced at Tran Van Ngo, who had turned away to deal with a problem concerning defueling the rockets. Tiger battalion was preparing to move out, since both batteries' locations had been compromised by their rocket firings.

Xuan said, "Do not worry, Tran's Russian is very poor." He didn't reveal that it was not nearly as poor as Gregarian's Vietnamese.

The Russian major drew a breath. "This is my first exposure to the tactics the Americans are using, but I studied the reports closely before my departure." Gregarian's tone was chiding. "The tracking radars should only remain on the air for short periods, only for that time necessary to acquire and shoot down the target. I sent such guidance from Moscow several weeks ago."

Xuan was displeased. Gregarian was concerning himself with trivia. The important thing was that the rocket forces had destroyed two American aircraft and had relentlessly driven other invaders down into the furious artillery fire.

"Did you receive my message?" Gregarian asked.

"Colonel Dimetriev passed it to us and I forwarded it to the battalions with my own remarks. Perhaps when you've seen more of our operation, you will understand why we sometimes keep our tracking radars on for longer periods of time."

Gregarian's voice filled with passion. "You'll only lose radars. We examined the missile parts you sent us three months ago and found they were indeed from a radar-homing missile. We'll know more when we get a missile in better condition, but we have enough information to say that if you shut off the radar the missile can no longer track its target."

"Perhaps," Xuan said, "but if you remember my earlier briefing, I told you of the importance of defending Hanoi. The rocket battalion at Vinh, for instance, is guarding a lower-priority area and is more vulnerable, so the commander there must be cautious and seldom turn on his radars. Here, we have many rocket battalions that can threaten the radar-hunters from all directions. This area is very important and must be protected. We cannot and often need not be cautious."

Xuan Nha did not add that he had never considered the radar-hunters as much of a threat. They had destroyed a few radars, but were more of a nuisance than a threat.

Gregarian was obstinate. "I noticed also a sudden blooming of one aircraft return on the radar scope, one I considered to be a radar-hunter. When I used tracking radars in Russia and watched aircraft firing missiles, I noticed the same phenomenon. The aircraft we saw today was launching a missile. Were any radars threatened by missiles today?"

Xuan was silent, then acknowledged, "A missile destroyed the radar antenna at Happiness three site." Two technicians and an officer had been killed there.

"Southwest of us?"

"Twenty kilometers southwest."

Gregarian said, "Then it was a missile launch I saw. Did you notice the flash on the commander's scope?"

Xuan wanted to grit his teeth and growl; instead he smiled. "No, I did not." He had heard the same claim from the area commander at Vinh, not believing him. He'd considered it a story made up and circulated too widely, with no technical basis.

"It is interesting, don't you think?"

I will send a notice to all radar operators to look for the blooming, and tell them they should proceed with caution when they see it."

Gregarian said, "I would be happy to help you with the message when I return from setting up the P-50 radar."

Irritated at the man's condescension, Xuan turned away. Lt Quang Hanh was talking on a field phone, its antenna wire now strung into the branches of a squat tree since the command van was being prepared for its move. Hanh replaced the receiver and hurried over. "Wreckage from five aircraft have been located."

"What of the American pilots?"

"Three are dead. One was alive. Rice farmers near Tuyen Quang caught him and beat him to death."

Such was often the case. That was why the People's Army tried to reach the downed Americans first. Sometimes the pilots were interrogated for intelligence, but mostly they were kept alive because Lao Dong party officials felt the pilots might be valuable bargaining material in the future.

"Two pilots are in custody. One was shot as he attempted to get away, and will probably die. Headquarters wants to know if you wish to gain information from the other one."

Xuan sometimes sat in on prisoner interrogations. Often obstinate, their intelligence was of questionable value. He was most successful when he led his own private interrogations. "Major Wu may attend the questioning if he desires."

"Yes, comrade Colonel."

"Anything else?" asked Xuan.

"The aircraft that was in trouble, that was hit by artillery fire? . . ."

"Yes."

"Several witnesses saw it descending toward the mountains. They claim that it likely crashed east of Than Uyen, in the Fan Si Pan. American fighters circled over the eastern ridge for more than fifteen minutes, and a listening post heard them talking on their emergency frequency. Their rescue attempt was called off, but we expect another one tomorrow at first light. A team is forming at Than Uyen to go into the area and capture the pilot before the Americans return."

The Fan Si Pan was a mountainous region at the outer limits of the American rescue capability. Few American pilots had been extracted from its eastern slope, for it was close to the heavy defenses deployed along the Hong River and the adjacent rail line, proving dangerous for enemy rescue forces.

Xuan Nha thought. "Tell Major Nguy to have the capture team assembled at Than Uyen, but tell them to wait. If the rescuers dare to come, we will provide a welcome. Then the capture team will have even more pilots to look for."

Quang Hanh's baby face twitched with a smile.

"Pass on that much. I'll coordinate the rest when we've returned to headquarters."

Quang Hanh went back to his field phone.

Xuan regarded Gregarian. "We should return to Hanoi so you can prepare for your trip tomorrow." He had heard enough of the Russian's criticisms.

"One other thing. The *mayor* failed to follow doctrine. He did not shoot when he had an easy target at twenty kilometers range, waiting to select a more difficult one when it was closer.

The system has a maximum range of forty kilometers, and is optimized for twenty kilometers, no closer."

"Perhaps he noticed something you did not."

They both looked about the site then, watching the men working at their feverish yet methodical pace to dismantle the site and prepare to move out.

A smile played at Gregarian's fleshy lips. "These rocket systems, wonderful as they are, must be used properly."

Xuan kept his silence.

27/1925L—Takhli RTAFB, Thailand

That Sunday the stag bar of the Takhli Officer's Open Mess rapidly came to life as the men straggled in from the dining room after finishing their evening meal. Mal "Bear" Stewart sat at the end of the dark bar holding a scotch in his left hand. He slowly shook a dice cup with his right.

"You really want to bet your motorcycle?" asked the Bear.

"Sure," said the Thai bartender, called Jimmy because none of the American officers could pronounce Phahakkhap-hap the same way twice. Jimmy looked about, enjoying the attention he was getting.

"Dammit," exclaimed the Bear, "this is serious stuff. Don't you go thinking if you win, you get your money back, but if I win, I won't take your motorcycle."

"I bet my Honda," said Jimmy, smiling.

"Jimmy, I'll take it this time," the Bear threatened. "I swear I'll take it."

"Yep." Jimmy grinned wider. He had already lost eight dollars in tip money and his next month's salary. "Dubble or nuthin."

"Okay, you get your money and next month's paycheck back if you win, right?"

"Yep."

"And I get your money, your paycheck, and your motor-cycle if you lose."

A crowd had gathered. Sam Hall leaned forward at the Bear's elbow, watching raptly. Glenn Phillips looked on with interest, carefully sipping a Manhattan. Tiny Bechler craned his neck to see over the group, watching the dice cup. Toki

Takahara and Jimbo Smith discussed their belief that all Orientals were consumed by the urge to gamble.

Mike Murphy, seated to the Bear's right, was not attentive. He was drunk and quietly growing sodden, cradling his head from time to time. He thought of Tommy Larkins, the captain in his flight who had been hammered out of the sky a few hours earlier. He'd been a friend; the others respected his sadness and did not interfere.

Sam Hall shook his head at Jimmy. "Don't bet him your motorcycle." Sam turned to the others. "He's proud of that motorcycle."

The Bear said, "He *wants* to bet his motorcycle. You ready, Jimmy?"

They clapped their dice cups onto the table and lifted. The game was zap aces, the quick and dirty favorite of fighter jocks.

Jimmy had two sixes and a wild ace. The Bear showed four natural deuces. Jimmy looked at the dice in disbelief. He scratched his head, then looked at the Bear with pleading moon eyes.

"Where's the keys?" asked the Bear.

Jimmy regarded the dice intently, as if he could change the spots if he just stared hard enough.

"The keys," repeated the Bear. He took them from Jimmy's slowly extending hand.

"Dubble or nuthin," cried Jimmy.

Sam looked at the Bear quizzically. "You're not gonna take his motorcycle, are you?" Sam was becoming intoxicated and was maudlin about Jimmy's plight.

"He bet it," the Bear growled. "He beat me out of twenty bucks the other day, and he sure as hell took that."

"Dubble or nuthin," insisted Jimmy.

"You don't have anything, Jimmy," the Bear said.

"Dubble or nuthin."

"I already got everything you own that's worth anything."

Jimmy thought. "I got two wife."

"I don't want your damn wives, Jimmy. I had *one* once, and that was too many."

"Maybe you jus' borrow my wife." Jimmy gave his impression of a leer, with only marginal success. Like most Thais, he liked the Americans. He was not displeased at the thought of sharing one of his wives, especially the older, louder one whom he had been obligated to take following his brother's death. The consequence of losing his Honda was serious.

"No wife."

"We talk about it."

"Let's talk about the money you owe me. Write me an IOU," demanded the Bear, holding out a ballpoint pen.

Jimmy's face fell a bit. He took the pen from the Bear and scribbled on a bar napkin, looking at it as he handed it over.

"Dubble or nuthin," he repeated.

Max Foley entered the bar, pulling off his hat before Sam could reach the gong to the bell that hung over the middle of the bar. If the bell had been rung in time, before the hat was removed, Max would have been obligated to buy a drink for everyone in the bar. An old fighter-pilot rule. You also bought drinks for the house if you got a phone call from a wife when you were in the stag bar, or just rang the bell by mistake. The protocols of the stag bar were stiffly enforced by ridicule. Reputation meant a lot to the group.

Foley burrowed his way to the end of the bar, where he motioned to get the assistant bartender's attention. He was thirsty. "Shit!" he proclaimed to no one in particular, glowering. "Nothing's gone right today." He had just arrived from the command post, where he had filled out his final reports from his long day as supervisor of flying.

Sam Hall called out to Max. "Anything new on Benny Lewis?"

"No."

"How about the others?"

"Nothing new."

The stag bar was filled. More than two dozen men crowded along the Formica and chrome bar, and the same number sat at tables. Others stood in groups, discussing and laughing and moving their hands as they reconstructed air battles. Jimmy's assistant was a skinny, dark man they called Pak, shortened from another impossible Thai name. With Jimmy busy gambling, he worked hard to stay even with the demand for drinks.

Max stood beside Doc Roddenbush, one of three flight surgeons assigned to the medical clinic at Takhli. He was nursing a Coke since he was on call.

"I heard about Captain Lewis," Doc said. "Too bad."

"Yeah," Max said. "Hopefully we'll get the chance to snatch him out of there tomorrow. One of the Jolly Green choppers had engine problems today, so they had to abort the effort."

"How about the others who were shot down today?"

"They went down in the Red River valley, Doc. The choppers can't go there because the ground fire's too intense."

"But Lewis wasn't in that far?" Roddenbush was genuinely concerned. Benny's easygoing nature made him popular with just about everyone.

Max thought for a moment. "Where Benny went down was just borderline bad."

Sam Hall nudged his bulk through the crowd to move in beside Max, his face bleak. Hall had been stationed at Spangdahlem with Foley and Benny Lewis.

"You gonna write Bets?" Sam asked. They both knew Lewis's wife.

"One of us should, I guess."

"You write her. I'm not good at that shit."

"Who is? Anyway, they may pick him up tomorrow. Colonel Mack's trying to get approval for an all-out effort at first light."

Hall shook his head. "The chances for a pickup aren't all that great. He made it past the Red, but he was still about twenty miles on the other side of the Black River. The Jolly Greens don't like going past the Black unless they absolutely have to."

Max hissed out a pent-up breath. "I saw the position on a map at the command post. The area looks isolated, but sometimes that's deceiving."

"Colonel Mack made a couple of low, slow passes around the area and didn't see any natives. The gomers'll send in search teams if they know the airplane went down, and they probably do."

"How did Benny sound on the radio, Sam?"

"A lieutenant in my flight took a hit and I had to chaperone him outta there so I didn't hear him, but Colonel Mack said Benny sounded full of piss and vinegar. Even when Mack told him about the chopper having engine trouble, and that he'd have to spend the night up there, he took it well. Course, how else you gonna take it? Big thing is he said he was okay, didn't have any broken bones or anything."

"Shit." Max sighed. "I'll write the damned letter. Tomorrow. After the rescue attempt, in case they get him out."

The lonesome sounds of "Lara's Theme" beat out of the jukebox, drowning the sounds of a dozen conversations because it had been turned up by one of the pilots. Sam waved somberly to Max, then returned to the group watching the Bear playing dice with Jimmy. They were looking with disgust at the bartender.

Glenn said to Jimmy, "Give me a bourbon Manhattan. I hope you're better at mixing drinks than you are at dice."

"I just won both of his wives for a month," gloated the Bear.

Sam was intoxicated. "Aww, you're not really gonna take his wife are you?"

"Both of 'em. See this paper," said the Bear. "I've got his IOU."

Toki Takahara leaned forward. "How do you know what it says? It's written in Thai."

"I trust him. He can't write very good in English. I trust you, Jimmy!"

Toki, a nisei from Honolulu, confided drunkenly to Tiny Bechler. "Jimmy shouldn't gamble. The Oriental mind is different. They can't help themselves."

Jimmy handed Glenn his drink, then set his jaw. "Dubble or nuthin," he pleaded, staring at the Honda key resting on the bar before the Bear.

"What you going to bet, Jimmy? I already got it all."

"My house? I got house in town."

"Aww," said Sam, "you really don't wanna be doin' that, Jimmy. Like Toki says, you shouldn't gamble." He turned to the Bear. "Give him back his wives. Maybe he'll stop."

"He can't help it, I tell you," said Toki.

"Dubble or nuthin," Jimmy said, his eyes shrewd. "My house."

Colonel Mack entered the side door, grimly looking about as he made his way toward the group.

"What the hell's going on here?" he joked.

"Just having a few drinks, Colonel," said Phillips.

"We got approval for the Res-CAP, so don't you characters get too carried away."

Phillips said, "Think I'll go over to intell and see if they've got anything new."

"You need me to come along?" asked the Bear.

"No. I'm just mainly restless." Phillips drained his glass and departed.

Colonel Mack ordered a whiskey and glanced about the crowded bar. He looked at Tiny. "How did you like flying with Phillips today?"

"It was hairy as hell, Colonel," Tiny said happily.

Colonel Mack paid his thirty cents and sipped his bourbon, listening to Tiny.

"We were setting up to make a bomb delivery on a SAM site Glenn found. I haven't seen that much flak in my last ten missions put together. Then two different SAM sites from downtown Hanoi hosed six missiles at us and we got a tour of North Vietnam from about fifty feet above the dirt. Phillips has balls bigger'n the Harlem Globetrotters'."

"You did okay today, Tiny," the Bear said. "You saw that fuckin' MiG before anyone else in the flight, and you were the only one able to stay with us through all the maneuvering while we were going after the site."

Tiny warily accepted one of the Bear's infrequent compliments. "Thanks." One of Tiny's several prejudices was against navigators, and Wild Weasel bears wore navigator wings. He would probably have liked the Bear if he was a pilot.

The Bear turned to Colonel Mack. "You saw the fuckin' flak up there today, Colonel. Intelligence said it was gonna be moderate. They ought to be up there runnin' around North Vietnam with all the guys who got shot down by their fuckin' moderate defenses. Somebody's gotta do something about those turkeys."

Colonel Mack said, "It's always been like that. At least since 1944 it has. Poor target intelligence is an Air Force tradition, Bear."

"Wonder why they call them intelligence," grumbled Tiny, "since they're so damned stupid."

Sam Hall, who had been listening to the conversation, shook his head. Sam thought the best of most people, even intelligence officers. "You guys are bein' hard on 'em. They do their best. I talked to DeWalt . . . you know, the intell lieutenant?"

"He's the dumbest of the bunch," said the Bear.

"He says they get shitty information from Seventh Air

Force that they try to straighten out before they brief us. He says the recce photos they get are usually old and out of date. The higher headquarters have to see them before they'll pass 'em down to the operational units. They work three or four hours every night to get ready for the morning mission, then all day when the missions are flying they're either briefing or collecting debriefings from the flights. He says they put in twelve- to twenty-hour days, seven days a week."

They all quietly reflected on Sam's revelations before the Bear disagreed. "You're too easy on 'em, Sam. They've gotta do their job better or we're going to continue to take dumb-ass losses because we aren't prepared."

Colonel Mack shook his head at the Bear's hardheadedness.

The bar was full to overflowing. A group of songsters led by Jimbo Smith and Toki Takahara gathered nearby and sang noisily. Mack, Sam Hall, and Tiny walked over and joined in as they started their next rendition.

"I love my wife, yes I do, I love her troooly," sang the men.

"I love the hole, that she pisses throoogh."

The bar was filled with a silly and incomprehensible feeling of nostalgia.

"I love her tits," they sang.

"And her nut brown aaasshole."

"I'd eat her shit—gobble, gobble—gobble, gobble."

"With a woooden spooon."

The bar was uncommonly quiet at the end of the profane song.

Mike Murphy had started to slide off his stool beside the Bear. He grieved for his friend and for his friend's wife, and at his inability to help. Sam guided him to his feet.

"Time to go to my trailer," said Sam. "I'll drop Mike off at his hootch."

The Bear also got up. "I'll go with you. Help you with Mike."

Jimmy the bartender became alarmed. "Dubble or nuthin," he cried as the Bear started away.

The Bear tossed Jimmy the Honda key. "You can use my bike tonight, Jimmy, but you tell them wives to perfume up, because I'll be by one day soon."

Jimmy adroitly caught the key and grinned.

CHAPTER FOUR

Monday, November 28th—0655 Local, Route Pack Six, North Vietnam

Bear Stewart

Mal Stewart looked out over the familiar valley as he listened to the radio.

"Stingers, we've got SAM activity from south of Yen Bai. Out of range. Nothing exciting yet." Phillips's voice was calm, although they fully expected trouble.

Their four-ship Wild Weasel flight had ventured out over the Red River valley to challenge the defenses and keep them occupied during the rescue. Tiny Bechler flew as number two. Number three was Toki Takahara. Four was Ken Maisey.

Twenty miles northwest of them, four flights of single-seat Thuds were approaching the area where Benny Lewis had gone down the previous afternoon.

The mission was a maximum effort to pull Benny Lewis from the ground before the North Vietnamese found him. There had been no JCS target tasking from Washington that morning, so the wing commander had called in debts from various friends at Seventh Air Force headquarters in Saigon; the rescue effort, officially called a Rescue Combat Air Patrol or Res-CAP, had been approved. The Thud pilots knew it could be any one of them down there surrounded by hostiles. The tanker crews sent them off with full tanks and a firm thumbs up. F-4C Phantom crews joined up from Ubon Air Base in eastern Thailand to provide protection from MiG's. Crews of the two EB-66 electronic jamming aircraft had volunteered to fly orbits a dozen miles north of the rescue area, to jam enemy radars that tried to interfere with the rescue.

The sixteen fighters led by Colonel Mack carried light loads for good maneuverability and longer loiter-time. Each Thud carried a 650-gallon fuel tank on centerline, two pods of 2.75, white phosphorous rockets, AIM-9 Sidewinder missiles, and a full can of 20mm ammunition for the Gatling gun.

"No activity," said the Bear in a pleasant tone.

"Too quiet," muttered Glenn. Neither SAMs nor MiG's had yet been noted near the area.

Glenn had called for heavier loads for his Wild Weasel flight. Aside from two Shrike radar-homing missiles, he carried four CBUs, the bomb-shaped cannisters that would pop open after release and spew out hundreds of grenade–like bomblets. The others in Stinger flight carried 500-pound Mark 82 bombs.

Colonel Mack repeatedly called Benny's call sign on the emergency channel as they zigzagged over the area into which he had parachuted.

"Kingfish lead, this is Hornet, do you read me?"

Silence followed his calls.

The Bear didn't know Benny Lewis well, but he liked what he had seen. The man's noteworthy traits were his fast devotion to his family and his loyalty to his fellow fighter jocks. Benny was a steady type who exuded a calming influence upon the other strike pilots. The Bear hoped they could pull the rescue off.

Alone over the Red River valley, the Wild Weasel flight maneuvered and watched for threats to the rescuers.

The Bear looked up from the IR-133, the sensitive receiver that displayed signals from enemy radars. He stared out of the cockpit at their two o'clock, then slowly swept his vision to the right. Tiny Bechler's single-seat Thud turned and jinked a thousand feet away. He continued sweeping his vision rearward until the ejection seat's headrest interfered, then craned his neck to peer at the limit of his vision.

"Kick your right rudder, Glenn." The aircraft yawed, allowing him to scan back to their six o'clock. "We're clear on the right."

Phillips only grunted in response.

The Bear scanned past Toki Takahara's weaving two-ship element. It wasn't that he didn't trust the other members of the flight to do their best in spotting MiG's, it was only that you could not be too wary when you flew over the valley.

"Clear on the left," he said.

"Kingfish, this is Hornet," called Colonel Mack, trying again to raise Benny Lewis on the radio.

Phillips slowly turned his flight southward, careful to remain between the rescue force and the threats in the valley. The Bear shared his fierce protectiveness, as he, too, was suspicious that the gomers were up to something.

The Bear again worked the IR-133, the heart of his Wild Weasel equipment, noting signals from two Firecan AAA radars; green spikes alternately grew and diminished from the grass at the bottom of the scope. He glanced at the radar homing scope, processing the signals from the radar. "We've got sweeping guns," he said. "Ten and twelve o'clock." He presented his information quickly, accurately, and understandably.

One of the two signals stopped sweeping and remained steady on the scope.

"One gun tracking at ten o'clock," the Bear said. "No threat," he added. The radar's signal was too weak and thus too distant for its 57mm guns to pose a threat.

"Nothing else?" asked Phillips.

"Nothing right now. You want to fire a Shrike at him to keep his respect? We're probably coming within range."

Phillips thought before answering. "Let's wait. There may be something better to shoot at later."

"Weeep, weeep, weeep . . ." An emergency locator beacon sounded.

"We've got an emergency beeper!" called Colonel Mack over the din.

"Weeep, weeep, weeep . . ." It sounded weak and distant.

"Weeep, weeep." The the beeper was turned off.

"This is Trigger lead." It was the F-4C MiG-CAP leader. *"I've got a fix on my radio DF from over in the valley, Hornet. That's not Kingfish."*

"Thanks, Trigger," said Colonel Mack. *"Keep up your visual lookout, Hornets."*

"THIS IS BIG EYE! LONGHORN AT ALPHA GOLF THREE! I REPEAT, THIS IS BIG EYE! LONGHORN AT ALPHA GOLF THREE!" The command-and-control aircraft had seen MiG's near Hanoi on radar and was broadcasting over Guard radio channel with so much power that their eardrums hurt.

"Keep an eye out for bogeys," directed Colonel Mack.

"Hornet, this is Wasp lead," came Sam Hall's voice. *"I'm seeing some flashes low on a hillside down there."*

A short silence followed, during which the fliers held their collective breaths.

A calm, distant voice sounded over the radio. *"Hornet, this is Kingfish."* Benny Lewis's voice!

Colonel Mack responded immediately. *"We're reading you three-by-five, Kingfish. Weak-but-clear."*

"I just flashed my mirror at a flight of Thuds that passed over. I moved west during the night, Hornet. Trying to make your job easier."

"We received the mirror flashes. Be with you in a minute, Kingfish. You got any company down there?"

"There's a road through the valley east of me that had some vehicle activity yesterday, but I haven't seen anything or anyone on this side of the mountain. It's mostly wild jungle here."

"What's your condition, Kingfish?"

"I'm sick and tired of running up and down these hills and ready to get out of here. Otherwise I'm fine."

Colonel Mack began to issue orders on the squadron common frequency. *"Hornet three, go to Crown frequency and get the Sandies and choppers on their way. Tell them the area seems safe, and that we've got a hell of a lot of fighter support for 'em here."*

"Roger, three's changing to Crown frequency."

"Wasp lead, keep Kingfish in sight."

"I've got a good visual on the area the flashes came from," said Sam Hall.

"I want everyone to keep a close look for any ground troops that might be moving into the area. Anything that moves near that valley is a threat to the Jolly Greens."

"Honeybee flight reads you."

"Skeeter flight, roger."

Colonel Mack returned to the emergency frequency. *"Sit tight, Kingfish. We're calling for rescue."* His voice sounded quietly pleased.

"Yes, sir," replied Benny, his voice calm. *"I've got three flights of Thuds in sight now."*

"Still no company down there?"

"No." Then, *"Damn!"* A long pause. His voice returned a moment later, high with new emotion. *"No humans, but I just*

*heard one hell of a roar from some kind of animal. Are there
tigers around here?"*

"You hear that?" The Bear said to Phillips. "It'd be shitty
if Benny got eaten by a fuckin' tiger while he was waiting to
be picked up."

Phillips agreed that would be shitty.

The Bear peered hard into the distance past Toki Takahara
and his wingman. "We got a bogey at our eleven o'clock,
level," he said. "It's still a long way out. Wait, it's turning. I
see two of 'em now."

"We got bogeys out over the valley, Stingers," announced
Phillips.

"Two."

"Three." Toki's voice was crisp.

"Four."

The Bear frowned. Four's voice contained an element of
panic he didn't like. Ken Maisey was a U.S. Naval Academy
graduate who let you know it in the first moment of discussion.
He was new, but there was something in the voice other than
new-guy caution.

*"This is Trigger lead, Stinger. Where'd you see the
MiG's?"* The F-4C Phantom flight leader sounded excited.

Glenn's voice was conversational. *"They're a few miles
northeast of Yen Bai, heading north in a slow right-hand turn.
And . . . I've got a visual on two more bogeys that are just
about over Yen Bai now, also heading east."*

*"Roger. Let's go burner, Triggers. What's your position,
Stinger? I don't want to get your flight mixed up with the bad
guys."*

The Bear growled over the intercom. "I don't trust those
F-4 jocks with their fancy fucking missiles."

Glenn chuckled, obviously happy he wouldn't have to
worry about both MiG's and SAMs all alone over the valley.
He radioed, *"We're turning west near the dog pecker, Trigger."*

"I got two bogeys in sight, Triggers!" announced the
excited F-4 Phantom leader. *"Eleven o'clock and very low.
Clean 'em up."*

White shapes tumbled through Stinger flight. It took a few
seconds before the Bear realized they were fuel tanks from the
high-flying Phantoms.

"Hot damn!" came Tiny Bechler's radio call. *"That was
close."*

Phillips sounded angry on the radio. *"Trigger, you dropped your tanks through our flight!"*

Trigger shouted gibberish as they chased eastward toward the MiG's. They changed radio channels and went off the Res-CAP frequency.

"I've got another tracking gun radar," said the Bear, eyes switching back and forth between receivers as he manipulated them. "Eight o'clock." He looked about the sky again for MiG's and saw one. "I've got a bogey at our three o'clock, closing, couple miles out."

Glenn must have also seen it, for he was banking hard into it. *"MiG-17 at three o'clock, Stingers!"*

The MiG pilot obviously saw them turning, for he dove toward the ground.

"Keep an eye out, Stingers," Phillips admonished, banking left now.

The flight members should have seen the MiG before it got that close. The Bear decided to razz their asses at debriefing.

"Stinger lead, this is four. My afterburner won't light."

"Bullshit," muttered the Bear. "I expected something like that from Maisey."

"I can't see in his cockpit, Bear. Maybe he does have a problem." Phillips switched to radio. *"Roger, four. Anything else wrong?"*

Four's voice came out quaking. *"I'm not sure. My fuel flow is awfully high. I'm burning between seven and eight thousand pounds an hour."*

"Roger," Phillips said, noncommittal.

"How the fuck's he know his burner's not working? We didn't go into burner. Maisey's problem's with his back," said the Bear. "His yellow streak's acting up."

"Maybe," Glenn said.

"Dammit, we need the second element."

"If his bird's acting up, he won't be much good to us anyway," Glenn said. *"Stinger three, escort four back home,"* he radioed.

"Ah, roger," came Toki's disgusted voice. The Bear watched the two Thuds turn west toward the green mountains. They were soon out of sight.

"How's your airplane, two?" asked Phillips.

Tiny Bechler replied promptly, *"Everything's in the green, Stinger lead."*

"Keep a good lookout, two. It's a MiG day."

Some days the SAMs and triple-A were all you would encounter. Other days, MiG's seemed to be everywhere. And some days there were both.

The Bear watched a SAM site's radar signal grow on the IR-133 scope. He tuned a cueing bar onto the signal to select it, then switched to another mode for analysis. He fine-tuned the inch-wide signal, fed in more attenuation, and measured its strength. The manipulations took a total of three seconds.

"We've got a tracking Fansong at five o'clock," he said, glancing out the window for visual reference. "Probably somewhere near that big U in the Red River."

The Bear selected, then transferred the SAM signal onto the small cathode-ray tube in Phillips's front cockpit. "This guy's a threat, Glenn."

Glenn banked the aircraft to put the strobe from the site at two o'clock on his attack scope. SAMs were easiest to dodge when they came from the right or left forward quadrants.

The Bear eyed the U in the river where he thought the site was located. Flat farmland stretched in all directions.

"Think we ought to engage him?" Phillips asked. The Bear liked that about Phillips. He knew it was not only his ass he was betting, and that it would be highly dangerous to attack a SAM site out over the valley with no terrain to dodge in and out of.

"He's close, maybe close enough to get a shot at the Res-CAP aircraft, Glenn."

"Yeah?" Phillips sucked in a breath, noisy on the intercom. "Well, let's have a go at him."

"Roger."

Phillips turned the Thud to line up for a Shrike missile shot, at the same time becoming a fat target for the SAM operator.

"He's looking at us now," said the Bear, constantly analyzing the signal on his scopes. As he'd anticipated, the radar's pulse rate doubled and the power level jumped. "He's in high PRF, preparing to shoot."

"Let's see if he's got balls," said Phillips, continuing to turn toward the site.

"Come right a couple more degrees," directed the Bear.

He had switched to the homing mode and was watching two steering bars on the scope, which were more accurate than Phillips's display. "A cunt-hair more. Yeah! He's at twelve o'clock, centered!"

"I'm tracking him with the Shrike needles," said Glenn. "Five degrees of depression angle. We're getting close."

The ACTIVITY button had illuminated and squeal in the Bear's headset. "He switched on his missile-tracking beam," he said.

"I've got . . . I just saw a SAM launch!" Phillips called the launch over the radio, telling Tiny to prepare for hard maneuvering.

The Bear switched back to the analysis function. He noted their position in the radar beam to doubly ensure that they were the intended target. "He's shooting at us. We're centered on his radar scope."

"Both beams?" Phillips asked. The SAM operators had to center them on both azimuth and elevation scopes to accurately measure their position and steer the missiles.

"Yeah," said the Bear, noting how smoothly the tracking radars kept the Thud centered in their respective beams. "He's pretty good, Glenn. Watch out for him."

Glenn Phillips

Phillips eased the stick back, and the Thud's nose came up. "I've got six degrees loft angle. That oughta do it," he mumbled. He had to be canny and quick. He depressed the trigger and felt the rumble of the Shrike missile.

"*Missile away,*" he called as the Shrike streaked from the pylon.

"*Stinger lead, break!*" came Tiny's desperate call.

Phillips banked hard right.

An explosion slapped the aircraft, throwing it sideways. Phillips reversed into a harsh left turn.

"*The second SAM's clear,*" called Tiny. Glenn knew it was, for the missile had passed directly over his cockpit a split second before exploding.

"*You got the third SAM in sight, two?*" asked Phillips.

"*It went wild, lead,*" said Tiny.

They were breathing hard, adrenaline pumping.

"Damn, I lost my visual sighting on the SAM site," muttered Phillips on the intercom.

"Shit!" said the Bear, echoing Glenn's disgust.

"I'm coming about to look for the Shrike impact," muttered Phillips.

"We got him!" said the Bear. "The SAM's radar signal dropped off the air. The fuckin' Shrike got him!"

Phillips quickly got onto the radio. *"Stinger two, I don't have a visual on the SAM site. We got a hit with the missile, but I don't see it."*

Colonel Mack's voice came over the radio. *Stinger lead, this is Hornet. How's it going out there?"*

"We've hit a SAM site with the Shrike, but I can't see the son of a bitch."

"Stinger, the rescue's coming along fine. The Sandies have just arrived on the scene, and the Jolly Greens are inbound. Keep their heads down just a bit longer and we'll have Kingfish out of here."

"Roger, Hornet."

Glenn, sighting something unusual, grew excited. *"Stinger two, set up for bomb delivery."*

"Two," came Tiny's immediate acknowledgment.

They climbed under full power, perching at 10,000 feet in an attempt to gain a visual sighting of the Shrike missile's impact smoke.

"See that clump of trees near those paddies in the curve of the river at our two o'clock?"

"Roger," replied Tiny after a slight pause.

"Well, I'd bet my maiden ass that's camouflage net and not all trees. I think I see smoke from the Shrike hit, too. Ready?"

"Two's ready."

Phillips rolled the big Thud up on its back and lined up on the target. He tucked the stick back into his lap and pulled into the dive. He turned to wings level in a steep dive. "Down the chute!" he said to the Bear.

"Stinger lead is in on a forty-five degree dive," he called to his wingman.

Phillips noted swarms of angry bees zipping upward. They were firing 37mm and 14.5mm. Sissy stuff, but it could get your attention. He did not call out the ground fire. The others probably saw it, and if not, nothing could really be done once you were in the middle of a dive-bomb anyway, if you wanted to hit anything. His eardrums popped repeatedly as they hurtled downward. He held his jaw forward to equalize the pressure in his inner ear.

"You're a bit steep," the Bear noted. "Almost fifty degrees."

"Compensating," grunted Phillips.

They pickled at 6,500 feet above the ground, very low for the steep dive angle, but he didn't want wide dispersal of the cluster bombs. Phillips pulled up to jink away from the target. He banked hard left suddenly, trying to sight the target visually.

"Shit!" cried the Bear. "The site's on the other side of the river."

Phillips quickly switched his vision and saw netting over there. The bomblets were going off on the near side of the river, sparkling like fireworks . . . useless fireworks! A shower of bullets streamed toward them, as if from a water hose, from the periphery of the real SAM site toward which they had turned in their escape maneuver.

The sissy stuff was trying to saw them in two!

"Damn!" yelled the Bear as the aircraft shuddered.

"We're hit!" Phillips pulled the stick, and the nose of the aircraft moved sluggishly upward. He continued his left turn, back toward the Red River.

They climbed up past the worst of the small-arms fire. Phillips tried to turn the aircraft to the right, gaining little response.

The Bear sucked in a breath, loud over the intercom. "Glenn, I can see holes in both wings."

"Yeah?" He was fighting even for limited control of the bird.

"There's a piece of metal sticking up through the left wing. Can't see how bad it is."

"*Stinger two, lead is hit. What's your position?*" called Phillips over the radio.

"*I'm at your five o'clock, coming up fast, lead,*" replied Tiny.

The aircraft lurched.

Tiny exclaimed, "*Lead, you're trailing smoke, and your left pylon just dropped away!*"

"*Roger,*" said Glenn, fighting hard at the controls.

"Bear," he cried out, "I don't think I can control it much longer. We're losing it!"

"Try to stay with it, Glenn," yelled the Bear. "We're still out over the valley."

Glenn's heart pounded wildly.

They crossed the Red River, headed for the hills.

Phillips groaned with his effort. The Thud was trying to enter a constant roll to the right. He held the left aileron and was kicking at the rudder pedals.

"Stay with it, Glenn!" encouraged the Bear.

Smoke was curling at Phillips's feet and his legs grew suddenly hot. He heard a crackling sound. "What's that?" he asked.

The Bear was coughing and gagging over the intercom. He tried to say something before starting to cough again.

"You okay back there?"

"Stay with it," the Bear whispered.

The thick smoke was impairing Glenn's vision. He wondered how far they had progressed past the Red River.

The Thunderchief bucked and shuddered in a rapid series of compression stalls.

"You're on fire, lead," called Tiny Bechler in a positive voice.

Glenn could see the fire in his mirrors. He wondered how the Bear was faring and started to ask.

"Get out!" Tiny yelled.

The engine quit and it was suddenly very quiet.

"Mayday!" called Phillips over the radio. He yelled one last time to the Bear over the intercom. "We're burning and I can't control it! We're gonna have to get out!"

"See you on the ground!"

"Take care, buddy!" said Phillips as the Thud began to slew sideways through the air.

"Get out!" called Tiny Bechler again.

"Shit!" yelled the Bear before coughing again. The expletive was a common one of aviators forced to bail out.

Phillips heard the explosion of the Bear's ejection seat. He then rotated his left ejection handle back. The hinges of his canopy released, thrusting up in the windstream. He tried to keep the aircraft upright by nursing the rudder one last time. Depressing the ejection-handle trigger, he immediately blacked out as explosive charges slammed the seat against his buttocks.

He returned to full consciousness a few seconds later, swinging in the chute, dazed and numb. The wind whispered as he floated earthward. He scanned the sky, but could not find Tiny. He looked down. Ahead he saw the impact of the aircraft in the green jungle. Dark smoke issued through the trees from the crash site.

He twisted and finally saw, at a considerable distance below, another olive-drab parachute. The Bear. He felt oddly serene, his eyes drawn downward. He peered at his right, lower leg. His foot was pointed inward and something white protruded through his flight suit, the end splintered and sharp. He stared in amazement at the broken bone.

It's going to hurt like hell in a moment. I'm in shock now, he calmly told himself, *but I've got to act quickly before the pain arrives and screws up my thinking.*

He tried to pull a survival radio from his vest. He failed the first time, but pulled off and discarded his flying gloves and was successful on his second attempt. He switched the radio to T/R, the transmit and receive mode.

"Weeep, weeep, weeep . . ."

All Phillips could hear on the radio was his activated emergency beacon.

"Damn."

He twisted and grasped the right parachute riser in his hand, released a canvas cover, then felt inside to switch off the beeper. He listened again on the radio. The emergency channel was clear.

"Stinger lead has ejected," he rasped. He remembered the Bear, but could no longer see the other parachute. *"Stinger lead Alpha and Bravo have ejected."*

28/0745L—People's Army HQ, Hanoi, DRV

Xuan Nha

Lt Col Xuan Nha was left in charge at the command center, as Colonel Trung was off inspecting damage done during the Yen Vien air attack. The atmosphere in the large, poorly ventilated basement room was electric with tension, as always during an air attack. The plotters and battle staff waited impatiently for more word about the American rescue mission in progress some 200 kilometers northwest of Hanoi.

Xuan was not overly optimistic. His boldest battalion, Tiger, reported that they had not had time to set up either battery in the area. They were languishing under hastily contrived camouflage nets on different sections of railroad north of Yen Bai. Success or failure lay with the command battery of Cobra battalion, commanded by Maj Nham Do, and in the dozen interceptors launched to nip at the edges of the rescue force.

Nham Do was new, too cautious and careful, too prone to precisely follow the complex Soviet doctrine for Xuan's liking. Xuan had radioed him as the fighters were still ingressing, to say that today he expected results. Xuan had hinted that he needed a commander at a remote listening post near the border, hoping to spur Maj Nham Do to his own philosophy of attack, attack, attack.

The Americans had come early. He had still been in his office when Lt Quang Hanh had advised that the listening stations were reporting their passage. Other reports arrived. About thirty fighters, a medium-scale effort, flew on a track north of their usual ingress route, in a line directly toward the Fan Si Pan and the downed American pilot. Xuan Nha had hurried down to the command center, made his radio call to Major Do, then sat back to see if his game of using the American pilot as bait would pay off.

The last word from Cobra had been that two Thunder planes Nham Do thought were radar-hunters had turned directly toward them, as if to attack. He was preparing to fire rockets at them.

Xuan's face was impassive, showing a mask of serenity, but his mind was churning with possibilities.

A radar-hunter aircraft! Cobra must succeed, so they could study the wreckage and question the pilot.

Major Nguy raised his head from one of the field telephones on his desk. "Colonel Nha, two American rescue helicopters are reported passing south of Than Uyen."

Xuan digested the news. The rescue effort was succeeding. They were probably picking up the pilot even now. He cursed inwardly, wondering if he had erred by not allowing them to capture the pilot.

There were too many American fighters to attempt to get

MiG interceptors through to the helicopters, which flew well below the altitude coverage of the rocket sites. He grew impatient for news from Cobra.

Lieutenant Hanh hurried up once more, excited with his message. "The radar-hunter fired a missile, hitting Cobra one. This time their missile did much damage."

"Go on."

"The explosion ruined the antenna van and fragments went through the command van. One of the radar operators was killed."

Xuan felt hot with anger.

"Major Do reports that one Thunder plane was hit by the artillery he'd deployed about the site. It was obviously crippled as it turned back toward the mountains to the west."

"That's all?"

"Major Do sends his deepest regrets about the damage to Cobra one. He is very upset, sir."

"He should be." Xuan Nha walked to the map table and motioned for Quang Hanh to follow.

The baby-faced lieutenant laid a finger on Cobra one's location, tracing a route directly westward toward the mountains south of the rescue effort. "The American fighter was last seen here trailing smoke and fire. It was definitely burning, sir. Major Do reports that it surely cannot remain airborne."

"He would say that, wouldn't he?"

Major Nguy joined them at the table. "Observers at Yen Bai have reported that a Thunder plane in trouble passed five kilometers north of their location."

Xuan Nha flickered a smile before springing into action. "Major Wu, please join us," he snapped. Then to Quang Hanh: "Get Colonel Thao Phong on the telephone line. I wish to speak directly with him."

Major Wu joined them, his cadaverous face strained.

"I am placing you in charge of the effort to capture the pilot of an aircraft believed to have just crashed a few kilometers east of Yen Bai," said Xuan. "It is imperative that we capture him. Use whatever resources are necessary. I *must* question this pilot."

Although Xuan was the husband of his aunt, Major Wu normally tried to avoid difficult tasks for the fruits of failure were often unpleasant. Xuan knew that, yet he also felt that Wu might be able to use his party influence to cut through any red tape necessary to capture the pilot.

"The pilot has probably ejected from his aircraft somewhere in this area." Xuan pointed to the rugged area between Yen Bai and Nghia Lo.

"It may be difficult with all the American fighters in the area," said Major Wu, his voice low. "Perhaps Major Nguy is more suited to this task, comrade Colonel."

Xuan Nha hid his impatience. "Major Nguy is busy with reports. Somehow we will deal with the American fighters. Concentrate on getting ground forces into the area."

"Yes, sir."

"Immediately!"

Major Wu hurried to find an unused radio phone so he could muster the ground forces.

Xuan Nha remembered something else and pointed a finger at Major Nguy. "Get in touch with the Russian, Major Gregarian. Tell him to stay at Yen Bai and not to move the new P-50 radar until we have completed the capture effort. Too many American aircraft will be roaming about up there."

"Yes, comrade Colonel."

Quang Hanh was holding a telephone toward Xuan.

"Do we have a listening post at Nghia Lo, Lieutenant?"

"Yes, comrade Colonel. I will check to see if they have sighted the burning aircraft."

Xuan Nha liked Quang Nha's initiative and quick mind. "Pass your findings to Major Wu."

Xuan took the telephone; his tone changed. "I took pity upon your sister and let her look upon my elephant's trunk," Xuan told Lt Col Thao Phong, air battalion commander at Phuc Yen.

"Your mother was most appreciative when I let her into my pilots' barracks last night," replied Thao Phong.

"Are your pilots ready to fly?" asked Xuan Nha. "I may have targets for them."

"There are too many American pirates flying, Xuan Nha. Both Phantoms and Thunder planes. I lost an airplane and a good pilot to a Phantom less than half an hour ago."

"They cannot fly forever without refueling," Xuan said. "I intend to watch very closely with my radars and listening posts and tell you precisely the moment the majority start to leave."

"Go on," Thao Phong said, his interest piqued.

28/0825L—North of Nghia Lo, North Vietnam

Bear Stewart

The fire had burned its way into the Bear's oxygen system. As he squeezed the ejection handle, he sucked in a lungful of hot, bitter smoke and began to choke. Then the explosive charge blasted him out of the aircraft and pure oxygen was forced into his lungs from the high-pressure green bottle attached to the seat. The little green bottle saved his life.

He clawed the oxygen mask catches loose from his helmet, but before he could gulp in a breath of fresh air he threw up black soot, mucus, and chunks of food through his nostrils and mouth. Then, through eyes awash with tears from the raucous coughing, he saw a small village below. Reacting instinctively, he located two red-marked lanyards on the rear risers and tugged hard. The canopy was reconfigured, with the air funneled out the back like a sport parachute. He was able to steer around the village a couple of miles farther toward the northwest.

He saw Phillips's chute, higher and southwest of him, dropping toward a large open field. The Bear steered around to land closer to the pilot, but cautiously so, for he was circling back in the direction of the village.

He looked at the horizon. The earth was verdant, with teak forests and lush jungle broken with patches of tall elephant grass. To the northwest were green mountains. Southward were rugged formations called karsts—series of honeycombed, sandstone cliffs. Behind him was the river and the heavily populated valley. Westward was freedom.

He choked again and more vomit gushed. His chest constricted with sharp pain as he panted. Closer to the ground now, he tried to pick an acceptable landing area, for he didn't wish to get tangled up in a 200-foot teak tree. He became so convulsed with coughing that he almost blacked out. Good fortune prevailed and he tumbled to earth in a small clearing. The camouflaged parachute settled in a heap over him.

He clawed his way free, pausing for another fit of coughing. He crammed his face into the nylon fabric of the parachute to muffle the sound. The spasms ended abruptly. He sat there on the ground, wondering if it was safe to pull the nylon from his face. After a few seconds he realized he must, for he couldn't simply sit and wait for the gomers to arrive. He sucked air into his lungs in a cautious, painful gulp.

Glenn Phillips

Phillips looked at the ground and saw he had little time. He pulled down on the left parachute riser, sluggishly steering away from tall trees toward an open field of grass. He prepared for a PLF, which would allow a fall in the opposite direction from the broken leg.

His instructors at the Fort Benning jump school would have been proud of their student's parachute landing fall that morning. Phillips lay quietly where he had landed for a few seconds, allowing the chute to collapse before him, increasingly apprehensive about disturbing the broken leg. When he finally moved, it was to remove his helmet and suck gulps of sweet air and to reassure himself that he had made it thus far. A numb leg, but at least he was alive, more or less functioning properly.

I'm in shock, he realized. The pain was about to come.

Bear Stewart

The Bear warily released the parachute straps, stood and looked, cautiously approached the inflated raft. He pulled his Buck knife with its eight-inch blade from the sheath on the g-suit leg and stabbed the raft several times. Then he dragged it, still hissing and deflating, behind a sprawling bush. Moving faster, he performed rough surgery on the parachute to remove a single panel of fabric, then cut off several strands of nylon parachute cord. He emptied the contents of the survival kit onto the panel, quickly deciding what was essential. With his knife and hands he dug a hole in the soft earth behind the bush, burying the excess with the flattened raft and remainder of the chute. He accomplished it all in a trancelike state, constantly fighting the urge to cough. It took less than fifteen minutes, but it seemed forever.

The Bear wrapped his treasures into the parachute panel, tossed the sack over his shoulder, and carefully looked around.

"Malcom old buddy, you're one hell of a long way from McAlester, Oklahoma," he said to himself, just so he could hear his voice. It did not give him confidence. Cautiously, and looking about as he went, he began to jog toward where he had last seen his pilot descending in his chute.

Glenn Phillips

He lay in tall grass, the parachute collapsed in a heap in front of him. The survival kit in its gray, fiberglass shell, had dangled a few feet beneath him during his descent and now lay at his feet. The bright yellow raft was propped upright in the elephant grass fifteen feet away.

The grass was good cover, he thought, but the damned raft was like a beacon. He had to do something about it.

His leg was beginning to throb with the first spasms of sharp pain. He remembered the syringe of morphine packed in the kit and hauled in the lanyard connecting him to the survival kit—with great urgency.

He heard the rumble of jet engines. The sound of hope. He switched on the emergency beacon so they could home on it with their direction-finding equipment. With the pain becoming so severe, he was surprised at his lucidity.

I must continue to think clearly! Can't allow the pain to take over. Got to stay in control.

The survival kit was now in his grasp. He fumbled with the catches, opened the lid, and after a moment found the syringe marked with a warning. He screwed the needle into place, hands shaking, then jabbed it into the muscle of his forearm. He squeezed half the contents into his system.

That should handle the pain.

The morphine effect was immediate. He moved as if in a dream, floating happily yet panting with exertion. Sweat ran down his face in tiny rivers as he pulled at the rubber raft's lanyard. He yanked hard and the raft flopped down flat. He continued to pull. When it was within reach he stabbed it with his knife until it was deflated.

He was exhausted.

The sounds of the jet engines grew louder. As he listened more intently, he could also hear chopping sounds and shrill, distant voices.

Bear Stewart

Dense forest was slowing his progress and every several minutes he'd have to stop to gag. It was frustrating, not being able to make better time.

He heard excited voices off to his left, moving parallel to his route, and knew they were coming for him. Cursing inwardly, he steeled his nerves, as he did when he flew into a heavy combat area. He burrowed into the protection of a thicket of bushes then he carefully placed the sack on the ground at his side, pulling his revolver from its shoulder-holster.

Should he fight or surrender? He mulled it over in his mind, then decided to be judicious and act according to the situation. The fits of coughing had robbed him of a great deal of spirit.

The voices were close when he felt the familiar heaving of his chest and realized he was about to vomit again. He did so as silently as possible, and when the stream of black puke abated, he buried his teeth into the nylon parachute fabric and bit hard to keep from coughing. He convulsed and choked, but remained quiet. He had to. His life depended on it.

The villagers passed by, their voices growing faint. The rush of exhilaration was followed by dark shame: they were headed toward Phillips. The Bear edged back, farther from their trail, and hefted the sack. He scrambled for ten minutes through particularly dense jungle, directly away from the path of the villagers.

The rumble of jet fighters grew loud.

Glenn Phillips

Despite the drug's effect, Phillips was filled with dread. The voices were getting closer. His rescuers had damn well better hurry. He lifted the hand-held emergency radio and switched off the emergency beeper. He carefully turned down the volume on the radio, lifted it to his ear, and switched to RECEIVE ONLY.

"Bee flight, check in!" he heard.

"Two!"
"Three!"
"Four!"

The sound amplified from his survival radio was loud. He was fumbling to turn down the volume when he heard another call.

"Stinger lead, this is Hornet. Do you read me?"

Phillips's emotions rebounded from despair to happiness. He turned the wafer switch to TRANS/REC.

"Hornet, Stinger Alpha reads you," he answered. *"I'm at the edge of a field of elephant grass. I can see you now. I'm at your eleven o'clock, four or five miles out."*

"I read you loud and clear, Stinger Alpha," came Colonel Mack's reply. *"We've got Sandies and Jolly Greens standing by to pull you out of there, partner."*

Phillips heard the Vietnamese voices again, more strident now. He pulled the issue .38 Special revolver from his vest holster and laid it beside the survival kit before raising the radio to his lips again.

He spoke his next words apprehensively, knowing they would call off the rescue if there was the potential for danger to the vulnerable Sandies and Jolly Green rescue helicopters. *"I've got company, Stinger. I can hear them coming."*

"How close are they, Stinger Alpha?"

Phillips tried to judge. *"Probably a couple hundred yards away and moving toward me, Hornet."*

The roar of the jets grew louder. He saw a formation of Thuds in the distance.

"You think they've got a fix on your location, Alpha?"

"Yeah," Glenn said. *"They probably saw me coming down."*

"Okay, Alpha, let's try something. Give me smoke . . . orange smoke."

Phillips hastily searched through the contents of the survival kit and lifted out a smoke flare. He pulled the initiator ring, waved the sputtering flare in the air until it spewed a steady steam of bright orange smoke, then held it as high as his arm would reach. The smoke billowed as the excited voices drew closer.

The two flights of Thuds changed to trail formation, one behind the other, and descended toward Phillips's smoke. The lead aircraft rolled into a slight bank while Colonel Mack adjusted course, then headed directly at the advancing Vietnamese at 300 feet above the ground.

Just as he passed over the Vietnamese, a loud B-R-R-A-A-A-A-T sounded as Colonel Mack fired his Gatling gun.

The second fighter imitated its leader, followed by the third, fourth, and so forth, each Thud flying low and firing a short, loud burst with the gun as it passed directly overhead. The roar of the engines and belching sounds of the Gatling guns were so loud that the earth seemed to vibrate. Nine aircraft each made one pass, flying the same racetrack pattern they would on a gunnery range. One aircraft's gunnery pass followed the the other in a noisy merry-go-round.

The aircraft finally pulled off high, forming back into individual flights. Tiny Bechler had joined them, for five aircraft were in one flight.

You'll do, Lieutenant, he thought.

Phillips listened carefully for sounds of the villagers and heard them crashing wildly in the distance, their sounds receding.

Glenn exulted. *"Hornet, Stinger Alpha. I can hear the gomers traveling away from my position."*

"Roger, Stinger Alpha, I hoped that might get their attention. The Sandies are inbound now." Colonel Mack paused. *"Stinger Bravo, can you hear me?"*

The Bear responded immediately. *"Bravo reads you five-by-five."*

The transmission was loud. The Bear had to be close by.

"Stinger Bravo, were you close enough to see Alpha's smoke?"

"Negative. I'm in a dense growth of brush. I was close enough to hear the voices though. The people are from a village southeast of my position. Alpha's west of the village. I was moving toward him when I heard the gomers going for him."

"I've got the village in sight. You're correct about Alpha's position," said Colonel Mack. *"How close are you to the village, Bravo?"*

"Maybe a mile." Bear Stewart ended the transmission with a fit of coughing.

"How about working your way a mile or two farther from the village, Bravo. Let's say northwest, directly away from them. That's pretty heavy jungle area, but there's a few small

clearings there. The farther you are from the village, the better the Jolly Greens will feel about attempting a pickup."

"Will do, Hornet."

"What's your condition, Bravo?"

"I'm fine." He coughed. "Swallowed some smoke and shit in the aircraft, but otherwise okay."

"How about you, Alpha?"

Phillips looked dreamily at the bone sticking through the g-suit. "I got a ticket home, Colonel. A bad fracture of the leg."

"Are you able to move around?"

"No, sir."

"Stick tight and we'll get you out of there."

"Roger."

"Hornet, this is Bravo. I'm ready to move out now. You won't hear from me for a while."

Phillips listened to the radio conversation as if he were a nonparticipant. Like he was watching a movie—or having a very bad dream. The morphine had put him into a euphoric state that scared him almost as much as the situation.

Bear Stewart

As the Bear walked northwest, stopping periodically to stifle the nasty fits of coughing, he had very pleasant visions of this being a short-term stay in North Vietnam. He thought up lines like, *Sorry, folks, but I just have to go. Got a lunch date with No Hab at the Club.*

Glenn Phillips

Phillips was startled awake by the angry, buzzing sounds of a propeller-driven airplane. He'd dropped off to sleep. An A-1H Sandy aircraft hove into view, banking over the clearing. He noticed then that his survival radio was crackling with sounds.

"Stinger Alpha, this is Sandy lead, change to channel delta on your radio. I repeat, change to channel delta." The stubby, tough little airplane flew around the periphery of Phillips's view.

Glenn selected D with a wafer switch on front of the hand-held radio. Woozy from the drug, he examined his work.

"This is Stinger Alpha on channel delta," he said into the radio. His voice sounded like he had a mouth full of soggy crackers.

"Good. I'm reading you five-by-five, Alpha. How bad is the leg?" Phillips saw a second A-1H holding in a nearby orbit. They made sounds like swarming bees.

Phillips looked down, mused, and cocked his head. *"Pretty bad. The bone's sticking through the side of the g-suit."* The leg was throbbing again.

"I think I've got you in sight, Stinger Alpha. Are you connected to the deflated raft down there?"

"Yes."

"Okay, I can see the raft with you stretched out beside it. Any company at the present time?"

Phillips listened hard. *"Nope,"* he said.

"What's your mother's maiden name, Alpha?"

Phillips thought, then said, *"Peters!"*

"And your favorite football team?"

"College or pro?" Phillips asked warily.

"Pro."

"Well it's certainly not the Browns."

"What is it, Alpha? What's your favorite pro football team?" The Sandy pilot sounded patient, not angry at him. He had a list of questions relayed to him by Red Crown. The downed pilots had to answer the questions correctly or the search could be called off.

"Go Dolphins!" Phillips chuckled at his cleverness, then grimaced in pain. The leg was beginning to really trouble him. *"My leg hurts,"* he whimpered.

"I understand, Stinger Alpha. Hang in there a little longer."

"I'm going to use the rest of the morphine," Phillips announced.

"Not yet, Stinger Alpha! The paramedics in the Jolly Green will take care of you. That'll be in about half an hour or so. You can handle it until then. We gotta keep you alert for the party, you know."

"Party?"

"We'll have a whing-ding party when we return to base. Three in one morning is a good score."

Phillips grimaced, fighting the growing pain in his leg. He looked up then and felt a moment of confused panic.

"Where's the F-105's?" he asked the Sandy driver.

"Hornet had to depart for the tanker, Stinger Alpha. They depleted their fuel running off your gomers down there. The other two Thud flights have refueled and are on their way back. Soon as they get here we'll get the show on the road and get you outta there. Don't fret, Stinger Alpha. We Sandies will take care of you. These old Spads may be slow, but they're tough."

"I see." Glenn thought about Benny Lewis. *"You say you got Kingfish out?"*

"Safe and sound. Old Jolly Green's got him almost back home by now."

"That's great!" Benny Lewis was out! Even with the pain Glenn felt good about that.

"Yeah. Stand by, Alpha."

Five minutes later Sandy lead came back on the air and reestablished contact. *"The choppers are just twenty minutes out, holding for fighter support. It won't be long."*

"Roger." Phillips felt heady with excitement. Very soon the terrible pain would be alleviated.

"Also, Sandy two just got a fix on Stinger Bravo."

The second A-1H Sandy was talking to the Bear on another rescue frequency. Glenn grunted his response from between clenched teeth.

Something in the distance drew his attention. He glanced at the Sandy buzzing about over the area and at the second A-1H circling to their north. He then peered hard at the sky. A glint of sunlight flashed off something to the east. He shaded his eyes, swatting at an incessant swarm of insects. He could just make out the shapes.

He scrambled for the radio.

"Sandy lead, you've got MiG-17's."

"Say again?" called the Sandy pilot, his voice still conversational. *"I was talking on my other radio."*

The lead MiG was descending directly toward Sandy lead.

"You've got a MiG at your five o'clock, Sandy lead!" cried Glenn.

The silver MiG opened fire at 3,000 feet. The A-1H immediately nosed over and slammed into the side of a hill.

The second Sandy saw his leader crash, watched a silver MiG-17 flash by, and transmitted a panic call on Guard channel.

"Mayday! They've just shot down Sandy lead! Mayday!"

"Damn, damn, damn," Phillips whispered. He turned his channel selector to emergency frequency, gritted his teeth with the pain, and transmitted, *"Get down in the weeds and turn, Sandy two. They can't hit you if you keep turning!"*

He watched as the Sandy fled, heeding Phillips's advice as he jinked and turned and hugged the hills. MiG's swarmed everywhere, making gunnery passes on the elusive, slow bird. Another formation of MiG's held high above.

The shooting gallery moved west and then it grew quiet. Glenn realized he was parched and remembered the drinking water in the plastic bottles sewn into his survival vest. The water was hot and tasted of plastic. He drained both bottles, trying not to think.

Bear Stewart

The Bear stared with disbelief as two silver MiG-17's flew directly over his position at 1,000 feet.

"Assholes," he ranted. "Fucking rotten, commie bastards!"

For the moment the rescue attempt was done for. There was no way they'd bring the Sandy back and without him the Jolly Greens wouldn't come. With trembling fingers he began to fashion a backpack from the parachute fabric and riser cord. Emotion gnawed as he prepared to leave behind his friend, close as a brother, to face the humiliated gomers. The Bear paused before strapping on the makeshift pack to head northwest toward the mountains he'd seen earlier.

Glenn Phillips

Phillips sighed mightily. He picked up the half-empty syringe, set it on his chest, and quietly lay back. He would not be able to think clearly after a second morphine shot, so he decided to get any heavy pondering over with now. He tried to relax, but couldn't with the pain shooting through the leg, spreading through his body.

He thought of his parents in Florida, how he should write more often and how badly he wanted to see them. He'd get his blue and white '62 Corvette out of storage in Las Vegas and drive east on Route 66. Take his time traveling across the South. Call his old girlfriend in San Antonio. If she wasn't tied up maybe they'd go out for a couple of drinks and a good time. Then on to Fort Pierce to surprise the folks. They'd like that.

Human sounds. Shouting and rustling from the field. Not much idle chatter this time. They knew exactly where they'd find him.

He gathered the survival radios together—four of them in all—and one by one smashed them on a rock until they were useless. He didn't worry about the noise.

The people were drawing nearer, moving cautiously as they closed in.

Perhaps they would be friendly. He couldn't remember a bombing raid near this area. No reason for them to hate Americans.

Sure, he chided himself, *a pocket of Democrats right here in North Vietnam.* Tears of pain coursed down his face.

He lifted the revolver, wondering if he should use it on either them or himself. He hesitated. *Bullshit!* he decided, drawing back. He threw it as far as possible into the tall grass.

Phillips waited until he felt their presence, then pushed the needle into his forearm, slowly depressing the plunger. He tossed the empty syringe aside.

Come on dope! he thought, gnashing his teeth in agony.

A villager wearing a coolie hat and loincloth emerged from the wall of grass, gripping a nasty-looking machete, staring inquisitively. A woman appeared at his side carrying a short, three-pronged pitchfork. The man spoke in a low tone and motioned abruptly at Phillips. The woman glared.

"Hello, motherfuckers," Glenn said cheerfully. The morphine was taking the edge from the pain.

The woman regarded him with cold hatred. When several more villagers arrived, she spoke in a shrill voice, gesturing at him. Her mouth looked filled with blood, from chewing betel nuts.

"Ugly," muttered Glenn as he tried to give her a charming grin.

The villagers surrounded him, looking, staring, and chattering excitedly about the bone that protruded from the g-suit. The woman approached, prodded at the bone, laughing. Phillips groaned at the dull pain. She probed more harshly, making Glenn Phillips shriek and wish he could die. He tried to curl himself into a protective ball. The woman kicked the leg and he cried like a baby. She jabbed the pitchfork into the leg and he puked up water and chunks of the candy bar he'd eaten for breakfast. He began to sob as she continued the relentless jabbing.

After a while the men rigged him to a strong bamboo pole and carried him to the village, where they stuffed him into a small cage, the bottom of which was covered with sweet-smelling shit.

More than sixty people inhabited the small village. They gathered to see him babble as the woman continued to probe his leg with the pitchfork. The men eventually tired of the game and went back to their bamboo huts. Other women and several children joined in the woman's fun, prodding with a variety of wooden sticks so they could listen to him scream.

Bear Stewart

From several miles away the Bear heard the keening from the village. At first he tried to think the sounds were made by a jungle bird. He knew better. He gritted his teeth; his rage building.

"You just hang in there and survive, Glenn," he whispered. "I'll do the getting even." There were a few tears, but they were ones of outrage at what they were doing to his pilot and of shame that he'd done nothing to help.

Late in the afternoon a truck drove into the village and several soldiers, wearing pith helmets and baggy green uniforms, shoved their way through the crowd. They stared at the American stuffed into the small cage. One pulled his ear to see if he was alive. Getting no response, he toed the broken, exposed leg bone and heard a low moan.

They dragged the pig cage to the truck and were in the process of lifting it into the truck's bed when a woman came running up, shrieking. She pushed them aside, shouting and brandishing her pitchfork, saying that all three of her sons had been killed by Americans in the south. A soldier threatened to shoot her if she did not desist.

The soldiers put the cage onto the truck bed, then shoved it forward until it rested against the cab. One made a short speech, grinning and pointing at the pilot, then crawled into the passenger's seat. Two others got in front while the rest gathered in back. One lounged with his feet on the cage as the truck was driven from the village.

Bear Stewart

He intermittently walked and jogged throughout the remainder of the day, placing as much territory as possible between himself and the village. At first he had to stop every ten or fifteen minutes. He was still coughing and spitting up soot and crud. By late afternoon the spasms had diminished, leaving only a raw throat and aching chest.

He drove himself relentlessly, crawling through brambles, scrambling up hillsides, slogging through marshes and streams. As the evening light waned, he was grasping for fingerholds to climb a 200-foot karst that blocked his way. He finished the climb in darkness, then descended a long, sloping hillside of elephant grass to enter a dense teak forest. After half an hour he stopped because he could go no farther in the pitch black of the jungle night.

28/1140L—Udorn RTAFB, Thailand

Benny Lewis

The A-1H Sandy aircraft were stationed at Udorn because that base was closest to the northern portions of North Vietnam where the majority of fighters were shot down. The medical clinic at Udorn was one of the best equipped of the forward bases, and many of the pilots were taken there by the Jolly Green helicopters after being picked up.

Rescue forces—the Sandy pilots and the crews for the big HH-3 helicopters called Jolly Greens—had to be convinced of the positive identity of the pilots they rescued, for they were the easiest targets in the North Vietnamese sky. They wanted to make damned sure they weren't being suckered into a flak trap, or into hovering over some gomer dressed up like an American pilot, so they asked questions no one but the pilot would likely know.

The personal data card on Benny was a capsule of his life:

```
N; LEWIS, BENJAMIN LLOYD, JR. / NN; BENNY / R;
0-3 / DOS; 12 JUN 59 / CMP; REGAF / SN;
FR69277 / DOB; 22 JAN 37 / POB; SANTA ROSA,
CAL / RC; CAUCASIAN / HT; 71" / WT; 185# / HR;
BLD / E; BLU / BL; O POS / DEN; METH / MS;
MARRIED, 02 SEP 61, ELIZABETH (NMN) DOWNEY,
2701 E. CHARLESTON AVE, LAS VEGAS, NEV - 2
CHILDREN, (1 M/1 F) / FATHER (L) - MOTHER (L)
(CONNORS) / Q; CHILDHOOD PET CHICKEN - MR
BUGS / Q; FAVORITE SPORT - SKIING / Q;
FAVORITE COLOR - RED.
```

"It would be the shits," the paramedic told Benny Lewis, "if we picked up some gomer and he said, *You make one mistake, Yankee dog. Take me home to Hanoi.*"

"Hell," Benny said, still euphoric over the rescue, "you almost know as much as I do about me."

"Almost?" said the wiry black sergeant who had gone down the cable and helped connect him to the tree penetrator device. "You forgot your pet chicken's name."

"I was close," replied Benny.

"Mister Flies is not close, Captain. Mister Bags was close. Mister Big was close. But Mister Flies? Not close at all."

"Flies are more closely related to bugs than bags."

"Admit it, Captain, you were shook up."

Benny had powerful arms, but he had struggled with the tree penetrator device they had lowered at the end of the cable. The diminutive sergeant had dropped down, secured Benny to the device, given the thumbs up to the cable operator, and held Benny in a tight embrace all the way to the chopper. He was a pro, and Benny was thankful they had men like him on their side.

"Hell," he said, "I'm lucky I remembered my name."

The paramedic sergeant laughed. "Good to have you home, sir." He glanced at the door. "I've got to leave now. Got a hundred reports to fill out because we were successful. If we hadn't been, I'd be at the club having breakfast right now. See how much trouble you caused." He grinned and nodded his head at the medics in the hospital examining room. "They'll take good care of you."

"Do you know whether they picked up the guys flying Stinger lead?"

"Our pilot said a real fiasco was taking place over there. You can find out when you go over to make your phone call."

"Phone call?"

"Yes, sir. When they let you outta here, head over to Sandy Control, that's the rescue command post here. If they got a free line, the guys there'll connect you to the nearest Air Force base and the base operator there'll connect you with home. Your family live close to a base?"

"Near Nellis, in Nevada."

"Shouldn't be a problem then, if they got lines open. The quality of the telephone system isn't bad, and I'm sure you'd like to let your family know you're okay."

"I'd like that. And Sergeant, thanks again."

"Just doin' my job, sir." The staff sergeant left.

A sallow-faced flight surgeon stared intently at him, as if trying to find something wrong with him that the X rays, blood, and urine samples weren't revealing.

Benny shrugged. "Honest, Doc. I'm fine."

"Never can tell," the doctor said gravely. "I'm not sure about the back."

"I feel good. A little stiff, but good."

"You'll get a Purple Heart, you know. You were wounded in combat."

"Wounded?"

"The hand," said the doctor. "I'll make sure the paperwork gets started."

"But I'm fine." Benny had cut the web of his hand between thumb and forefinger on the ejection handle, and had required three stitches and a splash of disinfectant.

"Take advantage of all you can, Captain. You deserve it."

Benny grinned again. It felt wonderful to be out of the hostile jungle.

"We're trying to decide whether to send you to the hospital at Clark Air Base for further observation," the doctor said.

"The Philippines?"

"This is just a field hospital, one step up from dispensary. Clark has the regional hospital. They're much better equipped than we are here. Better equipment, full lab facilities, well staffed."

Benny's mind was blossoming with another idea. He could finish whatever tests they wanted at Clark, then get a hop up to Honolulu and meets Bets for a week of fun in the sun before returning to Takhli. "How tough is it to get a hop to Hickam from there, doc?"

"They have med-evac flights going to Hawaii every day. Like I said, take all you can get."

"The paramedic said the command post could hook me up to my home phone."

"If the lines are available."

"How do I get there?"

While he waited for the rest of his blood and urine samples to be checked, he took a shower, ate a good meal, and even conned a hospital tech into picking up a new flight suit from the personal equipment shop. Even then he hadn't been cleared to leave the hospital.

He killed the time with thoughts about his family. It gave him a warm feeling, made him realize he had an anchor for the sometimes nomadic military life. He loved his wife, adored both his children. Bets was a bit high-strung, he sometimes thought, and had been spoiled and encouraged to spend beyond her means by her overindulgent father, but she meant well. And the kids were coming up straight and fine. Intelligent and sparkly-eyed children he could be proud of.

He tried again, finally talking the flight surgeon into letting him get away long enough to get the call through. A medic drove him to the rescue center.

Sandy Control was a hastily contrived wooden structure on the flight line. After showing his ID to the burly sergeant at the door, he entered the darkened room.

A major shook his hand. "Good to have you back with us, Captain Lewis."

"Thanks. By the way, have you got a status on Stinger lead? A Weasel crew shot down on my Res-CAP?"

"They're still up there," the major said, filling Benny in on the details of the day's Res-CAP mission.

Half an hour later Benny sat, with growing anticipation, at a small table in the rear of the command post. After several failed attempts they finally got a line through to the Nellis autovon operator, who placed the call. Benny listened hard over the static-filled line as the telephone rang on the other end.

After being shot down, losing two good friends, and

hearing about the Sandy pilot's death, he had become numbed by the accumulation of shitty luck. He was ready to hear the voices of home, to talk with the kids and tell Bets how much he missed her. He could hardly wait to tell her about meeting him in Honolulu. She'd like that.

Bets was not at ease with her role as a military wife, and their six years of marriage had been tough for her. He'd always told himself he would make it up to her someday; today seemed a good time to start. As the telephone continued to ring he savored his eagerness. It was after one in the morning in Las Vegas, so he wasn't surprised that she was slow answering.

"H'lo?" A male voice, thick with sleep or booze.

Damn! "Sorry to wake you. Wrong number," Benny said.

"Yeah, okay." The man hung up.

Benny motioned to the airman first class who had put the call through. "Got a wrong number."

"Hold on, sir. I've still got Nellis on the line, so they can just redial."

Benny listened as the call was placed once more, shaking his head in disgust. The previous night in the jungle he would have given anything to hear his family's voices. For a while he had thought he might never get the chance to do so again, or at best for a long, long while. He didn't appreciate the wrong number.

The airman motioned for him to pick up the receiver again. This time Bets answered.

"Hi, honey, it's Ben." The sound echoed over the many miles, but he couldn't keep the exultation from his voice.

"Ben? It's really you?" Her voice was husky.

"Yeah. Damn but it's great to hear your voice. Great!"

He heard her suck in her breath. "The line's awful, Ben. It's like you're in an echo chamber somewhere." There was a long pause. "You're not back in the States yet, are you?"

She was acting strange.

"No," he said. "I'm not in the States."

"Where are you?" she demanded. She had been drinking. He could recognize the fuzzy voice she got when she drank too much.

"I'm in Thailand." He started to tell her about the shoot-down, but decided against it. Something else bothered him, the edge of guilt he could hear in her voice. "Uh, Bets?"

"Yes?"

"How are the kids?"

"Fine. Why do you ask? Were you worried I wasn't taking care of them?" She sounded defensive, not at all happy to hear his voice.

"Of course not. Could I talk with them?"

"They're up in Oregon with my parents. Mom and Dad came down to visit. They took the kids back with them for a couple of weeks."

"I didn't know."

They were both quiet for a long pause.

"You, ah . . . you sound strained, Bets. Anything wrong?"

Silence.

"Want to talk about it?" he asked. His stomach was turning sour.

"No." Her voice was very weak.

He sucked in his breath, then exhaled it very slowly. "I didn't get a wrong number when I called a few minutes ago, did I?"

"Was that you?" she blurted.

"Yeah. That was me." Benny felt like he wanted to puke.

She paused for only a heartbeat. "No."

"No?"

"No, you did not get a wrong number. We certainly weren't expecting your call."

We? He felt numb. "Who is it? The guy who answered the phone, I mean."

"You don't know him, Ben."

It was his turn to pause. "What's his name?" He'd kill the bastard.

"Really, you don't know him."

"I see." He cleared his throat. "Have, ah, have you known him long?"

"Long enough. . . . Ben, let's stop this. I don't want it. I don't need it. I didn't mean for you to find out this way. I really didn't. But now you know, and that's the way it is. I was going to write and tell you."

Benny sat with his head covered by his hands. He shivered once, then cleared his throat. When he spoke next, his voice croaked.

"The kids . . ." His voice failed him.

"I'll be fair about them. You'll have time with them."

They were quiet for a long moment.

"I told my parents what I was doing, Ben. How it was getting impossible between us and all. They understand."

"I didn't know it was bad between us."

"I can't take it any longer. I couldn't take another tour in Germany, with you gone all the time. I don't want to go to Asia and be stationed in some godforsaken hole in Japan. I don't want the Air Force any more. You're happy whenever you're around airplanes, but I'm miserable every time I come near a military base. If I ever remarry, it'll be to someone who's there when I need him to fix the car or move furniture or mow the lawn." She was wound up, spewing out words like she'd been saving them.

"I see," was all that Benny could think of. He felt hurt and foolish. Another man was there, in *his* home, with *his* wife, listening to them talk.

"I don't think you really care, Ben. You've never . . ."

A voice cut in, saying "Priority call," and the line went dead. He depressed the cutoff button and replaced the receiver.

He walked in the tropical heat in a trance, so troubled that he ignored the men who saluted as they passed. The devastation was overpowering, attacking the very core of his being. He had been a part of something wonderful, and now, without warning, it was gone. What would become of him with his family gone? He felt very sorry for himself.

He found the O' Club. The lieutenant who had flown Sandy two that morning was there, distraught and intoxicated, drinking with his friends. Benny sat in a corner of the bar, oblivious to what was happening around him. He ordered a Beefeaters, straight and neat, and asked the bartender to keep them coming.

CHAPTER FIVE

Monday, November 28th—2200 Local, People's Army HQ, Hanoi, DRV

Xuan Nha

The day had started well.

At 0850 operators at the controls of Xuan's P-2 acquisition radars radioed the command center to tell them the American fighters were withdrawing, leaving the rescue forces at least momentarily unprotected. Lt Quang Hanh immediately relayed the word to the People's Air Force controllers at Phuc Yen airfield.

At 0930, Xuan endured a euphoric call from Lt Col Thao Phong, crowing that his pilots had shot down at least one, maybe two rescue aircraft, followed by a windy dissertation about the difficulties of shooting down propeller-driven aircraft with a jet. When Xuan hung up, he'd motioned to Major Wu, his wraith-thin intelligence officer.

"The American rescue forces are gone. Now get me the radar-hunter pilot!"

Xuan had returned to his office. For more than eight hours he'd waited for word from the command center, thinking of how he should interrogate the radar-hunter pilot. About questions he would ask.

What kind of training did they undergo? What kind of equipment did they have? How did they locate the rocket site radars? How did they launch their homing missiles? What were weaknesses that Xuan Nha's men could exploit?

When he returned to the command center, they had still not captured the pilot. Major Wu seemed relentless in his efforts to capture the pilot, issuing so many directives on the radiophones that even Xuan became confused.

Upon Wu's orders the men in the center had eaten only a sparse, soldier's meal: boiled rice and broth of dried fish. Xuan had arrived back in time to join them; the food stirred in his stomach. It was time to return to the field and reaccustom himself to leaner fare, he thought idly. He was not meant to be a clerk.

He thought how the Russian, Gregarian, was accompanying the P-50 radar into the mountains, disregarding Xuan Nha's request to stay at Yen Bai.

Time passed slowly. The likelihood of locating the pilot before civilians found and perhaps killed him grew slimmer with each passing moment.

"Ayyy, comrade Colonel!" exclaimed Quang Hanh suddenly. "They found the pilot."

Xuan started to smile, then repressed it. Quang Hanh appeared unhappy.

"He was captured by villagers and severely beaten."

"How badly beaten?" Xuan asked, frowning.

"He is not expected to live. That was what the soldiers who found him told the radioman at a unit they passed."

Xuan Nha's brows furrowed. "Go on."

"The soldiers found him placed in a small cage, being punished with sharp sticks and clubs. The soldiers had to force the villagers away from him."

"Will I be able to question him before he dies?"

"I ordered them to give him aid, but the radioman said the truck had already left, toward Cam Khe. There is a compound there where they hold prisoners."

"Fools," whispered Xuan Nha. "They won't need a compound for a corpse."

Others looked at him with drawn breath, for they feared him most when he grew quiet. He felt that fear was a good thing to generate in subordinates.

Major Wu hung up his own field phone and looked on, a silly smile on his thin face.

"You have let me down," started Xuan.

"I have more news, comrade Colonel," Major Wu quickly interjected.

Xuan looked at him, wondering how Li Binh could have such a fool in her family.

"Another pilot escaped from the airplane," Wu said hurriedly.

"I didn't know this was a Phantom."

"It was a Thunder plane," said Major Wu, "but there were two pilots."

Such had been reported before, but Xuan Nha had never fully realized the implication. Thunder planes with two cockpits had been reported by observers in Thailand, and had even been shot down. Were those the radar-hunters' aircraft? The thought of discovery excited him.

"Where is the second pilot?"

"He was seen parachuting into the same area as the other. The villagers didn't see him, but three different farmers saw two parachutes come from the airplane."

"Get him," said Xuan Nha in his quiet voice. He cast a hard stare at Major Wu. "And this time I want him alive and well so he can answer my questions."

"We will start at first light," said Major Wu.

"Not in the morning. Not even in an hour. Have them go after him now, tonight. I want him captured quickly, before he can be killed by civilians or worse, rescued." Xuan knew his words were reaching him—Wu appeared frightened. "You are responsible."

Major Wu licked his lips, his voice unsteady. "I will have a hundred soldiers take the field tonight."

Xuan spoke so quietly that Wu had to strain forward to hear. "You will send as many as is required. You will find the second pilot and have him brought directly to me."

"Yes, comrade."

Xuan Nha rose from his desk and looked about the busy command center, then strode away. He turned before reaching the door. "I will spend the night at home. Call me as soon as you find him."

29/0320L—Northwest of Nghia Lo, North Vietnam

Bear Stewart

The Bear woke with a start and peered through the darkness. Something had moved out there, not far from his hiding place. He carefully, quietly, pulled his revolver from its holster.

The rustling sound grew louder, then suddenly stopped as if *whatever-it-was* had sensed his presence. *Whatever-it-was* remained stationary. Periodically he heard a woofing sound, an exhalation of breath. Crickets that had been chirruping were silent.

God but it's dark, he said to himself.

He carried a small flashlight in his flight-suit pocket. It had both white and red-lensed lights, which was handy since red didn't screw up your night vision when you flashed it about a dark cockpit. His fumbling left hand found it, carefully pulling it from the pocket.

He hated to use up the batteries' charge—He had no idea how long he might have to evade—but he very badly wanted to know what was out there. He didn't even know if he should be frightened, for Christ's sake.

Probably a jungle rat, he told himself, or a monkey of some kind. He'd seen small monkeys scurrying about the branches during his day's trek; some jungle rats grew as large as small dogs.

What the hell would a monkey be doing on the ground in the middle of the night? he asked himself.

A jungle rat? Making a woofing sound?

Forget it and go back to sleep, he told himself. But he couldn't. There was no way he was going to sleep with Benny's tiger or maybe a foul-tempered jungle bear out there deciding whether or not to have a taste of him. He stood up slowly, holding the flashlight in his left hand, the pistol in his right.

He extended the flashlight and lined up the business end of the .357 magnum with where he thought the beam would strike.

Don't shoot unless the son of a bitch charges, he warned himself. He switched on the light at the level he imagined a Bengal tiger's body to be.

The light illuminated only the green forest.

He heard a snuffling sound and lowered the light.

A mean-looking little pig pawed at the dirt and grunted. Black, built low to the ground, it had sharp tusks that curled up. The eyes glittered red in the light's reflection.

"Holy shit," he muttered.

The boar shuffled to one side and tossed its head defiantly, eyeing him all the while. It half turned toward him, snorting.

He fixed the beam on the pig, and began to laugh silently. The light jiggled as his shoulder moved. The pig gave a final snort, then trotted away as if satisfied with what it had seen.

The Bear shivered involuntarily and gave another quiet, nervous chuckle. "Hell," he whispered, liking the confidence in his voice. "It was a fucking dwarf pig."

He slid the .357 magnum Smith & Wesson Highway Patrolman model revolver, his private weapon, back into the horsehide leather shoulder holster, a present from his grandma Bowes's people. He was accurate with the revolver out to more than seventy-five yards, a feat few could match with an issue .38 Special. He carried the big revolver with a familiarity that he especially appreciated in his present circumstances. He was damned glad he had taken the time, done the paperwork, and endured the headaches to bring it along.

By day the camouflage-colored parachute panel had served as his pack, loaded with the essentials from the survival kit. It was now spread out in a small pocket he'd burrowed between a thicket of bushes and the bases of two large teak trees that had grown together.

He wrapped himself in the parachute panel, carefully checking for a good seal to discourage mosquitoes and tiny insects, reaching for the flashlight from the survival kit. Its beam was much brighter than that of a small rechargeable one, which was why he hadn't used it. He had to assume the gomers had located his cache of survival gear castoffs, had picked up his trail, and were tracking him. He did not wish to be betrayed by a bright light, unnecessary sounds, or even his smell. Twice he had stopped his journey to daub himself with dirt and leaves to mask body odors. An old Cheyenne practice he'd learned from Grandma Bowes's side of the family.

The Bear grumbled to himself over his situation for a weary moment before succumbing to the waves of fatigue. Just before he slept, he heard once again in his mind, as he had a dozen times during the day, the piercing screams from the village. He wondered if it would have made any difference for Glenn if they'd been able to join up. He felt ashamed for running and worse about the jolt of elation he'd felt. One thing he'd decided after hearing the almost inhuman screams. If the gomers caught up, he would take as many of the bastards as possible with him.

Light was beginning to filter through the forest when he awoke. His fourteen-dollar Seiko showed it was 0630. He pushed his head out of the cocoon and listened for any sound that might seem out of place. Except for jungle birds making loud and screeching conversation, he could hear nothing.

He set about breaking camp as quickly and silently as possible. He tied the survival equipment into a tight bundle, using nylon risers and the parachute panel, and fashioned arm straps. He pulled on his survival vest, then donned the makeshift pack, stretching and adjusting the nylon cords for ease of mobility and comfort. Satisfied, he zipped the g-suit at his waist and halfway down over his legs.

The g-suit was made of tough canvas, and had a thick rubber bladder inside. When pulling positive gravity forces in the aircraft, the g-suit, worn snug about your legs and waist, inflated to keep the blood from rushing to your lower extremities. Now it served as chaps to protect his legs from stinging bamboo, razor-grass, thistles, snakebite, and other natural hazards of the jungle wilderness.

Prepared to move out, the Bear pulled the survival map from a pocket, cursed at its inadequacy, and made educated guesses as to his position. He remembered mountains a few miles to the west. He studied the map carefully and eliminated all but two possibilities.

He reasoned that they had passed beyond the muddy river for about a minute before ejecting, and then their forward momentum had taken them even farther by the time the chutes had opened. He had slipped his parachute beyond the village, probably for another westward mile or two. He added up the mileages, came up with ten or eleven, then added the distance he might have traveled and decided he was just nineteen miles from the river.

He held the survival compass flat, let it settle down, and again selected due west. The map showed a road five miles farther. The road meant civilization, and he would have to exercise special caution there.

He decided to slow his pace from the previous day's and to be more careful to eliminate traces of his passage. His goal was to get into an isolated area, then to get on the radio and set up a good, clean rescue. The area across the road looked like a good choice. Isolated enough and not too far away.

He gnawed a bite off a pemmican bar from the survival kit and drank a third of a bottle of water as he carefully looked the area over again, determined to leave no sign of his overnight stay. Satisfied, he put away the tasteless pemmican and snapped the canvas cover over the baby-bottle pouch, eye-balling a distant tree directly to the west. When he arrived at the tree he would take another sighting, choose another landmark to the west, and carefully continue once again. He would thus be assured of traveling only westward. He wanted to make the job of his rescuers as easy as possible.

By eight o'clock the Bear had neither heard nor seen signs of humans during his trek through the dense forest, and he was beginning to feel better about his situation. He was congratu-lating himself on his canniness and the increasing possibility of escape when he heard the deep rumbling of jets passing several thousand feet overhead. He cursed silently, remembering he had stowed the radios in the pack. He stopped to remove two radios, replaced them into their vest pockets, and continued on.

He paused at a creek and drank deeply. As he refilled the baby bottles, he heard distant engine sounds. Not jets. Vehi-cles? Carefully and quietly, he continued.

Less than an hour later he emerged from the thick forest. He looked around carefully, edging forward for another few cautious steps. His footing gave way. He tumbled down a five-foot embankment of red dirt, wet from recent rain, rolled to his feet, and crouched in a shallow ditch at the side of a well-traveled roadway.

Again he heard the rumbling sounds, closer and clearer now. Sounds of many engines gunning and gears shifting as vehicles labored up the grade toward him.

Heart pounding, he scrambled up the embankment, then scurried back into the protection of the foliage. He belly-flopped onto the ground and lay still, listening. He then wiggled, snakelike, peering cautiously around the base of a small bush. As the sounds grew louder, he flattened closer against the ground, wondering if he had been seen.

Stay cool, he told himself, *and don't worry about things unless they're real. Keep your eyes open and your head down.*

Part of him wanted to flee deeper into the forest, but he was too inquisitive. Gomer vehicle traffic normally moved only at nighttime or under the protection of a low overcast.

Time seemed to stand still. Finally a truck labored into view, traveling from right to left up the hill. It looked like an old Studebaker six-by-six, spouting black smoke from an exhaust stack as it picked up speed on the level section of road. In the rear were a score of uniformed North Vietnamese soldiers and it towed an S-60 57mm antiaircraft gun. Both truck and artillery piece were adorned with branches and netting to camouflage them from the air. Next came a Soviet armored personnel carrier, spewing up a plume of moist, red dirt. Several more six-by-sixes passed, towing S-60 guns and carrying troops and ammo. A flatbed passed, loaded with a dozen or more smaller 37mm antiaircraft guns.

What the hell, wondered the Bear, *are they going to defend up here?* He tried to think of a target of consequence in the hills west of the Black River, but could not. He edged forward to see better.

After the flatbed there was a long pause between vehicles, but he could hear more trucks laboring up the grade. A utility vehicle, jeeplike with sloping front end, pulled up and stopped immediately across from where the Bear lay.

Fuck! he said to himself, and flattened lower, face in the dirt but keeping an eye on the vehicle. He eased the big revolver from its shoulder holster.

The driver and his three passengers got out, stretching, oblivious of the Bear who watched from just thirty yards away. They wore green field uniforms with dark epaulets.

Two of them walked slowly toward the Bear, still stretching, and one said something over his shoulder as he unbuttoned his pants. Another man said "Nyet, nyet," and laughed.

The four were Caucasians, Russians, for Christ's sake!

The Bear sucked in his breath at the thought of lying on the ground in North Vietnam, watching Russians take a piss.

The banter continued between the men; all but one laughed boisterously as they urinated.

The Bear wondered what they were talking about. North Vietnamese pussy? He didn't wonder what he would do if they saw him, for he had decided he could take out at least two, perhaps three, before they could reach whatever weapons they might have in the vehicle. The fleshy one standing across the road and doing his business with his back to the Bear was quieter than the others and wore a single gold star on his dark shoulder tabs. A field-grade officer. One big star was probably a major. The others had smaller red stars on their tabs, most likely company-grade officers, lieutenants and captains.

Without warning, black puke filled his throat, choking him. He snorted involuntarily and dark fluid splattered out of his nostrils.

Damn! he raged inwardly, watery eyes fixed on the men at the sides of the road, ignoring the searing sensations in his nose and throat.

The Russian lieutenant nearest him had heard and was looking about. He cocked his head, waiting for further sounds. The Bear drew a long breath, muscles tensed, preparing to bring his revolver up. He would take out the major first, then the others. Rank has its privileges, he thought.

The Russian lieutenant stared into the forest, carefully scanning with narrowed eyes. The major on the other side of the road grumbled about something. The alerted lieutenant said something back, now staring at a point just above the Bear.

The sounds of approaching heavy vehicles grew louder.

The major started toward the utility vehicle and spoke gruffly over his shoulder, and the suspicious lieutenant looked abashed. They all buttoned up and hurried back to the vehicle. After a few grinds the engine started. The Russian jeep revved, then lurched away spewing red mud.

"You lucky assholes," said the Bear with bravado and a heavy lump stuck in his throat. His adrenaline subsided, making him feel lightheaded. He had come close to bagging a Russian, one of the real enemy. Or maybe they would have bagged him. He wiped away the strings of black spittle and coughed up some more.

A heavily laden, covered six-by-six passed, then a flatbed loaded with gray-painted boxes. A diesel roared and changed gears and hove into view, hauling a large trailer.

"A goddam Firecan radar," breathed the Bear. Next came another flatbed, with the Firecan's dish antenna stowed and lashed upside down on the bed and hauling a generator behind. Two fuel trucks passed, grinding along slowly, followed closely by a six-by-six loaded with Vietnamese troops who hunkered down miserably on the wooden benches.

"What the fuck's it all for?" he wondered aloud. "What's up here to protect?" Firecan radars were used to direct 57mm and 85mm antiaircraft artillery fire.

The next vehicle answered his question. A huge truck labored by carrying a tremendous framework of steel. It was the antenna for a radar that the Bear had studied closely. A Barlock command-and-control radar, the best the Soviets had, with long-range and precision capability.

This was an important convoy for the North Vietnamese.

*They must be in one hell of a hurry if they're moving in broad
daylight,* he thought.

He waited for half an hour after the final truck had passed
before he warily crossed the road. He found himself at the
bottom of a high, rocky ridge. The side of the ridge was
sparsely covered with scrub brush, so he considered waiting
until it was dark before proceeding up the hillside. *You can't
wait, Mal!* the feeling told him, *freedom is on the other side.*
He gnawed a bite off the pemmican bar and drank more water
before pulling out and testing the two radios. He slid one into
an upper pocket of his flight suit where it would be handy,
determined to contact the next flight of fighters he saw or heard.

God! he thought. *I need a cigarette in the worst way.* He
turned and started up the steep incline.

He was two-thirds of the way up the side of the ridge
when he heard the distant rumble of jet engines. He switched
the emergency radio to Guard channel and to TRANS/REC.

"*This is Stinger Bravo transmitting in the blind on
Guard,*" he radioed. He repeated the call, then added, "*I'm on
the ground and need a ride out of here.*"

Following his third transmission, an F-105 driver from
Korat, Beagle lead, returned his call. "*Read you three-by-three,
Stinger Bravo. Weak but readable. Do you have us in sight?*"

"*I can hear jets, Beagle. I can't see you.*"

"*Roger, Stinger Bravo. Hold down your transmit button
and we'll home on your position.*"

"*Holding down. Here is a series of short counts, Beagle.
One, two, three, four, five, four, three, two, one. One, two
three . . .*" The Bear continued his counting for two full
minutes, until he could see a flight of four Thuds at about
5,000 feet in the distance. His heart started to pound at the
sight.

"*I've got you in sight, Beagle, heading directly toward my
position.*"

"*Roger, Stinger Bravo. I read you loud and clear now.*"

"*Come right a couple of degrees, Beagle. I'm on the side
of the ridge, four or five miles at your twelve o'clock.*"

"*Any unfriendlies in your area?*"

"*None I'm aware of. I crossed a road a couple miles to
the east with heavy truck traffic. They were hauling a Firecan
radar, some fifty-seven millimeter guns, a Barlock radar, and
maybe a couple hundred troops. I don't think they could be set*

up this fast, but you might want to look out for them a few miles
to the southwest of my position."

"No one in your immediate vicinity, Stinger?"

"Negative." He paused, eyes fixed on the flight of
fighters weaving and jinking overhead. "Beagle, you just
passed over me."

"Roger, Stinger Bravo. I've got my number two calling
the rescue people now. We can't stay much longer, but we'll try
to get things in motion for you. Are you injured?"

"Negative, Beagle lead." The Bear nestled into an out-
cropping of rocks and surveyed the road far below. He could
see no traffic.

The Thuds orbited north of his position for a few minutes
before Beagle lead came back on the air. "Stinger Bravo, the
Sandies are alerted and they've located fighters to fly CAP.
We're Bingo fuel and have to depart. Sayanara and see you
later, buddy."

"Thanks for setting things up, Beagle," said the Bear. He
released a long breath. It had gone well thus far. When the Thuds
banked westward and departed, however, he felt awfully alone.
He started up the hillside again. He climbed for fifteen minutes
and heard nothing . . . neither in the air nor on the radio.

"Come on, Sandies," he urged.

He saw a delta-winged fighter swooping from high above
and hunkered behind rocks until he was sure that it was not a
MiG-21 but an F-4, with three other Phantoms in tow. The
flight swept past his position, banking into a lazy left turn.

"F-4's," he called, "you just passed over Stinger Bravo.
I'm directly at your nine o'clock position on the east side of the
ridge."

"Roger, Stinger, This is Pistol lead. We'll be MiG-CAP
for the rescue."

They're flying too damned low, the Bear thought.

"Pistol, there are some trucks hauling big guns on the
road a couple miles east of me. You may want to keep an eye
out for . . ."

An eruption of artillery fire streaked upward toward the
flight.

"Watch out, Pistols, they're shooting," called the Bear.

"Hot damn!" said Pistol lead. "I'm hit."

The F-4 trailed smoke as he climbed out of the area,
turning west. The rest of his flight moved in close, departing

with him. A minute later Phillips's Bear heard the distinctive sounds of two emergency beepers on Guard frequency. The pilots of the lead Phantom had ejected.

"Damn it!" he cried out, hoping this rescue attempt would not also be aborted.

After the F-4 beepers had been shut off there was no radio contact for five long minutes. Then the airborne F-4 pilots started to talk with one of the crew members on the ground. The Bear remained silent, still climbing the hill as they worked to locate both crew members.

Nearly an hour passed with the rescue attention shifted to the F-4 crew. He listened to them being picked up by a chopper, which he saw only once in the distance. The Bear continued climbing until he reached a relatively flat area near the apex of the ridge. There he waited, craving a cigarette.

A flight of Thuds arrived, homed in on the Bear's count on his radio, and reestablished his position. He called for them to remain alert because of the guns.

"Stinger Bravo, this is Red Dog lead," came Sam Hall's distinctive Southern voice. *"Just where are those guns located, Bear?"*

"Seven or eight miles north of my position, Red Dog."

"Keep your head down for a few minutes while we calm them down some, you hear."

"Yes, sir."

Bear watched as bombs were dropped into the valley from which the flak had erupted. Sam rolled and jinked away amid another flurry of shooting and bursting clouds of shrapnel.

"You see where the shooting came from, Red Dog two?" asked Sam.

"Roger. Two is in hot."

"Three is in hot."

"Four's in hot."

The Bear gave an exultant whoop. In the distance the valley erupted in a pall of smoke and fury as six bombs from each fighter were dropped on the gun positions. Yet even as the last aircraft was pulling off the target, streams of tracers continued to shower upward and bursts of flak pocked the sky.

A pair of Sandies appeared from over the ridge line and buzzed over the Bear's head.

"Stinger Bravo, this is Sandy one-one. While your buddies keep them busy over there, what say we try to get you out of here?"

"*Sandy one-one, I am all for that.*" Then the Bear began to laugh uncontrollably.

"*Go to button charlie on your radio, and give me some orange smoke if you've got it.*"

The Bear changed channels and reestablished contact with Sandy one-one. He then pulled a smoke flare from his survival vest, pried the cover off, and waved it around in the air to get the orange smoke going.

"*Stinger Bravo, I've got you in sight. A Jolly Green chopper's standing by. He'll come in for the pickup after you answer a couple of questions for us.*"

"*Roger.*" He was concerned that he wouldn't be able to remember what he'd put down on the rescue questionnaire.

"*What's your mother's maiden name, Stinger Bravo?*"

"*Uh, oh shit.*" Think, he begged himself. "*Bowes! It's Bowes!*"

"*How about your cat's name when you were a kid back in Montana?*"

"*I'm not from Montana, I'm from Oklahoma. And I didn't have a fuckin' cat.*"

"*Those're the golden words. By the way, Sandy one-two reports there's a group of about a hundred gomers down below you, coming up the hill, and I do believe they're after your butt. I want you to work your way over the ridge. That way the Jolly Greens will be masked from their small-arms fire.*"

"Shit!" the Bear exclaimed. He scooped up his pack and hustled away from the hillside from which he had come, running up and over the apex of the ridge. With a whoop of surprise he slid and fell twenty feet down a steep slope. He retrieved the radio from the dirt and limped on, cursing, then monitored again.

"*That's good, Stinger Bravo. Real good. Jolly Green five-one will be coming in from the northwest to attempt a very quick pickup.*"

"*I don't have him in sight,*" yelled the Bear, his words coming in a rush.

"*He'll be there just as soon as I make a rocket run on your buddies, Stinger Bravo.*"

The A-1H turned on a dime and disappeared from the Bear's view. He heard a whoosh, and then the sounds of exploding rockets. Immediately following the rocket attack he heard the *whop-whop-whop* of the chopper. Two Jolly Green

HH-3 helicopters were coming toward him. One held back, but the other continued in his direction.

"*Stinger Bravo, this is Jolly Green five-one. You got any more smoke?*"

He fumbled at a second flare, got it going, and waved it until it was billowing bright orange smoke.

"*I've got a positive, Stinger Bravo. This will be a damned fast pickup. Sandy one-two just reported the bad guys are getting close.*"

"*Roger, Jolly Green. I'm ready.*" Never been more ready in his life.

The chopper crew started to reel out a cable with a pickup device dangling below as they approached. The Jolly Green roared into position, and the Bear was almost knocked from his feet by the blast of air from the rotor-blades.

When the device was still ten feet overhead and the chopper was still stabilizing, the Bear began to jump to try to reach it. He heard one of the Sandies strafing the hillside, much closer. His greatest fear was that the chopper crew would weaken in their resolve and flee, leaving him to face a bunch of pissed-off gomers.

The pickup device was five feet above his head. *Come on, dammit!* He heard the rattle of AK-47 fire.

Finally it was within reach. He pulled down two lower arms of the device and clambered on, wrapping his arms around it, clutching it tightly so it couldn't possibly get away. As he reached down to fasten the safety belt, the chopper pilot decided enough was enough. He turned the craft westward, rapidly accelerating. The Bear hugged the pickup device tightly, maintaining a firm grasp on the pack with its supply of survival gear, just in case. He trailed along behind the chopper in the wind and downdraft.

After a couple of minutes the chopper slowed to a moderate speed so he could be reeled in. The reel operator and a paramedic pulled him inside. The pilot wasted no more time, and the chopper dipped and picked up speed.

"Hey Sarge," yelled the Bear, grinning at the reel operator who was frowning as he examined the ragged edges of a bullet hole in an aluminum bulkhead. "You got a fucking cigarette?"

30/1730L—People's Army HQ, Hanoi, DRV

Xuan Nha

Xuan Nha sat quietly at his desk, staring moodily out the window over the rooftops of the northern *quartier* of the city, watching the remnants of clouds in the otherwise flawless sky. It had been unseasonably wet this year. They should be well into the dry season and yet the mornings had been constantly cloudy, often rainy, for the past month. Perhaps that was changing; it had not rained for three days now.

Like many men who had faced death yet had inexplicably survived, he believed in the fates. As a warrior, he also felt he could influence the outcome. He had not done well with that during the past forty-eight hours.

Yesterday had not been a good day. The convoy carrying the new radar and guns had been bombed, and Nicolaj Gregarian, the Russian technical adviser, had received a concussion that had left him dazed and bleeding from one ear. He would require medical attention before returning to duty. The ultimate insult had been that the giant P-50 radar had been turned into a smoldering heap of twisted metal while the second radar-hunter pilot was being rescued.

That morning he'd received a curt message that General Luc and Colonel Trung, his superiors, wished to see him at 1800 hours, when they returned from discussions with the general staff. As Xuan prepared himself for the meeting, he wondered about the subject.

The possibility of disciplining him for Major Wu's ineptitude crossed his mind, but was was washed away. Generals did not concern themselves with such small matters. Anyway, Xuan Nha was their link with the world of technology—radars and complex rocket weapons—one of few who could understand those systems, pick out their merits and weaknesses, and adopt proper tactics. They needed him.

As for the destruction of the P-50 radar, Gregarian had ignored Xuan's suggestion to remain at Yen Bai. Nothing there to criticize Xuan Nha for. They would not be concerned about the rescue of the pilots. Under Xuan's guidance the People's

Air Force interceptors had destroyed a propeller-driven rescue aircraft, a feat never previously accomplished.

He was not likely to be faulted by the generals, for they didn't realize he was in error. But he knew. He had selected the wrong man for an important task, and for that he had trouble forgiving himself.

Major Wu had remained convinced that the second Thunder plane pilot was hiding in the forests near the mountain village. At Xuan's urging he'd called for more manpower, but instead of sending them out to find the pilot's escape route, Wu had 2,000 troops stumbling over one another around the village. When they unearthed the second pilot's raft and remnants of his parachute nearby, he had only grown more stubborn in his belief that they would find the pilot cowering within the dense foliage.

Then the captain commanding the troops with Gregarian's party had radioed, saying American aircraft were orbiting a few kilometers south of them. The captain recognized the unique patterns as a rescue effort, and was setting up antiaircraft guns to protect his convoy.

The second pilot had traveled more than twenty kilometers from the village. Major Wu had sat benumbed, his thin, cadaverous face twitching in disbelief.

Xuan had taken over, ordering the captain to quickly establish his defenses and send all remaining troops after the second pilot. Fifteen minutes later the captain radioed that his gunners had destroyed a Phantom and asked if they should try to capture those pilots instead. Ignore them, Xuan had ordered, and capture the second Thunder plane pilot.

The fighters were orbiting over a hilltop. Xuan had directed them to proceed up the hill, regardless of the danger, and capture the second pilot.

All contact was lost until a dazed radioman reported that the convoy had been bombed, that dozens were killed, and that survivors were staggering about, bleeding from eyes and ears. The captain, as well as Gregarian and the other Russian advisers, had been incapacitated, the radar destroyed. All aircraft, including the rescue forces, had departed, and the second pilot—his prize—had been rescued.

Major Wu had mournfully reported that thirty-eight men had been killed by rockets as they tried to scale the hillside. The fool did not understand that the capture of the second pilot would have been worth ten times that number to Xuan.

If they had been in the field, Xuan Nha would have summarily shot his wife's nephew. That he was unable to take any action against Major Wu annoyed him.

Lieutenant Hanh interrupted his thoughts, peering into the open office doorway.

"The wounded pilot you wished to interrogate is now at Cam Khe, Colonel Nha."

"His condition?"

"A bone was sticking out from his leg. They stopped at a village and found a man who knew about such things and he set the leg, but the soldiers feel the man is dying."

"They said the same in the beginning. Perhaps he might not die after all."

"The leg is badly swollen and they say the flesh is rotting. The villager cut away some of the leg and soaked the wound with alcohol, but they think it was too late."

Xuan could sense Quang Hanh was holding something back. "Why didn't they tend the leg earlier?" he asked.

The lieutenant drew in a breath. "The driver said they had been told to find the American, but not that it was important to keep him alive."

Another wave of irritation washed over Xuan, subsiding quickly. He glanced at Quang Hanh. "You have done well, Lieutenant."

"Thank you, sir." The lieutenant's baby face beamed. He bobbed his head happily and departed.

Quang Hanh reminded Xuan of himself when he was that age and had performed similar duties, albeit with fewer modern radio conveniences.

He went to the window and looked out at Ho Tay Lake in the distance, trying to forget about Major Wu's ineptitude, until it was time to leave for the meeting with General Luc.

Two large, gray concrete buildings housed the headquarters of the Vietnamese People's Army. In Xuan's building were headquarters for the Army Air Force, the Army of National Defense, and the small People's Navy. Those forces, with only rare exception, operated within the confines of the Democratic Republic. The other building housed the general staff, various organizations supporting the People's Army and Viet Cong in the Struggle for Unification, and representatives of the Pathet Lao, Khmer Rouge, and Thai/Burmese rebels. The planning staff there concocted the battles and dispositions of troops, the logistics staff coordinated the vast shipments of arms and men, and the command center in the basement was concerned with troop movements and ground fighting.

Xuan walked across the parade grounds at the rear of the buildings. The grounds, which once hosted formations of gaudily uniformed French Union Force soldiers from the various provincial forces of Indochina, now served as a parking lot. Soviet and Chinese tanks, armored personnel vehicles, and several hundred trucks were parked in neat rows.

He entered a side door, showing identification to an eternally suspicious group of guards, and proceeded down the corridor to General Luc's office. He waited a quarter of an hour before Luc's hawkish female secretary bade him to enter. He did so with a minor degree of apprehension.

Both Luc and Colonel Trung sat at one end of the general's office table. To Xuan's surprise, Lt. Col. Thao Phong, his friend from the VPAAF, was seated at the opposite end. Luc nodded curtly at Xuan and waved him into a seat beside Phong. There were no exchanges of pleasantries.

General Luc, wearing a guarded look, indicated Thao Phong. "This matter concerns both you and comrade Phong."

Thao Phong stared at the table, wearing a grave look. Xuan wondered if Phong might be in trouble, and began to think of ways to disassociate himself from his former friend.

"Colonel Trung and Thao Phong have made accusations against you. These have been taken up with the general staff, and have even received the attention of the party."

Xuan's feeling of concern grew. He feared no man in battle, but he was sensitive to criticisms from superiors, and anyone who did not respect the all-powerful Lao Dong party was insane. Yet wasn't it these, the Army and the party, that he served best? He willed his pounding heart to calm. "Accusations?" he asked.

"Yes."

"First," said Colonel Trung, glowering, "you left me with that smelly group of Russians at the embassy party."

"I humbly apologize, comrade Colonel." Xuan had already agreed that it would not happen again, and had considered the matter closed.

"I was forced to eat their cakes. Have you ever eaten such dry and tasteless garbage?"

Thao Phong looked at him sadly. "You accused my sister of being a common whore."

Xuan blinked his eyes, astounded. He knew Phong well, and although they joked about such things, he knew of no sister.

General Luc sighed. "There is little I can do but take action, comrade Xuan Nha. It has been decided by the general staff."

Xuan held his stare straight forward, waiting for the worst.

"I cannot disregard the desires of General Giap and the general staff, can I?"

"No, sir."

"Or the party?"

"Of course not, comrade General." Xuan steeled himself.

General Luc reached into his opened attaché case, paused dramatically, then tossed two new epaulets across the table to Xuan Nha. "You are promoted to colonel. General Tho has already informed Thao Phong, for he also has been promoted."

Xuan was stunned. "Thank you," he muttered, finding it difficult to share in his superiors' fun.

General Luc nodded gravely. "You are a good and loyal soldier, Xuan Nha. You will be placed in charge of all rocket and radar-guided artillery forces, and report directly to me."

"Tiger of Dien Bien Phu," said Colonel Trung pleasantly.

"Fornicator of small animals," said Thao Phong.

Xuan Nha increasingly relished the moment, smiling at his previous fears and wondering how he might tell Li Binh.

General Luc explained that Thao Phong would move from the air regiment at Phuc Yen airfield to Hanoi, to coordinate between the Army of National Defense and the Army Air Force. He and Xuan Nha would work closely together.

General Luc looked evenly at the newly promoted colonels. "Some do not believe you will succeed. You will have to prove yourselves through results."

Xuan smiled, now inundated with happiness. "We shall, comrade General."

"You will get to build the fence of steel you have talked about," said Trung, irony in his tone. Trung had continually discouraged him. But of course, Trung would never comprehend electron tubes, or that rockets traveling three times faster than a rifle bullet could be precisely guided.

But there was more, and Xuan Nha was startled by General Luc's next words. "The Russians have agreed to immediately provide seventy more MiG's, fifty new rocket batteries, and additional tracking radars and artillery."

"With one hundred twenty interceptors," exulted Thao Phong, "we will sweep the Americans from the skies!"

"There will be a price to pay the Russians for all of this," said General Luc.

Xuan and Thao Phong grew quieter, allowing General Luc to continue.

"Slowly, the Russians are gaining influence. Already they are supplying more weapons than the Chinese, and now we find we must construct our military around their use." He arched an eyebrow. "Neither of your new positions would be required if there were no such sophisticated weapons. Colonel Dimetriev and Major Gregarian urged us to take this action to better control the weapons."

"The face of warfare is changing," explained Xuan Nha.

Colonel Trung scowled. "Perhaps, but in the end it will always be the courage of the men manning their guns that drives the Americans away."

Xuan Nha disagreed. "Victory will take the expertise of technicians and the judgment of rocket battalion commanders. I would trade a hundred of your mindless gunners for one trained electronics technician."

Trung seemed unhappy.

Phong embellished on Xuan's statement. "I would exchange a thousand soldiers for a MiG, a pilot, and a well-trained jet mechanic. Now we will have more MiG's, and nothing shall stop us. We will defeat the Yankee air pirates."

General Luc shook his head at the fighter pilot. "No one can really *beat* the Americans. Not even the Russians or the Chinese. We should never believe we can succeed with only force of arms. If the Americans threaten us with their nuclear bombs or missiles, invade with their army, or use B-52 bombers to destroy Hanoi and Haiphong rather than often-empty jungles in the south, the Russians and Chinese will withdraw, leaving us to negotiate for peace. We would not go back to the hills to fight again, for that would mean losing everything we've gained since 1954."

The others listened silently.

"If we win this struggle, it will not be from military heroism or technical ability. It will be because the American politicians never develop the desire to win. That is the task of our diplomats and politicians, to prevent the Americans from getting that desire.

"Your task is to protect Hanoi, which General Giap often points out has been our political center since the beginning of our history. You must protect our vital industries, which the Enlightened One points to the pride. You must protect our supply lines from Haiphong and China to Hanoi, and then to our soldiers fighting in the south. You have both said you could stop the American fighters if you had the proper weapons. Now you have them. Now it is your turn to show us those were not just words."

30/2010L—Takhli RTAFB, Thailand

Bear Stewart

Mal Stewart sat dangling his legs off the side of the bed in the crowded little room. He wore hospital garb and was staring through new issue sunglasses, trying to get Doc Roddenbush to listen to his side of things.

Col B. J. Parker, the wing commander, was there. So were Colonel Mack and his ops officer, Johnny T. Polaski. They took turns congratulating him for escaping from North Vietnam and criticizing him for arguing with Doc Roddenbush.

"I don't feel bad," the Bear tried again.

"You admitted yourself you ingested a lot of smoke," said Roddenbush, who was both the flight surgeon assigned to the Bear's squadron and the major in charge of the clinic. "You probably ingested chemicals we can't even imagine. Imagine if we put you back on flying status and you had some kind of reaction when you were flying."

"I don't get to fly the fucking airplane much of the time, Doc. I'm in the backseat." He was growing irritated, frustrated that the doc refused to listen.

Roddenbush raised a hand. "Rules are the same for navigators."

Bear tried to set him straight. "I'm not a fuckin' navigator," he growled.

"You're not?" Roddenbush looked puzzled, glancing down at Stewart's records, which plainly said NAVIGATOR in the rating column.

"I'm a . . ."

Colonel Mack turned from a conversation with Parker and Polaski. "Quit giving him a hard time, Bear. Just plan on going to the Philippines like he says."

The Bear knew he had lost his argument.

Doc Roddenbush bobbed his head. "They've got facilities at Clark to give you a proper checkup. And," he smiled, "they have female nurses."

Takhli was an all-male environment, with no American servicewomen assigned to the wing. Male medical technicians did work usually assigned to nurses, and male administrators did work done elsewhere by secretaries.

"They've got female nurses at Danang now," said Colonel Mack.

"That's right," said Johnny T., grinning. He was the youngest and most brash button colonel on base. "The guys there ordered five hundred pounds of nurses, and the Air Force sent both of them."

The Bear tried one last time, keeping his voice low so the others wouldn't hear. "Doc, I'm not sick. I swallowed some smoke, but after I got on the ground up there my system went into a reject mode and got rid of it. They checked me over at Udorn and could hardly find a trace of the crud."

"You ought to go."

"Hell, I'll probably catch the killer clap or something there."

"We can cure anything you get. We've got antibiotics so good they can restore virginity." Roddenbush laughed.

Colonel Parker broke off his conversation with Mack and Johnny T. and came closer. He squinted an eye and pointed with his portable radio. "Do as Doc Roddenbush says." B. J. held the antenna directly at him, like the barrel of a pistol. "Anyway, you don't have a pilot."

"He probably doesn't think he needs a pilot," joked Johnny T. "Believe me, Bear, you need one."

"How about Benny Lewis," retorted the Bear. "He went through Weasel training. We could team up when he gets back." Benny Lewis had been sent to the Clark hospital for a thorough checkup of his back.

Polaski tried reason. "Then you should go to the Philippines and try to talk him into it. You guys crunched the last flyable Weasel bird so there's nothing for you to do here until we get new airplanes."

"You keep arguing," said B. J. Parker, "and I'll charge you for losing the airplane. How long would it take to pay off three million on captain's pay?"

Colonel Mack joined in. "You're better off quitting while you're ahead, Bear."

The argument was definitely lost. The Bear activated his optimistic side and decided it wasn't all that bad. He might even discover yet another fertile area to cultivate the joys of his bachelorhood. He turned to Parker.

"Sir?"

The wing commander leaned toward him. He'd flown fighters for a long time and was typically hard of hearing.

"How long before we get new Weasel airplanes?"

"Two weeks, maybe less," he said. "I forwarded a priority message to PACAF telling them it's essential to our state of combat readiness that we get replacement Weasel aircraft and crews. This morning I received a message that there are ten F-models being modified at McClellan Field. A couple will go to Korat, but we'll get the majority since we've taken the worst losses."

Sam Hall entered the room, towering over the others. "This the Bear's den?" he asked, an easy grin playing across his ebony features.

The Bear leaned forward and held out his hand. "Thanks for keeping the gomers occupied while they picked me up, Sam."

"Anytime, Bear," drawled Sam Hall, engulfing the Bear's hand in his huge one and shaking it. "We sort of enjoyed it."

Colonel Parker again pointed his radio and squinted one watery blue eye to regain the Bear's undivided attention. "I've got to go and check out a problem on the flight line, but I want one thing understood before I leave. You *will* go to Clark, just as the doctors say."

"Yes, sir," said the Bear.

"And you *will* enjoy yourself."

"Understood, sir."

The O' Club

An hour later most of the squadron—the Bear was restricted to the medical clinic—convened in the club. Four lieutenant colonels, Mack, Polaski, and the commanders of the two other fighter squadrons were playing liars dice. Quarters were stacked up before them on the bar while Jimmy the bartender watched and tried to worm himself into the game.

"Jimmy," deadpanned Colonel Mack, "you can't gamble, because everything you own already belongs to Bear Stewart."

"I don't remember," said Jimmy, looking sly.

They ignored him, continuing their game.

At the opposite end of the bar, the two surviving Wild Weasel crews were talking about how they were the last of the eight crews that had been flying from Takhli just three months earlier, and that there were no airplanes left for them to fly.

Andy Schumacher said he was having maintenance try to repair one of the badly damaged birds.

Les Ries, as the only remaining Weasel major, spoke with new authority. "There's too much battle damage, Andy. Let's wait for the ones they're preparing back in the States."

"The strike guys are having to fly with no Weasels to protect them," said Andy, "and I don't like it."

"Neither do I," said Les Ries, "but maintenance says there's probability of structural damage to both of those birds."

There couldn't have been more difference between men and styles than between the two Wild Weasel pilots.

Les Ries worried about the tiniest details. When he felt sure of something little in the world could change his mind, and Les felt sure about most things. With Glenn Phillips out of the picture, Les was the ranking Wild Weasel, and felt he should be listened to, even if Andy Schumacher was in a different squadron.

Andy was an easygoing and mellow sort who often wore a lopsided smile. While he was not out to challenge the world, he was very protective of the strike force when he flew. The pilots in his squadron liked him out there in front, trying to protect them from SAMs.

Andy said, "We've got maintenance working on my old bird, Les. If they can put it together, we'll take a look and see if it's worth taking the chance." He grinned his infectious, friendly expression.

"I don't like it," said Les Ries in his forceful tone. "You ought to wait."

On many of the Wild Weasel crews, the front- and back-seaters came to reflect each other's attitudes and preferences. Dan Janssen, who was Ries's bear, was assertive and sure. Larry Stark, who was Schumacher's, was quiet and reflective.

Janssen was speaking authoritatively about a new Weasel system being installed in the new birds back in the States. "It'll be able to correlate between two of the SAM radar's signals to tell us exactly which SAM site is firing," he was saying. "You guys wait on the new birds, and you'll be better off than putting together an outdated trash pile and trying to make it fly like an airplane."

Nearby, Tiny Bechler wagged his forefinger, a glass of scotch hidden in the massive fist from which the finger projected. He had consumed more whiskey than normal and was providing advice on many subjects. Sam Hall sat on the adjacent barstool, listening halfheartedly and approaching his own limit for intelligent conversation.

Sam stood almost six-five and weighted in at 235. Tiny was an inch shorter, but carried more weight. Both barely fit in the ejection seat of the F-105.

"You're my flight commander, Sam. You're supposed to listen to me and give me guidance." Tiny finished the drink and motioned to Pak, the assistant bartender, for another. "I say you're prejudiced."

"And I say you're a screwed-up lieutenant."

"You say you're not prejudiced against anyone?" Tiny asked slyly. "How about navigators? I'll damn well bet you're prejudiced against navigators."

"Bullshit."

"Would you want your sister to marry a navigator? C'mon now, Sam. A fat-ass navigator with glasses an inch thick, carrying a plotter and a big briefcase to his bomber every morning with egg dribbling down the front of his flight suit?"

"My sister's already married," Sam hedged, "to a farmer back in Alabama."

Two pilots from the pig squadron began to scuffle, yelling and creating such noise that Sam had to raise his voice to be heard. The 354th squadron commander looked up from his dice to see if his men were about to hurt one another. They were just being playful, so he returned to his game.

"So what are you getting at?" asked Sam.

Tiny Bechler stared at the clean glasses Jimmy and Pak had placed in neat rows on the long, narrow glass shelves. "I thought all navigators were a bunch of fat-asses, with no common sense or coordination. Then I got to know Mal Stewart, who's okay. He's ready to fight and die just about as well as we are."

Hall shook his head. "Bears go to navigator school, and then through some kind of electronics training. Anyway, the Bear volunteered for Weasels, knowing he'd be sent here and probably get shot down."

"That does take balls." Tiny thought about it and took a

drink. "But how the hell would I keep up my image if I started liking navigators?"

"Before this thing's over, you'll respect a lot more people. Bomber pilots, trash haulers, chopper pilots. War's like that."

"Bomber pukes?"

"They start bombing up in pack six, and that may be what it's gonna take to win this thing, you'll be saying they're great guys. Then when peace comes, there'll start up a whole new set of prejudices."

Tiny shook his head in wonder to think he could ever respect people like that.

The two pilots from the pig squadron had reconciled their differences and waved for everyone to join in a song. The button colonels delayed their dice game and chimed in to sing "The Camel Song." Sam joined them.

> *Oh, the sexual life of the camel,*
> *Is stranger than anyone thinks,*
> *For in times of amorous passion,*
> *He tries to make love to the sphinx.*

Tiny sang along in his booming, pleasant bass.

> *Singing—toora lie, toora lie, toora lie*
> *toora lie, toora lie—Ayyy!*
> *And after a week on the desert,*
> *He makes a mad dash for the sphinx*

> *But—the—sphinx's posterior orifice,*
> *Is clogged with the sands of the Nile,*
> *Which accounts for the hump on the camel,*
> *And—the sphinx's inscrutable smile!*

The men cheered. Sam ordered drinks for himself and Tiny.

"Think Phillips is still alive?" Tiny asked.

"You're just full of hard questions," said Sam.

"If I got shot down, I don't think I'd let 'em take me alive. Hell, who knows if those guys'll ever be released?"

Sam stared for a moment before he spoke. "You know who the last guy was who told me the same thing you just did? Glenn Phillips." Sam shook his head. "You get shot down, you don't know what you'll do."

CHAPTER SIX

Nicolaj Gregarian

Immediately upon his return from the mountains that morning Nicolaj had demanded that *Polkovnik* Dimetriev immediately arrange a meeting with senior North Vietnamese military officers. "Those who can make decisions," he had said.

When Anton Dimetriev had waffled, he'd said he would bring the matter to the attention of his general at PVO Strany; the chief Soviet adviser knew that Gregarian had influence there. The meeting had been arranged.

As the time for the meeting approached Gregarian became increasingly resolute.

Following his humiliation and close brush with death during the bombing, he had found purpose as never before. He hated the Americans, all Americans, with a newfound fervor.

As a child Nicolaj had been taught about the West's betrayal of their people. How they were decadent, tempting their workers with big homes and automobiles that in reality were available only to the rich. How these capitalists wished to expand their dominance until the entire world was their marketplace. How they were ruthless, not hesitating to use atomic weapons on their enemy in 1945.

He'd seen photographs of Appalachia and of Detroit slums. He'd read stories of the gangster bosses who ruled their cities, about the Mafia that ruled the bosses. He knew that they exploited black people and American Indians. The people cried out for justice, and Washington gave them oppression. Those

163

things had impressed Nicolaj as a boy, but as he had matured he had steeped himself in technical studies and had become so interested in them that political dogma began to bore him.

He'd come to realize the hatred directed at the decadent westerners was mostly propaganda to keep the masses from getting excited about shortages of food and goods at the state stores. It wasn't that he didn't believe the photographs and proof offered by the political indoctrination officers; he just felt that it was overdone. He wasn't interested as long as the Americans and British and Western Europeans were kept away from the Mother Country. His rocket systems helped do that. He was a patriot, but he simply wasn't very excited about the rest of it.

Now he had seen, firsthand, the cruelty and pain Americans were capable of. He had watched their war planes climb until they were almost out of sight, then dive and release their weapons.

He'd been several hundred meters from the first bomb impacts, watching with academic interest and ignoring cautions screamed by the Vietnamese. Then came the first series of concussive waves that swept over him like a terrible hand. He'd been thrown several meters, like a child's rag doll, eyes bulging and threatening to pop from their sockets, an eardrum bursting and seeping blood and mucus. He had been unable to function for several minutes, then slowly came to his senses as warm urine ran down his legs. He'd been deafened, and could only faintly hear himself screaming as he crawled to the roadside. For the remainder of the seemingly endless attack he'd huddled there, crying like an infant.

The attack on the convoy had jolted him to reality.

As if in a dream, he had drunkenly staggered closer to the impact area, where pieces of soldiers' bodies lay scattered about. One of the *leytenants* accompanying him had been killed by the overpressure. Nicolaj could still see him in his mind's eye: turned inside out, eyes popped from his skull, meat bulging from his ears, fat tongue protruding from his stilled mouth. The other *leytenant* had been taken to a rude hospital at Yen Bai, where he died. The two had been close to the bomb impacts; they had gone there to help camouflage the P-50 radar as the aircraft circled to attack. Of the advisers, only he and the *kapitan* had survived more or less intact.

Now, three days later, Gregarian's hearing had returned in

one ear, but he would never forget the attack. The Americans must be defeated, whenever possible killed. Here, in this unlikely land, he would prove that the Americans could be beaten by Russian defenses.

As he waited for the generals and colonels, Nicolaj gingerly massaged his ears.

Xuan Nha, new epaulets on his field uniform, entered the room and smiled at Gregarian, who had learned only that morning about the promotion.

"Congratulations, comrade *Polkovnik*," said Gregarian, calling Xuan by his new rank.

"Thank you, Nicolaj Gregarian. I am still amazed." Xuan spoke loudly, so that Gregarian could hear. He knows, Nicolaj thought, what bombing is like.

"You are very young to be a *polkovnik*," said Gregarian.

"Very lucky." Xuan held his smile. "You know about luck though, since you seem to have survived the bombing well."

He shuddered involuntarily, hoping Xuan Nha would not notice.

"What is the subject of your briefing for the generals?"

Gregarian hedged, not wanting to cover his subject twice. He was saved by the arrival of *Polkovnik* Feodor Dimetriev and *General-Mayor* Luc, and then a two-star general named Tho, whom Dimetriev introduced as the commandant of the People's Army Air Force. Nicolaj gave Xuan Nha a helpless shrug, to tell him the matter was out of his control.

A *kapitan* in stiff and correct dress uniform looked into the room and nodded to someone behind him, as if signaling that the room was secure. Only then did a squat, dour-looking fellow enter, wearing a linen uniform that sported the three-star epaulets and wreathed collar tabs of a *general-polkovnik*. His aide went to the rear of the room and assumed an alert position. The *general-polkovnik* nodded to the others, quieting them. He stared at Gregarian, measuring him, then turned to a young *polkovnik* wearing aviator wings who had entered the room behind him, motioning for him to turn on the overhead fan.

The three-star general settled back and nodded. "Begin," he ordered in Vietnamese.

"My Vietnamese is not good," Gregarian began. "Does everyone understand Russian, or should I get an interpreter?"

Polkovnik Dimetriev explained, and the three-star snorted angrily.

Dimetriev was red with embarrassment. He spoke tight-lipped to Gregarian. "Try speaking Vietnamese."

It was Gregarian's turn to blush.

The *general-polkovnik* was growing impatient.

Dimetriev introduced Maj Nicolaj Gregarian in Vietnamese which Nicolaj could barely understand. After a few more of Dimetriev's pleasantries, he motioned for Nicolaj to begin.

Nicolaj tried his Vietnamese. "Good morning."

The *general-polkovnik* nodded. "Good morning," he replied.

"I come from PVO Strany . . . headquarters to . . . help you . . . establish an . . . air defense . . . system . . . which will stop . . . the Americans."

The *general-polkovnik* raised his hand for Gregarian to stop. He strode unceremoniously to the door, then turned and gave Nicolaj a scathing look. "I will attend your next briefing, after you have learned our language," he said in Russian. He abruptly left, the aide scurrying behind him.

A heavy silence followed.

"Speak in Russian," the two-star People's Air Force general said, a trace of scorn in his voice.

Gregarian smiled, thankful but upset. To help them he had disrupted his life, traveled thousands of miles, and come close to being killed. It galled him to be treated shabbily by an Asian with a stone-age mentality.

"You have angered General Van Tien Dung," General Luc said in Russian, "second only to General Giap in the People's Army. It would be wise if you learned Vietnamese."

Gregarian's face burned.

"I will have a tutor assigned to the *mayor,*" said Xuan Nha.

"Go ahead with your briefing," said General Tho, impatient. "Hurry, for we have had two American attacks this morning and expect another this afternoon."

"I wish to build a sophisticated and impenetrable defensive network here in your country," said Gregarian. "And also to train your people to use it effectively."

The VPAAF two-star shrugged. "So do it."

"It will require a great number of dedicated resources."

"Such as?"

Gregarian began. "First, a P-50 command-and-control radar and a modern control facility. Second, a comprehensive communications control network, extending to all defensive units in the country. Third, a complete training facility, with a P-2 acquisition radar, a guided rocket system, one hundred of your best technicians and radar operators. All must be dedicated to do nothing but control all defenses and train your people."

General Tho grunted. "We already have a radar control system in place at Phuc Yen for our interceptors. We've also promoted one of our VPAAF commanders"—he nodded to the *polkovnik* pilot—"to coordinate with the rocket forces. We send our pilots and our radar controllers to train in your Russian schools. Why do we need more?"

"All of those are good first steps. The P-1 radar and your controllers at Phuc Yen are adequate for a small effort. The acquisition and targeting radars are good for the rockets and artillery for small efforts. But we are talking about stopping a determined, modern air force."

The general stared. "That is why we requested more interceptors and rocket systems."

"Now you will have hundreds of interceptors and rocket sites, thousands of artillery pieces. It must all be orchestrated or they will fail to act effectively. That is what I wish to do, give you a way to make all the pieces work together."

"And the training you speak of. Your own PVO Strany tells us they are providing us with the best training possible."

"The schools are very good at teaching fundamentals, how to engage enemy targets with fighters, rockets, or artillery, but they cannot teach you what I propose."

"Then you have not given us your best?"

"Our own people receive the same training. But then, comrade General, they go to their various units, where they are trained to work in their specific environments. The defenses at our Siberian and southern areas, for instance, are different from those of Moscow or Leningrad, so the training is different. What I propose is an air defense network so closely integrated and controlled that it is as good as the best in my homeland. So modern that our experts will travel *here* to learn. The training I propose would be like a graduate school, necessary because nothing will be found like it anywhere else in the world."

The Air Force two-star turned impatiently. "What do you think, Colonel Thao Phong?"

"The idea is good," the *polkovnik* pilot answered, "but we must hear more before we decide. Continue."

"I want to build a fortress, with a P-50 radar as the nucleus and a single group of controllers running the entire air battle, in charge of all interceptors, rocket forces, even artillery. With a sophisticated communications net," said Gregarian, "and Russian controllers—"

"No," interjected Xuan Nha. "We must have our own controllers."

"Our PVO controllers are accustomed to directing large numbers of aircraft and assigning targets to the appropriate defenses. Yours are not."

"They will learn."

"But first we should have Russians, or perhaps North Koreans, who have perfected a concept called *absolute control*. We will turn over the positions as your people learn."

Xuan Nha was the key, Nicolaj realized, but he seemed reluctant. The others in the room, including the Air Force general, were looking at him and deferring to his expertise.

"Let us build a shield through which nothing can pass," Gregarian said, now concentrating on Xuan Nha.

"But," said Nha, obviously enjoying the attention, "it must be a shield commanded by Vietnamese."

"Then you are not against Russian controllers as long as you have Vietnamese commanders?"

Xuan Nha thought for a moment. "Let us talk about it further tomorrow."

"I must contact my superior officers at PVO Strany quickly, so they will rush the delivery of another P-50 radar and prepare the controllers to travel."

General Luc sighed, becoming as impatient as the Air Force two-star. "I admit that the idea *seems* to have merit, but I must first have the reassurance that Colonel Nha is comfortable with it. Work it out between the two of you, then brief me and I will bring *Colonel Nha's* recommendation to the attention of General Dung."

"And I shall wait for Colonel Thao Phong's recommendation." The VPAAF two-star rose, grumbling that he had a war to run, and left.

General Luc pinned Gregarian with an unblinking stare.

"You should learn Vietnamese. General Dung remembers such things."

Gregarian ran his tongue over pudgy lips, discouraged at the nebulous outcome of the meeting. "Yes, *kamerade General*."

Xuan Nha raised a hand. "I will attend to the matter. Comrade Gregarian will be speaking Vietnamese like a schoolteacher within a few days." He turned to Nicolaj with a smile. "This evening, with your approval of course, we will move you to more appropriate quarters where you can learn without distractions."

Nicolaj nodded his agreement, realizing now that it had been a mistake to call the meeting without first consulting the Vietnamese *polkovnik*. General Dung and his generals had taught Nicolaj Gregarian just how recalcitrant and difficult the Vietnamese could be, but he still felt determined to succeed.

02/1425L—Clark Air Base, Republic of the Philippines

Bear Stewart

The Bear padded down the glistening hospital hallway searching for Benny's room, feeling silly in the bare-butt smock, robe, and paper slippers they'd issued him. The robe was too small, ending above his knees, and his long, bare legs made him look like a stork. After making several wrong turns in the maze of corridors, he found the room number he'd been given at the desk. He ignored the DO NOT DISTURB sign and peered inside. The tiny, two-man room was unoccupied.

As he started to back out, he saw a half-emptied B-4 bag at the foot of the furthermost bed. CAPT B.L. LEWIS was stenciled on its side. A set of crumpled shade-505 Class-B's were strewn on top of an assortment of civilian clothing.

"Benny, you're becoming a sloppy bastard," said the Bear to the empty room. He moved a canvas shave kit from the room's only chair and sat, idly looking about the room. It was identical to his own on the next floor. Ten minutes passed before the door opened and Benny entered, holding a candy bar and a half-empty Coke bottle.

The Bear leaned back in the chair, eyeing him. Benny's

expression was tired and a day-old stubble accentuated his frown. He looked like a wino coming off a bender.

"You look like shit," the Bear said cheerfully.

"Good to see you, too," Benny mumbled.

"How you doin', Benny?"

"This morning they told me you were coming. A nurse asked if I knew you. I told her I don't know a Malcolm, but I know Bear Stewart. She didn't understand."

Mal looked closer at his red eyes. "You really do look like shit."

"Didn't know you were holding an inspection." Benny's monotone voice matched his appearance.

"Someone *oughta* hold an inspection. You could scare people with a mug like that."

Benny changed the subject. "You come out of it okay?"

Stewart shrugged, dangling a skinny, pajama-clad leg over the arm of the gray, government-issue chair. "Breathed some bad smoke when the airplane was burning. My system didn't like all that shit in there, so it got rid of it."

"Where'd they take Glenn?" Benny asked. "I heard he was hurt bad."

The Bear looked surprised. "Take him?"

"What hospital's he in?"

"Glenn didn't get picked up."

"Shit," exclaimed Benny. He couldn't take much more. "Damn it to hell!"

"Yeah." The Bear saw moisture welling in Benny's eyes.

"They still trying to get him out?"

"The gomers got him."

"Aw shit, Bear."

"He was banged up pretty bad and there was a village right next to where we went down. He didn't have much of a chance."

Benny shook his head in agony.

It was hard to believe that a week before Benny had been the coolest fighter jock in the squadron. He changed the subject. "Doc Roddenbush said they shipped you here straight out of Udorn."

Benny said, "Yeah."

"Colonel Mack wants you to call the squadron if you need more time off. Said he'd authorize a couple weeks leave in the

States if you want, or he could set up an official TDY to Hawaii. He'll get the orders cut, he said."

Benny was only half listening.

The Bear waited for a moment before asking in an uneasy voice, "You okay?"

"Yeah, sure."

"You don't look so good."

"You sound like the doctors."

"How's that?"

"They keep saying I hurt myself. All I got was a scratch on my hand from the ejection handle and a sore back, but they keep trying to build it into something worse."

The Bear agreed. "The flight surgeons are all excited because I inhaled all that smoke and shit in the airplane. I think they're pissed off because they can't find anything left in there. Can't get them to believe I puked it all out."

Benny grew more talkative. "The doc at Udorn decided there might be something he didn't know about, like a broken back he couldn't see on the X ray, so he sent to Tan Son Nhut for a med-evac bird. I'd gone to make a phone call and hadn't shown up by the time the plane arrived, so he got all in a panic. Called the air police and told them to pick me up."

"The air police?" The Bear laughed.

"They were serious about finding me. I was at the O' Club thinking things over, and didn't know all the cops on base were looking for me. I guess the doc thought I'd crawled off somewhere to die, like an old Eskimo or something."

"They found you, I guess."

"I was with Sandy two, the guy who was talking to you over the radio. We were sort of incoherent, which irritated the hell out of the cops. Took me to the flight line strapped to a litter. By then the med-evac bird had been waiting for an hour. The doc told the flight nurse to keep me immobilized all the way here, because I might have a broken back."

The Bear shook his head in wonder. "Nice to have your own personal airplane and flight nurse?"

"I wouldn't know. I'd put away a fair amount of booze. Ended up sleeping all the way here." Benny's voice started to trail off, as if he was losing interest.

"I wasn't so lucky," said the Bear. "I got the scenic route through fucking Southeast Asia. Gooney birds, a C-54, C-130, you name it."

Benny was somber again. "I hate that about Glenn."

The Bear didn't answer.

Benny went to his B-4 bag and peered inside, too wrought up to regain control. His voice came in emotional spurts. "I finally got some of my clothes and gear from Takhli. Would you believe the laundry here lost the new flight suit they issued me at Udorn? Idiots."

"I carried that bag all the way from Takhli," the Bear said.

"Thanks."

"No sweat." The Bear pulled at a tiny bandage at the crook of his arm, examining the purple puncture hole. Upon his arrival a doctor had told him he needed a full lab workup; a vial of blood from the arm, a pinprick in his finger, a bottle of urine, and a smear of feces.

"I told them I'd gone through all the lab shit at Udorn, then again at Takhli," he lamented, "but they said I've gotta do it again. People who work in hospitals are deviates." He looked at Benny, determined to gain a response. "Give you those little bitty bottles and tell you to go piss in them just after you've taken a good whiz."

Benny's voice was sad. "So, you think the gomers killed Glenn?"

"I don't know. Probably." He was getting tired of all the gloom. "Benny, I don't mean to be disrespectful to Glenn or anything—I love the guy like a brother—but you and I are here and we're going to be able to fight another day."

"I don't know, Bear, I may hang it up."

"That's a shitty thing to say."

"I've done my part."

"You got a MiG kill and the guys in the squadron think you're some kind of hero. You go down in an area nobody thinks you can make it out of, but everyone works their asses off trying. Big Res-CAP just for you, and they pull it off. And here you are thinking of quitting?"

"Maybe."

The Bear was growing angry. "You should be celebrating, and you're standing there looking like shit and feeling sorry for yourself? What's this *hang it up* shit?"

"It's personal."

The Bear sucked in a breath. "Fuck you and your personal

stuff, Benny." He walked toward the door. "You're too busy feeling sorry for yourself to hear someone trying to help."

Benny followed him into the hall, put a hand on his arm. "I'm not good company right now. I need to sort some things out."

"Maybe so," said the Bear. He didn't know Benny all that well, but the fighter pilot with the barrel chest and neck like a rhino had always seemed rock solid. Now he just seemed weak.

"I feel shitty about you and Glenn getting hammered," Benny said again, and although his head was turned away, the Bear saw the glistening in his eyes.

"You didn't do it. We screwed up trying to kill a SAM site." He glanced at his watch and grunted. "I've gotta get going. Supposed to get the lab results and find out the score about this hospital drill. Maybe you do need a little time to get your act together."

The Bear shook off Benny's hand then, leaving him to drown in his personal sorrows.

02/1900L—Hanoi, Democratic Republic of Vietnam

Xuan Nha

Sergeant Ng let Xuan off at the door of the sprawling villa he shared with Li Binh and their six *political retrainees*. Few homes in Hanoi were more imposing.

Since the revolution, some of the larger villas had been transformed to multiple-family dwellings, hospitals, and even orphanages, but mostly for the consumption of visiting Westerners. Most of the high-ranking Lao Dong party leaders had come from wealthy families and were accustomed to such comforts.

Xuan's father had owned the villa and the French had placed his estate into a trust when he died, but after the Communists came to power and years of petitioning, the issue was finally settled in Xuan Nha's favor. He had been a war hero, a rising star in the People's Army, but it had been the influence of Li Binh's position that decided the issue. It was more proof that marrying her had been a most beneficial thing.

He entered the door and asked the elderly manservant, "Is Madame Binh at home?"

The man said she was.

Like the other domestic attendants, the manservant was a political retrainee, working in humble circumstance to free his mind of improper influences. Like the others he'd once been a person of means. Li Binh felt that those who had fallèn the farthest were the most agreeable to do her bidding without question. Xuan Nha didn't care who the servants were so long as they did as they were told.

An energetic Li Binh swept in. "You are early," she said.

"It has been a good day. Good days are the easiest."

"I heard bombs exploding south of the city."

"The Americans destroyed a few trucks, a few buildings, and they blew up three fuel tanks up north at Ha Ghia." He took his customary seat on the stiff chair made of strips of water buffalo hide. A soldier should never be too comfortable. He would grow soft and know comfort when the war was finished.

"We shot down at least eight American airplanes in all. Perhaps nine or even ten. More than ever before in a single day. It is hard to imagine what it will be like when we have all the new systems in place."

She smiled, glanced at her watch, and clapped her hands. A womanservant hurried into the room. "We eat in half an hour," Li Binh commanded, shooing the woman back into the kitchen.

She watched the departing servant with a pleased look. The woman had been the wife of a wealthy planter with household servants of her own. The government had taken over the plantation, and her husband now labored at the Tri Cau mines, hauling ore on his back alongside hundreds of other men and women of questionable political orientation. The woman was thankful for her job, eternally anxious that she might lose it and be forced to join her husband at the huge open-pit mine.

Li Binh was high in the hierarchy at External Affairs. That ministry and Defense were the two most important organs of the wartime government, and she liked to be reminded of her influence. The servants knew that and took time to flatter her and appear to attend to her smallest desires. The servants slacked off in the daytime when they were both away, and they secretly despised her. Sgt Van Ng, who lived in a small room in the garage, told Xuan so, and the aging, maimed sergeant was almost mystical in the ways he knew about such things. Xuan neither cared nor did he bring it to Li Binh's attention. His father's servants had done the same in their day, and he supposed that was the way they were.

"I must change for dinner," she said. "Would you care for tea while you wait?"

"Yes."

She clapped her hands once more. "Tea for the colonel!" she demanded, then gave him a flash of a smile before departing for the bedroom. Li Binh seemed happier with him; her anger over his scathing remarks about her nephew had begun to dissipate.

He still seethed inwardly about Major Wu's incompetence. If Li Binh had not been so adamant, he would have had the piece of pig's dung shot.

A servant brought tea. Xuan sipped it and reflected.

Before the series of endless wars had begun, Xuan Nha's father owned a company which manufactured exquisite, hand-crafted furniture. Like others exporting to the depression-gripped world, they came to be in trouble. In 1934, his father began a two year excursion to revitalize their markets, accompanied by his young bride. They would cast critical eyes and make suggestions for the homes of the world's *riche,* with surnames such as Chang, Giannini, Hearst, Huntington, Rockefeller, Du Pont, Roosevelt, Lilley, Benz, Krupp, and Rothschild.

Midway during the voyage the bride was impregnated, and in Paris they lingered for their son to be born. Seven days after, Xuan's mother had died of infections. Troubled by the thought of traveling with the demanding, chubby baby, his father welcomed assistance from his dead wife's relatives who lived in the growing Vietnamese community of Paris. They all felt it was wise to delay the infant's voyage until he was older. When his father departed for Hanoi, Xuan Nha was left behind.

The world war had intervened to delay his return.

His playmate was a cousin a year older than he, a precocious and lively-eyed brat named Li Binh.

Xuan had left Paris after the end of the war, a twelve year old stuffed with masculine ego, overjoyed at the prospect of meeting his father and new family. He thought of Li Binh as a pestilence and was happy to be rid of her.

His father had prospered during the war by expanding into heavy construction. In 1947, when his offspring by his first wife had arrived from Paris, he'd sagely advised his son to "Back the winner, and you will always be a patriot." During the war in Indochina he had befriended, in succession, the Vichy French, the Japanese occupiers, the Viet Minh rabble army, the British liberators, then the French Union forces who came to reclaim their empire.

Xuan Nha had been confused at his father's pragmatism, for in the Vietnamese community in Paris they'd talked of a new, free Vietnam.

With each passing day Xuan Nha had felt more ill at ease with his new family. They were rich and he wanted for little. His father's wife tried to be pleasant and the children were not allowed to be discourteous. But still he felt like an unwelcome intruder. He'd emerged from a past they seldom mentioned, and his father spoke to him only about the world of commerce. He grew to hate them all.

They owned a large villa in the central *quartier* of Hanoi, but Xuan Nha preferred the austere dormitory of his academy. His father's family never realized how he despised their influences with this or that high-ranking French officer, or with the *Bao Dai,* the French puppet emperor who ruled first from his mansion in Hue, then from the palace at Saigon.

On his fourteenth birthday he wrote to Li Binh about his parents, traitors to the cause of Vietnamese liberation. He hadn't expected an answer, and was surprised to receive a sympathetic response. There followed a series of letters, each confiding their darkest secrets. He wrote of his hatreds, she of her passionate beliefs.

He was fifteen when he joined the secret Young Socialists for Liberation of the People. By then Mao Tse Tung had succeeded in China and arms were pouring across the border to the Viet Minh. A call went out for volunteers, and like many fellow students he eagerly prepared to go to the hills.

He passed a message through the Young Socialists that he was ready. After an agonizing wait the Lao Dong party passed their wishes from their hiding place in the mountains. He was to visit often with his family and gain information from their friends.

Li Binh had also joined the Young Socialists, for the

movement was fast gaining influence among the Parisian Vietnamese. She spent her time passing out pamphlets on street corners and pleading with passersby, urging that French forces stop their bullying of Vietnam.

Xuan was distraught that everyone was doing so much and he so little, but he listened carefully as his father entertained and dutifully reported each conversation.

His father spoke about his future. The following year he would be sent to the United States, first to preparatory school, then to Harvard to study economics and business. After graduation Xuan would be placed at one of the firm's field offices. Xuan despised the concept of capitalism. Patriotism flowed hot in his veins! He yearned to fight and, after heroically killing a hundred French legionnaires, to die for his country. But he nodded dutifully and said *oui, mon père* in the enemy's language before returning to the academy dormitory.

The next night four friends from the Young Socialists took him along on one of their secret forays. They violated curfew, leaving the compound well after midnight, and ventured into a sleazy section of the southern *quartier*. There they crept into a decrepit building and surprised a French corporal who was drunkenly humping on a bored prostitute. They bound and gagged him, then forced the whore to chew off his testicles before ceremoniously killing them both. At first Xuan Nha was sickened by the viciousness, and only after they left did he realize he was sexually aroused. Back in the dormitory he'd been compelled to masturbate before he could sleep. The killing forays became a weekly ritual with the group.

He finished at the academy at the top of his class, and his instructors sent a note to his father recommending that Xuan attend university to study higher mathematics. The world is controlled by businessmen, his father snapped, and you *shall* study business.

He could take no more. Xuan Nha had spent his final evening in the villa entertaining the son and thirteen-year-old daughter of a high executive of the Michelin company who was staying in the guest house. At midnight he'd gone to the gate to speak with the security guard on duty. When the guard turned, he's skewered him with a thin sharp knife, up through the fleshy kidney area as he'd been taught, then motioned to the shadows where his comrades waited. He'd left the villa before first light, driving his father's American automobile through the awakening streets. Only once had he stopped, to mail a letter to Li Binh.

He'd driven out the Doumer highway, across the big bridge and twenty kilometers farther before pulling off the road and into a small village at the base of the mountains. Then he'd propped open the trunk of the Cadillac, and settled down to wait. An hour later, five suspicious Viet Minh soldiers had cautiously entered the village. The French executive, bound and blindfolded, kicked feebly in the intense heat as flies droned and settled on him. He'd proven to be a good hostage, for his company donated generously for his release.

In 1955, after the country was divided by decree of the major powers, the Lao Dong party had begun to prepare for the great Struggle for Unification. Lieutenant Xuan Nha, the Tiger of Dien Bien Phu, had been selected to travel abroad to attend the University of Paris.

At the 800-year-old Sarbonne the handful of students from the Democratic Republic of Vietnam studied mathematics and physics. If North Vietnam was to become industrialized, as was Ho Chi Minh's aim, they would require a core of people with technical expertise. The French were stupid, Xuan Nha thought. Beat them in a war and they'd still enroll you into their universities. Ask any Frenchman and you were likely to hear they were great admirers of Ho Chi Minh. Vietnam had become an American problem as that country poured more and more money and materials into the puppet government in Saigon.

Xuan had explored the Western culture by fornicating with their women, drinking with their workers, arguing with their intelligentsia, and debating politics with the students. He found French women to be bovine, the workers pampered, and French communists shallow in their belief. Foreign students, on the other hand, gave him a glimpse of the world, and he examined them carefully. He observed students from India, Africa, the Far East, the Americas, Europe, and England, as well as those from the old French Union empire of Vietnam, Cambodia, Laos, Algeria, Chad, Somalia, and Tahiti.

Fight anyone, he'd decided, except the Americans, for they believed too completely in their invincibility to be easily defeated. But because of the Americans' passion for fledgling democracies such as South Vietnam, he believed they would someday fight, so he spent a good share of his time observing them, talking with them, arguing about the similarities and disparities of the Marxist and American revolutions, and attending their movies at the campus cinemas. He'd even shared the bed of a long-haired California girl.

The more he learned of the Americans, the more he worried about their righteous enthusiasm. Only they possessed the means to stop the People's Army from taking South Vietnam by force of arms. With that thought in mind, he had come to despise them.

One Spring day in his third year, as he walked across the sprawling campus in the light rain, Li Binh appeared, saying she wished to talk. Her visit surprised him for she seemed remote whenever he visited her parents. She motioned toward a stone fountain, and they sat on a bench there. As the rain stopped she carefully furled the umbrella, mysteriously quiet.

"I have waited for you to visit again," she finally said.

She was skinny and angular, three inches taller than he, and had a long, drawn face. She also spoke too directly for the liking of the past generation of Vietnamese.

She said, "I was frightened that you would not like me. I'm scared right now that you will walk away."

"I won't," he said with a smile.

"I respect what you accomplished for our people. Did General Giap really call you the Tiger of Dien Bien Phu?"

"It was General Dung, his second in command."

"It is inspirational to speak with you, Xuan Nha," she flattered.

"Are you still a member of the party?"

Proudly she said, "I am now a full delegate to the French Communist Party."

He was impressed and told her so. After a while he confided, "I read your letters."

"And I read yours, Xuan Nha. I still have the one you wrote the night before you left Hanoi, when you told what you were about to do. I can not imagine anyone so dedicated."

"Did you tell your parents?"

"They would not understand."

"I despised my father. It was easy to kill him."

"And his wife and children?" She shuddered, but her eyes were on his face.

"They were traitors."

"The article in *Le Monde* mentioned your family, but they

dwelled longest about how the Michelin executive's wife and children had been mutilated."

He didn't mention what he'd done to the arrogant daughter. How he'd told her that no one should die a virgin. Only after he'd had his fill of the terrified girl had he carved her like the others.

"When he was ransomed, the executive didn't mention you as his kidnapper."

Xuan shrugged. "He was blindfolded and his eardrums punctured."

She studied him carefully with wide eyes before speaking her mind. "I've waited for you, Xuan Nha. I wish to return to Hanoi with you to help the party unify our country."

Upon later reflection, he realized that she'd carefully planned it all.

At many times like this Xuan had reflected on their beginning, but never had he been sorry. Marrying Li Binh had been his good fortune. Upon reaching Hanoi she'd used his status as a hero of the republic to gain access to government officials. Within a year she'd risen to a level within the Ministry of External Affairs that she no longer needed his influence.

That night, perhaps also thinking about their beginning, she came to him.

Neither of them were highly sexual with one another. She needed tenderness, Xuan to be stirred, and neither would give those things. They fumbled through the act, both careful to maintain self-control. He lay on her, thrusting silently, and she periodically grunted, her thin body protesting his weight.

When they were done they lay back as she told him about a project she was working on. "Last summer President Johnson proposed that we meet to discuss the American prisoners of war. I have prepared a response to be released to the International Red Cross. As long as the Americans continue their barbaric bombing, we will refuse to talk."

"That won't stop the bombing," Xuan said.

"Perhaps not, but we are aiming this at the American people."

"Prisoners disgrace themselves by allowing themselves to be captured," he said. "We should kill them all and eliminate the expense of holding them. Prison guards could be used to carry supplies to the south."

"Some day the American prisoners will be sold back to their people in exchange for something we want. For now, since they have not declared war, we call the Americans pilots criminals and say that we're justified in treating them like murderers. Some of their own people are beginning to listen."

"You deal with their traitors in America," he growled. "I try to convince them to leave by killing their pilots. If I kill enough of them, perhaps they will go home."

She changed the conversation. "So what do you think of your new adviser?"

"Nicolaj Gregarian is a fat and pompous *Tay* pig."

"You've never liked the Russians."

"They are egotistical over too little. This one is as bad as the others." He shook his head disgustedly. "Tonight I introduced him to your agent, the instructor who will teach him Vietnamese. He wrinkled his nose at her. He is no homosexual, or at least we do not think so, but he acted as if I had assigned a monkey to teach him."

Li Binh thought. "Perhaps he would prefer a *Tay*. I know of an Englishwoman married to a Vietnamese who was recently disgraced. She is a conniver. She denounced her country, but now she says that was a mistake and she wishes to return to England. Her case was passed to my office. I could tell her that if she makes the Russian happy and reports everything he says, we will let her return to England."

"I do need the Russian's cooperation."

"I will send her to replace the other agent."

"You would not have believed Gregarian today. He tried to speak Russian to General Dung, but the General walked out of the meeting."

"General Dung should be more diplomatic." Unlike most of the Lao Dong party elite, Dung was low born. Like many others, Li Binh disapproved of his crude mannerisms.

"Ho Chi Minh favors Van Tien Dung, for he is both a good general and a link with the peasants. Today he showed the Russians he is not enamored with everything they do."

"What did the Russian do when he walked out?" she asked.

"He just sputtered. Colonel Dimetriev was there and I thought he would faint. Dung showed them that we don't need them, for we can always turn to the Chinese. Of course he did not tell them that Chinese advisers *never* speak Vietnamese.

"I prefer the Russians," said Li Binh. "They are more useful for what I am trying to accomplish in America. They control the Communist Party in the U.S.A."

"Gregarian wishes to establish a centralized control for the defenses, and I agree. I've decided to set it up somewhere near the Chinese border, where the Americans are restricted from flying their fighters."

"Will you travel up there?"

"We leave Tuesday morning to select an appropriate location."

She thought before speaking. "Will you take my nephew?"

He sighed. "Yes, Li Binh, and I will keep him from harm."

"I know he displeased you, but he is my blood."

He started to tell her that her nephew was an inept fool, but held his tongue.

Her voice fell to a low whisper. "If anything should happen to him, husband, I would be upset beyond your wildest belief."

CHAPTER SEVEN

Saturday, December 3rd—1330 Local, Clark Air Base, Philippines

Benny Lewis

Benny eased the door open and peered in. The Bear was reading an old copy of *Stars & Stripes*.

"I showered and shaved so you wouldn't nag," Benny announced.

The Bear examined him. "You gotta do something about the eyes."

"You should try looking through them."

The Bear tossed the newspaper aside. "What the fuck's the problem, Benny?" A subtle soul he'd never be accused of having.

"It'll pass."

"Death in the family? Sick kid? Car and furniture repossessed? Wife fucking around?"

Benny winced. "Drop it, Bear."

"Wife?"

Benny felt a flash of irritation, then said, "Yeah."

"Hell, I thought it was something serious," said the Bear.

"How would you feel? You married?"

"Nope, but I've been there. Maybe you oughta feel a little shitty. Maybe. But you sure as hell shouldn't give her the satisfaction of *living* shitty."

It felt perversely good to share his misery.

"Kids okay?" the Bear asked.

"They're with her parents. Her folks think I'm some kind of military swine, but they dote on the kids."

"You've only one option, Benny."

"What's that?"

"You've gotta see how good life can be. That's sweet revenge."

"I feel like a failure, know what I mean?"

"I've been there."

Benny felt relieved, talking about it with the Bear. They hadn't been close at Takhli. But they were from the same squadron and it felt good to have a familiar face to talk to.

The Bear was grinning maliciously. "Let's get outta here and do something sinful. Maybe have a few drinks at the club? You didn't stop imbibing juniper juice when you gave up on women, did you?"

Half an hour later they had changed into short-sleeved knit shirts and chinos, and he was watching the Bear do his act at the hospital registration desk.

"What do you mean, we need a pass from a doctor. I've got nothing wrong with me, my friend's got nothing wrong with him, and we've got to get a damn pass before we can get out of this place? You ever heard of unlawful detention, lady?"

The middle-aged Filipina was unconvinced, her face stiff as she continued about her business of filing multiple-colored hospital forms. "Is too late today. You mus' get a Saturday pass sign by a doctor on Friday."

"My doctor's the little guy with the sissy mustache and bald spot. You got his phone number?"

She pursed her lips unhappily, refusing to discuss the matter.

The Bear muttered "Bullshit" and joined Benny, frowning.

Benny peered at the imperious Filipina. "I think she means business."

"I'm not done." The Bear stalked to a nearby bulletin board and moved his forefinger down the list of names on a hospital duty roster. He looked thoughtful for a moment, then brightened. "Be back in a couple minutes," he muttered, charging away down the well-scrubbed hallway.

Benny wandered to a nearby waiting area, then sat and read a five-year-old *Life* magazine under the occasional glare of the officious Filipina. Fifteen minutes later the Bear returned with a chunky nurse wearing major's leaves on her collar. She laughed heartily at something he said, waved him away, then stepped up to the desk where she curtly motioned to the Filipina, who immediately became more attentive.

The Bear sat beside Benny. "Head duty nurse," he said. "What's she doing?"

The commotion between head nurse and receptionist increased in volume, then subsided. The nurse approached and handed each of them a blue card. "They're temporary, just good until midnight. Can't get real weekend passes until I get a doctor's signature."

The Bear said, "I owe you, Marty."

Benny noted that the underarms of her uniform were wet with perspiration even though the hospital was air-conditioned and cool. She regarded the Bear with sharp eyes. "Yes, you do owe me." She turned to Benny. "Remind this lummox to meet me at the club at seven sharp."

Benny pocketed his pass.

She gave the Bear a secretive smile and spoke in a lower tone. "Dinner before TLC. We'll eat, then talk over old times."

The Bear winked. "See you at seven o'clock." He grabbed Benny by the arm. "Let's go get 'em."

"You two promise to take it easy," the nurse called as they walked toward the door.

"You will never be sorry for your gesture of humanity."

"Good seeing you again, Mal," she called.

As they walked outside, Benny asked, "You know her?"

"She was stationed at Columbus Air Force Base, Mississippi, when I was at Shreveport. I used to drive over on weekends to date her roommate. Small world, huh?"

They took a decrepit black and yellow base taxicab to the O' Club, which was built at one side of a huge, lush lawn area outlined by tall trees. Benny had once been told that before the Second World War, U.S. Army cavalry officers had played polo there. The building at the far end of the field had been an indoor horse arena where officers of means exercised Arabians they'd shipped in from the States. It now housed Thirteenth Air Force Headquarters, which provided logistics support for the flying units in South Vietnam and Thailand.

The O' Club's exterior looked weathered and drab, but inside it was gracious, with walls of mahogany, exotic rosewoods, and massive, tasteless paintings. Benny led the way into the large main barroom. They were the first customers of the afternoon. The Filipino bartender recommended strawberry daiquiris.

"Good stuff," the Bear said as they leaned back in princess chairs near the window, sipping the frozen drinks and watching officers' wives cavort around the pool in bright swimsuits.

Benny thought again about Bets. "Bear, life's kinda shitty."

"A couple of days ago when we were running around the fuckin' jungle trying to get away from the gomers, I might've agreed with you. Now it's only shitty if we let it be."

Benny stared out the window at a cute redhead with a shower of freckles and a well-rounded derriere.

"Nice," muttered the Bear, also staring. "Her pussy probably tastes like Dial soap, but I've been known to relax my esthetic standards."

Benny mused. "Know something?"

"What?"

"I didn't tell my wife I got shot down."

The Bear lit a cigarette. "Forget the bitch."

"We've shared most things. Seems strange not telling her."

The Bear regarded him thoughtfully. "She a good fuck?"

Benny felt a flash of anger, then laughed uneasily. "You're crazy, Bear. I ought to kick your ass, saying things like that."

"Trying to protect her good name?"

Benny felt anguish. The Bear was baiting him intentionally, trying to get him to loosen up. It wasn't working. "Come off it. She's the mother of my kids."

"Just tell me. Is she any good in the hay?"

"Not great, but she's okay. She just has trouble trying to be natural, know what I mean?" It surprised Benny that he could share such thoughts.

The Bear slowly nodded his head, wearing his I-thought-so look. "A lousy lay, right?"

"Not wonderful."

"It's the lousy lays who end up screwin' around, trying to prove it's not their fault they fuck like zombies. They think it's our fault they can't come, and that it'll be better with somebody else. Other guys are Prince fucking Charmings, ready to wait on them and be considerate and think their piss should be bottled by Chanel."

Benny grunted, wondering how the Bear had figured out his wife wasn't responsive in bed.

"I had a wife once," said the Bear. "Pretty girl. Not a scientist, but she was good-looking. When she was eighteen she was third runner up in the Miss Kansas beauty contest. She had tits so nice they'd curl your toes just looking at them, and I'm a breast man."

Benny studied Bear Stewart. He would be regarded as ruggedly handsome by women. Sort of a lanky Burt Lancaster with big ears. "How come *you're* not still married?"

"I enlisted in the Air Force when I got outta high school. Seventeen years old. Took my mother's signature before they'd let me in. Met this secretary in Denver when I was still going to the tech school. We got married a year later, after I'd been picked for instructor duty there at Lowry. We were awfully young."

"That makes it tough."

"I had a job all lined up when I got out, at Martin Marietta in Denver. They were going to help pay my way to get my double-E degree. I thought I was the smartest Injin around, and she thought she was always gonna be a beauty princess. But," the Bear rubbed two fingers together, "we had lousy sex."

"Too bad."

"After a while we didn't care what the other one thought, so we brought it out in the open. I told her she was a lousy lay, and she told me I was inconsiderate."

"Were you?"

"Sure I was, but I told her I'd try to do better. Anyway, she checked out a book on sex at the library. According to it, the secret to good sex lay in the ability of the male human to arouse the female human by providing appropriate attention to her pleasure points."

Benny caught the bartender's attention and indicated another drink for each of them.

"She read and I'd try to memorize everything about those pleasure points. Places like behind her knees, back of her neck, inside her thighs, the fuckin' arches of her feet, like that. Then she'd lay back and actually watch the clock when I was doing it, and when the time was up she'd say 'yeah that was good.' I was only inconsiderate if I didn't spend exactly the correct amount of time fooling with her pleasure points before I'd roll her over."

"Jesus."

"Then she told me she had the hots for the librarian who'd recommended the book. Told me she couldn't live without him, that he made her feel like a real woman. I said fuck it, gave her the furniture and car, and reenlisted to get money to pay for the divorce."

Benny paid for fresh drinks.

The Bear sipped his daiquiri and made a contented sound. "Best thing ever happened to me. I was stuck for six more years in the Air Force and wanted to do something else, so I put in for Officer Candidate School.

"You gonna get back with your wife?" the Bear asked. "No."

They eyeballed a woman in a bright blue swimsuit. The Bear caught his breath. "Abstinence is bullshit. Let's get out of here and find some female companionship."

Benny smiled wanly. "I just got screwed by a female, remember."

"Gotta get right back on when you get thrown. You know, Benny, I got a grandmother who's half Cherokee. She's always boosting the Cherokee side, saying the People's eyes see more, and their ears hear more and such, the People being the Cherokee of course. On my dad's side I got some Choctaw, which doesn't help Grandma Bowes's faith in me. But the Choctaw are big talkers and storytellers and I like them. My favorite of the bunch was my Great-Uncle Miles, who was cantankerous, couldn't read or write because he thought it was a waste, and thought people were generally no good."

"Sounds like a sweet fellow."

"Uncle Miles was shot by a cowboy over on the Canadian River when he was caught shagging the guy's wife. He was proud of it, too. Bragged about the scar on his ass until he died of colic and meanness at a very old age. He generally acted like you've been doing lately, except his disposition was better."

"Thanks."

"Uncle Miles told me something that helps when I'm having trouble making up my mind about things. He said, 'Mal, there's two kinds of people in this world. Those who get ulcers and those who give 'em. You got your choice of which kind you want to be.' That's what he said, Benny. Put another way—my way—there are fuckers and fuckees out there, and you've got to decide which way you want to go."

"Is that supposed to make me feel better?"

"Just telling you what my Uncle Miles said." The Bear stared out at the officer's club pool. "Looking at married pussy is frustrating."

"Your Uncle Miles say that too?"

"Nope. He thought marriage was just another part of the white man's plot. Said if we let them, the white man would keep on making rules and generating paper until they buried us in the stuff."

Benny laughed.

The Bear smiled to encourage him, then motioned at the officer's wife in the blue swimsuit. "Her tits remind me of Takhli."

"How's that?"

"They're both a little overwhelming." They had finished their second daiquiris and the Bear stood up. "Gotta get some female companionship."

"You know anyone here?" asked Benny.

"There's a major in Manila who works embassy duty. He's single, so he'd know a lot of women. How far's Manila?"

"Too far to get there and back tonight."

"You know anyone here?"

"I've got a buddy over at Thirteenth Air Force Headquarters, but he's married and a straight arrow, so I doubt he could help you."

"I've never been here before. Never went to snake school. They were in too much of a rush to get the Wild Weasels to Takhli." He referred to the jungle survival training most of the aircrews attended en route to combat. The school was located in the mountainous jungles behind Clark Air Base.

"It's a good school."

"When we were shot down, I sure wished I'd gone," said the Bear.

"Looks like you did okay without it."

"Yeah. Now where the hell do we find the women?"

Benny was starting to like the Bear, even if he was sort of crazy. "There's schoolteachers here," he said. "Or you could just wait for your nurse. She's lusting for your body, Bear."

The Bear's brow furrowed. "Marty'd fuck a billy goat. My lady friend at Columbus said you can tell when Marty's horny because she starts sweating. I haven't seen her yet when she wasn't."

The Bear suddenly stood up. "Be right back."

"I'll be here," said Benny, waving for another daiquiri.

After half an hour the Bear returned, looking like a cat about to feast on the family canary. "Let's go."

"Where?" asked Benny, feeling mellow.

"The base exchange."

Benny followed him toward the door.

"I made a phone call and got a date. I've gotta get her some candy or something so I can make a good impression."

They were outside the club, walking past senior officers' homes, quarters built by the U.S. Army Corps of Engineers before World War Two.

"See that building?" asked Benny, pointing to one of the large houses that was built on short stilts and had tropical screens instead of windows. A splash of red paint marked the rear of the dwelling.

"Yeah."

"When the Japanese captured Clark, they brought American officers there for interrogation. A Filipino told me the wooden floors were so permeated with blood they had to be replaced. They think it's still haunted by the officers who died there, and some nights they can hear the screaming of the men being tortured."

"Charming."

"The Filipinos are superstitious and they won't go near it."

"I thought the people here were good Catholics."

"They are, but it's their own brand. The Spanish ran into some problems getting the natives here to accept Christianity when they arrived back in the early 1500's. In fact . . . you remember Magellan from school?"

"Sure. First guy to go around the world. I had a girlfriend used to say, *you be good to me and I'll do a Magellan on you.*"

"He only made it halfway around. Only got this far before he was killed trying to sell the natives on Christianity on one of the islands south of here."

They were walking at a fast pace.

"The people here already had their own religion. They were animists, and believed powerful spirits lived in mountains, rocks, trees, and such. They were also afraid of the dead.

The Spanish priests were in a hurry to make good Christians out of them so they let the Filipinos continue with their old beliefs so long as they bought Catholicism too."

"So they're not just Christians."

"They *claim* they're good Christians, but most of them are mixtures of Christian, animist, and believers in old wives' tales. The mix is different according to the area they're from."

They walked on, turning the corner toward the base exchange.

Benny said, "I thought you didn't know anyone here."

"I called the operator and got a date. Told her I was shot down in Vietnam—a poor wounded veteran—and needed to talk to the horniest operator they had."

Benny's jaw dropped. "You're shitting me."

"Maybe I said the sweetest operator. . . . Anyway, one thing following another, she said I should talk with one of her friends. She said the girl was very pretty, and was separated from her cruel Chinese businessman–husband."

Benny shook his head in amazement.

"So I told the special girl my story, how I'd been without female companionship for a long time."

"And she went along with your bullshit?"

"I told her about the Purple Heart I'm getting."

"Jesus," Benny said in disgust.

"She said her father had fought in World War Two, and would love to talk with me. She also said her sister would like to talk, too. She was engaged to a Philippine Air Force fighter pilot who got killed.

"I pick her up at the main gate at six. She's going to take me home to meet Pop, and then we're going to dinner."

"You're crazy!"

"I told her there were two of us. She wants you to meet her sister."

"Bear, you really are crazy." For the moment he'd forgotten about his funk.

At the exchange they selected candy and small gifts: ornate cosmetics compacts, an inlaid jewelry box, tobacco, and a pipe. The girl had told the Bear her father spent most of his time just sitting about fouling the air with his pipe.

"Filipinos are sentimentalists," Benny advised sagely. "They'll love you."

"Us, you mean."

From the BX they took a black and orange taxi. At four o'clock they were at the main gate.

"Two hours to go, so let's not waste it," said the Bear. "How about a hotsy bath?"

They left the cab at the gate and made their way through the Saturday crowds of Americans and Filipinos. After a short search they found the Blue Diamond Bar and Swedish Massage Parlor. At the rear entrance they each paid three dollars to a taciturn old woman who showed a gaudy, gold front tooth when the Bear announced his displeasure at not getting her services. He settled for a plump nineteen-year-old who giggled at his jokes as she led him through a curtained doorway.

Benny's girl, slender and shy, was dressed in a miniskirt and an armless cotton blouse. She led him through the doorway and motioned to a bench. "You take off clothes," she said, handing him a towel. She then turned on steaming hot water in an old chipped bathtub at the other side of the room. "You want beer?"

She took a dollar from him and left the room.

He stripped naked, then wrapped the towel around his middle and sat on the bench, feeling heady with intoxication. As he sat waiting, he turned philosophical. *The Bear is right*, he thought. *Living well is the best revenge.*

The girl returned, barefoot and dressed in hot pants and a T-shirt advertising Coca-Cola, punctuated by erect nipples. She carried a bottle of San Miguel beer as if it were fine champagne.

He swigged the ice-cold beer and shivered. It was close to a hundred degrees outside, and the air conditioning was dismal. That, with the steam rising from the tub, had him sweating like a pig, but the beer chilled him as it trekked through his pipes.

The girl led him to the tub. "In." She pointed imperiously.

He inserted his right foot and withdrew it with a howl. "It's too damned hot!" he yelled.

"In," she repeated, bringing her hand to her mouth to giggle at the face he made. She pulled his towel away as he gingerly sat in the tub, sucking his breath as the hot water covered him to the waist. She scrubbed his back thoroughly with soap and water, and he felt muscular tensions easing away, as if he was being exorcised of mean spirits. She washed his hair, making the roots tingle as she shampooed and massaged his scalp with her knuckles, then used a rough washcloth on his chest, legs, and feet.

She stopped and giggled. He had an erection.

"You want special," she said, sliding her hand down and grasping him.

"No," he said, very badly wanting the special.

His refusal neither bothered her nor slowed her down. "Up," she said, motioning. He stood and let her towel him off, then lay on the massage table as she pummeled his back with relentless hands. She worked and kneaded his buttocks and legs, then pummeled again.

When he rolled to his back she modestly placed the towel across his loins. She rubbed and kneaded his chest, arms, and legs. Finally, she reached under the towel and touched him again.

He groaned out loud and flinched.

"Special?"

"No," he mumbled.

"Hokay," she said, willing to go along with his strangeness. She motioned for him to turn onto his stomach once more. "You like me to walk on back?"

He considered, since the doctors thought there could be something wrong with his back. To hell with it, he decided. "Sure," he said.

She crawled onto the table and, using the wall beside the table to steady herself, slowly and expertly trod up and down the muscles of his broad back.

"MM-mmm-mmm," he muttered involuntarily as she walked. It was delicious torture.

"You very strong man," she declared.

"MMM-mmm-MM-MMM-mmm," he moaned in his pleasure.

Thoughts of his wife's infidelity had been washed and pummeled away. For the first time in days, Benny Lewis felt human.

03/1715L—Takhli RTAFB, Thailand

Tiny Bechler

"One mechanical alarm clock," Tiny said.

"Check," Mike Murphy said.

"Another group of letters. Let's see . . . seven in all."

"You look them over?" asked Murphy.

"They're mostly from girlfriends. A couple were a little heavy, so I tossed 'em."

"Okay, seven letters, check."

Tiny held up a portable tape recorder. "One recorder. I checked the tape inside. It was from his parents."

"One tape recorder, check."

Tiny counted, then looked up. "Eight unrecorded three-inch reels of tape."

"Eight reels of magnetic tape, check."

Tiny Bechler looked about until he was satisfied, then began to secure the top of the box with strapping tape. "We're finished."

Murphy filled in the rest of the form, then signed Michael K. Murphy at the bottom, in the SUMMARY COURTS OFFICER space. He handed one copy of the inventory sheet to Tiny, who placed it on top of the contents before closing the last flap. Another copy was placed in a small envelope and taped to the outside. A third copy would go into the squadron files, and the fourth he would keep for his own records. As summary courts officer Mike was responsible for the return of his squadron mate's belongings to his family.

"Shitty job," growled Tiny Bechler. He had been volunteered by Colonel Mack to help. They'd lost two pilots in yesterday's strikes.

While Tiny checked to make sure the three other boxes of clothing and goods were properly taped, Murphy completed two other forms, then signed all copies of each.

"Well babes," Mike said sadly, "when the guys from shipping and receiving get here we turn these in and then we're done."

Tiny looked at the boxes. "Jimbo Smith was a good guy."

"Yeah." Jimbo had still been in his aircraft when it had hit the ground.

Colonel Mack came into the hootch.

"You guys done yet?" Mack asked.

"Just finishing," said Murphy, still examining the forms for accuracy.

Tiny looked at his handiwork before standing up.

"You checked the stuff over good before you boxed it up, right?" asked Mack.

"Yes, sir," said Mike. "He's clean. There was a lot of . . . ah . . . questionable stuff. Half-finished letters to girlfriends, stuff like that."

"And?"

"When she gets the stuff, his mother will know Jimbo lived like a saint."

"No use for Mom to think otherwise," said Mack. He looked at the boxes. "We'll all miss him."

Mike Murphy, who had been close to Jimbo Smith, did not comment, but kept looking over the paperwork. His eyes were moist.

Within the squadron, only Toki Takahara and Mike Murphy were openly sensitive to the loss of their buddies. The others also felt those losses but kept their feelings close inside. Too many had been lost to properly grieve for them all, so they'd developed hard shells. Tiny sometimes wondered how Toki and Mike could cope with grieving and still function.

Captains Bud Lutz and Toki Takahara walked down the aisle of the hootch toward them. They had been handling the personal effects of a major named Jack Rose who had only been at Takhli for four days when he'd been shot down. It was his second mission.

Tiny Bechler didn't like Bud Lutz. He was aloof and had never joined the others at the bar. He seldom saw him excited or rattled. A quiet type. Some of the guys said he was very studious. Tiny thought he was just scared shitless. He'd seen him reading from a Bible before a mission briefing once.

"We're done," said Lutz. Summary court duties were the least pleasant ones in a combat squadron.

Colonel Mack looked at Lutz squarely. "You forget something?"

"What's that, sir?"

Colonel Mack pointed at his shoulder. "Your date of rank as major was today. You oughta be wearing your new rank."

"I just didn't get over to the parachute shop to get them sewn on. I'll get it done tomorrow."

"You're out of uniform, Major."

"Sorry, sir."

"Shipping and receiving on their way over?"

Bud Lutz said, "Should be here any minute now. I told them seventeen-thirty."

As he spoke a staff sergeant carrying a clipboard entered the hootch and looked around. Two burly airmen followed him. They'd done this before, but didn't look like they enjoyed it.

"Remember you've got an appointment at the club. Gotta spend some of that new major's pay on free drinks, Bud. See you there soon as you're done."

Lutz solemnly went to the other end of the hootch and started with the shipping and receiving people.

Colonel Mack looked about with obvious satisfaction that the dismal job was done, then left.

"That Lutz is a real turkey, isn't he," said Tiny to Murphy.

Mike Murphy drew in a breath. "Tiny, just shut the fuck up unless you've got something better to say."

"Sorry," said Tiny, startled by the outburst.

"Bud Lutz is a lay preacher, doesn't smoke or drink or screw around on his wife. That why you call him a turkey?"

"Well . . ."

"You think all the real men drink and raise hell every night, like you and me? You think you gotta fuck whores to be a real man?"

Tiny felt uneasy.

"Bud, Jimbo, and I were in the same flight back in Wichita. Bud had already been here when Jimbo and I arrived a couple of months back. He got us assigned to the 357th so he could teach us what he'd already learned about flying combat.

"Night before last Jimbo and I went to downtown Takhli. Screwed around, got drunk, and started talking about the differences between us and Bud. You, me, the rest of us try to forget about being scared shitless, losing buddies, or screwing up and dropping our bombs a little long and maybe killing some civilians. We drink and sing songs and raise hell to forget, so we can fly tomorrow.

"Bud's different. He remembers his shortcomings and prays for the strength to do better."

Tiny looked closer at Bud Lutz, who was coming down the aisle with the shipping and receiving sergeant. The two airmen were carrying out the last boxes of Major Rose's things.

Mike pointed out Jimbo Smith's boxes to the shipping and receiving sergeant, and went over the tags to make sure they had Jimbo's correct address on their own forms.

Lutz glanced over at Tiny. "Thanks for the support, Lieutenant Bechler," he said.

"Glad to help, sir," said Tiny, in a quieter voice than he normally used.

"Guess we're done here now. Let's go to the club so I can buy some refreshments for you characters."

Tiny understood something he had not before.

03/1750L—Angeles City, Republic of the Philippines

Benny Lewis

When Benny emerged from the bathhouse the Bear was waving good-bye to the old woman with the gold tooth. He hefted the sack of gifts and followed the Bear out the door into the brilliant sunlight. Benny felt good. Red-faced from the heat of the bath, loose from the rub and scrub, and more than a little intoxicated, he stepped out with new zest.

"Hot damn," said the Bear. "I think I like the Philippines."

"Yeah."

"You get the special?"

"No," he quickly replied.

"A hotsy bath is incomplete without the special. My lady had magic hands."

They stopped at a stand and bought mangos wrapped in paper. They ate the fruit as they walked back toward the main gate, talking and wiping juice from their mouths with the coarse tissue. They were close to the walk-through gate, where the Filipino workers exited the base.

"She said she'd come through about six," said the Bear.

At 18:07 according to Benny's flying watch, a petite

Filipina dressed in neat slacks and a linen blouse passed
through the walking gate and casually looked about.

"That's Esther," the Bear said.

Benny shook his head. "Can't be." The girl had too much
class to be picked up with a telephone call.

"That's her. Yellow blouse and black slacks, like she
said." The Bear waved. "Esther?" he called.

She was slim and had rounded, pleasant features, including a petite nose and chubby cheeks. Her friendly smile
showed off perfect teeth. "You are Captain Malcolm Stewart?"

"Guilty," the Bear said smoothly. "You are lovely beyond
all expectations." Benny listened with surprise as the Bear
turned up his charm.

She wrinkled her nose. "My parents taught me to beware
of smooth-speaking men."

He held his arms out expansively. "I will be whatever you
desire."

She laughed pleasantly and turned. "You must be Captain
Lewis."

"Call me Benny."

"And what do I call you, Captain Malcolm Stewart?" she
asked, turning back toward the Bear.

He motioned to Benny. "My friends call me Bear."

"What do you prefer?"

The Bear was grinning at his good luck. "Bear is a special
name used for warriors, and in your presence the last thing I
want to think of is war. Call me Mal."

Benny groaned, but noticed that Esther sparkled. She and
the Bear spoke in conspiratorial tones as they made their way
through the mob of civilian workers exiting the base. Benny
was scarcely considered and felt content to trail along behind.
The day was warm, the girls they passed were pretty, and for
another moment he forgot about being miserable.

Bear Stewart

"Where to?" the Bear asked her.

"To my home to meet my family. Do you mind?"

"Not at all," he said. *No matter what the country, you got
to pay your dues,* the Bear thought.

"And you, Captain Benny?"

"That would be fine."

Damn, thought the Bear. Benny's mood was swinging like a gate. In the midst of his last retort, he'd started looking ill at ease. The Bear was determined to help his squadron-mate through his tough time.

"We will take a jeepney," Esther happily announced.

"Jeepney?" asked the Bear.

"A homegrown jeep," muttered Benny. "They build 'em here."

The Bear noted the sour expression. Perhaps meeting Esther's sister would help.

She was talking about her family. "You must be patient with my father," she bubbled, "for his memory fades."

They climbed into the back of a chrome and bright-red, backyard-manufactured vehicle with a Japanese four-banger engine sounding like a washing machine out of sync. From the front the jeepneys looked like World War Two jeeps, for they were fashioned precisely after that design. In the rear was a passengers' pit. Rows of gaudy lights rimmed the top of the vehicle fore and aft.

Esther gave instructions and bargained with the driver, then turned her attention back to the Bear. "It is not far."

The city was pulsing with life. Raucous honking, shouts, whistles, and laughter from both G.I.'s and Filipinos filled the air.

As they rode along the busy street, the Bear noticed several old Reo trucks and wondered if they, too, were replicas. Benny said they were relics from the war, left by the Americans in 1945. Some were built from the parts of several vehicles. You could tell because of the different colors of the various body parts.

Esther periodically attempted to draw Benny into the conversation, but he remained taciturn. After a moment she would return her attention to the Bear. *Pretty and intelligent,* the Bear decided, wishing she just had more in the tit department.

They rode for ten minutes though the town's congested center. Residential streets were crowded with a variety of homes: large stucco Spanish-style homes topped by red tile and frameworks of wrought iron to protect the windows; others less ornate, but still sporting the iron-framed windows; poorer homes built of plywood, with neither wrought iron nor fanciness; makeshift hovels crowded into the alleys.

They passed small buggies with drivers who tapped their crops on the haunches of small ponies, harnesses festooned with tassels and bits of bright metal. Esther called the gaudy buggies *calesas*.

The sun had dropped to the horizon, filtering red hues through the western sky. Evening shadows were invading the streets when they stopped. Esther paid the driver with change offered by the men and they crawled down. She led the way down a side street to a modest house identical to a thousand others they had passed. Hers was obviously not a prosperous family.

She opened the door and shouted, Americanlike, that they were there, then beckoned for them to follow. The clean, barren home consisted of three or four small rooms. Esther's mother, slender and graceful, greeted them warmly. She clucked and hovered, then shooed Esther to the kitchen to fetch bottles of San Miguel beer. The Bear fished around in the sack from the BX and presented her with the jewelry box and candy. She acted like it was Christmas, nodding her head at her good fortune and grinning, showing gaps in her teeth.

The mother showed the gifts to a white-haired man with a worn and deep-lined face. He was seated in a chair fashioned of frayed bamboo, clutching a gnarled walking cane. He smelled old, his breath sweet, reminding the Bear of his Uncle Miles. His chicken's neck was corded and wrinkled, and a dark scar ran diagonally across his Naugahydelike face. He spoke slowly, savoring and measuring his words.

"I am honored that you visit us," he said. "My daughter called. Our neighbors have a telephone," he added proudly.

"We are the honored ones."

"She said you fly airplanes?"

"Yes, sir."

"That you both escaped the enemy after being shot down?"

"Yes."

"American pilots were shot down during our war. They were butchered by the Japanese when they were caught. The Japanese used swords. They would have the pilots face the east and make our people watch as they forced them to bow down. Then they would cut off their heads. Our people tried to rescue American pilots before they were caught by the Japanese."

Everyone was quiet. Benny wore a troubled expression as

he watched the old man, but offered no words. The Bear broke the silence. "Esther said you were a soldier."

The old man was happy to talk of his military service. "I saw General Wainwright once," he said proudly, "when the Japanese marched the American officers through Tarlac."

"He was a great hero," said the Bear, trying to remember who Wainwright was.

"Yes," said the old soldier, "but he should not have told us to quit fighting when we still had guns and bullets. We could have fought longer, perhaps even until help arrived."

"Oh?" replied the Bear. He knew little about the war in the Philippines twenty-five years earlier.

"When the message arrived from Corregidor to stop fighting, many of us did not agree, but our officer said the order must be obeyed. We gave up our guns and bullets to the Japanese. We were taken to Tarlac in boxcars, marched to Capas, then on to the prison at Camp O'Donnel—the same place the Americans had trained us to march and fight. I spent ten terrible months there. Many died of starvation and sickness, both Americans and Filipino."

The Bear nodded. He had never in his life heard of Camp O'Donnel.

"I escaped. Not many did. I met with others in the hills and we wished we had the guns and bullets we had given the Japanese." He nodded gravely. "Some of us had to fight with only the cane knives we were given by field-workers."

The old man grew increasingly pale around his mouth and eyes.

"Rest now, Father," said a new feminie voice. The speaker, more girl than woman, came out from the kitchen. She glanced shyly at Benny and the Bear. Obviously this was the sister, quite similar in appearance except her figure was fuller at the breast and hips than Esther's. She wore a dark dress, cut severely and covering to her calf.

In mourning. *Ought to fit right in with Benny,* thought the Bear.

"This is Angela," said Esther. She introduced both men. A glance at Benny showed no emotion registering on his face as Angela warily greeted them.

"You have a fine family," the Bear said to the old man, who looked at his brood and considered. He nodded finally, as if agreeable but not really convinced.

After a few more minutes of small talk and presenting gifts to the women, the Bear brought out the briar pipe and tin of tobacco. He presented them to the old guerrilla fighter who took them with trembling hands and examined them closely.

"Thank you again for inviting us into your home," said the Bear.

The old man handled the pipe carefully, turning it over in his hands, then motioned abruptly as if having made up his mind. "My home is yours," he pronounced.

As the men spoke for a while longer, the mother pulled her daughters into the kitchen. *Probably telling them to keep their legs crossed,* the Bear thought.

When the girls emerged, everyone was smiling. After bows and handshakes, and a final nod to the old man, the four made their exit.

"Nice folks," commented the Bear as they walked up the dark side street toward the main thoroughfare. Esther stopped him and pecked him on the cheek. "The gift for Father was perfect," she said. "He will treasure it until he dies."

Angela walked quietly beside Benny, more careful to maintain her distance. "Thank you both," she said in English more halting than Esther's.

When they reached the corner, Esther giggled and clapped her hands. "Our parents are ashamed that neither of their daughters is happily married," she exclaimed. "They wish we would settle down and raise many babies."

"Esther!" exclaimed her sister.

"I was married for a while, to a Chinaman in Manila," said Esther.

"Divorced?" asked the Bear.

She shrugged noncommittally. "It is not so easy for us in the Philippines, you know."

"I see."

"Angela was engaged to a pilot," she said in a confidential tone. "They were to be married this month."

Benny was looking at Angela again. From the way he acted, he could be examining a turkey.

Angela interrupted the Bear's thoughts. "He was killed. . . ." She searched for the words. "In airplane crash."

"I'm sorry," he said.

"They were very much in love," said Esther with a dreamy expression.

The Bear placed his arm around Esther's shoulder. Angela looked around and glared at him. "We are not like the girls in bars," she said sharply.

Which translates, the Bear judged, *to no nooky for Benny*. He wondered about the Spanish influence injected during their several hundred years of rule. He'd been to Spain and seen how their religion restrained relations between guys and *nice* Spanish girls. He supposed the same traditions were impressed upon *nice* Filipinas.

"Your friend is good-looking," said Esther in a low tone, looking toward Benny. "He is troubled?"

"Yes, he is."

"How old are you?" they heard Benny ask Angela. "Eighteen," she answered. "I'll be nineteen soon," she added.

"That's very young," he said, and the two grew quiet again.

"How old are you, Captain Benny?" Esther asked.

"Twenty-eight, almost twenty-nine." He looked at Angela. "Does that seem old?"

"No," she decided. "Twenty-eight is a young man's age."

Esther broke in again. "But twenty-nine is very old, isn't it Angela." They all laughed.

After walking two blocks they located a jeepney that took them across town to a stuccoed, two-story building Esther claimed was the best restaurant in Angeles City. There they ate lush salads, tender steaks, a tasty *pancit* dish, and capped it off with desserts of sherbet and wafers that melted in their mouths. They drank a bottle of wine with the meal. Following the meal they had coffee liquer served in tiny porcelain cups, allowing them to relax and talk over flickering candlelight.

They left the restaurant and walked, careful to stay clear of the rowdiest bars from which loud music and lusty shouts emanated. They window-shopped and talked for a while, then the Bear slowed down, allowing the two couples to separate. He drew Esther into a storefront alcove where they shared a warm, wet kiss. The way she clung to him, his hope for the evening was revived.

When they emerged, Benny and Angela had stopped a short distance farther down the street. "You're a nice girl," Benny was saying as they approached, "and it really has been a nice evening."

"Do you want to kiss me?" she asked suddenly.

Benny hesitated, and the Bear was embarrassed for him. Suddenly he turned and staggered. The Bear hurried up and steadied him with a hand on his arm. "You okay?"

"Yeah. Too much to drink."

"Let's go to a nice bar and sit for a while. Esther knows one close by."

"I'm really bushed, Bear."

The Bear looked over at the two girls. "I gotta admit it doesn't look promising."

"I'm going back to the base. It's just too soon."

The Bear nodded. "Maybe so."

Benny motioned toward a parked jeepney. "See you tomorrow, okay?"

The Bear looked at him hesitantly, then glanced at the girls.

Benny gave him a wry look. "Remember what your buddy the nurse said about being back at the hospital by midnight," he said, "but have fun."

"Thanks for reminding me, asshole," the Bear said. It was past nine.

The girls were waiting. The Bear explained that Benny was going back to base.

Esther seemed upset. "Are you sure?" she asked Benny.

"I'm afraid so."

The girls were both curt as Benny said his good-byes. He finally broke away and walked toward the jeepney. The Bear watched him, then replaced his arm around Esther. "Let's find that bar you were telling me about."

They walked, the Bear's arm around Esther's waist.

"You think I am ugly?" Angela asked from the other side of Esther. She was frowning.

"You are very pretty," he said, steering them around a group of civvie-clothed airmen standing outside D' Big Bopper bar, from which loud rock music swelled. One of the group whistled.

A *calesa* with jingle-bells on the harness clopped down the street. "Let's take that," Esther said, waving to the driver.

"Is it that far to the bar?" asked the Bear.

When they crawled into the buggy, he ended up squeezed into the seat beside Angela, with Esther sitting knee to knee on a smaller seat opposite them. The driver flicked his reins, and the Bear watched the busy city pass by. Esther seemed

oblivious of Angela and his closeness, pointing and chattering.
As they drew into the darker back streets, he recognized some
of the large residences. The girls were on their way home.
What the hell? he thought.

"No drinks at a bar?" he asked.

He heard a snort from Angela.

"You have been a gentleman," murmured Esther. "Perhaps," she added with a smile, "you will be rewarded. Would
you like to hear more about Filipinos?"

"Sure," he said. *Some reward,* he thought.

"Filipinas are surely the most superstitious people in the
world. Our family is from Tarlac province, where people may
be the most superstitious of all."

Angela's hand was warm on his leg.

"The people from the various parts of the islands believe
in different things, but they are all frightened of the dead and
of ghosts." Her voice dropped. "Some think the dead return to
their loved ones five days after they die."

He laughed, but the girls did not join in.

"Angela and I are modern and intelligent women, don't
you believe?"

"Certainly."

She smiled vaguely, then her face was lost to him as they
passed into deep shadows. "These silly women believe that the
ghost will stay until a very strong person enters their life. Then
the ghost feels angry, and must depart."

"But you don't think so."

"Our mother believes, but she is from another generation.
For instance, she believes that if a woman goes to bed with wet
hair, she will go crazy. She also believes that Angela's dead
fiance has returned. She hoped that Captain Benny might be
Angela's strong man."

"Benny's having trouble with his own ghosts," he said.
"No reflection on Angela."

Esther directed the driver to stop at their lane.

"Do you have a dollar?" she asked him.

"I'll pay him when I get to the base," he said.

She looked exasperated. "Please?"

Bear started to argue, then gave her a dollar bill before
dismounting.

Esther chatted with the driver in Tagalog, slipping him the
dollar. When all were down the Bear bowed elegantly. "Thank

you, ladies, for a fantastic evening." He didn't show the sarcasm he felt.

"Walk us home, please," said Esther primly. Relucantly, he agreed. They'd gone less half the distance to the dark house when he heard the *calesa* pony clop away.

"Damn," he muttered.

As they grew close to her home, Esther pulled him closer. "Be very quiet."

Angela fumbled with the lock, then pushed slowly. The door creaked. Esther released him and slipped past, disappearing into the room.

"Thanks," he whispered in disgust. Turning to leave he felt Angela's hand on his arm.

"Please," she said in a low voice, tugging.

"Inside?"

"*Shhh,*" she said, closing the door behind them. The Bear felt awkward and wondered about her parents as she led the way. He bumped against something, the old man's chair he thought. From one of the back rooms he heard a stirring.

"Come," Angela whispered impatiently. Faint light from a window outlined the room, and he could barely make out a bed and a dresser. Angela closed the door.

"What are you doing," he whispered harshly. She came to him, gently drawing his head down so they could kiss. As her tongue explored, her breath quickened.

"Oooh," she moaned in the low voice, kissing him again. "You are so strong. There is no other but you."

The Bear was puzzled at first, then found himself grinning in the darkness. She was speaking for the benefit of the ghost! He thought fleetingly of Benny and how this should have been for him. He felt her hand grasping at his trousers, and all thought of Benny disappeared.

"Fuck off, ghost," he growled and let her pull him toward the bed. She was already moaning with false passion.

When they were done, he rose back, still in her, silently panting. The proximity of her parents bothered him. She hadn't been quiet about it, moaning and talking aloud the entire time. When he'd pushed to enter her, she'd bucked and convulsed wildly, almost throwing him off. The bed had creaked so noisily in an unmistakable tempo that he'd been amazed it hadn't collapsed. During her two orgasms, she had cried "Oh, oh, oh," in ever louder yelps.

Remembering the noise he whispered, "Your parents?"

"What about them," she said in an impatient voice. "Father is old, and doesn't hear anything once he's asleep." She stroked his back with her light touch, ready again.

"And your mother?"

"She won' complain." She pulled him closer to whisper. "The ghos' of my fiancé, remember?"

Angela held him captive between her legs and after a few more quiet moments began to slowly rotate her hips and move beneath him. "Oh, you are so strong, Cap'n Mal."

She was moving her hips in a sensuous circle, pulling and manipulating him with her vaginal muscles. *Look ma, no hands,* he thought crazily just before he forgot about jokes and noise and began to get serious about things again.

"Me on top," she gasped. "Oh, Cap'n Mal, you get me so hot."

He slowly rolled, perching her on top, and she began to lift and grind down on him, working those wonderful muscles. When they finished the second time, he started to relax as he had done before, but she would have none of it.

"I will help you," she said, slithering down in the bed. She helped him with butterfly hands and warm mouth until he was again at the edge, then clambered eagerly back on top, lifted, and wiggled to impale herself. She resumed her rocking and moaning.

He was spent. They lay entwined, panting in rhythm. *Three great fucks in record time!* he thought.

She kissed his chest and licked his nipples, trying to start again. "Oh, Cap'n Mal," she said. He groaned at the thought of another performance.

"Later," he pleaded.

After several more tries Angela accepted that he was unable to continue. Then, as abruptly as she had turned on her ardor, she rolled onto her side and dropped into peaceful slumber. The Bear blew a ragged breath of relief.

She drew back and he almost dropped off to sleep. The door creaked as Esther's dark shape crept into the room, startling him.

"Turn your head while I change into my nightclothes," she whispered. He closed his eyes, knowing he couldn't have felt lustful if she were Brigitte Bardot. He heard the sounds of a zipper, called himself a liar, and opened his eyes.

"I mus' be here when my parents wake," she whispered in her sleepy voice. He watched her nude shadow stretch and slip a short nightgown over her head. She had a trim gazelle's body. She shook a finger at him in the gloom, letting him know she was aware he'd been looking.

"I'll leave if you wish," he whispered. The bed was not very big.

"Shhh." She circled the small bed like a cat inspecting its nest, then slid in on the side opposite Angela as he raised an arm for her to lie on. She nestled her ass against his side for a moment, then turned and burrowed her face into his shoulder. The Bear cupped one of Angela's breasts in his right hand and one moon of Esther's trim ass in his left. Both women stirred, snuggling to adjust themselves to his grasp. Esther mewed prettily, her fingertips moving on his chest. She was breathing unevenly, as her finger slid down his belly and found him.

No one, the Bear told himself happily, *is going to believe this back at Takhli.* Amazingly, he was growing under the ministrations of Esther's fingers. He started to compose the story for Glenn . . . dammit! . . . for Mike Murphy, who was reputedly the foremost cocksman in the wing. Esther moved against his leg, breathing faster and making him forget all about Murphy. He stroked her, his hands and fingers playing across her body.

"So strong," she whispered. He released Angela's breast to pay better attention to her growing need.

At first they were stealthy and almost furtive. After he was in her, she moved her legs together, making herself fist-tight, and proved that Angela's magical manipulations ran in the family by lying very still and just using internal muscles. After several minutes of unhurried pleasure, Esther could not help releasing her first long, low shuddering moan. Not long thereafter he was ready to claw at the walls.

Later, as he lay there sandwiched pleasantly between the two girls, sleep washing over him like the tide moving onto a beach, he caught his breath in a flash of unpleasant remembrance. At first he could not recognize it, then he wished he had not. Glenn Phillips's face hovered, mocked him, opened its mouth, and emitted the shrill, haunting scream.

He had told himself he would cope with it at some distant, later time. Now the terrible noise grew louder. He felt a lump in his chest, making it difficult to catch his breath. He lay there, sweating profusely, his mind in turmoil, then carefully, methodically, he pushed the images and the sounds away until the memory clouded and was gone.

At six, Esther shook him awake, motioning urgently. She was clothed, her face serious. "You must go."

The Bear groaned. His head was pounding, his throat was sore, and his penis felt like raw meat. He had difficulty swallowing and tried to speak, but only incomprehensible sounds emerged.

"Mother says please to hurry. My father will be waking up."

He crawled out from the covers and sat on the bedside for a moment, scratching his head and chest, then searched the room for his clothing. When he'd finished gathering it, he was still missing his shirt, shorts, and one sock.

"Hurry." Esther beckoned from the door. He slipped on the pants without shorts and put the single sock in his pocket. He found his shirt wadded beside the bed and pulled it on, yawning and wondering if he looked as bad as he felt.

"My family mus' go to Sunday Mass. Please hurry."

He rose fully to his feet and, disoriented, almost fell.

"Shit," he croaked. His mouth was dry and held a bitter taste.

She pulled him by the hand through the house to the front door, her mother and sister silently ignoring him from the kitchen.

"Call me tomorrow," she said, then pushed him out and closed the door behind him.

In the bright daylight the quaint side street showed itself to be a dirty and sharp-smelling alley. Fine dust swirled up with each step. The modest houses lining the alley were shanties and lean-tos constructed of scrap plywood, cardboard, and bamboo.

He stopped to fish a cigarette from the crumpled pack in his shirt pocket. A yellow dog with a curled tail and an indelible grin sidled up beside him. The dog raised its leg and sprinkled on his pants' leg. He kicked at it, missing and almost falling. The grinning dog slunk away, leering back to make sure he wasn't being followed.

For a crazy moment the dog reminded him of the pig he'd met in the jungle. He lit the cigarette, coughed, and listened to the agonizing beat of blood in his forehead.

He emerged onto the larger thoroughfare and began to look for a jeepney. "God, but it's good to be alive!" the Bear yelled to anyone who might be interested, laughing as he waved at an approaching jeepney.

It was seven-fifty before he finally got back to the hospital room. He took a long, very hot shower, and pulled on the issue smock before happily padding toward his bed. Each step jarred his aching head.

"Dear God, do I need sleep? Yessir! Has it been great? Yessir!"

He was pulling back the covers when the door opened and Marty the nurse stood there, hands on hefty hips.

Oh, shit!

"Where in hell were you last night!" she demanded.

He thought quickly. "Didn't feel too hot, so I came back early. Sorry I missed you."

"Bullshit on that," she said, eyes glittering with anger as she pushed into the room. "I called back here from the club and had 'em check. You weren't here."

"I don't know about your people. Not very reliable," he tried.

"I know who's reliable, and it sure as hell isn't you," she said nastily. "I had a great dinner planned and you were out screwing whores. I've got a long memory, Mal."

This was Marty's turf and if allowed to continue her present mood, she would surely make his life miserable.

"No shit, Marty," he tried on a different tack, "Benny and I weren't feeling too good, so we came back early. I sat in Benny's room and we talked until real late. I even fell asleep on his chair, but we were back pretty early."

Her eyebrows lifted, and he knew she was considering his lie. What she might lack in sophistication, Marty the nurse made up for with sixth sense. "Bullshit," she said, her final judgment made.

He nodded toward the door, trying to smile. "Those things lock?"

She glanced at him, not understanding. "Of course not. It's a hospital, remember."

"Too bad." He shook his head, still grinning.

"You look awful, like you're about to drop from exhaustion."

He mustered all the charm he could, which was puny. "I'm not feeling well, nurse. Can you make it better?"

Marty didn't require much charm. She was smiling, eyes animated, chest beginning to heave dramatically. She touched his arm, perspiring mightily.

A full hour later Marty straightened her uniform and primped happily at the door as the Bear, now cross-eyed with exhaustion, prepared to drop off into well-earned sleep. She'd toiled hard, but had been able to rouse him twice to pay his dues.

God did he have a story to tell them back at Takhli. In his fog he started to build the story for Glenn's—not Glenn for Christ's sake!—for Mike Murphy's benefit.

"Mike, you may not believe this," he would tell him, *"but I had three different women a total of seven times in one night and morning."* Had it really been seven? He tried to recall. Mike might not believe him. He wondered how he could bring back proof.

The problem was too difficult. He fell into a deep slumber.

04/1845L—Takhli RTAFB, Thailand

The Takhli contingent of the composite strike force had consisted of eight four-ship flights, Korat providing eight more flights of F-105's, and Ubon four flights of F-4 Phantoms. The pilots had been briefed to ingress into North Vietnam in their individual flights, cross the Red River five miles south of Yen Bai, then turn due east toward Thud Ridge. When they had crossed Thud Ridge, half of the composite strike force was to swing southward, using the ridge as a shield while they approached the Yen Vien railroad siding. The remaining aircraft were to turn northward and bomb the Ha Ghia fuel storage area, fifteen miles to the north. Both targets were believed to be well defended by the North Vietnamese.

Both targets were also more meaningful than they normally were assigned. Yen Vien was a major siding on the northeast rail line. Korat had sent its eight flights of Thuds there. Large amounts of fuel were thought to be stored at Ha Ghia. The 355th wing, led by the 357th Tactical Fighter Squadron, and the F-4's from Ubon Air Base had gone to Ha Ghia.

Colonel Mack

Mack stood in a corner of the briefing theater, talking to Maj Max Foley and Lt Col Johnny T. Polaski, two of the luckiest men in the world. Foley and Polaski were both smoking cigarettes and drinking the rotgut mission whiskey handed out by Doc Roddenbush after the tough missions.

By all that was logical they should be dead, or at best sitting before Vietnamese interrogators with no whiskey or cigarettes and little hope.

Johnny T. Polaski had been leading the attack on Ha Ghia, his flight engaged by MiG-21's. Johnny T. had turned hard to engage a silver-colored, delta-wing MiG and had not seen the MiG's wingman. The second MiG had fired a heat-seeking Atoll missile from his six o'clock position and the missile had tracked straight and true. It had smashed into the tail of Polaski's F-105, but had not detonated. He had flown the Thud back home with the enemy missile buried, unexploded, in his tailpipe.

Foley had been pulling off the Ha Ghia target, still manuevering hard when he'd also seen MiG's. He'd called for his flight to drop their empty fuel tanks in anticipation of engaging. His fuel tanks had released, but one had somehow ended up wrapped about his right wing. He'd flown the aircraft all the way back to Takhli, the collapsed fuel tank still firmly affixed to the wing.

Mack listened, marveling at just how tough and resilient the Thud was. The formal debriefings with maintenance and intelligence were finished, and now Mack was just bullshitting with them, trying to find out things the others had not.

What was right or wrong with maintenance? Were there too many CNDs (could not duplicates)? Was the enemy doing anything different that they should learn to cope with? Were some new or better tactics evolving that would allow them to better cope with enemy air defenses? What could they do to minimize losses when they flew tomorrow? He discussed the small details that the debriefers might think were inconsequential, but that might save future lives.

Other than the loss of one aircraft—a new lieutenant named Ricard had bailed out and been picked up unscathed—it had not gone badly for the squadron. Red Crown had relayed that a total of twenty-four MiG's had been launched against the strike force. The EB-66's said eighteen SAMs had been fired. Still, the 357th squadron had placed their bombs squarely on a tough target, and they had suffered no casualties. The fact there were no secondaries from the target, which meant there had been no fuel in the big tanks, was not their fault.

Mack finally broke up the informal session and walked from the command post back toward the squadron, thoughtful as he gazed out at the ever-busy flight line. He watched as a crew chief fussed over his bird, like a mother over her child just home from a fight with the neighborhood bully. He'd only had to tell one chief that his airplane would not return. It had felt good to add that the pilot had been picked up and was just fine.

At the squadron he went into his office and picked the roster off his desk. Sergeant Hill had already updated it with the rescue of Lieutenant Ricard.

The roster reflected the changes of the last ten days.

357 TFS KEY PERSONNEL ROSTER	As of: ~~25 Nov 66~~	
Cmdr:	~~Lt col Lee, J.F.~~ (K)	MacLendon, T.F.
Ops:	Lt Col Polaski, J.T.	
A-Flt:	*Maj Hall, M.S.	
	~~Capt Smith, J.A.~~ (K)	
	Capt Huffmeier, C.L.	
	Capt Maisey, K.R.	
	Capt Meyer, J.C.	
	1/Lt Bechler, H.J.	Lt Radkovich
B-Flt:	*~~Maj Ralston, M.A.~~ (K)	*~~Maj Rose~~ (M)
	~~Capt Lewis, B.L.~~ (RW)	Capt DiFazio
	Capt Clark, C.R. (C*)	
	Capt Raymond, T.W.	
	1/Lt Rodriguez, G.M.	Lt Ricard (R)
	1/Lt Singleton, T.S.	
C-Flt:	*Maj Crawford, P.T.	
	**Capt Lutz, B.T.	
	Capt Murphy, M.K.	
	~~Capt Larkins, T.T.~~ (M)	
	1/Lt Mullens, M.W.	
	1/Lt Silva, J.S.	
D-Flt:	*Capt Swendler, O.A.	
	**Capt Takahara, T.	
	Capt Maier, R.L.	
	Capt Spalding, J.J.	
	1/Lt Brown, C.C.	
	1/Lt Capella, R.S.	
	(M)	

WW-Flt:	~~*Maj Phillips, G.P./Capt Stewart, M.S.~~ (RW)	
Atch:	Col Parker, B.J. (Wing Cmdr)	
	Maj Foley, M.T. (Wing Weapons Ofcr)	
Maint:	2/Lt Shilling, D.D./CMS Roberts, C.A.	
1st Sgt:	M/Sgt Silvester, T.S.	
Admin:	T/Sgt Hill, P.C.	
P.E.:	S/Sgt Perez, S.L.	Notes: 100 = Finished Tour
		C = Status Change
Flt Srgn:	Maj Roddenbush, D.L.	W = Wounded
		R = Rescued
* Flight Commander		P = POW
**Ass't Flight Commander		M = MIA
		K = KIA

Too many losses, he decided, for just ten days of flying.

During this time Mack had worked hard on the basics of combat flying. He had put up his old signs. "DON'T FLY BELOW 4,500 FEET," "JINK, JINK, JINK, KEEP YOUR AIRSPEED UP, CHECK SIX O'CLOCK," and talked with the men about low-exposure weapons-delivery profiles, MiG tactics, and how to dodge SAMs. He had personally flown with each flight commander, to make sure they put words into practice, then with each new man as he came aboard. He pounded the basics into their brains, and watched as they gained confidence.

The threats—SAMs, MiG's, and flak—the enemy was throwing at them were indeed becoming manageable. Give them another couple of weeks, he thought, and the 357th would be ready when the major shoot-out came with the North Vietnamese. And the shoot-out *would* come. The politicians would give them a meaningful target. They would go after it, and the enemy would try to deny it. Both the North Vietnamese and the Thud pilots would recognize it when it came, and after a bloody fight one would come out the winner. Only one would be left in command of the sky.

Book II

Today—Termite Hill, Democratic Republic of Vietnam

Precisely ninety-three miles west of Hanoi, the Da River, which flows southeast to Thanh Hoa, is joined by a small tributary from the southwest. In the V of the union is a low mountain, barren and desolate and pocked with deep craters.

American pilots once called it Termite Hill.

Tribesmen travel from the mountainous region near the Ma River in eastern Laos, down the untended road on the opposite side of the stream, and ford the Da near the intersection of the stream and in full view of the mountain. They take their meager produce to market to trade for essentials, as they have done each few months for centuries. But they are especially wary as they pass by Dead Mountain. It looks eerie and forlorn. The tribesmen believe it is inhabited by spirits.

Years before, the elders of the group remember, the mountain had been tall and proud, thickly forested and lush, loud with the busy sounds of monkeys, birds, and flying insects. Of course, the mountain had still been alive then.

When the War of Unification was raging and the Americans flew their fighters past here to bomb the Great Hong Valley, the tribesmen had astutely found another market, far to the west, and for several seasons had gone there. They had heard stories that the mountain had angered the Americans and that they were killing it, but few had believed they could succeed.

When the Americans stopped flying overhead, the tribesmen returned to their old trade route. They had been amazed at what they had seen when they looked across the tributary to the mountain. No sign of life. Quiet, except for an occasional stirring of wind across its barren and desolate ground.

Nothing grows there, now. During the rainy season the heavy downpours wash great amounts of red soil from the mountain, so much that the Da River changes to the color of blood as it flows past, and every dry season it seems that the

217

mountain has shrunk even more. They wonder if someday it will disappear altogether.

The tribesmen were puzzled so they asked the people at Bac Yen, the farm village nearest the mountain, what had happened. The villagers told them the American airplanes had dropped great numbers of bombs and sometimes would even shoot their guns at the mountain.

The tribesmen still wondered. On a subsequent trek through the village, they stopped again to discuss the subject. Why had they bombed this particular mountain, which seemed to be of little apparent use to anyone?

The villagers just shook their heads again, ridiculing the tribesmen, and said everyone knew the Americans were crazy. There had been no soldiers at the hill, no supplies or buildings there. There was no reason at all, but the Americans bombed it anyway.

The people from Bac Yen had been careful to avoid Dead Mountain after the Americans had started to bomb there. The intelligent ones still did, even though the planes no longer came. It was a treacherous place. Sometimes, when the wind blew the dust and the shape of the mountain was blurred in the shimmering heat, and there were distant moaning and the sounds of angry voices.

CHAPTER EIGHT

Monday, December 5th—1740 Local, Clark Air Base, Philippines

Benny Lewis

A sign was suspended near the cafeteria serving line: "This Food Has Been Inspected & Passed by 1Lt Marjorie Stubbs, Ass't Dietary Officer CABHR 23-12."

The patients snickered and sometimes even laughed, for the food's appearance and taste were such that it could, indeed, have passed through Marge's skinny GI tract.

Benny and the Bear sat in the crowded hospital dining hall, staring at food passed by Marge. The Bear toyed with crispy nuggets of meat that the menu described as braised beef tips. He laid his fork on the edge of his plate, admitting defeat. Benny, having previously given up on braised beef tips and nourishing vegetable—raw broccoli—retreated to dessert, trying a spoonful of tapioca pudding with the visual appeal and consistency of Lepage's paper glue. He made a face.

"Uncle," he declared.

"We should have gone to the club for dinner," said the Bear.

In two days they both would undergo flight physicals, required before they could be placed back on flying status. Until then they'd been authorized freedom to come and go at will. The only possible complications were a blemish on the Bear's right lung, a smudge on the X-ray film the flight surgeon said was diminishing in size, and an imperfection in the curvature of Benny's spine, which the doctors could not determine was harmful. If all went well, they would return to Takhli in three days. They were both anxious to get back.

219

Benny was beginning to grieve less over the split with Bets. He had started to change after a telephone conversation on the same morning the Bear had returned to the hospital with his wide grin. After talking awhile, he realized he didn't know this woman any longer.

"My friends here in Eugene," she had said, *"including my psychoanalyst, all agree that you are participating in an evil war."*

She told him about her close friends from preparatory school days who now held meetings and sent blood-splattered letters to congressmen protesting America's illegal participation in Vietnam's civil war. She had decided to join their effort, since she could provide valuable information on what it was like to live inside the fascist military machine. She would tell them about the mental aberrations of America's baby-killers.

"Ben," she concluded, *"get out of that silly war. Come back and regain your sanity. The men over there, including you and all your friends, will just end up being killed for nothing. Ben, no one cares. I don't know a single person here who cares if any of you get killed, or if you win or lose your war."*

His war?

Before he hung up he couldn't resist asking how long she'd known her new lover.

"You left in September," she'd answered simply, and had not offered more.

Benny emerged from his reverie. He placed his spoon down on the fiberglass tray, unable to stomach the tapioca.

"What did you do today?" asked the Bear.

Benny shrugged. "Not much. You?"

"I got a call a coupla hours ago," said the Bear, "from a friend who went with the airlines back in sixty-three. He's herding a Boeing 707 around the Pacific for TWA."

"Where'd you know him from?" asked Benny.

"Before I became a Weasel, I was in SAC flying B-52's. He was the copilot on my first crew. Parker Lindsey's his name. You probably wouldn't know him."

"Never been in SAC, and hope I never get the pleasure," said Benny.

"Not my style either," agreed the Bear, "but they got some good people."

"Why'd this Parker guy get out of the Air Force?"

"Dollars and cents. He's been with Trans World for three years now, so he's probably pulling down fifty thou."

"First officer?"

"Yeah. Says he'll be a captain in a couple of years."

"He probably makes double what we're getting. Depressing, isn't it."

"I'll bet all the bastard has to do is man the damned autopilot and get coffee," said the Bear.

"They've got stewardesses to get their coffee."

"Oh, yeah."

"And no one's shooting at him."

"He's got a shallow fuckin' perspective. All he talks about are his investments and money."

"I've got friends who made the same choice, and most of them are happy. Between layoffs they're happy anyway. My wife would have loved it if I'd gone with the airlines."

"Then you've thought about making the change?"

"Airline pilots and BUF pilots have an interest in aviation, but they don't like to fly. I'm a fighter pilot and I love flying. They could cut my pay, or make me a buck captain forever, but I'd still want to fly fighters."

The Bear toyed with a spear of raw and brittle broccoli.

"How about you, Bear. How come you aren't out making big bucks with industry? You could make a bundle with your knowledge of aircraft electronics."

The Bear thought before he replied. "I like the flying, the camaraderie, and knowing I'm doing something for my country a little better than the next guy."

Benny abandoned his food and brought the subject back around. "How'd your airlines friend find out you were here?"

"We've got a mutual buddy in Manila. The guy I told you about who volunteered for embassy duty? Parker Lindsey contacted him when he got in and found out I was here and how to get in touch. Says his crew's going to lay over in Manila and wondered if I could make it down there, maybe have a drink and talk over old times."

"You ought to do it. Manila's a nice city."

"I thought I might start rating Esther and Angela on their individual talents."

Benny groaned. The Bear changed the story to make it juicier every time he told it. "Don't start telling me about it again."

"Anyway," the Bear asked, "how do you get to Manila?"

"It'll take about an hour if you take a Rabbit."

"What the hell's a Rabbit?"

"That's the Filipino answer to Greyhound. The drivers are paid by the mile and by the numbers of passengers they haul. They stuff 'em in like sardines and drive as fast as the diesel engine will let them."

"Jesus."

"You still ought to go. Manila's a nice city. Hell of a lot better than hanging around this place." Benny remembered Manila as an illusion with glittering lights, fine restaurants, and modern hotels. A metropolitan oasis where the wealthy sucked the juices from the countryside.

The Bear got a wily look on his face, like he was trying to set a hook in a fish with a tender mouth. Whenever the Bear tried to be cagy, Benny thought he just became more transparent.

"You like Manila, I take it?"

"Yeah."

The crafty look again. "You want to come with me?"

"I'll tag along if you want the company." Benny had anticipated the question. It would be nice to get some quiet time in away from the base, perhaps even do some sight-seeing—and forget about what had happened. He wanted to be ready to fly and fight when they returned to Takhli.

The Bear grinned, as if he'd hooked his fish. "Let's go tonight. They're having the get-together at the Manila Hilton. Parker said there'll be people from the airlines and some embassy employees."

"I thought you were visiting your dusky harem tonight."

"Time for new and greener fields. It's a quarter to six now so if the ride takes an hour, we ought to be there by eight."

"We'd have to get off base and find the right bus." Benny paused. "Look, my buddy stationed here at Thirteenth Air Force said he had an extra car he'd loan me."

The Bear sneered at the food in his tray. "Then let's get your friend's car and get the hell out of here. I saw Marty the nurse a little bit ago and she's starting to roll her eyes around and sweat a lot."

05/2055L—Cam Khe, North Vietnam

Glenn Phillips

Phillips lay on the wooden deck that served as a bunk, curled into the same fetal position he had assumed when he had been cast into the room several nights before. *Two nights? Five nights?* He'd lost count. A leg-iron was clamped to his left ankle, the chain secured to the wall. It was unnecessary. He could have gone nowhere had he been unfettered and the door left wide open.

Periodically, a guard would come to the door and peer through an eye-level slot, mutter something in nasal Vietnamese tones, and after a few minutes grunt and move on. During each visit Phillips attempted, with great difficulty, to focus his sight and hearing on the guard's presence. He felt an exhilarating sense of achievement each time he was able to do so, for it proved that he was at least partially in control of his mind and senses.

Sensations from his mangled leg were severe, yet they were nothing compared to the way it had been at first, before he'd started dying. It was when the pain had begun to diminish that he realized his body was finally beginning the difficult process of giving up life. He was relieved that the awful pain was about to end. But then another instinct had glimmered in the recesses of his troubled mind, and he found himself struggling to live. That was when he'd started the focusing-of-senses game.

Phillips could remember only fragments of the days that had passed since ejecting from the Thud. He could recall the rescue attempt so rudely interrupted by the flight of MiG-17's, being surrounded by villagers, and sudden, searing pain. He had glimpses of taunting villagers, of being stuffed into the impossibly small cage to endure obscene cruelties, of vague remembrance of twilight consciousness as he bounced and excreted and shrieked in the back of the truck, still caged as they traveled along an endless and primitive cart path.

Much later he noticed the arrival of a new man, a guard he dubbed Fishface because his face resembled that of a carp. He remembered being extracted from the cage by Fishface and finding the energy to scream as a sad-looking Vietnamese medic pulled and tugged at his foot in an effort to reposition the protruding bone into a semblance of normalcy.

The following day, after trucking all night and stopping for the day in yet another tiny village, a teenaged boy had crawled up on the end of the truck bed and wielded a length of bamboo. He concentrated his energies upon the injured leg and elicited squeals of delight from the gathered mob as Glenn weakly howled, rolling about the truck bed in agony. The guards had looked on with little interest before Fishface had finally stopped the fun by wrestling the bamboo stick away and comically threatening to thrash the boy with it.

On his last night on the road he had been able to take food: bitter tea, rice, and scraps of dried, chopped fish. They had watched closely and chattered among themselves as he had wandered back into delirium. They had trussed him carelessly then, as if no longer concerned about an escape attempt, placed him in the truck bed with Fishface, and set out once again. Before dawn they had reached the holding camp.

Glenn Phillips heard the guard rattling the door, the muttered words. He peered hard at the door, and thought he could see the guard's face. Was it real, or was it his delirium? He concentrated harder, heard a sound, and saw an accompanying light. That was no delirium! He had seen and heard it! He tried to enunciate a croak of victory, but could not. He was able to groan though, and the sound startled the guard who had heard only silence on earlier rounds. The guard peered closer, and Phillips stared into glittering eyes. Fishface spoke in a rush of Vietnamese, then paused for an answer Glenn was unable to provide. He slipped back into darkness.

05/2100L—Manila, Republic of the Philippines

Liz Richardson

Liz Richardson sometimes related things to her brief and ignominious acting career. She'd started it as the female lead in the semiannual school plays in her last two years at York High School, and both family and friends had agreed she was surely the prettiest girl to ever graduate at Yorktown. She'd ended it in Richmond, where she'd been attending the University of

Virginia, when a lean, pipe-puffing, tweed-jacketed, thin-mustached assistant director at the little theater had advised her that she did not possess a glimmer of aptitude for the stage.

The assistant director had impressed her with his devotion to Shakespearean wit and seduced her with a bottle of inexpensive wine before he'd told her. She'd then fled his apartment in such a dramatic flurry of outrage, sorrow, and postvirginal tears that he'd almost changed his mind about her acting potential.

In her third year, she'd dropped out of college to answer a recruiting campaign for airline stewardesses. Such behavior was called headstrong at family gatherings and DAR chapter meetings, but her parents had supported her choice.

Now, more than 9,000 miles from Yorktown, Liz tipsily regarded the group of airline pilots, embassy workers, stewardesses, and hangers-on milling about the party suite. Any good director would complain. *Project,* he would tell them. *Settle down, empathize and project yourselves subtly into your parts. You're overacting.*

TWA and Pan American captains stood with practiced poise, discussing all subjects with unchallenged authority, existing on a stratum above the rabble of the world, which included everyone who was not an airline captain. They would be the brilliant doctors, ship captains, firm fathers, and never accept less than leading roles.

Small groups of stewardesses flirted with the captains, laughed at their puns, and hung onto their words, making it obvious they were available. No doubt as to their roles: the other women, whores with hearts of gold, well-scrubbed girls next door, vamps and tramps. The leading ladies were back home keeping house and looking after the captains' kids.

The trusty sidekicks were there. Cocksure first officers who mimicked the captains and talked endlessly about their lesser careers and achievements. About interesting things like how they enjoyed the accuracies of inertial navigational systems over the older Doppler systems. About the flight routes and how close they were to upgrading to captain.

Bureaucratic embassy staffers gathered into their own groups. Pipe-smoking, stiff and correct, speaking of the absolute corruption of Asians and offering instant remedies for ancient challenges. They moved in their own hierarchy, driven to ascend their diplomatic career ladders to success. If you called one a pompous ass, he'd tell you the official government position on pomposity and asses.

American and Filipino businessmen pushed through the mob with their stunning Filipina fashion models. The businessmen tried to gain favors from embassy staffers and investments from the airline captains. The Filipinas were given as prizes to whoever showed interest. The businessmen were the slimy bad guys, essential to any stage production.

Liz tired of her game.

She would never again take up with a male member of the human race. If, however, she chose to break the vow, she was resolved never to do so with anyone at all like the insufferable airline captains or the sidekicks standing conspicuously near them. Three months earlier her ex-fiance had been upgraded to captain.

On Friday afternoon, before driving to SFO for the flight over, she'd opened the window of his fifth-floor condominium and hurled his damned two-carat engagement ring into the parking lot. As she'd driven away, she'd felt perverse satisfaction watching him scramble about on hands and knees among the Porsches and Mercedes, looking for the ring.

Now it was Monday. Still angry and feeling sorry for herself, she strengthened her resolve. She picked a red wine from a tray borne by a white-jacketed Filipino. Normally she drank white wine, but Liz was determined to change a lot of things she normally did.

Two more men entered the suite. She looked them over more boldly than she would have the week before. One was tall, rugged-looking, obviously outgoing. The other was stocky, powerfully built and stoic. They stood together near the bar.

A Pan Am first officer named Jack, who obviously thought of her ex-fiance as a role model, approached her and tried a syrupy line. He was concerned about her, knew she'd been hurt by the breakup with Jeff, wondered if he could be of help. He knew of a quiet little bar a few blocks away that played American jazz. He was also a good listener.

"Cheat on your wife with someone else, Jack," she said, glaring, tossing back her wine in a single gulp.

Jack drew back, then wandered off toward a gathering of Pan Am stews. *Silly twit,* she thought.

Now the two newcomers were talking with a TWA first officer she'd met. The taller of the two looked a bit on the arrogant side, but he had a whimsical air about him, like he was trying to pull off a joke. Watch out for that one. The other, with the quieter manner, had no-nonsense eyes he pinned on whomever he was speaking to. Too confident to be first officers. Too young to be captains. Not stuffed-shirt enough to be embassy people.

She decided to guess their occupations, a pastime she shared with other stewardesses on the long Pacific runs. She studied them. Very erect, with short, neat haircuts. Military, perhaps Navy. There were two Navy bases nearby, Subic Bay and Cubi Point. She finished the glass of wine, her third of the night, satisfied she had them pegged.

The gregarious one glanced her way, gazing evenly, like he could read her mind. She had the eerie feeling that he could. He gave her a flicker of a smile and turned back to his friends.

Perhaps she should sink to the depths and take up with a military officer. They certainly looked to be in excellent physical condition.

Ridiculous. She sympathized with the growing antiwar movement, joining the ranks of those who wondered why America was fighting in an inconsequential country half a world away. If women ran things it would be different. There wouldn't be any wars. Men are all asses, she decided. Polygamous, pompous, silly asses.

Jeff was all for the war, yet was pleased with his exempt status. She felt he was only pro-war because more captains were needed to cover the added number of Pacific runs, a fact which had allowed him to be upgraded early. He was no better than a military war-lover.

She located a group of sister stewardesses and was starting toward them when the taller man broke away from his group and approached. *God,* she thought, wondering what she'd let herself in for.

"Hello there," he said with a grin. "You looked deep in thought over here by yourself. Why not come over and be thoughtful with us."

"I'm fine," she said, feeling the wine.

"Yes, I'm very sure you are," he said. His eyes swept

boldly over her and his mischievous smile grew. "Why not join us anyway."

"You're military, aren't you?" she blurted.

"I'll be anything you wish."

She thought that was a dumb line, but he did have a magnetism about him. "Navy?"

"I get seasick when I get within fifty feet of a boat."

"Oh," she said in a disappointed tone.

He looked at her empty glass. "Where's the wine?"

"Over there."

"I'm ready for one. What can I get for you?"

She hesitated, then decided to ditch him after he got the drink. "A red wine, please." As he left to fetch wine she looked back at the other one, with the broad shoulders and nice eyes. Her mother would say he had the look of good breeding.

Benny Lewis

Benny was attempting to carry on a discussion with Parker Lindsey, but had not gotten beyond the fabulous salary, the five-bedroom riverside home in St. Louis, a deal concerning two large rental properties, and the damn operations desk that had cheated him out of a thousand dollars the previous month because of a scheduling foul-up. Lindsey was now launching into a discussion of the merits of various aircraft assignments and routes that could reap the most money.

The Bear returned and interrupted, presenting a pretty redhead.

"Liz, this is Parker Lindsey, a first officer with TWA, and Captain Benny Lewis, my squadron mate."

Benny half turned. Almost as tall as Benny in her half-heels, she was surely the most striking woman in the room. *The Bear's done it again*, he thought wryly.

"Gentlemen, meet Liz Richardson. She has consented to put us out of our misery by adding a bit of sunshine to this otherwise mundane and hairy-legged group."

Benny grew nervous; she was staring directly at him. She was exquisite, with delicate features and flawless skin. Her hair shimmered with hues of copper and dark rust, and cascaded halfway down her back. Green eyes, moist and slightly out of focus as if she'd had a few too many wines, regarded him gravely.

"How do you do," he said, feeling awkward under the gaze. She reminded him of someone he knew and couldn't place.

Parker Lindsey interrupted his thoughts. "We've met before, Liz. You're engaged to a Pan Am captain, right? What's his name? Jeff something-or-other?"

"Mud," the redhead replied in a caustic tone.

"Yeah, that's it," mumbled Lindsey uneasily, as if Mudd didn't quite seem correct.

"I'm no longer engaged," Liz said. "I'm forever and ecstatically free." Her eyes returned to Benny.

Liz Richardson

She knew the tall one was trying to chat her up, so in defense she concentrated on the quiet one with the attractive eyes.

"How about you, Captain?" she asked. "Are you married?" She was taken aback by her own forwardness.

He hesitated. "Yes," he finally answered.

"Bullshit," said Mal Stewart.

Liz cocked her head, puzzled.

"I'm still married," he said, looking evenly at Stewart.

Stewart released an exasperated breath. "Whatever you say, Benny."

Liz decided his marriage was in the process of breaking up, and that somehow made her sad.

"So you're not Navy," she said to fill the quiet.

"Air Force," Benny replied.

"God, not a pilot."

"Guilty. I fly fighters."

Unlike the other one, he was not trying to hustle her, and somehow that seemed discouraging. She gave a tiny shake of her head, deciding not to like either of them.

He seemed uneasy under her stare, so she looked away to the taller one. Their eyes met. Was he mocking her? She felt the animal attraction, tingled and grew moist between her legs at the thought of being with him.

Silly. She was a woman on the rebound from the man she'd intended to marry. Likely if he had been a two-headed dwarf, she'd be equally attracted. Knowledge is strength, she told herself. She'd been well and repeatedly versed that uninhibited sex was a prime evil. After that one wild evening in Richmond with the assistant director, she'd kept herself in full restraint, never again losing control.

It was the wine. She must never again drink red wine. She avoided the tall one and looked again at the safer one introduced as Benny, listening to his pleasant voice.

The obnoxious first officer continued trying to impress Benny Lewis, and the fighter pilot refused to acknowledge her presence. *Damn you, pay some attention to me. Half the guys in this room have tried to hustle me and you just act like that bore is making sense and I'm not even here.*

The captain in charge of her San Francisco–based crew caught her eye, beckoning at her to join him at a nearby group.

It was time to get away and regain her senses. She lingered for another moment, deciding to make the fighter pilot jealous. Males disliked being deserted for another man for any reason. She tried to catch Benny Lewis's eye. "I'm being summoned," she said. He didn't seem to notice.

It was Mal Stewart who said he would wait, lightly brushing her shoulder with his hand. The electric feeling returned. "Thank God," she muttered as she walked away, but she was still tingling.

The Pan Am captain conspiratorially leaned forward as she approached. "They're putting us on the Tokyo run the day after tomorrow, Liz. That okay with you?"

"Sure." She was in no rush to return to San Francisco.

"You did a superb job on the flight over." He used the father image, patted his crew on their heads like good little people. "I'll buy dinner tomorrow night."

She was busy, she said, glancing back at the group she'd left. Mal Stewart was looking, but she avoided his eyes. Too much animal aura and promise of something she couldn't afford to respond to. The other one elicited an entirely different response.

Her closest friend waved from the clan-gathering of Pan Am stewardesses. Julie Wright was a junior stew who had been with Pan American for less than a year.

Julie detached herself and they met halfway.

"You've been busy," chided Julie, glancing at the men.

"Mm-hmm. Very boring."

Julie cocked her head. She liked to clown around in an earthy, profane manner. She had large breasts, a tiny waist, a sexy, whiskey voice, and attracted men like bees to honey. Her nose was too large and her hips too matronly, the other girls catted, but her total combination drove the guys wild. She didn't give them the time of day and that made it worse, for they regarded her as a challenge to their masculinity.

"Something serious?" Julie asked, lowering her voice as she saw that Liz was deep in thought.

"I acted like a fool joining those guys I'd never met before."

Julie laughed. "You're silly."

"See that guy there? Walking back from the bar toward the other two? The one with the cultured look?"

"Sure. The one you were just ogling."

"Not ogling," Liz said with distaste. "I just thought he was a gentleman."

"I was about to go over and join you in your misery, maybe rescue you by offering my bod in your place, when I saw you leave."

"It's not funny!" Liz stamped her foot in anger. "You know I'm not like that."

Julie laughed. "Sometimes you get silly with all your culture and breeding and what is or isn't appropriate."

"Don't you think there's such a thing as rebound, losing your head because you're emotionally vulnerable?"

"I might, but over Jeff? He's such a pedigreed ass. . . . Oh, hell, sorry Liz."

"You're right. Jeff is an ass. But it still hurts." She smiled a hurt look. "My mother's still talking about what a great catch Jeff was."

"What about this nice looking guy you're making moon eyes over?"

Liz Richardson looked across at the muscular fighter pilot and mused. "He's too short. He's what, maybe five-ten or eleven. I prefer men over six feet tall."

"Like Jeff?"

"God forbid." She took a breath. "No more moon eyes over the captain, okay?" She refused to mention the one who'd made her tingle.

"He's a captain?"

"They're in the Air Force, stationed somewhere in Thailand."

"You're kidding me."

"That's what they said. They fly fighters. Anyway, no more leers."

"Too bad. You were more human as Miss Hot Pants."

Liz grimaced.

Julie was eyeing the two military men. Regardless of her jokes about men, Julie Wright had seldom seemed serious about the guys she met. As if searching for something she hadn't found. Even her interested look was out of her normal character.

"Did I ever tell you," Julie said, "that my father was Air Force?"

"I remember you complaining about living in all those different places."

Julie was still staring.

"Dammit, Julie," Liz hissed, "now it's you with the big eyes."

"Hon, it's not my big eyes the guys are after," she joked in a sultry voice, and Liz couldn't help laughing.

"Look," Liz whispered, "they're coming this way."

As the three men approached, Liz prepared to make introductions, but they walked past. They stopped before a smooth, thirtyish man with a Clark Gable mustache who stood guard over a girl who looked like she was still in her teens. Mal Stewart and the TWA first officer addressed the guy like an old friend, but he didn't seem that happy to see them.

The girl was barelegged and wore a skimpy skirt and a clinging, see-through blouse. Untethered breasts moved as she talked and her dark nipples jutted sharply into the fabric. Surely, Liz thought, there were laws against being so obvious.

The men passed pleasantries, then to the horror of Clark Gable the girl attached herself to Benny Lewis's arm, rubbing her breasts sensuously against him as she told him something that made him smile. Mal Stewart looked on like a bull ready to paw the dirt. Liz despised them both for their male weakness. Couldn't they see the girl was a low-class tramp?

"I was introduced to the slick guy with the mustache," said Julie. "He's a major on the military attaché staff at the embassy. The girl's the horny daughter of some biggie in the Australian embassy. She said she just dearly loves military men, and she obviously wasn't lying. She's sure laying it on heavy with your guy."

Liz shrugged. "Not my guy."

"You don't care?"

"No." Liz kept her eyes averted from both men.

"See you around," said Julie, and walked toward the mustached major. His friend clung to Benny's arm, rising on tiptoes to whisper another private joke. She grasped Mal Stewart's arm, to include him in her attentions, as Julie arrived.

"Hello, Major. Remember me?" asked Julie in her huskiest voice.

"I . . . uh . . ." the mustache replied. His attention was on his date, who was giggling and tugging at both Stewart's shirt and Benny's arm. The oblivious Trans World first officer tried to carry on a conversation with the mustached major, whose attention was glued to his date.

"I've just got to show you Manila while you're here," the girl was gushing, "and you've got to tell me all about fighting the war. Fighter pilots! I can't *wait* to tell my friends." She sounded thrilled by their proximity.

Liz followed Julie, intrigued.

"Julie Wright, remember? Best damn stewardess in the world." Julie turned her smile and attention to the two Air Force men. "And you gentlemen?" she asked rather loudly, reaching out and grasping both men's arms. She had sucked in a breath and the spectacular breasts promised to burst from the thoroughly crammed blouse. The males shifted gears from the teenager and gawked.

"I don't think I've had the pleasure," Julie murmured.

Liz slid in beside Julie, feeling wicked as she edged the Australian girl away. "Julie, this is Captain Benny Lewis, and his friend there is Captain Mal Stewart, who is also called . . ."

"Bear," he said.

Julie smiled, still displaying her spectacular figure and giving her world-class come-on. "Hello, Benny and Mal Bear."

" 'Scuse me," said the military attaché as he grasped his date's arm. "Gotta get this young lady some sustenance. Good seeing you, Mal. Uh, nice meeting you too, Captain."

The two men worked to keep from staring at Julie's endowments, hardly noticing that the attaché had pried the girl's hands away. "Yeah, see you." "Nice meeting you," they muttered to the fleeing attaché. Mal Bear's eyes were pulled back to Julie's spectacular bosom.

The obnoxious TWA first officer followed behind the

embassy major, trying to make a point about investments as his
audience hustled his date toward the door.

"Liz was telling me you were a couple of fighter pilots
from Thailand?" asked Julie.

"No ma'am," said the awed Bear. "He's a fighter jock.
I'm but a poor and honest EWO. We're in the same squadron
at Takhli." He pried his eyes away to look at Liz, obviously
puzzled at the turn of events. Liz felt easier with them now that
Julie was there.

Mal Bear was indeed a ruggedly handsome man. Precisely
the kind mother and family told her to beware of. Her
emotional danger flag went up again. When she regarded the
one called Benny she felt much easier, almost a kinship.

Julie laughed from deep in her throat. "Can't kid me,
Cap'm. Ain't no electronic warfare officers in fighters."

Mal Stewart turned his head back toward her, opened his
mouth to speak, then reconsidered. Liz didn't know what Julie
was talking about, but it was obvious she'd mentioned something sensitive because he was no longer looking at her
magnificent boobs.

"What do you know about pilots and EWOs?" he finally
snapped.

"Why nothing, Cap'm. But my father did. About fighters
and pilots and EWOs and all of that. He was a very cagey chief
master sergeant who ran the tightest flight line in Europe."

"Wright," muttered Benny. His face brightened and he
snapped his fingers. "Chief Wright?"

"You knew my father?"

"Of course." Benny said. "He virtually ran the maintenance effort at Spangdahlem Air Base. Sure I know your dad.
And you're wrong. He's the best flight line supervisor in the
world, not just Europe. Chief Wright could write books about
airplane maintenance."

"No more. He died last year of a heart attack."

"Chief Wright?"

"Surprised us, too. Daddy always seemed too organized
to have something like that happen. Had his first attack just
after we got back to the States, and he had to retire. I think he
was disgusted at the slipshod way the heart attacks were
scheduled. He died after his fourth one last year."

Benny turned to the Bear. "Chief Wright was one of the
immortals of the Air Force, like gooney birds and Jimmy

Doolittle. We used to joke that Chief Wright was sent by big brothers Orville and Wilbur to make sure things were done right." He glanced at Julie with a frown. "Sorry. I didn't mean to make light of his death."

"No offense taken," said Julie. She shook her head wistfully. "I still have a love-hate feeling for the Air Force. My father was away from home a lot, traveling or working two and sometimes three twelve-hour shifts in a row during exercises and deployments. He was always gone at critical times. It was miserable holding late Thanksgivings, Christmases, and birthdays."

"The Air Force," said Benny wistfully, "takes a lot of understanding."

"I remember good times, too," Julie said.

Liz felt like an outsider. As Julie opened up, Liz realized she was really learning about her for the first time. Mal Stewart noted she was being left out of the conversation then and patted her arm warmly. The tingle . . .

"Daddy warned me," Julie said, somberly regarding Benny Lewis, "never to have anything to do with a fighter pilot. He said fighter pilots were sex maniacs who'd tell you anything to have their evil way."

"Is that true?" Liz asked.

Benny Lewis shrugged and looked innocent. "No one's perfect."

She laughed. Their eyes met and they shared their first meaningful contact.

"Daddy never said a word about electronic warfare officers though," Julie said, shifting to Stewart.

The Bear leered mischievously. "Good thing he never hear of Emil ze EWO, eh."

"There were EWOs at Spangdahlem, Germany, flying in the EB-66's." She wrinkled her nose. "Daddy didn't warn me about them."

The Bear retorted darkly, "I'm not in EB-66's."

"Aren't you?"

The Bear mumbled something, obviously upset.

Liz saw his discomfiture. What in the world was an EWO?

Benny said, "He's a fighter pilot, no matter what he says." He meant it as a compliment, but the Bear glared at him too.

It was all very confusing to Liz.

Bear Stewart

The Bear was a casualty of Julie's jibe. He felt another twinge of anger when he realized that Julie was steering Liz's attention to Benny.

The beautiful redhead was ready. He'd known that when he'd first seen her across the room. Like you could tell when you saw a high-strung filly pacing and walleyeing a stud horse in the next corral. She'd known it, too. Once she got going, she was the kind who would claw down walls. But Julie had maneuvered Liz next to Benny and stood guard between her and the Bear.

Benny was a good guy and a friend, but the Bear hated to give up on the redhead. *Give up, hell!* he told himself.

He reached for Liz's arm and gave her the slow, penetrating look. "Let's go find a real bar downstairs where we can talk and maybe dance a little," he said in a confidential tone.

"Great idea," piped up Julie Wright. "Thought you guys would never ask."

The four of them found the lounge on the mezzanine floor of the hotel, where they sipped exotic rum drinks and cracked crab claws. They listened to a rhythm and blues group imitating American songs popular several years before. They danced periodically, relaxing and cuddling to a slow dance or moving with a slow rock tune. It was a good time, and the Bear tuned in again with the redhead. It was going to be an outstanding night.

It was the buxom pest, Julie, who screwed things up.

The Bear had leaned forward in the stuffed leather couch to talk to Liz. She'd stared back at him for the first time and without words they both knew. She moistened her lips. It would be like spearing a fish in a barrel, he decided. He started to reach for her hand to dance to a fast one when Julie grabbed his arm and motioned toward the dance floor.

"C'mon, Mal Bear. Let's boogie."

"Sure," he finally said. Dancing with Julie and watching all that firm flesh moving against the blouse had its fine points.

Approaching the dance floor, Julie raised a finger. "Just a sec." She hurried over and whispered in her friend's ear, drew back to give her a serious look, then returned to the dance floor.

"Everything okay?" asked the Bear.

"Oh yeah." She shook it all.

The Bear grinned. "Oh yeah!"

He didn't grin a moment later when he saw Liz and Benny motion that they were leaving.

Julie Wright came closer, still moving. "Guess you struck out, big fella."

The Bear felt shitty enough without her remark. "C'mon," he said sourly, "let's sit."

Back at the table he regarded Julie closer. "What was that all about?"

"What's what all about?"

"All evening you've been pushing me away from Liz."

She pegged him with her eyes. "She's a friend. Maybe I don't want to see her get screwed up by you. You're just out for one thing, and that ain't visiting the zoo, big fella."

"You think Benny's not out for the same thing?"

"Your friend Benny is one of the most hurt men I've ever come across."

"That part's true. He got screwed royally by a real bitch."

"Well, Liz just found out her fiance was making it with some of her best friends. Now she's found someone else she's attracted to. I doubt either of them are up to turning things into a good situation, but I wasn't about to let you foul things up."

"Thanks," he said caustically.

"I think you would've scored. She's vulnerable, and I don't think she'd do anything about it if someone like you gave her the rush. Anyway, she's not for you tonight, big fella."

He realized he was pouting, which in turn made him smile.

"Am I wrong?" Julie asked.

"I'll go along. Benny needs something."

"I'm glad you finally see things my way."

"You're a tough lady, Julie. Care to dance?"

She stared at him. "No."

"You call it."

She continued to appraise him. "If you want to come up to my room, I'll have one drink with you, no more. I'm not feeling vulnerable. You get the booby prize, Mal Bear."

The Bear considered the booby prize and was impressed. Mal Stewart was a devout bachelor, and he especially enjoyed the challenges of the life.

Benny Lewis

In the elevator, Benny stared awkwardly at the dark, lacquered-wood interior. When he turned toward Liz to say something, she started nervously.

At the eighth floor she pointed to the right. "I'm in eight-forty-two."

He led the way. "Got the key?"

She nodded, still skittish.

At the room she fumbled with the lock. The door swung open and Benny stepped around her, peering about inside. "All clear. No gremlins or madmen."

She stood, hesitating and biting her lip, waited several seconds like that.

"Are you all right?" he asked.

"No," she whispered, fleeing inside. She muttered, "Good night," and closed the door abruptly in his face.

Benny was confused by the change in attitude. Starting down the hallway, he stopped to regard her door once more, then turned and continued to the elevator. *A strange one,* he decided. Again, she reminded him vaguely of someone else.

Back at the bar he was surprised to find that Julie and the Bear had already left. He retrieved his bag from the bellboy, checked into the hotel, and went up to find his room. He was turning down the bed linen when the telephone rang. He answered, expecting the Bear.

"Hi." The voice was small.

"Liz?"

"I called to apologize about the way I acted when you walked me to my room."

"Don't worry about it."

"I do though." Her voice caught, betraying both her emotion and her intoxication.

"We're both tired."

"I acted silly. You were a perfect gentleman."

He cleared his throat to speak, then decided to remain quiet.

"Are you going back to your base early tomorrow?"

"Not until day after tomorrow."

"Well, if we see each other again," she said, "I promise not to act like a fool."

"Well, if we see each other again," she said, "I promise not to act like a fool."

"First, you didn't make a fool of yourself." Benny paused thoughtfully. He had not made a date in years. "Second, how about breakfast?"

"I'd like that."

When Benny hung up, he felt a pang of guilt. Like rules of flying, he'd taken marriage seriously, and it wasn't easy to change. He pulled off his clothes, hung them neatly, and crawled into the inviting bed. Then, as he had every night, he thought about Bets, the kids, and his fractured life. The heaviness returned. He tossed and thought and prepared for another miserable night.

Just before dawn he woke up, and it took a moment before he realized that he had been dreaming. The woman he'd been with wasn't Bets. He tried to drift back to sleep and recapture the pleasantness. He thought about the girl called Julie, Chief Wright's daughter. He had felt so damnably at ease and comfortable with her.

CHAPTER NINE

Tuesday, December 6th—0945 Local, Takhli RTAFB, Thailand

Colonel Mack

The crew chief drew his hand sharply across his throat. Mack MacLendon responded by chopping back the throttle of the big turbojet engine.

He pulled off his helmet and head-sock in time to hear the compressor blades of the engine clattering to a stop. The specially fitted helmet had cost him $150, but it was worth it to be able to shut out the loud ambient sounds and clearly hear the radio. Many of the pilots who flew the Thud, with the loud J-75 engine and the air turbine motor screaming away just beneath them, chose to dip into their savings and pay for the special headgear. Those who continued to wear the issue helmet would grow increasingly deaf. Hearing specialists called it the "boiler room effect."

The commander from the 354th fighter squadron was taxiing by, leading the afternoon mission. Same target, different players. Mack waved and gave him the finger. The squadron commander responded by extending the F-105's air refueling probe, which itself looked very much like an extended middle finger. Mack pointed his forefinger grimly eastward, toward the enemy, and made a pistol of his gloved hand.

The 354th commander nodded, acknowledging that he understood. They were shooting like hell up there around the Yen Vien rail yard.

"How'd it go, sir?" Chief Master Sergeant Cas Roberts, the squadron maintenance chief, had climbed up the yellow

240

ladder propped on the side of the huge fighter. He took Mack's helmet and handed him his go-to-hell hat.

Mack carefully penned a red hash mark on the snapped brim of the hat, regarded the growing row of such marks on the hat with grim satisfaction, then put it on before stretching.

"Tolerable, Chief Roberts, if you discount the fact that we lost good people and airplanes."

"How many this time, sir?"

"Three of our birds aren't coming home."

Roberts nodded, not rushing him, knowing that he would continue at his own pace. He had known MacLendon for some seventeen years, since Cas had reentered the service following a four-year stint as an auto mechanic in Toledo. Like Mack, this was Roberts's third war.

"Lieutenant Mullens, my number four, got it over the target."

Cas Roberts knew the lieutenant. A farm boy from Arkansas with a slow grin, freckles, and unruly blond hair. "Did he have a good parachute?"

Mack glanced at him, then carefully adjusted the go-to-hell hat squarely onto his head. "No chute, Cas. Lieutenant was into his dive-bomb when he got hit by flak and went straight on in with his airplane."

Roberts expelled a breath. "Quick."

"Yes, mercifully so."

The crust chief master sergeant cleared his throat of the awful Takhli dust, restraining the urge to spit. "Who else, sir?"

"Whiskey three, Captain Murphy's aircraft, was also hit over the target. SAM we believe. His aircraft was heavily damaged, but he was able to nurse it back to Udorn and land. I'll check his status when I get to the command post, but his bird looked all chopped up. You'll have your work cut out for you on that one. You may want to send a survey team to Udorn to see if the aircraft's repairable."

"Yes, sir. I'll put the team together."

"And then there was Captain DiFazio. New guy. Talked with a Boston accent. Hardly got to know him. This was only his fifth or sixth flight. First time in pack six, I think."

"Yes, sir?"

"He was Red Dog three. Went into the dive-bomb and forgot to move it around much. Must've looked like a fat target to the gomers, Cas."

"Yes, sir. Bet he did."

"He was hit by flak over the target. Probably fifty-seven millimeter, because there was a hell of a lot of it, and fifty-sevens put up a lot of steel. He went on and released his bombs, streaming smoke, then pulled off the target, still flying straight and level. I was yelling over the radio for him to jink."

"Damn."

"He just continued climbing out straight and level, and when SAMs were launched at his six o'clock he just kept climbing, calm as you please, looking like a DC-Six at Podunk International."

"Damn," Cas Roberts repeated. He backed down the ladder to make way as Mack dismounted. Feet back on the ground, Mack bent over to relieve the pressure and disconnect the tight crotch and chest straps of his parachute. His mind was still plagued by the mission.

"Half the strike force was watching him, yelling for him to jink, that SAMs were coming, telling him he was on fire and that he'd better bail out. Then he got drilled by all three SAMs, one after the other. It was a nasty sight."

"Any word on Whiskey four? Crew chief there says he's a no-show too."

"He probably landed at Udorn with Whiskey three." Mack grunted with relief as the crotch straps were released and he could properly stand.

"Yes, sir. Makes sense that he would do that." Chief Roberts scribbled a note on his clipboard. They walked around, looking at the aircraft that had brought Mack home.

"How's Evie, Cas?" Mack unzipped his survival vest to half-mast to allow a cooling breeze in, if one should ever come.

"She's well, sir."

It was a part of the ritual. Evelyn Roberts was Cas's wife of some sixteen years. Mack MacLendon had dated her a couple of times before she had met Cas, and he joked with Roberts that he had stolen her away.

"When you get done with this carnival act, drop by my office and bring me up to speed on the aircraft situation, okay Cas?"

"All right, sir." Roberts gave a mirthless grin, "We're gonna have trouble making the schedule until we get replacement birds in here next week."

"We keep losing pilots like this, we won't have anyone left to fly 'em anyway, Cas."

"Yes, sir," said the sergeant with eight stripes on each arm and as much responsibility as any man on base. "We all feel it pretty damned heavy when a bird doesn't come back. It's hard to forget the officers we salute and send out to fly. I know I've tried to just concentrate on the airplanes and forget about the pilots in every war I've been in, and I've failed every time."

"Message received, Cas."

"I got two guys I've gotta watch pretty close, because they're starting to act strange. Both of them were chiefing too many birds that went down. One guy, a damn good man, he's lost four airplanes now that Red Dog three's down, and he was already close to going over the brink, sir."

"Can't let that happen."

"No, sir. I can keep them together for a while, because they're good men, but it's tough on 'em. These guys, couple of my best, are gonna end up vegetables unless we get 'em relief."

"Thank a good R and R to Bangkok or the Philippines might help?"

"Can't hurt."

"Send me the names and I'll cut the orders."

"Appreciate it, sir."

Mack started toward the crew van that had pulled up twenty feet distant, then turned back to Roberts. "Keep 'em flyin', Cas."

"Yes, sir. You can plan on it."

06/1250L—Manila, Republic of the Philippines

Benny Lewis

As they entered the hotel, Liz waved to get a bellboy's attention. "It's almost one in the afternoon," she said in an aside to him. "It seems earlier, doesn't it?"

Benny nodded quietly.

Liz gave the bellboy, an aging Filipino, a few pesos. "Could you take the packages," she asked, indicating the armload Benny was carrying, "to room eight-forty-two? And please be careful."

Benny watched appreciatively. Liz Richardson was an entirely different person from the unsure and frightened woman she'd seemed the night before. Today her manners, poise, and confidence matched her beauty. All morning both Filipino and American men had stolen appreciative looks at her, regarding Benny with a mixture of jealousy and respect. He'd responded with a feeling of guilt, like they'd caught him doing something wrong. The feeling was silly, but he couldn't shake it.

The bellboy took the parcels containing silver and capis shell jewelry and other appropriate junk souvenirs. "Would ma'am like anything else?"

"No, thank you." She turned to Benny. "I'm starved."

They lunched at the ground-floor cafe with its lush tropical garden setting. Wrought-iron chairs and glass-topped tables were set amid tumbling waterfalls, hanging orchids, and birds of paradise. Liz talked about life in San Francisco, and encouraged Benny to talk about himself. But it was like a barrier was drawn about his current life.

As they waited for the check, she reached back to the only breakthrough she had discovered. He found it easy to talk about Benny Junior and Laurie with her.

"You told me the kids' names, but what do you *really* call them?" she asked.

"He's Little Benny. I'll have to change my pet name for Laurie because she's starting to resent it. That's natural, I suppose, because she's almost three."

"What is it?"

"Puddles."

"Puddles?" She started to laugh.

"Yeah," he said. "She deserved the name when she was a baby, so we called her that."

"That's awful." She laughed so hard that tears formed in her eyes. He found himself chuckling along.

"What else do you call a kid who can soak her way through half a dozen diapers in a single afternoon?"

"She's two?"

He nodded.

"And Little Benny's four? What delightful ages. Just listening, I can tell you love them very much. Kids can sense things like that. They'll adjust."

With her efforts, his mood swings were less extreme. He fished through pictures from his wallet. "Here, that's them. I'd have gotten better ones of Laurie, but she kept squirming."

"She's a little ham, isn't she?"

"She's a flirt, too. I'd better get her into a convent in another couple years."

Liz laughed.

They heard a yell and looked around to see Julie Wright approaching, bubbling with enthusiasm and waving her arms. Benny instantly felt the warmth he'd known the night before.

"You'll never guess, Liz! We went over to Corregidor. The place is simply beautiful, and so full of history it reeks."

"Nothing like reeking history," growled the Bear as he followed Julie up to the table. "Damn if I've ever walked that far in my life."

Liz stiffened as the Bear spoke. She avoided looking at him.

"That where you were?" asked Benny. "Corregidor?"

"Yeah. We were at breakfast by seven-thirty and on our way by eight." He groaned. "Hey lady, I'm supposed to be an invalid. I'm going to get a Purple Heart, remember?"

"You'll deserve another one if you don't order us some coffee pretty quick, big fella. I'm caffeine deficient." Julie turned to Liz. "Want to take a hike to the girls' room?"

"Sure," said Liz. "Excuse me, Benny." The women left, chattering.

"How you doing?" asked the Bear, sitting. He was staring, like he was trying to peer into Benny's skull at what he was thinking.

"We went to Makati and looked at the big buildings, then over to some shops in Chinatown. Saw a lot of junk, and she bought most of it."

"Make out last night?" The Bear looked at him as if he expected details.

"Didn't even try." Benny frowned. God, he thought, here comes another of the Bear's efforts to lift him out of his mood.

"Hell, I get you all set up and you screw it up every time."

"What do you mean, set me up?" Benny wished the Bear would leave things alone, but he knew he would keep trying to get a reaction, thinking he was doing him a favor.

"Well, you know," the Bear continued in a malicious

tone, "I got her hot to trot last night, and you were supposed to take over from there. What's wrong, couldn't get it up?"

"Bear, you can be a real asshole sometimes."

The Bear didn't let up. He nodded at the direction the women had taken. "Guess I'll have to do her for you, old pal. Nasty job, but someone's gotta satisfy the poor girl."

Benny knew he was being baited. "You're right, I think she was horny last night. May still be. I'm sure you'll find out." He abruptly rose, tossed five dollars onto the table, and started to walk away.

"You going to walk away from reality again?" The Bear shouted his question.

Benny sighed, feeling weary.

Bear Stewart

People at adjacent tables turned to stare as he marched up behind Benny, grabbed his arm, wheeled him around, and glared. Psych 201 hadn't worked, so he'd let him have it with both barrels. *Get pissed off, Benny. Anything's better than feeling sorry for yourself.*

"Remember? I was one of the stupid shits that bet my ass trying to get you out of North fucking Vietnam. I'm the one tried to get your mind straight at Clark. Then I tried to hustle Liz last night, but goddammit, when it sunk through that you were interested, I felt happy. I'll bet you just gave her the old sorrow bullshit. Tell you what, Mister Sorrowful, you take a flying fuck at the next doughnut that rolls by. Me, I've had it with your shit."

Both of their faces were flushed with anger now.

The Bear raised a rigid finger and pointed it at Benny's face. "I was even considering flying with you. That was fucking trust in your ability. But buddy, I take it all back. I don't fly with crybabies! I don't even want to fly in the same sky with you!"

The Bear stalked back to his seat, ignoring the open-mouthed people. It would take him time to calm down.

He opened a menu and stared as if he was interested.

Benny returned to the table. "Fuck you too, Bear."

"Ah hell," muttered the Bear, "I shouldn't have been shouting that shit."

"You do have a wonderful way of pissing people off."

"You get pissed off?"

"Yeah."

"Good."

Benny shook his head. "I understand what you're trying to do and when I'm more objective I'll probably appreciate it. For now, Bear, no more social worker, okay?"

"Yeah. I'm not after the chaplain's job."

Benny gave him a mock glare. "And keep your ugly paws off Liz. You can't have all the women in the world."

At last Benny was beginning to act human, and thanks to his missionary work.

"Hell, that Julie's enough of a challenge," he said. "We had a good time over there today. She kept me laughing. She's tough, too. Tries hard to keep me in line."

"She's tackled an impossible task."

"She thinks I'm a pussy cat."

"Thought you were a breast man?"

He laughed lightly. Benny was loosening up. "What do you think of those knockers?"

"Cool it, Bear." Benny looked embarrassed.

"Gotta be size forties, and every inch is real." Benny stared over the Bear's shoulder, like he saw something there and shook his head as a signal to hush.

The Bear wasn't going to fall for it. "Julie's got enough bazooms for two women."

"Did I hear someone mention my name?" asked a tiffed voice from behind him.

The Bear, red-faced, scrambled to his feet, and helped with her chair.

Julie sat stiffly. "Sorry 'bout that," mumbled the Bear.

Her jaw was firmly set. "You should be."

The Bear glanced at Benny for support. None was forthcoming. Finally, the women began to chatter and things started to get back to normal. He wondered if they noticed the change in Benny, who was now looking on with quiet, casual interest.

After coffee the four walked together down the wide streets, trying to avoid money changers offering to sell Philippine pesos at black-market prices.

After a short while they split up. Julie couldn't resist seeing Chinatown for herself. Liz wanted to return to the hotel to try the pool. Benny agreed to join her. He seemed to be rising, Lazarus-like, out of the gloomies.

After they slid into the backseat of a taxicab, Julie asked the Bear about the subtle change in Benny. But the Bear was tired of worrying about Benny.

"Is Benny a good fighter pilot?"

The Bear couldn't help but respond. "He got a MiG just before being shot down, and he's supposed to be one of the best stick-and-rudder men around. If he tried to fly combat with the attitude he's got right now, though, he'd just get himself killed."

"He'll get it back."

He steered the talk back to them. "You seem to know about divorce. You been through it?" he asked. She looked too young, maybe twenty or twenty-one.

Julie spoke soberly. "No. I just listen to friends who've been there."

"I did it once. Went through a divorce I mean."

Julie refused to get off Benny's problems. "What's Benny's wife like?"

"I never met her, but from what he said she's being a real bitch about it all. I think we're getting close to Chinatown. See the storefronts, the Chinese words?"

"They're obviously just not right for each other. That's why I've been awfully selective. Finding someone who's worth getting serious over isn't that easy. How about you, Mal Bear Stewart? Are you selective?"

He felt uneasy. "Sure I am."

She laughed, teasing him. "Liar. You've got some of the worse lines in the world. Do they really work?"

"We were talking about Benny, remember?"

She laughed again, like she knew she was making him nervous.

"We're about to head back to Takhli," he said, "and he won't have any time to get his shit together there. The fuckin' gomers aren't very selective about who they shoot down."

She drew back and looked at him. He'd caught her doing that several times that morning. "Stop cursing," she said quietly.

He regarded her with caution, recognizing the gleam of possessiveness.

"I like you," she said, "but I'd feel better if you'd stop cursing, Mal Bear Stewart."

He looked out at the buildings they were passing. "That's why you wouldn't make love with me last night?"

Now it was she who changed the subject. "I didn't like hearing you discuss my bra size, either. I'm sensitive about my breasts."

"Hell," he snorted appreciatively, "you should be proud of them."

"You like me?" she asked, suddenly coy.

"I told you I liked you."

She looked away. "That's good, because you turn me on."

"So answer the question. How come I ended up spending the night on the couch alone holding my busted nuts?"

"Talk like a gentleman."

"Is that why? 'Cause I didn't act gentlemanly enough."

She released a breath. "No."

"Then why?"

"You've heard about girls who don't go to bed on their first dates?"

"Oh."

"No, listen. I don't go to bed with a guy on fifteenth dates, either." She paused. "I'm what you might call . . . inexperienced."

He regarded her with mounting awe as it began to sink in.

"Sometimes I come on strong when I'm with the gang, joke about guys and talk like a hooker, but I don't take the mating game as lightly as some of my friends do. I'm twenty-two years old and I have never gone all the way with a man."

The Bear sat back. "You gotta be shitting me," he whispered.

"I am not." She grabbed him by the ears then, and shook his head.

"What'd I do?" he howled.

"You cursed again. I refuse to lose my virginity to a man who won't stop cursing when I ask him to."

The Bear looked at her in amazement, ears still clutched firmly. "You refuse to what?"

"Oh, shut up." She pulled him forward and kissed him.

"Leggo my ears," he pleaded.

She kissed him again. "I made up my mind last night when you were being such a jerk over Liz. I wasn't about to let you anywhere near her because she was screwed up, and I was afraid you might enjoy consoling her too much. Too bad, big fella."

Was this woman serious? "Let go, dammit!" She yanked and he howled, only half kidding. His ears hurt!

"So you aren't going to curse any more today, and maybe sometime soon you can show me what I've been missing."

She was looking at him with a soft but calculating expression.

He remembered her remark about the mating game and felt a surge of bachelor's panic. "I've been married. It wasn't any good so I'm never going to get that involved again," he warned. He couldn't believe he was making excuses.

"You're foolish to say never," she said smugly.

He remembered how heated the mutual mauling had gotten the night before, how responsive she had been. "Maybe we can work out a compromise," he said.

"First, tell me you'll stop cursing like a truck driver when you're with me."

"I can't make that promise." He thought of her body, of being the first with her.

"Will you try?"

"Yeah, I'll try." His voice was gravelly. He was becoming so aroused he'd have agreed to anything short of treason.

Julie Wright released his ears, sighed, and smiled demurely. "Then the rest is up to me, isn't it."

The Bear rubbed his ears gingerly as she traced his face with a gentle finger. He felt butterflies in his stomach as he worried about what he might be getting into.

06/1640L—Bac Can, Democratic Republic of Vietnam

Xuan Nha

Xuan found himself slipping into one of his infrequent black moods as he arrived two hours late at the city of Bac Can. The mood had been detected by his staff officers who judiciously kept their silence and distance. They had been witness to them before.

Theirs was a small convoy on the heavily traveled highway. Xuan Nha led in his utility vehicle, with the chief

Russian adviser and his intelligence and communications officers seated behind him. Following was an armored personnel carrier carrying Quang Hanh's communications platoon. Next was Tiger battalion's rugged command vehicle, a Soviet-built APC with Xuan's logistics officer accompanying Maj Tran Van Ngo. Strung out behind were three six-by-sixes carrying a company of combat engineers ready to survey what they were now calling the Wisdom complex.

Xuan disliked being out of radio contact with the Hanoi command center, especially with the improved weather conditions and the probability of American bombing raids. That was one reason he had ordered Sgt Van Ng to drive faster. He disliked idle time, and just north of Thai Nguyen they had been delayed by road construction gangs. The road was in poor condition due to heavy truck traffic from the Chinese border. They had been bounced about and bruised by the increased speed, but when Major Gregarian suggested they slow down Xuan told Sergeant Ng to drive even faster.

They slowed finally as they drove into the heart of the small city, then into a town square with administrative buildings on one side and three military barracks on the other.

An assemblage of people had gathered near the entrance of the most imposing building, preparing for some event. A welcoming party? They drove up before them.

Xuan pointed to the barracks closest to the large government building, issuing orders to Lt Quang Hanh. "Set up your radio in there and establish contact with headquarters. Immediately."

As the utility vehicle came to a stop, Quang Hanh jumped out and hurried back to the APC hauling his technicians and radio equipment.

Xuan looked at the gathering. When he had picked this area for the training site, he had told Major Wu to research the backgrounds and credentials of the local politicians. He turned toward Wu directly behind him.

Major Wu leaned forward. "The fat one is the mayor, a recent appointee. He comes from Cao Bang, near the Chinese border. The party approved the appointment, but said we should scrutinize him closely, especially if we are to establish an important facility such as Wisdom nearby. The choice will be yours, comrade Colonel."

Xuan grunted. "Is his loyalty questioned?"

"A widower. He married a young Chinese woman last year. She and her family are practicing Christians, and the party believes she is in contact with church organizers."

Xuan examined the obese mayor, then nodded. "Go on."

"The mayor's assistant is from Saigon, an immigrant from 1954. There was not much to learn about him. Too little in fact. He will be replaced."

Xuan Nha didn't comment. Major Wu was well aware of his leader's displeasure over failing to capture the second pilot. Perhaps this was the reason he had done a good job with his latest task.

Still seated, Xuan nodded stiffly at the fat and officious looking mayor, then at his council assembled at the bottom of the steps to the building.

When his men were out, he dismounted and stretched, then turned to face the officials, still feeling ill-tempered. Local politicians were insufferable, hiding in the confusing maze of bureaucracies within bureaucracies instilled by ancient Chinese mandarins and continued by the French. Xuan despised their vast tomes of regulations. They could never expedite the simplest things, but they were very good at hampering any slight sign of progress.

"I am Colonel Nha," he announced to the bureaucrats. "My men will be staying here for the next few nights. I assume those are government quarters?" He gestured at the barracks.

One of them cleared his throat grandly. "We are sorry, comrade . . . uh . . . Nha, but we cannot provide the guest quarters as you requested in your call. They are being used by others."

Xuan frowned at the mayor. "I have fifty men here who must be housed. Those are barracks for soldiers, so we will use them."

The mayor winced at Xuan's rudeness, then curtly nodded to his spokesman. The assistant was lanky, tall, and effeminate. He cleared his throat again before continuing. "If you had let us know much earlier we might have accommodated you. We get many such requests from military convoys passing through the area, and cannot provide support for you all."

Xuan sighed, weary from the day's journey. He maintained a tone more reasonable than he felt. "We do not tell civilians of our movements because we are soldiers. Although the war has not previously impacted you here in Bac Can, that is about to change."

The administrator glanced at the mayor, received a nod, and spoke in a tone meant to discourage further discussion. "I am sorry, Colonel. If you must stay here, have your men make their camp outside the city. Perhaps we can find quarters for your officers if you apply to my office in the morning."

Xuan spat out words like bullets. "All of my men will be billeted here . . . tonight . . . now. Like all patriotic Vietnamese, you will be expected to do your part to bring victory. You are obligated to provide us with quarters and food."

"That is quite impossible."

Xuan ignored him. "Who is occupying the government quarters?"

For the first time the mayor spoke. "We have an important delegation from Hanoi, an industrial development group sent by the minister of economics." He spoke with authority, his voice rich with musical Chinese accents common in cities not far from the border. His voice grew sly. "Perhaps you would like to take the matter up with the ministry in Hanoi?"

"My men will take the barracks." Xuan started to turn away, the matter done.

The mayor glared. "You cannot do that," he said loudly.

For a moment Nha betrayed his rage with a terrible look, but just as quickly he regained the serene look. He spoke quietly. "I would like to speak with you alone, comrade."

"I am sorry, but we are leaving for a meeting with the industrial delegation. They are waiting for us in the hall next door. Perhaps later. Perhaps after," he added nastily, "you and your men have set up camp outside the city."

Xuan felt the excitement of impending confrontation. He sighed, his look sad, then he spoke to one of the mayor's advisers. "You."

"Yes, Colonel Nha." The man was obeisant. Perhaps he had heard of his reputation.

Xuan motioned to the toadying administrator. "Go and begin your meeting with the group from Hanoi. Local industrialization is important to the war effort, and the meeting should not be delayed due to the incompetence of your mayor."

Both the mayor and his assistant looked aghast.

Xuan turned to Major Wu. "Get two good men. Armed."

The mayor tried to object, but Xuan Nha ignored him. Wu picked two combat engineers and looked to Colonel Nha for reassurance.

Xuan nodded. "Direct the other men to move into the

barracks. Move the delegation's belongings onto the street. I'm sure they will be able to find other lodging."

"Yes, comrade Colonel," said Wu, his thin lips curling to a smile.

"I'll be with you shortly, after I speak with the mayor."

Majors Wu and Tran Van Ngo began to organize the move into the barracks.

The mayor still argued but now was noticeably nervous.

"We shall proceed to your office," said Xuan. It was not a request. He motioned the two soldiers toward the assistant who had addressed him. "Bring that traitorous dog." The two armed men cut the assistant from the council members, roughly shoving him forward. When the mayor looked about for support, a municipal policeman judiciously looked away.

"You!" Xuan snapped at the policeman. "Keep everyone out of the building. No one shall enter while we are talking."

"Yes, Colonel."

Xuan Nha nodded abruptly at the mayor. "Lead the way!" he barked.

The mayor walked up the steps of the administrative building, trying to muster as much dignity as he could. Xuan, the two soldiers, and the assistant followed. At the top of the stairs Xuan motioned for them to wait, then turned to the council. They stood gawking, their composure and aplomb lost.

"Go about your business, comrades."

The group hurried away toward the meeting hall.

They went inside to the mayor's sumptuous suite. A male secretary gawked at the armed men from his desk in the mayor's outer office.

"Out!"

The secretary fled.

Xuan turned to the two men holding the arms of the assistant, who was trying to show a conciliatory smile. "Keep the traitor dog out here waiting. I'll tend to him shortly."

Xuan closed the private office door behind them, facing the mayor with sadness. He took his time lighting a Salem cigarette with a Zippo lighter he had taken from the body of an American pilot his men had shot down. It was one of the few trophies he'd allowed himself.

The mayor blustered, his voice rising. "My appointment as mayor was approved by First Minister Pham Van Dong."

Xuan filled his lungs with smoke, then slowly exhaled.

The mayor regained a degree of boldness. "I was not told about you, Colonel, that you could come here and tell my council what they are to do, how to conduct meetings, who should be removed from the guest quarters!"

Xuan quietly let his mood smoulder.

"It is difficult enough to manage . . ."

Xuan jerked his pistol from its holster and placed it on the desk. The mayor's mouth snapped shut and he stared at the scarred automatic, a Chinese 7.62mm Tokarev.

"So you will remember in the future," Xuan said evenly, "I am Colonel Xuan Nha of the People's Army, commandant of rocket and artillery forces."

The mayor started to speak again, but again Xuan interrupted. "We are surveying the area north of Bac Can to establish a military installation for purposes which are none of your concern. I am sure you will cooperate." Xuan motioned for the mayor to sit.

The mayor settled slowly behind the old French desk as Xuan fingered the pistol and stared down at him with his lazy eyes. "While we are in Bac Can, and every time we visit you in the future, I will expect appropriate treatment both for my men and for myself."

The mayor followed the pistol as Xuan slowly pointed it at the mayor's right eye. He sucked in a great breath, mouthed a fearful "O."

Xuan slowly lowered the pistol. "I do not like interference in my official duties. You do, in your wisdom, understand me?"

The mayor nodded vigorously. "Yes," he said, gushing words. "You will receive our very best hospitality, Colonel. I apologize for any misunderstanding."

Xuan mused, knowing he must train this bureaucrat well to avoid future problems. "Bring him in!" he bellowed to his men outside.

The soldiers opened the door and pushed the mayor's assistant inside. He stumbled, bobbing his head in deference to both Xuan and the mayor.

Xuan raised his pistol, again aiming for the right eye.

The assistant began a shriek. The roar in the closed room was deafening. The body dropped like a sack, convulsed, and drummed its legs mightily. Blood splattered against the walls, furniture, and the mayor's desk.

The mayor cringed into his chair, his eyes bulging in shock. Xuan motioned and his men departed. He bent, picked up the ejected cartridge, and examined it closely. The firing pin had indented the very center of the primer. He was pleased, for his armorers had recently worked on the pistol.

"I will expect my men to be provided for. Perhaps you could find some women to cook and serve them a good, warm meal."

"Certainly, Colonel," the mayor whispered, trying to smile, ignoring the body as if it were not there. "What else do you wish, Colonel?"

"I will now meet with my officers. Please ensure that the food is ready in, perhaps, one hour."

The mayor jotted a note with a badly shaking hand. "Yes, yes."

Xuan's black mood was diminishing. He was quite enjoying himself. "My men will stay at the barracks."

"Of course."

"I will stay at your house."

"My house?" The mayor's face dropped, his fat jowls quivering, then he fought to recover. Quickly he said, "I would be honored to have you as our guest."

Xuan absently tapped the Tokarev against his leg. "My officers and I will join you for dinner. We will eat precisely half an hour after the men are fed."

"Your officers?"

"There will be me and five others. One is a Russian. He's a pig like all *Tay,* but he is necessary."

An attempt at a smile. Words came rushing forth. "I will inform my wife. Her aunt is staying with us, helping during my wife's pregnancy. I will tell them to prepare special dishes."

"Nothing special! Remember the brave men fighting in the south who have so little to eat. We are soldiers and our needs are basic. Rice. Perhaps a little fish. Wine. Meat for the Russian. He's a pig, so give him pork."

The mayor wrote on his desk pad, which was sprinkled with blood. "We will do our patriotic duty, Colonel. It is an honor to have an important officer such as yourself staying with us." He was sweating, although the day was a relatively cool one.

Xuan looked at him and decided that he was likely waiting to get a messenger off to Hanoi regarding his and Xuan's relative powers. He drew a folded paper from the pocket of his uniform jacket and spread it before the mayor.

"Please note that I have unlimited power."

The mayor read the letter signed by General Luc ordering provincial officials to provide support as demanded by Col Xuan Nha. The letter read that his activities were vital to the defense of the people, and that noncompliance would not be tolerated.

The mayor bowed his head in the old act of obeisance.

Xuan reholstered his pistol and recovered his letter. "You will meet us in front of this building to escort us to your home."

In the nearest barracks, Xuan found Major Gregarian and Major Wu sitting at a table, chatting. Xuan had instructed his men to speak only Vietnamese in his presence, but the Russian's halting speech was difficult to comprehend. Fortunately, Gregarian could understand it better than he spoke it.

Lieutenant Hanh's radio paraphernalia was set up at one side of the barracks lobby, a thick wire strung outside to a generator and thinner ones out to various antennas. Xuan was briefed. The morning raid on the Yen Vien rail yard had been followed by another in the afternoon, and the marshaling yard had been left in ruins. Hundreds of tons of war materials destroyed or damaged. Carrier-based planes had attacked fuel barges being towed up the Hong River from Nam Dinh, and twelve of those had been lost. At least two aircraft had been shot down, both of them by antiaircraft artillery. One pilot dead at Yen Vien, and two Navy pilots being pursued near Binh Luc. Two other aircraft had been hit, but it wasn't known if they had made it back to their bases.

Xuan grunted. Only two enemy aircraft destroyed? Increasingly, bombs were being released on target as the Americans learned to cope with the defenses. The tremendous number of promised rocket systems and MiG's would surely make a difference when they arrived, but Xuan Nha believed that the real difference, the thing to break the back of American air power, would be the concept they were calling Wisdom.

Xuan Nha walked to the table where Gregarian and Wu

talked and took a seat. "The mayor had graciously invited our officers to eat at his house," he said.

"Your conversation with him was convincing," said Major Wu, showing a careful smile. Xuan Nha felt more gracious toward his wife's nephew as the foul mood continued to abate. He thought about the glowing messages that Wu sent about Xuan Nha's achievements to Lao Dong party headquarters. If another political officer were assigned, would he be as helpful?

Xuan looked at the map spread before them, and listened as they continued to discuss the red X's that Xuan and the Russian had made before they had left Hanoi. All would make good locations for the new command and control complex.

"The nearest location is here, in these flowers," said Nicolaj Gregarian, his finger on the map.

Wu shook his head. "Trees, Major, not flowers."

"Yes. Trees."

Xuan looked at the map location. "I believe that one will prove best."

Gregarian agreed. "The P-50 radar can go on this elevation here, and the command-and-control building here. We can place the P-2 acquisition radar on this elevation, and," moving his finger again on the map, "hide the engagement radar and rocket launchers in the trees."

"We should look at other locations for the rocket battery," said Major Wu, "perhaps even prepare them all so we can provide mobility training."

Xuan was impressed. Wu's statement was worth considering.

"No," the Russian argued. "The location for the special rocket site must be perfect, and we must camouflage it well. So well the Americans will never suspect it is there."

Xuan baited him. "When we shoot at the American aircraft with the Wisdom rocket site, they may try to find us, regardless of restrictions." Wisdom complex would be sited inside the restricted flying area near the Chinese border.

"That is why we must never shoot rockets!" said Gregarian, in his excitement reverting to Russian. "Except to protect Wisdom itself. The radar vans will have duplicate scopes for training and measurement systems to show how closely the operators can track targets. The instructors will be the best technical talent from Russia. The rocket system operators who

graduate will form the core of your rocket defenses. It would
be wrong to expose such a valuable battery just to shoot down
a few aircraft. And if the command-and-control site were
found? . . ."

"But if the complex *does* come under attack?" Xuan
asked.

Gregarian sighed. "Then all would be lost, and the special
rocket site must be used to defend the Wisdom complex as best
as possible. I plan to take every measure possible, though, to
ensure they do not find Wisdom."

The Russian's request to PVO Strany Headquarters had
said the systems, controllers, and instructors they sent would
be safe from attack.

Technically Gregarian was very good; with systems he
bordered on genius. But Xuan sensed that the Russian looked
down on his Vietnamese hosts' unsystematic approach to
combat.

Xuan watched as Major Wu and the Russian adviser
pulled out large-scale maps to plot the various routes they'd
take during the next two days to examine locations for the
Wisdom systems.

Capt Nguyen Pho, his logistics officer, entered the barracks lobby and cornered Quang Hanh. They were talking
about their favorite subject, women.

Captain Pho joked about a girl he had seen looking at
Quang Hanh. His men liked to talk about the young women of
the various villages, but Xuan made them adhere strictly to the
principle that General Giap had long ago laid down against
taking advantage of the people. There were to be no murders,
no theft, and no rapes committed by his soldiers against the
people. Swift execution was the most merciful judgment Xuan
rendered in such cases.

Of course there was no such protection provided for
"traitors" and "enemies of the people." Periodically, especially when his men had been deployed away from home for
several months, he would make judicious decisions about the
questionable patriotism of a few comely women in the area.
His men liked that.

He thought about his officers. They were all different, yet
except for Major Wu, they shared two common denominators:
technical skill and success in combat. Judging from the
knowledge Wu was exhibiting in his conversation with Gre-

garian, he might soon be included. If he could turn Wu into a success, it would greatly please Li Binh and her family.

Maj. Tran Van Ngo, the ambitious commander of Tiger battalion, entered the room. It was his company of engineers they had brought along to help survey sites for the Wisdom complex, and like any good commander, Tran had been making sure his men were taken care of.

"We dine with the mayor," Major Wu announced to the group.

Tran Van Ngo grinned at Xuan. "It is good to know the mayor had a change of mind."

Xuan shrugged. "He is becoming a true patriot. He will escort us to his home in ten minutes."

Tran Van Ngo looked pleased. "The men are being served in their quarters by young women. I almost stayed." He made an appreciative, clucking sound with his tongue. "You should see them, comrade Colonel. I would bet that some have never seen the great elephant."

"I'm sure Major Van Ngo will try to change that," said Wu.

"Not me. I put the party, the people, and my men before myself. That is the secret of our great social revolution, isn't it?" Tran grew thoughtful. "Still, I suppose I should always be an example for my men."

"I shall duly report your enthusiasm for the people's revolution," said Major Wu with an uncharacteristic smile. "The party will be grateful for your patriotic interest in females."

"Ha," said Tran. "I might worry, but you'll likely be the first to wave your elephant's trunk at those poor girls."

Lieutenant Hanh laughed. He was the baby of the staff.

Tran Van Ngo shook his head. "Just wait, Quang Hanh. One of these days your trunk will rise up just like the big boys'."

"Enough," said Xuan. "Let's go and enjoy the mayor's hospitality."

"Comrade Colonel," said Tran Van Ngo in a more serious vein, "Captain Pho and I had some city workers dispose of the mayor's assistant. I told them he was a traitor to the great struggle for unification, and that his body should be displayed at the front of the administrative building for three days and then tossed into the city's refuse dump. His wife was creating a disturbance, so I gave her a lecture about patriotism and how she should have reported his antirevolutionary ideas."

"He scared the dirt out of her," added Capt Nguyen Pho.

Major Wu grinned at Major Ngo. "I suppose you also offered to console her."

"She is a delicate flower. I hoped that reeducation might be in order."

Xuan nodded curtly. "You handled the matter properly."

Major Wu agreed. "They will begin to remember all the unpatriotic things the assistant has uttered in his despicable life."

"Let us go to dinner," said Xuan. "As we walk I will tell you how to behave. There is more teaching in store for the mayor to make him an even better patriot."

Xuan and his officers ate well at the mayor's house, the former residence of a forgotten French provincial official. They devoured offerings of curried rice delicately laced with fish and chicken. Surprisingly, the mayor had found two bottles of French wine. The mayor ate little, but he was politely attentive to their conversation. His wife, her aunt, and two servants served the group without sitting, rushing to provide more food whenever necessary. The Russian adviser ate his boiled pork and greens quietly, wrinkling his nose at the smell of their fish.

As the mayor had said, his young wife was obviously pregnant. She was a small woman, plain, with features almost indistinct in the roundness of her chubby face, but she was cheerful and pleasant. When she smiled she showed large, strong, beautiful teeth, so white and even they looked as if they were carved of new porcelain. She was obviously proud of them for she smiled a great deal. They transformed her into an almost pretty woman.

The meal was nearly completed when the officers began, as Xuan had briefed them to do.

"Your excellency," said Tran Van Ngo, using the French term, "you are on a diet?"

The mayor nodded, noticeably pale from the afternoon's events.

"You will be as trim as Major Wu before long, and all the females like him."

Wu, thin as a wraith, laughed.

The wife smiled prettily. Xuan noticed that Quang Hanh was staring at her.

"Or is it the size of Major Wu's elephant's trunk they like so much?" asked Capt Nguyen Pho.

The wife's smile drooped, suddenly puzzled. Xuan wondered if she'd ever heard soldier's slang.

Maj Tran Van Ngo grimaced. "No such talk in front of the maidens, please." He gestured in mock modesty at the aging aunt. She was in her mid-thirties, bony and thin.

"Oh," said Captain Pho. "Perhaps the maidens have not seen an elephant's trunk. Would you care to see the major's trunk, old aunt?"

Both women's eyes were downcast. The two servants entered, bringing hot tea, saw their expressions, and stopped dead-still.

"The mayor's wife has certainly seen an elephant's trunk," said Tran Van Ngo. The other officers laughed loudly.

The mayor, not knowing what to do, laughed politely, but he was growing red with embarrassment. Xuan leaned back in his chair, thinking that the mayor knew what they were talking about, yet the man just sat there without complaint.

"Major Van Ngo, you are coarse," said Xuan.

"Yes, comrade Colonel. I may never get to admire her lotus blossom if I speak like that," said Tran.

"Major Van Ngo!" Xuan exclaimed in mock horror.

"Tran's family is from the south, Colonel. We must forgive him," said Captain Pho.

"How about you?" Tran Van Ngo asked Lieutenant Hanh. "You're just a baby. Wouldn't you like to see the mayor's wife's lotus blossom?"

The youthful officer grinned.

The mayor's wife scurried to the kitchen, embarrassed. The two servants followed her.

Colonel Gregarian looked confused and started to ask what was going on. He shrugged, then continued to stuff chunks of boiled pork into his mouth.

After a moment, Xuan looked penetratingly at the mayor. "Call her back."

The mayor drew a breath, then whispered, "She is five months with a child."

"I have eyes."

The mayor called his wife back into the room. She

skulked in, then hurried to the mayor's side, making herself small beside his protective bulk.

"Lieutenant!" Xuan demanded. "Major Van Ngo asked a question. The major is a hero of the people. Surely you should answer."

"I asked the lieutenant," repeated Tran, "whether he would like to see the woman's lotus blossom."

The lieutenant grinned a soft, embarrassed look, staring at Tran and avoiding the woman. "I guess so."

The mayor looked with beseeching eyes, first to the lieutenant, then to Xuan Nha.

Xuan sat back, regarding the mayor. He pursed his narrow lips and slowly dropped his hand to caress the handle of the Tokarev.

A look of terror spread over the mayor's face. His voice quavered. "Please," he begged Xuan.

Xuan stared back with soft eyes. He grasped the handle of the pistol.

The fat mayor jerked his head around to his young wife. He whispered, "Go with the lieutenant." The aunt gasped.

Van Ngo laughed.

The wife looked on in disbelief. She stepped away from her husband, eyes darting back and forth between the officers.

"Be gentle," said Tran Van Ngo, "because I want to let her compare my elephant when you are done."

"Stop." Xuan raised his left hand to his men.

The woman looked at him, catching her breath.

"I have decided that whatever is good enough for my officers is good enough for me."

Van Ngo laughed uproariously.

"First!" he added.

Neither the mayor or the woman understood. The mayor, in his confusion, showed an expression of gratitude, thinking the ordeal was over. The Russian, finished with his meal, looked on with a bored expression. He belched loudly.

Xuan stood, stretched, and nodded toward the outside door. "I am sure the mayor would enjoy providing my officers with a personally guided tour of his city."

"Of course," rushed the mayor. "I would like you all to see Bac Can."

"Meanwhile, I'm going to rest," said Xuan.

Van Ngo laughed again.

The mayor's wife visibly slumped in relief as the officers stood, believing that her trial was over. She tried an awkward smile and with her still-horrified aunt started toward the kitchen.

Xuan motioned at her aunt. "Take her with you."

"Of course, comrade Colonel," said Major Wu.

As the men started to leave, the mayor looked perplexed. Tran Van Ngo guided him out the door with a hand on his arm. Captain Pho grasped the aunt's elbow and firmly propelled her in the same direction. The mayor's wife tried to follow, but Nguyen Pho pushed her back, pointing to the colonel. She froze.

"Show me to my room," said Xuan, stretching again.

Tran Van Ngo and Wu pushed their heads back inside. Tran was first. "About the assistant mayor's wife, sir. Shall I comfort her?"

"That is your patriotic duty, Major Ngo. Perhaps the others would care to join you." He smiled. "Perhaps even the mayor. In fact, I insist upon it. The mayor will be last, of course."

Major Wu appeared intoxicated. "And the old aunt?"

Van Ngo laughed. "I am sure she would enjoy a tour of the barracks, Colonel."

"As you wish." Xuan indicated an unopened bottle remaining on the table. "Take the wine and provide yourselves and the mayor with a drink before he returns . . . in the morning."

Van Ngo grabbed the bottle, grinning as he closed the door behind him.

Xuan said politely to the mayor's wife, "Please show me where I can rest."

It was an arousing night for Xuan Nha, for he had been appropriately stimulated.

After they had reached a physical understanding much too gentle for his liking, he rolled off her and napped. He awoke to find her off the sleeping palette creeping toward the door, so he dragged her back. This time he grasped her hair and forced her head down to introduce her to the French way. She resisted by twisting away. He hit her hard, then while she sat spraddle-legged and dazed, he retrieved the Tokarev and pulled back her lips with his fingers.

A short while later he slept, at peace with himself. The black mood had long evaporated.

06/2030L—Officer's Club, Takhli RTAFB, Thailand

The men who came to Takhli to fly F-105's into battle did so with the knowledge that their contract was for one hundred missions, at the end of which they would be obligated to throw a balls-out party for the rest of the guys, and then be reassigned to the States. Less than forty percent of the strike pilots of Takhli achieved that goal, so the hundred mission parties were a very big event. The pilots attending would look at the man wearing the red, white, and blue *100 Missions, North Vietnam* patch, with *F-105* printed in the center, with a mixture of awe and encouragement. The wearer of the patch was living proof that it could be done.

Tiny Bechler

The hundred mission party for Capt J. J. Spalding was a success. The bar was rowdy and loud with songs the men were singing, which was the way they all liked it.

Tiny sat talking with Chickenplucker Crawford and Swede Swendler about the day's mission when Andy Schumacher and Larry Stark quietly came in the back door. The Weasel crew from the 333rd squadron had attempted to fly with them that morning to help shield them from the SAMs.

"You chickenpluckers come over here and have a drink with us!" yelled Crawford.

Andy grinned his lopsided look, and shook his head sadly. "We tried."

Chickenplucker laughed. "I hear you landed in a tree, Andy."

Schumacher's grin faded. "Took me twenty minutes to get down. It's not that easy. You ever bail out, try not to land in a tree."

Andy had cajoled maintenance into trying to repair the least battle-damaged Weasel airplane, worried about the strike force having to fly without Weasel support. The F-105F had made it as far as the tanker, then abruptly slewed sideways and started to come apart. Both men had successfully ejected and were picked up in the Laotian Plains des Jars.

Tiny Bechler, having decided that he liked flying with the Wild Weasels because of the action, had been flying on their wing. He joked, "That was the only tree around for ten miles, Andy. How come you didn't try to steer your chute away from it?"

Andy tried a glower. He was too pleasant-natured and just looked like he was grinning wider. "I did try. The damned tree was like a magnet."

His bear, Larry Stark, quietly accepted a beer. "You both okay?" Chickenplucker asked him.

"I'm fine. But Andy got skinned up shinnying down the tree."

J. J. Spalding, who was paying for it all, raised a glass and yelled for silence unsuccessfully. He was too intoxicated.

Sam Hall stood on a chair, waving his arms to quiet the room. "J. J.'s got some words of wisdom he wants to pass on while he's still coherent," he said.

Spalding, the new hundred mission patch bright on the shoulder of his flight suit, mounted another chair and held out his arms grandly, swaying dangerously.

"Chickenplucker!" yelled Crawford.

"I just wanned to pass on th' secret of my success, havin' single-handedly brung th' gomers to their knees," said J. J.

"What's that, asshole?" shouted Swede, his flight commander.

"Th' secret . . ." Spalding grew glassy-eyed and wavered, then crumpled. Several of his 357th squadron-mates caught him and carried him to a chair at at table in the corner of the bar, where they propped him against the wall.

"Guess that was all he had to say," quipped Swede Swendler.

"Damn," said Tiny, peering above their heads at J. J., his mouth gaping. "Wonder what the secret was?"

07/0545L—Bac Can, Democratic Republic of Vietnam

Xuan Nha

"Enter," he called out.

Maj Tran Van Ngo rudely guided the mayor inside, then stood behind him.

Xuan was looking into the bureau mirror at himself, pulling his uniform neatly into place. He waved Van Ngo out the door and smiled pleasantly at the fat and panting mayor.

"Your hospitality was complete," said Xuan politely. He strapped on the pistol belt and adjusted it for comfort.

The disheveled mayor looked about for his wife. Xuan beckoned curtly and the woman come out of the closet where she had been kneeling, shining his boots with a cotton cloth. He took the boots, inspected them, and sat down on a chair to pull them on. She stood beside him, eyes lacking spirit, older and wiser and no longer the merry wife the mayor had left behind. Her lips were puffed, bruised black from use.

Xuan rose, reached into his pocket, and handed her several aluminum-alloy coins. "Show your gratitude, Christian whore!" he ordered. She grimaced wide, displaying her toothless mouth.

The mayor uttered a croaking sound.

"Your patriotism is no longer in doubt, comrade mayor," said Xuan. "You have provided me and my men with a warm welcome."

The mayor nodded, his head moving in jerks.

Xuan started to leave, but stopped as he drew abreast of the mayor. "Tonight my officers and I will sleep in the field. We will leave most of the engineering company in the barracks here for a day or two. Take care of their needs as if they were your sons."

The mayor nodded again.

"Next time we send a message that we will visit, I expect to receive proper treatment. The war is coming to you, and we will protect the people. It is your duty to support us."

Xuan glanced back. The mayor's wife was frowning stupidly at the coins in her palm. He leaned toward the mayor confidingly. "You should get rid of that unfaithful piece of Chinese dog meat," he said. "She confided to me this morning that she is a practicing Christian. A patriotic mayor deserves better."

He walked out to the veranda and met a waiting Van Ngo. Xuan took a deep breath of morning air. It was already warm. The late rainy season had gone and they could expect dry, hot days for a few months. He felt very good.

"Where is the old aunt, Major Ngo?"

"She was in the men's quarters when I saw her last, comrade Colonel. It seems she left a mess in some of their bedrolls, so they had her clean them."

They left the mayor's home and walked casually toward Xuan's utility vehicle. Sergeant Ng held the door open for him. "The other officers?"

"They are eating, Colonel."

"Did they all console the widow of the traitor?"

"She bit Quang Hanh, but he consoled her anyway. They all would have made you proud, Colonel. Even Major Wu. He tired himself teaching the old aunt how she should act with the men. He must like aged meat." Van Ngo laughed.

"The Russian?"

"No. He went back to the barracks early."

"And the mayor?"

"It took surprisingly little persuasion. He consoled his assistant's wife quite energetically."

Xuan laughed.

"Then I took her to my men's barracks and had her join the aunt. She was there when I arrived this morning, helping with the bedrolls."

Xuan and his officers crawled into the vehicle as Sergeant Ng started the engine. Even the old, scarred veteran looked happy this morning.

Xuan mused. "Perhaps now we can get on with business, and prepare to kill more Americans."

They started with the location farthest from Bac Can, then worked their way back in, observing each potential site carefully, weighing the merits and problems with each location.

On the second day, as they approached the closest site—the one they were sure they would prefer—Xuan looked far up in the sky and observed two American EB-66's, the Pesky planes fitted with electronic jammers in their bellies. Around the bombers swarmed several Phantoms, agile fighters that protected the bombers from Col Thao Phong's MiG interceptors.

He watched for a long time, remembering the headaches they had given his radar operators. Nicolaj Gregarian joined him.

Xuan pointed. "Those are the Pesky planes that jam our acquisition radars," he said. "They set up their orbits here, sixty kilometers from our nearest rocket battalions."

Gregarian grunted, straining to follow them with his eyes. "That will be very close to our Wisdom complex," he said.

"They use electronic receivers to triangulate the position of our radars," said Xuan.

Gregarian cursed. "Then even here we are not safe."

"I moved a rocket battery up here once to shoot them

down. They jammed the radars and got away, then moved their orbit for a while, until we moved the battery."

"Are they that effective?" said Gregarian.

"When they are close to the radar, they are. Could Wisdom shoot them down?"

Gregarian watched the Pesky planes and slowly nodded his head. "The rocket site will have an optical tracking device that is not affected by jamming."

"Then it could shoot them down," said Xuan.

Gregarian frowned. "I would not want to expose the special rocket battery to their bombs."

"Pesky planes do not bomb. They fly above our artillery at ten thousand meters, jamming our radar and warning the Thunder plane pilots when we fire our rockets," he said.

Gregarian shook his head. "What about the Phantoms?"

"Those Phantoms do not carry bombs."

"You are sure?"

"I interrogated two different Phantom crews who had escorted Pesky planes. They carry only air-to-air missiles to fight our interceptors."

He measured Gregarian's reaction and knew he was thinking hard.

Xuan went on. "If we let the Pesky planes continue to fly here, then Wisdom may be compromised."

Gregarian finally shook his head. "No. We can't do it."

Xuan was quiet. He had set Gregarian to thinking and that was enough for now.

Major Wu

Major Wu stood a few meters distant, observing Xuan Nha and the Russian. Colonel Nha turned once to glance at him, and Wu fought to keep his face impassive.

Never let him know what you are thinking, he admonished himself. He peered up at the specks in the sky far above, and when he looked back Nha was doing the same. He thought then about the notebooks he kept, and felt pleased. He was documenting everything, just as his beloved aunt, Li Binh, had told him to do.

Throughout the trip, he had been careful to please Xuan Nha; only once had he lied to him. That secret he would guard closely until the time was right.

CHAPTER TEN

Wednesday, December 7th—0900 Local, Manila Highway, Republic of the Philippines

Bear Stewart

Benny deftly navigated between the largest potholes as they weaved their way back up the concrete highway toward Clark Air Base.

"You're a great driver," said the Bear, holding on. "I think I'm gonna puke."

"We hit a big one and the car won't survive. This thing's almost as old as I am."

They slowed to a crawl behind two children perched on the backs of carabao, young boys dwarfed by the huge, docile creatures with their tremendous, sweeping horns.

"Every once in a while," said Benny, "a carabao turns its head to bite at a fly and a kid riding on its back gets impaled. I wouldn't ride one of those things if my life depended on it."

"Looks sort of like fun."

"You ride horses?"

"Where I'm from, if you don't ride horses they think you're queer. Most expensive thing I owned before I went in the Air Force was a roping saddle. I even tried bronc riding at the local rodeos until I left home. You ride?"

"Not much. We lived just outside of Santa Rosa when I was a kid. Some of my friends lived on ranches and farms, and sometimes I'd go riding with them."

"Julie said Santa Rosa's a nice place."

"I'll probably go back there when I retire."

"I plan on going back to McAlester some day."

"Your folks alive, Bear?"

"My dad died when I was eight, and Mom worked in the general hospital as a practical nurse. We were poor, even by east Oklahoma standards. Talk about grim."

"I'll bet your mother's proud of you."

"Yeah." The Bear stared out at the lush countryside. His mother was in the cancer ward of the hospital she'd worked in for thirty years. When he'd visited her before leaving to fly combat she hadn't recognized him. Old Grandma Bowes had told him his mother would live to see him back, but he didn't think so. He didn't like thinking about it.

"Nice girls back there," said the Bear, changing to more pleasant thoughts.

Benny nodded. "Very nice."

"You seemed to hit it off with Liz."

Benny nodded again, but didn't comment.

"I told Julie I might be able to see her on my next R and R. She thought that was a great idea."

The Bear thought about the present she'd offered, and about his response. He wouldn't broadcast the fact that he'd turned down a real, no-shit virgin. If it hadn't been for the double-decker with the Filipinas, and if he'd been positive that neither was carrying the Philippine killer-clap, it would have been different, he told himself.

It was not easy to forget the stewardess with the awesome mammaries. Funny, likeable, and a virgin to boot. But he wasn't about to lose his mental block about getting "serious" with any woman.

Benny drove on in the silence. A large pothole came out of nowhere. He swerved hard. The Bear grabbed the door-hold and hung on. "Hi-yo Silver," he said.

"You were pretty vocal yesterday about me being an asshole," said Benny.

He shrugged. "I was out of line. It's your life."

"You really pissed me off. I feel a lot better today so maybe that was what I needed."

"A lot of us have been where you are, Benny, but the timing for you was awfully shitty. It's traumatic enough being shot down, but then the wife thing on top of it? Hell, that would get to anyone."

Benny looked at Bear for a long second. "You still want to fly together? Yesterday you had reservations."

"Yesterday I was trying Psych two-oh-one and got carried

away. But, sure, if you've got your act back together and really want to, I'd like to fly with you. Just don't do it because you think you owe me. Any of the guys in the squadron would have tried to help. I just happened to be here."

Benny had obviously been thinking about it. "The other day at breakfast Glenn Phillips was saying we've got to do something about the defenses. If the Wild Weasel thing doesn't work, and the North Vietnamese threat just keeps getting worse, the strike pilots won't be able to fly up there at all."

The Bear grunted unintelligibly as they slammed into another pothole.

"So let's go and try to make a difference, okay?" Benny added.

"We'll have to be damned smart to really make a difference. Glenn and I were pretty good, but we never did get to actually drop bombs on a site. We shot a lot of Shrike missiles and banged up some of their radar antennas with them, but it takes more. We won't really scare the bastards until we start bombing the shit out of their sites."

"It's been done before."

"Not often," the Bear replied. "Al Lamb and Jack Donovan killed a site with rockets and bombs back about a year ago, when the Air Force was trying to see if a concept like Wild Weasel could really work, but I'd bet not more than two or three SAM sites have really been destroyed with bombs since then."

They talked about tactics and what they would do together on the remainder of the trip back to Clark Air Base. When they were coming into the outskirts of Angeles City, Benny held his hand out and the Bear took it. They shook hands.

"A team."

"Yeah," said the Bear. "I'm ready."

"Well, I'm not. You're going to have to be patient while we practice together and I come up to speed. It's been a while since I went through Wild Weasel training, and I've forgotten the little bit they tried to tell us there."

"Wouldn't help if you'd gone through it yesterday," said the Bear. "We'll have to build our tactics as we go along. No one has ever faced all the shit we're about to get into."

"A hell of a challenge."

"That's the only kind that's worthwhile," said the Bear.

08/1600L—Takhli RTAFB, Thailand

As the C-130 Hercules taxied toward base operations, the Bear was at a window, peering out at the long rows of F-105's as they passed the 357th squadron area. He sat beside Benny on the nylon web and aluminum frame seats lining the sides of the cargo aircraft.

"They're here," he said. "F-105F Wild Weasel birds looking all shiny and new. Bet they've got a new-car smell. Want to take a look?"

Benny felt his enthusiasm. "Sure."

They hauled their B-4 bags with them as they walked down the ramp. The sky was blue and faultless; the heat hovering about the hundred-degree mark. Aircraft and men only a hundred yards away were indistinct, shimmering in the thermal waves that rose from the tarmac.

The three Wild Weasel aircraft were parked in a single row, buttoned up, with cockpits closed, sleeves on pitot booms, engine covers over intakes, and chocks in place. They still carried travel pods—discarded fuel tanks from old fighters redesigned to hold the personal belongings of the aircrews who ferried the aircraft across the Pacific. The birds had obviously just arrived.

Benny and the Bear scrutinized each one. The tail numbers were 277, 301, and 315.

"Beautiful," said the Bear. "Want to see the equipment?"

He opened the canopies on number 277 and crawled into the rear cockpit. Benny leaned in beside him, listening as the Bear described each receiver in detail. A few of them were new. They had the new APR-26 to correlate SAM launches with specific sites, and a two-band ER-142 to replace the single-band IR-133 receiver. The Bear went through the actions he had to take in the backseat to isolate a radar signal, then how he would transfer the information to the front seat so Benny could line up in the rough direction of the radar.

"Best of all," exulted the Bear, "it's got the new Azimuth-Elevation system. When you get close, I switch to AZ-EL and bright dots ping on your combining glass, precisely on the SAM radar. It's a new idea called 'heads-up' display, so you don't have to look inside the cockpit when you're attacking."

Benny was trying to digest it all. The AZ-EL hadn't been covered in his training.

"Problem is, whenever I send a signal up to you in the front cockpit, I'm blind. Can't see if other SAM sites are launching missiles at us."

"And that's when they're most likely to launch SAMs."

"You're right. And that means we can't stay in AZ-EL mode for long. We'll practice until we get the hang of it."

Benny was maxed out for the day. He crawled down, then the Bear closed the canopies and came down himself.

"I've got a lot to learn," said Benny. "First I've got to start thinking Wild Weasel again."

"We'll get there. Just remember, there aren't any real expert Weasels yet, no matter what Les Ries or anyone else says. The equipment is great, and the aircraft are like new, but no one has figured out good, solid tactics."

"Brand new engine on this one," said Benny as he examined it.

"No one's figured out a great way to kill SAM sites and survive," repeated the Bear, trying to press the point home to his new pilot. "That's what we're going to have to come up with. Shooting missiles at 'em makes us a nuisance, but when we learn how to bomb the bastards off the face of the earth, and return to do it to another one the next day, then we'll have the SAM operators shaking in their boots and things will start to get easier for everyone."

"Sort of a private war, isn't it."

"That's a good way of thinking about it. It's between the SAM site commander and us. He's got a hundred technicians and specialists helping him. All you got is me, my receivers, and your balls."

"Looking things over?" asked a voice behind them.

They turned and saw a skinny, sun-bronzed man, shirtless and wearing only fatigue pants and boots.

Benny grinned and shook his hand. "Bear, meet Sgt Jerry Tiehl, best crew chief at Takhli. You chiefing this one now, Sarge?"

Tiehl shook the Bear's hand and nodded. "My second Weasel bird. I got a wreck and tried to put it together a week ago, but we had to rush it too much. It lost oil pressure when

Major Schumacher and Captain Stark were just going onto the tanker and went down."

"They get out okay?"

"Yes, sir, no thanks to me."

"Bull," said Benny. "You can't take on that kind of responsibility."

"It was my bird, sir." The matter was a simple one of responsibility for Jerry Tiehl.

"Get ready to paint our names on this one," said the Bear, looking up at the aircraft.

Tiehl looked at them both, then at the aircraft. "Chief Roberts said the squadron would assign crews and send him a list of names."

Benny spoke up. "Get them to hold off on this one until we get the okay from Colonel Mack, Sarge. I'll try to get two-seven-seven assigned to us."

"Will do, sir."

"Is it a good airplane?"

"If it's not, it will be. I won't lose another one to a malfunction." Tiehl spoke with such determination they knew it would be true.

They reported in to the squadron. Their belongings had been transferred from the hootch to one of the new, modern concrete buildings the pilots called "Ponderosas." One of the sprawling, windowless buildings had been assigned to each squadron. Theirs was air-conditioned, and had a dayroom equipped with a combination kitchenette and bar. Each of three hallways led off to a pair of two-man bedrooms and a bathroom. Compared to the old hootches, the Ponderosa provided gracious living.

Benny and the Bear had been assigned to the same room, which made them suspect that someone in the squadron had known they would team up. When their gear was squared away, the Bear caught a ride to the club. Unlike the old hootches, the ponderosa was a quarter-mile away.

The Bear ate dinner with Toki Takahara and Ken Maisey, who had been in the Weasel flight the day he and Glenn had been shot down. Maisey was a ring-knocker, quick to let you know he was an Annapolis graduate and not one of the rabble from lesser commissioning programs.

Toki told him there were a lot of new faces in the squadron since he'd left.

The Bear ordered his third choice, Salisbury steak, from the waitress, then turned back to the conversation. "Hell, Toki, I was only gone for eleven days."

"We lost Jimbo Smith, Tommy Larkins, Mort Mullens, and two new guys you wouldn't know. J. J. Spalding and Tip Singleton both finished their hundred missions a couple days ago."

"Jimbo Smith?" The Bear's chest felt heavy. Jimbo and Mike Murphy had been his closest buddies. They'd joked around, drank, and chased women in Takhli village together.

"Is it true you and Benny Lewis are going to be flying together?"

Word traveled fast at Takhli. "We're gonna give it a try, Toki."

"We sure as hell need some help from somewhere. The defenses are worse than they've ever been, Bear. And Intell says it's going to get tougher, that the North Vietnamese have a bunch of new SAMs coming."

A group of new guys were sitting at two tables nearby, wearing stateside Tactical Air Command shoulder patches and generally looking ill at ease. "Who're they?" the Bear asked, thinking he knew.

"The Weasel crews who brought in the F-105F's."

"I oughta kiss their feet for bringing us airplanes," said the Bear. He studied the new Weasels, thinking one looked familiar. The group stood, glanced around awkwardly, then left toward the bar, talking animatedly among themselves.

"Hell," said Toki, "I'll kiss their asses if they help with the defenses."

Sam Hall, Chickenplucker Crawford, and Swede Swendler—all flight commanders from the 357th—stopped by the table on their way to the bar.

"Good to have you back, Bear," Sam Hall said. "Hear you're teaming up with Benny. Great idea."

"Hi, chickenplucker," said Crawford. Pete had once been chastised by B. J. Parker for indiscriminately calling everyone 'chickenfuckers'. He now substituted 'chickenpluckers,' but everyone knew what he meant.

"Get your ass strapped back into an airplane and get back in the air so you can take care of us guys," said Swede Swendler.

When he'd finished eating, the Bear strolled into the bar. He'd planned this entry at Clark. He looked around for Mike

Murphy but he wasn't there. The Bear looked on as the new Weasel crews were being introduced around.

He wondered how many would survive. No Weasel crew had yet finished a hundred missions at Takhli. It was a hazardous occupation, being a Weasel.

A short captain, one of the replacement Wild Weasel pilots, approached him with his hand out.

"Hi. I'm Henry Holden," he said. "I hear you flew with my roommate from the Academy."

"Roommate?"

"Glenn Phillips. We bunked together when we were cows at West Point."

"Yeah," said the Bear. "I flew with him."

"Too bad about him getting hammered. Never was coordinated, though," Holden jabbed a thumb at the room. "My backseater says he knows you."

The Bear bristled at the offhanded remark about Phillips.

"Pudge, you getting settled in?" asked Colonel Mack, who joined them.

"Yes, sir."

"You met the Bear, I see."

"Hell, I heard all about Bear Stewart two months ago when Glenn wrote and told me to get my ass into Weasels."

During the next few minutes the Bear learned that Henry "Pudge" Holden had married Glenn Phillips's younger sister and was thought of as a brother. He also found Holden every bit as pompous and cocksure as Phillips had been. Perhaps, he thought, they put bullshit into the food they served at Hudson High.

"Glad you're going to be joining the 357th," said Colonel Mack, who also appeared to be a friend of Pudge Holden's. "Have you met Benny Lewis yet? He'll be your flight commander."

That was the first time the Bear had been told who the new WW-flight commander would be.

"I knew Benny at Nellis," said Pudge. "He's a damn good man."

"Hello, asshole," said a voice at the Bear's elbow. He turned to see a captain almost as short as Pudge Holden holding a drink in each hand. The newcomer pushed one of the drinks toward the Bear. "You still drink horsepiss scotch?"

The Bear took the drink, then placed him. "Lyle Watson," he said. He was the one who had looked familiar in the dining room.

"You got it. Best fucking EWO in the world."

Watson and he had vied for the pleasures of the nurse at Columbus Air Force Base who had roomed with Marty. Each had vocally disliked the other, and had maneuvered to cut the other out. Although separated, Watson had been considered married and unavailable, and the Bear had commuted from his base in Louisiana, so both had a disadvantage.

"How's Marilee?" the Bear asked.

"Screwed her brains out last time I saw her. She sends her love."

The Bear grinned maliciously. "She get over the infection?"

Watson frowned. "Are you the bastard who gave it to her?"

"Nope. I just shared her misfortune and got the hell away."

Watson shook his head. "I had some fancy explaining to do when I got back together with my wife."

"Same with my girlfriend back at Barksdale."

"I want to call things even between us, Mal." Watson looked around the room. "I figure I'd better make friends now, because I hear you're considered the best Weasel EWO in the wing."

"I'm not holding a grudge. I'll teach you what I can."

Watson laughed. "Teach me? I just don't want you feeling bad when they find out I'm twice as good as you are."

The Bear was amused. "You'll be lucky to get five missions in before you get hammered."

Watson motioned toward the already noisy barroom. "Good guys?"

"The best you'll ever meet."

They sipped their drinks. The Bear knew Lyle Watson drank gin, even remembered his brand, because their common friend Marilee had kept it stocked in her apartment. He noticed that the drink Watson had bought him was Johnny Walker Black. Funny what people remember, he thought.

Mike Murphy came in and beelined for the Bear. "Hey, babes. Good to see you're back from the ravages of the Philippines. Any of the fifty-cent whores take pity and give you a little for five bucks?"

"All the women in the P.I. are now walking around bowlegged."

"Probably because Benny Lewis was there, babes. Fighter pilots do it better and you oughta know that by now."

"I can outjump, outfight, outrun, and outfuck any pilot alive." The Bear grinned. "Meet Lyle Watson. He and Pudge Holden over there are new Weasels in the 357th."

They shook hands.

"You guys know each other from before?" asked Murphy.

"We had a lady friend in common who gave us both a nice gift. Says *something* about his judgment."

"But not much," Mike said. "Good to see you back, Bear. Nice meeting you, Lyle. I gotta talk to a guy." Murphy left.

Two other captains walked up. Watson introduced them as Bill "Shaky" Anderson and Fred Norman, new Weasels destined for the 354th squadron, where Les Ries reigned as the WW-flight commander. Anderson appeared nervous, although he'd not yet flown a combat mission. Norman, a short and gnomelike EWO, was already intoxicated and obnoxious.

"The Thais call the 354th the pig squadron," explained the Bear. "They see the emblem in front of the squadron building with the mean-looking bulldog and it confuses them. They never saw a bulldog before, so they think it's a pig."

When Mike Murphy returned, the Bear took great pains to *almost* accurately describe the night in the Philippines when he'd gotten in *thirteen* good fucks with *three* beautiful women. Murphy didn't believe him but he liked the story, and that was almost as good to the Bear.

"Babes, that's gonna be a hard one to beat," said Murphy, thinking. Mike had an aw-shucks approach and an air of naiveté that women adored. They wanted to mother and take care of him, and he just smiled helplessly and didn't discourage them.

Andy Schumacher and Cinnamon Bear Stark came over to welcome him back, and he remembered the story he'd heard about them losing oil pressure and bailing out over Laos.

"I landed in a tree," Schumacher griped to Benny, showing his lopsided grin. "Only damned tree for miles around."

The Bear noticed they were nervous and laughed over inconsequential things. He wondered how long they would last now that they'd used up their confidence.

Maj Les Ries and his EWO, Dan Janssen, came over and Les clapped Benny Lewis on the back.

"I hear you're a Weasel again, eh Benny?" Ries said. The two started to talk, and the Bear stepped back, out of the conversation.

Janssen followed him, crowing. "Remember when Les and me rolled in and bombed that site last month, Mal? When our bird was shot up?"

He remembered. Whatever it had been that they'd bombed had been so well camouflaged and the photos so poor that it was hard to tell if Ries had bombed a SAM site, a formation of guns, or even a small village in a thicket of trees.

"Colonel Parker's putting us in for a DFC. We put the hurt on that bastard, Mal."

The Bear thought for a moment. "I hear things went pretty badly with the strike pilots while I was gone."

Janssen looked at him with a trace of belligerence. "Yeah, but Les and I have some new tactics figured out. Colonel Parker named us lead Weasel crew for the wing after you and Glenn got shot down. We're going to hold weekly Wild Weasel meetings and tell the new guys how it's done. You and Benny, seeing you'll be flying together, should be there too."

"Good to hear you're going to share your vast expertise, Dan." The Bear was being sarcastic but Janssen didn't notice.

Lyle Watson approached them, his hand out to Janssen. "Hi, I'm Lyle Watson."

"Dan Janssen. I'm the head Weasel EWO," said Janssen proudly.

Head Weasel EWO? Disgusted with the conversation, the Bear went to the jukebox and played a dollar's worth of quarters, repeatedly punching the buttons for "Lara's Theme." He took a seat nearby and enjoyed the plaintive sound. His thoughts turned to Julie, and he felt a wave of nostalgia mixed with bachelor caution.

Lt Col Johnny T. Polaski, their squadron ops officer, came over and sat down, listening to the music with him.

There came a pause between playings.

"Good to have you back, toad."

"Good to be back, sir. Damn good."

13/1340L—Route Pack Six, North Vietnam

Benny and the Bear were aloft together for the first time, flying as number three and leading the second element in the Wild Weasel flight led by Maj Les Ries and Capt Bad Bear Janssen. Benny said he would feel more comfortable if they didn't take the lead position until he'd picked up a few pointers.

Once again the strike force's target was the Yen Vien railroad yard, and Polaski was mission commander. He had admonished the strike pilots that this time they were to get *all* their bombs on the target.

"This time let's take 'em out so they *stay* out for a while," he'd said, full of himself for getting to lead a strike mission for the first time.

The Bear felt that Ries had postured and preached a lot at the mission briefing before he got down to business. Finally, he'd told the audience he intended to locate and bomb the SAM site that intelligence had labeled Lead 3, on the northern edge of Hanoi. Johnny T. had been impressed.

"You Weasels keep them busy," Johnny T. said, "and we'll be okay. We've pounded the defenses around the Yen Vien rail yard so much in the past couple weeks that they've got to be hurting."

Later, when they'd broken up for the individual flight briefings, Ries had told the Weasel flight that he just wanted them all to stay out of his way while he located the site and then he'd lead them in on a dive-bomb attack. The Bear had asked Ries if he wanted them to announce SAM launches he detected on his equipment as a backup, since the equipment in the Weasel birds was new to both Bad Bear Janssen and himself.

Janssen had quickly butted in. "You guys just hang on and try to keep up. I'll pick up all the SAM launches and Les will make the calls. There can't be two flight leaders."

The Bear had shut up. Afterward, when they arrived at aircraft number 277 and were beginning their preflight, he'd told Benny that he thought both Polaski's and Ries's planning was faulty.

"We're going to see a lot more defenses than they're planning on," he'd said. "If they've been pounding away at

the same target there won't be less defenses, there'll be more.
The gomers concentrate SAMs and guns where they think
we're going to bomb. And if Ries thinks he can just fly in there
and bomb the SAM site without more planning than that, he's
dumber'n I thought."

"Maybe so, Bear," Benny had replied, "but I'm here to
learn and if Les has something to show me, I'll hang on and
watch. This is their show. When we're flight lead, we'll do it
our way."

The Bear begrudgingly agreed.

As they approached the Red River, the Bear found himself
fumbling with the new ER-142 receiver and wishing he had
spent more time studying it. The scopes were smaller, and now
he had to worry about two of them rather than one. He almost
told Benny they had a tracking gun radar, then realized it was
the elevation beam of a Fansong, the SAM radar tracker. He
analyzed it closer, watching as it swept around, then told
Benny as the Fansong started to track their flight in earnest.

Benny acknowledged.

Ten seconds later, when they were over the dog-pecker,
the SAM signal was even stronger. Ries had still not advised
the flight.

"Janssen must be having trouble with the new receivers
like I am," said the Bear. "You'd better call him about the
Fansong. It's got us centered and I think it's about to launch."

Benny disagreed. "He said he didn't want any calls."

The SAM signal jumped in power and doubled its pulse
rate. Then the HIGH PRF light came on, confirming the Bear's
analysis.

"Benny, he's about to launch missiles."

"You sure?"

"I wouldn't say it if I wasn't sure," he barked, unaccus-
tomed to being questioned.

The APR-26 squealed, the launch light lit, and the
ER-142 showed them centered in both beams.

"We've got a valid launch," said the Bear, "and it's at
us."

"Tomahawk three has a SAM launch," called Benny, not
waiting longer.

There was silence from Tomahawk lead; the Bear glanced
over and saw Janssen still bent over his scopes.

Benny rolled the aircraft up on its right wing, then pulled back hard on the stick. "I see a—"

The aircraft bucked gently as the first SAM went off just to their left.

Benny reversed hard to the left, still in the slight dive and gaining energy.

The other two SAMs went wide to their right and above them.

"Shee-it!" cried the Bear.

"You okay?" asked Benny.

"Yeah."

Tomahawk four called. *"Thank you, Tomahawk three."* It was an implicit criticism of Ries.

Benny turned and started a climb to rejoin Ries and number two, who were at their eleven o'clock high.

"Tomahawk three, this is lead. We didn't have a launch indication on our equipment. Go ahead and call 'em if you see 'em first."

"Roger, lead," answered Benny.

The SAM signal was off them and tracking someone else now. Les Ries wasn't talking to the strike force to keep them advised of the SAM threat, which made the Bear grumble.

They flew on toward Thud Ridge, where they hugged up against the ridge so the SAM radars couldn't see them. They flew down the ridge, then turned and flew north, away from the target, still tight against the mountainside.

"What the fuck are they doing?" asked the Bear.

"What do you mean?"

"Ries briefed we were gonna pop up, find the Lead three site, and try to bomb it."

Benny grunted as they pulled g's.

"We're not doing the strike force any good hiding here next to the ridge," said the Bear.

"Tomahawks, I'm going to turn and fire a Shrike," called Ries.

On the radio they could hear the strike force as the flights approached the target, ten miles south of Tomahawk flight.

"Shee-it," said the Bear again, disgusted.

The flight went into a sudden, soaring right turn. When they stabilized there were no strong radar signals directly in front of them. The Bear wondered what the hell was going on.

He saw a flash of fire as a Shrike missile streaked away from one, then the other of Tomahawk lead's pylons.

Five seconds later Johnny T. Polaski, Hatchet lead, said he was climbing to position for his dive-bomb delivery.

"Can you tell if they've got SAM activity?" asked Benny, talking about Polaski's flight.

"Not from this far out," answered the Bear, again cursing Ries for his stupid tactics. "I've got a couple SAM signals, but we're too far away to tell if or where they're shooting."

"Too bad."

"Ries is not doing anything like he said in the flight briefing," the Bear grumbled again.

Benny was silent.

The radio erupted with a melee of warning calls, curses, and the strained sounds of pilots' voices as they pulled g's.

"What the hell?" asked the Bear, who often flew with his radio turned low so he could concentrate on the radar signals.

Benny filled him in. "The mission commander just took a SAM hit. Hatchet two said it went off in his cockpit."

When they landed, still carrying their bombs and missiles, the Bear was so furious he could hardly talk. He remained quiet during most of the flight debriefing, staring coldly at Ries as he explained what his tactic had been.

"I wanted to get a few miles away, turn, and fire a couple Shrikes back into the area just before they went into their dive-bomb. I figured if a SAM radar came on the air the Shrikes would home in on it."

The Bear interjected. "Might've been nice if you'd shared some of that philosophy with the rest of us before we took off."

Ries snapped around and glared hard at him. "You got a complaint?"

The Bear's voice was harsh as he rose to his feet. "I'd bet Colonel Polaski's got one."

Ries exploded. "What the hell do you mean by that?"

The Bear ignored him and walked out of the room.

Later Benny found the Bear reading a letter in the Ponderosa dayroom. "It's from Julie," he said.

"You came close back there," Benny said.

The Bear peered up with a quizzical expression.

"Ries could take an insubordination charge to Colonel Parker."

"Let him. He's an incompetent bastard. Didn't do a fucking thing he briefed. Even worse, he didn't give Polaski any support, just let him get killed."

"He thought he did the right thing. You're arguing he should have used different tactics, but like you told me, there aren't any tactics in the books yet and we're having to try a lot of different things."

The Bear kept his voice quiet. "Tell me, Benny, what do you think about what the Wild Weasels did up there today?"

Benny didn't hesitate. "We were ineffective. You and I will do it different, and I hope a lot better, once I get up to speed."

"God, I hope so. Benny, I counted six different SAM radars and five triple-A radars on the air at one time. That's more than I've ever seen before. We're talking about very directional radar beams, so there's no telling how many were really operating. We keep doing as bad as we did today, we won't be able to fly up there much longer. We gotta start coming up with some good, smart shit."

"You've got to learn to keep some of your criticisms to yourself, Bear, or you're going to end up in deep shit before we have a chance to even think about our own tactics."

The Bear released a pent-up breath of exasperation. Benny was right. Tactics were the prerogative of the flight leader, and it had been thoughtless of him to blame Les Ries for Polaski's death. It was time to shut up and act like a good soldier.

He found Ries in the bar and apologized. Les was noncommittal, nodding abruptly before turning away, as if the Bear's opinion wasn't worth his time. The Bear apologized to Janssen too, and received the same coolness.

The Bear kept his head during the apologies, then bellied up to the bar and got wobbly-kneed drunk with Lyle Watson. He told him about his high-scoring night in Angeles City.

"Fourteen times?" asked Watson. "Naw. That's not humanly possible."

"S' possible," slurred the Bear.

13/1600L—People's Army HQ, Hanoi, DRV

Xuan Nha

Col. Xuan Nha's staff were still in the command center, exultant about the day's events. Three attacking aircraft had been shot down: a Voodoo reconnaissance jet by artillery, a Thunder plane by a direct rocket hit from Tiger one, and a Phantom by artillery. Nicolaj Gregarian watched from the rear of the command center.

"We are a good team, Russian," said Xuan Nha. "Your equipment, my men. We are starting to improve our fence of steel, don't you think?"

Gregarian smiled. "But it will be much better when we have Wisdom."

"It will be better, but already it is very good. The added numbers of systems are making life miserable for the Americans."

Gregarian agreed.

"Anyway, site leveling of the Wisdom complex will be finished tomorrow and we will be ready to start putting it together. When will the systems arrive?"

"Perhaps a week. A ship will bring the communications systems, vans, special rocket radars, and personnel to Haiphong. The P-50 radar will come by train from China, as the other one did." Nicolaj paused, likely reflecting on that first P-50. "My people at PVO Strany Headquarters are supportive but cautious, Colonel Nha. They will watch us closely and want us to take no chances with the equipment or the experts they are sending."

"Wisdom shall succeed. Then we shall celebrate again, but now we are happy for what we did today. The Americans are beginning to tremble when they fly. I interrogated a pilot flying from Thailand yesterday, and he said they are afraid. We've put fear into their hearts, Russian."

Major Nguy

At one side of the command center, Major Nguy, Nha's quiet and capable executive officer, had been cornered by

Major Wu, who hoped Nguy might have a solution to his latest dilemma with the colonel. He had reassured Xuan Nha that the wounded pilot captured in the mountains west of Yen Bai was recovering, albeit slowly, and that shortly they would be able to interrogate him. But when he had gone to view the prisoner, he'd found that again the damnable pilot was dying. Wu had been afraid to tell the truth, and now Xuan Nha was pressing for a time to see the pilot.

Reluctantly, Major Nguy swore to keep Wu's secret from Colonel Nha. Then he asked if there was any hope at all of the pilot's recovery.

Major Wu bit his lip apprehensively. "I spoke with an officer at Hoa Lo prison, and he does not believe so. The prisoner remains delirious."

Nguy found it difficult to feel sorry for the intelligence officer. Wu was moody, acted aloof from the rest of the staff, and was especially difficult whenever Nguy was placed in charge. Yet, as the colonel's second-in-command, Nguy felt he must try to deal with personal problems that might affect the performance of the group.

"Is there still infection?" he asked.

"No," replied Wu. "At least the doctor I sent to visit the prisoner didn't believe so. He had been treated with sulfides and penicillin. He said some butcher had carved a portion of the muscles from the leg, but that there was no infection."

"Then why does he not get better?"

"The doctor is not sure. He knows the leg is healing incorrectly. He gave him drugs so the prisoner could rest better but then he was not coherent. And lessening the drugs only made the pain more intense. He cried and babbled nonsense." He added, "Other wounded prisoners have arrived at Hoa Lo in much better condition, and they died within a week or two. It is a prison, not a hospital."

"Offer the colonel other prisoners to interrogate. We have identified at least four others at Hoa Lo who were likely flying the radar-hunter mission."

"The colonel is determined to interrogate this particular man. He is very definite about it. It makes my position difficult, comrade Major." There was a plea in the voice.

Major Nguy sighed at Wu's solicitousness. "There is perhaps a solution."

"What is that?"

"There is a Russian surgeon at Bach Mai Hospital who is very good. He saved the life of one of our officers who was severely wounded during a missile attack on Steel two battery. Our doctors thought he did not have a chance, but the Russian operated and saved him. He might be able to repair the prisoner's leg. But," he paused, thinking, "it is unlikely we can get approval for him to operate on a prisoner."

They tried to think of how they might be able to get the American pilot onto the doctor's operating table and finally gave up. The bureaucracies involved were too difficult.

"Perhaps," said Major Nguy, "we should ask the colonel to help."

"No!" said Wu, unsuccessful at hiding his fear. "I will find another way."

Major Nguy was inundated with paperwork and had to return to his office. As he climbed the stairs, he reflected on Wu and his problem. Colonel Nha had softened his display of disdain toward Wu following their trip to Bac Can, but Nguy could tell there was still something wrong there. He also thought it likely that Wu was running to his aunt, the well-known Li Binh, to seek her support and advice. She would probably fix things for her spoiled and incompetent nephew once again. She might even be able to get the Russian surgeon to see the prisoner.

When he thought more about Wu and Li Binh, he decided there was possibly more going on between them than Colonel Nha, or even he, had suspected. The nephew was about the same age as the aunt, and he spoke of her reverently. Nguy hoped, for the group's sake, that if Wu was exercising more than familial love for his aunt, the colonel would not find out. It would be best, he thought, if Wu were transferred away.

He decided to look into that option.

He transferred his thoughts to the discussion he'd had earlier with Col Xuan Nha.

Following his promotion, the colonel had decided to retain the same offices and his old staff. Xuan Nha joked that it was a shame he only had a major for an executive officer, and that one of his men was most deserving to become a lieutenant colonel. Major Nguy was quietly proud that he was about to get the promotion he'd worked so hard for. He decided that Xuan Nha had been definite enough with his hints that he could pass the happy news to his wife tonight.

He stopped worrying about Major Wu. Only much later would he realize his fatal error.

13/2100L—Takhli RTAFB, Thailand

Colonel Mack

Twice each week, wherever Mack MacLendon was in the world he took time out to write to his wife. They had been married for twelve good years, but in his heart he had known her forever. She was his solace, his pillar, a part of him like his right arm, and he could not imagine life without her. Unlike some of the other men, he never hesitated to tell it to her the way it was. From the first she'd wanted to know about the events in his life, and war was no exception. By writing her, he released something that it would have been unhealthy to keep inside.

Tuesday
December 13th

Dear Alice,

Hope your cold is getting better. It does not seem that long since you were ill the last time, so you had better start taking better care of yourself. Make sure you see the doc out at the base on a regular basis, hon.

It has not been a good day here. You may have heard by the time you get this, but today we lost Johnny T. Polaski. He was hit over the target and was likely killed. We had become close since I took over the squadron.

His wife Amy will need your support, so get a letter off quickly to her. I will write her one from here too.

You have had to give so much support to so many wives lately, and I am sure there are going to be more friends lost in this war.

Johnny T. was talking to me yesterday, saying he felt the SAM threat was overstated, that the men were overreacting to them. I tried to tell him that he had to weigh all the threats, and to worry about them equally for they were all lethal. I guess I should have talked to him harder.

Benny Lewis (remember him from Spangda-hlem?) came to me a few days ago and asked if he could fly a very dangerous but necessary special mission called Wild Weasel, and I agreed. At first I had asked him about Bets and the kids, wanting him to think about them before making his decision, but he was abrupt and guarded with his answers. I believe they are having marital trouble of some nature.

Too many of our friends' marriages seem to be going onto the rocks lately. Wish there could be more like you, but they broke the mold.

Well hon, in my first war I was given a cot in a squad tent to sleep on. In Korea it was better, because I was given a bunk in a barracks. This war they've given me a single bed in an air-conditioned trailer. Wars seem to be getting better and better.

I love you,

Mack

CHAPTER ELEVEN

Friday, December 16th—0800 Local, Dong Hoi, Route Pack One, North Vietnam

Benny Lewis

The Bear and Benny were flying together for the third time, but it was the first time they'd really been able to work on their own tactics. They were leading the Weasel flight in the lower panhandle of North Vietnam, supporting several flights of Thuds flying armed reconnaissance missions. The strike flights were looking for supplies and troop concentrations and attacking targets of opportunity in the more sparsely settled areas near the demilitarized zone separating North and South Vietnam. The Weasels were there to protect them from radar-directed threats.

The Bear detected only a few, weak signals from enemy radars well north of them. "No threats," he said over the intercom, meaning there were no radars close enough to do harm.

Benny surveyed the flight of single-seat Thuds they were leading. It was a no-brainer, an easy counter that the jocks savored after the peril and confusion of pack six. There were a few clouds in the area, but the visibility was generally good.

"Okay," said Benny, wishing to make the best of things, "line me up on a radar."

"All we've got are the radars from our own ships."

"I'll safe my weapons switches so there won't be any goofs," said Benny. They flew southward at a lazy 450 knot airspeed.

The Bear told him what he was doing as he tuned to a sweeping Navy signal and isolated it on his main receiver. "Now I'm transferring a radar signal to your scope. See it?"

291

"No . . . Oh yeah! It strobed then disappeared again."

"The operator's sweeping his radar beam around the sky, looking for MiG's."

"There it is again, at our nine o'clock."

"That's it."

"I'm turning left," Benny said. He had trouble lining up on the signal, which intermittently blossomed on the small attack scope.

"Come left five more degrees," said the Bear as they flew out over the South China Sea.

Benny made the adjustment.

"That's good."

"The signal's steady now," said Benny.

"He saw us turning toward him," said the Bear. "We got his interest, so now he's tracking and trying to sort us out. You get so you know what the radar operator's thinking."

The signal jumped in power, the strobe immediately growing from one to three rings.

"Now he's increased his signal strength so he can track us better. He's not worried because we got our IFF on and that tells him we're friendlies. But he's interested. Select a Shrike missile station and line up on him using the needles."

"I got him." Benny corrected again, using steering needles that got their information from the Shrike missile. "He's dead ahead now, and the needles show him low, like he should be." He nosed over slightly and read his dive angle. "He's a couple of degrees down."

"Probably fifteen, twenty miles away. Well out of the normal launch range for your Shrike. You'll have to use your Shrike tables to get the distances. See any ships up ahead?"

"Yeah, three of 'em dead ahead." Benny referred to notes on his kneeboard. "At our altitude and with him four degrees down, we're . . . uh . . . sixteen miles from the radar."

The Bear sounded satisfied. "You're doing great. Now, if we were going to bomb him, I'll show you one of the things I could do. First, I fine-tune the signal on the Weasel receiver, then I switch to AZ-EL. Is your steering dot doing anything?"

Benny watched the dot pinging on the combining glass. "It's jumping all over hell."

The Bear fined-tuned some more. "How's that?"

"It's better, but it's still not settling down enough to bomb accurately with."

"Ahh hell. I'll get the avionics shop to work on it. Let's try using the attack scope."

"F-105's ten miles southwest of Dong Hoi, this is Jasper. Discontinue your present heading! I repeat, discontinue your present heading!" came a call over the emergency frequency.

"What the hell?" said the Bear angrily. "They know we're friendly aircraft. They even know what aircraft we're flying."

Benny banked and turned starboard, and the flight followed. "The ships out here carry missiles, and they might get really stupid and shoot if we continue inbound."

"Navy assholes," grumbled the Bear.

"Let's find something to drop our CBUs on," said Benny. He switched to radio. *"Let's green 'em up again, Razors."*

"Razor Two."

"Three."

"Four."

The responses came as they passed back over the coastline and rearmed their switches.

They dropped down to 4,500 feet and trolled, hoping someone would shoot at them so they could knock out some guns. They had flown for ten minutes when Benny circled over an intersection. Below were several trucks stationary on the dirt road.

"Razor flight, take a hard look at that intersection," called Benny.

"Razor lead, Razor three. I think it's a flak trap trying to sucker us in."

Three's voice—that of Ken Maisey—was tremulous.

The North Vietnamese were known for placing burned out trucks in open view on the roads to try to entice the Americans into bombing them. Then they would open up with their guns and attempt to shoot them down. Numerous pilots had fallen for the ruse. But the Weasels were carrying the right weapons load to deal with a flak trap.

Benny called, *"Razors, listen up. Three and four, hold high and keep a good lookout. Lead and two will go down and try to draw some fire. Let's see where they're shooting from and what they're made of. Razor two, jink out to the right. I'll approach from the west, you come in from the south."*

Three and four soared higher, leaving them. Tiny Bechler, flying Razor two, swung out to the right, then reversed back toward the trucks. Benny began a shallow dive, nose directly toward the intersection.

Both aircraft continued toward the target. As they came into range they began to jink, weaving and dipping, waiting for groundfire.

Streams of small-arms and 37mm cannon-fire erupted from thickets of jungle at their one o'clock.

"Fucking amateurs," snorted the Bear. The 37mm was not aimed, but was simply fired into the air over the intersection where the gunners hoped they would fly. The 14.5mm, streams of bees, were aimed directly at them, not leading them, and went far behind the aircraft. White puffs formed above the flak trap, but both aircraft had already broken off their attacks.

"You get a good visual on the guns, Razor three?" asked Benny.

After a long pause Maisey answered in the tremulous voice. *"They were shooting pretty good down there, lead."*

"Dammit," muttered Benny. *"Did you note their positions?"* he radioed.

"I'm not sure, lead. I think the gunfire came from several sources."

Benny was joined by Tiny Bechler, who gave him a thumbs-up. They climbed to gain altitude for weapons delivery. Benny wondered if he should believe Maisey. If the guns were bunched together as he'd thought, it would make things easier, for they could concentrate on that one area. He then saw the second element a mile away and waggled his wings in greeting.

He decided to believe him. *"Razors, we're going to drop our CBUs on the guns. Let's release high enough to get good area coverage. Follow my lead."*

His delivery was a good one. Benny was pleased when he rolled over and saw the bomblets sparkling throughout the target area. Tiny Bechler's CBUs were also well delivered. After the CBUs stopped exploding, the ground fire had diminished to a few trickles of 14.5mm bees fired wildly about the sky.

The Bear announced his pleasure. "Shit hot."

"Where's three and four?" Benny asked. He looked about for the second element.

"No telling," said the Bear caustically. "Three's Maisey, remember?"

Benny looked more but still could not find the second element. *"Razor three, say your position,"* he called.

He was answered by silence.

"Razor three, this is Razor lead. I repeat, what is your location?"

After another moment Maisey radioed. *"I've got a problem with my utility pump, lead. I'm five miles south of the target, holding in an orbit."*

The Bear grumbled from the backseat. "It's his same old bullshit all over again."

Benny held his tongue. If Maisey had an emergency situation with his hydraulics, he should not be dive-bombing. Anyway, the flak trap was not a priority target. *"Razor lead copies. Razor three and four, safe your switches and let's head home."*

The Bear went off the intercom so he could release his mask on one side and have a cigarette. When he came back on intercom it was apparent he'd been thinking about things.

"You know," he told Benny, "I got a feeling we're going to sting 'em good."

16/1200L—Bach Mai Hospital, Hanoi, North Vietnam

Glenn Phillips

Glenn knew he'd been drugged, for he was mercifully oblivious to much of the terrible pain. It was still there, but it had become a throbbing, bearable sensation. Everything about him seemed fuzzy and indistinct. He looked down toward the bent leg, healing at a ten degree outward angle, but couldn't see it. He had been clothed in a hospital smock and was covered by clean sheets. Aside from the fact that he was floating on a giant marshmallow, it was a pleasant change.

Was he at home, returned from the dream? He was unable to reason it out so he stopped trying. He tried to move his marshmallow arms, but they were too heavy. Was he strapped down? He thought so.

A doctor in frameless glasses and wearing a green gown bent over the leg, speaking in a strange language to an assistant. He probed the leg with a metal instrument. The language was not Vietnamese and the doctor was not Oriental. Glenn tried to sort that out in his mind.

He blinked, more awake now, and looked around the room. Things were quite clean, as if back home in a stateside hospital. Out of the corner of his eye, however, he saw a stern-countenanced female nurse and a uniformed Vietnamese officer, very thin and familiar-looking. A glimpse from the prison cell?

Sunlight flooded through a nearby window, so he knew he was not in any part of the prison he'd previously noticed. It was eternally gray and sunless there. *Where am I?* he wondered.

Not in heaven, he decided. *The angels are too ugly.*

Glenn Phillips, he told himself, *you've got a silly, marshmallow mind*. He giggled, causing the doctor to look up, startled. He said something to the stern nurse. Glenn giggled again, because they didn't realize the world had turned into a marshmallow.

Noises from beside him. He was unbuckled from the bed, lifted and placed on a gurney, and strapped down once more. Someone wheeled him down an endless hall, stopping outside double doors.

The doctor appeared again. He held one of Phillips's eyelids open, peering into his soul as the assistant depressed the plunger of a syringe taped to his forearm. Phillips faded into a pleasant dream, where he watched himself driving on a long stretch of straight, wide highway in his Corvette. Periodically the doctor would hover magically, pull back the eyelid, and say something into his cloth mask in his strange language.

The Bear appeared beside him in the Corvette, fiddling with the instruments and saying "no threats." When Glenn tried to respond, he was gone, replaced by Pudge, his roommate at the academy, wearing a gray uniform, laughing and calling him a turkey. The doctor returned, lifted the eyelid, and grumbled something. Glenn's mother appeared, looking tight-lipped and stern.

"I'll be good, Mom."

It was pain that woke him. Niggling pain that made him uncomfortable. Nothing like the searing pain that had stolen his mind. The only illumination in the room was filtered from an open door to a dim hallway. He could see darkness outside a window on the other side of several occupied beds. One of the patients moaned a lot. He dropped back to sleep but was again awakened by the pain, worse but still bearable.

He lay there for half an hour before he heard footsteps in the hallway.

The light was turned on and the assistant he'd seen before came in. He took Glenn's pulse and blood pressure, muttering words to someone. The same skinny officer as before peered over his shoulder. Soviet-style collar tabs. A major.

Phillips sighed, wondering what had happened, thankful he could endure the pain.

The doctor entered with a squat Vietnamese officer with a sharp bird's nose, speaking again in the guttural language. Russian, maybe.

Bird-beak crowded up to the bedside and leaned over, peering at his face, wearing a friendly look. He wore the epaulets and collar tabs of a full colonel. He turned away to speak with the doctor, who motioned at Phillips's leg, then displayed and explained a fifteen-inch, shiny metal rod. Looking satisfied, Bird-beak then spoke with the familiar, skinny officer. He clasped the skinny major's arm and nodded, speaking softly and giving approval of some sort.

Still foggy-brained, Phillips tried to observe Bird-beak closer, and was drawn to the soft eyes. A compassionate man? Glenn thought about that, finally deciding he was more of an actor.

The doctor spoke and the assistant administered another shot. As he drifted back to sleep, he could feel the soft eyes boring into his mind with questions, and he began to understand why they had tried to repair him and end the mind-searing pain. It was going to present him with a new challenge that he didn't want to think about just yet.

Major Wu

Wu was happier than he had been in more than two difficult weeks. As he watched Xuan Nha leave the hospital room, he had visions of things returning to normal.

The colonel had made him a major. It had been rumored that there was room for a lieutenant colonel on the staff now that Xuan had been promoted. He decided to ask his aunt about it. He felt uneasy over the growing file on the dangerous colonel's activities. The patience his aunt had suggested was difficult to maintain.

He turned to observe the sleeping American pilot, the source of much of his recent unhappiness, and his eyes narrowed with loathing.

The Russian doctor looked up from the bedside. "Your colonel is happier now?"

"Yes, thank you."

The doctor nodded at the sleeping pilot. "The leg will never be strong due to the muscle loss, and he will limp badly because the leg is now two inches shorter than the other one. There was no way to make them the same length."

"But he will live?"

"Oh, yes. In pain for a long time, but he will live. I will recommend a rehabilitation program involving extensive physical therapy and when he can walk, special shoes."

Major Wu shook his head impatiently. "Never mind that. When will we be able to question him?" Xuan Nha wished to personally conduct the interrogation.

The doctor rubbed a speck from his eyeglasses, thinking. When he spoke he did so with a trace of distaste. "He should rest for a day, recuperate for another day or two, and then slowly be withdrawn from the drugs. A week?"

Wu's eyes flickered to the sleeping body. "We do not have that long."

The doctor was upset. "It's not just the broken leg and the bone's acceptance of the rod, but also the repairing of the muscle. Until his body has generated sufficient scar tissue, he will remain in constant pain and must be sedated."

"What is the minimum time we must wait? Tomorrow?"

"You would be talking to a beet, a radish. Be patient and he will be ready."

Wu could not be patient because Xuan Nha would not be. He sensed that the Russian doctor was being protective of his patient. He thought of Colonel Nha's schedule, and then his own. During the next three days Xuan would be working on a logistics report for a general staff meeting. Wu had important matters to attend to at Bac Can.

"The colonel will speak to him on Tuesday morning. That will give you more than three days to prepare the prisoner for interrogation. Forget about therapy. Just make sure he is awake and that he can answer questions."

The Russian doctor wore a troubled expression. "And after the interrogation?"

"He will be returned to Hoa Lo prison." Wu smiled. *"They* will take care of his rehabilitation."

Wu left the university hospital, pleased with the way things were going. He thought about the possibility of being promoted. His aunt had arranged the prisoner's operation with a single telephone call. Even a general would have had difficulty doing what she had done so easily. Her manipulative fingers seemed to extend into every source of power in Hanoi. Surely she would have no trouble arranging the promotion for her loyal and loving nephew.

But first he had the things to do at Bac Can.

19/2100L—Hanoi, DRV

Xuan Nha

Xuan sat in his leather-strap chair, his reading glasses perched forward on his nose, frowning as he pored over the report he'd briefed to the general staff. With only minor exceptions his suggestions had been approved.

Li Binh sat nearby, also reviewing paperwork, hers from the Ministry of External Affairs. Xuan looked up to find her gaze fixed upon him.

"How was your briefing received by the generals?" she asked.

He shrugged. "We prepare for days to make a presentation to get approval we know they will give. A waste of time."

Her eyes were cool tonight. "How is my nephew doing?"

"I have not seen him for the past two days," he said.

"He has been working on a project for the party," she answered.

He paused, but it appeared no more would be disclosed about Wu's activities. Li Binh held Lao Dong party business closely to herself and Xuan knew not to delve. They both were allowed their own secrets.

"And the Russian? The chief adviser?"

"Gregarian?"

"Yes, how is it going with him?"

"Since he was given the Englishwoman yesterday, he's

seemed much happier. I believe he is in heat for her smelly
body."

"And what happened to the young schoolteacher?"

"I questioned her at some length. She did not have much,
but she told me about some discussions Gregarian had with
some of the other advisers who visited him."

"Is she still presentable?" asked Li Binh.

He snorted. "The Russian fornicated with her twice in as
many weeks. Other than being crushed by his weight and
cursed at for daring to fidget about while he toiled, she is fine."

She indicated the reports she'd been reading. "The
Russians have been helpful to me."

"Oh?"

"The Communist party in America is more closely
aligned with the Russians than the Chinese whom we worked
with before. The Russians have placed me into direct contact
with a woman in America, the daughter of the leader of the
party, and I no longer must send my information through the
Chinese. Things go more smoothly and quickly now. She
travels to the campuses, arranges for the activists to lead
demonstrations at just the right times for us to gain political
impact, and has arranged contacts within the black power
movement and other revolutionary groups."

He was mildly interested. The same raised, clenched-fist
salute symbolizing Vietnamese unity under communism was
now used by American blacks as a symbol for power to the
people. Was it coincidence?

"We are also gaining influence among the Jesuit Catholics
in America. If we are successful they will be in the forefront of
the fight against the recruitment of American soldiers." She
looked directly at Xuan. "Some were reluctant to help at first
because of reports that our Lao Dong party was anti-Christian.
We are trying to convince them of our tolerance."

Li Binh was seldom subtle. Was she trying to make a
point?

"The Catholics?" He grimaced, remembering how hypo-
critically devout his father and stepmother had been. "The
Enlightened One has said we must never allow the subversion
of the people's loyalty by the *Tay* religions."

In 1955 and 1956, Vietnamese church leaders had been
executed alongside wealthy landowners and merchants, and
hundreds more had fled south to the haven offered by Catholic

president Diem's regime. Ho had called them dangerous and issued orders to treat them no differently from others who opposed them. The Catholic Church had been forced underground with the other *Tay* religions. Former priests and nuns remained, but under close scrutiny by the party, and they were prohibited from pursuing converts.

"I have received no new orders regarding the Catholics," said Xuan.

"A directive was issued that all matters concerning the church were to be handled with discretion. It was distributed by Lao Dong representatives to all military units. My nephew told me he passed the word to all your battalions."

Xuan could not remember. The mandatory briefings were usually exhortations to excel and defeat the evil Americans and the slothful southerners. Xuan considered them useful for his men but a waste of his own time.

Li Binh continued. "The new directive demands that actions against Catholics must be approved by the party."

Xuan Nha became cautious as he remembered Bac Can, the mayor's wife. He had not mentioned the episode to Li Binh.

"If you ever have cause to discipline Catholics, I suggest you be discreet."

Xuan carefully removed the eyeglasses and lit a cigarette. He stared at her over the ember and spoke quietly. "Where are you leading with this conversation, Li Binh?"

"Learn to exercise caution, my husband. The lines of combat are not always drawn as clearly as you might believe."

He exhaled smoke through his nose, thinking. "What have you heard?"

"A committee report from an economic development group visiting Bac Can mentioned certain actions you took there two weeks ago."

"Was the report critical of me?"

She looked thoughtful. "More cautious than that. They were upset that your men took over their living quarters, and one statement mentioned mistreatment of women. There is also an investigation report which I have asked to be destroyed."

Xuan shrugged. "When we find treacherous civilians, it is within my authority to take action as necessary."

"Oh, there was no criticism of the actions against the assistant or his wife. It was the degradation of the mayor's wife and her aunt because of their Catholic religion. If they had been accused of being spies or traitors, it might have been different."

Xuan felt a flush of embarrassment. He wondered fleetingly if she knew of other times and other women he had disciplined.

"A letter was prepared by the wife's aunt and sent by messenger to a Catholic priest at Lang Son, where the mayor's wife and her aunt were from, saying she and the Christian wife had been raped and the wife disfigured because of their religion."

"Ridiculous." He felt anger that the old aunt had acted so brazenly in the face of his authority.

"Perhaps, but if such a letter found its way to the wrong hands, it could harm our efforts. I can assure you, husband, if that were to happen, the party would destroy your career. Perhaps worse. Neither of us could keep them from taking action. Your military achievements would be meaningless. Even General Luc would demand your head."

Xuan was shaken. "Politics are often forgotten in the field," he said lamely. He looked at her, feeling shame at having to ask. "What course should I take, Li Binh?"

She flashed her look of triumph. Li Binh enjoyed parading her power. "I passed information regarding the letter to my nephew, and he has discreetly handled the matter."

Xuan raised an eyebrow. "Wu?" He was instantly suspicious.

"Now there is no letter, and no messenger. The mayor's wife and her aunt have disappeared while on their way home to Lang Son.

"Then it is over?" He felt relief.

"Their bodies will be discovered in the rubble of the Ha Ghia fuel-storage depot where the Americans bombed. I will advise the French news services that the Americans bombed pregnant women and church workers, and even show them pictures and give them names."

Relief flooded through him.

"You should think of a way to show your pleasure at my nephew's discretion. While he asks for nothing, certainly such devotion should be rewarded."

Xuan rubbed his jaw, confused at the turn of events yet

pleased that things had turned out so well. He wondered how
they could possibly have found out about the aunt's letter, yet
knew that the party had its ways. He was lucky to have Li Binh
at his side, and, begrudgingly, he felt indebted to Wu.

"I'll think of something for him," he muttered.

"I'm sure you will," she said in her confident tone.

The next morning at seven o'clock, Xuan Nha arrived at
the Bach Mai Hospital room. Major Wu and a sour-
expressioned sergeant were already there, sitting quietly and
staring at the American pilot. Other patients in the room, all
intelligence officers planted by Wu, had been removed.

Xuan first glanced at the men, then turned his attention to
the pilot. "I will talk to the prisoner," he said.

Wu stood. "Alone, comrade Colonel?"

"Yes. For a while, at least."

"The sergeant is from Hoa Lo prison and he speaks
English."

Xuan gave him a fleeting smile. "I need no interpreter. I
studied English in Paris. I was not happy with my progress
until I was able to talk an American student into coming to my
apartment. For weeks I spoke her language, but then I learned
that Americans speak very poor English and that my grade had
suffered." He laughed at the memory. "The *Tay* sow was
insatiable and my reward was poor, but I learned to speak
English like an American."

Although Xuan had told the story many times before, Wu
laughed.

"I've handled several interrogations of American pilots,"
said Xuan, "but I have particularly looked forward to this one.
Have you talked with him?"

"We waited for your guidance."

Xuan nodded. "Good. The information I asked for?"

The sergeant hurried over and gave him a folder, trying to
grin ingratiatingly but only succeeding in looking more dour.
"I hope you find it complete, comrade Colonel," he mumbled.
"We gained the information from the other prisoners after
much work. Some were reluctant to—"

Xuan held up a hand to silence him. "Return in an hour."

They left. Xuan walked to the bedside, noting that the
pilot's eyes appeared alert.

Xuan glanced at the closed door, then carefully pulled on

his eyeglasses. The reading glasses represented physical weakness, and he was careful not to use them around his men.

For another moment he read from the sheet, then spoke in English, slowly, because he wished to be clearly understood. "Your name is Glenn Parnell Phillips. Your rank is major. Your serial number is FR67115. I already know those things, so please don't insult me by repeating them."

There was no response, only a narrowing of the eyes.

Xuan cocked his head, looked at the man, then leafed through and read from another sheet. "You are from a place called Florida, and your parents still live there. You are thirty-one years old. You are not married. You were stationed in Germany, at . . . I cannot pronounce it. While you were there you sat in an airplane loaded with an atomic bomb, and your target was in the Democratic Republic of Germany. Would you have dropped the bomb if your superiors told you to, Glenn Parnell Phillips?"

There was no answer. Xuan had anticipated none at this stage.

"You were stationed in America at a base called Nellis. There you flew on an acrobatic team. Next you attended a school for pilots. What did they teach you?" Xuan looked up from the sheet of paper and waited for a reply.

The pilot's jaw quivered, as if he found speech difficult. "My name is Phillips, Glenn Parnell. My rank is major. My serial number is FR67115."

"That was not my question, Major."

Phillips was surprisingly brusque. "That's my answer, Colonel."

"Ahh, so you can speak. I'm surprised you can tell my rank. Most Americans cannot."

The pilot was quiet.

"You fly Thunder planes."

Silence.

"Two-seat Thunder planes. Your mission is to fire missiles at our artillery and rocket site radars. There is a pilot in the front seat to fly the airplane and a pilot in the backseat to fire the missiles. Which one are you, Major?"

Silence.

"Those men who just left? The major and the sergeant? They want to talk with you, but I told them first I wanted one hour alone with you. When they return they will not be gentle.

If you refuse to talk to me I will order them to remove the bandages and to break your leg again, and they will do it."

A look of fear crossed the pilot's face, and he was unable to compose himself. "Please?" He gasped. "No."

"Talk to me, Major."

The pilot closed his eyes and sucked in a breath. "My name is Phillips, Glenn Parnell. My rank is—"

"I know all that!" hissed Xuan.

The pilot was quiet.

"Would you have dropped your atomic bomb on innocent civilians in Germany?"

Silence.

"Open your eyes, Major."

The pilot's eyes flickered open.

"If you do not answer my questions, my men will break the leg again. I also promise they will keep you alive for a long time, and that you will suffer even worse than before."

The pilot swallowed, tears brimming in his eyes. Was he ready to talk?

"For the last time, would you have dropped your bomb?"

The pilot hesitated, likely thinking how harmless the question actually was. He nodded then, and a tear trickled down the side of his face.

Xuan relaxed. This one was easy. The mutilated leg had, after all, been fortuitous.

"What did you learn in the school in Nevada?"

Another hesitation.

Xuan snapped the folder closed. "I am not a patient man. I am going to walk out, and later you will pray for me to return so you can answer my questions." He turned as if to leave.

The pilot caught his breath. "Please," he pleaded.

Xuan stopped. "I already know the answers to my questions, Major. They were given by other prisoners. Don't you think it is ridiculous to be quiet now, when you will beg to talk to me later?"

Silence.

"This is your final opportunity. What did you learn at the school?"

The pilot's throat was dry, his voice weak and defeated. "Air-to-ground gunnery."

"It says here that you learned radar bombing, dive-bombing, skip bombing, and loft bombing."

"Yes."

"Was that all?"

The pilot hesitated before giving his response. "I also learned air combat tactics. And about the M-61 cannon. How to strafe targets at both low and high angles."

"Did you fly in the front or the back of your Thunder plane?"

After a pause, "The front seat."

Now to verify that the pilot was telling the truth. "What was the name of your female friend when you were in Germany?"

Hesitation. "Which time? I was there twice."

Good. "The second time."

"Her name was Nicole."

"A German girl?"

"French. She was from Lyons."

The information checked with the sheet. Xuan was pleased.

"What is the missile that you shoot at our radars?"

A sigh. "It's called an AGM-45A Shrike."

"How far away can you fire this . . . Shrike . . . and hit a target?"

"Twenty miles? I'm not sure."

Xuan exhaled sharply. "I'm out of patience."

"Please," the prisoner whined. "The other pilot fires the missiles. I just go where he says."

"What is the name of the backseat pilot you fly with?"

Hesitation. "I fly with different pilots. We're not trusted to fly together with the same one all the time."

That made sense, although the sheet said it was a man named Malcolm Stewart. "What was the pilot's name you were flying with when you were shot down?"

"A guy named Malcolm."

That was correct enough. "How does he fire this Shrike missile?"

"I don't know, I don't like the damn things. They don't work half the time, and when they do they don't hit much of anything. Sometimes they just explode right there on the airplane's pylon. I lost a good friend like that once, but when I asked my superiors about it they told me to be quiet and I was afraid to ask more."

"Your superior officers are cruel?"

"Yes."

"What are the names?"

"General Roman is the worst. I think most of the men who work for him are homosexuals or fly bombers or something."

"What about your backseat pilots? How are they trained?"

"They don't tell me things like that. I don't like the backseat pilots anyway. They act so damn superior, but they don't know what they're doing. I think they may get some sort of training, but it can't be much."

Xuan smiled at his triumph. This prisoner would tell him anything he wanted to know. The pilot continued to babble about the stupidity of the backseaters until Xuan stopped him.

"Tell me more about the Shrike missiles."

The pilot sighed. "I'm only a major, but I heard they've discovered sabotage from one of the factories. An electronic module in one of the missiles they received was fouled with chocolate. They think it was from a factory near a place called Hershey, Pennsylvania."

Again Xuan stopped him, but he made a mental note to tell Li Binh about the possibility of sabotage at a munitions plant in Pennsylvania.

"How do you know where to fly so your missiles will hit the radars?"

"Other pilots see the guns or missiles and radio the backseat pilot, and he tells me to go there."

"How does the Shrike missile find the radars?"

"I don't know. Maybe it goes after the heat from the radar. They don't tell me things like that. They don't trust majors. They have to force us to fly, you know?"

Xuan leaned forward. "What do you mean?"

"All night long they encourage us to drink whiskey and sing patriotic songs, and when we're very drunk they tell us to fly. Some of us don't want to, even when we're drunk, so they threaten our families."

These insights were new to Xuan Nha. He continued his questions with mounting glee, periodically interjecting a question to check the pilot's veracity. He asked how many pilots and aircraft the Americans could call upon, and was told the numbers were endless. He asked about American politicians and was told they were corrupt and power-hungry. He asked if the two-man Thunder planes could actually locate the rocket sites, and was told they would never be able to find them. He asked about American women and was told they were silly and promiscuous. He asked about B-52's, and was told they could carry hundreds of bombs and would be virtually impossible to shoot down. He asked about the negroes in America and was told they were all lazy and lay around eating watermelon. He asked how atomic bombs were made and was told that aside from having something radioactive in them, he only knew they were dangerous.

From the responses and his own knowledge about Americans, Xuan Nha knew the pilot had told the truth. He asked the questions again and was told the same answers. As the end of the hour drew near, he carefully pulled off his eyeglasses and wiped them before replacing them in his pocket. He was satisfied that his rocket sites were much safer than he had dared believe from the bungling two-man crews flying the radar-hunter Thunder planes.

When Wu and the sergeant reentered the room, a fearful look came over the prisoner's face. Xuan studied him one last time and again concluded that he'd told the truth.

Wu was smiling solicitously. "Another success, comrade Colonel?"

"Did you doubt me?"

"Of course not, sir."

"He would have sold his mother. He is a poor and very unpatriotic soldier."

Wu laughed. "Should we question him further now, or wait until we get him back to the prison?"

Xuan contemplated what should be done with the prisoner. He considered the pilot his private trove of information and felt that others might dry up his well through mishandling.

"No more questions for now," he finally said. "Let him heal for a while here, and when he is stronger, return him to the prison and put him with new pilots we shoot down."

The sergeant said it was their policy to keep the prisoners isolated.

"If I decide to interrogate him again, I want him to be aware of what is happening."

"Of course, comrade Colonel," said Major Wu with a glare at the sergeant, as if Xuan's statement was the most intelligent thing he had ever heard.

Xuan turned a withering stare upon the sergeant. "Watch over him and do not let him die."

The sergeant groveled and swore to follow the colonel's instructions.

"When I'm finally done with him, you can do as you wish. I feel unclean in his presence. He is a coward, a traitor to his country, but his information is valuable."

As he left he failed to notice the pilot's flicker of a smile, or know that he was trying hard not to laugh about chocolate missiles.

20/2305L—Mu Gia Pass, Laos

Bear Stewart

It had been a busy few days for Benny and the Bear. They had flown two more missions to the lower route packs, and now the two-ship night mission in support of a B-52 mission to the Laotian side of Mu Gia Pass, which straddled the North Vietnamese border. Mu Gia was a favorite bombing area for headquarters planners for it was a narrow valley through which the meandering Ho Chi Minh trail was funneled.

Benny and the Bear never saw the bombers. The B-52's flew their "Arc Light" missions at much higher altitudes. The F-105 Weasels were escorts, tasked to attack any SAM threats that might appear. SAM sites had never deployed into the areas the B-52's bombed, but the Americans couldn't take the chance of losing one of the big, expensive bombers.

When the bombs began to explode in the distance they watched in awe.

"My God," exclaimed Benny. "I've never seen so many bombs going off."

They watched as one long string of bombs after another flashed and danced brightly in the eerie darkness of the distant valley. Each bomber released more explosives than an entire flight of F-105's. The Bear wondered aloud why the hell the big bombers weren't being used up north in pack six.

"I don't think they believe the BUFs could survive there," answered Benny.

"Maybe," said the Bear, "but it would sure as hell give the gomers something to think about. The B-52 radar navigators are damned accurate. One string of those bombs would take out any of the targets we pound on for days. I flew in 'em, but I never actually saw what they could do from a ringside seat like this."

He looked at his scopes. "No threats, Benny. I think they've taken the night off."

"No threats," Benny radioed on a blind frequency, then turned back toward North Vietnam, fifteen miles distant. He returned to their conversation on the intercom. "You were an EWO in a BUF. You think they could survive in pack six?"

"They'd have to change some things. Their war plan is to fly up there in three-ship cells. Ten cells of bombers one behind the other across North Vietnam. They'd drop their bombs, then make a nice right-hand turn and leave."

"Sounds crazy."

"Amen. If they ever bomb up in pack six they'd better either change their plan or prepare to lose a lot of aluminum and men. The crews know that, but they're being led by generals who flew in World War Two and never saw a SAM."

Benny returned to business. "Any threats?"

The Bear surveyed his scopes again. "Not a peep. I've got a long-range radar, but it's not generating enough power to be a Barlock like the one I saw when I was running around on the ground. I guess Sam and his flight destroyed it."

"Can you tell where the signal's coming from?"

"It's probably the old Token radar they've got up at Phuc Yen."

They were quiet for a while as the Bear observed the multiple signals of the distant radar rise and fall on his analysis scope.

"You hear from Liz?" he asked.

"Once. Just a nice letter saying she enjoyed her time in Manila."

"I got one from Julie. She's a hoot. Wants me to stop my fuckin' cussing."

Benny laughed. "Watch your ass. I think she could be a determined girl."

"Yeah? That's what she says, too. She wants us to meet them in Bangkok." The Bear became uncharacteristically quiet. "No threats," he finally announced.

21/1900—354th TFS Pilots' Lounge, Takhli RTAFB

Maj. Les Ries watched the last men enter the pilots' lounge. The group included the Wild Weasel crews from all three squadrons of the wing. Les nodded for Dan Janssen to shut the door, then told everyone to get a beer and take a seat.

"This will take a while," he said when they'd all settled, "so let's get started. Everyone here?"

Andy Schumacher and Larry Stark were there from the 333rd, as well as the two new crews in their flight. Ries looked out at his own squadron-mates: Shaky Anderson, Fred Norman, and another new crew. "My guys in the 354th are here."

"I've got them," said Janssen, who was taking notes for the meeting.

Benny gave a wave of his hand. He was the 357th WW-flight commander, with Pudge Holden and Lyle Watson, Dave Persons and Dutch Hansletter in his flight.

"The 357th is here," said Janssen, writing the names.

"Let's get started," said Ries.

The Bear sat beside Benny, sipping a Coors and examining Ries from behind his sunglasses. Ries reminded him of a strutting tom turkey. Arms crossed on his chest, moving around in front of them with a grand air of importance. Benny had told him to cool his open criticisms. Regardless of how hard the Bear tried, it was difficult to like Ries.

Ries went over and took two documents from Janssen, then waved one at the group.

"This is an intelligence estimate from Seventh Air Force. It's very sensitive, because of the sources they used to get the information. What it says is that the numbers of MiG's and SAMs are being effectively doubled at this time. More than fifty new MiG's either have been or are in the process of being flown from Russia into Chinese bases, and are being prepared for deployment to North Vietnam."

A couple of the Weasel pilots grinned. "Good. More targets," they muttered.

"Also, two or three SAM batteries are arriving every week at Haiphong and are being transported to Hanoi. There they are married up with new crews and trucked off to the countryside. That means that an entire new battalion is being added to the SAM network every week."

"Jesus," the Bear muttered. It was worse than he'd believed.

Ries held up a message. "This is a Seventh Air Force message, asking our opinions about how to best mount an offensive against the air defense system. The discussion we're about to have is classified at least Secret, maybe even Top Secret, so I don't want any talk in unsecured areas."

The Bear's mind churned. He'd been an advocate of a balls-out offensive against the air defenses since his first week of combat. Now they were being forced to come up with something, or face sure disaster. "Shit hot," he growled.

Ries agreed. "I think that's the consensus of all of us older heads. We've been wanting something like this. It's just too bad we've had to wait this long. Now it's going to be doubly hard to try to take on this number of defenses, but at least headquarters agrees that something has to be done."

He read from the message: *"Recipients will consider coordinated attacks on both air-to-air and surface-to-air defenses."*

"Sounds ambitious," said Andy Schumacher.

Andy, noted the Bear, *is getting cautious.*

Ries continued. "The message asks for representatives from each F-105 and F-4 base to meet for three days at Seventh Air Force Headquarters in Saigon and present their plans. Colonel Parker, Dan, and I will be the representatives from Takhli. The wing commander at Korat will bring along his Weasel reps, and there'll be some guys from the F-4 wings at Danang and Ubon. We'll talk about the best way to take out SAMs and MiG's, and present our ideas to General Moss, commander of Seventh Air Force."

The Bear swigged his beer, grinning about the possibility of slugging it out with the defenses instead of being encumbered with having to protect a strike force.

"What are you going to suggest, Les?" he asked.

Ries glared his way, and he could tell from the look that he had not been forgiven.

The Bear ignored the look, for the matter was too important to him. "I've put a lot of thought into how we could do something like this."

Ries's voice was icy. "We all have. You'll get your turn.

Now, let's start with the 333rd. How about you, Andy? You've been here since creation itself."

The Bear bit his tongue. He and Phillips had arrived at the same time as Schumacher. As Andy Schumacher began expressing his cautious views, doubts began to niggle about Ries's ability to put together a good plan.

After several had spoken and the meeting had made little progress, the Bear stood up during a period of silence.

"I think we should start by spending a week with the best recce photos we can get. No strikes that week, just lots of recce missions, with the recce birds protected by F-4's and Weasel Thuds. We study every search, command-and-control, and acquisition radar up there, and target every one of the bastards."

Ries looked on in exasperation, but the Bear continued. "Then we start phase one. We send in a bunch of F-4's, maybe seven or eight flights of them, flying the same speeds and medium altitudes as the Thuds normally do. The gomers launch their MiG's, thinking we only got a bunch of bomb-heavy Thuds, and our F-4's wipe them out. Right on their heels, while the F-4's are still shooting MiG's, we send in our guys. By then the gomers will have their command-and-control and acquisition radars on so they can fight the F-4's. A Weasel leading each flight of Thuds, using all the Weasel and strike birds we've got here and at Korat, and we bomb the shit out of those radars."

"Which ones?" asked Cinnamon Bear Stark.

"The acquisition and search radars we targeted the week before."

"What about the SAM sites?"

"We ignore them. They come on the air, we pop a Shrike missile their way, but we just concentrate on the long and medium-range radars. We put out their eyes."

"Okay," said Ries. "You've had your turn. Next idea?"

"I'm not done," said the Bear. "When their eyes are out, we attack their SAM sites with every jet in Asia that can carry a bomb. With the command-and-control radars gone, we could even use B-52's, but if the generals don't like that, we do it with Thuds and Phantoms. Bomb nothing but defenses for a couple weeks and get it over with. Every time a SAM comes on the air, have three or four Weasels and bombers ready to pounce on his ass."

Andy Schumacher spoke up in a dubious tone. "We could lose *our* asses, too."

"We're already doing a good job of that, Andy. What I'm talking about is putting the bastards off the air so permanently you could fly across North Vietnam in a Piper Cub."

Ries was glaring. "We've got other people in the room, Captain Stewart, and some of us have studied tactics for more than the few months you've been in fighters." He glanced around the room, and his eye lit on Pudge Holden, who had been holding his peace.

"Pudge, you taught tactics at Nellis. You have any ideas?"

Pudge shrugged and slowly rose. "I heard Andy say we ought to launch more Shrikes, and Shaky say that we ought to use terrain-masking better, and I heard you say something about rolling back the threat, right?"

Ries nodded for him to continue.

"I heard someone say we ought to use a low-level ingress now and then, and someone else say we ought to try lofting bombs. None of those things make up a campaign. They're just tactics. Maybe they're good tactics, but I'll bet they've all been tried already, and you haven't eliminated the air defense system with them. Now the defenses are about to get a lot worse, right?"

"So what's your point?"

"My point is, when Bear Stewart stands up and makes a pitch for the only real campaign we've heard about here, let's listen. Then maybe we can criticize and change it to make it better, but he's making sense, so let's start by listening."

Ries looked angry. "I've got to listen to everyone. Stewart's not the only one with ideas."

"You asked, so I told you what I thought." Holden sat back down.

Ries folded his arms again and looked at the group. "I've worked out an approach to solving the problem with my bear. It's called a "roll-back" campaign. Instead of one Weasel flight on every mission, we use two flights. One flight protects the strike force, just like now, and the other Weasel flight bombs or shoots missiles at the outermost SAM site, then the next one and the next one, until we've pushed the bastards back to the sea."

"What about the acquisition radars the Bear was talking about?" asked Lyle Watson.

"Too hard. We'd never find the search or acquisition radars. Hell, we have trouble locating the SAM sites, and they're big."

"How about his idea to have an all-out, dedicated campaign?" asked Watson.

Ries shook his head, irritated. "That would take coordination between recce, the other fighter wings, and maybe even the B-52's. They'd never buy it at headquarters."

"Sure to hell won't if you don't try," muttered the Bear.

Les went on. "We'll be preparing our position paper during the next few days. Any of you want to look it over and comment or play devil's advocate, see either Dan or me. Now, let's go around the room one more time."

The Bear had heard about Ries's and Janssen's roll-back campaign idea before, and had always thought it was a dumb one. He started to stand, but Benny put his hand on his arm and pulled him back down.

"Forget it for now, Bear," he said. "You're just pissing uphill, and you oughta know by now where the pee's going to land."

When the meeting broke up, the Bear left with Benny, Pudge Holden, and Lyle Watson.

"The dumb shit," muttered the Bear. They all knew who he was talking about.

"I disagree," said Benny. "Ries's and Janssen's roll-back idea isn't all that bad, and by the time all the staff pukes and the brass and the guys from the other bases put in their two cents in Saigon, nothing's going to be recognizable anyway."

The Bear tried to cheer himself. "At least the brass are starting to understand we've got a problem with the defenses."

CHAPTER TWELVE

**Thursday, 22 December, 1966—1700 Local, 357th TFS
Pilots' Lounge, Takhli RTAFB, Thailand**

Tiny Bechler

Tiny arrived at the pilots' lounge ten minutes before the
squadron meeting called by Colonel Mack was scheduled to
begin. He was enjoying a cool beer with Mike Murphy and
Bear Stewart when Sam Hall and Chickenplucker Crawford
walked in and joined them.

"What are you chickenpluckers talking about?" asked
Crawford.

"The Bear says he and Benny are going on R and R to
Bangkok with a couple stews they met in Manila," replied
Murphy.

"Hell," joked Crawford, "they just got back from their
last boondoggle."

"When you guys going, Bear?" asked Sam.

"We'd like to take off a few days over New Year's," the
Bear said.

"I'll make a note of it," said Sam. As acting operations
officer until a replacement for Johnny T. Polaski was assigned,
Sam approved R and R requests.

They watched as other pilots came in and gathered into
cliques. Swede Swendler joined them. "What's the meeting
about, Sam?" he asked.

Sam shrugged. "This one's Colonel Mack's show."

"Any word about when they'll name a replacement for
Colonel Polaski?"

"Not that I know about," replied Sam.

"It's probably someone from one of the headquarters,"

316

growled Chickenplucker Crawford. "Some toad the generals want to get promoted."

"You're the one who deserves it, Sam," said Swede, and the others agreed.

"I'm happy with the A-Flight commander's job."

Benny Lewis came over with a captain in tow. "Sam, like you to meet Dave Persons, one of our new Weasel pilots. Dave, this is Sam Hall, our ops officer, Pete Crawford, C-Flight commander, and Captain Swede Swendler here has D-Flight. You've met the others."

"I'm just acting ops officer," Sam corrected as they all shook Dave Persons's hand.

"I've been telling Sam he deserves the job, permanent," said Swede.

A handsome lieutenant named Willy Dortmeier joined them and Chickenplucker introduced him as a new member of his C-Flight. Dortmeier had arrived the day before from Bitburg Air Base in Germany and was still groggy from the time change. Tiny knew him from the Air Force Academy. His father had been an ace in the Pacific in World War Two, and Willy was motivated by family tradition. Maj Gen Bill Dortmeier had retired the year before, but Willy had inherited his steady hand and keen eye.

Colonel Mack came in, and Chickenplucker bellowed, "ROOM TEN-HUT!"

"As you were," Mack said, and went to the refrigerator.

"What's the meeting about, boss?" called Swede.

Colonel Mack pulled out a bottle of beer and opened it. "Drinking beer and flying fighters. Isn't that enough?"

Mack leaned against a table, tilted his head, and took a long swig, then casually regarded the group. "Might as well get started. I suppose everyone's here that's going to be." He looked about the room. "Lots of new faces. Flight commanders, go ahead and introduce your new people."

The flight commanders called out the names and each new pilot raised his hand so the others could make their catcalls. When they were finished, Mack welcomed them to the 357th.

"We're here to win another war," he said, "but you guys know that. You're all adults, and I'll treat you like that. We'll try to get you a few indoctrination missions in the lower packs before we send you up to pack six, but there's no guarantees. Each one of you will have the pleasure of flying on my wing on one of your first missions to pack six. That doesn't mean I'm the best—"

"He's the best," said Crawford in a loud voice, "and don't you chickenpluckers forget it!"

Mack waited for the hooting to subside. "Like I say, I may not be the best, but I generally know how to get there and back and maybe I can show you a couple of things."

The consensus of the muttering between the old heads and the newcomers was that the boss would show them the no-shit way it should be done.

Mack read from notes. "Maintenance is asking that we write things up better when we land. They're complaining we're in too much of a hurry to get through the debriefing. Slow down and write properly so they can troubleshoot the problems and fix the birds. They're also asking that you not give the debriefers a hard time. You got a problem with maintenance, take it up with Lieutenant Shilling or Chief Roberts and let them straighten it out."

A discussion arose about maintenance having too many CNDs. "I've had a radio problem three flights in a row," said Ken Maisey, "and the answer's always the same: 'could not duplicate.' I'm getting tired of it."

Tiny heard Bear Stewart mutter something about Maisey's family lineage.

"Like I said," repeated Mack. "Take it up with Lieutenant Shilling or Chief Roberts."

Maisey continued with his complaint. "I told Chief Roberts and he said that no one else can find the problem, like I'd made it up or something."

The Bear snorted loud enough for everyone to hear.

Lieutenant Shilling, the overworked and harried maintenance officer, raised a weary voice. "I'll look into it, sir."

"I hope so," griped Maisey.

Mack moved to the next subject. "The air cops are raising hell about one of our finest, who has now reaped four tickets for parking violations and two for speeding. This same individual has also been singled out by the motor pool for damage to our squadron van."

Tiny tried to act nonchalant, but the old heads knew who Mack was talking about, and they turned malicious grins on him.

"Thirty-five miles per hour on base, ten miles per hour on

the flight line, and don't park in the colonels' designated spots even if you know they aren't around. The base commander says that no more tickets will be tolerated from this squadron." Colonel Mack paused. "To fix the problem, I've assigned Lieutenant Bechler as squadron vehicle control officer. I'm sure things will improve under his astute guidance."

They all hooted at Tiny, who glared about sheepishly.

Mack took a drink of beer and waited until the laughter stopped. "Now let's talk about jobs."

The room grew quieter.

"We've got so many actors, we could put on a play. We've got an acting ops officer and two acting flight commanders. I just came from wing headquarters and it's official," he said, then paused for a long moment, looking about.

He grinned. "Sam Hall is your new ops officer, and I expect everyone to give him the best support possible."

Cheers.

"Does that mean we can't call Sam an asshole anymore?" called Chickenplucker Crawford.

"Not any more," yelled Swede Swendler. "Now he's *asshole, sir!*" The pilots roared.

Mack then announced that Bud Lutz and C. R. Clark would take A and B flights, Crawford and Swendler would keep C and D flights. Benny was confirmed as WW-flight commander.

After the meeting closed, they stayed in the squadron lounge to celebrate and shoot the bull. Tiny watched and waited for his turn to congratulate Sam. He felt good about the movements in the squadron until he started to think about the losses that had made the changes necessary.

Bear Stewart

The Bear talked with Mike Murphy again about the upcoming R and R.

"You guys will have a good time," said Mike. "Bangkok's a good R and R town. Mike grinned. "But watch your ass. You've been talking a lot about this Julie."

"She's a nice girl, Mike."

"That's the scary kind, babes. First thing you know you'll be getting serious."

The Bear grinned. "I've got a built-in fear of serious

relationships. Acts like a warning receiver and tells me when to back off and run."

Mike looked out at the room. "Most of these guys are married. You ever think maybe they've got something we don't?"

"Yeah. Every time I think about what happened to Benny when he called home and found his old lady in the sack with a guy, I think about how lucky I am."

Mike Murphy turned to the Bear. "What's she like, this girl of yours?"

"She's not my girl."

"What's she like?"

The Bear thought. "Nice kid. She's got her act together. Bazooms so big you wouldn't believe. She's sexy and pretty."

"Good in bed?"

The Bear paused. "I don't know."

"You haven't taken her to bed and you're meeting her a second time?"

The Bear didn't answer. He was having a hard enough time trying to think things through for himself.

The redhead looked at him very seriously. "Sounds like you need some advice on how to handle her. You haven't been around a nice girl in a while, and you shouldn't treat her like you would some round-heel. You gotta treat her special."

The Bear waited, suspicious.

"First, get a real nice hotel room. Fancy. That'll put her in a nice frame of mind."

Mike was trying to help after all. "Yeah?"

"Then get some bath beads, you know, the kind they have in Europe that will leave her skin nice, and make sure you have some nice bath oils and cologne water."

"Uh-huh."

"Then have her take a nice, slow bath and get herself all relaxed and oiled and perfumed . . ." He paused.

"Go on," said the Bear.

"Then open the door and let me in, because she sounds too good for you."

"Asshole."

24/0655L—Vinh, Route Pack Two, North Vietnam

Benny Lewis

The Bear said the commander in charge of defenses at Vinh was good. In fact, the Bear said, he was likely the best of them all.

The city of Vinh was located at the mouth of the Ca River, 150 miles south of Hanoi, which meant the gomer commander was isolated from the mutual protection offered by the redundancy of SAM, MiG, and AAA defenses in the Red River valley. He also had to make do with far fewer assets, because they kept the most and the best to defend Hanoi and Haiphong. But the Bear said the guy improvised and did his job all too damned well.

He said the Vinh commander normally had only one SAM site to work with, sometimes two, and only had two Firecan radars to aim his antiaircraft guns with. But by the use of patience and good tactics he was able to keep the Weasels from finding his radars and he still bagged more than his quota of airplanes.

As they flew just south of Vinh, with only a single, distant Firecan radar monitoring them, the Bear explained more about his begrudging admiration for the unseen commander.

"When the war's over," he told Benny on the intercom, "I want to come here and shake the bastard's hand. He's that good. The MiG's are too chickenshit to come down here to protect him, he doesn't have a bunch of other SAM sites around to help take the heat off, and he can't leave his radars on the air for long or the Weasels would have his ass."

Benny grunted as they made a sharp turn. Tiny Bechler was on the right, and Pudge Holden led the second element on the port side.

"He's the only gomer commander who's really got us figured out," the Bear said. "Somehow I think he's found a way to tell the Weasels from the strike aircraft, because he never attacks when we're around. It's only when we get low on gas and start for home, or if there are no Weasels fragged on the mission, that he shoots."

"Interesting."

"Then he waits for one of our guys to screw up, like letting his airspeed bleed down too low. He turns on every radar he's got, starts shooting artillery like hell, every gun he's got, and gets our guys stirred up, climbing to get out of the flak and bleeding off even more airspeed. A second later he fires SAMs and gets his kill. He doesn't waste missiles because he doesn't often miss. If all of them were as good as him, it would be bad news. You'll see what I mean."

They were protecting a small strike force that was fragged into the area to bomb the Vinh ferry, which was very difficult to find.

"Where's that gun?" asked Benny, talking about the Firecan radar.

"Three or four miles north of Vinh, at your ten o'clock. Try turning toward him, and I'll show you what I'm talking about."

Benny called the flight. *"Red Dog flight, we'll be maneuvering."*

He went into a sharp bank and turn to the left, pulling enough g's that the Bear groaned on the intercom. Benny dropped wings level, heading toward the steady strobe on his attack scope.

"The guy's good. Watch."

Benny selected a Shrike station and began to center his needles. "He's still on the air," he said, thinking that this time the Bear was wrong.

"Try firing a missile at him," said the Bear.

Benny lined up precisely with the Firecan, using his needles, and dipped the nose of his aircraft until the needles were centered, to check how low the target was on the horizon. He referred to a card clipped to his kneeboard. If you knew the dip angle and your altitude, you could determine the distance. "He's in range," he said, pulling the nose of the aircraft up to toss the missile at the radar.

The Shrike missile was ten feet long and eight inches in diameter. If launched at the correct airspeed, distance, and loft angle, it would be tossed into the radar's beam and steer itself into the antenna, where the forty-five pound fragmentation warhead would detonate.

"You're lined up okay," said the Bear.

Benny depressed the red trigger button on the stick. The Shrike missile whooshed off its pylon, streaking upward in a

long arc. Twenty seconds to impact, he guessed. A second later
the strobe disappeared from his attack scope.

"Where'd it go?" asked Benny.

"He shut down his radar."

"Damn," said Benny, thinking about the wasted missile.
With no radar beam to home in on, the Shrike would likely end
up making a mess of some confused farmer's rice paddy.

"He's not as cool as he usually is. Normally he'll let the
missile fly out for a few more seconds before shutting down,"
said the Bear.

A flight of strike aircraft led by Chickenplucker Crawford
called out intense barrage fire from guns near the mouth of the
river. It was obvious that they had not located the ferry, and
that the gunfire made it difficult to get in closer for a better
look.

Another Firecan radar came on the air, this time from their
five o'clock.

"It's from over near the beach," said the Bear.

When Benny started a hard turn to his right to line up on
the second AAA radar, that one went off the air and the first
Firecan came back on.

"Shit!" he exclaimed.

"I told you he was good."

Benny turned east, then shook the control stick. "Fly the
airplane," he said, pawing around in his canvas bag, "while I
look at my map."

"I've got it," said the Bear, taking the controls.

Before taking off, Benny had looked at a photo of what
could possibly be a camouflaged, mobile SAM site set up in a
crook of the Ca River fifteen miles west of Vinh. The photo
interpreters at Udorn had not been sure, but had annotated and
illegally bootlegged a glossy print to Takhli for their possible
interest at the same time they'd forwarded the film to Saigon.
Lieutenant DeWalt had hurried over with the photo before the
mission briefing and had shown it to the Bear, who'd growled
and told him to suck wind with his old photos. Ignoring the
Bear's grumbling, Benny had studied the photo and copied the
coordinates onto his map.

He stared longer at the map, glancing out at patchy
clouds. "Let's take a look at that crook in the river."

"Waste of gas, Benny. If anything was there, it's moved.

The guy's just too good to let one of his sites get caught like that."

Benny shook the stick and took back control. "DeWalt said this one was photographed yesterday."

The Bear was quiet for a moment before grudgingly giving DeWalt a compliment. "Well that's the least incompetent he's ever been."

They flew up the Ca for another minute before Benny called out the bend in the river. "We got any signals on the air?"

"Just the one gun north of Vinh. If there's a SAM site over here, he's got his radar shut down."

Benny flew down to 4,000 feet and started a run toward the bend in the river.

As they passed, the Bear whooped. "Trucks!"

"Yeah."

"Red Dog lead, I saw a bunch of trucks down there next to the bend in the river," radioed Pudge Holden.

Benny pulled the aircraft up and around to his right. *"Roger, Red Dog three. I counted ten or more trucks and that's where the SAM site was supposed to be."*

"Trucks, big cannisters, and a couple vans down there," said the Bear on intercom. "He's loaded up and getting ready to move."

Benny didn't hesitate. *"Red Dogs, it's a SAM site preparing to vacate the premises. Let's take 'em out, Red Dogs!"* They were carrying hard bombs rather than CBUs for the flight, since headquarters hadn't though they'd find defenses to bomb down here. Benny wished they had the CBUs.

He led the flight up and around, to attack from the east so the morning sun would be in the gomer gunners' eyes. The others dropped into trail, one behind the other, like ducklings.

"Red Dog lead, I didn't notice any shooting as we went by," called Pudge Holden.

"Don't believe it, three. They'll shoot," called Benny, his voice positive.

He set up a shallow, thirty-degree dive-bomb pattern to give the pilots longer to sort out the target. As they approached, the loaded trucks and vans grew more distinct. At 5,000 feet the Bear called out small-arms fire, which Benny saw from a corner of his eye. He concentrated on the largest van, which was crawling toward a group of trees. He saw

37mm bursts. Ignoring them, he pressed on straight and level to 3,500 feet before pickling the six bombs off. He felt the familiar lurch as they released, and pulled back on the stick to jink away from the target.

They both grunted, pulling g's, then Benny rolled the aircraft over so they could see the target area.

Explosions rent the ground as their eyes focused. The truck was thrown straight up into the air, and the van tumbled end over end. Another smaller van rolled several times.

"Whooo-eee!" yelled the Bear.

Tiny Bechler's bombs impacted, bursting the larger van and making the smaller one roll several times more. The Bear whooped again, and then again when Pudge Holden's and number four's bombs exploded into the pile of missile cannisters. Large, bright-orange secondary explosions erupted, followed by several fireballs. One missile escaped, blown free from its cannister, and slithered and spewed smoke as it snaked across the ground.

The 37mm and 14.5mm small-arms fire continued, but when Benny checked, no one had been scathed.

"What do you think?" he asked the Bear as they were climbing out and the others were joining up.

"I think," the Bear said, "I owe DeWalt a fucking beer. That was the cleanest, easiest SAM site kill in the history of the Weasels."

"Yeah," Benny said with deep satisfaction.

Pudge Holden radioed, excitement in his voice, *"Red Dog lead, I thought you said killing SAM sites was difficult."*

Benny laughed. *"You complaining, Red Dog three?"*

"Not a bit, lead."

The banter continued as the flight patrolled the Vinh area for another fifteen minutes before leaving for the tanker.

The Bear was quiet.

"Something wrong back there?" Benny asked.

"Not wrong, just different. We killed the bastard and I loved it, but it doesn't add up. The gomer commander here is too smart to let that happen. It's like he's left someone else in charge."

"From what you say about him, I just hope he stays on leave or R and R or wherever he is."

25/1300L—People's Army HQ, Hanoi, DRV

Nicolaj Gregarian

Gregarian sat quietly in the rear of the meeting room, observing the twenty Vietnamese officers sent to help set up Wisdom complex. These were the best. Controllers from the P-1 command-and-control radar at Phuc Yen credited with two or more aircraft kills. Key area, battalion, and rocket battery commanders who had proven themselves by shooting down large numbers of Americans. The most knowledgeable electronics and missile technicians.

Their tactics and abilities were proven, and today they would begin sharing their practical knowledge with the twenty Soviet advisers who had arrived in Hanoi the day before. Of course, the Russian *leytenants* and *kapitans* waiting in the adjacent room would be even better than the Vietnamese, for Gregarian knew that Russians were technically superior to Asians in any endeavor.

His superiors at PVO Strany Headquarters had tempted the finest and brightest young radar controllers, engagement commanders, and electronics and rocket technicians by promising preferential treatment and assignments after the six-month tours at Wisdom site. They did not really have to offer so much, for the men were enthused with the idea of engaging an enemy in mortal combat on a daily basis and teaching the Vietnamese to win against their American oppressors. They would return to Russia as combat-proven experts in their fields.

Nicolaj was overjoyed that it was finally beginning. From this two-day meeting would emerge an outline of exactly how Wisdom complex should operate, the procedures they would use, and the communications structure they would need. From the outline they would develop a detailed plan for Wisdom complex, and also the seeds of syllabi for classes and practical exercises to train future commanders. In five days they would travel to the site to share more insights and supervise, so that everything would be optimal when the equipment arrived for installation.

He looked about again at the Vietnamese in the room.

A combat controller from the Phuc Yen command-and-control radar was there, cocky, with five American aircraft kills to his credit. He would share insights with the four Soviet controllers, and together they would supervise the installation of the new P-50 radar's control center north of Bac Can.

Two lean MiG pilots sat quietly in a corner, periodically surveying the room with the steady looks that fighter pilots like to give to non-fighter pilots. Both had killed two aircraft. One had been introduced by his nickname of "Captain Doom."

The area commander from Vinh, a quiet, unassuming *podpolkovnik,* was speaking with his counterparts from Haiphong and Hanoi. Xuan Nha disliked his caution, but his record spoke for itself. Eighteen kills, eleven of them with rockets, and no losses of rocket sites or radars until yesterday when he'd been en route to this meeting. A mobile rocket battery had been bombed and destroyed while preparing to move to another site.

The commander was anxious to return to Vinh, but Gregarian was too interested in what he had to offer to permit it. He spoke of ways to identify radar-hunters by observing their distinctive tactics, and could tell when targets were most vulnerable by observing their profiles. Those were things to be shared, regardless of Xuan Nha's new information that the two-seat Thunder planes posed no real threat and his continuing desire to have his commanders attack, attack, always attack.

Two battalion commanders were there, *Mayor* Tran Van Ngo from Tiger, ambition glittering from his eyes, and a meticulous *mayor* from the permanently sited rocket battalion on the north side of Hanoi. They were, Xuan Nha had said with pride, his best.

Three rocket battery commanders attended, both young, bright *kapitans*.

There was an antiaircraft artillery *mayor* entrusted with more than 700 big guns dispersed throughout the Haiphong area, and a *kapitan* from Hanoi. Although Nicolaj considered artillery an archaic method of engaging supersonic jet fighters, their success continued to exceed that of the more modern defenses, at least in number of aircraft destroyed. Gregarian knew that ratio would change when the success rates for both MiG's and guided rockets were enhanced by the Wisdom complex.

The others in the room were bright, technically canny

communications experts, siting engineers, radar technicians, and rocket personnel.

Nicolaj liked what he saw here, but he was more concerned with the men in the other room. His military future would be imperiled if harm should come to the young officers from the Soviet air defense system. One was the son of a Soviet general, another a grandnephew of Leonid Ilich Brezhnev, first secretary of the party. Such was the importance PVO Strany had placed in the success of the Wisdom project that they had entrusted him with the future. There was no room for failure.

Mayor Nguy, Xuan's hardworking executive officer, came to the back of the room and sat beside Gregarian. Nicolaj nodded and voiced his greeting.

His grasp of the Vietnamese language had improved with the assignment of the stout British woman as his private tutor. He smiled, remembering the previous evening's lesson, then hastily returned his thoughts to the room and matters at hand. He was growing anxious for the meeting to begin.

"I believe," he said in his child's Vietnamese, "it is time to bring in my people."

"In a few more minutes," said *Mayor* Nguy. "Colonel Nha wishes to speak with each of our officers to express the importance of the Wisdom complex. He will demand full cooperation with your people." Nguy paused. "Then the great Tiger of Dien Bien Phu will threaten them to gain their cooperation."

Nicolaj heard something new in the voice. Suppressed anger? He withdrew the thought, for the staff officers were all direly afraid of Xuan Nha. Yet there was something different in the way Nguy spoke of his colonel.

"It's an exciting day," said Nicolaj.

"Yes, I suppose it is," replied Nguy, and Nicolaj knew something was indeed amiss.

They were joined by *Kapitan* Nguyen Pho, the logistics officer. "I have the final equipment lists for Wisdom. I will provide copies to you both."

Nguy said something to Nguyen Pho in a low voice. They both looked at Xuan Nha as he spoke quietly with the controller from Phuc Yen, the friendly smile playing across his sparrow's features. Nguyen Pho quickly looked away, but Nguy's eyes lingered.

Something is happening that I don't understand, Nicolaj thought. "Is something wrong?" he asked.

Nguy gave him a feeble grin. "What could possibly be wrong? You have your experts, and now your equipment is approved and will be arriving very shortly. All that remains is to make it all work, and I'm sure you can do that."

Nicolaj was concerned, for the success of their endeavor depended greatly on the cooperation of Xuan Nha's team. "We, comrade. I cannot do it alone. We must work together to make Wisdom succeed."

Nguy nodded, still distracted. Nguyen Pho gave him a nudge, and they turned toward the doorway.

"Here's *Lieutenant Colonel* Wu," Nguy said, his expression flat as he spat out the new rank.

Nicolaj watched the intelligence officer enter the room. The man was preening like a rooster, he thought, and he then understood the dismal tone of Nguy's voice.

The week before *Polkovnik* Nha had told Gregarian that he had authority to promote one of his men, and that he intended it to be *Mayor* Nguy, his second-in-command. He had indicated as much to his men, for they had joked about it with Nguy.

Gregarian sympathized with the executive officer's jealousy, but the man should not be surprised. As it was in Russia it was here. The party favorites were considered first. When he looked again, now with wiser eyes, *Mayor* Nguy's expression was glum, and Nicolaj wondered if the schism that was forming would hurt his project. He decided to speak to Xuan Nha about the matter later, then changed his mind. He respected Nguy's abilities and the stability he lent to the others on the team. Xuan might overreact as he had done in the past, which would make matters even worse.

Xuan Nha motioned to him from the front of the room, and Nicolaj Gregarian went out to bring in the Russian experts. He forgot about Nguy and concentrated on the challenge of taking the Wisdom complex from the planning table to actuality.

28/0610L—Ponderosa, Takhli RTAFB, Thailand

Bear Stewart

He came awake slowly, looked out from under his blanket, and blinked sleepy eyes. He wanted to go back to sleep.

"Wake up, Bear." Benny shook his shoulder again.

The Bear sighed. He'd been dreaming of the two Filipinas, and things were going great with both of them. Then Julie Wright had showed up and screwed everything up because he'd dropped the two others and was chasing her. You're too late, she'd said, walking away. He'd pleaded with her, but she'd kept going, saying she didn't have time for him now. She was just walking and he was running, but he couldn't catch up.

"Les Ries called. Wants us to come over to the 354th so he can show us their briefing. They're leaving at oh-eight-hundred for Saigon."

Ries and Janssen had been working day and night on it, but the Bear couldn't get excited about their grandstand briefing. He grumbled while he showered and dressed, wondering what Ries really wanted them for.

They arrived at the pig squadron at six-thirty, and the Bear poured a coffee for himself as Benny and Ries started going over the briefing. The Bear yawned, watching them.

Ries motioned him toward a spare copy. "Take a look. If you see any errors, let me know. Too late to change much content, but look for typos and such."

Ries was as gruff as ever.

The Bear thumbed through the document marked SECRET. The concept briefing was based on three phases, and stressed elimination of the entire radar net. It was his concept, refined and made better, combined with elements of Ries's roll-back plan.

"Do you like the basic theme?" asked Ries.

The Bear nodded silently.

"Thanks for the input," Ries said simply. He was no more friendly, but he said the words as if he meant them.

They found a few grammatical errors and Ries penned in the changes. Afterwards, Benny and the Bear left for breakfast.

"Where was Janssen?" asked the Bear as they trudged down the long boardwalk toward the club.

"Les said he worked most of the night on the briefing." Benny left it at that.

The Bear's mind was busy. "What the fuck's wrong with Ries? He acted like he hated my ass, disagreed with everything I said at the meeting the other day, and now he's gonna take my plan to Saigon and present it to the generals?"

"Not just yours. He combined all the ideas, like he said he was going to do, and came up with a damned good briefing."

The Bear was quiet.

"And as far as his being bitchy to you, he's been like that to everyone. It really got to him when Johnny T. got hammered while he was supposed to be protecting him."

"I suppose," muttered the Bear, "but I still think Ries screwed it up."

"Maybe, but it was the best he could do that day. Dan Janssen was having trouble with the new equipment and their flight coordination wasn't great, so he decided to change from briefed tactics. No one's good all the time."

"The hell you say," mumbled the Bear under his breath.

They ate breakfast, then wandered down to see the Takhli delegation off. The total complement consisted of Col B. J. Parker, Ries, Janssen, and Capt Swede Swendler, who had been submitted for an Air Force Cross for nursing a flight of shot-up Thuds back to safety and killing a MiG trying to pick off a cripple. General Roman was going to be in Saigon for the last day of the meeting and would pin on the decoration, which ranked just below the Medal of Honor.

Parker got onto the T-39 Sabreliner last, tossing a salute toward a group of maintenance men. As the T-39 taxied toward the active runway, Benny and the Bear walked back to the 357th squadron. They were flying in the afternoon go.

28/1415—Route Pack Five, North Vietnam

That afternoon they flew an easy counter to pack five, the bulge of North Vietnam west of the Red River valley. The Weasels patrolled the area between the threats and the four strike flights on their road-recce mission, roaming about the mountain roads looking for supply convoys and other targets of opportunity.

Tiny Bechler had again volunteered to fly on their wing while Pudge Holden and Lyle Watson led the second element, learning as many secrets as possible before leading their own missions.

The Bear watched as Holden maneuvered his element up to fly line abreast of their first element.

"What's he doing?" he asked.

"Pudge likes to fly up forward like that. You get too many MiG's to handle, you split the flight into two independent elements. That's easier when you fly line abreast."

"Air-to-air tactics, huh?" The Bear thought it would be nice if he could get in on shooting down a MiG. Even more though, he wanted to roll in and bomb more SAM sites, like they'd done near Vinh on Christmas Eve. "Wish we could do something like that with SAM sites," he said.

Benny was quiet for a long while as they patrolled.

"You up there?" asked the Bear after a full minute of silence.

"You just said a mouthful, Bear."

"I just asked if you were still there. Thought you might've gone somewhere," he quipped.

"I'm thinking about what you said about using air-to-air tactics on SAM sites."

"SAM sites don't fly, Benny. You're not going to start trying to shoot down the missiles, are you?" He laughed. "You start dogfighting with SAMs, I'm staying home and drinking beer."

"Listen. They limit us to one Weasel flight for each strike mission, right? But now that we've got more Weasel birds, we can always put a Weasel flying in number one and number three, like we're doing today."

"That's so if one Weasel's equipment goes out, the other one can take over," the Bear replied.

"Let's say the equipment on both Weasel birds is good. We fly in toward a site, split the flight into two independent elements, and come at them from two directions. When they shoot at one element, the other bombs 'em. What do you think?"

"Maybe."

"No maybe to it. I think it'll work."

The Bear thought about it. "What if there's three or four sites shooting?"

"Then you've still got two Weasel flights for them to worry about, and it's easier to maneuver with a two-ship element anyway." He sounded excited.

A Firecan radar came on the air. *Back to work,* thought the Bear. "We got a tracking gun radar at ten o'clock. Powerful," the Bear said.

"That's Yen Bai. They're starting to shoot."

They watched flak clusters over the town.

"Take him out," urged the Bear.

Benny turned hard right, to gain separation. After a minute, he swung back in a 180-degree turn to prepare to fire a Shrike missile at the radar.

"Hatchet flight," he called, *"we're on the attack."*

29/0630L—Thanh Hoa, Route Pack Four, North Vietnam

Benny Lewis

On Thursday they led the Weasel flight to Thanh Hoa, a city forty-five miles south of Haiphong at the mouth of the Ma River and North Vietnam's second busiest port city.

It was a maximum effort, an all-out attack on the petroleum storage area at Thanh Hoa, and quite a different mission from the day before. The Weasels flew high, well in front of the force, presenting a fat target for the SAM operators so they would fire their missiles at them rather than the strike force. The Bear was calling threat signals as fast as he could digest them. Benny spent his time jinking, turning, diving, and pulling up to evade the SAMs and flak.

"Gun radars at two and six o'clock. SAM at nine, tracking. He's no threat yet. Still have the gun at twelve, Benny. Oops, new guy at five o'clock. He's coming on strong."

"SAM?"

"Yeah. Still getting stronger and we're centered in both beams. He's looking at us."

"SAM activity at five o'clock, Red Dogs," called Benny.

"High PRF," said the Bear. The SAM commander had doubled the pulse rate of his radar so he could track them more precisely. "Missile beam's on. . . . Okay, we got a valid launch at five o'clock!"

Benny reefed the stick, turning hard right. *"SAM launch at five o'clock, Red Dogs,"* he grunted over the radio. *"Get ready to take it down."* "Take it down" meant he was about to perform a violent split-S maneuver to evade the missiles.

"Another tracking Fansong, Benny. Six o'clock, going to seven."

"Shit!"

"SAM launch at seven o'clock!" said the Bear.

Benny saw missiles coming up from their three o'clock and knew he had to worry about them first. He kept turning and put them at two o'clock, watching them closely, nose slightly down and in afterburner. The airspeed jogged through 600 knots, increasing.

"I got a visual on the SAMs at our eight o'clock," said the Bear. "They just dropped their boosters. Tracking true."

"Shit," Benny muttered again. *"Get ready to maneuver, Red Dogs,"* he radioed. He waited for a few seconds more, then rolled over on his back, continuing to watch and wait as the first covey of missiles accelerated smoothly through the sky toward them. They were damned close! He sharply pulled the stick back until they were diving, beginning the split-S maneuver. The Thud was shuddering under the strain.

Three seconds later Tiny Bechler called, *"Missiles are clear, Red Dog lead!"*

Benny abruptly rolled wings level and, breathing hard into the oxygen mask, looked for the covey from the other site. The first missile was abeam them and had no chance. He saw the second missile close up, skidding through the air as the computer down below transmitted intercept corrections. He yanked the stick and kicked the rudder into a gut-wrenching right turn, causing his g-suit to inflate tightly against his legs and abdomen. The second, then the third missiles slid by, not detonating until past them.

He leveled again. "Point me at that last one!" he yelled.

The Bear grunted, working his controls, then said, "Okay, he's on your attack scope."

The strobe flickered on his scope and he corrected toward it. The Shrike needles activated and he followed them, correcting again, then dipped the nose to get a quick approximation of the depression angle, so he could compute the range of the SAM site. Needles centered.

"Tracking SAM at nine o'clock," said the Bear. "Signal's getting stronger. He's going to launch missiles."

When they landed back at Takhli, Benny felt cheated. They had launched their two Shrikes, and Dave Persons, flying number three with Dutch Hansletter, had also launched two radar-homing missiles. But the entire time they had been on the defensive, and the Bear said none of the missiles had hit. No wonder, Benny thought, for he had been too busy dodging missiles to take time to properly launch the Shrikes. Just as the last SAMs had launched, Benny and the flight had dumped their bombs on a concentration of 85mm guns. He felt shitty about that too, wishing they could have found a better target.

29/1000L—Takhli RTAFB, Thailand

Colonel Mack, who had been mission commander, saw them coming out of the intelligence debriefing and clapped Benny on the shoulder. "I hear you guys are going on R and R in the morning?"
"Yes, sir."
"You deserve it. You and the Bear did good work up there today, Benny."
"I don't know, boss."
"We got good bombs on a tough target with no losses. You kept 'em off our backs. That's good work, Benny. My flight didn't have a single SAM launched at us. How many'd you have?"
"I counted four sites. That's twelve missiles. Bear thinks there was another launch we didn't see."
Colonel Mack grinned. "Feel like a magnet for SAMs?"
"Yes, sir."
"But you kept them off our asses. You may not be happy about it all, but I'll fly with you anytime, Benny."
When Mack had left the room, Benny turned to the Bear. "What do you think?"
"I think we dodged a shitpot of missiles."
Benny agreed. "Every time I tried to find out where the missiles were coming from, they'd either shoot like hell or fire more missiles."
They were outside now, and watched a U-2 make its

laboriously long, straight-in approach. The U-2's were part of
the covert operations going on across the field, where the Air
America C-130 operation was also set up.

"What're we gonna do, Benny? They shoot the fuckers,
we've got to dodge 'em. That may take some heat off the strike
force, but it'd take heat off everyone if we could kill the sites."

Andy Schumacher approached, wearing his habitual grin.
"How'd it go up there today?"

"In a word, shitty."

"We're leading the Weasel flight back to the same area
this afternoon," Andy said.

They went back inside and found a table where they could
spread out a map.

"Thanh Hoa's tough." Benny explained the defenses
then, marking the general locations of four sites on the map.

He tapped one of his marks. "I had this guy's location
down pretty good. I was getting set up to bomb him when we
got a SAM launch from another site and had to break off."

"Awfully flat over near the coast," Andy said. "No Thud
Ridge to hide behind there."

"Every radar in the world can see you," Benny agreed.

"Well"—Andy's grin was more nervous than before—
"guess I better get started with my flight planning. Thanks for
the information."

"Wish I could be more help."

After Andy had left, Benny thought for a moment. "Let's
find Pudge Holden. He's damned good with air-to-air tactics.
I'd like to work some on that split formation."

Holden was in the squadron lounge, drinking soda and
bullshitting with Lyle Watson.

Benny sat down beside them, thinking about his idea.

The Bear mumbled about having to get some things to
take on their R and R to Bangkok, then he and Lyle Watson
took off in the direction of the on-base Thai market.

"How'd it go?" asked Pudge.

"The missiles were thicker than flies up there. We were
up against six or eight SAM sites today, and so many Firecans
it'd raise your hair."

Pudge shook his head in wonder.

"We've got to come up with a way to protect the strike
force at the same time we find and bomb the sites."

"What about Ries's trip to Saigon? Maybe the brass will approve his plan."

"Maybe, but I don't think we can just sit around waiting for something that *might* happen. The SAMs keep getting thicker every week. We've got to destroy some of the sites, Pudge. We didn't scare anyone up there except ourselves today."

Benny put three coke bottles on the bar counter to simulate SAM sites, and they began to wave their hands like airplanes and try to come up with new tactics.

Mike Murphy came into the lounge and saw Benny. "Where's Bear Stewart?"

Benny told him.

"Tell him he owes me thirty bucks for some earrings I picked up for his girlfriend. I dropped 'em off in his room."

"Will do."

Murphy said he was flying in the afternoon strike.

"Watch your ass. There's a hell of a lot of defenses up in that area today."

"No sweat, babes. Tell the Bear I'll get my thirty bucks tonight. I gotta tell him more about how to act with a nice girl. He's not great in polite company." Mike waved and left them.

"Who's leading this afternoon's Weasel flight?" asked Pudge.

"Andy Schumacher. I told him about the defenses."

"Andy's a good man," said Pudge. "I've known him a long time. They've got eighty missions now. That's more than any other Weasel crew in the wing."

"They'll be the first to finish with a hundred missions," said Benny. "No one else has made it."

"Let's talk tactics." They turned back to the Coke bottle SAM sites on the bar.

29/1430L—Thanh Hoa, Route Pack Four, North Vietnam

Andy Schumacher

"The SAMs are clear, Ragman lead!" called the wingman.

Andy watched the SAM's deadly orange and black

blossom and yanked the nose of the aircraft farther around to the left and steeper into the dive.

"Launch at six o'clock!" came Larry Stark's voice from the rear cockpit.

"Ignore it," said Andy.

Benny's marks on the map had been accurate. They had fought their way through the continuous hail of missiles. Andy could clearly see the site below, a pall of smoke from multiple SAM launches hovering above it.

They were doing 570 knots and were passing through 9,000 feet. The dive angle was forty degrees.

"We're fast and a little shallow," he muttered.

Black flak bursts popped thickly around them.

Andy corrected his sight picture, bunting over and pulling the pipper down. He would release a bit low.

Larry's voice: "We've got a—"

An explosion! The airplane was wrenched sideward in the sky, coming apart, no longer flying.

The g-forces were tremendous. He grunted and strained to inch his right hand down, trying to find the ejection handle. *Damn it!* The g-forces tried to push his hands up, away from the ejection handles.

With great effort he located the handle, slowly rotated it, heard the roar of the windstream as the canopy left, then pulled the trigger. *We're going too fast!* was Andy Schumacher's final thought as the explosive charge blasted him from the cockpit.

Mike Murphy

"*Weeep, weeep, weeep!*"

"*Ragman lead is down!*" called someone. Mike glanced at the lineup card on his kneeboard. Andy Schumacher and his bear. More disjointed chatter told him they would get no SAM support from the rest of the Weasel flight.

Mike was leading Copper, approaching the target area behind the first strike flight.

"*Watch for SAMs, Coppers,*" he radioed.

He was climbing to the offset point, glancing out to his left, when he heard the chatter of a SAM radar on his threat receiver. The sound had been almost constant since they had ventured out over the valley, but this one seemed stronger and more insistent. Then he heard the squeal in his helmet and saw the bright LAUNCH light.

The SAMs wouldn't be able to track him through the dive-bomb maneuver. Just a couple more seconds and he'd be ready.

He eyed the target, then rolled the aircraft over on its back. Two of the big fuel storage tanks were still billowing smoke from the morning's attack, but two more looked to be intact. A string of bombs from the flight in front of him ruptured one of the two. It spewed fire in slow motion, then erupted in a mighty explosion.

He hesitated for another heartbeat, then remembered the SAMs and called, *"Copper lead is in."*

"Copper lead, we got—"

A SAM explosion to his right, close by, and the Thud shuddered mightily.

Damn!

A searing pain in his chest!

He tried to tuck the nose down, for it was lazily wandering about, but the controls refused to respond. He thought about how quiet it was, then realized the silence was due to the fact that there was no engine noise. Slowly, and with effort, he unfastened his oxygen mask, coughing hard, spattering red onto the gauges.

Mike looked over to his right to see his wingman moving in an S-maneuver, trying to slow down with him. His bird was slewing about wildly, refusing to respond to the controls, wandering in its own crazy path. Descending now, directly toward the city of Thanh Hoa. No chance to control the aircraft so he could glide out over the water. No more options.

Mike coughed again and saw the red spray. *Messy.*

He depressed the radio button, gasping. "Gotta get out. I'll see you, babes."

He rotated the handles, pulled the triggers, and scarcely felt the hard kick.

Mike Murphy watched dreamily as the parachute canopy billowed and flapped, filled with air, and jerked him up short. He floated earthward.

He thought of trying to steer his chute out over the water.

Streams of bright machine gun tracers arced through the sky, searching for him. He tried to twist away. The streams of fire found and settled upon him.

28/1635L—Command Post, Takhli RTAFB, Thailand

Benny Lewis

The right wing of Maj Andy Schumacher and Capt Larry Stark's aircraft had been torn away by an 85mm round as they were dive-bombing a SAM site. Both ejected, but they were going so fast that the parachutes streamered. The wingman had made a single low pass and thought he saw one of the chutes hung up in a tree with a body hanging underneath. It was the only tree around.

With no Weasels to draw the SAMs, the strike force had lost two more aircraft.

Mike Murphy had taken a SAM hit from the site Andy Schumacher had tried to bomb. He had ejected over Thanh Hoa, and the other pilots had watched tracers crisscrossing near the chute.

The other Thud pilot, a lieutenant named Capella, had made it out over the water before he'd ejected and was subsequently picked up by an Air Force SA-16 amphibious rescue aircraft.

After their debriefing, Benny talked to the crews about the mission, about the god-awful numbers of SAMs and guns, and how they'd been lucky to suffer only the losses they had.

He gritted his teeth, knowing something had to be done.

He found the Bear at the Ponderosa, packing away some things he'd bought at the Thai market.

"Mike Murphy got it," he told him evenly.

The Bear looked up at him and stood still for a long moment. "Mike?"

"Yeah."

The Bear paused for another heartbeat before going back to packing his B-4 bag. "How'd it happen?"

"Schumacher and Stark were going in on a site and got shot down. The site launched SAMs and bagged Murphy. He ejected right over the target, and they were shooting like hell. No one believes he had a chance."

The Bear nodded slowly.

"Just before he ejected, he made a radio call. He said, 'I'll see you, babes.'"

The Bear was quiet.

"Before he took off he said to tell you he'd gotten some earrings for Julie. Said he left 'em here in your room."

"I found them. Mike's better than me at knowing what women like. These have black star sapphires in them."

"He said they cost him thirty bucks."

The Bear nodded, continuing his packing.

They went to dinner, and afterward to the bar. At nine o'clock, when the full crowd had gathered, the Bear stood on a barstool and yelled for them all to quiet down. A few did.

"I owe Mike Murphy thirty bucks. Drinks are on Mike tonight!"

The Bear gave Jimmy the bartender thirty dollars and told him to keep passing out twenty-five cent drinks until the money was gone.

That would teach Mike, he told Benny, to get himself shot down.

Benny nodded, but he wondered. The Bear had lost yet another close friend, but he was acting as if none of it were real.

Was it real? he asked himself.

CHAPTER THIRTEEN

**Friday, December 30th, 1966—0815 Local, People's
Army HQ, Hanoi, DRV**

Major Nguy

He knocked at the door and stood stiffly in view of Xuan
Nha. The colonel was busy scanning the daily report he had
prepared. He finally glanced up and nodded abruptly for Nguy
to enter.

Nha pursed his lips inquiringly. "You knock? You are my
executive officer. Come in and take a seat, old friend." He
looked down and continued to read.

Nguy sat stiffly, eyes ahead and no smile on his counte-
nance. He was normally well groomed, for he was an orderly
man, but today he had prepared himself meticulously. He wore
a crisply ironed green uniform. His Hero of the Struggle for
Independence and Shining Valor badges were gaudy on his
chest. Two small blood-red stars indicated severe wounds he
had suffered in combat. He wore the Soviet-style collar tabs
recently adopted by Giap for his officers' uniforms.

"A good report," Colonel Nha summarized.

"Thank you, comrade Colonel."

Nha scratched his heavy jaw. Major Nguy remarked to
himself that the sparrow had aged during the past weeks. He
had followed this man for five years now and had always
respected his dedication and quick mind. The respect had
wavered only in the past week with Wu's dramatic increase in
influence. He wondered if Nha knew that all of his staff were
increasingly unsure.

"So?" Colonel Nha put his question simply.

"I very respectfully request to be transferred to a combat

342

unit, comrade Colonel." Should he add that he could no longer properly accomplish his duties? Perhaps, he told himself, when the time is more appropriate.

Nha arched an eyebrow in surprise. He tapped the papers before him. "But you do a superb job for me, old friend."

Nguy wished Xuan Nha would drop the charade of friendship. Perhaps once, when they had arranged defenses together during field trips to the southern or western provinces, but no longer were they comrades-in-arms. The colonel no longer seemed to need friends. Even Thao Phong, the fighter pilot colonel, and Maj Tran Van Ngo, his handpicked replacement at Tiger, had noticed his distance during the past week. Both men had asked Major Nguy what was troubling Xuan Nha, for he was normally the one to know such things, and he'd been at a loss to answer.

Now Xuan Nha looked at him with a brooding, troubled look, and in the silence Major Nguy realized he must tell his superior officer what bothered him. He was a dutiful person, and it was his job to keep Xuan Nha informed.

He blurted, "My duties as executive officer, your second-in-command, can no longer be carried out, comrade Colonel. I am under the constant scrutiny of the chief intelligence officer."

Nha sighed. "It is one of the ironies of our great socialism that even the heroic and most capable officers remain under the watchful eye of the Lao Dong party. Even me. Even General Luc. Perhaps even General Dung. None are exempt."

"I can no longer give an order when you are gone which is not scrutinized and often reversed." He started to continue, then remembered his wife's terror and grew quiet.

"When the struggle for unification is won, we soldiers will reap our true rewards. Remember the time following our glorious struggle for independence? When we went from village to village to ensure the loyalties of the people? We held limitless power. It will be so once again when our country is unified. There will be great need for capable administrators such as you. Stay with me and I promise you will be rewarded."

Nguy wanted to believe him. "I have tried to serve you well, comrade Colonel."

"And you have."

Major Nguy hesitated, wondering if he should go further.

The previous morning his wife had been taken from their modest quarters before their children's eyes by four men wearing the nondescript uniform of the Internal Affairs secret police. Terrified, she'd been driven to an unmarked building near the river and taken to the basement. Blindfolded and questioned throughout the morning about her husband's acquaintances and activities, even about their intimacies and private discussions. Throughout, she had heard screams of terror and agony. She was rudely released in Ba Dinh Square and left to make her way home. Although she hadn't seen him, she had recognized one of the interrogator's voices.

"It is best if I am transferred, comrade Colonel." He decided not to tell Nha about his wife. Nha was either ignorant of or in collusion with Wu and what had happened. Perhaps it was Wu and Nha's wife, Li Binh. Regardless, Major Nguy would likely gain no support from Xuan Nha, who was not political.

The colonel steepled his fingers beneath his chin. "I am submitting you for promotion. You know that, do you not?"

"Yes, comrade Colonel."

"Be patient. It will come. In the meanwhile, I will speak with Lieutenant Colonel Wu. He should not interfere with your duties."

Nguy grew alarmed. "Please, sir, do not do that."

Colonel Nha was obviously interested in his outburst.

"I would like to return to one of the rocket battalions."

Xuan Nha smiled. "We all would like to return to combat. We in the staff also serve, you know. At least that is what they would have us believe. You are my right arm here."

Nguy was not to be deterred. "I am weary of headquarters duty. I cannot tell you how much I would appreciate it if I could return to combat."

Colonel Nha nodded thoughtfully, perhaps remembering the good times they had shared. Perhaps the time Nguy had shielded his superior from harm and bomb fragments with his own body during a Thunder plane attack west of Hanoi.

"I will continue to serve you well in the field."

"And your promotion? A rocket battalion is commanded by a major."

"I will wait for another day."

"And you are sure you wish to do this?"

"Yes, comrade Colonel."

Xuan Nha stood and walked to the window, then stared without expression out at the rooftops, toward Ho Tay Lake. He nodded finally. "I have a certain position in mind which would require all of your talents."

Major Nguy waited.

Colonel Nha wagged his head tersely toward the door. "Return to your duties. I will call you later in the morning and tell you of my decision."

Major Nguy turned and left the room. Wu was in the outer office, speaking with old Sgt Van Ng. Wu smiled a superior look at Nguy. "You look like you are dressed for a parade, comrade Major."

Nguy fought down an angry rebuttal and gritted his teeth. He wondered if Wu had overheard the conversation.

Lieutenant Colonel Wu narrowed his eyes. "Is there a problem, Major Nguy?"

"No."

Wu raised his eyebrows.

"No, *comrade Lieutenant Colonel,*" muttered Nguy.

Wu nodded, happier. He went into the colonel's office then. Before the door was closed, Wu heard him saying, "There is a matter of concern, comrade Colonel."

Major Nguy saw the one-eyed sergeant looking at him as he strained to hear more. He hurried out into the hallway.

You've won! he pleaded inside his mind to Wu. *Leave me alone.*

Xuan Nha

Wu was far too cocky with his newly bestowed rank, Xuan thought as he listened to the man's report on the activities of Major Nguy. It was apparent what his wife's nephew was aiming for as he almost openly made his bid for the executive officer's job. He spoke of Nguy's growing incompetence and said that others on the staff were as concerned as he.

Xuan raised a hand. "I have known Major Nguy for several years. I read his reports daily and see his work, and I am happy to be able to leave my post and know it is in competent hands."

Wu bowed his head in feigned humility. His mouth was twitching with a smile, Xuan noticed.

"Perhaps the Colonel is speaking of the Major Nguy we had a month ago. I assure you he is a different man today."

"How is he different?"

A smile of camaraderie. "I have received certain reports from the party. What makes this especially worrisome is the sensitivity of his position, his access to so many secrets."

"Are you saying he is a spy?" Xuan asked incredulously.

"Not that. It's just that a person in his position must be entirely reliable."

"What have you found?" asked Xuan, knowing that Wu did not have to answer anything involving Lao Dong party business.

Wu was evasive. "Perhaps no single thing that is terribly wrong, but there are little troublesome things which may provide reasons for his increasingly suspect activities. Did you know his wife is Chinese?"

Xuan smiled. "Your own name is Chinese. Have you wondered about yourself?"

Wu's smile was erased and his look grew more cunning. "My family is the same as your wife's, comrade Colonel."

"I know, and it is an honorable one. The Chinese have been here for five thousand years now. Those with such names may have been purified with good Tonkinese blood after that long, don't you think?"

"Of course, comrade Colonel. But Major Nguy's wife's family immigrated in 1937, less than thirty years ago."

"Have you considered that Major Nguy is a Hero of the Struggle for Independence?"

"So long ago, comrade Colonel. It also came to the party's attention that he was a prisoner of the French Union Forces."

"He led a prisoner's revolt and was severely wounded in a daring escape."

"I assure you, the party is concerned about him."

Xuan Nha started to argue further, then hesitated. He was reluctant to speak against the Lao Dong's wisdom, even with this relative of his wife's. Wu could say the party disliked green pigs, and who was he to say that green pigs were not enemies of the people if the party said they were.

Wu saw his hesitancy. His smile returned.

Xuan cleared his throat. "Perhaps you are correct."

The smile widened.

"I will send Major Nguy to the Wisdom complex. I will say that I've selected him to be in charge of construction there."

"A wonderful idea, comrade Colonel! Of course I must assign a very competent party representative there to keep an eye upon his activities. The party will require it since his loyalty has been questioned."

"I will tell him today that he must go."

Wu's eyes glittered.

"But of course I must also think of someone to replace him."

"If I can be of help in any way, comrade Colonel, I would be happy to serve."

"I have never doubted that, not for a minute."

30/1630L—Bangkok, Thailand

Julie Wright

Pan Am had a contract for their crews to stay at the Princess Hotel in Bangkok, and Liz had been able to get reservations and special rates despite the holiday season. The two women sat in the lobby, waiting for the men who were more than an hour late.

Julie saw them first and stood, waving her large handbag. "There they are," she said in her husky voice. Liz stood up behind her, not nearly as excited.

As the two men approached, Julie began to fidget and run out of patience. When they were ten feet away, she hurried over and hugged the Bear, ignoring the fact he was toting a well-stuffed B-4 bag. "I missed you, Mal Bear," she said.

He gave everyone an awkward smile as he endured the hug.

Liz was more subdued and stood her ground as Benny put his bag down and gave her a kiss on the cheek. "Good to see you again," he said.

The other two could act as properly as they wanted. Julie just wanted to cling a little longer and savor the fact that they were together again. She was quite unable to turn the Bear's arm loose. They walked and she held on, not caring what anyone thought.

"We're all on the third floor," she told him. "Liz and I have a double room. Separate rooms for you guys. We figured you were the big spenders."

"We're later than we thought we'd be," said Mal Bear. "Waiting for a plane, then trouble getting here from the airport. There's a bunch of marines in town from Vietnam."

"You had to take an airplane?" she asked. "I thought your base was nearby."

"Takhli is two hundred kilometers by highway," he said. "A hundred and twenty miles. Takes four or five hours by bus, because the drivers stop and leave a gift at all the Buddhist spirit houses, and there's one every couple of miles. Last week it took one of our guys seven hours to get here by bus because of a herd of elephants."

"Elephants? Like in wild elephants?" asked Julie.

"They've domesticated them. Use them to haul lumber, pull plows, lift things, stuff like that. Anyway, this guy was in a bus and they got behind a herd of elephants on the highway. Things got pretty fu—— . . . pretty ripe back there behind them, so the driver tried to pass and they slid off the road."

Julie giggled joyfully, feeling alive. "Don't tell me!"

"Yep. They skidded on the sh—— . . . on the elephant dung. Anyway, we thought it was best to wait for the afternoon airplane to Don Muang airport."

The women laughed. He was trying so hard not to curse that Julie felt like kissing him and telling him what she felt for him right here in the lobby. She was tired of holding back.

"You been to Bangkok before?" the Bear asked her.

"Liz has, so she's our tour guide. All I've learned is that Bangkok's real name was some Thai word meaning City of Heaven, and that the big attraction here is the Green Buddha."

"The Emerald Buddha," corrected Liz. "I remember, because emeralds are things I could easily grow fond of." She batted her eyes.

Julie squeezed Mal Bear's arm before finally releasing him. She was a private person and had never imagined that she'd allow Liz to see her like this. Of course, Liz would likely not realize the enormity of her feelings. She was too self-centered to think much about others and so poised and so damnably stunning she could get away with it.

It was impossible to keep the happiness from bubbling into her voice. "We start tonight with dinner on a floating restaurant. Then we sightsee tomorrow. If it's in Bangkok, we'll see it. Four days' worth," she said.

"We may not be able to stay that long," said Benny.

"Oh?" Liz was looking at him.

"You've probably heard that President Johnson called a bombing halt for New Year's, but we don't know how long it'll last. We'll have to head back if the bombing's resumed."

"Let's enjoy while we can," said Julie with false bravado. She didn't want to think about the Bear returning to danger.

The two men went to the desk to register.

"I forgot just how nice Benny is," whispered Liz.

Julie watched Mal Bear closely, unable to tear her eyes away. She had just made her irrevocable decision, damn the torpedoes and straight ahead, and was ready for whatever lay in her path. She turned to Liz, realizing she had been saying something about dinner. "Did you say reservations at eight?"

"Eight-thirty. That'll give everyone time to go up to their room and relax. Perhaps take a nap and try to catch up on the time difference. We can meet the guys at seven-thirty, have a drink here at the hotel, and still make our reservation time."

Julie didn't want to waste any of the time she could spend with Mal Bear.

Benny finished at the desk and approached. Liz touched his arm, an intimate gesture with a hint of sensuousness. Julie wished she had more of that sort of composure.

Liz said, "I was just telling Julie. We can all go upstairs and relax for a bit, then meet down here for a drink at seven-thirty before we go out to dinner."

"If you two want to, go on upstairs," said Julie. "I'll wait here for Mal Bear." She wanted to be alone with him but couldn't appear *too* obvious about it.

"We'll wait for you," said Benny, being polite.

Damn! said Julie to herself.

Julie listened with half an ear as Liz and Benny chatted about the canals, the floating restaurants, markets, and other Bangkok sights that lay in store.

Mal Bear joined them, showing his smile.

"Shower time," he announced. "We flew down here in a very old gooney bird. The fu—— . . . the thing growled and groaned all the way, and we sweated and got dirty as hell . . . excuse me . . . from thirty years of accumulated dust and grime. Dunno about you folks, but I'm going to clean up."

"Last time I was here the water was turned off in the middle of my shower," said Liz.

Mal Bear grimaced at the thought and hefted his bag.

Liz explained the schedule again as they went up to the third floor together in the small elevator. She pointed down the hallway toward the rooms. Benny was in 37, Mal Bear across the hall in 38, and both women in 33.

"See you at seven-thirty," Mal Bear said, and after a single backward glance disappeared into his room.

Benny placed his bag in his room, came back out, and embraced Liz lightly. He included Julie in his warm look. "Great seeing you both again," he said. "Just great."

Inside their room, Liz gushed. "I didn't remember how nice he was. He's a real gentleman. The people back in Yorktown would love him."

Julie was nervous as a cat and about to break out in hives, and Liz wanted to talk about people in her hometown?"

"They're trained to be officers and gentlemen," she said archly.

Liz looked thoughtful as she fluffed a pillow. "I think I could really get to like him, except for the war thing." She picked up a paperback, lay on her bed with the pillow propped behind her head, and began to read.

Julie sat at the small desk, trying to concentrate on her own book. After rereading a single paragraph for several long minutes, she put the book down and walked to the window. A sculptured garden below was bathed in the golden glow of the waning sun. A Thai gardener busily walked around with clippers, pruning things and staring critically at his work.

Horrible thoughts came to her. She'd all but offered herself to the Bear in Manila, but he had said the time wasn't right. She'd listened and loved him more for his strength. Now the thought of that self-restraint began to bother her.

Why had he hesitated after coming on so strong the first night? They'd been together long enough after she'd decided to lose her virginity, so why hadn't he been overpowered by his lusts? She looked down at herself and didn't wonder as she thought of how dowdy she really was.

She tried to think positive about the guys who constantly

came on to her. But she wasn't interested in any of them. Her guy was the one who'd shown the forbearance, who just fifteen minutes ago had gone into his room with hardly a backward look.

God, but she was miserable! The doubts grew. Why hadn't he turned back to her at the door as Benny had done with Liz? He could have at least given her a smile.

She stalked slowly, miserably to the door.

Liz lowered her book. "Where are you going?" she asked.

Julie trusted herself to mumble, "Out," before she hurried into the hallway.

A stew went by, dragging her suitcase behind her down the hall, and Julie averted her head. A moment later she rapped lightly at number 38.

No answer. She sucked another breath of courage and knocked again, louder, and heard movement inside.

He peered out through a crack, then held the door open for her. She saw he was still wet from the shower, clad only with a towel wrapped around his middle.

She threw her arms about his neck and pressed against him, sobbing.

He held her tightly and nudged the door closed with his foot.

"Now," she said.

"Are you sure?"

"Oh God yes!"

"I can't make any promises."

"I know."

It was better than she had ever imagined it could be. He was gentle; she was the wild one. She could only respond to his lead for she was inexperienced, but she did so energetically and it was wonderful. When they were done and lay entwined together, she felt so utterly fulfilled and content that she cried.

He grew concerned.

She said she was happier than she had ever been in her life.

He told her she was special to him.

She said she loved him.

He only smiled, but with such tenderness and warmth that she knew.

She asked if he wanted her to move her things into his room, and he thought about it for a while.

"No," he finally said. "It wouldn't look right."

"They'll know," she said. "I won't be able to hide what I feel for you, Mal. I don't care what anyone thinks. I just want to be near you."

"It's not what they think, it's what they know. What they might say about you."

She snuggled against him, savoring his smell. He put his arms about her and she felt protected and content.

30/1730L—People's Army HQ, Hanoi, DRV

Xuan Nha

Xuan called in the *Tay*, Nicolaj Gregarian, and told him of his decision to appoint Major Nguy as commandant of the Wisdom complex.

Gregarian was exuberant. "An excellent choice," he said in Russian. Despite his general success in getting him to learn Vietnamese, Xuan Nha had been unable to dissuade the Russian from speaking his own language when they were alone.

Gregarian regarded him with a sudden frown. "But the *mayor* is also a very good executive officer, is he not? How will you replace him on your staff?"

"I've not yet decided." He looked at the Russian. "Perhaps Lieutenant Colonel Wu?"

Gregarian was silent too long, so Xuan Nha went on to other things. "The Americans will observe a two-day bombing halt beginning tomorrow. Five convoys are positioned to move the equipment to Bac Can: two from here and three from Haiphong. The trucks will depart tomorrow at nightfall and travel all night, then again the next night."

"Will that be long enough? We have included sensitive monitoring equipment in the shipments, which must be transported very carefully. And the movement must be covert."

Xuan was patient. "Two nights will be enough. We are good at such things. Tonight and tomorrow the roadways will be improved. As each convoy sets out, three hundred men will go before them to ensure the way is clear of obstacles and that holes have been filled. All equipment and men will be in place at Wisdom site before the sun rises on January second."

"Good." Yet the Russian still appeared worried.

"We must assume the Americans will resume their bombing on the second. I have asked my wife to try to get more time, even long enough for us to complete the installations and testing at Wisdom, but Li Binh says we should not plan for longer than that."

Gregarian nodded.

"We also know the Americans are up to something and that it may happen when they resume bombing."

"They will try something new?"

"Our sources say they have sent delegates from all their air bases in Thailand and from the Phantom bases in the south to a meeting in Saigon. The headquarters people who direct the bombing campaign will all be there. Something important is being planned. Perhaps something is changing in the way they make their air attacks."

"What could it be?" asked the Russian. He was a worrier, thought Xuan Nha.

"We don't know, but I do not have to tell you that our rocket battalions are more vulnerable while our best commanders are busy setting up the Wisdom complex."

Gregarian's large brow was still furrowed as he pondered what the Americans could be up to. "Could it be a massive attack on the rocket defenses?" he wondered aloud.

"My wife's office will encourage the Americans through all means available—the Swiss Red Cross, the Russians and Chinese, our embassy in Paris, the United Nations, and more—to extend the bombing halt."

"All equipment must be in place at Wisdom before the bombing is resumed."

Xuan felt exasperated. "I tell you it will be." The Russian had a fixation on a single problem when there were so many.

Xuan continued. "I do not worry about Wisdom's effectiveness. Our plan is good. I am concerned about other things. Most of all, that our defenses remain effective for the next few weeks while we are setting up the equipment."

"It will be worthwhile. When the integration is complete, your defenses will work together like the pieces of a clock. You will have a *true* fence of steel."

"I hope," said Xuan Nha, "we can convince our superiors

it is worthwhile if something goes wrong. Every good plan
costs something. The cost of this one is this period of increased
vulnerability."

When Gregarian left, Xuan Nha received a disturbing
report that confirmed his fears. Thunder planes had attacked a
barracks complex fifteen kilometers west of Hanoi. Boosters
from rockets launched at the Americans by Tiger two site had
somehow fallen precisely on the military post the Americans
were bombing. The large armory at Viet Tri was destroyed,
some 200 militia had been killed, and more than 1,000 more
were without quarters. It was unclear which had caused the
greater damage, the bombs or the battery's own rocket boosters. Worse, the Thunder planes had escaped without a single
loss.

It would never have happened if Maj. Tran Van Ngo had
not been away from Tiger.

General Luc's office called, asking for a complete report
on the rocket booster incident. Xuan assigned the task to
Lieutenant Colonel Wu: the man had proven himself to be very
good with excuses.

Xuan wondered if more mistakes might be in store. He
called his friend, Col Thao Phong. After they had exchanged
their customary insults, he asked the disposition of the interceptors.

"We will be ready by Monday when the bombing halt
ends. Much more ready than we've ever been, Xuan Nha."

During the past three weeks, while the interceptor forces
had been refurbished and undergone improvements, the rocket
sites had been used as the vanguard of defenses. Large
numbers of VPAAF MiG fighters had been shuttled across the
border to Ch'in Hsien airfield in China, to join the seventy new
ones from Russia. All were to be examined from nose to tail
and fine-tuned by Soviet maintenance technicians. At the same
time, Thao Phong had coordinated a series of briefings for his
aviators at Ch'in Hsien, conducted by Russian, Chinese, and
North Korean fighter pilots.

The MiG's were to be ferried back during the next two
days, when the skies would be clear of American air pirates,
and more than 100 MiG interceptors would be dispersed in
camouflaged revetments at the various bases. Twenty eager
North Korean pilots would fly with VPAAF pilots and provide
further instruction and support.

"How soon before your people will actually be ready to fight?" Xuan asked.

"As I said, my pilots will be ready to fight on Monday when the Americans return. A longer delay would be bad for their morale."

"Good," said Xuan. "Could your MiG's carry the entire load on Monday? I would like to give the majority of the rocket forces a few additional days to repair their systems and move to new locations. Many of the systems are in need of maintenance. Also, I have too many of my best commanders preoccupied with Wisdom to feel good about things."

"Are you getting soft on your men?" joked Thao Phong.

"I am also concerned about the Americans. Our intelligence sources tell us that certain agreements were reached at their Saigon meeting, but we cannot find out what they were. I believe they may be preparing for a large-scale attack on my rocket forces, and I want to be prepared."

Thao Phong disagreed. "I received the briefings about the meetings, too. I believe that somehow they have learned about our VPAAF efforts, our new interceptors, our training, perhaps even our plan to improve command-and-control with Wisdom."

"Then you are also concerned?"

"I am happy they know. They realize our interceptors will beat them now. If they have heard what we are preparing for them, they will fly very cautiously."

"Then you agree to send your interceptors up in force Monday?"

"Of course! Our pilots are more ready than ever and our airplanes are finely tuned. General Tho will be pleased. He asked for just this sort of thing, as quickly as possible."

Xuan Nha allowed some of Thao Phong's exuberance to wash over him. "We will meet tomorrow and finalize our agreement, as I've already advised General Luc. I will support you with the permanent Hanoi rocket sites and all of our antiaircraft artillery, but otherwise you will have the entire sky to your interceptors."

"I would love to see the Americans' faces when they see us coming. We will sweep them from the sky."

30/1900L—Bangkok, Thailand

Liz Richardson

The loud rapping sound merged with Liz's dream. She awoke slowly, fighting it, groggy from deep slumber. She stretched languorously, trying to ignore it, then started as she realized someone was at the door. It was Julie, who'd forgotten her key when she'd gone out.

"Guess I dropped off," said Liz, yawning wide. "I was sleeping like the dead. What time is it?"

"It's already seven o'clock. I've been beating on the door forever. We've only got half an hour to get ready."

But Julie did not look troubled about it at all. In fact, she was smiling serenely as she went to the vanity. Liz blinked away more sleep, then stood back to look at Julie.

"Hurry," said Julie.

"I'll make it." Liz considered herself a quick-change artist, but just now she was interested in Julie. There was a different air about her friend, something she'd not noted before.

"Okay, what is it?" she finally asked. "You've been gone for two hours and now you come back looking like you've won a lottery."

Julie shrugged and continued her mysterious smile. "The magic of Bangkok?"

"Baloney. Where've you been?"

"Oh, just exploring." Julie looked about the vanity, found her brush, and began to carefully stroke through her hair, which was damp as if she'd just washed it.

Aha! thought Liz.

"Come on, we've got to hurry," urged Julie.

Liz was still intrigued, but her friend had slipped into a quiet mood, her mind elsewhere as she looked in the mirror and brushed, the smile lingering.

"Okay, be that way."

They were twenty minutes late meeting the men. The Bear joked about their tardiness as Benny pulled out their chairs.

Both men wore summer sport jackets and open-neck shirts, but any similarity ended there. Their dress reflected their personalities. The Bear's jacket was pleated and boldly cut, with Western-style pockets. He wore a heavy gold bracelet, a garish ring with a chunk of uncut turquoise, and a gold-colored watch. Overstatement. Benny was conservatively dressed in a simple blue jacket and white shirt. His only jewelry was a fashionably worn Rolex watch. A study in understatement and assurance, Liz decided favorably.

The lobster dinner at the floating restaurant was superb. White-jacketed waiters scurried and hovered, and a chef periodically darted from the kitchen to survey his audience. A small string combo played soft background music.

"They've played for the king," Liz said. "At least that's what the cultural people at the embassy say."

"King Bhumibol," said Benny, "plays a mean clarinet himself. He loves jazz and even writes his own music."

"Benny," said the Bear to the women, "is like a walking travelog. He's our Chet Huntley of local history and color."

Liz looked at Benny. "Maybe you should be tour guide."

"I've never been here before. You have, which means you're stuck with the job."

"Tell us more about the king," said Julie, snuggled beside Mal Stewart. She would alternately bubble with excitement, then grow quiet and content. Liz couldn't bring herself to believe she could be serious. He lacked refinement. Surely Julie could see through him.

Benny told them about the king of Siam, who was born in the States and educated at Harvard, and whom the people idolized like they did rock stars in the States.

"So he runs the country?" asked the Bear.

"They have a strongman who does that. An ex-general named Kittikachorn. He makes the tough decisions and takes the blame when things go wrong, while the king writes his music and plays his clarinet."

"Fascinating," said Liz, impressed.

"Strongman doesn't sound like such a great job," the Bear said. "Sounds like this Kittycorn does all the work and gets none of the glory."

"It's not all bad," replied Benny. "He just announced that he might accept the winner of the Miss Thailand contest as his next wife. He's fifty-five years old and she'd be wife number twenty-one, if I remember correctly."

"Can you imagine twenty-one women waiting in line to

nag you when you get home?" said the Bear, shaking his head in awe.

"Thai women are exquisite," said Liz, looking at a nearby table. The beautiful woman there met her expectation of the exotic East. She could picture her in golden Siamese trappings, dancing gracefully. "They're so delicate."

The Bear examined the young woman seated beside an older man. "Nice looking. Bet you a buck she's a who—— . . . a high-priced prostitute."

"Why would you say that?" asked Liz.

"He's treating her too well. Thais don't treat their wives that nice. Mama's probably at home taking care of the kid. Maybe several mamas are home taking care of a lot of kids. That one's either a hooker, a mistress, or he's courting her to add her to his collection of wives."

"Men!" said Liz, only half joking. She suspected Mal Bear was being either mean or purposefully crass, and she didn't appreciate him bringing the subject up.

"How about you, Mal Bear?" murmured Julie.

"I don't care if he's got a concubine on the side."

"You know what I mean. How many concubines have *you* got?"

"Gotta be married to have a concubine," he replied evasively.

The Bear's joke heightened Liz's already dark assessment of him.

"I'd hate to be a wife and have to put up with other wives and mistresses," Julie said, twitching her nose in repugnance.

"Better not get serious over a Thai, then," said the Bear.

Julie laughed, and snuggled to his arm. "I won't."

"What do you think about the wives and concubines?" Liz asked Benny.

Benny shrugged. "Different culture is all. For instance, if your brother or close friend dies here, it's taken for granted that you'll take on his wife, raise his kids and all. They've got a healthy outlook about it. They think the Western cultures are the strange ones."

"Aren't there a lot of men left over?"

"A great number of Thai men take vows of abstinence and become Buddhist monks. It's also traditional that if a man can't afford a family, he can't marry. It all balances out."

Before they left the restaurant, Liz announced the next

day's schedule. In the morning they would explore the klongs, the network of canals that prompted visitors to call Bangkok the "Venice of the Orient." They were fast disappearing, being filled in to make room for modern, glass buildings, products of wealth brought by the war in Vietnam. In the afternoon they would visit the Grand Palace, which the first king Rama had dedicated as the center of the universe, and view the Temple of the Emerald Buddha.

"Culture," quipped the Bear, "is the bane of the working class. Let's go find a bar."

Liz despised his attitude. She concluded there were two classes of military officers. There were gentlemen, like Benny and those who were sent to VMI, West Point, and the Citadel, and then there were others, like Mal Bear.

They discovered a small place called the Red Room, with a mahogany bar and quiet tables. As they ordered Irish coffees, Liz noted that Julie remained quiet and attentive to the Bear.

While they waited for drinks and Mal Stewart talked about how lonely Christmas at Takhli had been, Liz studied Benny Lewis. There was a cauldron of emotion bubbling within her that she had never allowed to surface. After Jeff, she had decided that the next time she made love should be when she was safely married. She was not sure she could continue to keep her desires in check if they were ever truly released.

So why had she started taking birth control pills again? The thought bothered her during the cab ride back to the hotel.

Mal Bear and Julie decided to have a drink at the hotel bar by themselves. As Liz and Benny took the elevator up, he told her about the Bear losing his closest buddy at Takhli.

"That's terrible," she said, thinking how awful it would be. "Have you lost close friends?"

"Yeah, quite a few," he said simply.

"How does it feel to be so close to death?"

"It makes you happy you're alive, that it's them and not you. Then you feel guilty about feeling that way."

She felt sad inside.

They stopped at her door and chatted for a moment before he leaned forward and gave her a pleasant kiss. When they drew apart she wasn't ready for him to go.

"I've got some mini's inside," she said. "Care for a drink?"

"Sure," he said and followed her in.

They had time, she decided. Julie would go to Mal Bear's room. She'd had that look about her, like she would be happy to curl up near him.

She showed Benny the collection of miniature bottles she and Julie had taken from the airplane coming over. "Your choice," she said.

"Gin. Be back in a minute." He took the ice bucket and disappeared, and she wondered whether she should encourage things to go farther. She still hadn't decided when he returned.

She fixed him a martini and poured herself a red wine. They sat on the edge of the bed and sipped their drinks as they talked. He told her more about his base and the terrible losses, and she listened, not daring to tell him that he was reinforcing her antiwar sympathies.

After a while she asked, "How's the situation with your wife?" She sounded almost too casual, but she wanted to know.

"I signed the separation agreement last week and sent it to her lawyer."

She shook her head sadly. She was very pleased.

"By the way," he said, "thanks for the moral support back in the Philippines."

She thought his voice was a little thick with emotion. He was going to make a pass. She wondered how to most gently put him off. But should she?

She abruptly made her decision. The time *was* right and they would not have long together. She leaned toward him. He put his glass down and held her tightly. She enjoyed the sensation as they kissed. When they broke for air, she felt her breath coming faster and with some effort slowed it. *Be sensible, Liz*. Even if they made love, she must remain in control of herself and the situation.

She savored the aftertaste of the kiss. "Mmmm," she said, and put her arms around him. They kissed again and she sensed he was becoming aroused. *Don't act as if you enjoy it too much,* she cautioned herself.

Benny groaned and his hand gently cupped her left breast. "A long time," he whispered.

She stiffened and the hand dropped away. She was acting too coldly. Ease up. It was what he needed. The fact that he needed her made her warm. She reached over and turned off the bedside light, leaving only the glow from a single small lamp.

This time the kiss was wet and more intense. Her own tongue explored and she carefully arched her body toward his, allowing him to feel her against him. *God, what a build the man had!* They slowly lay back on the bed, pressed tight. She felt him hard against her abdomen and tried to repress the flood of warmth.

Liz tried to pull back just a little to catch her breath, but he was holding her tightly and she found herself losing her composure, heard herself crooning an involuntary moan.

"My room," he whispered.

He started to roll away, and she cried, "Don't go." *Julie wouldn't be back for hours.*

She was unbuttoning his shirt, then kissing his chest and shedding her blouse. He fumbled, so she guided his fingers to the bra release. She sensed it when he crossed the threshold separating caution from lust. They kissed wildly, and he felt her and she ached even more. He pulled a hand from her breast and reached down.

"I'll do it," she said. She worked his belt buckle free, then slowly loosened the catch and zipper.

He fumbled with her slacks and she twisted to get out of them. He pulled her bikini panties to her knees and caressed and probed her moistness with his hand, leaving her to push at the panties with feet and toes.

"Just a second," she said brightly, and drew back to remove the panties, fighting again to recover her senses. She moved gracefully, then repositioned herself, slightly drawing up one leg, knowing she looked appealing in the glow of the dim light.

They caressed and petted, and each time she felt her heat mounting, she would think of unpleasant things, like serving dinner aboard a crowded stretch 707 in turbulence, so she wouldn't lose her self-control. When he finally crawled onto her, she guiding him, she knew she was back in command of herself. Now to endure.

He entered her slowly, pressing lightly while he kissed her and explored with sure hands, moving relentlessly yet without haste. The heat grew in intensity until she felt she was being consumed, focused there, flushing upward to her face, her nipples tingling and her senses keen.

Liz cried out suddenly, tossing her head about wildly on the bed. She raked his back with her fingernails and gripped him about the waist with knees up and legs locked about the small of his back. She wanted to pull him entirely into herself!

For that one grand moment she was maddeningly, deliciously, totally out of control. An orgasm of shuddering intensity began to build . . .

Voices and laughter from outside. Sounds of the door handle moving.

"Oh, God!" she cried out. Benny withdrew.

"Get out!" called Liz toward the door, twisting away in horror as the door opened wider. She saw shapes. "Get out!"

The door closed and Liz huddled on the bed, burning with embarrassment but not wanting it to end. Then she looked at Benny, who was already dressing.

She wanted to tell him to come back, that she wanted to feel the wonder of it again. But she just lay there, chest heaving and clutching herself, too proud. Finally, she retrieved a shorty nightgown and pulled it on, trying to think of what she should say at a time like this.

Benny was quickly dressed, and finished by brushing his hair into place with his hands, the whole time avoiding looking at her. His face was flushed.

Liz stood, face flushed with humiliation but not wanting him to leave. There was nothing in her training that told her what to do.

He started to go, then turned to her, looking at her strangely.

Should she embrace him?

"See you tomorrow," he mumbled, and was gone.

She huddled on her bed miserably for a long time, thinking, before Julie finally came back to the room. She came directly over and sat beside her.

"Liz, we didn't see a thing."

That wasn't what worried Liz. There was nothing she could do about whatever Julie and Mal Bear had or had not seen. Her sadness was about Benny and the way he'd left.

"It's not just you," she said sadly. "What's he going to think, Julie?"

Liz noisily blew her nose. Her throat caught in a hiccup, then she blew again.

Julie didn't know that they hadn't finished, and she wasn't about to tell her. She'd probably been across the hall having multiple wall-crawlers with Mal Bear the whole time she'd been lying here feeling so miserable.

"He's probably as embarrassed as you are," said Julie.

Liz walked over to the mirror, where she dabbed her eyes dry and then heaved a sigh. "I guess I've known it since I first met him. He's awfully perfect for me, Julie."

"Then go after him, Liz. Considering everything you've got," Julie said, observing her, "that shouldn't be difficult."

As Julie was about to turn off the light, she told her about what Benny had said about Mal Bear losing his friends.

"I know. He feels responsible for every one of them." Julie went on. "He doesn't feel he's doing his job as well as he should, and it's tearing at him inside."

"He feels responsible?"

"Their jobs, Benny's and his, are to protect the other guys. Now, let's get some sleep so we can do Bangkok tomorrow."

When Liz finally drifted off, the matter of her feelings about Benny was happily resolved in her mind. She was a little concerned that some of her friends might consider him a warmonger, and that her parents might think her a blithering fool for settling on a man whose background she knew so little about, a divorced man at that, but that would be worked out.

They spent the next two days sightseeing, shopping at gem and jewelry markets, and trying the city's cuisine and nightlife. Once, at the women's urging, they ventured into what the men called a GI bar, and Liz was intrigued as they observed the sexy, doll-faced prostitutes hustling soldiers on rest and recuperation leave from Vietnam.

Liz tried to attract Benny by using various wiles. She was attentive and warm. He was friendly. She tried cool and proper. So was he. She tried sensuous and suggestive. He was shy and quiet. Nothing seemed to get his attention. At night, when it came time to drop her at her door, he'd kiss her and she'd respond enthusiastically, but then he would draw back, smile, and say good night. As she prepared for bed, she would think of his coolness, and it became difficult to imagine that the first night they'd coupled like wild demons.

When she turned off the lights to sleep, alone for long hours—for Julie dawdled late with the Bear—she would lie awake and try to make sense of it all. Now that she knew what

she wanted, she didn't know how to fight to get it. Life was
infuriatingly complex.

She had thought it out very wantonly. When she got her
chance she would satisfy him as he'd never been satisfied
before. She'd learn his darkest desires and make them come
true. She knew men liked to be aroused orally, and once when
she thought of doing it, she found herself writhing about in
bed. She stopped and lay still, embarrassed, for it was Mal
Bear she had been fantasizing about.

On Monday they wandered through the silk market.
Exquisitely brocaded Thai silk was fast becoming known as
one of the world's finest fabrics. The prices at the market were
modest, a tenth of what she would have paid in New York or
Paris, but Liz found it hard to become excited, even when Julie
bought four yards of beautiful white-on-white silk for an
evening dress she would have made by a great tailor she knew
in San Francisco's Chinatown.

That morning she'd confided to Julie that she had utterly
failed with Benny. Tomorrow their time together would be
over, and he was still acting cool. Julie was sympathetic, but
she was not herself these days and didn't offer a solution. Her
radiant, fulfilled look made Liz's situation even more madden-
ing.

After the silk market they ate dinner at a small, clean
restaurant they'd found. They ordered Thai beef, strips of lean
meat with greens, curry, herbs, and hot, green peppers over
white rice. They had learned to eat the extremely hot Thai food
slowly, both to savor it and to allow their taste buds to recover
between bites. They drank ice-cold Singha beer to help cool
off.

"Robert Mitchum was here a short while back," said
Benny, coming up with another of what Mal Bear called
useless nuggets of information. "He wolfed down a plateful of
hot curried beef. Said it was sissy stuff compared to the
Mexican food he got in the border states."

"Whooo-eee! Call me sissy," said the Bear, taking a
mouthful of beer and blowing.

At least, Liz thought jealously, Julie had certainly enjoyed
the trip. She acted utterly happy. Liz wondered just what Mal
Bear did that kept her glowing like that.

It was dark by the time they arrived back at the hotel.
They went to the bar for a last round of nightly drinks together.

This time Mal and Julie left early, and Liz was left with Benny, who sat brooding in a sort of melancholy. He ordered another round for them both.

"It's been fun," he said.

What was this, the thank you note? she wondered.

Getting no response, he added, "It's been relaxing."

Liz looked at him with mounting irritation. She'd given up on playing the various roles. "So what did you think of Bangkok?" she asked.

"Dirty, smelly, old, good food, gentle people."

She realized that this was the first time she'd really had him alone to herself. Except of course, on the frustrating trudges to her door. She looked at him squarely, without demureness, and observed him closely. He met her eyes. *Perhaps* . . .

"Uh, sorry about that first night, Liz," he mumbled. It was the first time either of them had mentioned it.

"What?" she asked dumbly. "Sorry?"

"The first night we were here."

"You're sorry?" She could not help herself as the dark rage that had been festering bubbled to a boil.

He nodded.

"You're sorry we made love?" She didn't care that the two businessmen at an adjacent table looked at her with surprise. *"You're sorry?"* Her voice was growing shrill.

"You're taking it wrong," Benny said, uneasy and obviously surprised at her outburst.

"I heard *exactly* what you said, Benny Lewis." Her Virginia accent grew more distinct as her anger grew. She stood slowly before erupting. She stamped her foot and squealed.

His mouth drooped.

After being so frustrated, it felt wonderful! She did it again, just stamped her foot and squealed out her anger even louder. Then she marched off toward the lobby.

The elevator was busy. She hmmphed, and started up the stairs. She huffed upward, her anger rising with each step. *The goddam idiot fool!* She stopped at the second floor landing, blew out a breath, and squealed again, this time so loud her throat ached. She felt a hot flush on her face, knew she was beet-red and unattractive, and didn't care.

At the third floor she stormed out through the stairwell

door toward her room, fuming. Benny waited at her door, holding the purse she'd left at the table. She stopped in front of him, puffing from the effort of the stairs. "Now"—she blew a breath—"now what . . . am I . . . supposed to say? . . . 'Thank you nice man . . . for your wonderful . . . manners?' "

She angrily grabbed the purse, upended it, and scattered the contents onto the floor. Tissues, keys, various lipsticks, two compacts, birth control pills, aspirin, cologne, loose change, hairpins, and a wallet went flying. She saw it all lying in disarray and aimed a kick at the wallet.

"You're sorry, huh?" she snorted.

He was standing quietly. The fool had a grin on his face! She shrieked, stamping her foot yet again, then knelt to start collecting her things, unceremoniously throwing them into the purse.

"Just stand there and watch!" she stormed.

"Want some help?"

"I'd kiss a warty frog before I'd ask you for help."

A man pushed his head out to see what was happening in the hallway. Liz glared at him so nastily he pulled his head back like a turtle.

She continued to collect her things, slowing down as her anger subsided.

Another door opened. The Bear looked out questioningly, saw her and Benny, and asked if he could help. Julie said something from behind him.

"Go to hell!" Liz yelled.

"Wow," said the Bear, and closed the door.

Benny knelt and picked up a compact and some hairpins. "You're upset," he said.

"God, but you're observant."

"Sorry."

"You already said that!"

He looked exasperated. "You know what I mean."

She started to speak, then stopped herself. She took the things he had gathered, dropped all but her room key into the purse, and snapped it shut.

As Benny rubbed his jaw thoughtfully, she found her key and opened the door, angry because her hand was trembling. She stormed inside, tossed the purse onto the bed, and went to the vanity, where she angrily poured a glass of red wine.

02/2308—Bangkok, Thailand

Bear Stewart

The Bear heard it on the radio, threw on his pants, and hurried over to Benny's room. He knocked lightly, so as not to disturb his friend if he was in there consoling Liz. *Whoo-ee, had she been mad!*

He called Benny's name.

"Yeah?" called Benny. He was awake.

"The war's back on," called the Bear.

Benny padded to the door and let him in. He was alone. The Bear went to the bedside clock-radio and tuned to the Armed Forces Radio station. A few minutes later the announcement was repeated, and they both grinned as they listened.

F-4's had entered North Vietnam, flying at the same altitudes and airspeeds as the heavily laden Thuds, and had destroyed seven MiG's. They were calling it a *MiG sweep*.

They were exultant. "Shit hot!" whooped the Bear.

"We'd better get back to Takhli," said Benny anxiously.

The Bear shrugged and indicated the radio, his smile drooping. "Listen."

The announcer said that despite the day's successful air missions, the bombing ban was being extended in the hope the North Vietnamese would reconsider the president's terms for negotiation.

The Bear made disparaging remarks about politicians, not excluding his commander in chief.

"We'd better get back anyway, Bear," said Benny. "Maybe the ban will be lifted right away."

"You got more faith than I do, old buddy," said the Bear. "Julie's leaving. What's holding you?"

Julie was joining a Pan Am crew that needed a junior stewardess on the morning Tokyo run.

The Bear shrugged. "I've got a friend stationed at Seventh Air Force Headquarters who'll be in town tomorrow. He wants to get together so he can pass something on. Says it's pretty sensitive information, so he's set up a secure room at the embassy."

"Then I suppose you'd better stay," said Benny.

The Bear didn't really want to delve, but Benny had been acting strange, like he had in the Philippines.

"What's with you and Liz?" he asked. "Up until tonight she was giving you the big come-on, and you were acting cool as hell." Liz planned to take a series of deadhead flights back but had made it clear that she could stay if Benny wanted to spend an extra day.

"You know something, Bear. They even have the same name."

"Who?" he asked, but he knew.

"Bets and Liz. Elizabeth, even spelled the same way. When you guys walked in on us the other night, she went half beserk, yelling for me to get out, just like Bets would have." He shook his head angrily. "Then she started playing games to make up, like Bets used to do."

The Bear was quiet, thinking a lot of women would get excited if people walked in while she was bareass with a man.

"She damn near asked for my pedigree papers.

"Julie says she was raised like that. Well-to-do family with old money. She says Liz can be a jerk, but she thinks you're doing a great job turning her into an American."

"She'll have to do it by herself. I'm going back to Takhli."

"It's your call," the Bear said.

"You seem to be getting along well with Julie."

The Bear nodded. "Nice kid."

"She's awfully serious, Bear."

The Bear nodded again, not knowing what to say. He knew Julie was serious, but he hadn't made the slightest attempt to extricate himself. He knew he should make a move soon, because he didn't want to hurt her. He wished his mind was clearer about it all.

"I'd better get on back," he said. "Just thought you'd want to know about the F-4 MiG sweep."

He went back down the hall and let himself in.

Julie was sitting up in the bed, her breasts covered modestly. "Was he alone?" she asked.

"Yeah," he said. "Things aren't good with those two."

He looked at her and saw again the wondrous expression on her face. Emotion stirred in his gut, like a knife twisting there. He had to make a move to let her down gently.

She held her arms out to him, and the sheet fell away. He stood for a moment, savoring the sight before he turned off the light.

03/0845—Bangkok, Thailand

When Julie left on the Pan Am crew bus the next morning, the Bear stood outside in the heat, watching her wave until the bus turned the corner. He watched a bit longer, then returned to the hotel lobby deep in thought, only to run squarely into Liz Richardson.

"Excuse me," he said.

She regarded him evenly. It was obvious she had been waiting for the others to leave. "It's time we talked," she said.

Dark rings under her eyes betrayed her lack of rest. Something in her voice, in the purpose of her expression, made him believe she wanted more than friendly conversation.

CHAPTER FOURTEEN

Tuesday, January 3rd, 1967—1000 Local, People's Army HQ, Hanoi, DRV

Xuan Nha

The tribunal of generals had been hastily called, and it was not a pleasant one. General Dung presided, barking questions and glowering whenever answers were given slowly.

Eight MiG interceptors had been destroyed. Seven in the air and another upon landing at Phuc Yen airfield. Two more had been badly shot up. None of the American air pirates had been destroyed or even damaged.

"Why did you send out MiG interceptors after the Phantoms, when you knew they were so dangerous?" Dung had been over the same questions several times.

The major in charge of the P-1 long-range radar at Phuc Yen said the VPAAF had requested intercept information. His controllers had seen the aircraft ingressing, flying the same altitudes and airspeeds as Thunder planes. Following Col Thao Phong's directions, they had radioed the information to the interceptor units at Phuc Yen, Hoa Lac, and Kep. The radar controllers had then directed the MiG's toward the invaders using normal procedures.

Dung was stone-faced. He waved the major from the room and turned to Xuan Nha. "Why were so few guided rockets fired at the Phantoms?"

It was Xuan's turn in the hot seat. He stood straight as a rod and spoke cautiously. "The equipment and weapons of the mobile rocket battalions were in need of repair and maintenance. After coordinating with Colonel Phong, I directed the mobile battalions to shut down and perform all necessary repairs. That left us with only the Hanoi and Haiphong area batteries, and the Phantoms stayed well out of their range."

General Dung's eyes glittered with animation. "Under whose authority was this done?"

"My own, comrade General." He had fully coordinated the stand-down with General Luc, but to say so would be inappropriate.

Dung nodded abruptly, without the slightest sign that he was willing to excuse him. "So you left the interceptors to their fate. That was quite presumptuous of you, Colonel."

There was nothing for Xuan Nha to say. Dung motioned angrily as he sat down. Dung turned back to Col Thao Phong. "Once again. Why were so many of our interceptors destroyed?"

Thao stood quickly. "By the time our interceptors could tell that the attackers were not Thunder planes with bombs, but Phantoms with only missiles, they had seen many of us, comrade General."

"And your pilots could not get away?" A sneer in the tone.

"No, comrade General. It was a dishonorable and cowardly trick the Americans played."

Dung snorted. "How many of our pilots were lost?" He knew, of course.

"Four killed. Two injured. The rest are well."

"Good pilots?"

"Major Tan was one of our finest, another was a North Korean adviser pilot. The rest are easily replaceable."

"As you are, Colonel?" General Dung waited for the pilot colonel to pass his own sentence.

Thao Phong slumped slowly, looking resigned and weary. "Yes, comrade General."

General Dung coldly nodded to General Tho, commander of the VPAAF, who sat at his elbow.

Thao Phong drew a short breath of anticipation.

"You will return to your former unit at Phuc Yen," said General Tho, "and assume Major Tan's duties." He rudely held out a hand. "Your epaulets."

Thao Phong's eyes were impassive and militarily correct, but his fingers trembled as he handed the epaulets to General Tho.

"You were promoted too quickly, before you proved yourself in the defense of the homeland. I must suffer for that poor decision, although I must say I had misgivings about the promotion from the first. Now *you* will lead the interceptors into the fight. Perhaps that will teach you to properly coordinate future decisions with your superiors."

The People's Army Air Force general looked contemptuously at Thao Phong, even though all in the room knew that Tho had enthusiastically endorsed the request to send the MiG interceptors out to fight alone.

"Leave us, *Major* Thao Phong," he said, with a disdainful flick of his wrist. The VPAAF's shame was expunged. A scapegoat had been blamed, dishonored, and demoted.

General Luc, Xuan Nha's superior officer, looked on with interest, obviously waiting for a similar nod from General Dung so he could deal with his own colonel. Colonel Trung, Xuan's former superior, sat at General Luc's side wearing a satisfied expression.

Dung's look made Xuan feel exceedingly uncomfortable.

"This Wisdom thing you are building. A complex of highly sophisticated radars?"

"Yes, comrade General."

"Is it the reason your rocket sites were not prepared to fire?"

Xuan Nha hesitated, trying with difficulty to organize his thoughts.

"Well?" Dung's voice was loud.

"It is one of the reasons, comrade General."

Dung leaned toward him. "Tell me this, Xuan Nha, when Wisdom is completed, will it stop such things as happened yesterday from happening again?"

Xuan's voice emerged in an alien, pleading tone. "We will be able to work better with all our forces, not just with interceptors, rockets, or artillery. At the present we must assign the air to one or another. With Wisdom, we will work with them all."

"Is that an answer?"

"It *will* ensure that such things do not happen again, comrade General."

Dung looked at him, the animated eyes still angry. He turned suddenly to General Luc. "For the present, let him proceed with Wisdom."

Luc nodded respectfully.

Dung returned to Xuan Nha. "If we do not see results very shortly, we will know you personally have failed."

Xuan's heart pounded.

"You do not have long."

"A few weeks is all I will need," he tried to reason.

General Dung grunted disdainfully, as if that was out of the question and Xuan Nha was no longer worth listening to.

The generals rose together and filed stiffly from the room. Colonel Trung followed without a backward look at his former subordinate.

As he walked back across the huge parade ground toward the VPAND building, Xuan stumbled twice but recovered gracelessly. He could cope with battle, even with the certainty of impending death. Without his self-esteem, though, what would be left of a man such as he?

Xuan saw himself standing before the generals in disgrace, as Thao Phong had been forced to do, and he shuddered. Like warriors of all times and all lands, honor, courage, and pride of achievement had come to mean everything. The thought of being scorned by his men and fellow officers was a specter far worse than anything else he could imagine.

Fear churned within the pit of his stomach. There was so little time! The Wisdom complex was his only chance of salvation, but it would be weeks before it could be completed. If only . . .

Could it be hurried? He must drive his men, even the Russians, to work faster.

03/1500L—Takhli RTAFB, Thailand

Benny Lewis

The Weasel crews met at the pig squadron to listen to Ries and Janssen recount how things had gone at their Saigon meeting. Les was enthused, and within a few minutes he had the others excited.

The atmosphere was upbeat.

Bear Stewart was still in Bangkok, but Benny wished he was here. If he could observe Les Ries when the pressure was off, perhaps he'd drop some of his criticisms.

Ries and Janssen alternately described the meeting. "General Roman didn't show up until the last day, and that was only to look good and pass out medals. The meeting was General Moss's own show."

Roman was the big cheese for all the Pacific Air Forces. Moss, commander of Seventh Air Force, headquartered in Saigon, had the responsibility of running the air war. The lines of authority between the two were sometimes vaguely drawn, with the resulting friction felt down to wing level. Roman was a four-star and Moss was a three-star, but the guys preferred Moss. Although he acted like he shit sacred pellets, at least his background had been in fighters. All Roman knew or cared much about were his B-52's and bomber pilots. On the other hand, Moss knew fighters and didn't make bones about distrusting bomber people.

"General Moss seemed interested," interjected Janssen. "He listened hard, said that by God something's got to be done about the buildup of defenses."

Ries resumed. "The air-to-air guys were up first. They started off with an intelligence briefing that showed some of the MiG's had been flown out to southern China where all the new MiG's from Russia were being outfitted. The spooks had intercepted radio traffic saying one hell of a lot of MiG's would be flown in by Tuesday morning. There was a big F-4 delegation there from Ubon. They gave their pitches about flying the flight profiles of Thuds with their Phantoms to fool the gomers, and got approval from General Moss. Then they went to work planning the MiG sweep."

"They done good," said Pudge Holden, "for a bunch of ham-first Phantom drivers."

A generous amount of good-natured ribbing was normal between F-4 Phantom pilots and F-105 Thunderchief jocks. Yet the F-4 pilots respected the Thud pilots for their guts and tenacity, and more than one F-105 pilot wished he could be fighting MiG's in the more maneuverable F-4's.

Pudge asked, "They got theirs, now how about ours? Are they going to turn us loose on the SAMs?"

"I'll get to that," said Ries, waving a hand.

"You damn betcha they're going to," said Janssen, unable to hold it in.

Ries waved his bear into silence. "I gave my briefing on

the second afternoon. Told 'em we had to do something about the defenses besides acting like targets for SAMs."

"What did the Weasels from Korat have to say?" asked Benny.

"They were supportive." Ries turned to Janssen. "Didn't you think so?"

Janssen agreed. "They were a lot more cautious in their approach, but they agreed in principle. Their main thrust was that the strike force should start flying in larger formations to concentrate the jamming power from the ECM pods."

The bears started mumbling among themselves. Some liked the ECM jamming pods, but grumbled that the power output was too low to be really effective. Others said the jamming just screwed up the radar detection gear so you couldn't tell when a SAM was launched at you.

Dan Janssen shook his head. "At Korat they've got more faith in pods than we do. They're even saying if everyone's got their jamming pods turned on, you don't care if they launch SAMs because they can't hit you. They want the strike force to fly up higher, straight and level. No jinking or moving around because that screws up the jamming."

"What did their wing commander say about that?" asked Lyle Watson.

"I think he may go along with it. Said they had to do something better than they're doing now to reduce losses."

"What did B. J. Parker say?"

"He said Takhli is going to wait and see the results from the tests they're running back in the States. They're supposed to finish flight-testing at Nellis sometime this month."

"What about *your* briefing, Les?" asked Pudge.

"I told them the Takhli Weasels want a campaign to take out the radars and SAM sites in a methodical fashion and gave our pitch. I believe General Moss was in favor, especially when the Weasels from Korat agreed it was a good idea."

"Did he give us a thumbs-up?" asked Pudge.

"Not in so many words. We had to completely change his mindset. I think we got about as good as we could expect."

"Yeah," said Janssen. "When we walked in there the general was about to rule that since the Weasels are critical resources, and there are so few of us, we can't fly except on the important JCS strikes. No more support of road recce in the southern panhandle or pack five. No easy counters. Only strike support, and mainly in pack six."

"Shee-it," said Shaky Anderson. "No one could survive that kind of pressure. It would take a year to get a hundred missions, and come to think of it, no one would *ever get* a hundred missions."

"No Takhli Weasel crew's survived a hundred missions yet," complained Lyle Watson. "Sounds like the general wants to keep it that way."

"We talked him out of that," said Ries. "At the end of my briefing, I told him that regardless of whether he approved the SAM campaign, we had to have a few easy missions to train the new guys and work out tactics."

The group vociferously agreed.

"Yeah," said Shaky. "I want about a hundred easy training missions."

Laughter.

"General Moss thanked us for our insights," said Ries.

"After Les's briefing he got up and shook our hands," said Janssen. "Said it was great to have the word direct from the field."

"How about the campaign to eliminate the SAMs?" asked Benny.

"When I was done, Moss had his staff guys take our briefing viewgraphs. Told them to do a study of how we can all work together to make it happen. A lieutenant colonel named Gates who said he's a friend of Bear Stewart's expects they'll call us back in a couple of weeks to go over the plan."

They all talked about the briefing, asked questions of Ries and Janssen, and were generally happy about the way things had gone.

Cpt. Dave Persons spoke up. "What'd I hear about a party?"

"Not *a party*," said Janssen. "*Two parties* on New Year's Eve, one after the other."

"President Nguyen Cao Ky showed up at the New Year's party at the club and handed out Vietnamese service medals," explained Ries. "Then he invited us to the bash at the palace."

"A country run by a thirty-year-old fighter pilot can't be all bad," said Pudge Holden.

"He's a little guy," said Dan Janssen. "His wife's a good-looking broad, but she wasn't at the party long. Took off real quick after saying something to Nguyen. I think she caught Swede Swendler looking at her with lust in his eyes."

Laughter.

"Hell," said Pudge, "Swede probably thought she was just another LBFM."

LBFM was a slang term given the local bar girls. *Little brown fucking machines.*

Pudge Holden and Lyle Watson came over to Benny when the meeting started to break up. Benny said he was pleased with the results, but Pudge withheld judgment. "I'm sure Les gave a good briefing," he said, "but I've worked at headquarters before. Unless you get a general's approval right there when you're nose to nose with him, you've got a problem."

"You don't think we'll get approval?"

"I'd say you were right before. We should be working up our own tactics. No matter what General Moss says, he's going to trust his own staff officers more than anyone out here at the bases. Also, the Wild Weasels are beginning to capture imaginations and get attention from the Pentagon on down. Too much attention means too many interested generals."

They watched the Weasel crews congratulating Ries and Dan.

After thinking about it, Benny agreed with Pudge. "Let's just keep working on our tactics," he finally said, "and assume we're going to have to do it all ourselves."

03/1700L—People's Army HQ, Hanoi, DRV

Nicolaj Gregarian

The Russian stood with Nha before the wall map of the Bac Can area, looking at the pin-flags. Different flags showed the locations for each system and building: the P-50 long-range radar, the communications building, the adjacent command-and-control center, the P-2 acquisition radar, the experimental, electro-optic/electronic rocket system, and the two SON-9b artillery radars. Two more showed barracks areas, one for foreign advisers and visitors, the other for the Vietnamese specialists and technicians.

When Nicolaj had received the summons, he'd been at the Russian compound holding technical discussions with a group of important Soviet civilians. Scientists and systems engineers from the advanced rocket-design group at Kuybyshev. Interested in the experiment taking shape around the innocuous village of Bac Can. So prestigious a group that Soviet diplomats worldwide had been ordered to somehow get the Americans to delay resumption of bombing until the group was safely in place at Wisdom. Their Vietnamese hosts must be wondering why they were receiving such vigorous diplomatic support. They would be equally confused when such support was withdrawn later in January, for the group then wished to observe Wisdom in operation under actual combat conditions.

Nicolaj had been concerned when *Polkovnik* Feodor Dimetriev had spoken to him earlier about the generals' tribunal, but he hadn't suspected the extent of the impact upon Xuan Nha. Any sign of anxiety was out of character for the short Annamese *polkovnik,* but Nha was so nervous, pacing and jumping at the slightest movement, that Gregarian wondered about his mental health.

Gregarian nodded a friendly greeting as *Mayor* Nguy entered the office. Nha glanced at Nguy noncommittally, although a moment before he'd shouted to *Serzhant* Van Ng that he wanted him. Shouting was not Nha's normal way. Neither was ignoring *Mayor* Nguy, the man he had entrusted with their project.

"Status?" Xuan Nha breathed, still staring at the map.

"The P-50 radar has been inventoried and is ready for installation," Gregarian said. "Site alterations and construction of the buildings are almost completed. Next come site inspection, installation of equipment, bore-siting, and testing. Then completion of the communications net and final systems testing, and the deployment of the dummy radars that will make it impossible for the Americans to locate the P-50 with their electronic systems."

Xuan Nha stared at Nguy. "You are ready?"

Mayor Nguy was to depart for Bac Can with a contingent of fifty combat engineering personnel drawn from a coastal defense project at Haiphong. More than 200 other civil engineers, taken from other projects, were already in place.

Nguy nodded. "We shall be there in five hours. The road is still very good."

Although the tribunal in Dung's private meeting room had been conducted secretly, *Polkovnik* Dimetriev had been told, and in turn he'd told Gregarian. He described the demotion and disgrace of Thao Phong, adding that Xuan Nha's own time clock was running and that he'd been given little time to obtain results.

There was no way for the Soviet advisers to help Xuan Nha with his personal problem. The Vietnamese were vulnerable to certain pressures, due to the vast military support from the Soviet Union, but the Vietnamese were adamant that they retain control of their people. In the past they had not hesitated to discipline other technical personnel. Xuan Nha might be no exception.

Gregarian worried not only about losing Xuan Nha as his key supporter for the Wisdom complex, but also about damage that Xuan might cause because of his mental state.

"What is the *earliest* the installation can be completed?" snapped Xuan to Nguy.

Gregarian interrupted. "Let us not hurry so much that we make mistakes."

Xuan erupted. "In two weeks the commanders must return to their units."

The outburst had come in the midst of quieter discussion and was startling. Xuan Nha's pleasant mask was stripped away, replaced by a drawn and anxious look.

The Tiger of Dien Bien Phu was gone, taken away by *General-Polkovnik* Dung, the man who had given the nickname so long ago. Gregarian wasn't surprised at the turn of events, for little the strange Asians did surprised him, yet he had not been prepared for this. Xuan's face worked with ugly emotions, fought to calm itself, then grimaced horribly again, like some alien flesh with no human owner.

"We *must* have results," Xuan repeated in the strained voice.

Quang Hanh came in, saw Nha's face working, and stood quietly. Xuan had kept the young communications officer running since Gregarian had arrived, and many of the tasks had been frivolous ones.

Xuan Nha turned to the window and stood for a moment. Gregarian thought he heard a muffled choke.

"Comrade Colonel?" addressed Quang Hanh, very quietly.

They heard a grunt of recognition.

"We have official confirmation that the Americans have

agreed to extend the bombing halt for at least a week, I was told."

"What office told you?" asked Xuan Nha, still turned to the window.

"Your wife's office in the Ministry of External Affairs, sir."

Silence.

"It was what we wished for," said Gregarian, testing the water.

"One week? I must have more. I told her that *I - must - have - more - time.*"

"That would be ideal," agreed Gregarian.

They all waited for what seemed an eternity. Then, abruptly, Xuan Nha turned from the window back to them, his mask back in place. A smile, the sad eyes, the look of friendship.

"I am sure my wife and her people are doing everything possible to gain us more time. Now, is there anything else we can be doing? I will find more people if you feel they are necessary, Major Nguy."

"There will be nearly three hundred engineering experts working with three thousand laborers, comrade Colonel. That will certainly be enough. If there are more their efforts may be counterproductive."

"Colonel Nha, there is something else," said young Quang Hanh.

"Does it concern this effort?"

The *leytenant* looked at the others in the room. "Yes, sir."

"I have no secrets about the Wisdom complex from these two," said Xuan Nha, so serene and calm that it seemed impossible that he could have been so upset a few moments before. "Proceed."

"A complaint was forwarded from the Ministry of Internal Affairs."

"Complaint?"

"They say our people at Bac Can have conscripted craftsmen and government workers and are using them as common laborers."

"Are we doing that?" Xuan asked *Mayor* Nguy.

Nguy looked discomfited. "Your order was to get to work immediately, comrade Colonel. You said to get laborers from the cities, the farms, anywhere. I relayed that word to our engineering personnel there and they did as you said."

Again the mask lifted, but this time only for a flash of an instant did they see the horror. *What are we seeing?* Gregarian asked himself.

"We do not need complaints just now," whispered Xuan Nha. "Not from any source."

"Yes, comrade Colonel," said *Mayor* Nguy in his correct tone.

"Fix it for me when you get to Bac Can, old friend."

Nguy nodded.

The mood swung once more. Xuan Nha began to pace the floor, glancing periodically at the map. "So little time," he muttered.

Gregarian tried again, pointing at the map. "Wisdom is a good idea. We have a very good plan. We will have results very shortly."

Xuan Nha was incited by the words. He turned to Nguy. "Fourteen days! I will give you two weeks to complete the Wisdom complex."

Both Gregarian and Nguy stared. Even with swarms of laborers working relentlessly, ten days of work lay ahead just to place, bore-site, and calibrate the several permanent radar installations, and then at least another week to tie everything together. The commanders could return to their units then, but yet another week would be required to test the sensitive monitoring and communications equipment. Dummy transmitters had to be installed and harmonized with the P-50 so they could electronically mask its presence.

"Be reasonable!" blurted Gregarian.

Xuan Nha's jaw twitched and he stared at Gregarian with hate pouring from eyes no longer soft. Gregarian grew quiet, even fearful. The man was capable of anything.

"Fourteen days, Major Nguy. This is the time you have to build the system. Then the commanders and men must return to their units, and Wisdom must be activated."

Nguy looked to Gregarian, then his colonel. It was a near-impossible task.

I will hold you responsible, Major Nguy. You . . . ah . . . you know of certain irregularities in your recent behavior we have discussed."

Then Gregarian saw what Xuan had already seen. *Pod-*

polkovnik Wu stood outside the doorway, looking in somberly, his wraith-thin figure resplendent in his crisp field uniform.

Mayor Nguy saw him also and openly flinched. He nodded his head dutifully to Wu, then turned back to Xuan Nha. "I must go now and begin, comrade Colonel."

"Results," breathed Xuan Nha, glancing at Wu in the doorway. "We must have results."

"You shall have them." *Mayor* Nguy's face was drawn.

Xuan Nha spoke in his low voice, and they listened hard. "Remember, traitors can be found *anywhere*."

His words captured everyone's attention.

04/1300L—Command Post, Takhli RTAFB, Thailand

Benny Lewis

Les Ries and Dan Janssen came into the command-post briefing room and nodded curtly to Benny and the Bear, who had just recently returned.

"You guys wanted to talk?" asked Les.

"The Bear had a meeting with a friend of his at Bangkok, and he says it's important we share what he learned," said Benny.

Les looked evenly at Bear Stewart, his stare showing little warmth. He was obviously still holding the old grudge. He and Dan Janssen sat down and waited.

The Bear was acting odd upon his return from Bangkok, quieter and looking like something weighed heavily on his mind. Benny supposed it had something to do with Julie and kept out of it.

"I met with an old friend named Pearly Gates at the Bangkok embassy," said the Bear. "He's a lieutenant colonel stationed at the headquarters in Saigon."

"I met him at our briefing," said Dan Janssen.

"Yeah, he told me about it. Said you guys gave a good pitch."

"General Moss liked it," boasted Janssen.

"What have you got?" Les asked impatiently.

"Pearly said the gomers shipped in some new equipment of some kind, and wants us to keep a lookout for anything new up there."

"They don't know what it was?" asked Les.

"He says it was offloaded at night at Haiphong and secretly trucked out. He said the highway to Hanoi was smoothed, like they might be carrying something delicate."

"So what do they think it is?"

"They didn't know. That's what's bothering them at Seventh Air Force. Pearly wants us to keep our eyes open for new radar signals, anything that seems different."

"So whatever this thing is, is in Hanoi?"

"They're not sure of that, either. He said the photos of the roads north of Hanoi look like they were smoothed out, too."

"How far north of Hanoi?"

Les Ries was barking his questions impatiently, and Benny could tell the Bear didn't appreciate his tone.

"They're not sure of that either," answered the Bear. "The road was smoothed over all the way up into the Chinese buffer zone."

"So we're supposed to look for they-don't-know-what, and it's they-don't-know-where? Sounds like a bunch of crap."

"Colonel Gates wouldn't have wanted to meet me like that if he didn't think it was something important."

"Why the hell isn't he back in Saigon working on our plan like General Moss told him to do," asked Les, "instead of boondoggling off to Bangkok to see some captain and tell him a bunch of horsecrap?"

"And how come he told you, and didn't tell us when we were there in Saigon?" asked Dan Janssen.

"He was in Bangkok on other business, and I'm someone he knows," said the Bear, heating up. "He can trust me to get the word out."

"This is clearly a waste of our time," said Les Ries, getting to his feet.

Ries and Janssen left without further word.

Bear Stewart shook his head in disgust. "Hard to tell those guys anything," he said.

Benny agreed, but didn't say it. "What do you think it might be?" he asked the Bear.

"Got me, but if Seventh Air Force is concerned, don't you think we ought to be?"

Colonel Mack came into the briefing room with Sam Hall in tow, carrying several classified messages. They sat down at a table and Mack began to leaf through them.

"How come you two came back from R and R early?" asked Sam.

Benny answered. "I heard about the MiG sweep, and thought they might call off the bombing halt."

"According to the message traffic we've been getting," said Mack, "it'll be a week or more before we go back to pack six. We'll be supporting a joint ground operation called Cedar Falls, going on around Saigon."

"You guys could have taken more time," said Sam.

"I was ready to come back," Benny said, grinning at Sam, "but the Bear got in an extra day."

"Take every bit you can, Bear," said Sam.

Benny noticed that Mal Stewart didn't smile.

CHAPTER FIFTEEN

Friday, January 13th—0830 Local, Takhli RTAFB, Thailand

Col. B. J. Parker

The weekly message from Seventh Air Force was the long, chatty kind Lieutenant General Moss liked to send. Often they directed a new strategy or imposed a new restriction. Seldom were old strategies or restrictions scrapped. New strategies were explained as being "in the context of" or "to meet the exigencies of" existing ones. Restrictions were added to the top of the existing list.

B. J. Parker, wing commander of the 355th TFW, examined the message.

Paragraph 1 was a structure breakdown of air combat forces, subparagraph 1b covering forces based in Thailand. The Thai government had authorized B-52 bombers to be stationed at U Tapao when construction was completed there. Another F-4 squadron was slated for Ubon Air Base. RF-4C's were to replace the old RF-101 Voodoos at Udorn.

Paragraph 2 discussed the current status of *Operation Cedar Falls,* an Army sweep near Saigon. Allied ground forces were encountering stiff enemy opposition, but were expected to wrap things up within the week. B-52's would fly Arc Light missions to destroy enemy strongholds and troop concentrations. IN-COUNTRY AIR FORCES (meaning the guys stationed in South Vietnam) WILL CONTINUE TO PROVIDE CLOSE AIR SUPPORT FOR THE OPERATION. OUT-OF-COUNTRY FORCES (meaning Thailand-based aircraft) WILL CONTINUE TO ATTACK SUPPLY ROUTES TO ISOLATE THE NVA AND VIET CONG IN THE IRON TRIANGLE,

385

AND KEEP THEM FROM REINFORCEMENT AND RE-
SUPPLY.

Paragraph 3 stated IT IS ANTICIPATED THAT TACTI-
CAL FORCES WILL RESUME ROLLING THUNDER
COMBAT STRIKES ON 15 JAN 67 AS OPERATION CE-
DAR FALLS WINDS DOWN. MULTIPLE, PREVIOUSLY
SELECTED JCS TARGETS ARE ANTICIPATED, AS ARE
MAXIMUM EFFORT STRIKES.

Subparagraph 3c discussed and reinforced the numerous
restrictions.

Subparagraph 3d was directed toward the Iron Hand
flights. "Iron Hand" was the headquarters' code name for Wild
Weasels. It was brief, and referred to a second message, from
PACAF Headquarters, which had been forwarded to Takhli and
Korat, where the Weasels were based. The subparagraph ended
by saying ADDRESSEES WILL ENSURE COMPLIANCE
TO GUIDANCE CONTAINED IN THE HIGHER HEAD-
QUARTERS MESSAGE.

B. J. noted down the date-time-group of the second
message. He called to the master sergeant sitting at the admin
desk in the outer office to locate and advise Maj. Les Ries that
he wished to speak with him right away. He turned his attention
back to the message.

Subparagraph 3e intrigued him, if only by its ambiguity.
AUTHORITY IS BEING SOUGHT TO ATTACK SEVERAL
NEW JCS TARGETS, DESIGNED TO CRIPPLE THE
NORTH VIETNAMESE INDUSTRIAL BASE, AND WHICH
MIGHT BE VIEWED AS ESCALATIONS TO THE WAR
EFFORT. MORE INFORMATION WILL BE FORTHCOM-
ING.

The last paragraph discussed the allocations of funds
authorized for the various units and referred to yet another
message.

B. J. called out again to the master sergeant and told him
to get him the two referenced messages. He waited and read
through General Moss's message once more while the sergeant
contacted the communications center.

He then called the base commander, said the authorization
of funds message was in, and suggested that they get together
at 1000 hours to talk over the dollar amounts they had been
authorized for various projects.

The base commander controlled the facilities, the air

police, food services, personnel center, chaplains, lawyers and medical people, services people, the civil engineers, even the control tower, base support aircraft, and noncombat pilots. Other colonels, called deputy commanders, supervised logistics, maintenance, and fighter operations.

B. J. was the man in charge. As wing commander he was responsible for it all, the one who got ultimate credit or blame.

"Base CO at ten-hundred!" he called out to the admin sergeant, who acknowledged the time of the meeting.

Maj Les Ries arrived, saluted smartly, and B. J. had him take a seat.

"Happy Friday the thirteenth, sir," Les said cheerfully.

Parker knew Les Ries as a perfectionist. He did his utmost to make things go right, even to the point of disregarding his personal safety and career. He was at his happiest when things were going right. When things went wrong he grew testy and sharp and tended to look at problems as personal failures. Few in the wing knew that Ries was also a genuine, died-in-the-wool genius, with an astonishing memory and an IQ of immense proportion. Most saw only the egotist, unable to realize that the man was inhibited by a mind that saw a different picture than they did.

Colonel Parker had mixed emotions about the man's capabilities as the leader of his Wild Weasel contingent. He would have preferred someone more concerned about his career, who would make himself, the wing, and of course, B. J. Parker look good.

"We finally got the message you've been waiting for. They're bringing it over from the command post now."

Ries smiled in anticipation.

"You did a good job briefing in Saigon. General Moss was so impressed with the whole show that he says he wants to set up something like that on a regular basis."

Ries glowed with the compliment.

The master sergeant came in and handed the messages to Parker. B. J. put the allocations message aside, then studied the one titled IRON HAND FORCES UTILIZATION.

"They cover everything we wanted, sir?" Ries was fidgeting, like a high-strung child.

It was a half page of print, and to the point. He read it thoroughly before looking up, then wagged his head slowly from side to side.

"PACAF says the Weasel aircraft are expensive, critical assets, and must be conserved. They feel that losses to date have been far too high."

He looked down and read the message for another moment before continuing. *"Iron Hand assets will be employed only against the highest priority targets."* He looked up. "Only against JCS targets, I think they mean."

Les was growing pale.

"It also states that PACAF/CC . . . General Roman . . . is concerned with the ratio of SAM sites destroyed to losses of Iron Hand assets." He looked up again. "They want more sites killed and fewer losses."

Les sadly shook his head.

"In the last paragraph, they say that due to a complaint received through *diplomatic channels from the People's Republic of China*—let's see—*a strong protest of indiscriminate missile attacks*—*Iron Hand forces must have positive target identification before firing Shrike missiles."*

"They can't do this," breathed Ries, his face flushed with color.

"It's not the first time we've gotten a message from headquarters we've disagreed with, and I can assure you it won't be the last."

B. J. was concerned that Ries was about to come unglued. He listened patiently for a moment as Ries began to ramble.

"They can tell our pilots to go out and hit two-bit targets with millions of dollars of airplanes and bombs. They can tell us to spend the lives of the best men in America, but make damned sure they tie our hands so we can't win. They can tell us to watch our friends get shot down by MiG's, but not to shoot MiG's on the ground because that would be cheating. They can tell the Weasels we're critical, so we only get to fly on the most dangerous missions. They can tell us we should kill more SAM sites, but we can't have a campaign to kill SAM sites. They can . . ."

"Snap out of it, Major!"

"What can't they tell us, sir?" Les whispered.

Parker glared at Ries, not because he was wrong, but because he was out of line.

"We read about how Congress is beginning to listen to a bunch of dirty, long-haired, doped-up anarchists. Who's listening to us? Who gives a damn, Colonel?"

There followed a silence so complete they could hear the admin sergeant's typewriter clacking out front. Finally, "You through?"

He was not. "I tried to tell them what we needed when we went to Saigon." Ries's voice caught. "I guess I didn't get my points across."

"This message isn't from General Moss's people," B. J. said. "It's from their higher headquarters."

"Still . . ." started Les.

B. J. sighed. "Call a meeting of all the Weasels and read them the PACAF message. Let them know the message was not specific. We'll comply with the intent for a couple of weeks and only let the Weasels fly on pack six missions. If we don't get clarification by then, we'll make our own judgment of what a priority mission means."

"But sir?"

"You're dismissed, Major."

When Ries had left, B. J. tried to turn his attention to the funds allocation message.

It was strange, he thought, that so much was being done for morale and living conditions, but that so many pilots' lives could be squandered because of the lousy restrictions. But what could be done? In the course of his career, B. J. had seen the men who tried to fight the dragons in the system. The system always won—it had to win or the system itself would be threatened. He was no dragon-fighter. If he raised his voice he would be replaced in a heartbeat, and who the hell would listen to a washed-up colonel?

B. J. rose quickly, for he had to get out and clear his mind of rebellious thoughts. He went to the outer office and got his hat. "I'll be at the command post," he told the sergeant.

"Base commander at ten-hundred, sir," the sergeant reminded him.

"I'll remember," he said.

B. J. went outside and stood, letting the intense heat wash over him. His radio crackled. The first aircraft would be landing in two minutes.

He looked up at the cloudless sky, waited, then finally saw the first flight approaching in echelon at 350 knots. Needle-nosed, sleek, and clean. One by one the four aircraft pitched left, perfect in their five-second timing, to fly a tight arc. They were evenly spaced on the downwind leg, then dropped out of sight as they began their turn to final.

A good visual overhead pattern. He started to walk, arrived at the door of the command post, then turned to watch yet another flight arrive over the field. Another good pattern. Regular Thunderbirds, those guys.

Les Ries's complaints were forgotten. It was not that he didn't care, just that the Wild Weasel restriction was just one more they had to learn to live with. He had to concern himself with fighting a confusing and difficult war, and somehow get through it all with his wing and his career intact, while losing as few men and aircraft as possible.

He entered the command post to get the status report.

15/1310L—Takhli RTAFB, Thailand

The target was a barracks a few miles west of Hanoi. They had bombed the area once before, and it had been tough. Colonel Parker, the wing commander, was mission commander for this first strike to pack six in the new year.

Hit the barracks, he'd said, but for God's sake don't hit this white building. He'd pointed to a picture of the target area on the wall. The large building was marked with a red cross on top, and Seventh Air Force Intell said it was a new hospital.

Sam Hall, who was leading one of the first strike flights on target, had raised his hand, and Parker had recognized him.

The gomers probably have something in there, boss, he'd said. Sam questioned that it was really a hospital because of its location and lack of windows. Probably a warehouse for guns or SAMs or something, he'd said. He said he'd bet the barracks would be empty and the hospital/warehouse would be full of supplies.

Col. B. J. Parker said if someone made a mistake and hit the hospital he'd have his ass. No one doubted he meant it.

Benny Lewis

They were in the arming area at the end of the active runway, engines idling as the quick-check crew and the armorers scrambled carefully about the aircraft to check weapons and fuses and ensure that down-locks and *Remove Before Flight* pins had been pulled.

Last of all, the armorers pulled the pins that armed the bomb fuses. When armed, only a short length of wire attached to the pylon kept the weapons' timers and sensing transducers from activating and setting off the bombs. When the bomb dropped away the wire was pulled out. The times would start ticking and the sensors start sensing. The same procedure had been used since the first aerial bombs had been dropped from balloons.

Benny and the Bear were flying number 277. CAPT B LEWIS and CAPT M STEWART was painted in yellow block letters on their canopy sills. Tiny Bechler was their wingman. Dave Persons and Dutch Hansletter were flying as number three in the Weasel flight, and Willy Dortmeier was flying on their wing.

Benny sucked a drink from the tube to the ice-water bottle behind his seat, and looked over at Chaplain Black, who approached the side of Bechler's jet. The padres did their duty in the arming area, showing their presence to beef up morale. Poor attitudes were their enemies, and they searched them out and tried to defeat them wherever they might be. Captain Black, the Protestant chaplain, looked and acted like a B-movie rendition of a mortician. Benny wondered if he ever smiled.

The Bear's laugh came over the intercom from the backseat. "You hear about Lyle Watson and the two sisters?"

"What's that?" asked Benny.

"Last Monday we went downtown. He decided he'd try two, like I did that time in the Philippines."

"You bears trying to start a trend?"

"Anyway, he talks these two LBFMs into going with him for twelve bucks, because that's all he's got. Ever since, all he's done is bitch about it. Said there were the two of 'em laying there about as lively as two-by-fours, talking in Thai and giggling every time he tried to get it up. Not a tit or a good fuck between them, he says, and all he could think of the whole time was how they'd taken his last nickel. Then when he leaves, he realizes it's almost curfew time and he's got to find someone to borrow money from so he can get back to base. Finally he finds Sergeant Tiehl, who's down there in a pickup trying to find his assistant crew chief, and cons him out of a ride home."

"He's lucky."

"A couple days later he starts hurting. Every time he takes a piss he thinks he's gonna die. Yesterday he got guts enough to go to the clinic. Doc Smith takes one look, shakes his head, and tells him he's got a world's record case of gonorrhea. *Killer-clap!* Stuff that eats penicillin like candy."

"Jesus."

"A double dose, so to speak. Doc Smith joked with him about the two girls being the infamous clap-clap sisters, and told him he'd be lucky if it didn't fall off within a week. Just kidding, but now Lyle's scared to fly."

"Is he okay?" asked Benny.

"Doc Smith pumped him up with every kind of antibiotic imaginable. Says he couldn't catch a cold. Says his warts'll fall off." The Bear laughed. "But Lyle's scared. Says if he got shot down, he couldn't get more antibiotics and he'd die of terminal gonorrhea."

"You got a strange sense of humor, Bear." Benny had never had a venereal disease. He shuddered at the thought, then went back to memorizing the Shrike launch tables as they waited for the armorers to finish.

15/1420—Route Pack Six, North Vietnam

The Weasels approached the target area first, a dozen miles in front of Colonel Parker, who liked his Weasels well out before him. They got their first SAM launch from a mobile site set up in a new location on the east side of the Red River.

"Valid launch, ten o'clock," said the Bear, his voice starting to rise because there was a lot of radar activity.

Benny spotted the dust and smoke from the SAM launch, and then the first two missiles. He warned the strike force about the SAM site, advised Dave Persons to swing out wide with the second element, then told his wingman to prepare for some hard maneuvering.

Noses slightly down, they lit their afterburners to pick up speed and maneuvering energy. They waited until the first missile was close, almost until the markings on the thing were distinguishable, then Benny broke up and left.

The first SAM flashed by without detonating. Two others followed.

Benny reversed hard right, still nose-up but with his energy level still high. He glanced back and saw the missiles detonating high above them. The explosions were white, not the orange-black color they made when they were in thicker air closer to the earth.

"You're hot, Benny!" yelled the Bear.

"I've got a visual on the site," said Benny. He called, *"Follow me in, Eagle flight, we're on the attack."*

"Two!" said Tiny from their wing position.

"Eagle lead, three's also got a good visual on the site," called Dave Persons.

"Good man," Benny muttered as they were soaring to set up for delivery of their CBUs. *"Eagle three, you come in from the north. We'll deliver from the south,"* called Benny.

"Eagle three, wilco."

Benny nosed over and began his dive. He jinked twice, then steadied the aircraft and centered the pipper on a position short of the target. The camouflage was good, so he had to guess a little. The pipper was drifting upward smoothly, toward the offset release point.

"Valid launch, three o'clock," called the Bear, telling him more missiles were being fired at them. Benny ignored them and concentrated on his geometry problem.

He pickled a little high to get good dispersion of the bomblets, then broke away last from the heaviest concentrations of flak bursts.

A few seconds later, Benny dipped a wing and they looked back. CBUs winked and blinked, dancing brightly about the area. Nothing exploded.

"Damn," said Benny, thinking he'd missed.

Then the bright, orange burst of a SAM warhead exploding! A second missile went slithering across their view.

"Shit hot," yelled the Bear exuberantly.

Their aircraft bucked upward. They ignored the hit and stared as Tiny Bechler's bombs impacted and a van was blown apart. The camouflage netting was down, and they could see the SAM site clearly.

Dave Persons's CBUs sparkled. Another missile detonated, still on its launcher. Bombs from Willy Dortmeier's airplane completed the destruction.

"Scratch one SAM site," said Benny over the radio, unable to keep the rush of pride out of his tone.

The strike force was working on the target with their bombs. Colonel Parker's voice came calmly over the air, telling his flight to rejoin to the south.

"Whoo-ee, look-it that baby blow," called someone. Sam Hall's voice? Benny didn't have long to think about it.

"Eagle four is hit," came a lonesome call. Willy Dortmeier.

"Eagle four, you're trailing smoke," called Dave Persons.

"I got a tailpipe overheat light," called Eagle four.

"You better get outta that thing, four."

"I'll fly it back a little farther."

"You're burning. I can see the flame, four. Get out!"

"Just a little more."

Benny saw Dortmeier's Thud, trailing black smoke as he flew westward, trying to make it back across the Red River. The white flame at the bottom of the aircraft was burning brightly.

Benny called, *"Eagle four, this is lead. Get out. You've got a magnesium fire going and it's hot."*

"I'm almost to the river now. Just another few seconds."

They were too far south for that, thought Benny. He'd have to fly for thirty more miles to reach the hills, and there wasn't time.

"Get out, Eagle four. Now!"

"Just a . . ."

The airplane torched and blew apart, disintegrating into large chunks of metal. From the pieces a streaming parachute emerged. The chute opened.

"Weep, weep," cried the emergency beeper.

They circled the chute once. Benny couldn't tell if Willy was moving as he swung beneath the parachute, but the eerie sound of the beeper shut off.

"He turned off his beeper," called Dave. *"Shall we set up a rescue attempt, lead?"* Persons's voice was hopeful.

"Negative, three," replied Benny, *"too many people down there. Our best bet is to leave him to them, not try to rile 'em or get 'em excited."*

Benny waggled his wings while still in Willy Dortmeier's sight, to say good-bye, then turned back toward the strike, which was still in progress. They still had Shrike missiles, and there were a lot of threat radars on the air.

"Two-ring Firecan at three and another at ten. Fansong at

eleven o'clock," growled the Bear over intercom, his voice having a rough edge to it. Benny remembered seeing him at the bar with Willy Dortmeier the night before.

"Let's get a Shrike off at the SAM," said Benny.

"Turn left five degrees," said the Bear, his voice returned to normal.

When they'd fired their Shrikes and the last strike bird was off the target, Benny saw two MiG's to the north coming toward them. He turned the flight hard right. They engaged afterburners, but the MiG's dove toward the ground and fled.

15/1525—Udorn RTAFB, Thailand

They missed the rendezvous with their tanker because Brigham, the ground radar at Udorn, had trouble giving them proper directions and couldn't join them up. Low on gas, the flight landed at Udorn.

They were on the ground, parked in the transient aircraft area and walking around the aircraft, when Benny saw the black smudge on the aft end of the fuselage.

"Felt it back there when we were coming off the target," said the Bear, eyeing the smudge.

"Me, too." Benny looked closer and found a small piece of shrapnel lodged in the metal skin and a couple of jagged holes.

The transient area crew chief said he'd look it over closely.

"Unless you find something wrong," said Benny, "we'll fly it on back to Takhli." The crew chief looked dubious.

He joined the Bear, and they walked over to Tiny's aircraft, which had been parked beside them. Tiny was still in the cockpit, pulling off his helmet. He complained, as he did about most things, that the helmet fit poorly, and now he briskly massaged his scalp before coming down the ladder.

"Good bombs, Tiny," said Benny. "We took the site out clean."

Tiny nodded, then shook his head sadly. "Too bad about Willy. He was a classmate at the academy."

"That's what he told me last night," said the Bear. "Said you were just as much of an asshole then as you are now."

Tiny grinned like he considered the remark a compliment,

then remembered about Dortmeier and grimaced. "Willy was a good man."

"He said he just got married," the Bear said.

"He's a general's son and his wife's an NCO's kid," said Tiny. "Same girl he took to his high school prom over in Weisbaden, Germany."

"I didn't know you guys were friends," said the Bear.

"I guess I kind of thought he was a little weak, what with his father being a general and all. Maybe," said Tiny awkwardly, "I was wrong about him."

A blue Air Force pickup pulled up nearby, and two officers in flight suits got out to look over the wounded Weasel bird.

Dave Persons taxied into place beside Tiny's aircraft and shut down his engine. He gave them the thumbs-up, but looked wistful. No one liked losing a wingman.

The two officers, a major and a captain, were still looking over the Weasel Thud. "You fly that?" the major asked. He pointed at 277.

"Yeah," said Benny. He jabbed a thumb at the Bear. "With him."

"Weasels?"

"Yeah."

"Where's your wheelbarrow?" asked the captain.

Benny gave him a questioning look.

"To carry your balls in."

The crew chief came over from 277. "Better not chance flying it until we look it over closer, sir. Got some shrapnel in there. All kinds of hydraulic lines there, and there's fluid in the bay. Maybe nothing serious, but it shouldn't be flown until we know."

"Damn," said Benny.

"Sergeant Tiehl's going to be some pissed off when he finds out we hurt his bird," said the Bear.

"You guys want a ride?" asked the major. He wore an F-104 patch. Udorn's squadron of small, fast interceptors was assigned the mission of providing protection for various aircraft, such as the tankers, when they flew out over the Gulf of Tonkin, and for Big Eye, the airborne command post. The problem with the F-104's in Southeast Asia was that they couldn't carry many bombs and didn't have legs long enough to fly the lengthy missions over North Vietnam.

"Maintenance is sending a van," said Benny. "We've still got to debrief."

"We'll take you," said the major. "Want to hear how you guys do it and survive."

Benny rubbed his jaw. "We don't always do that," he said. "You notice we're flying a three-ship."

Dave Persons and Dutch Hansletter came over. "Something wrong?" asked Persons.

"Our bird took a hit. Looks like we'll be spending the night. You guys can refuel and go on back to Takhli."

Tiny looked dejected.

"What's wrong, Tiny?"

"I never spent the night here."

"Well, come on. We'll find a reason. Not often we get to lay some hurt on a SAM site like that. It's worth a bit of a celebration."

Persons and Hansletter returned to Takhli. Benny, the Bear, and Tiny Bechler spent most of the night at the club, talking with F-104, RF-101, and Sandy drivers. Not once did they pay for their own drinks.

16/1030L—Takhli RTAFB, Thailand

Bear Stewart

The F-105F Wild Weasel aircraft carried a KA-71 strike camera embedded in its chin so the crews could make their own bomb damage assessment after each mission. The camera came on when the pickle button was depressed, clicking away and capturing the world before, beneath, and behind them in panoramic fish-eye views.

Before they landed at Takhli in 277, which the maintenance people at Udorn had examined and released for a one-time, straight-and-level flight home, Benny passed a message to the photo lab, asking the lab to quickly develop their 70mm film. The Bear's receivers had indicated launches of SAMs they hadn't seen, and he thought they might be on the film.

They went through a belabored maintenance debriefing, enduring Staff Sergeant Tiehl's critical questions and worried looks as he kept interrupting the debriefing team to ask questions. Jerry Tiehl was an exacting crew chief and a worry-wart about his airplane. The Bear tried to explain that 277 had done great things—had destroyed a SAM site and brought them home after taking a nasty flak hit—and while that mollified him some, Tiehl was still unhappy.

"You guys try to take better care of it up there, okay?"

When they had escaped the maintenance shack, and Sergeant Tiehl had hurried back to the wounded Thud, they proceeded to the command post. There they sat through yet another intelligence debriefing, giving the same answers to questions they'd been asked at Udorn.

When they had answered the stock questions about the shootdown of Willy Dortmeier, Lieutenant DeWalt queried them about the interceptors they'd seen.

"They were MiG-19's," said Benny.

DeWalt looked at him incredulously. "There aren't any MiG-19's in North Vietnam."

The Bear looked on quietly.

"We saw two of them," said Benny.

"You sure they weren't MiG-17's, sir?"

"I got a good look at one of them, and it was fatter than a MiG-17, like a MiG-19." The silhouettes of the two Mikoyan aircraft were much the same, but MiG-17's had only one engine and no afterburner while MiG-19's had two engines, both equipped with primitive afterburners.

"I hate to put that down, sir. You sure you want me to? Higher headquarters says there's no MiG-19's in North Vietnam."

"Then you'd better tell them. Flame was shooting twenty, thirty feet out the tailpipes. Russian afterburners look like that, and MiG-17's don't have afterburners."

"I dunno, sir," DeWalt hedged.

Benny started to fill in the written narrative about Lieutenant Dortmeier's shootdown and probable status, and he asked the Bear to take over answering the debriefing questions.

DeWalt winced. He disliked working with the Bear, who sometimes ridiculed his intelligence estimates. The Bear grinned maliciously.

"Seventh Air Force says there are only MiG-17's and MiG-21's in North Vietnam," said DeWalt warily.

The Bear was patient. "Well, let's not argue with higher headquarters."

"I agree, sir."

"How about putting down that it was a MiG-17 with two engines and afterburners?"

"That would be a MiG-19, sir."

"That's what the hell he was trying to tell you!"

Lieutenant DeWalt sulked, but he wrote it down.

"What size antiaircraft artillery?" DeWalt asked.

"Fifty-seven, eighty-five, small arms, a guy throwing rocks, you name it."

"Would you describe it as heavy, medium, or light?"

"Heavy."

DeWalt filled in the blanks on his form, then read again. "How accurate was the flak?"

"Two out of four aircraft got hit, for God's sake," said the Bear. "One was shot down."

"Yes, sir, but how accurate, just generally, would you say the flak was?"

"They were accurate twice. Since they fired several hundred rounds at us, and since I guess you want the average, you can put down that it was inaccurate flak."

That made Benny smile as he finished the narrative and pushed it toward Lieutenant DeWalt.

"Dumb shit," said the Bear as they walked outside the debriefing room and stopped at the Coke machine.

"Dumb questions," corrected Benny. "Higher headquarters sends the questions and those guys just fill in the squares."

They saw Les Ries walking toward the command post door, a frown heavy on his face, and Benny hailed him. He came over and they both saluted. Dan Janssen joined them, and he did not act any friendlier than Ries. The Bear guessed they were still sore about the silly-assed PACAF message.

"We got a site up there yesterday, Les," said Benny. "Saw the missile launch and dive-bombed the smoke."

Les looked unhappier yet.

"You sure, Benny?" asked Janssen in a belligerent tone.

The Bear's jaw drooped.

Dan Janssen continued. "We flew up there yesterday morning, before you guys did, and we didn't see a site where Dave Persons said you guys bombed. There was one in the same general area, but it wasn't that close to the river."

Les spoke then, his voice brittle with irritation. "I took a look at Dave's film. He thought it was a SAM site too, but like

I told him, I think you guys got a couple of triple-A batteries. You're just not used to seeing SAM sites yet. They're hard to see."

"We saw SAMs exploding on the ground," reasoned Benny.

"Probably a pile of artillery rounds. They were indistinct in Dave's photos. Too much smoke and dust to tell for sure, but it wasn't a SAM site."

The Bear found his voice. "Are you calling us liars?"

Les gave him a withering look. "I'm just trying to tell you something, and that's often hard to do, Captain."

Janssen seemed to be gloating. "Everyone makes mistakes. You too, Mal."

"We're not wrong on this one."

"I think you are," said Les.

The Bear's temper flared hotter and his voice rose angrily. "Well, I'll tell you both what I think—"

"Back off, Captain," said Ries. He glared harshly, nodded to Janssen, and the two of them walked into the command post.

"What the fuck was that all about?" exploded the Bear.

Benny returned his look of disbelief. "They've got the rag on for some reason."

The Bear burned all over again when he thought of Janssen's smug look. Benny motioned back toward the command post. "I want to talk to Max Foley about the MiG's. I'm positive they were MiG-19's."

"I didn't get a good look," the Bear said, smoldering.

"It's not a real big deal. MiG-19's won't be hard to handle, but we should at least be prepared for them."

The Bear watched him go inside, then began to think. He walked to the squadron and checked out a crew van, then drove to the photo lab, ears hot with anger. Their film was hanging in long strips, drying before a fan.

"Only be a minute or two more, Captain Stewart," said a cheerful photo interpreter.

"You get a look yet?"

"A quick look. You'll be interested."

After a short wait, the PI took the strips down, cut off a few frames, and imprisoned one with clips on a light table.

"See here," said the photo interpreter showing him a

frame of two cylinders with brightly glowing tails. "Surface-to-air missiles," he said.

"Can you see where they came from?"

"Somewhere off to your right. They're at the rear of the photo, so they're behind you."

They looked at several bunches of flak bursts and muzzle flashes from the ground. There was no sign of a SAM site in the early frames. Just tree thickets and rice paddies.

"Keep going," said the Bear.

Several frames later a photo showed the bomblets going off, pinpoints of light, some in the air where they collided, then the majority where they detonated on the ground.

"Keep going."

A bright detonation.

"Keep going."

A SAM appeared on the ground, burning on one side, being propelled wildly sideward.

The Bear grinned. "Cut that one for me."

"Yes, sir."

In the next frame some of the camouflage netting was missing. The Bear traced a part of the Star of David–shaped road network between missile launchers and what the PI identified as a loaded missile launcher.

"Cut that one, too."

Benny Lewis

Benny was in the command post, deep in discussion with Max Foley and Pudge Holden about the best ways to cope with MiG-19's. Max had opened a volume of TAC Manual 3–1, the classified fighter tactics bible, and was going over the differences between the performance of the two MiG's when the Bear came in and interrupted.

"Where's Ries and Janssen?" the Bear snapped.

Benny drew back and looked around. "They were here a few minutes ago."

Max shook his head. "Ries mentioned something about going over to his squadron."

"Thanks." The Bear turned and started to leave.

"Where you going, Bear?" called Benny.

"I got something to show 'em."

"Film?"

"Yep."

"Wait up. I'll go with you."

Benny left Foley and Holden, both still nose-deep in the books, and joined the Bear. "What'd the film show?"

The Bear showed the frames to him.

"Great!" said Benny. He looked up at the Bear and cocked his head, knowing he was up to trouble. "You want to show these to Ries and Janssen?"

"Sons of bitches called us liars."

"So now you know they were wrong. Why press it?"

"I want them to know."

"Wait until you've calmed down," said Benny.

"Wouldn't be half as much fun then."

It was only two buildings down the flight line to the 354th, so they walked. Benny resolved to keep the Bear out of trouble.

They found Ries and Janssen at the duty desk. Things quickly got beyond Benny's control.

The Bear walked up to Les and flung the frames onto the counter. "Want to see pictures of a SAM site? Probably the first one you guys have seen, so take a good look."

Ries glared harshly, ignoring the photos. "I just want to see you get the hell out of here, Captain."

"Let's see the photo of that SAM site you say you bombed last month and compare." The Bear was hot with anger.

Benny grasped his arm. "C'mon Bear. You're going too far."

Ries's face was stiff. "You're insubordinate, Captain."

The Bear shook his head. "Fuck insubordinate. I don't like posturing assholes calling us liars."

Les's face went white with rage. "I won't stand for this!"

Janssen was gritting his teeth, holding back his own anger, fists formed stiffly at his sides.

"Try me," said the Bear in a menacing tone.

"Bear!" said Benny clutching the arm tighter. He pulled the Bear around to face him and saw that he was shaking with fury. "Go on outside. I'll be right there."

"Dammit . . ."

"Go on!"

The Bear glared at both Ries and Janssen again, then stomped off toward the door.

Benny turned back toward Ries. They had once been

friends, when they had been stationed together. "Les, why the hell did you start this? It's not like you."

"I don't enjoy being questioned, Captain."

Benny felt his frustration grow. "You're wrong. Look at the photos, for Christ's sake."

Les's features were hard. He pointed his finger like a pistol and started to jab it into Benny's chest.

Benny's voice was whisper-quiet. "I don't know what's wrong with you, Les, but one touch of that finger and I'll tear off your head." He retrieved the photos and left.

Later, over dinner, he felt discouraged. "We're not just fighting the North Vietnamese and the stupid restrictions. Now we're fighting among ourselves."

"Les is a grandstander and Janssen is tagging along saying *me too,*" the Bear said. "They're assholes."

"No, they're not. Dammit, they're heroes, just like most of the guys here. Les Ries"—he shook his head as he remembered—"has the nicest, sweetest, most loyal wife in the world and three daughters he thinks the world of. The youngest one is retarded, Bear, and Les dotes on her. Don't tell me he's a bad guy."

The Bear shut up.

"It was a good kill," Benny said.

"Yeah. I loved it."

The Bear changed the subject and asked if he'd heard from Liz Richardson. Benny told him she'd written a few times.

Liz wrote almost every other day, the letters posted from locations all over the Pacific, and he enjoyed her commentaries about the various places. Some were colorful and funny; all were informative. Except for one short paragraph in an early letter apologizing for her silly tantrum, she kept her words light. She offered to help out any way she could, like handling anything he needed done in the States. He'd decided to write in return.

"Hell," he leveled with the Bear, "maybe I made a hasty judgment. And something I forgot. She said to say hi to you and tell you thanks for the great advice, and you'd know what she meant. I guess you ran into her after I left?"

The Bear gave him a sheepish look. "Yeah, I saw her," he mumbled. Then, "You're going to see more of her, I take it."

"Maybe. I treated her pretty shabbily in Bangkok. Just looking for a reason to stay pissed off at all women, I guess." He looked at the Bear. "How are you doing with Julie?"

The Bear nodded without comment.

"She still serious?"

"Yeah." He looked troubled and like he wanted to say something. Benny started to ask what was bothering him when Sam Hall joined them.

"You guys talking about anything important?" asked Sam.

"Females," muttered the Bear darkly.

"My wife writes that women in the States are wearing skimpy little skirts and nothing underneath," said Sam.

"I can handle that," said the Bear.

"How's life as ops officer, Sam?" asked the Bear.

"Tolerable. I hear you and Les Ries had a run-in."

Benny shrugged. "Difference of opinion is all."

"He's making some loud sounds. Stay away from him and it'll pass. Les is acting strange these days." Sam looked meaningfully at the Bear. "He's mainly pissed off at you. You stay away from him . . . period."

It was an order and required no further explanation.

"Sam," said the Bear, changing the subject, "I hear you bombed the fuckin' hospital yesterday."

Sam's eyes opened wide. "Me?"

"That's what I hear."

"I missed the empty barracks, that's all. Maybe a couple of my bombs went near the white building. Sure to hell wasn't a hospital though. The thing is *still* blowing up. I guess they had a lot of explosives stored there."

"Was Colonel Parker pissed off?" asked the Bear.

"He chewed on my ass for a little bit, but he wasn't really mad. If it had really been a hospital it would have been different. I told him I made an honest mistake, but I don't think he believed me."

"*No one* believes you, Sam," said the Bear.

A waitress arrived and took their orders. Sam ordered his usual bottle of Louisiana hot sauce. He would use a third of it on the single meal.

16/2000L—Mack's Trailer, Takhli RTAFB, Thailand

Colonel Mack

Chief Master Sgt Casper Roberts knocked on the door of Mack's private trailer. When he saw that Maj Pete Crawford was already with him, he tried to beg off.

"Nonsense, Cas, come on in." Mack motioned him into a chair.

The squadron commanders' trailers were double the size of the other field-grade officers' trailers, but were still compact. MacLendon's consisted of sleeping quarters on one end, a bathroom in the center, and a living room–kitchen combination at the other end. The three men sat around the small dinette table, and Mack poured Scotch.

Mack nodded from Crawford to Cas. "Guess you already know Chief M. Sgt. Cas Roberts, woman thief and maintenance man."

"Woman thief?" asked Crawford.

"Colonel, you promised."

"Okay, Chief. No more sniveling." Mack grinned. "Anyway, the major here broke one of your aircraft all to hell, Cas. He just got in from Udorn on the gooney bird, and says he doesn't know if the bird is fixable."

"My maintenance team leader just called back from Udorn. It's class twenty-six material, Colonel. Broke a wing spar. Major Crawford's lucky it didn't come apart in the air. It would be a waste of time to attempt repairing the aircraft."

"Thought it was bad," said Crawford lamely. He'd flown too low delivering his bombs on a target in pack five and hit a treetop.

"Okay, let's see the rest of your figures, Cas. Show me the total sad story."

"Yes, sir." Roberts spread his paperwork out on the tabletop.

"I think I'd better go, sir," said Crawford, rising. "Sorry about the bird."

"Just pull out a little higher next time."

"Will do." He closed the door quietly behind himself.

Chief Roberts raised an eyebrow at Mack.

"He's good. Listens hard when I talk about tactics, then he tries them and comes up with improvements."

"He'll be even better once he stops flying into trees."

"He knows he pressed too close. I brought him in here so I could chew his ass in private, then gave him a drink of your good whiskey to take out some of the sting."

"I brought more," said Cas, pulling another bottle of single-malt Scotch from a plain brown bag. "Thought you might be running low."

Mack stowed the bottle in a cabinet. "Know what Crawford said?"

Roberts shook his head.

"Said he wouldn't mind dodging SAMs and MiG's and flak so much if he thought Washington was serious."

Roberts sipped the smooth whiskey and sighed appreciatively.

"You know who we need for president? A goddam kick-ass-and-take-names NCO. We keep getting all these ex-officers, but when have we ever had an ex-NCO for president?"

"Not once that I know of, thank God," said Mack.

A rapping at the trailer door proved to be B. J. Parker, the wing commander.

"Hello, Mack. Chief Roberts."

"Come in, sir," said MacLendon. "Cas and I were just going over the airplane situation."

Colonel Parker's eyes narowed and he pointed his portable radio's antenna at the distinctive three-sided bottle. "We commoners have to settle for rotgut, while you squadron guys drink good stuff."

"Just poor working men laboring well into the night, Colonel."

Parker watched as Mack filled the bottom third of a tumbler. He picked it up and carefully sloshed it from side to side, making a show of it. "Okay, Mack, where do you get it? There's no Glenfiddich this side of Bangkok. Maybe none in Bangkok."

"Sure there is. You're drinking it." He turned to Chief Roberts. "Maybe if we told the colonel, he'd approve an R and R to Australia. You remember that beach outside of Sydney where the women go topless?"

"Topless? I don' remember anything like that."

Colonel Parker grinned. "That's because the women put on their tops when they hear a sergeant's around."

"Colonel Parker, you are a cruel man. I was having a hard time coping with Colonel Mack here, and upon your arrival I felt that the hardworking enlisted men in this wing might finally receive some support."

"Support? I remember when you stole Mack's girlfriend back at Seymour-Johnson. I was there, remember. Saw the whole sordid affair."

Cas Roberts shook his head sadly. "We poor noncoms receive no justice at all." He reached across the table and grasped the bottle of Scotch.

"Hey!" cried out Mack. "Where are you going with our bottle?"

"Our bottle, sir?"

Mack gave Parker a grin. "Now you know, Colonel. Our NCOs get all the good whiskey. Periodically Cas makes a mercy trip by my trailer."

"Sounds sinister."

"Only when he doesn't show up with the Glenfiddich. Do you realize the power this man wields?"

Parker chuckled. They had periodically run across one another at the various fighter-bomber bases since being stationed together in North Carolina in 1950, when Parker and Mack had been captains.

Parker sipped his drink and sighed. "Helps one forget the eighteen-hour days. How do you get this stuff?"

Cas smiled. "Don't question, sir. I'll have a couple bottles sent over to your trailer. Cost you four-fifty apiece."

Parker sighed. "Nary a question will be asked, Chief."

They were quiet, staring at the amber liquid and relaxing. Cas Roberts finally glanced at his watch.

"Sorry, gentlemen, but I've got to check how things are going at the avionics maintenance shop. We've got two birds with weapons release system problems."

MacLendon followed Chief Roberts to the door, spoke for a few moments about aircraft problems, then let him go. As he returned to the table where Parker sat, he wondered about the visit. The wing commander made few unofficial calls.

"How's it going with your squadron, Mack?"

"Losing too many good men. Sometimes I wonder, what

with our losing so many of our really fine officers, what's going to become of the Air Force in a few years."

"That's when the ones who are staying out of the shooting war will show up to take over. Who do you think's going to be promoted first, a guy with a master's degree who was stationed at the Pentagon, or a fighter jock with a combat tour?"

They were silent. B. J. Parker finally raised his glass. "Here's to the silly bastards who dare to fight."

Mack muttered, "The dumb shits," and tipped his glass forward to toast.

They drank.

As Parker was leaving, he paused. "Just wanted you to know I think you're doing a hell of a job," he said. "Don't get discouraged because of the losses. With these threats, that's going to happen. You've welded together a good group of fighting men. When the flag goes up, I'm confident your squadron will be ready."

"When do you think that might be, sir?"

"Just as soon as someone up there gets as serious about the war as we are."

When Parker was gone, Mack pulled out the roster Sergeant Hill had typed for him before he'd left the squadron. A month ago he'd thought he needed two weeks. Now, due to the additional SAMs and MiG's, his men were having to learn all over again, and adjust.

He went down the list of names.

357 TFS KEY PERSONNEL ROSTER		As of: 25-Nov-66
Cmdr:	Lt-Col-Lee, J.F. (K)	MacLendon, T.F.
Ops:	Lt-Col-Polaski, J.T. (K)	Hall, M.S.
A-Flt:	*Maj-Hall, M.S. (C)	*Capt Lutz (Maj)
	**Capt-Smith, J.A. (K)	
	Capt Huffmeier, C.L.	
	Capt Maisey, K.R.	
	Capt Meyer, J.C.	
	1/Lt Bechler, H.J.	Lt Radkovich
B-Flt:	Maj-Ralston, M.A. (K)	*Maj-Rose (M)
	**Capt-Lewis, B.L. (RW)	Cpt-DiFazio (K)
	Capt Clark, C.R. (C*)	Cpt Pierce
	Capt Raymond, T.W.	Cpt Jones
	1/Lt Rodriguez, G.M.	Lt Ricard (R)
	1/Lt-Singleton, T.S. (100)	Lt Ricard (R)

C-Flt:	*Maj Crawford, P.T.	
	~~**Capt Lutz, B.T.~~ (C)	Cpt Hicks
	~~Capt Murphy, M.K.~~ (M)	Cpt Michaels
	~~Capt Larkins, T.T.~~ (M)	Cpt Whitelee
	~~1/Lt Mullens, M.W.~~ (K)	Lt Washington
	1/Lt Silva, J.S.	

D-Flt:	*Capt Swendler, O.A.	
	**Capt Takahara, T.	
	Capt Maier, R.L.	
	~~Capt Spalding, J.J.~~ (100)	Lt Ziegler
	1/Lt Brown, C.C.	
	~~1/Lt Capella, R.S.~~ (RW)	~~Lt Dortmeier~~ (M)

WW-Flt:	~~Maj Phillips, G.P. / Capt Stewart, M.S.~~ (RW)	
	*Cpt Lewis/Cpt Stewart	
	Cpt Holden/Cpt Watson	
	Cpt Persons/Cpt Hansletter	
Atch:	Col Parker, B.J. (Wing Cmdr)	
	Maj Foley, M.T. (Wing Weapons Ofcr)	

Maint:	2/Lt Shilling, D.D./CMS Roberts, C.A.
1st Sgt:	M/Sgt Silvester, T. S.
Admin:	T/Sgt Hill, P.C.
P.E.:	S/Sgt Perez, S.L.

Flt Srgn: Maj Roddenbush, D.L.

*Flight Commander
**Ass't Flight Commander

Notes: 100 = Finished Tour
      C = Status Change
      W = Wounded
      R = Rescued
      P = POW
      M = MIA
      K = KIA

He'd never seen, or even imagined, defenses as dangerous as they faced after the enemy had increased the numbers of defensive systems. But they were learning to cope in spite of them. His Weasels were beginning to knock out SAM sites, his pilots killed the occasional MiG that dared to engage them, and his men were putting their bombs on the target.

The only thing that could stop them now was the remote possibility that the North Vietnamese had something else up their sleeve.

17/1800L—People's Army HQ, Hanoi, DRV

Xuan Nha

Xuan was sick with concern over the losses of two rocket batteries. One had been bombed on the fifteenth, another just that morning. Tiger two, the second battery of Maj Tran Van

Ngo's mobile battalion, had been pulverized. One hundred and thirty-three technicians and support people killed. All of this despite the fact they had reported, upon setting up the previous night, that their camouflage had been flawless. Today Happiness one, a permanent rocket battery just seven kilometers from the People's Army headquarters, had been hit by a Shrike homing missile and then bombed. Destruction of Happiness one had not been as complete as that of Tiger two, for the hundreds of guns in the area had driven the attackers away, but more than thirty men had been killed and two launchers destroyed. Both attacks had obviously been the work of the radar-hunters, whom Xuan was growing to hate.

If they had only waited a precious few days, neither attack *could have* happened.

During the extended bombing halt, Wisdom complex had been frantically driven toward completion. Major Nguy had worked the battalion and battery commanders, the Soviet advisers, the civil engineers, the soldiers, and the thousands of workers to the verge of exhaustion. Today the commanders were en route back to their battalions and batteries. All defenses would be placed under the control of Wisdom at midnight.

Communications were completed. For the three primary MiG interceptor bases, a land-line was strung to Kep, and highly directional microwave towers relayed voice transmissions to Phuc Yen and Kien An. Remote transmitter towers had been erected, and radio directions spoken by the controllers at Wisdom would never be broadcast from Wisdom complex, but instead from those distant towers. When the Americans used their sensitive receiver installation at Da Nang to triangulate the source of transmitter power, their equipment would be confused by dual, simultaneous transmissions, and they would never suspect the Wisdom location. The method had been used by the Russians before to baffle the Americans.

The radio transmitters and receivers at the various radars, interceptor bases, rocket batteries, and antiaircraft artillery centers were also special, using the same L-frequency band as used by the Western world for different types of maritime and aircraft navigation systems. The transmitted signals were powerful, and the pulse recurrence rate of the carrier wave was jittered across a hundred-pulse-per-second spectrum. The received signals were decoded using a key that was electronically reestablished every thirty seconds.

The communications system, manufactured in the German Democratic Republic, worked flawlessly. The directions of the Wisdom controllers sounded crystalline clear, from Vinh to Haiphong to Dien Bien Phu, with only a high ping every half-minute to signal the code change. Two other channels of the same triple-tiered signal carried encoded target intelligence. The East German installers of the system were understandably proud of their work.

The well-camouflaged command-and-control center, with its two-meter-thick concrete walls, was located in a small clearing in a forest thicket under a maze of camouflage nets. It was of modest size, some fifty meters square, but inside there was room for twelve men working at consoles. There were adjacent barracks where Russian, East German, Czech, and North Korean specialists would stay until the Vietnamese were well trained in the idiosyncrasies of modern air defense control. Other barracks were hidden farther from the center.

Near the control center was the P-50 long-range radar, radiating in S-frequency band, its two huge, stacked antennas slowly turning, the six powerful beams picking up every aircraft, even large birds, from as far away as the western border. It observed the fleet defense fighters patrolling about the three American aircraft carriers in the Gulf of Tonkin, the COD utility aircraft shuttling back and forth toward Saigon, even the helicopters hovering about the carriers when aircraft were launched or recovered.

Dummy transmitters were being put into place, which would radiate synchronized, false signal patterns from locations to the northwest and east to confuse spy planes. They were the only link of the operation not yet completed. Xuan had ordered that final effort to be delayed, so they could concentrate on the rest of Wisdom. When operational in another two weeks, the dummy transmitters would make all efforts to electronically triangulate the position of the P-50 radar utterly impossible.

Fifteen kilometers west of the command-and-control building were the highly advanced defenses: the experimental rocket site, with electro-optic tracking devices slaved to the radar antennae, and new rockets with larger control fins and canards. The system was to be used in defense of the Wisdom complex and to train North Vietnamese engagement commanders and radar operators. The rocket system's oversized command van had dual positions and controls for hands-on training by advanced students. Here they would be taught to work through enemy jamming, and most importantly, to interpret the instructions of the Wisdom site controller.

The special rocket site was considered so deadly in the hands of the Russian instructors, the technical cream of the Soviet PVO Strany rocket forces, that the elite force at Wisdom felt invulnerable. That, combined with the fact that they were in the no-flying area adjacent to the Chinese border, gave them a sense of security they could have nowhere else in the North Vietnamese countryside.

Two SON-9a antiaircraft artillery radars were located near the rocket site, but they were there for training purposes only. No firing batteries were colocated with the SON-9a's. The Russians felt that antiaircraft artillery was archaic stuff that should have long ago been discarded in favor of rockets.

Wisdom would be placed in operation tomorrow, and would take control of the air battle from its single, all-seeing vantage point. That was none too soon for Xuan Nha. He was out of time, for his superiors were about to pull their support, completely and utterly. The harbinger of the bad news was his old superior, Colonel Trung, who would be the one to benefit most if he failed.

He had received the ominous call that morning, soon after the attack on Happiness one battery. Trung had said that General Luc had heard the bombs going off at Happiness one, the closest rocket site to the headquarters, which General Dung had enjoyed showing off to visiting dignitaries as a model of North Vietnamese technical skills. The general demanded to know when Xuan would provide the results ordered by Colonel-General Dung.

Xuan Nha had reverted to a careful attitude of obeisance, for Trung's proven, cautious ways were rapidly regaining credence with the general staff.

"Tonight Wisdom is completed, comrade Colonel," he'd said.

"Results. That is all the general is after, Xuan Nha. For the past three days the Americans have bombed and only two aircraft have been shot down. General Dung is beginning to think of it much as I do, as a Russian game, and sometimes wonders why you are so eager to turn our defenses over to the Russian controllers."

"The general will have to wait no longer for his results. Also, please advise him that one of my people, Major Nguy, will be in command of the controllers. The foreigners will be replaced in a very short period of time."

"But how much longer, Xuan Nha, until we get the results you promised?"

"Within the week you will have results so convincing that even you will be happy, comrade Colonel." Xuan's stomach was sour and he could not restrain a great belch, leaving the taste of puke in his mouth.

"There is talk . . ." Trung left the words hanging when he hung up, and Xuan Nha knew that no more time would be given. His hand trembled, and he hurried down the hall to the latrine where he was able to vomit without being observed.

Nicolaj Gregarian

Xuan Nha had called for him, and they sat in his office. The Vietnamese *polkovnik* leaned forward in his seat, edgy, as if he were about to bolt.

Leytenant Quang Hanh's report came from a rocket battery several miles southwest of Haiphong, where the Americans were again bombing. Steel two had been damaged by a Shrike radar homing missile launched from a U.S. Navy Intruder jet.

"See," said Xuan Nha. The man was perspiring heavily. Gregarian had never before noticed the phenomenon, even when they'd been in the terrible heat of the jungle. He had wondered if Xuan ever sweated as he did. Now Xuan Nha's forehead was beaded and his uniform was soaked, although a fan circulated air in the room.

"The Americans are successful again. No Thunder planes were shot down today, and they have attacked twice, destroying a barracks and warehouses at Viet Tri. Now carrier airplanes are attacking the petroleum reserves at Nam Dinh and none have been reported shot down."

"Tomorrow you will be successful as never before," said Gregarian with glowing confidence and pleasure that the enemy was succeeding. It would show the vast difference when Wisdom became operational.

"You are right, Major Gregarian. I have supported Wisdom from the beginning."

Xuan Nha was obsequious in his attitude. Since his change, Nicolaj had lost his fear and respect for the man. Nha was on the verge of being purged for incompetence for things out of his control. Nicolaj even wondered how he would react under the same circumstance, yet he increasingly loathed the man.

"Tomorrow your country will thank you, *Polkovnik* Nha."

"Perhaps. But I must give the generals something spectacular, something more than just shooting down a Thunder plane or a Phantom."

Gregarian knew what was coming. He had anticipated it and had worked the solution out with his superior officers.

"I have already bowed to your demand to make the P-50 radar operational before the dummy transmitters are in place to mask it. No more, please."

Nha looked at him, imploring. "We must shoot down the Pesky planes that orbit near the Wisdom complex."

Gregarian had studied the aircraft thoroughly since they had discussed its orbit, so close to Wisdom. The Americans called it by different names—EB-66E, A-3, the Destroyer—and it was ponderously slow and underpowered. But the converted bombers did pose a problem for Wisdom and he was prepared to deal with them. First he toyed with Xuan Nha.

"Their jamming is not so powerful, *Polkovnik* Nha. Your radars can see through it."

"We must shoot at least one down. Another one if they continue to fly around the Wisdom area. We've never been able to do it before with our rocket sites, although we moved a rocket system up there and tried once."

The Russian narrowed his eyes dramatically, then sighed in a display of reluctance. "You wish to use the rocket battery at Wisdom?"

"Yes." Xuan Nha's voice was pleading. "Without the dummy transmitters in place, they could triangulate the radar emissions from the Wisdom P-50 and accurately locate it. Their orbits are very close to Wisdom. The best way to hide

Wisdom is to shoot down a Pesky plane so they will no longer fly there."

Gregarian raised an eyebrow, as if he did not know that to be true. The EB-66E's would be flying almost overhead, and posed a definite problem.

Xuan Nha continued. "Since the Pesky planes jam the rocket site radars, it is difficult to shoot them down with our regular rocket batteries using radars. The electro-optic system of the special rocket battery would allow us to shoot them down without turning on the tracking radar."

Gregarian nodded. Just as he and his superiors at PVO Strany had decided.

"That is, if the system really works as you say it does."

The Russian refused to be baited. "I can assure you it does work."

Xuan Nha lowered his voice. "Help me, comrade Gregarian. We are in danger of losing it all. Wisdom, our ideas, all of it."

Xuan must realize that he was groveling, but he did not even attempt to restrain the catch in his voice. Gregarian allowed a moment of silence before he spoke. "We will do it, Xuan Nha. Only this once, but we will do it."

"I will not ask you to endanger Wisdom again. Only to rid ourselves of the Pesky planes, and so I can show the general staff their results."

"When do you want it done?" asked Gregarian.

"As soon as possible. I have no more time. Wisdom has no more time, for Colonel-General Dung is out of patience. I believe he is about to dismantle the Wisdom complex, bring all rockets back under the area commanders, and put Colonel Trung back in charge."

"We cannot have that," said Gregarian. "Tomorrow we will integrate the defenses for the first time and will undoubtedly find problems. I do not believe the Americans could find us in a single day."

"We may have no longer than that. Colonel Trung is anxious to see us fail and he has the general's ear."

Nicolaj nodded abruptly, as if those words convinced him. "We will do as you wish and shoot down an EB-66 as soon as they fly in the orbit near Wisdom. I will command the shootdown myself and assign my most expert Russian operators and technicians to assist me. Your men are not yet ready.

It takes a great deal of skill and judgment on the part of the operators." He filled his words with disdain, so Xuan Nha would know that his Russians were superior.

But Xuan Nha was listening to inner voices and did not recognize the slur. "Please keep this conversation confidential," he asked nervously, "until we are successful."

Gregarian nodded. "When I succeed, I will leave the announcements to you and allow you to take full credit for the planning and execution." Except, of course, for the glowing report to his own hierarchy.

That pleased Xuan Nha greatly. The North Vietnamese *polkovnik* smiled for the first time in days, but it was one of abject humility. "Is the Englishwoman pleasing you?"

Nicolaj narrowed his eyes, wondering if Nha had somehow heard about the beating he had administered to quiet the woman's constant harping. "She is acceptable," he finally said.

"There are other *Tay* women available. A certain one comes to mind. She was born here, the product of a French official's promiscuous daughter who was placed in an orphanage. She is young, perhaps fifteen, but fully developed."

Nicolaj was interested. He was tiring of the Englishwoman with her sharp tongue. She was *too* reminiscent of his wife.

"Do you want the French girl?"

Nicolaj shrugged, enjoying his growing power over the squat Vietnamese. "Send her to me when we return to Hanoi," he said, as if it were a matter of puny consequence.

They were to leave Hanoi at nightfall in a blacked-out convoy and would arrive at the command center north of Bac Can before midnight. They would be there when Wisdom took charge of the morning battle.

"I can have her sent to a country villa we commandeered near the Russian barracks at Wisdom, if you wish," said Xuan Nha.

Nicolaj nodded condescendingly. He liked his new relationship with Xuan Nha and had finally discovered something the Vietnamese were good at. They were acceptable procurers.

"Tomorrow we will show the generals, Nicolaj Gregarian, and teach the American pilots a lesson they will never forget."

Gregarian laughed. "There will be few of them left to

either remember or forget. There has never been such a concentration of sophisticated defenses, anywhere, and now Wisdom will provide them with eyes and a brilliant brain."

Xuan Nha stood, looking out at the growing darkness. "Shall we prepare to go?" He was eager to get started.

Book III

Today—Termite Hill, Democratic Republic of Vietnam

Precisely ninety-three miles west of Hanoi, the Da River, which flows southeast to Thanh Hoa, is joined by a small tributary from the southwest. In the V of the union is a low mountain, barren and desolate and pocked with deep craters.

American pilots once called it Termite Hill.

Tribesmen travel from the mountainous region surrounding the Ma River in eastern Laos, down the old, untended road on the opposite side of the stream and ford the Da near the intersection of the stream and in full view of the mountain. They take their meager produce to market, as they have done for centuries, but they are wary as they pass by Dead Mountain, for it is inhabited by spirits.

The tribesmen were puzzled about what had happened and why the Americans had selected this particular mountain—which seemed to be of little apparent use to anyone—to kill. Twice they had asked the people at Bac Yen, the farm village nearest the mountain.

The villagers told them the American airplanes had dropped great numbers of bombs and sometimes would even shoot their guns at the mountain. There had been no buildings or soldiers on the hill, no supplies stored or hidden there. There was no reason at all, but the crazy Americans killed it anyway. The people from Bac Yen still avoided Dead Mountain, for it was dangerous and they heard strange sounds from there.

Finally, in search of truth, one of the tribesmen searched out a cousin, a hunter who had lived not far from the mountain when the Americans had flown there and dropped their bombs, and after a while he brought up the subject.

He said there were still live bombs there that had not gone off when they had hit. Scavengers sometimes went there to dig up metal and gather bullet casings to sell in Hanoi, for both were plentiful, but they had to be very careful. Sometimes they were killed when they detonated unexploded bombs and small bomblets by treading in the wrong places.

He also said the villagers were wrong, that there had once been a listening post on the mountain and a small barracks on the opposite side. The soldiers had watched for aircraft flying overhead and reported them by radio to Hanoi. But one day there had been parachutes from an airplane, and then the Americans had come with helicopters and fighters. That day the Americans had killed the soldiers, and the outpost was never reoccupied.

After that, the cousin said, the Americans had dropped their bombs on the mountain so often that the mountain seemed to change shape almost daily. He agreed that Dead Mountain was inhabited by spirits. He said sometimes, when the wind was right, you can hear a faint, angry voice calling from the mountain in what is surely the American language.

CHAPTER SIXTEEN

Thursday, January 19th—1945 Local, Takhli RTAFB, Thailand

The morning's target had again been in the area immediately west of Hanoi. While one Thud had been lost to AAA, the pilot had been picked up near the Laotian border. The afternoon strike had been against another old target, the Yen Vien rail yard near Hanoi. Two strike aircraft, a Weasel bird, and an EB-66 had been downed in the afternoon. No crew members had been rescued.

All day the defenses had been relentless, almost flawless. When the command post people had queried Korat and the F-4 wings, the story was the same. A couple of days before, the defenses had been mean as hell. Now, suddenly, the gomers were twice as good and things were twice as bad.

The afternoon disaster had been a 354th squadron strike. They lost a newcomer captain to a MiG on the way in. The MiG appeared out of nowhere, picked off the only straggler, and disappeared. An old head, an experienced major, was shot down by AAA after diving to dodge a SAM over Yen Vien. The AAA had seemed to open up at just the right time, to shoot at just the right acre of airspace.

Les Ries and Dan Janssen had been in the barrel to lead the Weasel flight on the afternoon mission. They'd lost their number three, one of the new Weasel crews.

Inside the O'Club, the strike pilots drank quietly. Ries and Janssen sat together at the end of the bar, periodically staring about with moody looks. Through flying and working so closely together they'd developed similar personalities, as most good Weasel crews did. Matching scowls even made them look alike.

EB-66 crews were at their customary tables at the far end of the barroom. They had lost six of their good men to, of all things, a SAM. Poor form for an EB-66 crew, with all those jammers aboard.

Tiny Bechler was sitting at the bar talking to Sam Hall. On the other side of Sam, Swede Swendler played a dice game with Bear Stewart and Lyle Watson.

"Sure getting hard to make up my mind about things anymore, Sam," said Tiny.

"How's that?"

"I got out of the Academy at Colorado Springs thinking anyone who hadn't graduated from one of the service academies couldn't be much of an officer. Then I got here and ran into guys like Max Foley and Benny who hadn't been anywhere near any of the academies, and you can't find better officers than they are."

"The school doesn't matter. It's what you do after you get out of pilot training," agreed Sam.

"How about you, Sam?"

"Tuskegee Institute, class of '50," said Sam.

"See what I mean. You're a good officer, and you didn't need West Point or Annapolis to become one."

Sam drank from his glass, thinking Tiny was pretty smart for a lieutenant.

"And there's Colonel Mack who didn't even finish college."

"He's a good leader," Sam agreed.

"So I realized I was wrong about the academies, but I knew there were plenty other people I was better than."

Sam Hall nodded. "Likely you're right."

"I said to myself that egotistical asshole Glenn Phillips isn't worth a damn, that he's all smoke and mirrors and bullshit. Then I flew on his wing a couple of times and he turned out to have bigger balls than anyone I'd ever known. He never boasted to anyone."

"Glenn was cool."

"Then I got to know a few of the Weasel backseaters, and they're okay and they're navigators. So I was wrong about navigators, or at least some of them."

"What's your point?"

Tiny shook his head. "I didn't think tanker crews were worth much, until I was coming out of pack six on fumes and my flight lead radioed ahead to say I couldn't make it to the tanker. A tanker crew put me on a free channel, told me to keep transmitting on my radio, and to stand by while they came and got me. They came all the way into North Vietnam, Sam. I met them just on this side of Na San, charging in like they were in a fighter, just to save my ugly ass. They had me plugged in and taking gas while they were still turning around to get out of there."

"Colonel Parker put the whole tanker crew in for Distinguished Flying Crosses," said Sam. "Told SAC it was for some silly reason he thought they'd buy, like 'made all radio calls on time and passed a lot of gas,' because he knew they'd hemorrhage little bricks if they knew the crew took one of their tankers into North Vietnam."

"Hey, that's great," said Tiny. "Anyway, I was wrong about the tanker crews. Those guys saved my ass, and you gotta admit they work like hell to get us refueled as smoothly as possible every day."

"They're pros," muttered Hall. Sam was always happy to say complimentary things about those he felt deserved it, which was most people.

Tiny looked at the rear of the room where the EB-66 aircrews drank together, sitting around their customary tables.

"I used to make fun of those guys, tell 'em they oughta fly where we operate and get some real action. But hell, look at what happened today. Makes me feel shitty for what I said."

Sam nodded, thinking he should feel shitty.

Tiny looked sad. "I don't think there's anyone left I wanna be an asshole to."

"You still giving Sergeant Perez in the personal equipment shop a hard time?"

"Sometimes, but we've got a deal. He lets me blow off steam, and I make sure he gets to keep one of the squadron pickups for his shop. He's a good guy."

Sam smiled. "Like I told you before, it's hard to hate much of anything except snakes, commies, hippies, queers, and Wallace."

The Bear, seated at his customary barstool, was situated between Lyle Watson and Swede Swendler, playing liars dice and fending off the Thai bartender's pleas to get into the game.

"Jimmy, I've got IOU's on everything you got and everything you're gonna get in the next ten years. Maybe in your whole life."

"Dubble or nuthin!" demanded Jimmy.

"Then I'd get everything your kids would ever own. Forget it. You oughta stop gambling." The Bear vowed to ignore him for the rest of the evening.

The bar was quieter than normal, and his words carried.

"Gloomy, isn't it," said Lyle Watson, looking out at the men in the bar.

"You remember what it was like up there this morning? Getting tough to make it back, Lyle," said the Bear. He rattled the dice cup and plopped it onto the bar.

"No one's singing or anything. It's like they just want to get drunk and forget things."

"What's that?" asked the Bear, motioning at Lyle's drink. "Your second or third in the last half hour?"

"Yeah, guess so."

The Bear peered under the cup. "Three fives," he said.

"You're lying." Lyle lifted the cup and showed three sixes.

The Bear raked in the nickels, leaving one. "Ante up," he said. The other two pushed a nickel from their meager stacks. The Bear was winning.

Swede grumbled. "C'mon, give someone else a chance."

"Get Watson to stop challenging me every time. Tell him I never lie unless I have to." The Bear clopped the dice cup down again and peered.

Swendler turned to Lyle Watson. "He says he don't lie. Believe him, okay?"

"Four twos," said the Bear.

"Okay, I believe you." Watson took the cup and looked between his cupped hands. His face fell. "Jesus."

"Dumb shit," said the Bear.

Lyle showed a six and shook the rest inside the cup. He pushed the cup toward Swendler without looking. "Four threes," he said with obvious, false bravado.

Swede lifted the cup and showed a pair of sixes. The game was now between him and the Bear.

"You hear about the EB-66?" asked Lyle. "F-4 pilot that saw it said the missile speared it like a fish. Went halfway through and then exploded."

"Where'd you hear that?" asked Swede.

"Our command post called the command post at Ubon. A guy there said the F-4 pilot only saw three chutes. There were six guys on board."

"Damn," said Swendler.

"Shake the dice," said the Bear. He liked to hurry when he was winning, slow things down when he was behind. "What bugs me is, we've never seen SAM sites up there where the missile came from. Not ever."

Swede slapped the dice cup down, looked, and grinned. "Pair of sixes."

"Not ever?" asked Lyle.

"Not so far as I know," said the Bear. He took the cup, looked, kept a pair of fours outside and shook the cup. He looked and grinned. "Four fours."

"Liar." Swede lifted.

"I told you I don't lie." The Bear raked in the nickels.

"I wanna play," said Jimmy.

Les Ries left the club, the pained look still on his face. He had drunk several beers but looked sober. The Bear watched him go.

"Those two've sure been acting strange lately," said Lyle.

"Assholes," said the Bear.

"Maybe," said Swede, "but they're our assholes."

"True. Ante up." The Bear shook.

Lyle spoke. "It must be tough on 'em, losing their number three like that. You know that the pilot, Rick Taylor, was one of Ries's closest friends?"

"Yeah, I heard."

"Les doesn't take to failure," said Swede. "He thinks everything's his responsibility, like he's gotta carry it all on his own shoulders. He gives it his all and doesn't understand why sometimes things still go all to shit."

"Three sixes," said the Bear, thinking it was time to try to talk to Ries and Janssen and end the silly feud.

Half an hour later, the Bear made his way down the bar and confronted Janssen. He sucked in a breath, determined to try.

"Dan, why don't you come on over and join us," he said.

Janssen was intoxicated, stared at him with expressionless eyes.

"Come on, for God's sake. I'm trying to make peace." He felt better after saying it.

"Fuck off."

"I was wrong, okay. I shouldn't have said some of the things I did."

Janssen reached out and tried to shove him away, but the Bear sidestepped him. He went back to the other end of the bar.

"I tried," he said.

"I saw," said Lyle, who'd been saving his seat. The bar was filling with people, but the atmosphere was still downbeat.

The Bear, as befitted the winner of the dice game, ordered drinks.

"Chickenpluckers!" Pete Crawford yelled loudly as he entered the bar. He joined Sam Hall and the Bear.

Sam was talking to the Bear. "Where'd Benny go? This morning he got a long distance call at the squadron and wouldn't tell me who it was from. Then about five I answered a call from a round-eye who said she was at the gate. When I saw him leave, he was with Tiny Bechler in the squadron van going about mach two."

The Bear shrugged, feeling very unhappy as he thought about Benny and Liz together.

"Where'd he go?" asked Sam. "Chickenplucker says Colonel Mack's looking for him."

"The girl's up here visiting so I guess they're in town. I'll tell him about Colonel Mack when he gets in."

"Who is she?" asked Chickenplucker.

"A Pan Am stew he knows. Prettiest girl in Takhli town right now." He ought to know, he thought.

Chickenplucker was about to ask more, but they were interrupted by Colonel Mack, who tapped the Bear on the shoulder.

"Yes, sir?" asked the Bear, standing straighter and wondering how the squadron commander had slipped up on him.

"You sober?" Mack was not smiling.

"Sober enough, sir."

"There's a classified message at the command post I want you to read over. Mentions some changes the North Vietnamese are suspected of making. Where's Captain Lewis?"

"Downtown, sir."

"Then you do it. I want a briefing at the command post in an hour."

"I'll get over there right now."

Colonel Mack left.

"You want me to come along?" Lyle Watson asked the Bear.

"Sure. You better sober up some, though. Go splash some water on your face or something." The Bear looked over and saw Janssen looking at him with a question on his face.

An hour later, Mack MacLendon showed up at the small briefing room where the Bear and Watson had gone to review the message. He had both the major in charge of wing intelligence and Maj Max Foley, the wing weapons officer, in tow.

Heavy stuff, thought the Bear.

Mack leaned back against a table. "What do you think, Bear?"

The Bear pointed to the message. "They've finally integrated their defenses."

"What do you mean?"

The Bear explained. "We've been expecting something like this, Colonel. That's why Les Ries's briefing at Saigon meant so much to us Weasels. The defenses have been building and building, and now they've got a choir director. There's a new long-range command-and-control radar called a Barlock that we've detected the last few times we've flown up there, and it's probably running the whole show. They'll tune the system a little here, tweak it a bit there, but it's already about as bad as it can get."

"What can we expect next?"

"Since I got here I've heard guys saying it can't get any worse. I keep telling them it could. Well, sir, I finally agree with them. The North Vietnamese are at the limits. They've got all the SAMs, MiG's, and guns they can cram up there, and now they've got good command-and-control. It can't get worse."

There was a moment of quiet as the men digested the impact of his words.

Mack broke the silence. "Can we locate this new radar?"

The Bear thought hard. "Not with the Weasel gear. Our receivers are designed to go after tracking radars that lock onto us. The Barlock only paints its target every fifteen, twenty seconds." He brightened. "The EB-66's can triangulate it accurately with their receivers, but only if they get close enough."

The intelligence officer shook his head. "After the one was shot down today, PACAF Headquarters sent a message saying EB-66's are not to fly anywhere close to pack six."

"So much for that idea," mumbled the Bear.

"Keep thinking, Bear," said Mack. "The wing commander says he wants something done. He wants it done fast, and he's picked us to do it."

"You think headquarters might approve our campaign to kill defenses like Les Ries asked 'em?"

"No, I don't. An all-out effort to eliminate defenses would take too many assets. We'd lose aircraft and pilots we could be using to knock out targets."

"Two things come to mind, sir. First, it would have been a lot easier to eliminate the defenses before they were integrated. Second, knocking them out even now and taking our losses would still be a hell of a lot better than a slow hemorrhage while we keep flying up there."

"Forget the campaign, because you're not going to get it. What else can we do?"

The Bear paused, thinking hard, wishing he'd had fewer drinks and more time to think about it.

"My guess is we should work on the basics. The strike pilots have ECM pods and good radar detection equipment. They should learn how to use them to get the best results."

"Go on," said Mack.

"We know how to dodge missiles, and we can handle the MiG's. We ought to make sure everyone knows how to do those things well. The guys ought to know what the Weasels are doing out there, and they can help us knock out SAM sites. We make as few mistakes as possible and take out as many MiG's and SAM sites as we can, maybe we can get ahead."

Mack spoke up. "What about the new ECM pod formations they tested in the States?"

The Bear had taken a long look at the briefing viewgraphs sent from Nellis Air Force Base. "If the ECM pods were better, maybe we could consider it, but they're weak powered and only work half the time."

Max Foley added his agreement, "And if we fly in a king-size gaggle like that, there'll be less opportunity to maneuver against SAMs or take the offensive against MiG's."

Mack played devil's advocate. "Korat is going for it. They're going to fly straight and level in a single, big formation, with their ECM pods turned on."

The Bear shook his head. "Even if they get their pods working better, they'll lose the same numbers as we do. But it's probably good if they do things one way and we do it another, Colonel. It'll keep the gomers on their toes trying to figure us out."

"I agree," said Max Foley.

Colonel Mack got to his feet, like he'd made up his mind on something. "You and Benny flying tomorrow?"

"Yes, sir."

"I'm taking you off the schedule for a week. I want you two to come up with a group of guidelines for the strike pilots. What they should look out for, how to detect SAM launches, and how to dodge the SAMs without getting shot down by the guns. Major Foley, you work on tactics to use against the MiG's."

"Yes, sir," said Max.

"When you guys are done, set up a briefing for every pilot in the wing. And remember, I don't just want our guys to learn how to stay alive. I want everyone thinking of killing MiG's and SAM sites, like the Bear was saying."

Max Foley and the Bear agreed.

"I'll let Colonel Parker know what we've come up with and what you guys are doing."

As they broke up the meeting, the Bear asked for a minute of Colonel Mack's time.

"Sir," he started, "this might get sort of awkward, what with Les Ries being a major and all, and being the ranking Weasel. Shouldn't he be in on this?"

"Do you see him here, Bear?"

"No, sir. That's what . . ."

"Colonel Parker said I could pick anyone in the wing to work on this, and I'm choosing you and Benny. You two get together with Major Foley and get on with it."

"Yes, sir."

As he left the command post, the Bear found Lyle Watson waiting outside. They fell into step and walked back toward the club.

"You did good in there," said Lyle.

"Benny's gonna shit when he finds out what I've signed

us up for. This is a hell of a night for him to be downtown screwing off."

"I thought you'd be all for him. Getting to see his girl like that."

The Bear didn't answer. How the hell could he have known that Benny was going to change his mind about Liz? It didn't help to remember that he had said no when she said she wanted to see him again, or that he'd had to endure one of her tantrums.

When he thought about Julie, he felt even worse. He'd been reading her daily letter this morning when Liz had called the Ponderosa from Bangkok. Julie's pages had been filled with her steady kind of devotion, exactly the kind of thing he hadn't wanted to deal with.

But on the phone Liz had told him something that might change a lot of things. He had to do some heavy thinking.

19/2100L—Takhli Village, Thailand

Takhli was a small, ancient village built on the banks of the Yai, a minor tributary of the mighty Chao Phraya River. It lay only fifteen miles east of the Chao Phraya, situated on the main arteries of the north-south railroad and the highway from Bangkok.

The old village featured a bustling market square, a railroad depot, a number of stores, and a lumberyard built on the road going east toward the big military airfield.

In the market were entrepreneurs selling wares of all descriptions. Bolts of cotton, synthetic, and silk material. Live and slaughtered pigs, goats, ducks, and chickens. Baskets of betel nuts. Woven wickerwork. Vegetables and fruit. Bins of tubers, peppers, bright saffron, and curry. Tubs of river fish and eels. Cheap radios, tape recorders, and watches. Brooms and dusters. Dishes made of metal, pottery, and wood.

Buddhist monks went about the market, their eating cups their only worldly possessions. Old people and cripples begged there. Women walked around shopping wisely, munching on deep-fried chicken feet. Many of their mouths were bright red from chewing betel nuts, teeth black and falling out from the strong, addictive juice. Sometimes the men would gather, hunkering down to watch and wager on a battle between a cobra and a jungle rat, which usually ended in a standoff. The women averted their eyes and shuddered as they passed by the bloating bodies of thieves—usually once-rowdy teenagers— left to rot for a few days in an open area as reminders of what could happen if . . . Men looked to see if they recognized them. The bodies weren't there often, only when thieves were caught.

Bars, massage parlors, restaurants, and shacks had been hastily thrown together on the road leading to the base. Whores, hotsy bath girls, musicians, and entrepreneurs from Bankok lived there, working at night, lying around or visiting the market during the daytime. Thieves, samlor drivers, and beggar kids hung around there. American and Thai military policemen kept order at night on the strip, but they generally allowed the servicemen to do their thing, which was to whore and drink and enjoy themselves. American doctors from the base worked out programs to examine and treat the whores for syphilis and gonorrhea. Except for the overworked police force, no one minded much, for the action was mostly confined to the strip.

Liz Richardson

Liz had hired the taxi in Bangkok. She'd had trouble finding the right combination—a driver who appeared honest with an automobile that looked sound enough to make the trip—but had finally made the deal for thirty dollars.

What she was doing was taking all her courage. Even talking to Mal Bear hadn't been easy. She'd called him from Bangkok and explained that she was in Thailand for a five-day layover and what she wanted to do. He'd been hesitant at first, sounding guilty. At least he had that decency about him. He had not been at all happy about what she wanted to do, hadn't been helpful at all until she'd told him about Julie.

Julie would kill her if she ever found out she'd told Mal Bear.

After Liz had told him, he'd sounded dazed. Eventually he explained how she might go about getting to Takhli and finding Benny.

She'd gotten over her hatred of Mal Bear for rejecting her before they'd left each other in Bangkok. All that long night he'd played her body like a maestro might a piano, matching her hungers, teaching her new ecstasies, making her feel like a beautiful queen of passion. He'd repeatedly told her how desirable she was as he'd driven her to new heights, and she'd believed him. But then, at the end, he'd told her that he wouldn't see her again.

For a week there had been a different man at every layover. She'd tried her new wings and experienced pleasures that had only been fantasies before. But that wasn't really her and it had been easy to stop. She'd also come to realize that Mal Bear had been right, that they were not for each other. But if he'd asked she'd have tried. It had been that good.

She'd started writing letters to Benny Lewis because of his proximity to Mal Bear. Then she'd remembered that he really was a nice guy, that he was interested in places and history. She realized writing to Benny pleased her.

After the morning call to Mal Bear, she'd had the hotel operator place a second call to Benny at his squadron. She'd been brief, telling him she was in Thailand touring with a group and was coming up in a taxi to see him, and that she'd call him when she got to Takhli. She had not given him time to refuse her, but had excitedly rushed her words before hanging up.

After the long, bone-rattling cab ride, she'd called again from the base gate, using the phone provided by the droop-mouthed air policeman. The appreciative look on the airman's face was a tonic for her ego.

A huge man in an Aussie hat dropped Benny off from a blue van. Benny looked good in civvies, slacks and a cotton shirt that showed off his muscular build.

Civilians weren't allowed on base without special permission, he'd said, so they'd gone downtown in the taxi.

This time he hadn't kissed her when they met, and that was fine. They'd had a single drink at a sleazy club filled with bar-girls who Benny said were waiting for the night action to begin.

It was dark when they left the bar. When they were getting back into the taxi, she saw airmen in civilian attire getting off buses and out of samlors and starting to filter toward the different bars.

"The zoo's about to open," he said.

"It's a different world."

"Not much to it," said Benny. "Glitter and grime."

An airman whistled.

"And they don't get to see many round-eyes." He appraised her and looked appreciative. "You look spectacular, Liz, especially considering you've ridden for hours in the heat and dust."

"Thank you." No need to mention the time she'd spent getting fixed up before calling his squadron.

"Let's eat Thai food tonight," she said. "I'm famished."

He directed the way. As they rode he asked again why she'd come.

"I wanted to see the real Thailand, and I thought this might be the best way. Just rent a taxi and go north. I'm going to have the taxi driver drop me off in a city a few miles from here called Nakhon Sawan. I've got a reservation at a hotel there. Tomorrow morning I get on the train—it's called a *Roog-fry,* something like that—and go up to a place called Chiang Mai."

"I've heard about it. It's an ancient walled city up north. You're going alone?" He sounded surprised.

"I'll be with a group of our Pan Am people, mostly stews and a few agents here on vacation. I'll meet them tomorrow on the morning train. I just got a head start."

"Sounds like it'll be fun."

"Our Bangkok office manager says you haven't seen Thailand until you've experienced Chiang Mai. They don't allow motor vehicles in town, and he says it's unbelievably quiet. The prices are supposed to be great, and you can live like royalty. He says the silver market there is out of this world."

"Will he be with your group?"

"Nope, only girls allowed. I can only stay in Chiang Mai for two days. I'll take a small plane back to Bangkok on Sunday, then I'm working flights to the Philippines and on back to the States."

"You're going to be busy," he said.

"Now that you know everything, you can tell me what you've been doing."

"First, I'll show you our lovely metropolis and we'll find the restaurant."

They drove around the village for ten minutes, then found a dimly lit Thai restaurant with an unpronounceable name. The food was good, as good as the Thai food they'd had in Bangkok, but was so hot they had to pause even longer between bites. Benny talked some, but they spent a great deal of quiet time.

"How's your flying going?" she asked.

He answered with a noncommittal shrug.

"The news we get in the States is sketchy as far as you guys are concerned. Every now and then they just say that there was a raid on the Hanoi area and that more planes were lost."

"I don't think they want much publicity. Too many hush-hush agreements. For instance, we're not supposed to talk about how we get from here to North Vietnam, because there aren't any official overflight agreements."

"Are you still losing friends?"

"A lot of good people don't come back."

"Julie doesn't talk about it very much, but she sure misses Mal Bear." She didn't tell him the revelation that Julie had confided. Anyway, as she'd told Mal Bear, one missed period could easily be a false alarm.

"They seemed to get along well," Benny said, but he had a stern look about him when he said it.

She agreed, then remembered the next part of her plan. "Would you like me to give your family in Santa Rosa a call when I get back next week? I'm sure they'd like to hear that you're doing well."

"Would you?"

"Of course. Anyone else?"

He thought. "No."

She got his family's address and phone number, which she already knew, then they had a discussion about how his divorce was going (he was over his ex, she could tell), and (bitterly) how he'd not gotten a letter or any word about his children. By the time he was ready to return to the base in the taxi, she'd agreed to call his sister in Sacramento and to periodically send him news (he liked the *Examiner*) of what was happening back in the Bay Area.

At the gate, he was reluctant to leave. He dawdled and talked about the guys, how he and the Bear were doing well together, and then, how tough the flying was getting. Finally he gave her a long, pleasant kiss.

"I'll write more," she said.

He mumbled something about being sorry he hadn't replied and said he had a letter half written that he would finish. As the taxi drove away, he stood there for a while. At last he waved.

19/2330L—Hanoi, DRV

Li Binh

Xuan Nha was exultant, strutting about the house like a royal peacock. "Eight airplanes today," he gloated. "Eight!"

Always before his boasting had been done quietly, as if it were his destiny to succeed. Not so today. He was childlike, and Li Binh thought that his exuberance, much like that of her servants, was gratitude for his reprieve.

"General Luc was briefed tonight about the shootdown of the Pesky plane. He sent me his personal congratulations, Li Binh. He asked if I would join him tomorrow in his staff meeting, as I did before. That was why I hurried back to Hanoi."

He had just been deposited at the door of the villa, fresh from the field.

"It is like it was before, Li Binh. Just like before."

Nothing is ever like before, she thought archly, but did not tell him so.

He was still strutting, hands on his hips. "Tea!" he commanded, and the servants made noises from the kitchen area to let him know they had heard.

He sat in his leather strap chair, but his energy was still apparent. "It was like a concerto," he said. "From the Wisdom command center we see a complete picture of the air battle, and no airplane can escape our scrutiny. We see where the enemy is and know where our own forces are. I can look at the radar returns and know what the enemy is thinking!"

"And you have gotten results."

"Thirteen enemy shot down with Wisdom, and it has only been two days!"

"And the radar-hunters?"

"We shot one down today. It is apparent what they are doing, easy to tell who they are now. If the radar operators are observant, we can even tell when they fire their homing missiles."

"The American prisoner who gave you information about

the radar-hunters. Is what he said true? Are the Americans fearful?"

"If any are not, they shall be. Li Binh, we have won the air battle. All that remains is to shoot them down as fast as they come. Thirteen in two days, eight of those today, and we have captured eleven pilots."

As he continued to babble, she thought that she was fortunate not to have invited her nephew to the villa tonight. That should be a lesson for her, she thought. With Xuan's unpredictable schedule, popping in and out from his frequent visits to Wisdom, she could no longer have her nephew visit during his absences. From now on she would go to him.

She missed him almost as much as she was growing to detest Xuan Nha.

20/1000L—Hoa Lo Prison, Hanoi, North Vietnam

Glenn Phillips

Someone lifted the viewing hole cover, then the key rattled in the lock. Fishface came into Glenn's cell and glared as he hobbled painfully to his feet and bowed at the waist. Bowed low like they wanted, to please Fishface.

The kid gloves had come off soon after his return from the hospital. They'd tied his elbows behind his back and hooked ropes to his hands, hoisted him up, and stretched him until his feet no longer touched the floor, pulling his shoulders from their sockets. Then, after he'd hung there for an hour, they'd jogged him up and down for a while and dropped him to the floor. They had bent him two days later, showing him other things they could do with his body with their ropes. That was when he'd learned to bow. Other prisoners he saw in the exercise yard and washup area had been bent worse.

Fishface grunted, his normal sign of recognition, then turned and motioned. Another guard brought in a new prisoner, one he couldn't recognize who was still in his flight suit, and dumped him on the floor. Glenn bowed again as they left.

They were gone.

It was the first time he'd had a roommate, but the guy didn't look good. Glenn examined him closely. Unconscious, hoarse breathing, fetid breath—but whose wasn't—and bad

facial burns. Torn and charred flight suit with subdued lieutenant's bars on the shoulders, and blood at the right shoulder.
He stripped his fellow prisoner carefully and pulled him onto
his bunk.

He heard rapping on the wall. Several quick ones to clear
things, then five, pause, two. He went through his mental
gymnastics. He wasn't good with the tap-code yet. The
alphabet was divided into fives, with the K removed. A, F, L,
Q, and V started the rows. Two across in the V row. The letter
was W.

He knocked once. Received.

The knocking continued at a rapid rate then. "Who is new
guy?" was the question from the captain in the adjacent cell.
The brass among the prisoners had determined that the most
important thing they could be doing, besides resisting the
enemy, was to account for each and every POW who came to
jail. Whenever they got a name, it was everyone's responsibility to spread the word and add it to the memorized list.

He tapped a question mark, then returned to the man on
the bunk. As he looked him over more closely the lieutenant
groaned. A good sign?

The shoulder was cut, but not too badly. Glenn carefully
turned him and examined him closer. Burns on the neck, face,
and hands. Scaling, blackened skin with pink, tender flesh
beneath.

"Where?" the lieutenant's voice was weak.

"Hanoi Hilton. You're in jail. I'm Major Glenn Phillips."
Glenn whispered, since the Americans weren't allowed to talk
to one another, upon penalty of beating or bending with ropes.

"I thought . . ." He groaned. "They really hurt me.
Brought me in . . . and then really hurt me. Ropes."

"They like rope tricks."

Silence. The new guy turned his head painfully to try to
look at him and cried out in pain.

"When did they get you?"

"Five days ago." His breathing became badly labored.
"NVA got me . . . when I . . . came down in the chute."

"You're lucky it wasn't civilians. What's your name?"

He held his head rigidly in position. Apparently it pained
him when he moved it, and every few words he paused for
breath. "First . . . First Lieutenant . . . William Dortmeier, sir. Three-fifty-seventh at Takhli."

"My old squadron. You hurt anywhere? Anywhere worse than others, I mean."

"My face hurts like hell. I hurt my neck and my back in the ejection, but wasn't too bad until I got here. They hurt me with ropes. . . . God did they hurt me."

"The guys who brought you in here?"

"Yes, sir."

"Fishface likes to make us yell."

"I don't feel my legs now—I mean, I feel something, but not really." He whimpered, gritted his teeth, shifted a bit, and cried out. "My neck hurts!"

"You General Bill Dortmeier's son?"

"Yes, sir," he whispered, still gritting.

"No feeling at all in the legs?"

"No, sir. . . . Something's wrong . . . with my neck."

The tapping came again.

"Just a second. Be right back."

Glenn had tapped out *D-O-R-T-M-E-I-E-R– –W,* and was about to terminate when he heard a noise. He turned to see the lieutenant trying to see what he was doing. He slumped and made a final gurgling sound, his head slipping to an odd angle. Glenn hurried back in time to be at bedside when Dortmeier stopped breathing. Artificial respiration didn't help.

They didn't take the body away for two days.

23/1520L—Vinh, Route Pack Two, North Vietnam

Chickenplucker Crawford

They were flying at 6,000 feet over the flat land west of Vinh. With the mounting losses in pack six, the mission to the lower-threat area had thus far seemed a respite. Crawford's radar warning receiver was quiet, and he'd heard nothing about threats from the others in his flight.

The mission objective was to again eliminate the elusive Vinh ferry, which reconnaissance photos showed had been rebuilt and placed back into operation.

It was a large, bargelike ferry they would be looking for, and the recce photos had shown it loaded with trucks full of supplies. Hundreds of barrels of something had been stacked on the Vinh side of the wide Ca River, waiting their turn.

On some previous missions they had found other Vinh ferries and destroyed them. On other missions they had not found any sign of the ferry. It was thought that the present barge-ferry was somehow flooded and sunk during daylight hours, then raised and used at night and during bad weather to carry supplies and people across the wide river.

Today, Chickenplucker was leading the first flight on the target. There was no flak suppression flight, for the defenses would not be as concentrated as they were in pack six. There were no Wild Weasels, for they were presently banned from flying on anything but pack six strikes.

Too bad, thought Crawford. The Vinh SAM site was infamous for its trickery. He didn't worry much, because he had great faith in his own ability and in the discipline and resourcefulness of his fellow fighter jocks. Still, he would have felt easier if the Weasels were roaming about up there, trying to sniff out and preoccupy the radar defenses.

A gun radar came on from somewhere up north of Vinh and chattered on his radar warning equipment. It posed no threat to his flight, so he ignored it.

He saw the muddy Ca River at his eleven o'clock and adjusted his course slightly to fly toward its mouth.

"There's the river up ahead, Tonka flight," he radioed. *"We'll make a fast pass south of the ferry's last known position, then make a one-eighty out over the water and come back for a better look. Keep the speed up. I don't want to be caught lollygagging around Vinh."*

"Two!"

"Three!"

"Four!"

He felt buoyed by the precision of his flight's response. They were ready for the cagey Vinh commander Benny Lewis had warned him about before takeoff.

Only the steadily tracking gun radar was on the radar warning scope. Periodically, he heard a beep and saw the flicker of a single strobe from his left, but he ignored that one too because it wasn't ready and tracking.

The river loomed and grew. He kept it off to his left, staring hard to search for the ferry. Nothing he saw resembled the barge in the photos.

They approached the coastline and no one had yet seen the ferry. *Damn, if they hadn't hidden it well.*

He led his flight farther out over the water, the single Firecan gun radar still tracking them, the periodic beep in his headset still annoying him.

Crawford pushed his radio button. *"Lead and three'll be making a right turn in one minute, Tonka flight. Tonka three, you and four continue out another ten seconds before you start your turn. I want you back a couple miles when we're inbound. When we coast in I want four sets of eyeballs glued onto the south bank of the river. Look for the barge, camouflage, even a shadow in the water, and call out anything that looks suspicious."*

"Two!"

"Three!"

"Four!"

He turned right, waited for his wingman to settle into position, and adjusted his throttle so they were flying at 420 knots true airspeed. It appeared safe enough to fly at the slower speed.

He held the course, aiming for a point that would carry him a couple of miles to the south of the big river. Another Firecan radar joined the first one, making a buzzing sound in his helmet's earphones, showing two strobes now on the small scope. Both showed that the radars were well to his right, across the opposite bank of the wide river.

He could still define no threat to his flight.

He flew over the coastline and began his visual search.

What happened then was so fast that he never really could reconstruct it or get it straight in his mind.

A squeal and a red light. LAUNCH. The headset rattled. He looked and saw a chattering strobe, so powerful it illuminated a segment of the scope. He looked at two o'clock, in the direction of the strobe, and saw a missile already dropping its booster off, accelerating, close. Damn!

"SAMs! Break!" his wingman yelled. He nosed over and started a hard right turn.

The missile was upon him, then exploded. For a split second he was engulfed in the copper-red fireball. The engine gave a giant belch, causing the airframe to shudder.

He kicked the right rudder, and the Thud responded. Then it was no longer flying. He tried to determine where he was, realized he was heading for the ground too fast, rotated the handles, and pulled both levers. A giant kick in the butt!

He swung in the parachute. Watched the Thud impact the ground. Felt he must be in a dream. Disoriented. Looking about wildly, finally seeing the ocean to his left. Before him was a large field pocked with deep craters from naval shelling, with a half-destroyed shack at one end. He twisted about and saw, behind him, the river. It was only a mile away.

He released the right catch of his oxygen mask and let it swing away, and tried to prepare for his parachute landing fall.

Tracers shooting up from behind him. The ground racing up at him. Yellow, inflated life raft beneath him. The raft hit first, then he fell in an awful PLF, ended up on his side, his head and shoulders, then completed the somersault and landed flat on his back.

"Damn," he muttered. The chute was still floating, billowed by gusts of warm wind, white against the blue sky.

He determined he was okay after lying there for a few seconds. The chute billowed higher and tugged at him. He found the catches and released it, shucking off the parachute harness while he was about it.

Which way's the water? He was disoriented.

A Thud soared overhead.

His beeper was still on. He found the harness, fumbled around, and turned off the emergency location beeper.

He looked around and saw the building in the distance, a shack really. Uninhabitable? People inside? He remembered its position from his look while in the chute. The water was straight in front of him!

How far? It had looked to be three or four miles. A long way to haul the raft.

He grabbed his tether to the raft and started to pull it behind him. He got hung up when the survival kit he was also inadvertently pulling along snagged on a bush.

"Calm down, dammit," he muttered.

He pulled the kit and the raft into one of the craters he'd seen from the air. The hole was ten feet across and half as deep.

Yelling in the distance. Vietnamese voices. Crawford hunkered down in the crater so he couldn't be seen.

He pulled out a radio from his survival vest, switched it to Guard channel, then to REC ONLY. Nothing. He switched it to TRANS/REC and broadcast.

"This is Tonka lead. I'm down." There were no side

tones, no static. It wasn't working. He examined it quickly, then tried again with the same results. He tossed it aside.

A Thud flew low overhead, and the sound was loud.

He pulled out a backup radio and tried again. Static now. *"This is Tonka lead."* Side tones, so it was working.

"Ah, roger, Tonka lead. This is Lionel lead." Sam Hall's familiar Southern voice.

A soldier in a ragged uniform was suddenly there at the crest, peering down and aiming his rifle at Crawford's head.

"Hands up!"

Crawford almost pissed his pants. He was caught, and his damned gun was still in its holster.

As he slowly raised his hands, the radio came alive again. *"Say your condition, Tonka lead."*

The soldier became very excited, and Crawford felt he was about to shoot. He dropped the radio and stretched his hands higher yet. He tried grinning, but the soldier just kept yelling "hands up" over and over until more soldiers arrived.

He eyed them warily. "Hello, chickenfuckers," he said. This time there was no brass around to complain.

There were a half dozen of them, and they kicked him and beat him with heavy rifle butts as they stripped him of his survival vest, g-suit, flight suit, watch, wedding band, dog tags, and boots. Then they kicked and shoved him a couple more times to encourage him to walk, and finally holed up with him in the deserted shack until the Thuds had departed. They kept the muzzles of their guns aimed at him, but didn't mistreat him badly.

He heard bombs exploding in the distance, and was surprised that their concussions could be felt even here. The rickety building rattled and shook.

At the first shadowy signs of the falling sun they led him away, walking on a roadway pocked with so many craters they were hard to circumvent.

They walked for an hour, and he wished to hell they would give him his boots back. All he wore was his skivvies, socks, and T-shirt. When he motioned to one of his captors that he wanted something, the soldier hit him in the belly with his rifle butt, then was upset because of the delay while he doubled over to regain his breath.

It grew darker as they walked. He started to think of escape. He'd been schooled to attempt escape as soon as possible after capture. That was when you had your best chance.

The gomers must have read the same book, because they stayed close.

They came to the river and a small village there. He was herded toward a bamboo cage at the side of a small hut. He was pushed inside, and the door tied behind him. It was relatively dark, but he could see someone else huddled into a corner of the cage. A Vietnamese?

A soldier looked his work over, shaking the door to make sure it was secure. The gomers withdrew, leaving him behind to stand guard.

"Howdy," said the other guy.

Relief flooded him. Another American.

The guard came over and spoke excitedly in Vietnamese.

"Fuck off," said the other American.

The Vietnamese jabbed inside the cage with the barrel of his rifle, an old Garand, and the guy yelped with pain. The gomer didn't like them talking between themselves, Crawford decided.

A while later the guard was relieved by another soldier, much younger and not very intelligent looking.

Chickenplucker tried this time, keeping his voice very low. "Major Pete Crawford. Thud driver from Takhli."

The guard overheard and looked over at them, grumbled once, but didn't do anything.

"Captain Red Williams. Misty Fac. F-100's out of Binh Hoa." He was a forward air controller flying F-100 Super Sabres from South Vietnam.

"Good to see you, Red."

"I was shot down south of here, near Dong Hoi. Lucky bastards got me with small-arms fire."

"Got me with a SAM."

"I saw it. Ringside seat right here. The gomers like to leave you out in the sun."

"How long you been with them?"

"Five days now. I tried to escape the first night. Almost got out of the hut they had me in, but then I heard them coming so I got back inside and acted like I was sleeping."

"They keep this cage? Take it with them when you travel?"

"No. I think this is a regular route for their prisoners.

They take you from place to place, walk at night and hole up during the daytime. They walk you about every other day, tie your hands, and put a rope around your neck, like you're a dog."

"Damn," whispered Crawford. He didn't like the sound of that.

"When they move you, you walk all night. I see they took your boots like they did mine. It's hard on the feet, walking with no boots."

"I'll get used to it," said Crawford. "I went barefoot back in Tennessee so long they had to run me down and shoe me like a horse. My feet'll toughen up."

"They'd better," whispered Red. "They don't like you walking slow. I've stubbed my toes about fifty times, and my feet feel like hamburger."

The guard grew restless, walked over to them, then once around the cage. He was young, unenergetic, and not very interested in what he was doing. He went back to the front of the hut and lounged against it. They both watched him closely.

"I call them names, like the seven dwarfs. This guy's Dopey, and if we're gonna get out of here, I figure he's our best chance."

"He doesn't look very motivated."

"Two of the other guards, I call them Happy and Sleepy, they're not much better. The rest of 'em are more alert. Watch out for Doc. He's a real little guy, but he's mean."

"How many of them altogether?"

"Seven, like the dwarfs. Maybe more now they've got you. I figure if we can get out of here, we should either try to walk out to the west, or try the water. How far are we from the ocean?"

"Three or four miles."

"Thought we were still close, 'cause you can smell the salt water. Where are we?" asked Red Williams.

"That's the Ca River, and Vinh's just across. We were looking for the ferry when I got hammered by the SAM."

"It's bad when they take you through a town. The civilians come out and poke you with sharp sticks and throw rocks and things, spit on you."

"Well," said Crawford, his mind churning, "let's try to

get out of this thing as quick as we can. When do you figure is our best chance?"

"Hard to tell. You don't know when they're going to change guards. Sometimes it's every couple of hours, sometimes longer. Our best bet's probably as soon as possible after guard change."

"Maybe we won't be here much longer if we pick the right time. Like now? I think we can untie the door without making much fuss." Crawford didn't like the idea of being in the cage, not at all, and Dopey did not appear alert. He was slumped against the side of the hut and only periodically shifted around to look at them.

"Maybe so," said Red, "except it's almost feeding time. They only feed you once or twice a day, and not much."

"I think we oughta take our chances getting to the water, maybe somehow make our way to the Navy ships out there." Crawford slowly edged toward the cage door, but that was when the guard came alive, stretched, and walked over to them and peered inside. Like he was trying to appear alert.

Another soldier came around the corner of the hut and spoke in Vietnamese. He was carrying bowls of food.

"That's Doc," whispered Red Williams.

The new guard heard him, rushed over to the cage, and berated the prisoners. He chewed out young Dopey, who stood with an embarrassed look, then had him hold his rifle on the prisoners as he opened the door to shove in small bowls of rice and some water. He carefully retied the door and motioned for Dopey to leave.

Doc was more alert, nervously pacing about and glaring at them as they quietly ate their pittances of food with their fingers.

Red tried to whisper something a little later, but with his first syllable, Doc rushed over, screeching angry words and jabbing him savagely with his rifle barrel.

The opportunity for immediate escape was lost. Following Red's lead, Crawford curled up and tried to sleep. They should stay rested and retain as much energy as possible. With the meager diet, they would rapidly lose weight and muscle tone. When their time came, they'd need every possible edge.

He finally dropped off into intermittent, troubled sleep, thinking about escaping to the coast and what they should do once they got there.

CHAPTER SEVENTEEN

Wednesday, January 25th—1935 Local, Takhli RTAFB, Thailand

Bear Stewart

The wing was going through pilots as fast as they got them in and the maintenance crews hardly had time to patch up an airplane before it was again holed by flak.

Since he and Benny had been working on the tutorial directed by Colonel Mack, Pudge Holden and Lyle Watson had been flying in their place, and that fact had kept the Bear grumpy. Tonight, though, he felt proud of the Weasel crew. A few hours earlier they had found and bombed a SAM site in pack six.

It seemed a tiny ray of light in the bleakness, so he and Benny had dropped their work on the briefing and come to the club to help them celebrate.

Benny Lewis bought the SAM-killers a round. Max Foley, the wing weapons officer, came over and clapped Pudge on the back. "Nice work up there."

"Thanks." Pudge beamed, and they all knew he was justifiably proud.

Someone started singing Sammy Small—a favorite—and everyone joined in. They sang it loud, because they were tired of being gloomy.

Oh my name is Sammy Small—
Fuck 'em all
Oh my name is Sammy Small—
Fuck 'em all
Oh my name is Sammy Small, and I only have one ball,

448

but that's better than none at all—
   So fuck 'em all.

They continued with several verses, about poor Sammy, who had shot a man in the head, *with a bit of fucking lead.* Now Sammy was *going to swing, what a silly fucking thing. Fuck 'em all.*

The Bear looked around. Les Ries and Dan Janssen were at the other end of the bar, near the outside door.

Lyle tried to interrupt his thoughts. "Just call me Super Bear," he said, not trying for a modesty award. "Told you I was the best, Mal." He was inebriated.

The singing continued. *Sammy Small was going to swing from a silly piece of string. The parson would come, with his tales of kingdom come, he could shove 'em up his bum. The sheriff he'd be there too, with his silly fucking crew, they had fuck all else to do. So fuck 'em all.*

Ries and Janssen were awfully quiet down there, thought the Bear, like they were in a different world or something. Ries saw him looking at them. He stared back for a moment, then spoke with Janssen.

"It was easy," said Lyle, still at his side and still mouthing off about killing the site.

"If it was so fucking easy, how come you were so pasty-faced and out of bullshit for an hour after the mission?" asked the Bear.

"I was just reflecting on things." Lyle was grinning. "Just call me Super Bear," he said again. "I like the ring of it."

The ballad was ending sadly. Sammy Small was being marched to the gallows. *He saw Molly in the crowd, and he felt so fucking proud, when she shouted right out loud: FUCK 'EM ALL!*

Lyle was talking to the wing munitions officer, a major big enough to throw fear into the Green Bay Packer line who had become an undisputed hero the week before.

It had started when a 750-pound bomb had refused to release when Capt Toki Takahara tried to pickle it off over the target. Neither would it release when he repeatedly tried to drop it on the way out or in the jettison area east of Takhli. Yet when Toki had landed his Thud, one lug had capriciously released, the fuse wire had been pulled out, and the armed

M-117 bomb had skidded along underneath the aircraft in a shower of sparks.

Toki was lucky that the bomb hadn't been set off, or that the timer did not expire while he braked the aircraft to a halt, decamped over the side, and ran like hell.

The bomb had a time delay fuse that was impossible for the enemy, *or anyone else,* to disarm as the timer counted down. The problem—aircraft and armed, enabled, ticking bomb—was left with the munitions officer. He and his EOD team had done the impossible. They had downloaded, then disarmed the bomb by removing the extraction-proof fuse.

He had considered it *interesting.* The fighter jocks thought he was brave but crazy. That was okay, because he thought they were just crazy.

The big munitions officer grabbed Lyle, zipped down the top of his flight suit, and in red ink drew an "SB" on the chest of Lyle's T-shirt.

Lyle turned toward the room, chest puffed out. "I told you I was Super Bear." He nudged the Bear. "You should call me that from now on, Mal."

The munitions officer spoke in his gruff voice. "The SB stands for Sloppy Bastard. You were spilling your drink all over me the whole time we were talking."

The Bear laughed. "Sloppy Bastard?"

Max Foley was nearby, talking to Pudge, Benny, and Toki Takahara.

"They announce it in the morning. No one can fly within five miles of Hanoi. Not for no reason, nohow. Another rule straight from the big man at the top."

"Just fucking wonderful," bitched Pudge Holden. "No one?"

"Not unless you're in hot pursuit of a MiG," said Max Foley.

"So what's Hanoi?" asked Toki Takahara. "They mean the center of Hanoi or the edge of Hanoi?"

Foley looked puzzled. "I think the city limits."

"How do we tell where the city limits are?" asked Pudge Holden. "It's not like there's big red marks painted on the ground."

"I've had it with you haole Americans," said Toki Takahara, the nisei from Hawaii. "You've got too many restrictions. I'm joining the other side. I'll fly MiG's and shoot at you guys. If I screw up and get shot down, I'll just wave to the local folks from my parachute and go get another jet to fly."

The Bear was grousing about the new restriction in his mind when he was surprised to see Les Ries and Dan Janssen making their way toward them through the crowd of pilots.

"You guys having a tactics conference or something?" asked Ries, smiling.

Max told him about the new restriction.

"The restriction doesn't apply to the Weasels," said Les.

"How's that?" asked Pudge Holden.

"They say you can overfly Hanoi if you're in hot pursuit. It doesn't specify 'hot pursuit of MiG's.' If a SAM's fired at us, we can go in to take out the SAM site, because that's hot pursuit. I ran that by Colonel Parker, and he said the idea's got merit. I don't intend to ask further, because he might say no."

"Good thinking," grinned Pudge.

Ries looked at him thoughtfully. "Congratulations on killing the SAM site."

Watson beamed and puffed out his chest. "Call me Super Bear."

"Sloppy Bastard," corrected the Bear.

"And you, too, Benny, even if I'm a bit late," said Ries. "That was a good kill you got the other day. I was being hardheaded."

Benny returned Ries's compliment. "I hear you did some good work up there this morning."

"They're tougher than I've ever seen them. More than thirty SAMs were fired just on this morning's mission." Les appeared tired.

"You flying tomorrow, Les?" asked Benny.

"Tomorrow afternoon."

"We got eighty-eight missions now," said Janssen, speaking to the Bear, "so it won't be long before we're finished."

Ries and Janssen had been flying every chance they got and their total counters were adding up fast. Headquarters said you could only fly one pack six mission per day, but they got around the restrictions by volunteering to be spare. When another Weasel aborted, they would take off in its place and get another counter. Ries and Janssen would be the first Weasel crew at Takhli to get a hundred missions. Benny and the Bear were a distant second, with sixty-seven missions, and were

being delayed further by their work on the tutorial. Tomorrow
morning they would start giving their briefing, and when they
were finished in two more days, they could go back to regular
flying.

Ries maneuvered Benny away from the others, then
motioned for Dan and the Bear to join them.

"Tomorrow I'm going to try that tactic you and Pudge
have been working on," he heard Les say.

Benny looked unhappy. "It's premature. Why don't you
hold off for a few days? Colonel Parker said the Weasels can
start flying a few missions down in the lower route packs
again. Let's try the tactic down there and iron out the wrinkles
before we use it up in pack six."

"Dan and I've been working on something, and we can't
put it off. We think we've got a way to take out their big
radar."

"The Barlock," said Dan.

"Our receivers aren't built to handle that kind of radar,"
the Bear interjected.

"I've been working with the guys in the avionics shop,"
Dan said. "We've peaked a receiver so it's able to pick up a
whisper. We're going to try to home in on the Barlock."

"But," added Les, "we can't leave the strike force
unprotected, so we're going to break up into two elements. The
second element will stay with the strike force while we head up
north of Hanoi and find the Barlock."

"Remember when the Bear talked about the gomers
moving something fragile?" asked Janssen. "We think it was
the Barlock radar and command-and-control equipment."

"That could be it," mused the Bear.

"What do you think, Benny?" asked Les Ries.

"I dunno, Les. That wasn't the way I'd envisioned using
the tactic. I was thinking of the two elements supporting one
another."

"One reason we're telling you is we plan to use two-
seven-seven."

"You're using our airplane?"

Dan Janssen spoke up. "I had the avionics shop check all
the birds and their receivers, and yours were in the best
condition."

"I'm even going to use your wingman," said Les. "Tiny
Bechler says he's willing."

"You really think this is going to work?" asked Benny.

"Won't know unless we try," Les said grimly.

"Sergeant Tiehl is gonna shit if you hurt our airplane," joked the Bear.

Les threw a hard look at the Bear, and he realized he wasn't entirely forgiven.

Ries shifted his stare back to Benny. "If something goes wrong, I want you to take over as head Weasel. Give Colonel Parker the straight word about what's happening with the defenses, tell him what the guys need, all that."

"Well, thanks, but . . ." Benny looked uncomfortable.

As Les and Janssen walked off toward the dining room, Benny nodded at the Bear. "What do you think about their idea?"

"If they've got the receivers peaked sensitive enough, it just might work." The Bear wagged his head then. "But I don't like Ries's talk about getting shot down. They keep that kind of attitude, they'll get hammered for sure."

"It's just a passing thing. He'll get over it."

"Maybe," said the Bear.

26/0945L—People's Army HQ, Hanoi, DRV

Xuan Nha

The last air pirates from the west had left.

Since the activation of Wisdom, twenty-nine American planes had been shot down, almost double the number during comparable previous periods. The Pesky planes had been withdrawn to distant orbits and were no longer effective. Another week and the dummy transmitters would be operating, and there would be no chance at all for the Americans to locate the P-50. Xuan was pleased.

The after-action report arrived. A rocket battery west of Thanh Hoa had damaged an Intruder. Two other rocket batteries had fired in concert on a Phantom and shot it down. An artillery battery east of Yen Bai reported damaging a Thunder plane. A Phantom from Thailand was downed by a combination rocket/artillery engagement.

A good morning, but the day's critical gamble was yet to be played out.

This afternoon his rocket forces would have a reprieve, for Wisdom would be controlling only MiG interceptors and artillery radars. The action, only reluctantly approved by General Tho of the VPAAF, would prove that Wisdom could indeed improve the coordination and control of the MiG forces.

The interceptors would be directed entirely by Wisdom controllers. The pilots could no longer rove the skies in allotted airspaces, and randomly attack. As of today, they would be placed under the *absolute control* of Wisdom.

Wisdom had shown it could control rocket and artillery forces. Now they must show their flexibility by changing the players. This afternoon MiG-17's, MiG-19's, and MiG-21's would be vectored to the attacking force's rear positions, fire their heat-seeking AA-2 missiles, then immediately break away. No dogfighting or even tarrying to watch their victims go down, just clean assassination of the most vulnerable American aircraft.

It would be vindication for the terrible beating the MiG's had been given by the Phantoms. The controllers would be North Koreans, who had developed absolute control tactics to a fine art. Vietnamese MiG pilots had practiced with them, both in China and during bombing lulls, and claimed they were ready.

Thao Phong would lead the MiG interceptors from Phuc Yen to engage Thunder planes in the west. Another major who had participated in the January debacle would lead the MiG's from Kien An against the Intruders from the carriers. It was time for vengeance. It was also time to prove what Wisdom could give them, and what the Russians and North Koreans had done for air discipline with the rigid absolute control tactics.

Xuan Nha would be vulnerable, as Thao Phong had been during the last MiG-only day. It would be regarded as his decision, and his alone.

In case things went badly, he had instructed one-fourth of the rocket battalions—his best—to remain on alert. In the event of disaster, they would be prepared to come on the air in an instant. He hoped he would not need them, but he held a deep distrust of MiG interceptors and their capabilities.

His private telephone rang.

"Good morning, my friend," said Thao Phong. "And how is your sister?"

They had not talked since Thao Phong's disgrace. He

almost retorted in kind to Thao Phong, but reconsidered. Was this a contrived conversation? Were they being monitored?

"Good morning, comrade Major," he finally replied, trying to sound neutral.

A pause. "I am flying today."

"I know that, comrade Major." He felt a tugging in his chest as he realized what he must do. Thao Phong had been a loyal friend.

"It is my chance to prove many things, Xuan Nha."

Fool, he thought, *the party is listening.* "Address me properly, comrade Major Phong," he barked. "You know that the party has instructed us to use the title of 'comrade' at all times." His tone was icy. That should show the party he was faithful to their dictates, that he did not traffic in foolish conversation with those in disgrace.

"I understand, comrade Colonel."

The paranoia continued. "That is much better, comrade Major. Today I expect you to do your duty for the glory of the party."

"And for your sister and mother, comrade Colonel, who have both pleaded with me to exercise my elephant's trunk in their many and sloppy orifices." The line was disconnected.

Xuan's mind swam with horror as he hung up. Had the party been listening?

He called for Lieutenant Colonel Wu, but was told by Sgt. Van Ng that his executive officer was busy with other matters and would meet with the comrade colonel later. Sergeant Ng was now Lieutenant Colonel Wu's man, and made no excuses for it. Although he might not have a month earlier, Xuan Nha now understood implicitly.

Lt Quang Hanh came in. Wisdom was ordering selected rocket sites to shut down and begin major maintenance and overhauls.

It had begun. The defenses were left to the interceptors and Wisdom. Xuan Nha waited with mounting nervousness, both for Lieutenant Colonel Wu and for the afternoon attack.

26/1345L—Route Pack Six, North Vietnam

Les Ries

They left Takhli with a full-grown gorilla. Thirty-six Thuds loaded with 750-pound bombs to take out the highway overpass across the Red River from Hanoi.

When they arrived at the dog pecker in the Red River, Les called for the split.

The second element, led by Shaky Anderson, silently maneuvered southward, and Les and his wingman altered slightly northwest.

"How's our Weasel gear working, Dan?" he asked over the intercom.

"It's so damned sensitive I could hear a needle drop down there, but believe it or not, I don't have a single Fansong radar, Les. It's spooky."

"You're sure your gear's working right?"

"It tests out great. I'm picking up the Barlock just fine, by the way."

Les made his radio call. *"Eagle lead has negative SAM activity."*

"Eagle three has the same," called Shaky.

"Makes me wonder," said Dan from the backseat.

"Yeah, me too."

"Come left five degrees," said Dan.

Max Foley

The first indication that something was amiss came from the Weasels, flying far out in front of the strike force as the boss liked them to, just after Les Ries split up his flight. He heard them call that the SAMs were quiet. They were out there east of the Red River, and the defenses should have been damned active.

The SAMs had not been silent for a long time, and the sudden change sent up warning flag. The gomers had been firing multiple coveys of missiles every time the strike force came close to the valley, but today they were eerily quiet. He watched his own equipment. Only a periodic beep, and the

Bear had told him what that meant. The long-range command-and-control radar was painting him.

His warning flag stayed up as they continued the ingress. The MiG's had been cautious since the F-4's had cleaned their clocks on the second of January. Was it finally going to be a MiG day again?

The first verification came from Shaky Anderson, who led the second element of the Weasel flight. There was a confused transmission that no one could understand, then a flurry of yelling and shouting. It was a poor display of flight discipline, but it was easy to be sympathetic once you realized what was going on.

First the confusion over the radio.

Shaky Anderson shouted, *"This is Eagle three. Eagle four is down! I repeat, Eagle four is down."*

"Ah roger, Eagle lead," called B. J. Parker, who was leading Hawk, the chopper flight, and was next in line behind the Weasels. *"Calm down and give us a status report."*

"Eagle four?" Shaky called in a trembling voice.

Silence.

"Aww shit, I'm hit."

Big Eye loudly and repeatedly announced MiG's in several quadrants.

"Mayday! Eagle three is hit! We just had flameout!" yelled Shaky in his excited voice. Then the squeal of so many emergency beepers at one time that the radio was impossible to listen to until Max shut off emergency Guard channel.

Shaky and his bear, along with their wingman, had been shot down. MiG's, he bet, although Shaky hadn't said.

Max called, *"Eagle lead, this is Crossfire lead. You got MiG's up there with you?"*

"I don't see MiG's," came Les Ries's steady response, *"but I heard Eagle three and four go down south of us."*

Les Ries

"How you doing back there?" he asked Dan over the intercom.

"I'm starting to pick up the back lobes."

Janssen was starting to pick up the command-and-control radar signal even when the antenna was pointed away from them. The Barlock radar van and antenna moved around in a continuous, circular sweep and was only powerful when its six beams swept through them every twenty seconds. Janssen had only the bit of energy leaking out the back of the antenna to work with.

"It's weak, but I'm picking him up," said Janssen. "Turn left ten more degrees."

Ries responded, snapping into a quick turn and stabilizing. For the most sensitive of Janssen's receivers to work properly, they had to remain wings-level. They were flying northeast on a heading of 040 degrees.

"I think it's up in the Chinese buffer zone, Dan."

"Shit."

"We're going after the bastard."

"That's bad about number three and four getting shot down."

"It's a MiG day. Hope the rest of the guys keep a good lookout."

"Think we ought to swing back south and protect the strike force?" asked Dan.

"No. The best possible protection we could give them against MiG's would be to knock out the command-and-control. Let's keep homing in on that sucker as long as we can."

Les swung his vision off to his right, where Tiny Bechler flew, then looked forward again. He could see Thud Ridge up ahead.

Max Foley

"Eagle lead, this is Hawk lead," called B. J. Parker to Ries, *"do you have SAM activity yet?"*

"No SAM activity. Watch out for MiG's."

Max listened with mounting curiosity, then two glints up ahead materialized into a pair of silver MiG-17's. They were co-altitude and went into a cloud. He called them out to the others. *"This is Crossfire lead. I think everyone had better be on the lookout for MiG's. I just saw a couple duck into the clouds at my ten o'clock."*

He looked on his kneepad. Eagle three was Shaky Anderson and his bear. Eagle four was Capt Joe Meyer, an exceptionally sharp young fighter pilot. Both down, and the mission was still young.

"*Crossfire three, move out another couple hundred feet. Keep a good lookout at our six o'clock.*" Max's flight was tail-end-Charlie, last in the strike, and most vulnerable.

"*Crossfire three, roger!*" called his second element leader.

There was chatter on the radio as other flight leads followed his example.

The radio talk about the loss of the two aircraft was also continuing. *Did anyone see chutes? No reason to set up a Res-CAP effort since it's past the Red. What's the nearest landmark?*

Max tuned them out and concentrated on looking for MiG's. He didn't think it was over. He scanned the sky constantly, scarcely glancing inside his cockpit at all.

He turned the Guard channel back on. All three emergency beepers had been shut off. That meant that all three were likely alive and well enough to turn them off.

Out over the flat now. They crossed the Red River. The radar warning receiver was still silent, except for the periodic beep. A Firecan AAA radar came on the air, warbled, then began to track. No big deal, because his flight was jinking and weaving.

There was a long break in the clouds and he could see the next flight, Rifle, three miles in front of them. He also saw a pair of MiG's, low and at Rifle flight's six o'clock.

"*Rifle flight, you've got MiG's at your six o'clock!*" he quickly called.

"*Say again for Rifle,*" someone said in a calm voice, but he could see that two of the Thuds broke to their left.

A flash of light winked from the first MiG-17's wing, then another from the second MiG.

"*Atoll! Atoll!*" he yelled "*Break, Rifles!*" Atoll was the Soviet-built copy of the American Sidewinder missile.

Rifle lead broke hard left, as his second element had done, but his wingman had already torched brightly and was immediately nosing into a dive.

The MiG's were diving for the deck.

"*Crossfire flight, burners now!*" Max called.

He dropped the nose of his Thud toward the MiG's.

Les Ries

They were approaching Thud Ridge now, and Les tried to tune out the confusing radio babble as the strike force engaged and were engaged by MiG's.

Another Thud, Rifle two, had been lost. If they could only locate the Barlock radar and take out the eyes that were steering the MiG's, he could stop the carnage.

"Eagle four, let's go to button six," Les called, and they changed to a private frequency. He didn't want distractions as they concentrated on trying to find the Barlock.

"I got him dead ahead at twelve o'clock," muttered Dan from the backseat.

As they drew closer to Thud Ridge, Les turned fifteen degrees right and started a shallow dive. He intended to skim over the ridge-top, then hug close and follow it north. Their aircraft would be impossible to discern from the mass of the ridge on a radar scope. Then, when they were abeam the radar, they would turn east to home in and attack it. They would only be vulnerable as they dashed from the ridge to the radar.

Les studied the terrain at eleven o'clock, beyond Thud Ridge. Flat, with interspersed patches of trees and farmland. It was there somewhere. He glanced out toward Tiny Bechler.

"Drop back into trail, Eagle four. I'm pushing it up and we'll steepen our dive."

"Four!"

Les eased the throttle forward. The tape climbed until it indicated they were traveling at more than 600 knots.

26/1354L—People's Army HQ, Hanoi

Xuan Nha

Xuan had listened hard to the reports relayed by Lt Quang Hanh and twice had been on the telephone with Major Nguy.

Once again he spoke with his commandant at Wisdom.

They had not yet had time to assess it all, but so far they had confirmed three Thunder planes shot down by the MiG interceptors. It was definitely going well, except . . .

"Two aircraft have continued to fly in our direction since crossing the Hong River, Colonel."

"Radar-hunters?"

"I believe so. They are separated from the other aircraft, and we have no MiG's in position to intercept them."

"How far away are they from you?"

"Eighty kilometers and closing, still flying directly toward us. They have increased their airspeed and are descending."

Xuan cursed, wishing he had the dummy transmitters working.

"Seventy kilometers at two-twenty degrees and still closing, Colonel. Should we shut down the P-50?"

The P-50 was critical for the MiG's, both to direct their attacks and so they could elude the Thunder planes, yet its survival was also crucial. He must decide.

"Is the special rocket site tracking them?" Xuan asked.

"Major Gregarian is at the rocket site, Colonel. They are still well out of optics range, but he has them on his P-2 acquisition radar. He is reluctant to use the special rocket site and asks that we shut off the P-50 radar."

"No!" Xuan Nha had decided. He must not fail today and he needed Wisdom on the air to ensure success. "Tell him the P-50 will remain on the air, and that he *must* engage the radar-hunters with the special rocket site to protect it."

"The radar-hunters have turned due east and are now diving toward the mountains, Colonel. Perhaps they are not attacking after all."

Xuan thought of the terrain and the location of the fighters. "They will try to hide in the mountains as they find your location. Tell Gregarian that he must use his rockets, and he must operate in optical mode only."

"Yes, comrade Colonel."

"And quickly."

26/1358L—Route Pack Six, North Vietnam

Tiny Bechler

Tiny watched Major Ries's aircraft, now a couple of hundred yards in front of him, as they leveled from their dive and flew close beside the ridge. Thud Ridge was not as high or rugged as it was farther south, he noted.

They were getting close to the Chinese buffer zone.

"Uh . . . Eagle two, how's your IFF transponder?" Ries called.

The Identification, Friend or Foe system would tattletale on them when they passed into the restricted area thirty miles from the Chinese border.

"It's broke, lead." Tiny called, shutting it off.

"Roger," said Ries, a happier note to his voice.

Tiny heard a shrill sound, and a glance showed the ACTIVITY light was illuminated on his radar warning receiver. That meant a SAM guidance beam had been activated. There was no rattlesnake sound or flickering strobe to show the direction.

"Disregard the SAM, three. False alarm," said Major Ries.

"Roger, Eagle lead," he responded, feeling easier with the knowledge.

Ries had briefed that when they hugged up to the mountains as they were doing, the SAM radars couldn't see them, but it helped to know that his bear confirmed they weren't being tracked.

They flew closer yet to the mountainside, wingtips passing within yards of craggy outcroppings. *Jesus we're close,* he thought, eyes glued on Ries's bird. He dropped back farther until he was 500 feet behind, then stabilized and concentrated on his flying.

This was what the Thud did best. It was the most stable aircraft in the world at low level. They were traveling at 650 knots, just under the speed of sound, and everything to the sides appeared as a blur.

Ries called, *"Eagle four, we'll be turning starboard in about—"*

Tiny's eyes were riveted on Ries's Thud when it exploded and crashed into the mountainside.

Max Foley

Max felt low. He'd gunned down the first MiG-17, his wingman the second. He still felt like hell.

The gomers had shot down two more Thuds. Capt Tuck

Jones, number three in B. J. Parker's flight, had not rejoined the colonel's flight when they'd come off the target. No one had seen him go down or heard a beeper. And then Tiny Bechler had called in a shaken voice that he was exiting across the valley alone and that Les Ries and his bear had been shot down by something, he didn't know what, even though his eyes had been on their Thud when it happened. They had been shot down halfway between Thud Ridge and Kep airfield. No chutes or beepers.

Capt Bob Maier had been the one Max had seen get shot down by the MiG. He'd landed in the valley, well beyond the Red River. He'd talked to him on his radio and Bob had been in good spirits down there. He knew they couldn't rescue him where he was, so he planned to escape and evade all the way to Laos if need be to get rescued. He'd said he was presently wallowing around in rice paddies.

Next they talked to Eagle four, Capt Joe Meyer. It was a bit confusing in Max's mind, since Bob Maier and Joe Meyer had last names that sounded similar.

Joe was matter-of-fact about it all. He said he was going to go off the air and run like hell to the west, and he'd see them the next day. Like Bob Maier, he was in good spirits.

Colonel Parker had talked to Shaky Anderson, who was calmer on the ground than he had been in the air. His bear had landed smack in a small village not far from his own location. He said some people were coming out of the same village and heading his way. They didn't hear any more from Shaky, so Max figured he'd boogied in the opposite direction from the villagers.

The strike force was unduly quiet all the way back to Takhli.

The only one they heard from on the radio again was Bob Maier. He kept evading and trying to make it out across the heavily populated valley. For two long weeks Rifle two would call to the fighters passing overhead and say he was still making progress, still heading for the distant mountains. He had the entire wing rooting for him. The last time they talked to him he was almost to the Red River. They didn't hear from him again.

26/1620L—People's Army HQ, Hanoi, DRV

Xuan Nha

The results were before him, yet he could hardly believe them. Three Thunder planes shot down by the MiG interceptors. One other shot down over the target by artillery. A fifth shot down by Gregarian at the special rocket battery. Fantastic results in the west! One Intruder and two Phantoms shot down in the east. Superb!

That two MiG's had been shot down in the west and one in the east did not matter. They were expendable, so long as they got results.

He was in his seat in the command center, numbed by the extent of Wisdom's and his success. General Luc sat beside him, smiling broadly at the results, acting as if he'd known all along that it would be like that.

General Tho was on his way to the command center, a captain reported. He had relayed congratulations to Xuan Nha and said he wished to coordinate more days with his MiG interceptors taking the lead of things.

As always, Xuan thought, the pilots felt they could do it without his rocket forces. But now he, Xuan Nha, also controlled the key to success for the MiG's, for he had Wisdom!

He had met with Lieutenant Colonel Wu and reported Thao Phong's indiscretion. That report would be forgotten now, and things would even get back to normal with his old friend. Thao Phong had been credited by Wisdom with destroying two thunder planes. Like Xuan, Thao Phong was a hero.

He wished to be among the first to congratulate him. He would start by saying something outlandish about his mother, or even better, his wife. A smile crept onto his face as he thought of what he might say.

Thao had killed his Thunder planes. Xuan had again become indispensable, a hero of the Democratic Republic. It was likely that they would both receive another medal. Xuan felt he could expect a palm for his Red Star of Gallantry.

Colonel-General Dung's office called General Luc. Dung

and Giap, together, were asking for more information to include in the glowing reports they were preparing. General Luc handed the telephone to Xuan Nha, who answered the staff officer's queries in a calm and professional voice.

When General Tho of the VPAAF arrived, Xuan was still on the telephone. Tho was told the purpose of the call and looked impressed. He took a seat at the table with them and remained quiet until Xuan hung up.

They talked of more days for the MiG interceptors to show their true stuff.

Another report arrived, handed this time to General Tho. He read it carefully, thought for a moment, then sadly shook his head. He looked at General Luc.

"A hero is dead."

Luc looked back at him questioningly.

"*Colonel* Thao Phong was a credit to us all."

The tightness returned to Xuan Nha's chest, the same feeling he'd had when he'd spoken so tersely to his friend.

27/1215L—The Ponderosa, Takhli RTAFB, Thailand

Bear Stewart

The Bear sat in the dayroom, writing Julie a letter:

I need your answer pronto so I can finish my planning from this end.

Tiny Bechler came in carrying a helmet, furtively looked around the dayroom, then hurried back toward his bedroom. He'd only been at the Ponderosa for the past week, but Tiny made a difference wherever he went. Probably, thought the Bear, because of his size and unquenchable enthusiasm, as well as the constant intrigue he caused because everyone wondered which of his bigotries he would focus on next.

Tiny had already tried to convince the Bear that he couldn't be a navigator because he disliked fucking navigators. He'd also tried to tell Silva he wasn't really Portuguese. Next thing you'd know he'd try to tell Sam Hall he wasn't black, thought the Bear.

He went back to writing his letter. *Things are going so hot and heavy here that I probably won't be able to get off for long, but I'll get off for long enough.*

Swede Swendler came into the dayroom from one of the back halls and got a beer from the refrigerator. He was opening it with a church key when Ken Maisey came in the door carrying his A-3 bag, the big canvas sack the Air Force provided to hold all the paraphernalia they issued to fliers. He plopped it down at the door and looked around at the room with an air of nostalgic excitement, like a kid about to go to camp.

"Hi, Swede," Maisey said in a cheerful voice.

Swendler took a swig of beer and looked at him coldly.

"How're you doing, Bear?" Maisey asked.

The Bear neither liked nor disliked Maisey. He just didn't trust him in the air. "I'm doing fine, Ken. How about you?"

"For the first time in a long while, I feel great." He grinned mysteriously at the Bear and Swede and went back toward his room.

"You don't want to even talk to that cowardly shit," said Swendler.

"What do you mean?" asked the Bear half-attentively, trying to think of a way to put his next sentence to Julie. He wanted to get his words just right.

"Maisey quit."

The Bear looked up, puzzled. "What do you mean, quit?"

"He went to Colonel Mack yesterday and told him he wouldn't fly any more."

"He just . . . quit?"

"Yeah. Colonel Mack told him to think it over. Said he'd take him off the schedule for a while, even give him a few easy missions, but Maisey said he just flat-assed wasn't going to fly any more. Said if he flew again, no matter where he flew, he'd get killed and he knew it."

"You can't just quit."

"Colonel Mack told him to sleep on it and report back in the morning."

"And?"

"This morning he told Colonel Mack the same thing as last night. Said if he flew combat again he'd get killed, so he wouldn't."

"I'll be damned," said the Bear.

Maisey came out of the back, hauling a duffel bag and a B-4 bag. He dropped them at the door beside the A-3 bag.

"Where you headed, Ken?" asked the Bear. He still

couldn't believe it. Maisey was a naval academy graduate, always acting gung-ho military.

"Clark Air Base," came the response.

Tiny Bechler came from the back hallway and looked at them all with a too-innocent expression. He went to the refrigerator, got a beer, and stood beside the scowling Swede.

"What you going to do in the Philippines?" asked the Bear, still unable to believe it.

"I told them I wouldn't fly combat anymore, so they're sending me to the Clark hospital for psychiatric evaluations."

"What for?" asked the Bear.

"Got me," said Maisey. He opened the door, awkwardly hefted all the bags, and put them outside.

"See you," said the Bear, not knowing what else to say.

"I don't think so," said Maisey. He wrinkled his brow, as if he had figured something out. "They're sending me for psychiatric tests, but know what?"

They all looked at him.

"You guys are the ones who're crazy."

Maisey shut the door and they all just stared after him, then slowly looked around the room at one another.

After a bit, Tiny went to the door and peered outside. He grinned. "You guys ever notice that Maisey's got a big head?"

Swede glared at the door. "Got a fuckin' dick for a head, you ask me."

"Show you something," Tiny said. He went back to his room, and returned with the helmet he had come in with before. "See this beauty. Made by Sierra Industries, and it fits perfectly." He tried it on. Tiny had bitched a lot about his issue flying helmet being too small.

"I got his helmet," crowed Tiny.

"You're awfully damned lucky, I'd say," said Swede, wearing a suspicious look.

"No use it going to waste, is there? He won't need it unless he gets back to flying."

"Cowards like him don't get back to flying," said Swede Swendler.

"I didn't like what he said there at the last," said the Bear uneasily. "About us being the crazy ones."

"I think he was looking at you when he said it, Bear," kidded Tiny.

C. R. Clark, the captain who commanded B-Flight, came

in from outside. "You guys see Ken leaving with all his bags?"

"Yeah," said the Bear. "He quit."

Swede told him the story.

"Wish I'd kicked the bastard in the balls," growled Clark.

"He don't have any balls to kick," said Swede.

"You guys quit talking about my buddy," said Tiny, fondling the helmet.

"You," said Swede, "probably talked him into quitting so you could get that helmet."

"I did not," said Tiny. "I just knew he wasn't very happy up there flying. Son of a bitch has let us down a lot. You remember that time just before you and Glenn got shot down, Bear, and he ran away from the fight saying he had something wrong with his airplane?"

"Yeah?"

"Well, there wasn't a damned thing wrong with the airplane. I checked with Chief Roberts and he said they couldn't duplicate the problem and that it was just fine when they flight-checked it. Maisey did that sort of thing a lot."

"We all knew that, Tiny."

"So all I did was just suggest that if he ever did get shot down, not to wear his helmet, cause I'd like first dibs on it."

"And he up and quit?"

"I guess maybe I said it to him a lot."

Tiny showed off his new helmet, trying it on several times and marveling at the fit. Swede sat down and worked on officer evaluations for the pilots in his flight. Clark told jokes he'd just heard from some of the new replacement pilots. The Bear tried to finish his letter.

They all kept thinking and joking about what Ken Maisey had said about them being crazy, not him.

Maybe he was right, the Bear thought. But Maisey was the one who would remember this day for the rest of his life. He felt sorry for the poor bastard.

CHAPTER EIGHTEEN

Monday, February 6th—0130 Local, 10 miles north of Vinh, North Vietnam

Chickenplucker Crawford

As Red had told him, it was no fun being taken through the villages. The cities were even worse. They'd marched through Vinh two days before, where rocks had been thrown and kids had taunted. Women had screeched insults. An old man had cackled with delight as a thirteen-year-old boy poked a long, sharp stick into his belly, drawing blood.

Crawford had not cried out. He'd just narrowed his eyes and endured it, contemplating how nice it would feel when he got even. The guard, Grumpy, who'd been leading him by the rough rope around his neck, had finally yelled at the kid and made a halfhearted effort to chase him off. It was then the teenager poked the stick at Crawford's eye, causing him to twist away. The sharp point went into his cheek and broke a tooth. That hurt worse than the hole in his belly.

Tonight they were in a thatch hut, hands still tied behind them, and after thinking things over, Crawford decided it was time.

"Tonight we do it," he whispered.

Red said he was ready.

"I got a start on the knots. Maybe you can help."

Red moved so they'd be back to back. He worked for a long while. "Don't think so," he finally said.

Red's energy had been noticeably waning the last few days. The gomers weren't feeding them enough. Crawford was skinnier than Red, who was barrel-chested and heavy-boned, and figured he needed less, so he'd tried to give some of his

469

own food to Red. The F-100 jock had indignantly refused, saying he needed to lose weight anyway. Probably improve his golf game, he'd said. Red was like that.

"I'll work on 'em some more." Crawford pulled away from Red, stopped struggling, and just relaxed. He'd read a book once that escape artist Harry Houdini had been able to relax his muscles, go into a sort of semi-coma, then very slowly work his way out of anything. Crawford tried it himself.

He didn't know if that was what did it for him, but half an hour later he'd shucked off enough slack to get his fingers on the knots. It went much easier then. He finished with his own bonds, then worked to free Red.

"Good thing you're skinny," whispered Red.

"It ain't the dog in the fight, it's the fight in the dog," said Crawford.

They both stretched and rubbed their wrists in the darkness, then crawled quietly toward the back of the hut. Crawford lay flat and felt around on the back wall. The hut was built of thatch tied onto a bamboo pole frame with strips of woody fiber. It looked flimsy, but as he felt it he realized the wall was quite tough and resilient. Tearing it or taking it apart would be both difficult and noisy. He picked his spot and started to dig in the earthen floor with his fingers, carefully brushing back each small accumulation of residue with his hands.

Red tapped his arm. "I found a stick."

Crawford felt around and found Red's hand. It was a piece of bamboo an inch in circumference and several inches long. He began to dig quietly with it and made better progress.

"Someone's coming!" Red urgently whispered.

Fumbling at the door.

They scrambled back to their previous positions and feigned sleep, lying curled, hands held behind them away from the door.

It was Sleepy, with a flashlight that cast a weak glow. He opened the door wide and stood there, peering into the gloom. They were immobile and looked to be still bound. He left, apparently not concerned that there was a small mound of dirt on the floor in the back of the room or that the rope that had bound Crawford was lying there in plain view.

They waited for a few minutes longer.

"Dumb shit," whispered Red.

"Did you see if he had a gun?"

"Sleepy likes to leave his rifle propped up somewhere, because it's heavy. He carries an old French Mauser."

"Sleepy ain't exactly a ball of fire when it comes to work," said Crawford.

They felt their way back to their excavation. Crawford dug slowly and methodically, while Red pulled the residue back. He was careful to spread the dirt more evenly behind them, in case Sleepy returned and was more observant.

Half an hour later they had a hole big enough for Crawford to get his head through.

He looked around carefully, eyes adjusting to the bright moonlight, and could see a thicket about thirty yards distant. There seemed to be no one about back there. Still he waited. A movement to his left. He discerned a shape. A man was sitting just five feet away, leaning against the side of the hut, his head nodded over. Crawford looked longer yet, until he saw the shadowy shape of the guard's rifle.

He slowly pulled back inside, and drew Red over to the center of the hut to whisper in his ear. "There's a guard sitting on the ground back there. It's a wonder he didn't hear the digging."

"Shit. Who is it?"

"Can't tell. Hopefully it's Sleepy and he's alone. He's leaned up against the hut, head bent over like he's sleeping."

"Sounds like him. Sleepy can even nod off standing up, long as he's leaning against something."

"We're going to have to deal with him to get by."

"Going to have to be awfully quiet about it."

"I'll go out first. Soon as I start to take him out, you dig like crazy and get out of here yourself." Crawford drew in a breath, then went back to the hole in the floor and silently began to dig again.

Ten minutes later the hole was big enough for Crawford's slender body to slither through. He did so very cautiously.

He was out, crouching. He could hear the guard's even breathing. He approached him slowly, then crossed his hands carefully under the chin and paused. It was Sleepy.

Had to do it.

He clutched the cloth firmly and twisted his hands, the hard muscles of his fists gouging into the throat, as he'd been taught by the martial arts instructor at survival school. The hold would immediately cut off the flow of blood and oxygen to the brain.

Sleepy flailed. An arm beat once against the side of the hut, and Crawford pulled him away, maintaining the tight grip.

After fifteen seconds the struggling grew feeble.

After thirty seconds Sleepy slumped, a dead weight.

Two minutes later he was dead. Crawford counted to himself and relentlessly kept up the pressure before silently releasing Sleepy onto the ground.

Crawford crept back to the opening and crouched. "Come on," he whispered.

Red was digging frantically. A long minute later he wiggled his way through.

Crawford retrieved the French Mauser. He was familiar with it for it was similar to hunting rifles he'd had. Still, he hoped he wouldn't have to operate the gun in the darkness. He motioned to Red, and they carefully made their way toward the thicket, then beyond, in the direction they knew the sea had to be.

Crawford knew he wouldn't really feel safe until they were in a boat, maybe not even then, but he felt a lot better than he had when they'd led him around like a dog.

06/2030L—Ponderosa, Takhli RTAFB, Thailand

Benny Lewis

Monday, Jan. 30th

Dear Benny,

Received your letter today. For your information, it took six days for it to get here. Please let me know if it takes about the same time for mine to get there, so I'll know what you've read of my letters when you're writing yours (if you think that sentence was hard to read, you should try composing it!).

The days have been chilly here in the city. The high temperature today was fifty-two degrees. Up in your area (Santa Rosa), it got up to fifty-seven.

Highlights of the news today:

—In New York, the U.S. Court of Appeals ruled that draft boards can't punish Vietnam War protest-

*ors by reclassifying them to one-a draft status (just
heard that on the six o'clock news).*

*—In Washington, several peace marches are
planned over the next few days to put pressure on the
president and Congress to end the war—tomorrow
it's a group of religious people (some organization I
didn't have time to write down) who plan to starve
themselves on the White House (or Capitol building?) lawn.*

*—In Saigon, Bobby Kennedy is holding meet-
ings with several western leaders about ways to end
the war (he has dreamy eyes, but I wouldn't trust him
too far if he wasn't from such a good family).*

*—In Berkeley, another protest last week, not a
big one, but very newsworthy because of the combined free speech, legalize pot, and antiwar themes
(if you're on dope, like to curse, are gay, antiwar,
dispossessed by the capitalist establishment, poor,
pacifist (even if violently so), prefer whales to
people, or if you're a graduate student, the news
people here are likely to publicize your side—they
seldom have time for anyone else (funny I didn't
notice that before—Julie says I'm in the process of
growing a brain!).*

*—In San Rafael, a fire in a warehouse de-
stroyed an antique car collection valued at ???
(missed it, but the cars were old).*

—In Santa Rosa (nothing on the news today).

*—In San Francisco, this reporter was shocked
when her friend and confidant Julie (nee) Wright
announced that Mal Bear has proposed marriage.
Why didn't you tell me???*

*—In San Francisco today, Julie (nee) Wright is
busting her buns trying to get a YES answer back to
Mal Bear by the fastest means possible. So far she
has sent a telegram, mailed a letter with about five
dollars postage, and tried umpteen times to telephone (without success).*

*—In San Francisco today, this reporter has just
gone over both the* Chronicle *and the* Examiner *and
has nothing else to report.*

I think the news about Mal Bear and Julie is the

stuff of romantic novels. Meet in Manila, fall in love in Bangkok, propose by mail, get married at the U.S. Embassy. None of her friends believe it's real!

As you asked, I contacted your sister in Sacramento yesterday by telephone. She'd been away to L.A. on some government assignment. She said the California bureaucracy is alive and well, and that she's been promoted to assistant department manager. She sounded very happy to hear that you're okay. She said to tell you your niece has the measles and she hopes she doesn't get them from her.

I've got to run. Going to make a couple back-to-back Tokyo runs on the evening express. Lots of businessmen going to Tokyo these days. Interesting point: most believe the Japanese are doing well with their small item manufacturing, cheap imitations, etc. A few even say Japan is where it's at for new manufacturing techniques, and that it won't be long until they make a concerted, government-supported effort to penetrate the U.S. automobile market. Sounds crazy to me, but who knows? They are certainly doing well in the stereo field.

Gotta go. Love ya. I'll post a letter from Tokyo. No telling how slow that one will be in getting to you.

Liz

p.s. Julie asked and I've agreed to be maid of honor. See you at the altar.

Benny reread the letter to make sure that what he thought he'd read was really written there. The Bear getting married? His first thought was an angry one—that it had to be a ploy of some kind by the Bear to use Julie. Then he wondered, because the Bear had been moody since returning from the Bangkok R and R.

Julie was cheerful and fun-loving, a sweet and open girl, and the Bear was so damnably jaded when it came to women. He remembered him bragging about the two Filipinas and about other women. But he had never once mentioned taking Julie to bed, and Benny knew he had. Was Julie different for him?

He started to go and find him, confront him. But then he

realized how ridiculous that would make him appear. He decided to wait and let the Bear break the news.

07/1300L—Command Post, Takhli RTAFB, Thailand

Benny Lewis

From February 7th until the 11th, the president of South Vietnam had announced a truce for the observation of Tet, which was the Vietnamese Christmas and New Year's rolled into one. The classified message received at the Takhli command post added that the Operation Rolling Thunder bombing halt would last for even longer, that there would be no bombing of North Vietnam before the 13th. That meant there would be six days off, and the pilots in the wing were grateful for the respite.

But they weren't idle.

The 355th Tactical Fighter Wing used the Tet stand-down to prepare for the next fight, for they knew it would come all too quickly. Maintenance men worked hard to refurbish their airplanes. The fighter jocks worked to hone their skills.

Benny, Max Foley, and the Bear had finished their tutorial the week before, but had only been able to give it to small groups of pilots between combat missions. Now they were given the chance to do it right, one fighter squadron at a time in the command post briefing theater.

Today they briefed their own squadron, the 357th clit-lickers.

Colonel Mack introduced them, telling the pilots to clear their minds of preconceived ideas about tactics, and that they could argue like hell, but only at the end of the session.

The briefing started with a rundown of the antiaircraft artillery situation in North Vietnam, and Benny covered each type of weapon, its effective altitude, and the weakest links of each system. Although 37mm fire was nimble and easily slewed, it had short range and the rounds were small and not easily fused, so they generally were preset for specific altitudes. In contrast were 57mm rounds, which could be quickly fused to explode at different altitudes. S-60 guns had a fast rate of fire. Less nimble was 85mm, etc.

He finished the threat briefing, then they went over jinking and tactics to use when AAA was present.

Max spoke next, and the jocks listened intently. Not only had he been an air-to-air instructor at Nellis, he had now proven himself by killing a MiG. He spoke of the differences between wing-loading and energy of the Thud and the various MiG's, and about the differences in fighting doctrine. He told them they must see the MiG's while they were still setting up and know precisely what they were going to do before they made their first moves. He said that the Thud had the advantage of speed and firepower, and while it wasn't the most maneuverable jet in the world . . .

SAMs were last. Just the missiles. The Bear talked about the SA-2 sites, how they were set up with the command van in the center with six outlying missile launchers, and how the SAM batteries looked like a Star of David from the air. Then he talked about the timing once the missiles were launched. How when you changed your heading and airspeed, it changed the point in space where the missile was being guided, and how it took time for the radar to tell the analog computers, and for the computers to compute a new intercept point, and for the data-link to tell the missile and for the missiles to tell the stubby little wings to change position. He talked about how the stubby little wings couldn't really change the course of a Mach three missile very quickly.

Then Benny told how you could take advantage of all that by maneuvering when the missiles were close, and how if you had your energy up and maneuvered hard, the SAMs couldn't keep up with your . . .

Next the Bear talked about the various radars. How the long-range Barlock had six beams which together could give the gomers your position, altitude, and heading. How the mid-range Spoonrest fed target information to the tracking radars. How the Firecan radars had a little dish antenna that wobbled around and kept you centered and were linked to the guns. How the Fansong was really two radars, one for azimuth and one for height, and how it was linked to the SAMs.

The finale began with a description of how the gomers worked the entire system, coordinating MiG's, guns, and SAMs. It ended with a synopsis of how the pilots' tactics should be geared toward defeating that entire system, not just one threat or another.

The pilots argued and added insights of their own. The tones of voice would heat up, die down, then flare again. The planned ninety-minute briefing stretched to two, then to three hours, and when they finally broke up they all felt wiser.

As the last pilots filed out, Max Foley grinned at Benny. "Feisty bunch, aren't they?"

"I'm glad they're on our side."

The Bear was collecting the viewgraphs and looking sour. He had been going around like that a lot lately.

"You look like you aren't happy about the way it went, Bear," he said.

The Bear shrugged and took the classified viewgraphs into intelligence for safekeeping.

Max Foley watched him depart. "Something heavy on the Bear's mind?"

"He takes the briefing seriously," said Benny, but he knew it was more than that. The Bear hadn't yet mentioned what was going on with Julie. He hadn't wanted to talk about Ries and Janssen being shot down going after the Barlock, or the mounting losses among the strike pilots. He didn't even want to talk about Ken Maisey quitting. Whenever Benny tried to talk about anything other than the briefing, the Bear simply grew surly and less communicative.

Benny had decided to follow the Bear and try again to get to the root of the problem when Colonel Mack stuck his head into the door. "Good job, you guys."

They started talking about the briefing session and improvements they could make before they tackled the next squadron tomorrow.

07/1600L—People's Army HQ, Hanoi, DRV

Xuan Nha

Two dummy transmitters had been placed into position.

"Very good," he told Major Nguy on the radio-telephone.

"Major Gregarian is happy that we will not have to use the special rocket site again."

"He is an old maid," said Xuan. "Is he there at the center?"

"He is out with the teams setting up the last two dummy

transmitters, comrade Colonel." Nguy laughed. "I suggested it, for he is continually worrying about this or that procedure or piece of equipment. I don't think he believes it is working as well as it is."

"Our controllers must concentrate on learning from the Koreans and Russians."

"They are, comrade Colonel. Soon we shall no longer need their help."

"There must be nothing but good news from now on, Major Nguy. Wisdom must break the backs of the American air attacks."

"We shall, comrade Colonel. I have no doubt of that at all."

09/1030L—Takhli RTAFB, Thailand

Benny Lewis

Thursday was a revealing day. They learned more about what had happened to Ries and Janssen, and Benny learned what had been bothering the Bear to make him so moody.

From Monday through Wednesday they'd given the dog and pony show to the pilots of the three squadrons. On Thursday they had the day off. After eating a leisurely breakfast they wandered back to the squadron building to find that Colonel Mack wanted to see them ASAP.

When they reported to his office, Colonel Mack looked stone-faced. Tiny Bechler sat opposite him, looking nervous. Mack curtly waved Benny and the Bear inside and growled for them to close the door behind themselves.

"Lieutenant Bechler has something to tell us," said Mack, "that he's been holding inside for two weeks."

Tiny looked miserable.

"I've impressed on him that by not telling, he may have placed the lives of his squadron mates in jeopardy."

Tiny grew white-lipped.

Mack went on. "I've called you two in because I thought you needed his information more than anyone, since you have to deal with defenses." He eyed Tiny. "You want to tell them?"

Tiny looked Benny in the eye. "Ries didn't get shot down

near Kep, like I reported. We followed Thud Ridge up north into the Chinese buffer zone. They got shot down there."

The Bear started coming to life. "What got them, Tiny?"

"I dunno. It was like I said. I was watching them when their airplane came unglued. Came apart in a big, bright orange explosion."

"Orange? Like a SAM warhead going off?" asked Benny.

Tiny nodded, looking miserable.

"Was it a SAM?"

"We got a SAM activity light, but Ries called to disregard it."

"How come no one heard any of that on the radio?" asked Benny.

"We went to another frequency. Major Ries didn't want any distractions." Tiny looked miserably at Colonel Mack. "And when we went into the Chinese buffer zone, I guess he didn't want anyone overhearing us."

"Did you have a SAM light?" asked the Bear. "Or see a radar strobe on the scope?"

"No, just the activity light," said Tiny.

"Can you show us where it was on a map?" asked Benny.

"Not precisely. I'd say we'd just crossed into the buffer zone. We were up beside the ridge, doing better than six hundred knots. Probably six-ten."

"How close to the ridge?"

"Fifty feet or less. We were hugged up as tight as you can get."

The Bear spoke then. "Could they have hit the ridge with a wingtip?"

Tiny reflected for a moment. "I don't think so. There was the orange explosion, then the airplane came apart and hit the ridge. It happened so quickly I hardly had time to think, but I don't think they hit anything. Something got them."

Benny shook his head slowly. "Going that fast, and that close to the ridge." He turned to the Bear. "Could a SAM radar have been tracking them?"

The Bear stared out the office window, talking mostly to himself. "The Fansong is a good radar. Both beams use a Lewis scanner, and it picks out the moving targets from the still ones . . . but if they were flying that close to the ridge, they were in the same resolution cell as the ground." He shook his head slowly. "As far as I know, there's no way they could pick up an airplane flying that close to the dirt."

"What could it be?"

The Bear shook his head. "I don't know. Maybe something new to protect the Barlock and their command-and-control center?"

"You guys done with Tiny?" asked Colonel Mack.

"I can't think of anything else," said the Bear.

Benny nodded his agreement.

"I want everyone in this room to forget what was said here."

Benny and the Bear agreed. Tiny became tight-lipped again, because Colonel Mack was regarding him evenly with his hawk's eyes.

"Lieutenant, if I *ever* catch you lying again about something that might cost us lives and airplanes, I promise you I'll bust you so low you're looking up to crabgrass."

"Yes, sir," whispered Tiny.

"Now get the hell out of here."

Tiny was plainly shaken as he left the office.

Mack looked at Benny and the Bear questioningly. "You guys have any idea about what could have got Ries and Janssen?"

"It's hard to believe Ries ran into the ground," said Benny. "He was one of the best low-level pilots around."

The Bear shook his head. "And if Janssen said there was no SAM radar signal on the air, there wasn't one. He was a damned good EWO. Anyway, Tiny says he didn't have a SAM signal on his radar warning receiver."

"What the hell could it have been?" asked Mack.

"If it was a SAM, they were being tracked by something that doesn't show up on our receivers. Maybe a radar outside our frequency coverage? Electro-optics?"

"What do you mean optics?"

"Like television. You track something by using the contrast between the target and the background. Our people are testing a system like that to guide bombs."

"You think that's it?" asked Benny.

"You guys get out of here and let me get back to work," said Mack. "If you come up with anything the rest of us ought to hear about, let me know."

They went to Intelligence and started going over photos of

SAM target-tracking systems. After half an hour of looking and brainstorming, Benny glanced up at the Bear.

"You done with your shitty mood?" he asked.

The Bear was staring at a photo of something Intell called an E-variant Fansong radar, with what *might* be video sensors mounted at the sides of the vertical antenna trough.

"You were after me to get rid of my gremlins," said Benny. "Now you've got them."

"It's nothing," the Bear replied.

"Something to do with Ken Maisey quitting?"

The Bear looked up, shocked. "You think I'm turning chickenshit?"

"No, but you've been acting strange."

"It's personal."

"Like you told me in the Philippines, fuck personal. What's wrong?"

The Bear shifted his gaze up from the photos. "The gomer defenses are whipping our ass, Benny. Ries and Janssen were two of the best Weasels in the wing. Hell, maybe they *were* the best. And they got shot down by a SAM?"

Benny let him talk.

"Any jock here would feel like shit if he got whipped by a MiG in a dogfight. I'm a Weasel electronic warfare officer, and I feel the same way about SAMs and radars. First an EB-66 with all that jamming power, then a good Weasel crew. And the way the gomers are chopping up the strike pilots?" The Bear shook his head.

"I thought you were pissed off at me."

The Bear looked surprised. "Aw shit, sorry about that."

Benny asked, "Do you think we would have been shot down like Ries and Janssen?" He raised an eyebrow, and the Bear stared back.

The Bear finally blew out a sigh. "I don't know. Even if it was some kind of optical tracker, they should have known *something* was happening out there. I think Ries was busy flying the airplane, so he couldn't look out for missiles. Maybe Dan had his head down in the cockpit, working with his receivers when he should have been looking for SAMs." He shrugged, then looked harder at Benny. "You thinking of us going up there after the Barlock?"

"Not until we learn more about what we'd be up against. For now, let's just warn the guys to stay away from that area.

We're going to have our hands full trying to deal with the defenses we know about. We can't go up against some new kind of SAM system located in an area we're not even supposed to fly in."

"Sooner or later," said the Bear, "I've got a feeling we're going to have to take it on." The Bear's voice was quieter and less angry than it had been.

Benny felt the Bear hadn't told him everything that was bothering him, but it was a good start and they were getting back on track.

CHAPTER NINETEEN

Friday, February 10th—0305 Local, 16 miles north of Vinh, North Vietnam

Chickenplucker Crawford

They had been on the run for four days, huddling during the day in rice paddies and bomb craters, at night probing cautiously, trying to make their way to the sea. Whenever they thought they were getting close to water, they either saw or heard soldiers moving about, searching. Each time they had drawn back, farther inland, to seek a hiding place before daylight arrived.

Periodically they saw U.S. Navy recce aircraft flying overhead, but they could only watch and wish, for they had no way to signal their presence without alerting what seemed to be half the people in the world.

They both knew that if they couldn't get to the beach soon they had better start walking in another direction, for there were just too many people. They felt they had been tremendously lucky to carry it off and remain free for as long as they had.

Pete Crawford could hardly believe the number of people who inhabited the area. From the air it appeared mostly deserted. Down here there seemed to be farmers, fishermen, road work gangs, soldiers, children, and animals everywhere they turned.

They'd been seen several times, but only once at close proximity. That time it had been by a very old man returning to his stilted farmhouse from an adjacent field. He'd stopped and looked at them, lying there half-submerged in the muddy water of a rice paddy, and had actually tried to talk to them.

Either he'd finally decided they weren't real, or he'd been so feebleminded he forgot them. With a single shout of alarm he could have ended their freedom. Instead he had simply, painfully, continued to hobble toward the farmhouse.

They'd stayed there, not knowing what else to do in the daylight with people everywhere, and almost suffered cardiacs as they watched a group of soldiers in an aged weapons carrier stop and talk to the old man. He'd acted confused and just kept shaking his head. There was no telling what the old man had been thinking or saying, and they were so benumbed by the event that they didn't try to make sense of it. When dusk came they were not slow in moving out.

On the fourth night they were trying once again to make their way to the sea.

"It feels right, Pete. It just feels right."

"I hope so, Red. My stomach's gnawing on my backbone."

"If we don't get something to eat pretty soon," said Red, "they're gonna be able to pound me in the ground and use me for a fence post."

Their hunger jokes were getting feeble. So far all they'd had to eat were a few gecko lizards and a red frog that had made Crawford puke. All they'd had to drink had been brackish and salty water from irrigation canals.

"Little, tasteless salamanders," Crawford said disgustedly as he bit into a gecko.

Red told him geckos weren't salamanders. "Newts are salamanders. They got those in Korea. Geckos are just lizards that eat insects," he said. They agreed that regardless of what they were, the tiny creatures didn't have much substance and tasted like mud.

"I want a snake," whispered Red as they crossed a path and headed for the beach a mile north of their last attempt. "A big, fat snake."

"I saw a rat back in that rice paddy."

"You eat the rats, I'll eat the snakes," Red said. "Rats carry diseases. They've still got the plague over here, you know."

"I got my plague shot. I'd settle for a pudgy old pack rat."

"Snakes are cleaner."

They crept on in silence, cautiously making their way around a row of dark houses on stilts.

They'd become close in their eighteen days together. Each knew the other's home town, college, the first names and habits of his wife and children, his hobbies, where he'd been stationed, and the different aircraft he'd flown. They shared a common thirst for freedom. They both felt they would succeed, and that by God if they didn't make it this time they would try again. Each lent the other his own courage.

"You smell bad," whispered Crawford. "Like a gecko tastes."

"I've eaten so many geckos I'm starting to snap at flies and make funny sounds."

"We're getting close to the water, Red. Hear the surf?"

"Yeah. I can hear it. Notice the soil is turning to sand? We're close, Pete."

"Let's stop for a minute or two and listen."

They dropped flat on a rise of sand and looked over it through a thicket of weeds. They had been this close before.

They waited for a long time, listening, looking for movement. They heard the roar of a diesel truck engine far behind them. There was a paved road there, its bomb craters filled level with sand and rocks by work gangs they'd seen.

"You hear anything?" asked Crawford, impatient but fearful now that they were this close.

"I saw something move a little bit ago. I think it was an animal of some kind. Maybe a dog?"

"I think so. It went over toward the left. See that house over there?"

"Yeah."

They were wary. Twice, dogs had created a racket when they passed close to farmhouses. Little yellow, shorthaired dogs with their tails curled up behind. They were loud, and each time they'd barked, humans had come out to see what was there. Red told him in South Vietnam they raised dogs like that to eat. He said they tasted like stringy pork.

"Let's give it another minute or two," whispered Crawford.

Finally they moved out another hundred yards to the next crest. The sea was louder now, with the distinct sounds of breakers against the shore. They watched and listened again.

Nothing. The next rise was farther yet. The house loomed dark a few hundred yards off to their left, but there seemed to be no one up and about.

They went slowly, cautiously, Crawford clutching the old rifle and leading the way.

They could see it now. The black of the South China Sea, the water swelling and white-capping as it neared the beach. The moon was a sliver now, but they could see the dark shapes of boats drawn up on the shore. Fishing boats, probably twenty feet long, narrow, with high prows. A dozen or more of them.

"Luck's with us."

"I love it. We're gonna make it, Pete."

"You know anything about boats?" asked Crawford after a pause. "I went deep-sea fishing down in Florida a few times, but I don't know anything about launching boats."

"I thought maybe you knew about 'em. I'm from Kansas, for God's sake. I almost drowned at water-survival school."

"Well, by God, we'll learn."

They lay there, looking at the sea and thinking of the freedom it offered.

"Say," whispered Red. "We'll be the first ones to escape from North Vietnam after being captured."

"I'd like to be first, but mainly I don't like being a prisoner. I didn't like that cage even a little bit. See anything?"

"Nothing."

"There's that dog again."

The dog ran down the beach from the direction of the house.

"Son of a bitch."

"That's what he is, a son of a bitch."

They watched as the dog ran and played, chasing a long-legged crab that scurried out to the safety of the surf.

"It's getting light," said Crawford. "We'd best be making our move."

Red agreed, but felt caution as he watched the yellow dog.

"Let's go. Slow and easy, okay?"

Red followed him, hunkered down and running toward the boats. The dog stopped still, watched them for a moment, then ran toward them.

"There's food," whispered Red as they continued their run. "I could eat that sucker."

The dog stopped short, looked at them, and cocked his head. Then, as if he'd understood Red's threat, he growled and started backing away.

They reached the boats, then stopped and looked, trying

to decide what to do next. The craft were fifty yards from the water.

"Fucking low tide," muttered Red, "and now it's starting to come in. That's not good, Pete."

Crawford was examining the boats. "They look heavy as hell."

"Maybe if we turned one over. I think that's how they get 'em to the water. Turn 'em over and drag 'em."

The dog started barking at them. The sound was shrill and loud, even with the roar of the sea.

"Jesus!" said Red.

"That one looks lightest," said Crawford, and he grabbed his choice and began trying to turn it over. "Weighs a ton!"

Red grabbed hold with him, and they started making progress. The boat tipped up slowly as they huffed and pushed.

"Keep thinking first, Red. We're gonna be first."

"How sweet it is!" Red groaned.

They continued to lift and push. The dog was barking louder, coming close, then backing off and generally raising hell.

The boat finally teetered, and after a final shove turned over. Beneath it were oars and a great mound of fishing nets with glass floats.

"Oars," said Red. "We can't forget the oars!"

The dog darted in and tried to bite Crawford, who took a kick at it. The dog backed off and continued to bark with vigor. Crawford grabbed oars and oarlocks and put them in the boat, then added the old French Mauser.

"Let's go," he said unnecessarily, for Red was already shoving on the boat.

"I think someone's coming," said Red, panting and looking toward the house.

"Push!"

With both of them heaving they inched the boat forward. Crawford eyed the distant figure and judged he was indeed coming toward them. "Keep pushing!"

"I am!"

The boat slid forward a foot, then stopped. They would push, and the boat would move. Heave! Slide. Heave! Slide.

"Shit!" said Red. The dog had nipped him on the leg.

Heave! Slide. Heave! Slide.

"We're halfway."

Heave! Slide. Heave! Slide.

"The guy's getting closer," said Red.

They were both nearing exhaustion.

Heave! Slide. Heave! Slide.

The prow of the boat slid into the water.

The man, possibly the owner of the boat, was shouting at them.

"That's enough!" Puffing, Crawford lifted the old rifle from the boat and waved it about. Then he aimed at the man.

The man ducked down behind a sand dune but kept yelling. The dog continued to bark.

Crawford tossed the gun back into the boat and rejoined Red in his effort. The front of the boat bobbed as a wave washed in, turning the boat sideways.

They both waded in and pushed to turn the boat.

"Push it straight into the waves," yelled Red.

They tried, this time making better progress. The boat bobbed.

"Get in!" yelled Crawford, and Red did. Crawford stayed in the water and pushed, scrambled around to one side to stop the boat from washing back on the beach, then pushed and shoved again. Red jumped out of the boat and helped again. This time they made it farther out, met the next wave squarely, and the boat only came back a few feet. They pushed harder.

"Get in and row!" yelled Crawford.

"You get in, I'm bigger."

"Crawford scrambled, then finally flopped into the boat, banging his shin on a gunwale. His eyes watered with the pain. Red was still trying to keep the boat straight but was making poor progress.

Crawford found an oar, then an oarlock, and tried to get them together.

Red succeeded in pushing the boat out farther. The water came to his chest during the swells.

Crawford couldn't find the second oarlock.

The boat was turning again, so he rowed with the single oar and the boat corrected.

"Way to go!" shouted Red, still pushing. He grabbed the back of the boat and tried to swim and propel it.

They were twenty yards out now, and a big swell was coming.

"Get it squared with the wave!" yelled Red.

"I'm trying." The wave was on the wrong side to use the oar with the oarlock, so he grabbed the other oar and paddled.

The prow of the boat rose high, higher yet, then slid sideways and came back around.

"Shit!" yelled Red, now flailing with his feet to correct the boat as Crawford lost the oar and just tried to hang on.

"It's going over!" Crawford yelled.

The boat teetered on its side, then turned completely over. Crawford felt he would drown before he finally came up, and when he did the free oar bobbed up and hit him hard in the side of the head. He saw stars and almost lost consciousness.

Red grabbed hold of him and pulled him from the surf out onto the beach.

They watched glumly as a wave hit the capsized boat and rolled it over onto its side. The next wave beached it, still rolling up on its side.

They were exhausted.

"Shit," panted Red.

Crawford stood there, hands dangling, mouth open and gasping for air, and watched the boat wash farther onto the beach.

The fisherman was still yelling at them from over the sand dune, standing now since he was no longer threatened by the rifle, which had been lost in the surf.

"Gotta—try—again," panted Red.

They staggered toward the boat and when they got there, stood panting, hardly able to stand.

Yelling in the distance joined that of the fisherman.

The two men pushed the boat over again, tugged it to turn it, and finally got it nosed toward the sea. They pushed and shoved and got it floating. This time both of them held onto the back of the boat and swam, pushing it before them. They made it through a wave, then through another.

Crawford's legs were leaden.

He heard the crack of a gun.

"Fuck 'em," yelled Red.

Another gunshot.

They kept kicking and pushing and Crawford was so tired he began to sob.

The prow of the boat rose, higher and higher, and they kept kicking. The boat was almost on end, only the rear quarter still in the water. It swung wildly then, and as before rolled with the wave's impetus.

As he came out of the surf, coughing and snorting out the water, the soldiers were there before him. Red was still in the water, hunkered over, chest heaving.

They were marched, stumbling and falling, for several miles northward along the beach, then on a roadway. The soldiers didn't smile. The beatings didn't start until they arrived at a house, where they were strung up to the rafters. Pete Crawford had thought he was too tired to care if they beat him. He found that was not true.

10/2015L—Takhli Village, Thailand

Bear Stewart

With the tutorials completed, and with Benny bugging him to get into a better mood, the Bear decided that the bombing pause should be put to better use than to screw around with doing laundry, writing letters, or even to work up improved tactics, like Benny was doing. He ate dinner at the O' Club, refueled with a couple of Scotch whiskeys at the bar, and talked Sloppy Watson into accompanying him to town. Watson came along reluctantly, remembering the awful time he'd had getting rid of the dose he'd been given by the clap-clap sisters.

"Okay," he'd finally said, "but no talk about screwing women. I'm gonna be faithful to the wife. I'm a married man, Bear."

"Thought you two were separated."

"We're back together this week. At least we were the last letter I got from home."

"Sloppy, I will not speak about sex once while we're downtown. In fact I don't plan to partake of their fair maidens either."

Lyle thought about that after they'd boarded the base bus and were making their way toward the main gate. "You used to be the big cocksman. I remember that time at Columbus when my wife and I split up for a while and I met Nurse Marilee. She was telling me how great you were in the sack."

"Smart girl," said the Bear.

"She said she gave you an eight. Said only one guy rated better."

"You, of course."

"Certainly."

The base bus stopped at the Ponderosa, and Dave Persons and Phil Yost, two of the new Weasel pilots, got on. They were followed by Lt John Radkovich, a strike pilot new to the Bear's squadron who went about with a very serious look on his face.

Sloppy went on. "Then when I got here, you were all the time talking about women and how you made out, like the three women in one night in the Philippines."

"It happened."

"I haven't seen you screwing around for a while."

"Hell, I'm cured, Sloppy."

"Cured? Of women?"

"I found one I like a lot."

"Me, too. About a hundred I like a lot."

"You'll find out what I'm talking about some day. That broad you're married to?"

"Jackie?"

"Whatever. She's not the right one for you, Sloppy. You keep breaking up and getting back together all the time. If she was right, you'd be hopscotching on your head just to keep her around."

Lyle thought about that. "Stop calling me Sloppy, okay?" he finally said.

"You've been named. How can you not be called by your name?"

"I'm Super Bear, remember?"

"Bullsh——, damn!"

"What was that about?"

"My girl doesn't like me cussing all the time. If I get in the habit it's hard to stop, so I'm trying to cut down. I'm going to be seeing her pretty soon."

"You're getting to be a regular holy man. You ought to get yourself an orange robe and a cup, like the Buddhist monks here."

"They're saffron-color, not orange. You think I'd look good in one?" he joked.

"If you shaved your head."

They arrived at the gate and watched a full two-baht bus

depart for town, so they took samlors. After haggling the drivers down to three baht for the trip, they crawled into the seats behind the drivers and were pedaled away toward town.

Lyle got his driver to pull up abreast of the Bear's samlor so they could talk. "So you're really serious about that broad—what's her name?"

"Julie. Yeah I'm serious. No, she's not a broad. And no, I'm not nice about it if anybody calls her anything but a lady."

"So I'm sorry. I'll call her Lady Julie from now on."

They were quiet for a while in the darkness. Both samlors had dim front and tail lights, powered by little generators that rubbed against the tires, but the sliver moon was down low in the sky. A few lights from other samlors were visible in front and behind them, all bobbing along toward Takhli. The samlor drivers' legs made a swish-swish sound as they pedaled. They were both scrawny little guys with big guys in the back, but they made good time.

Lights of the strip hove in the distance.

"Doesn't seem real, does it?" asked Lyle.

"It is though. All of it."

They entered sin-town and went directly to the Takhli Villa, the officers' hangout.

They dismounted and tipped the drivers. "You guys wait here," said the Bear to the two drivers, motioning for them to stay put, "and we'll give you mock-mock tips."

"Good idea," said Sloppy.

"Sort of like having a cab wait for you," said the Bear.

John Radkovich arrived in his samlor, the sad look still on his face.

"How you doing, John?" asked the Bear.

The lieutenant frowned.

Radkovich had flown his first time in pack six two weeks before, on Ken Maisey's wing. It had been a tough mission and they'd seen a lot of flak, and when they landed, Maisey had quit. Then, the day before the Tet bombing pause was announced, he'd been flying up in pack six with an old head captain named Tom Raymond. They had been shot at by SAMs and during the evasion maneuver the old head captain had been shot down by 57mm flak.

Ever since, Johnny Radkovich had worn his frown. He thought he was a jinx to whomever he flew with.

The three of them went inside and picked a table.

They all talked for a while, and again the Bear heard how Radkovich felt he was responsible for Maisey quitting and for the captain getting shot down.

Radkovich was a skinny, nervous young guy, and the weight of his guilt was heavy.

"You're not responsible," he tried telling Radkovich, who would have none of it. He just sat, staring at the girl singing *Moo Reevah, Widah than a miiii,* sipping his whiskey sour and looking forlorn. His sad look attracted a bar-girl, who sat with him and conned him out of a dollar bar drink. Takhli bar-girls enjoyed the easy ones like John Radkovich.

Sloppy peered across at Radkovich's girl, and after another drink could no longer stand it. He waved to a bar-girl who looked pretty in the near-total darkness. He bought her a drink and she giggled, sat on his lap, and whispered to him about a fantasm short time. *"Fantasm!"* she kept saying.

Radkovich told the Bear he'd been a copilot on C-135's, and how he loved the huge airplanes. "We had turbofans on our new birds. Got rid of the gas-guzzler turbojet engines,"

"How the fuck—oops, sorry," said the Bear.

Radkovich looked at him strangely.

"How'd you get in fighters, you like trash haulers so much?" asked the Bear.

Johnny Radkovich didn't know. He shook his head sadly and drank his whiskey sour.

"I'll be back in a little bit," said Sloppy, getting intoxicated and smitten with the saucy farmgirl.

The Bear glanced at him. "Remember the clap?"

Watson bolted to his feet, dumping the girl from his lap. She scurried away, indignantly cursing in loud Thai.

"Bastard," muttered Sloppy to the Bear. "You didn't have to say that." He looked after the girl with a forlorn look.

"I'm saving you for your wife," the Bear reminded him before rising. "See you, Johnny. Why don't you take your girl in back and let her make you feel better?"

Radkovich even looked sad about that.

The Bear walked toward the door, and Sloppy followed.

Outside, Sloppy Watson brooded, then spoke up. "Doc Smith says not many of 'em have the clap."

"Maybe," said the Bear.

They got into the waiting samlors and took off up the street toward the Blue Moon massage parlor.

After a hotsy bath and a couple of beers, they went out to the samlors again, refreshed and getting drunk.

"In back," said the Bear to the samlor driver. He motioned and argued for a moment, and finally the driver crawled in back. The Bear climbed on and started pedaling. He wobbled a little at first, then got the hang of it and pedaled slowly down the street. Shortly Sloppy caught up, also in front and pedaling while his driver rode.

"See the Black Orchid down there?" yelled the Bear, indicating a distant set of lights.

"Yeah."

"Race you there!"

Sloppy didn't wait and dug in so hard that the bicycle wheels of his samlor squeaked, sort of like burning rubber in a street rod. Then they were both pedaling like crazy, neck and neck, first one and then the other drawing ahead.

The Bear won by leaning way out forward and humping away on the pedals.

"Cheat!" cried Sloppy.

They left the belly-laughing samlor drivers and went inside.

The Black Orchid was a hangout for black enlisted guys, and they were the only whites.

They got a table and ordered a drink, then waited a long while for it to come. Larry Hughes, a staff sergeant from pig squadron maintenance, came over and spoke quietly with Sloppy, then left. Their drinks arrived, brought by a pretty Thai waitress.

"What'd he say?" asked the Bear.

"Said most of the guys here don't like honkies drinking in their bar. Said he told 'em who we are and that we're okay."

"Nice of him."

"Sergeant Hughes is a good guy. A good crew chief, too."

The Bear looked sad. "We lost our bird, you know?"

"What's that?"

"We had number two-seven-seven. Sergeant Tiehl's our crew chief. He'd just painted two SAM missiles on the side of the airplane. Ries and Janssen were flying our bird when they went down. Sergeant Tiehl is still upset about it."

"You don't have an airplane now?"

"We're changing to three-fifteen. Sergeant Tiehl said it's a good bird, like two-seven-seven was, and today he had our names painted on the canopies and the two missiles on the side, one for each site we've bombed."

"I've gotta get a missile painted on our airplane like that."

"Yeah, makes you feel good, seeing the kills displayed there like that. Anyway, Sergeant Tiehl says he doesn't like other people flying our airplane."

Sergeant Hughes came over again, and this time he sat. "You gentlemen mind if I join you?"

"Not at all. And thanks for putting in the good word, Sarge," said the Bear.

Hughes leaned forward. "How long's this bombing halt going to last, sir?"

Both of them said they didn't know.

"I'd like it to be a long one," said Hughes. "I get tired of seeing birds not come home."

The Bear shook his head. "Yeah, maybe. But I like it when I'm flying every day. We get to know the defenses that way, know where the sites are and how they're acting."

Sloppy agreed. "I wonder what kinda surprises they're cooking up for us right now."

"I dunno," said the Bear, "but you can be sure there's something. Of course, we'll be laying some surprises on them too. Benny and Pudge have been working hard on their tactic. You know the one I'm talking about."

Sloppy nodded.

Hughes frowned. "I was just hoping you officers would know more about when we'll be flying again, so we could plan some. My airplane has a lot of delayed discrepancy work. Mainly just little things, but it'd be nice if I knew I could plan some down time, maybe a couple days of not flying so I could take care of them."

The Bear thought. "Today's Friday, Sarge. We won't be flying in Vietnam until Monday, for sure. Maybe a sortie or two to Laos, but nothing heavy. You could take tomorrow and Sunday for your work."

"Thanks," said Hughes, rising. "You guys have a good time. Nobody's gonna bug you. They give you trouble, I'll come over." He nodded and left, then wrapped his arm around the pretty waitress who had served them and whooped it up with a couple of his buddies at the bar.

They left after another drink, got back into the driver's seats of the samlors, and cruised down toward the main part of town. They stopped at a sleazy little bar they found on a back street of Takhli old-town, near the market. This time they invited the drivers inside, for it was that kind of place, not a GI hangout like on the sin-town strip. Here the clientele were very poor Thais and no one spoke English.

They bought drinks for the bar, drank Singha beer, and chased it with rotgut Mekong whiskey. The place smelled bad, like old sweat and bad booze.

"Whoo-ee," exclaimed Sloppy.

When they had ordered again, the Bear confided. "I'm getting married in three weeks."

Sloppy Watson stopped cold, his jaw drooping. "You?"

"Yeah. Thought I'd mention it, you being a good buddy. Even Benny doesn't know."

Sloppy was still dumbfounded. "You're kidding me, aren't you?"

"Nope."

The second rounds arrived and they saluted the samlor drivers in the room. "Numbah one," exclaimed one of the drivers, a mean-looking guy whose nose had been squashed flat on his face in some sort of accident.

Sloppy was shocked. "Married! God, Bear, that sounds awfully final for someone who enjoys his freedom like you. Why?"

The Bear shrugged. He sat, brooding.

"You better think it over good. Damn, man, you can get serious without getting married."

No response.

Sloppy shook his head. "You wanna talk it over?"

No response.

"Mal!"

The Bear jolted, came awake.

"You sleeping?"

"Naw." The Bear blinked his eyes, then drank his beer and chaser, realizing he couldn't feel his toes. "I'm gonna puke."

He went outside and made it a few steps farther before vomiting up the booze, beer, and part of his dinner. Sloppy came out, watched for a moment, then turned and also puked.

They stood, bent over, heaving and drooling.

"Shit," said the Bear.

Sloppy gagged a few times more, then sighed. "I'll be best man," he announced out of the blue.

"Benny's going to be best man. You can be second best man."

Sloppy blurted, "I'm not second-best at anything," then dry-heaved.

The Bear spat for a while, then sucked in a breath and straightened. He frowned at his friend, feeling very drunk but much better. "I've also got something awful heavy to tell Benny, and maybe then he's not going to want to have anything to do with me." He shook his head sadly.

"What's that?"

The Bear just kept shaking his head. "Nothing good. Nothing good at all."

Sloppy got the hiccups, and the Bear pounded on his back until they finally went away and Sloppy was pleading for him to stop.

They went back inside. The samlor drivers were laughing at them. "Numbah one!" the ugly one said again.

"Thai numbah one," said the Bear.

"Mellican numbah one," said Ugly. He grinned, which made him uglier, took something from around his neck, and somberly handed it to the Bear. "Mellican numbah one." He motioned with his hand and made a roaring sound like a jet engine.

It was a crude, hand-fashioned stone Buddha, with a thin copper filigree wire carefully wrapped around it. A prized possession of an incredibly poor but devout man.

The Bear made a show of removing his Saint Christopher's medal and giving it to the ravaged samlor driver. "Thai numbah one," he said, meaning it.

They had one last beer and whiskey chaser.

They retrieved their drivers, went back outside, and pedaled back toward the strip. It was only ten minutes before curfew time. At two in the morning the Thais shut everything down, the idea being that only Communist terrorists would be on the streets thereafter.

The air felt good on the Bear's face as he pedaled.

They stopped at the Takhli Villa just as the bartender was locking the door to observe curfew. They retrieved Johnny Radkovich, who had passed out at his table. His girl was long gone and his wallet free of cash. Ignoring the objections of the bartender that he owed for a drink, the Bear steered Radkovich out, with Sloppy supporting the lieutenant's other shoulder.

They dumped Radkovich into the seat beside the Bear's driver, got back on, and started pedaling toward the base.

They saw the headlights of a police patrol and huddled at the side of the road to hide, looking away like ostriches would. They continued on when the patrol had passed.

When they got to the base gate they gave the samlor drivers five bucks apiece, which was more than they would normally earn in a week, and ignored the complaints of the air policemen as they let them in. Johnny Radkovich came awake and grew belligerent with the cops, but the Bear cooled him down and he slipped back into his comatose state.

They walked the mile to the Ponderosa, supporting Radkovich a couple of times when he tried to lie down to sleep on the side of the road. When they got there, they dropped Johnny onto his bunk. The Bear went to bed, and Sloppy, knowing he'd never be able to find his way to his hootch in his condition, spent the remainder of the night on the dayroom couch.

12/1300L—357th TFS, Takhli RTAFB, Thailand

Benny Lewis

"It's damned important we start taking out the SAM sites, Pudge. We can't get to the command-and-control radar, so we've got to concentrate on protecting the strike force. The best possible way to do that is to knock out the SAM site that's closest to the target area."

Pudge agreed. "Maybe they'll start to use more caution about firing missiles if they think we're going to pounce on their asses every time they do."

Benny was with Pudge Holden in the squadron pilot's lounge, verbally polishing the new tactic to deal with the SAMs. The same one that had worked with such disastrous results on the day Ries and Shaky Anderson had tried it.

Rule one, they decided, was not to use the tactic unless both Weasel crews had good working receivers. Rule two was to confirm there were SAM Fansong radars on the air, and that it was not going to be an all-MiG day. Rule three was that even though they were separated, the elements must support one another.

Benny said, "Let's say I'm lead and you're number three. After we cross the Red River, you swing out about a mile off my left wing, on the side away from the threat. We fly across the valley like that. Then as we approach the target area, I call the split and you swing out even farther, okay?"

"Yeah. I move out a couple more miles so we got the target between us."

"You've got to be out even farther. Maybe seven or eight miles. Far enough that we look like separate flights on the SAM radars. We approach, keeping the target area defenses between us. Then the target area SAM shoots at one or the other of us, and that guy takes it down. The other guy watches the smoke and dust from the SAM launch and goes in and bombs the site."

"And the first guy dodges the SAMs, then pulls back up, and covers the guy bombing the site."

"You got it. But before we do something hairy like we're talking about, I want to make damn sure we've practiced and got it down right."

The next morning, they'd just been told, the single-seat strike birds would all be flying down near the DMZ along the Ho Chi Minh Trail, trying to put a stopper on the massive influx of supplies and troops that had started pouring from Hanoi to South Vietnam during the bombing halt. The Weasels would patrol the area between the interdiction targets and the threats to the north.

Pudge left to return to his hootch, and Benny found the Bear at the duty counter. As they walked toward the club for lunch, the Bear was quiet. He had lost much of the morose manner he'd displayed during the previous week.

"I'm getting married," he said as they walked.

"So I heard from Liz."

The Bear looked surprised. "You two still writing regular?"

"She's been helpful, handling the home front and all."

"We'll try to hold the wedding on the fifth of next month," said the Bear. "That's a Saturday. I called the embassy in Bangkok and reserved their chapel."

Benny nodded, head down as they walked, thinking about it.

"Will you be best man?"

"You sure you want to do this?"

"I told Lyle Watson, and he said the same thing. What the hell is this, Mother the Bear Week?"

"Remember when you told me about your other marriage, and how you weren't ever going to do it again?"

"This time it's different."

"I'll say. You knew your first wife before you married her."

The Bear sighed. "I want a lecture, I'll go to Father O'Brien."

"Catholic wedding?"

"Julie's a Methodist, and I don't feel like signing anything saying we've gotta raise our kids Catholic. Father O'Brien won't marry us, but he'll give us his private blessing. We'll get married by a Protestant minister."

"We'd better ask Colonel Mack for the time off."

"Then you'll do it?"

"Of course. I just think you're rushing things."

"I've changed my perspective some. Julie's gonna be a good wife."

Benny felt a strange lump in the pit of his stomach. "She's young."

"She's pretty, smart, socially aware, and knows what she wants. I'm hooked."

"Can't it wait until we finish our hundred missions?"

"She's also pregnant. You tell anyone I said that and I'll break your knees."

Benny felt inexplicably angry at the Bear and hurt about something else he couldn't quite define. He cleared his throat finally. "She could get an abortion."

"Fuck that. It's our kid. You didn't know, but she was a virgin when we met. That's also something private."

The lump in Benny's stomach pained him now. "Then I guess you better get married."

The cool tone got the Bear's attention. Benny hadn't meant for that to happen. It was just the thought of Julie being a virgin, and now pregnant. He wondered why he cared so much, and why the lump wouldn't go away.

"We gotta talk about something else, Benny." The Bear looked grim.

"Go ahead." The cool tone again, even though he hadn't wanted it there.

Max Foley yelled from in back of them, hurrying to join them.

"If you guys are going to lunch, I'll join you."

Benny told him about the tactic he and Pudge Holden had been coming up with to use against SAM sites in the target area.

Max grinned at him. "I think the best way to handle the SAMs is from as far away as I can get, but I guess you guys look at it different."

Just before they entered the club doors, Benny remembered that the Bear had wanted to tell him something and asked him what it was.

The Bear glanced at Max thoughtfully, then finally shook his head. "Forgot. Couldn't have been anything important."

13/1315L—Vinh, Route Pack Two, North Vietnam

Benny Lewis

The frag order directed them to protect strike flights bombing the trails and mountain passes of the Ho Chi Minh Trail, staying between the bomb droppers on the trail and the threats to the north. The Weasel sortie was precautionary only, so they flew in a two-ship flight. The strike aircraft that normally flew their wing were added to the numbers of aircraft trying to put a stopper in the heavy flow of supplies.

There were small arms and visually aimed artillery on the trail, but Wild Weasels were designed to counter sophisticated radar threats, and none of those had yet been encountered there.

After making a single pass through Mu Gia Pass and determining there indeed were no radar-directed threats there, they wandered northward to work on the tactic. They left the southern panhandle and ventured up to pack two, toward Vinh.

Benny wanted to be able to practice on *some* sort of enemy radar, and hoped the Vinh commander would oblige them by bringing up a Firecan AAA radar or two. It was hoping for too much to imagine he might try a SAM on them.

They progressed northward, Benny leading and Pudge

Tom Wilson

flying line abreast about a mile out to his left. Neither had a wingman, so they had to simulate that part.

They tried some line-abreast maneuvering to limber up on.

Pudge turned first, ninety degrees starboard, standard hard-rate-turn. Benny waited for ten seconds and turned. When he rolled out, Pudge was a mile out to his right now, and they were still line abreast.

"That worked slick," said the Bear.

"Yeah."

They tried an in-place one-eighty, both aircraft wheeling about rapidly toward the opposite direction. They rolled out, and Pudge was now on Benny's port side, still a mile out.

Another starboard turn, Pudge turning first, Benny extending. A little ragged, but after some adjusting, it turned out okay. Again they were headed for Vinh, but now Pudge was on his right.

"What you guys trying to do, get the backseaters to puke?" asked the Bear.

"Not a bad idea," retorted Benny. "Any radar signals on the air?"

"The Barlock search radar up north, but the signal looks funny, Benny. The azimuth is jittering, shows a different heading each time it sweeps. They must've put in dummy transmitters. The Soviets do that when they're trying to screw us up. Gonna be a lot harder for anyone to home in on the radar signal like Ries and Janssen tried."

"Well, that rules that idea out."

"Yeah. I'm also getting a peep every now and then from one of the Vinh gun radars. I think they're tweaking it up or something. It'll probably come on stronger when we get closer."

"Do they know we're here?" asked Benny.

"Oh yeah. There's a Spoonrest acquisition radar at Vinh that we can't pick up on the Weasel gear. I figure that's one reason the Vinh commander is so damned good, because he coordinates all his information and has figured out what we've got. Also, we're within the range of the Barlock, and like I told you, they're all talking together now."

"You're sure they get the Barlock information this far south?"

"Benny, you do the flying and I'll do the thinking, okay?"

Benny grinned into his mask. They were beginning to work smoothly together, like a well-oiled machine, knowing what the other was thinking with a minimum of verbalizing.

A Firecan radar rattled in his earphones, and a two-ringer strobe danced on Benny's attack scope.

"Gun at twelve," said the Bear. "No threat yet."

"Red Dog two, we've got a tracking gun at twelve o'clock," Benny called to Pudge.

"Red Dog two confirms, he's at our ten o'clock," called Pudge Holden.

The Bear and Sloppy had insisted that the first tracking radar contact must be confirmed between the two element leads, to show the Weasel equipment was working in both aircraft, before they split the flight. The idea was to split at twenty miles, well before they reached the eleven-nautical-mile optimum firing range of the target area SAMs. The Bear said SAM Fansong radar scopes had range marks etched in meters, and that Soviet doctrine said to fire missiles when targets were inbound, at twenty kilometers. That was between ten and eleven nautical miles. No one asked how the Bear knew about the etch marks on Russian radars.

"We're about twenty-five miles out," said the Bear.

"Yeah," said Benny. "That's what I've got, too."

When Benny figured they were at twenty miles, he radioed, *"Red Dog two, extend,"* jogging the aircraft left.

"Shit," mumbled the Bear, complaining about the hard turn. He never complained when they were maneuvering to dodge missiles or attack a target, only when they were lollygagging around the sky, or practicing. "Excuse me," he said then, remembering he'd cursed.

"Red Dog lead," came Pudge's radio call, strained under the g-forces of his turn, *"we got a second gun on the air."*

"He's right," said the Bear, still grumbling.

"Red Dog lead confirms," called Benny.

They rolled out back in the direction of Vinh. Benny could see the mouth of the river, the hills against which the city of Vinh was built, and the coast immediately beyond.

Pudge Holden would also be ingressing toward Vinh, far out to his right.

Both aircraft crossed over Vinh, collecting a smattering of 37mm fire.

They wheeled around the sky, talking to one another and trying to improve their coordination.

The AAA radars were well coordinated, blinking on and off every twenty seconds—the average flight time of a Shrike missile—but they seemed confused in selecting a target. First they would track Benny, then when he banked away, they would track Pudge Holden. Then Benny would reverse back inbound and they would slew between the two targets.

"You got them nervous," muttered the Bear. "They don't know how to handle two Weasels trying to pounce on their ass."

Benny lined up on a radar and fired a Shrike just as it came on the air, but the radar blinked off in time and the Bear grumbled that the missile had missed. They heard Red Dog two also miss with a Shrike.

Benny thought about what the gomers were doing then, trying to put himself in their place, like the Bear said. He lined up with the most distant Firecan, which shortly went off the air. The other one came on to track Pudge Holden. Benny stayed lined up, waited ten seconds, watching the second hand of the cockpit clock, then pickled and the Shrike rushed off the pylon, trailing its wisp of rocket smoke. Benny turned away.

"What the hell were you shooting at?" complained the Bear, for there was no radar signal there.

Then the gun radar came back on the air, tracking them. Five seconds later the strobe disappeared.

"I'll be damned," said the Bear.

"You think the Shrike got it?" asked Benny.

"I know it did. I can tell by the way the signal drops off the air when the missile hits the antenna. Damn." The Bear sounded impressed.

Benny laughed. "I played his game. We've got them confused, Bear. They don't know which way to look with two separate Weasels looking down their throat."

Benny and Pudge rejoined south of the city, and they practiced with the line-abreast formation again.

They flew back to Mu Gia Pass. There they were assigned a FAC, flying around in his O-1 Bird Dog spotter plane, and on his cue, dropped their bombs on a suspected concentration of troops under a canopy of trees. A few rounds of 37mm fire popped ineffectively below them, and the Bear ridiculed the inaccuracy of the gomer guns.

"For us it isn't much," said Benny, "but how'd you like to be in that little Bird Dog."

"No thanks."

They were very low on fuel, and sighed with relief when they hooked up behind the KC-135 tanker and began to receive precious fuel.

"You guys ready with your new tactic?" asked the Bear before they landed.

"Yeah," said Benny, "but we're going to keep practicing."

For more than a week they doggedly executed the simple split tactic as the strike force continued to be fragged against the targets on the Ho Chi Minh Trail. Even though it became humdrum and boring, they continued, because they wanted everything to be second nature by the time they went back up north to pack six.

CHAPTER TWENTY

Saturday, February 25th—1130 Local, Command Post, Takhli RTAFB, Thailand

Colonel Mack

Mack had been called to the meeting in the command post briefing room with the deputy commander for operations, deputy commander for maintenance, the wing ops staff, and the other two squadron commanders. The subject was not announced. They had just been told to show up.

At precisely eleven-thirty, Colonel Parker took the podium, flashed the ten-dollar grin he usually reserved for visiting generals, and began, a tremor of emotion thick in his voice. "We've very possibly got a very important target."

B. J.'s hands clutched the podium as he explained. Washington had been incensed at the way the North Vietnamese had taken advantage of the Tet cease-fire. The president had angrily requested that CINCPAC, the four-star admiral based in Hawaii, suggest a target that would, if destroyed, gain the undivided attention of the North Vietnamese. CINCPAC's first choices had been important government targets in Hanoi, but backchannel reports said they had been rejected due to the president's advisers' fears the Chinese might become sufficiently angered and enter the war if their diplomats were subjected to bombing.

"His second choice was the Thai Nguyen Iron and Steel Works, located here," Parker pointed at a location just east of Thud Ridge, "precisely thirty-five nautical miles north of the center of Hanoi. Indications are that they'll go for it."

There was some low muttering from the staff officers. The location was in the heart of the defenses. To bomb in the Thai

506

Nguyen area, the pilots would have to fight their way across the valley and through the worst of the defenses, hit a target swarming with SAMs and guns, then fight their way out.

"Headquarters Seventh Air Force has just alerted us to study JCS target numbers seventeen and nineteen, in detail, so we can prepare ourselves should it come."

Colonel Parker motioned to Lieutenant DeWalt, the young intelligence officer, who quickly gained the podium and nervously adjusted the microphone. He spoke from notes and gave a thorough overview of the targets.

Aerial photograph of a complex of buildings. Huge structures at each end, with a maze of smaller, connecting buildings and a long elevated rail with a large, overhead derrick running in between. A superimposed rectangle, outlining the critical buildings, covered an area more than two miles long and half a mile deep.

The Thai Nguyen steel mill was North Vietnam's showpiece, the pride of President Ho Chi Minh, the first product of his touted industrial modernization program. In fact, it was the only real success of his five-year plan.

The North Vietnamese had made no progress with the electrification of rural areas. The rail system was not yet upgraded, and it still ran on the old narrow gauge. The government program to efficiently allocate irrigation water through a new network of reservoirs and canal systems had not gotten off the ground, and they still used the ancient Chinese distribution system. But the North Vietnamese leaders were proud of the steel mill.

The ore from the great mine at Tri Cao, near Thai Nguyen, was extracted by use of crude, manual techniques, but the steel mill itself was a technological wonder when compared to the primitive industries in the remainder of the country.

Construction of the mill had started in 1960 using equipment and expertise from both the Russians and the Chinese, and involved some 20,000 workers. Its goal was to produce 200,000 tons of iron per year when completed in five years. The first blast furnace was operational in a little over three years, and in 1964 it had produced almost 100,000 tons of pig iron, cast iron, and steel.

That was all very impressive for a country which was ninety percent agrarian, nine percent stone age, and one percent Communist leadership.

War or no, construction efforts were continuing. So was production. Aerial reconnaissance photos showed ongoing work on a second blast furnace and sprawling new buildings housing more of the plant. The issue of the steel mill was loaded onto special railcars at the adjacent, modern loading facility and shipped both north to China and south to Hanoi. The DIA people couldn't tell them how much the mill had produced in 1965 and 1966, or even what the output of the mill was used to produce. They guessed at such things as bullets, mines, and trade credits with China.

The steel mill complex itself was JCS 19. JCS 17 was the sophisticated rail-loading facility.

A second photograph showed the loading facility. A maze of parallel railroad tracks and two huge loading docks. Red rectangle superimposed over a building in between the loading docks, smaller red squares over small structures beside the tracks.

The rail facility was semiautomated, using equipment from Czechoslovakia and East Germany. More efficient than anything found in Red China, the facility had a maximum loading capacity of 1,500 tons of iron and steel per day, which meant it would easily be able to keep up with the output of both blast furnaces when they were running at full bore.

The staff accepted Lieutenant DeWalt's briefing with stony silence. Colonel Mack gazed intently at the detailed map on the wall as Colonel Parker replaced DeWalt at the podium, his mind busy with ingress routes and tactics.

"Well?" asked Parker, casting his blue eyes about the room.

Maj Max Foley stood. "When do you expect the frag order, sir?"

"Seventh Air Force doesn't know yet, so I certainly don't. I just wanted you to be ready. I want you to start preparing bomb loads you think would be appropriate for a structure of that size. Then if we don't agree with the weapons loads specified on the frag when it comes in, we'll know what to argue for."

Max grumbled. "No matter what we suggest, they keep directing us to use M-117's." M-117's were World War Two–vintage 750-pound bombs stockpiled by the hundreds of tons in the States. They were meant to be carried in bomb bays, and were fat and bulky and created too much drag for the sleek and superfast Thunderchiefs.

But B. J. was in no mood for complaints, so he stared at Max Foley without comment until he sat back down. He glanced about the room brightly then.

"Any more?"

Getting none, he pointed to his deputy commander for maintenance. "Give me a quick rundown on aircraft availability."

The DCM stood, peering down at his notepad. "Seventy-four F-105D's on-station. Sixty-four flyable, but twelve have notable discrepancies."

"By tomorrow morning?"

"Are we going to fly this afternoon?"

"A sixteen-ship mission to pack five. An easy target, and I don't anticipate losses."

"I'll have sixty-eight flyable by morning, and we'll have most of the discrepancies corrected."

"Not good enough. I want *everything* ready. This may be an extended effort, and I don't want us running out of flyable airplanes. Put your guys on long hours. What's the *most* you can squeeze out of the men?"

The DCM looked unhappy, and Mack sympathized. Maintenance was already worked into the ground at Takhli. "Seventy flyables," he said finally.

"And *no* major discrepancies," said B. J. pointedly. He looked at the DCO, the other squadron commanders, then over at Mack, whom he studied for a longer moment. He glanced away.

"Squadron commanders, I want you to put together a tiger list. Pick out your top sixteen pilots and tell them they'll have to stay available for the next four days. None of them go downtown or on R and R. The minute we receive a frag order for either JCS seventeen or nineteen, I want them ready to fly. I want our best pilots flying on our first strikes at the steel mill, and I want results."

Lieutenant DeWalt slipped back into the room and hurried to the podium with a note. Parker's face worked for a moment, and finally turned into a grin. He looked up and slowly scanned the room. "It may happen sooner than I thought. No one here is to breathe a word about this target until it's released. Mack, stay here. The rest of you are dismissed."

As the others filed out, Mack wondered at the reason for his being held behind.

The second the door closed behind the last of the men, B. J. grinned again, but it was a nervous look. "We've been alerted for a morning strike on JCS seventeen, Mack."

A butterfly fluttered in Mack's stomach.

"The Thai Nguyen rail loading facility. The goddam commander of Thirteenth Air Force is coming in tomorrow morning, or I'd be leadng it myself."

"I understand, sir."

"This information just came in by courier. It's *that* goddam big, Mack. There's a lieutenant colonel from Seventh Air Force outside that door who has to brief me and the mission commander on the specific instructions and restrictions laid on by the generals."

"Who's going to be mission commander, sir?"

"I've picked you."

The butterflies started to settle, and Mack unconsciously narrowed his eyes as he thought about the upcoming melee. At least he would get to lead his men into the fight.

Lieutenant DeWalt led a lieutenant colonel wearing a Class-B uniform into the room, then swiftly departed.

The button colonel shook both of their hands. "Lieutenant Colonel Gates," he said, "Seventh Air Force plans and programs directorate."

He fished into his briefcase, brought out an Air Tasking Order marked SECRET, and handed it to Colonel Parker. "Your frag's in there. General Moss ordered me to visit all the bases involved in the strike. He wants to make sure this one goes off as smoothly as possible."

Gates gave a brief pitch. The president had directed the strike on the rail siding, but he'd made it clear they were not to damage the steel mill. They were to destroy the railroad siding as a *threat* to the steel mill. They were to render the loading facility into splinters, but they were not to harm the mill, not even to overfly it. If the North Vietnamese didn't respond to the threat, further direction would be forthcoming.

The button colonel made sure both men had received the message loud and clear.

"I've got the general's plane waiting at base ops. I'll visit Korat and Ubon, give them the word, then head back to Saigon to report to General Moss that you've all been briefed."

Parker chewed his lower lip. "Tell the general that Takhli is honored to be first on the target."

Gates started to say something, thought better of it, and departed.

Mack had noted Parker's fidgeting and said in a reassuring voice, "We'll make it a clean strike, Colonel."

Parker's voice was strained. "I want the pilots to know that if any man hits any part of the steel mill, I'll have his ass. Jesus! Both Seventh Air Force and PACAF would hold a witch-hunt. You'd get the hatchet as mission commander and I'd get it as your boss, but by God, I'd have the man's ass first!"

"Message received, Colonel."

Parker said, "I wish to Christ I didn't have to meet and greet the weak-dick three-star from Thirteenth Air Force tomorrow. This mission's important to the brass. Hell, it's even important to the president."

Parker paced, glancing periodically back to his squadron commander. "I'm putting you in charge of it because I know you'll do things right, Mack."

There was more pep talk, more nervousness, and Mack found himself continually reassuring B. J. Parker that they wouldn't screw it up.

Mack had his own concerns. *Was the Thai Nguyen steel mill as well protected as he imagined it would be?* The butterflies in his stomach returned.

B. J. studied him closely. "Mack," he finally said, "I'm putting you up for colonel with the strongest recommendation possible. A damned good evaluation report, and I've recommended a confidential attachment on top signed by General Moss. I think that will override what that wing commander at Yokota did to you."

"Thanks for the confidence, sir." But Mack's mind was not at all on the possibility of promotion.

25/1950L—Hoa Lo Prison, Hanoi, North Vietnam

Glenn Phillips

Glenn was beginning to feel that they thought he was a doctor or something, for periodically a badly wounded or terribly beaten prisoner was dumped into his cell to die. It had happened twice now. Tonight the guards dumped another one on him.

He knew this one. Against all odds it was yet another guy from the 357th squadron, and like the others, Pete Crawford was in terrible condition. From his head to the soles of his feet he was in bad shape.

He'd known Crawford in the squadron as a feisty guy from Tennessee, a pilot with a quick mind and good flying ability. He'd been C-Flight commander. But what they brought him was something that had been Pete Crawford, something with a bent and broken body and, it seemed, no mind at all.

At least this time his patient had been cleaned up and changed into prison pajamas.

He putzed around and examined him carefully before tapping out that Maj Pete Crawford had been placed in his cell. Bad shape.

He went back to the bunk and examined Pete closer. Abscess of his cheek, several broken teeth, bruises all over him, another bad abscess on his belly, arms wrenched and pulled so badly out of their sockets he was fearful of trying to push them back into position. Testicles swollen to the size of grapefruits. Anus swollen. Blood dried where it seeped from an ear.

He laid him out flat and after sucking a breath, pulled the limbs back into proper position. The eyes came partially open, but there was no other reaction, although the pain must have been excruciating.

He hurt for Crawford, and his anger smouldered for a moment. It would have been more compassionate if they'd gone ahead and killed him. But that was their way, he'd learned. They would torture you until you didn't care, until you wanted to die, but they wouldn't let you slip over that edge. They made you live with the awful pain and indignity.

They seldom tried to get military information. They just wanted to bend you and hurt you, to make you feel like you were no longer a man.

He prayed for Crawford, talking to God like the friend he had become.

A query tapped from the adjacent cell. Glenn went over and tapped out V-E-R-Y– –B-A-D.

He carefully massaged Crawford's bunched leg muscles.

The captain in the adjacent cell relayed an unnecessary response from the brass. *T-R-Y- –T-O- –H-E-L-P–.*

He tried to give some water to Crawford. Finally he forced it, pouring measured amounts down him. The throat constricted and Crawford drank. He was wasted and skeletal, like the guys in the photos of Dachau when it was liberated.

Crawford went through mild deliriums that night and through the next day. He was weak and obviously on the verge of death. He talked clearly once, although Glenn had to hunker down and put his ear close to Crawford's mouth. He talked about bird hunting back home and about his dog. It was a child's voice.

Glenn was able to force small amounts of rice with flecks of dried fish down Crawford's throat.

On the third day, Crawford muttered something that Glenn thought might be lucid.

"We were first, weren't we?" he asked.

"What do you mean?" Glenn responded.

"Push it out square with the waves, Red."

That was all there was for a day, for Crawford grew silent. When he finally spoke on the following day, he did so with his eyes open.

"It's you, huh."

"Yeah."

"We gotta get outta here."

After a few more sentences, Glenn learned that Crawford thought he was someone called Red. Since a pilot named Red Williams had arrived at Hoa Lo Prison the same day as Crawford, Glenn thought he understood.

That night Crawford talked again with his eyes open, and Glenn tried to tell him that Red Williams was also there in the prison, but in another cell. After telling him several times, he got through.

"We didn't make it. We tried," said Crawford.

A while later, Crawford recognized Glenn and called him by his first name. He told him about Bear Stewart, that Bear was now flying with Benny Lewis and that they were giving 'em hell.

That was the first time Glenn knew that Mal Stewart had made it out of North Vietnam alive. He'd presumed the Bear was dead. He happily tapped out a message to take Malcolm

Stewart off the mental lists of Americans known to be in North Vietnam.

Crawford went through another bad time then and cursed about a stupid, heavy boat.

That same night Crawford had a small bowel movement, his first since being dumped in the cell. He did it on the bunk, in his pajamas, and Glenn had to clean up the mess because Crawford wasn't able to move much and wasn't lucid enough to know he'd done it. But his body was starting to function, and that was good.

Glenn prayed, telling his friend that he was thankful that Crawford had shown that little sign of improvement.

26/0435L—Takhli RTAFB, Thailand

Colonel Mack

When Mack walked into the briefing theater, he noticed the board.

February 26

Takeoff	Time:	0630L/2330Z
	Altimeter:	30.02"
	Temperature:	31C
	Weather:	Clear
Primary Target	JCS 17:01	
	Thai Nguyen Rail Siding/Loading Facility	
	Air Refueling:	Green Anchor
	Tgt Coord:	21 -33'-21"N
		105 -52'-12"E
	Tgt Alt:	245'
	TOT:	0050Z
	Altimeter:	30.05"
	Weather:	Clear/Scattered
	Defenses:	Medium AAA/SAM
	Execution Word:	ALLEY CAT
Alt Tgt 1	Dong Hoi Barracks/Supply Depot	
	Air Refueling:	Blue Anchor Ext.
	Tgt Coord:	17 -25'-05"N
		106 -34'-00"E
	Tgt Alt:	50'
	TOT:	0035Z to 0050Z
	Altimeter:	30.01"

Weather: Clear/Scattered
Defenses: Light AAA
Execution Word: BULLDOG

Alt Tgt 2   Suspected Truck Parks
Air Refueling: Blue Anchor Ext.
Tgt Coord: Area of 18 -19'N
                        104 -55'E
Tgt Alt: 1750' to 2400'
TOT: 0015Z to 0045Z
Altimeter: 30.05"
Weather: Clear/Scattered
Defenses: Small Arms
Execution Word: COLLIE

"Got a good one today, boss," said Benny Lewis as he stared at the board.

"Yeah." Mack made a few notes from the board.

"If we go to the JCS target, I'd like to make a change in our normal Weasel tactics. Pudge Holden is going to be my number three, and we'd like to try something we've been working on."

"That's an odd flight lineup," Mack said. "Both of you guys are lead qualified."

"We plan to operate in two independent, yet supportive elements, like we'd do against MiG's."

"Like Ries tried?"

"He didn't get the chance to practice like we've been doing. We've got it worked out pretty well."

"Will it affect the strike mission?" asked Mack.

"We think it'll help you guys. It'll give us a better chance to take on the SAM sites."

"Dangerous?"

"Maybe, but it can't be worse than the way we were doing it before."

Mack thought for a moment. He liked for his men to be innovative, but he also wondered if this was the right time to try something new. "Tell you what, Benny, you go ahead and brief it to the crews when it comes your turn, and I'll either give a nod or an aw shit."

A few minutes later Lieutenant DeWalt came in, scribbled ALLEY CAT on the board, and gave a thorough overview of the JCS 17 target. He was careful when he talked about defenses.

"One SAM site and several dozen guns known to be

active in the target area," DeWalt said. "There may be more we don't know about." He added that an RF-101 recce bird had been shot down near the target area the previous afternoon.

Capt Smiley Boye said the weather would be good. Possibility of a few high, scattered cirrus clouds. Nothing at their altitude or below.

They launched into the mission briefing.

The EB-66's would be orbiting out over the water, thirty miles beyond Haiphong, trying to set up screen jamming of acquisition radars. The EB-66 briefing officer knew they could not do much good for the strike force at that distance.

A flak suppression flight would precede the strike flights to soften up the guns in the target area, scattering CBUs around the periphery of the siding. Colonel Mack would be leading the chopper flight.

Capt Swede Swendler would lead the next flight, the first to lay hard bombs onto the rail siding. Then Capt Bud Lutz and Maj Duffy Spencer, Pete Crawford's replacement as C-Flight commander.

Next would come the 354th squadron, with their most experienced and steady pilots leading their three flights. Finally the 333rd, with their squadron commander and his two best majors.

Benny Lewis would be out front, leading the Weasels.

The deck was stacked. B. J. had told the squadron commanders that he'd wanted the craftiest middle managers who were still damn good pilots, and he'd gotten them. Mack figured he had a hell of a lot of steadiness and moxie in the group.

He carefully spelled out the target timing and bombing assignments. Two flights to the north side, two to the south side, and the remaining five flights in the center. Anyone who was not positive he was going to hit squarely into the target was to pull off dry. No long bombs would be tolerated.

Benny Lewis briefed his new split-the-flight Weasel tactic, and after hearing it all, Mack gave him a nod. He and Pudge had thought it out well, and anything that might keep the SAMs off their backs while they concentrated on their bombing was okay by him.

Before the meeting broke up, Mack impressed on the guys that the brass wanted no screwups, that they were not to harm a single hair on the metal head of the steel mill.

* * *

There was a foul-up at the tankers. First Brigham, the radar at Udorn, had trouble getting the right fighters with the right tankers. Then Green Anchor 21 was unable to deliver fuel due to a pump system malfunction. That meant that eight fighters were held up, because they had to shift to another KC-135 tanker. They all delayed, finally dropping off the tankers fifteen minutes late, so then they had to push up their throttles in an attempt to make up the time. They had to, because the strike force from Korat was hot on their heels.

As they passed over the TACAN station at channel 97, on the Laos/North Vietnam border, a Thud in Mack's flight, flown by the lieutenant on his wing, came down with fluctuating oil pressure, so Mack told him to return to base alone. If it hadn't been such an important strike, he'd have sent someone with the lieutenant.

Then, as if that wasn't enough, Toki Takahara, in Swede's flight, said he had a fuel feed problem. He bounced his aircraft around a little, though, and the system seemed to correct itself.

The gremlins came and departed early, satisfied, for the rest of the mission was textbook perfect.

They went charging out over the valley with all the jamming pods turned on, jinking and turning, Weasels out in front eight or ten miles calling out the SAMs. As they passed over Thud Ridge, the target stood out clearly, like it had a neon sign on it, and just when Mack led the flight into the pop-up, Benny and Pudge both launched Shrike missiles into the target area at a SAM radar from different directions.

Mack led his two tigers down the chute, and they got their CBUs off just at the right altitude. As they jinked away, he saw sparkles going off and the gun-flashes diminishing.

He led his flight north a few miles, then reversed, just in time to see bombs from Swendler's and Lutz's flights impacting, gouging big craters in the tracks and tossing open-top cars around. Then Duffy Spencer's flight added to the smoke, dust, and turmoil by taking out the big loading platform.

About then someone called SAMs, but Pudge Holden was launching his Shrike and trying to follow up with bombs, and the SAMs went wild, zipping straight past them to exlode like spectacular, bright-orange fireworks. Benny Lewis was bombing a SAM site south of the target area. The air was clear of

SAMs while the superb pilots of the pig squadron made hash of the rail siding.

Benny Lewis

He turned up his right wing and watched Tiny Bechler's bombs exploding in a short string across the site.

"No threats!" yelled the Bear. "Pudge must have put the other guy off the air, because there's no signal."

But flak was still thick over the site they had just bombed, so Benny kept jinking hard.

"Red Dog two, we're at your two o'clock," he radioed for Tiny's benefit, and he watched him bank hard in their direction.

"No threats," the Bear repeated.

"We got signals from Hanoi?" asked Benny. He still had one Shrike missile left.

"Two SAMs, out of range," said the Bear.

"Let's get a Shrike off at one of them, and get the hell out of here."

"Come right twenty more degrees."

Benny reefed the stick against his right leg, watched his heading, and steadied on a course toward Hanoi. He jammed the throttle full forward and pulled the Thud's nose up ten degrees.

"That stirred 'em up, Benny!" the Bear called. "I'm putting a tracking SAM on your attack scope. Watch him, he's preparing to fire missiles!"

A three-ring strobe stuttered on his attack scope at their twelve o'clock. Benny centered his needles. Close enough. He pickled, watched the Shrike streak away from the pylon, then pulled the aircraft hard right and down.

"SAM launch, but disregard." The Bear grunted under the stress of the g-forces. "He only had time to center us in one beam."

They both panted as Benny pulled out of his maneuver and they sped toward the protection of Thud Ridge.

Maybe, thought Benny, *the bastards aren't ten feet tall after all.*

Colonel Mack

It was going damned well when Mack led his chopper flight outbound, back toward the west. Two 333rd squadron pilots were hit over the target by 57mm guns, but they both made it back. In the poststrike report, the radio calls to Red Crown were upbeat. Bombs on target.

The Weasels reported that Pudge Holden had hit a SAM radar with one of his Shrikes. Benny Lewis had done the same, then had followed his Shrike missile in and bombed the site, reporting a clean kill. Pudge said he may have hit a SAM site with his own CBUs, but didn't put enough confidence in it to take credit for a kill. But the SAM radar had not come back on the air to launch missiles at the strike force, and that was damned good. The Weasels had done a fine job and Mack congratulated them.

Target BDA photos showed they had pounded the siding to pieces, that Korat had done the same fifteen minutes after Takhli had departed, and that U.S. Navy A-6's had then further pulverized the target, turning it from rubble into mulch. Estimates said it would be a minimum of a week, perhaps even longer, before the siding could possibly be placed back into partial operation. The East European–supplied automated features of the loading facility would be out until new equipment could be brought in and installed.

Also very important was their report that, as directed, no one's bombs had landed anywhere close to the steel mill.

Mack came from the debriefings feeling good. The target had been an important one, yet they had destroyed it and lost no one. He tempered his elation when he remembered that Takhli would be striking the same target for the next few days, to drive home the president's, or whoever's, point with the North Vietnamese.

Today they'd had their best pilots at work, and it was obvious the gomers had been surprised by the major strike at Thai Nguyen. The defenses had been substantial, but certainly not what they would bring to bear if they knew the Thuds would return. He wondered how determined the enemy would become to protect their steel mill?

Mack stared out at the flight line from his office, sipping coffee. Somehow, then, he knew that the showdown had begun, and he worried, wondering if he had done nearly enough to prepare the men. Then he questioned if anyone could prepare for what they might be about to face.

27/1600L—Iron and Steel Works, Thai Nguyen, DRV

Xuan Nha

Xuan stood back a kilometer distant and surveyed the massive steel mill, the hordes of workers who were returning to their various duties after the all-clear siren had sounded, and the big trucks beginning to arrive again with their loads of ore.

He had just come from the rail loading facility, where he'd witnessed the carnage of two days of intensive bombing. Sixteen special cars, designed by the Soviets to carry heavy loads of steel plates, angle-iron, and crude ingots, were now mangled and ruined beyond repair. Loading docks, now rendered to splinters. The modern central control booth, an electronic wonder of Czech origin, now unrecognizable. Switches and boxcars, skilled and unskilled workers, forklifts and cranes, several kilometers of parallel tracks, now a jumble of metal, flesh, lengths of wire, and wood.

This time the intelligence gatherers of the Minister of External Affairs had not told them the strike was coming. They must be encouraged to do better.

The Minister of Industry, a favorite of the Enlightened One, had been visiting Thai Nguyen when the Thunder planes had first come to bomb the rail loading facility. It was providential that his party had not been there.

Upon his return to Hanoi, the minister had complained, with fearful look and dazed expression, that the loss of the rail facility seriously crippled their ability to transport the output of the great Thai Nguyen mill. Heavy trucks must be diverted to the mill until the siding was rebuilt, and they were more vulnerable to attack than the railcars that had been moved under cover of night.

The minister had looked horrified, and asked the generals if they could now expect attacks upon the steel mill itself.

The Enlightened One had been terribly upset after being told of the attack. He had sunk into a bout of gloom, even asked once in a very old man's voice whether anything could be worth losing everything they had gained and built.

It was a flagrant escalation of the war of terror, said the Enlightened One's prime minister and friend, Pham Van Dong. He wondered if they should move their timetable forward and begin bickering about negotiations, as they planned to do later, to stop the bombing. General Giap argued that they were not ready for such political maneuvering. The military forces in the south were slowly regaining footholds in the countryside, lost the previous year and during the recent Operation Cedar Falls, but it would take time to consolidate any degree of control.

Ho Chi Minh, ill and grievously melancholy, had under advice of his physician retired early. Pham Van Dong and Giap had gone to Giap's offices and argued through much of the night, both wishing to avert disaster.

This morning Dong and Giap had joined together to dissuade the Enlightened One from taking precipitous action. But when they left him, knowing how he treasured the steel mill, they had immediately called a meeting of party officials, ministers, and generals. There they quickly devised a twofold plan of action. The Ministry of External Affairs was to bring renewed international pressure on the Americans to stop the bombing. Secondly, they would seek a military solution.

Then the generals had called for Xuan Nha, for the second option called for his expertise. They asked, *Was it possible to drive the American air pirates away, to make Thai Nguyen and the vastly important steel mill complex invulnerable to air attack?*

Xuan Nha, swollen with pride at their attention, had told the truth—that no target could be made invulnerable to air attack. That was the way of things. But, he had gone on, they *could* make the target so extremely expensive that no rational human would dare to return there.

He asked for authority to make that happen.

They told him he could bring in whatever defenses were required and leave other areas, except Hanoi and Haiphong of course, undefended if necessary. He could ask for more systems from the Russians if he thought them useful, and they would back him without question. He could do whatever else was necessary and they would support him, but he must act quickly.

His orders were to discourage the Americans from making

further attacks in the Thai Nguyen area, and at all costs to avert serious damage to the steel manufacturing complex.

Defending Thai Nguyen was to be considered as crucial as the defense of Hanoi.

The generals used flattery, telling him they relied utterly upon his expertise. He who had driven the Pesky planes away, who had given them so many air victories, was asked to defend Thai Nguyen, the pride of the Enlightened One.

He vowed to succeed. He would build such a deadly concentration of defenses at Thai Nguyen that the Americans would be forced to desist, and he would begin immediately.

Colonel-General Dung had looked at him very solemnly then, and had quietly spoken of faith he had never lost in the Tiger of Dien Bien Phu. Then he'd hinted that there was room on his general officer staff for a man with his technical genius.

When Xuan Nha had left the generals to hurry back to his office, he'd trembled with pride.

He had radioed Major Nguy, commander of Wisdom complex, and Maj Tran Van Ngo, commander of Tiger battalion, and they and Xuan Nha had rushed to Thai Nguyen. As the parties traveled, there were three more air raids all targeted at the Thai Nguyen railroad loading facility.

Now the all clear sirens had sounded and they stood staring at the sprawling steel mill.

Xuan Nha slowly lifted his hand, pointed, then swept his hand from left to right. "That is what we must protect." He told them of the generals' decisions and of their faith in them.

They decided to immediately bring a full guided rocket battalion, with its three rocket batteries, into the immediate area. Two more mobile rocket battalions would be placed at strategic approaches to the area. Fifty radar-directed medium- and heavy-artillery batteries would be emplaced throughout the Thai Nguyen area, one hundred more at the approaches. Automatic weapons and light artillery were to be packed into the area so thickly that the gunners would be stumbling over one another.

That would give them 162 missile launchers, 700 antiaircraft artillery guns, and 10,000 small arms within sixty kilometers of Thai Nguyen, almost half of them to be in place by the end of the next day.

Four more mobile rocket battalions and thirty more medium-artillery companies would be moved from south of

Hanoi and Haiphong and placed on reserve status in Hanoi, ready to be rushed into the fight.

After agreeing upon each resolution, they would walk together to a nearby house where Lieutenant Hanh's men had strung the antenna and placed a noisy generator for a mobile radio. There they relayed the decisions back to the Hanoi command center for immediate implementation.

Hanoi confirmed when units had been alerted and were preparing to converge on the area.

Although it would present a difficult fire coordination problem for Wisdom, Major Nguy said it would be done. He advised Xuan that while he was sure they would efficiently destroy enemy fighter-bombers, he also felt the concentration of defenses would make them vulnerable to attacks, especially by the radar-hunters, and that he anticipated losses.

Xuan told him to make special efforts to destroy the radar-hunters, but that reasonable losses would be deemed acceptable.

Xuan also revealed that Maj Tran Van Ngo would stay at Thai Nguyen as the new area commander. He would immediately begin to survey the best possible sites for the many defensive systems. Tran was enthusiastic at the prospect of so many enemy targets.

Xuan told both Nguy and Tran Van Ngo that they were promoted to lieutenant colonel. "It was part of my initial request to the generals."

They thanked him.

He stared at the surroundings: the two vast buildings housing the blast furnaces, the buildings and shops, and the huge derrick hovering on its tremendous elevated track. He felt strangely emotional.

"It will all end here. It is our Dien Bien Phu."

They looked puzzled.

"Do you both realize that there has never been anything like this? No target on earth will be as well defended as this mill. Not Moscow nor Leningrad, not Washington, D.C. nor New York, not any place on earth."

The others looked with him, quieter as they contemplated.

"Here we will prove that in this modern day, with our sophisticated rockets and radars and computers, we can shield a target so utterly from attack that the entire concept of using aircraft in combat will be changed. This will be a historic time, perhaps the decisive chapter of the war," said Xuan Nha, still gazing out at the huge mill.

"Will the Americans come again?" asked Major Nguy.

"They will come. I feel it. They will return to bomb the loading facility."

"Again?"

"To show us they can. They are trying to frighten us."

"But it has been destroyed."

"They will return to the loading facility, and if we do not drive them away there, then they will come here to the steel mill."

"We must stop them," said a fiery Tran.

"Do not worry. Here at Thai Nguyen we will finally and decisively break the back of American air power."

Xuan slowly walked over to Quang Hanh and told him to relay that he wanted Lieutenant Colonel Wu to call in the staff and have them all prepare to stay around the clock at the Hanoi command center. He would do the same when he returned.

Xuan looked out at his two majors. He felt a special warmth for them, especially now that Thao Phong was gone. Upon those two, the battle for Thai Nguyen would succeed or fail.

He watched as Tran Van Ngo stretched, obviously alert and ready. *He moves like a cat,* thought Xuan, *a true warrior.* On the other hand, Major Nguy looked deep in thought, as he often did. *A steady and intelligent leader.*

He was lucky to have those two.

The two men stared at the steel mill, quieted by the enormity of their task, wondering.

"Can we really stop them?" Nguy asked Tran.

"If we kill enough of them, we will stop them," said Tran Van Ngo in his cocky and confident tone.

Chapter Twenty-One

Sunday, March 5th—1000 Local, U.S. Embassy Housing Compound, Bangkok, Thailand

Liz Richardson

The chapel was not large, but it was nicely done with natural woods and stained glass inserts in the windows. The pastor was young and outgoing and the service was correct, even if the military attendees were somewhat intoxicated.

Benny and several of the Bear's friends were there, having come down from Takhli in a military bus. Three other of Julie's stewardess friends had also made it, and the Air Force guys were giving them the once over and vice versa.

As the nuptial vows were said, Liz felt all mushy inside for her friend. Alternately she felt envious of Julie.

The Bear kissed the bride, and his friend, the one called Sloppy, edged him aside and laid a grandiose smacker on her. Then a really big guy called Tiny picked Sloppy up, set him aside, and, towering over her, gave Julie a more gentlemanly kiss. Benny was next and was nice about it. A grinning, brown-haired fellow they called Colonel Mack was next in line. He told the others that they didn't know what they were doing, and to watch carefully, then did a scene like Valentino.

Two of the guys wore blue Air Force uniforms, one called Pudge wore a white uniform tuxedo, and all the others wore civilian tuxes they'd hastily rented from a shop near the embassy grounds. They had gotten in late the previous night, so they had been forced to hurry things.

Benny had told her the bus was heading back to Takhli late in the afternoon and that a lot of them were on the schedule

525

the next morning. He'd said they were flying a lot of missions, and his grim attitude indicated they were tough ones. He'd added that the Bear was getting another day off and didn't have to return until tomorrow afternoon.

"How about you?" she'd asked, careful not to press him.

"If you want, I'll stay."

"I want."

He'd looked pleased.

The Bear returned from visiting with the preacher, probably giving him his customary tip, and someone yelled it was time for the reception.

Reception?

They all went out and crawled onto the Air Force bus. The driver was the big one called Tiny and he wasn't allowed to drink, but the others had a case of cold beer they'd gotten from somewhere and started popping them open and partying. When they were all aboard, Tiny began to struggle through the traffic, amid the squeals and honks and clamor. He would glare hard at errant drivers and look mean, but the Thais ignored him and continued to squeal around in their small Japanese cars.

The one called Colonel Mack had given away the bride, insisting that, by God, Chief Wright's daughter was going to be treated properly. He'd shaken his head and said he didn't know what the world was coming to, what with a fine young flower like Julie being given over to the clutches of someone as depraved as the Bear, and if she needed someone's shoulder to lean on, she shouldn't hesitate to call on him.

He welcomed her back into the Air Force fold.

"As you know, we take care of our own, Julie," he said. "I don't suppose you remember my wife Alice from back in Spangdahlem, Germany."

Julie said she'd been pretty young then.

"Well, she remembers you. What were you, about fifteen, sixteen?"

"Yes, sir."

"She led the Sunday teen group Bible study."

Julie remembered.

"In her last letter, Alice said for you to write and tell her how you and your folks are doing. Benny told me about your dad, but you ought to write her and tell her about your mother."

The guys were drinking the cold beer, and Liz took one

for herself. Benny, who had maneuvered to sit beside her, was talking to the one called Pudge about airplanes, and they were making flying motions with their hands.

It was all loud and boisterous and good fun.

Sloppy was sitting in the seat ahead of her, and he turned and tried to chat her up. A withering glare and curt word from Mal Bear caused him to quickly turn around and try with another stewardess, who was already being smooth-talked by a fighter pilot someone had called Swede.

They arrived at the Siam Intercontinental, a luxurious new hotel, and went to poolside, where Colonel Mack said one of the guys called Duffy had gone to set things up.

Duffy? It couldn't be! She remembered a night in Guam, and a guy she'd met by chance on Agana beach, just down from the hotel. A major, he'd said, on his way to fly combat. Unmarried but very innovative when they'd gone to her room. She had gone wild that one week of her life. *It just couldn't be,* she told herself again.

How many guys were named Duffy?

She had a sinking feeling as she followed the group, trying to casually answer questions that Benny Lewis had asked about things back home, thinking about the Duffy she had met. *Please, God, don't let it be him.*

Standing there, talking with a Thai bartender at a cabana bar they'd set up beside the pool, was Duffy. *The* Duffy. He turned and grinned at the approaching group, singled her out with his eyes, and did a double-take. He gave her a look of recognition and a pleasant nod.

Oh God! Had Benny seen?

He was the only Air Force person she'd adventured with except for Benny. And Mal Bear, but that didn't count because he wouldn't tell. Her world felt like it was about to collapse.

As the party got under way, she waited with leaden heart for Duffy Spencer to approach her.

Several chilled bottles of champagne, punch, and even a huge wedding cake were already set up in the cabana. Colonel Mack made another speech, telling them to drink up and enjoy, that it was all paid for out of their squadron party fund.

Benny stayed close by her side, because she was drinking too much. She laughed nervously when the men gathered around the Bear and grabbed him, then trundled him to poolside and tossed him in, tux and all. Julie clowned, leaning over at the poolside and shaking her finger at him. The Bear held his arms out to her. She laughed joyously and jumped in, came up sputtering, and they sank together, kissing. Next, a couple of the other stews went in, so Liz withdrew to safer ground. One at a time the guys were tossed in by friends.

Then, with Benny and everyone else except her and one other stew in the pool, Duffy Spencer stopped talking to the Thai bartender and came over to her.

"A good party, huh?"

Her heart was lodged in her throat. She nodded.

"You look good, Liz."

"Please?" she asked, feeling tearful. If she could only do it all over.

"I see you're with Benny. You guys serious?"

A "yes" was all she could get out.

He looked to the pool, where the exuberant group were splashing and dunking one another. "Benny Lewis? I wouldn't have guessed. He seems awfully tame for you."

She didn't comment.

"He's a good guy, and one hell of a good pilot, but I never figured him to be much of a hell-raiser."

"He's not. Don't tell him about us, please?"

"How about the guy off your crew who was in your room when I went back the next day?"

"He was our captain. He wanted to talk about the next leg of the flight."

"Hey, Liz. I saw him coming out of the shower with a limp dick, remember. Don't shit me, okay?"

She was quiet again, unable to suppress a quiver and a few tears.

"Maybe we can get together sometime here in Bangkok. Maybe in a couple of weeks?"

"No!"

Duffy Spencer grinned as if he knew better and walked away toward the pool. Then with a mighty leap, he jumped in to join his friends.

The cake cutting was next, and the bride and groom kept dripping water onto the icing. Finally Mal Bear did his chore, trying to be neat as he fed Julie. The fighter pilots walked up to the cake, disgusted with him. They each reached in and grabbed a handful of cake, frosting and all, and ate, licking their fingers. They cleaned up by throwing each other into the pool again.

Before the guys left in the Air Force bus, Colonel Mack presented the Bear with a key to the hotel's bridal suite, and said that had also been paid for out of the squadron party fund.

"Can't afford for any more of you characters to get married," he said, grinning.

Everyone hooted at the Bear, and Liz found herself giggling and forgetting about Duffy Spencer.

"Mal, if you need any help," said Sloppy as he climbed onto the bus, "just give me a yell."

The bus departed from the hotel, and left them—Mal Bear and Julie, Benny and herself, and the three stewardess friends—waving at the curbside. Liz was the only one who was still dry. The Bear and Julie mumbled apologies, grinning at each other like children about to get a treat, and walked toward the hotel. He held a possessive arm around her waist, and she had the same silly, glowing expression she'd worn in Bangkok.

Liz watched them go, unable to contain a smile of her own for Julie's happiness. She turned to Benny. "Where's your room?" she asked him innocently.

"I don't have one."

"Well, it so happens that I do. I'm over at the Princess Hotel. Come on along and we'll get you dried off."

Bear Stewart

They were in the suite.

"You're not showing yet," he said, looking her over at arm's length.

"A little. You haven't seen me with my clothes off yet."

"I was going to mention something about that."

She bit her lip. "Are you really sure about all this, Mal?"

"Having second thoughts?"

"Of course not. I meant you."

"I've never been more sure of anything."

"Sometimes I feel like I trapped you. Not with the pregnancy, because you didn't know when you asked if I'd marry you."

"You're the one who ought to feel trapped. You heard Colonel Mack say I'm depraved."

She tilted her head. "You better feel depraved tonight, big

fella. Ba, ba, ba, ba, boom!" She made sounds like strip-tease music and weaved back and forth, reached around for the catch at the back of the wedding gown.

"Let me do that," he said.

04/1030L—Takhli RTAFB, Thailand

B. J. Parker

Once a day over the course of a week, someone—either his 355th wing, or the wing at Korat, or the Navy A-6's—was tasked to return once again to Thai Nguyen to bomb the damn railroad siding and loading facility that had already been destroyed.

His 355th had rendered the facility unusable the first day they had gone there. Had done it well, with no loss of lives. Had pulverized the damned thing without doing any harm to the steel mill, just like the politicians and generals had wanted them to do.

He'd known they would be going back to prove a point to the North Vietnamese, but by the time they had gone back for the fifth and sixth times, he'd begun to wonder about the sanity of the whole thing. Every day *someone* went back to bomb it again, and the defenses were becoming formidable there.

B. J. went to the command post and called the Seventh Air Force deputy for operations, a two-star he'd known for a long while, on the scrambler telephone.

After beating around the bush for a while, he finally came out and asked the major general why they were having to go back, since they'd knocked out the target and it seemed like they should've gotten their point across to Hanoi.

Parker added, "The North Vietnamese have brought in about half the goddam guns they've got in the whole country. Another day or two, they'll have them all there."

"Don't second guess, B. J.," he was told on the wavering, squealing scrambler line. "This one's right from the big man himself. He's making a point with Hanoi."

So B. J. did not question further. He led that afternoon's mission, the wing's sixth trip to the Thai Nguyen rail siding.

04/1340L—Route Pack Six, North Vietnam

Sam Hall

Mack was away in Bangkok with a few of the squadron pilots, seeing the Bear married off to Chief Wright's daughter. Sam would have enjoyed going, but he'd encouraged Mack to take the time off and help the Bear do it right.

Colonel Parker, as mission commander, was flying as leader of the flak suppression chopper flight. Sam and Bud Lutz led the two 357th squadron flights, and today theirs would be the last strike flights on the target.

Dave Persons and his bear, Dutch Hansletter, were leading the Weasel flight, and Sam could hear them out front, trying to give the gomers hell by launching their Shrikes at the target area SAMs as they ingressed.

It sounded busy up there.

"Ford flight, we've got bogeys out at nine o'clock low," he heard Bud Lutz calling to his flight a few miles behind him. *"Keep your energy up!"*

"This is Red Dog. We count at least three SAM sites in the target area," called Dave Persons. Then in a more excited voice: *"Valid launch, Red Dogs!"*

"Ramblers, keep a good lookout for MiG's," Sam cautioned his own flight.

"Red Dog lead's hit!" called someone.

"Weeep, weeep, weeep!" came on distant beeper. Then a second one came over the radio, creating an awful cacophony. *"Weeep-eep, weeep-eep, weeep-eep."*

Sam switched off his emergency channel, to be able to hear other radio chatter.

Two strobes chattered on his radar warning gear, announcing the presence of guns and a SAM site.

Sam glanced out at three o'clock and nagged at his wingman, Rambler two, a sad-eyed lieutenant named John Radkovich, to move around more.

"Chevy three is down in the target area." It was Colonel Parker making the call.

Damn, thought Sam. So far the gomers had hammered a

Wild Weasel crew and a member of the chopper flight, and those were the first two flights in the target area.

Sam's Rambler flight made it through to the target with no SAMs fired at them, but the flak over the railroad siding was thick.

Sam went into his pop-up by feinting right, then soaring up to his left toward the offset point.

"Rambler two, swing out wider," he snapped at Radkovich, who was following too close.

"Two."

Sam topped at 12,000 feet and peered down into the smoke and dust thick over the target. Damn, but it was hard to see anything there. He looked, floated, and finally spotted the rails where they snaked into the siding. He began to wing over.

Something bright flashed at his three o'clock, and he glanced over toward his wingman.

Radkovich's Thud had been hit, half the wing torn off by 85mm flak. The wounded Thud began a constant roll.

"Bail out, Rambler two!" Sam yelled.

The canopy came off and fluttered away in the wind as the bird began to plummet.

"Eject, Rambler two!" he called. Two more 85mm rounds went off close enough to rock Sam's aircraft.

Radkovich's Thud continued downward, but there was still no chute.

"Get out!" he yelled one more time, still circling.

A strobe chattered and the SAM light illuminated, followed by the familiar, red LAUNCH light.

Sam nosed his bird over and started his dive-bomb attack on the already destroyed railroad siding.

04/1755L—Takhli RTAFB, Thailand

Sam had just finished with the debriefing when Col. B. J. Parker approached him.

"Sorry about your wingman, Sam."

Sam had never grown accustomed to losing a member of his flight. He never would.

"We've got a reporter on base, and I've got to make him happy. Seventh Air Force told him he could come out to the bases and get a story. Something about how our black officers are coping. I talked with him before we took off, but he wants to get it firsthand."

"It's not a good time, boss. Mack's gone and I'm in charge of the squadron." He also had to come down from the emotion of the combat mission.

"I know, and I told the reporter you had just landed, but he wants to get his story so he can get back to Saigon on the morning interbase flight."

Reporters were sent out to the bases every now and then by higher headquarters, and no one liked to talk with them. They kept looking for sensational stories that backed their own beliefs, and you had to stay wary and on your toes. They dealt in snapshots, quick judgments, and in quotes from "reputable sources," which was usually some enlisted clerk. Thus far Sam had avoided them.

Colonel Parker waited for his answer.

"Where is he, sir?" Sam finally growled.

"I sent him over to your squadron."

Sam left the command post and trudged back toward the 357th squadron building.

"The things a guy's gotta do for his country," he muttered.

Sam found him waiting in the pilots' lounge, which was otherwise deserted. He was a thin guy with hair down to his collar, and he wore a short-sleeved, mustard-colored outfit. The shirt had pleated pockets and military epaulets. He carried a writing pad in a weatherbeaten, brown leather cover. Sam wondered where they got their uniforms. There was probably some place in New York that sold them for outrageous prices. Either that or they bought them from Boy Scout outlets.

The guy was seated at one of the barstools in the empty room.

Sam sat down nearby. "Help you?"

The reporter glanced at his pad. "You are—ah—Marion S. Hall, the third?"

"Major Hall will suffice."

"Well, Major Hall it is then." He looked at his pad. "I see you flew a combat flight today."

"Yes."

"Is it tough?" he asked in a sympathetic voice.

"Is what tough?"

"Flying here as a black."

"It'd be tough flying here if I was pink, blue, or green."

"But it must be difficult. Your black brothers are demonstrating back in the United States, you know."

"Yeah. Some are."

"Are you saying you don't support what they're doing?"

"I didn't say that."

"Do you support them, Major Hall?"

Sam rubbed a sore spot on his cheek where the oxygen mask had chafed. "Sometimes. I'm for equality."

"But a black man here, flying for the white man's government? Isn't that difficult?"

"What are you doing? Trying to piss me off?"

"I assure you—"

"I'm a major in the United States Air Force. When I fly jets, I'm a very good fighter pilot. I'm here fighting for my country. If my country is a little screwed up about some things back home, then I'll help change it when I get there. But here I'll fight for it, because it's my country and it's at war. Something you don't ever want to do around me is poor-mouth my country. Now, is that all you've got?"

"I'm not trying to be antagonistic. I was trying to explore your perspective, that of a black officer in a white man's environment."

"I'm a major. I'm a fighter pilot. I'm an American. Forget I'm black, okay?"

The reporter read something from his notes.

"Do you believe we should mine Haiphong harbor?"

"Ask the generals," Sam snapped. "I just fly and fight."

"Surely you'd like to see changes in the way they're running the war."

"Sure. Have 'em lift the restrictions and let us fight."

The reporter was smiling and writing. "And who made those restrictions?"

"Got me. Some politician somewhere, I guess. And while you're at it, have 'em give us better targets. We'd win the war in a month or two and get to go home."

"What kind of targets would you like to bomb?"

"Airports, industry, the docks, the dikes, things like that."

The reporter nodded slyly, not writing that down. "And you're willing to drop bombs on your brown brothers in North Vietnam?"

Sam sighed, reached over and took the reporter's pad. He ripped out the top page, where the man had written his notes.

"I didn't mean to anger you, Major Hall," the reporter sputtered.

Sam stood slowly, dropped the pad back onto the bar minus the page, and forced a smile. "Is that all?"

The reporter opened his mouth to speak, but Sam raised a large, threatening finger to his face.

"I just flew to a place in North Vietnam where they're shooting like hell. I saw a kid no more than twenty-four years old get killed. A sad kid, who'd worked like hell to pay his own way through college so he could fly jets."

"And was he black?" eagerly asked the reporter.

Sam stared at him incredulously.

The reporter stared back.

."You don't really want an interview. You're just here trying to make trouble."

The reporter began to look frightened as Sam continued his withering stare. If he'd been able to read Sam's mind he would have known his feeling was warranted.

They heard loud laughing outside just as Sam thought of a proper ending for the interview. He leaned close to the reporter's face and said in a low voice, "Don't write something dumb about me or any of my friends here, or I promise you I'll get in touch with my friends at the NAACP and tell them you're a prejudiced honkie bastard. Once that word's out, you'll never get another story from a black *anywhere*."

Sam didn't know a soul connected with the NAACP. But the reporter's jaw dropped, and Sam knew he'd gotten through.

"Now, get the hell out of my squadron, because you piss me off!" he roared.

The bus had just returned from Bangkok and the Bear's wedding, and several pilots came in wearing civvies, looking hot and dusty from the ride.

Pudge Holden tried to say something to the reporter, but he was too busy trying to get out the door.

Mack came in and grinned. "How'd it go today, Sam? We still got a squadron?"

Sam went to the refrigerator and took out a beer.

07/1830L—Takhli RTAFB, Thailand

Colonel Mack

Mack had been about to leave the squadron to go to dinner
when Colonel Parker's admin sergeant rang him and told him
the wing commander required his presence at the command
post.

As Mack clapped on his go-to-hell hat and started toward
the command post, he guessed at the subject. He'd seen a silver
T-39 Sabreliner land ten minutes earlier and it had been all
shined up, like a general's aircraft.

He saw Colonel Parker entering the command post then,
and with him was the same lieutenant colonel who'd announced the attack on the first Thai Nguyen target. Mack
shook his head grimly, and continued to walk.

The same group was assembled that B. J. had brought in
before the previous *big mission* on Thai Nguyen. This time,
though, they were quieter.

The lieutenant colonel from Saigon had just made his
pitch.

"Any questions?" Parker asked the group.

"I've got one." The deputy for operations looked angry.

"Yes, sir?" asked Lieutenant Colonel Gates.

"What the hell are we doing? For ten days we've gone
back and forth to the rail siding, hitting them with everything
we've got, until now they've brought in every gun, SAM, and
MiG in North Vietnam just to protect Thai Nguyen. 'Don't hit
the damned steel mill!' they told us, so we threatened the pilots
with everything from court-martials to closing the club if they
harmed the steel mill. Now you're telling us the pilots are to
bomb the steel mill, with only a one-day pause? Goddammit!"

Mack glanced at the wing commander. Parker never
allowed this sort of arguing. Tonight, though, he simply stared
at the button colonel and waited for his answer.

"Well, sir," said Gates easily, prepared for just that
complaint, "I can't answer for the president, and this target
was directed by executive order. I can tell you that the
argument you just made was passed to CINCPAC, with an info

copy forwarded to CINCUSAF. Since I can't speak for them either, I can't answer your question, sir."

"We've lost twelve birds since we started hitting Thai Nguyen," said the maintenance colonel. "It would make more sense if we could get a few days of down time to work on the aircraft. I've had my men working fifteen-hour days to try to keep up."

"And then," growled the operations colonel again, "a week of bombing other targets so they'd move some of their damned defenses out of Thai Nguyen."

Gates looked at Colonel Parker. "Both Korat and the Navy have asked to drop the first bombs on the steel mill, sir, but the general was adamant that Takhli get first crack at it."

Silence. At times like this, Parker normally would crow about his wing's capability.

Gates continued, "Your pilots always come through with results."

Parker nodded, but did not smile as he usually did when he heard his wing applauded by headquarters.

"The general also knows you've taken considerable losses at the rail facility target, and that the enemy has built up formidable defenses at Thai Nguyen. I'm sure he'd be sympathetic if you requested to forgo being first this time and let someone else soften up the target defenses."

Parker stared back at him. "We'll be first on target, like always."

"But Colonel—" started the deputy commander for operations.

Parker pinned him with his stare. The matter was resolved and he was back to his old self. "We'll discuss it after Colonel Gates leaves." He turned back to Gates. "When you get back to Saigon, thank the general for his confidence and tell him we'll get the job done. Do you have anything else?"

"No, sir." Gates handed the Air Tasking Order to Parker and departed.

Later, when the meeting was finished, Parker kept Mack behind as he had done the previous time. Colonel Parker was going to lead the mission, so Mack wondered why.

Parker remained at the podium as the room emptied, staring at the big map of North Vietnam. Finally he turned to Mack. "What do you think?"

"It's going to be tougher than the loading facility. The

mill's a large, sturdy target. It's going to take a lot of sorties to take it all down, and they're going to fight to protect it."

"Do you think I was wrong in not asking for someone else to go first?"

Mack sighed. "That's too hard a question, Colonel. I'm paid to prepare my pilots to fly and fight."

"The DCO was right, you know. They've got half the weapons in North Vietnam gathered at Thai Nguyen to protect that one target."

"We'd have to fight it out some day, anyway. Sooner's probably better than later. And somehow I think the guys like being first. At least we've got tomorrow to prepare."

Parker nodded abruptly.

"I'd better go and make sure my men are ready."

"You do that, Mack." Parker stared at the map again, eyes riveted on the city thirty-five nautical miles due north of Hanoi. "Keep it quiet about the steel mill."

"I will, but they always seem to know when a big mission's coming."

"Well," said B. J. Parker grimly, "this time they've got a no-shit big one."

CHAPTER TWENTY-TWO

Thursday, March 9th—0440 Local, Takhli RTAFB, Thailand

Colonel Mack

Mack watched as the men filed into the mission briefing theater with their steaming coffee cups. B. J. Parker would be mission commander, but Mack had been unable to stay away. It was not morbid curiosity, but the protectiveness a commander feels when his men are in jeopardy.

They'd called in the all-star chorus, the same group that had first bombed the rail loading facility. As they came in and read the target on the board, most of them grew thoughtful and drew into themselves. There was little of the usual bantering.

When Lieutenant DeWalt entered and wrote the execution word for the Thai Nguyen steel mill, there were a few mutters. Then it grew quiet as the pilots wrote down the code words and flight information on their lineup cards. Too quiet, thought Mack. A pilot coughed and the sound seemed obscenely loud. He could hear the pencils scrawling on the cards.

Finally the Bear broke the silence. In his loud baritone, he told Benny Lewis that he wished to hell they'd change the term *EXECUTION* WORD.

A pilot told the Bear to quit acting like he could read and to go back to his comic book.

The Bear said he'd wanted to be a fighter pilot, but he couldn't qualify since his parents had been married to each other when he was born.

Duffy Spencer told his second element leader that they were going to swing around north as they exited the target area, because he'd like to look for MiG's up there.

539

Swede Swendler told Toki Takahara that he had hated fucking steel mills since he'd been a kid in Detroit, and that he'd always dreamed of bombing the damned things.

The gossiping and tactics talk grew louder, the jokes more obscene.

Tiny Bechler joked that the Bear should probably be replaced on the schedule because he was probably weak from all that honeymoon fucking.

The Bear told Tiny Bechler to yell a lot when he got shot down, because he would have his recorder going and that would add a little drama to the boring tapes.

They're okay, Mack said to himself. They'd taken their lumps at the rail facility, had lost some good comrades there. Now they were going back to Thai Nguyen, but this time they were going after a good target. That fact made the difference. Their excitement mounted, and the noise level in the room continued to rise.

A flight leader from the 354th squadron recapped some of the things they had discussed during the tactics tutorial, and that especially pleased Mack.

Lieutenant DeWalt took over the podium, waited nervously for quiet, then gave them the target overview. He briefed them that this morning they were to concentrate on bombing the southernmost building, the first huge blast furnace of the mill. When that was destroyed, they would concentrate on the middle structures. Last, they'd take out the northern building, the new blast furnace still under construction. Headquarters felt it would take numerous bombing sorties before the target was leveled.

Mack kept out of it, just watched the individual pilots in the room who were about to go out and bet their asses on a fast airplane and their skill. He decided to leave before Colonel Parker took over and the mission briefing got down to the gritty details.

Back in the big war, he'd had a commander who would get up before them now and make a speech about duty, honor, and country, about the importance of the contribution they were about to make, about how America was depending on them. In Korea, he'd had a squadron commander who led a prayer before each big mission.

Instead, Mack walked casually toward the door, then

stopped. He turned to glance around at them, then grinned and growled loudly, "Kick 'em in the ass!"

09/0500L—Thai Nguyen, DRV

Lt Col Tran Van Ngo

Yesterday's quiet, with no air strikes at Thai Nguyen, had not served to refresh Tran. He had only fretted and wondered when the Thunder planes and Intruders would return. During the ten days since he'd been placed in charge of the siting, provisioning, and care of the three full battalions of rocket batteries and dozens of artillery companies, he had worked night and day and was near exhaustion.

Official word of his promotion to lieutenant colonel had been sent from the People's Army headquarters to his make-shift office at Thai Nguyen soon after Xuan Nha had returned to Hanoi. Then Tran had craved action to show them all that the promotion was warranted. Now he longed for respite.

He was *Commandant of Area Defenses for Thai Nguyen*, of equal position with the area commanders at Hanoi, Haiphong, and Vinh. A grand title for a man who reeked of sweat, dirt, and toil like a rice farmer. For ten days he had not dared to waste time with such luxuries as bathing. He'd worked relentlessly, visiting each of the batteries, companies, and support units often, determining their needs, exhorting them all to move quickly and react boldly to Wisdom's guidance, returning to his office to plan, coordinate matters and send reports, and to capture bits of sleep. He'd ignore the others working in the room, unceremoniously unroll a mat at the corner of his office, and collapse upon it to immediately succumb to exhaustion.

Major Nguy had been promoted the same day as he, and was now *Commandant of Absolute Control*. It was a new title, meant to show the new way of things. Nguy had remained his old, steadfast self throughout the ten-day ordeal. Whenever Tran Van Ngo made yet another call for support, reliable Nguy had been there. It was unlikely that Nguy was getting more rest than he.

The combat had been obscenely frantic, yet now the calm seemed even more unnerving. Yesterday the Americans had bombed west of Hanoi and south of Haiphong, and had carefully avoided Thai Nguyen.

Was it over?

Xuan Nha had sent a short message from Hanoi, saying it was probable they had driven the Americans away. The enemy had likely counted their losses and decided the price of attacking Thai Nguyen was too high. He had intimated that the steel mill was now a less likely target, for the Americans were not as willing to give their lives for their cause. He praised the defenders at Thai Nguyen, but exhorted them to remain vigilant.

The last was unnecessary. The radar operators and rocket technicians were depressed and sick with worry about the next attack. They were made so alert by their fear that they could only sleep when utterly exhausted. Tran Van Ngo knew he should worry more about their fatigue, but he could not because he was like that himself.

In the ten days of their defense of the Thai Nguyen rail facility, three rocket batteries had been bombed unmercifully. Terror missiles had homed on and destroyed four other rocket site antenna vans and three SON-9 artillery radars, including one of the new training models brought down from Wisdom. Thirty-seven S-60 medium and eight KS-12 heavy artillery guns and their gun crews had been destroyed by bombs. Some seventy-five other guns had been damaged by cluster bombs and their crews killed.

He estimated that more than 1,400 men had been killed manning the defenses. The wounded had been taken into fields to await truck transportation as they bled from their mouths, eyes, and ears, and from terrible wounds. Tran did not know how many of those there had been. There was no official accounting, or at least none that he knew of. The Lao Dong party would not permit such pessimism. In times of military hardship they tended to hold massive victory celebrations at Ba Dinh Square in Hanoi, outside their party headquarters.

As each battery, gun, launcher, or van was destroyed, Tran Van Ngo had rushed other units in to replace them, whether in daylight or darkness, during an attack or a lull. Replacement operators and technicians were tight-lipped and nervous, some wide-eyed with fear.

Eleven men at a KS-12 85mm artillery battery had suddenly run, bolting when a Thunder plane attacked. The radar operators at a rocket battery had deserted their command van and fled when they'd come under attack by a radar-hunter. Dozens of men, at various times during the raids, had simply stopped working, curling up into protective balls on the ground.

Those who had not been summarily executed by on-scene commanders had been brought to him bound with ropes, examples of cowardice, and he had done his duty. One of them, a very young, bright radar operator who had once worked for him, had been incoherent and had trembled uncontrollably. Tran spoke soothingly to calm him before remembering that he had no reason to. He spat contemptuously then and told the party representative to shoot him with the others who had been brought to him that day.

But they had destroyed many enemy aircraft, more than ever before in such a small area and short time, and Tran forwarded daily reports of the heroism of his men, never mentioning their frailties.

Was defense of the railroad loading facility, bombed again and again after it was already destroyed, worth the loss of so many men and the shooting of once-brave soldiers?

He thought not.

They should have committed their forces more cautiously, bided their time, and waited until the Americans came to bomb the steel mill. He knew they would come, regardless of Xuan Nha's message. Now they would have no surprises for the enemy. The Americans knew what they had, for they'd laid it all out before them as they'd come back each day to drop more bombs on the mangled rail siding.

Where, Tran wearily wondered, would they drop their bombs this morning?

09/0545L—Takhli RTAFB, Thailand

Benny Lewis

He taxied into position at the end of the active runway and waited until Tiny Bechler pulled in beside. They lowered canopies, and Benny's ears popped as the cockpit began to pressurize. Throttle forward and the engine revved. His gauges were normal. Throttle to idle.

"You ready back there?" he asked.

"There you go," joked the Bear, "waking me up again."

The tower called, *"Red Dog, you're cleared for takeoff. Climb and maintain five . . ."*

He pushed the throttle forward, then outboard to A/B, and released brakes. The big fighter began to roll.

09/0620L—Thai Nguyen, DRV

Tran Van Ngo

Thirty minutes earlier observers near the two Thunder plane bases in Thailand had reported that very large numbers of aircraft were being launched with full combat loads of bombs. Their targets were unknown.

Tran told his communications officer, a lieutenant who worked at his radios set up on a table near the door, to wake him when the Americans were closer, but only if it appeared they might be coming to Thai Nguyen. He curled up on the mat and slept dreamlessly.

09/0715L—Route Pack Six, North Vietnam

Bear Stewart

They were out five miles in front of Colonel Parker's Eagle flight. He'd harped at them some, said he liked the Weasels farther out in front, but Benny and Pudge had convinced him their new tactic worked best when they were closer and they could start working over the target area defenses just as the strike force arrived. He'd relented.

Given the capability the gomers were showing with their integrated defenses, the Bear was thankful they weren't flying twenty miles out in front, like they used to do. He was not so happy, however, with what he was seeing on his scopes.

Benny had just called for the flight to split. They'd swung south, Pudge and Sloppy north, and suddenly it seemed the whole world was looking at them.

"We've got Fansongs in all directions, at seven, nine, ten,

one, and three . . . the one at ten acts serious. Tracking. Lots
of Firecans. I'm not going to call guns anymore."

"Roger."

"The SAM site at seven is probably just north of the target
area. We'll see when we turn back inbound."

"We're turning now."

09/0720L—Thai Nguyen, DRV

Tran Van Ngo

The lieutenant was shaking him. As Tran shook his head
to clear it, the communications officer returned to his table to
listen over headphones and repeat the important messages.

Tran stood and stretched, aching and still weary. The
lieutenant, looking increasingly grave, told him the Thunder
planes were crossing the great Hong valley. They had not
diverted southward as they had the day before, and now
approached the narrow, rugged ridge of mountains that on the
maps pointed like a giant finger from China to Hanoi.

The Americans were less than thirty kilometers distant
when Wisdom alerted the Thai Nguyen and Hanoi areas that
either area could come under attack.

Tran walked to the doorway of the house he'd appropri-
ated and stared out at the rugged mountains in the distance. He
could hear the lieutenant's words grow more excited. Two
Thunder planes had swung northward, two others to the south.

The radar-hunters, Tran decided. It was a new tactic some
of them had been using.

09/0723L—Route Pack Six, North Vietnam

Bear Stewart

Benny radioed, *"Red Dog lead is turning back in."*

"Red Dog three, roger and ditto," called Pudge, then,
"Red Dog three has a valid launch."

"We got activity too," the Bear said to Benny. "The site
at our one o'clock is serious."

"I've got a launch light," said Benny.

"Disregard," said the Bear. He was manually tuning and examining the signals with his sensitive and accurate receivers, a more exact procedure than the analog computer of the radar warning receiver could provide.

"The one at ten o'clock is in the target area. Line me up," said Benny.

"Come left ten degrees. There . . . you've got it on your attack scope."

Benny muttered as he tried to get the signal on his Shrike needles.

"Come left five degrees more!" said the Bear.

Benny immediately responded, then momentarily went wings level to work with his Shrike needles.

"Hurry with it, Benny. I'm blind back here when I give you a signal."

"Yeah," muttered Benny, still trying to pick out the signal with his needles. "Aha! I've got it on the Shrike now."

The Bear switched out of the blind mode and tuned to the signal. "Shit. We got a valid launch at two o'clock!"

"Red Dog lead, Red Dog two. We got missiles at two o'clock." Tiny Bechler's voice confirmed.

Benny launched the Shrike at the SAM radar he was lined up on, stood the aircraft up on the right wing, and pulled hard into the missiles.

09/0724L—Thai Nguyen, DRV

Tran Van Ngo

Tran nodded slowly at nothing, looking out at the rugged blue-gray mountains.

A terror-missile firing had been detected from the southernmost radar-hunters. Wisdom directed a rocket battery radar to shut off, another battery to fire three rockets in manual tracking mode.

He saw specks over the mountains. Turning and twisting in the sky as they grew closer, coming fast.

"Control says that Thai Nguyen is the probable target," said the lieutenant.

Wisdom was warning his area.

"Attack alert?" asked the lieutenant.

"Yes."

The lieutenant spoke into his microphone. Almost immediately sirens began to wail in the distance. The lieutenant lifted toggle switches, monitoring his several radios.

Tran watched hopefully as rockets streaked from a battery north of the city toward the distant aircraft.

09/0725L—Thai Nguyen, Route Pack Six, North Vietnam

Bear Stewart

The Bear saw a Guideline missile coming at them fast, and cringed small in the ejection seat. The missile roared past the canopy, close. A second one was approaching.

Benny continued to pull, then as quickly reversed hard left. Neither of them saw the third missile, but when enough time had passed, Benny turned back toward the target area.

The Bear glanced out. "Tiny's closing back up, looks okay."

"What's happening?"

SAMs at eleven, ah, two, six, and . . . that's eight o'clock. The one you fired at is off the air, but I don't know if you got it. My receivers act funny when we're upside down," he joked.

They heard Swede Swendler call that Hawk three had been hit and was going down. *Toki Takahara,* remembered the Bear. *Damn!*

09/0726L—Thai Nguyen, DRV

Tran Van Ngo

He watched as the specks climbed for altitude, still twisting and turning to evade the gunners below. The Thunder planes had indeed returned to Thai Nguyen. The rail yard again?

Three rockets erupted upward in ragged unison from the site twelve kilometers south of them, dropped their boosters, then sprang forward again as their sustainers fired.

The lead Thunder plane rolled onto its back, hesitated,

tucked downward, and went into its dive attack. Col. Xuan Nha was wrong. The Americans had not been frightened away.

"Control reports a Thunder plane has been shot down on the other side of the ridge."

Tran nodded vaguely, still watching as all three rockets missed the airplanes.

He watched the first two sleek fighters swooping down, then their bombs releasing, four from each airplane, flying neat and orderly formations of their own, then opening like peeled bananas and showering out bomblets that began to explode in the air as they touched one another. The bomblets would wreak havoc on his gun crews when they hit the ground and sprayed out showers of fragments.

The target was the steel mill, as he had suspected.

09/0727L—Thai Nguyen, Route Pack Six, North Vietnam

Bear Stewart

Eagle flight had delivered their CBUs to knock out the guns, and the first strike flight was in their delivery.

The Bear glanced over at the target area, saw flak in multiple layers, and aimed fire in clusters of fours and sixes up over the blankets of barrage fire. A volleyball-sized artillery round blasted up between them and Tiny.

"Jesus!" he yelled. "You see that?"

"Hundred millimeter," said Benny. "It's inaccurate."

"Thank God."

"Line me up again."

"Got one at two o'clock, going to three! Strong signal, he's about to fire at something."

Benny cranked the Thud into a hard right turn.

Pudge announced he was firing his second Shrike at a tracking SAM radar.

"Come right ten more degrees," said the Bear. "Woops, the bastard's stepped his power and he's gonna fire."

"I'm picking him up on the needles."

"Got another SAM launch at our five o'clock. Not at us! Not at us!"

"Roger. I'm shooting." Benny launched his second and

final Shrike. Now they were on the prowl for something to bomb.

"I got a visual on the SAM at five o'clock."

"SAM launch in the target area! Heads up!" radioed Benny, since no one had called the launch.

09/0727L—Thai Nguyen, DRV

Tran Van Ngo

The din of the guns was like constant thunder. White bursts from 37mm, fuses preset to common times, formed in layers. Flashes of explosions, closer to the Thunder planes, reaching out with their patterns of gray and black puffs to find the elusive fighters. Fifty-seven and eighty-five millimeter rounds.

He saw a white line against the blue background of the sky, arcing over him and downward.

Terror missiles!

"Tell Tiger one to cease transmitting!" he yelled.

Bombs erupted five kilometers away at the steel mill. First flashes and geysers of debris, a pause, then the rapid, muffled POOM-POOM-POOM-POOM-POOM-POOM sounds of the individual bombs exploding. Another series of sounds as a second group of bombs hit.

"Tiger one does not acknowledge, sir."

"Advise control that the target is the steel mill," said Tran.

He could see more of the fighters, climbing high, poising, then diving toward the steel mill.

His communications officer was in contact with Wisdom on their secondary channel. "Control has lost contact with Tiger one and Black Dragon seventeen."

One rocket and one artillery battery.

The third group of aircraft was delivering its bombs. The second of those was hit by tracking artillery fire, jettisoned its bombs, and flew erratically, almost drunkenly, back toward the mountains.

The house was constantly trembling, occasionally shaking violently, from explosions, concussive waves, and noise. The lieutenant was white-gilled with fear as he listened and spoke on his radios.

Good for you. Lieutenant. Does your concentration on your radios give you your only excuse for not running? Yes? Then, you are human.

09/0730L—Thai Nguyen, Route Pack Six

Bear Stewart

They were well south of the target area now, but the defenses were still relentless.

"See the site?" asked the Bear. They were staring out at the southern suburbs of Thai Nguyen.

"I'm looking. Oh hell! Is that it? Yeah."

The Bear looked in the general direction. Flak flooded the sky there. He hesitated before allowing himself to breathe.

"Yeah, me too," said Benny.

"Get the bastard," said the Bear finally, his voice thick.

"Let's give it a go. Ready?"

"Get him."

Benny turned hard, pulling more than six g's, then bent it back in the other direction. They were both groaning and puffing, g-suits swollen tight with air, pushing back the blood trying to go to their guts and legs.

More gentle jinking then, so Benny could make his call.

"South of the city, Red Dog two. See the smoke?"

"I got it!" said Bechler.

"I'm going left, you swing right. Low angle attack, no pop-up."

"Red Dog two reads you." The Bear watched Bechler jink out to the right. With all the guns firing, it would have been deadly to follow them down the same chute.

The SAM and LAUNCH lights illuminated. The Bear quickly examined the signal on his receivers. "Ignore the launch."

"Roger." They were in a shallow, thirty-degree dive-bomb attack.

Radio calls. Another aircraft shot down, this one by the furious flak over the target.

Benny pickled, the aircraft jolted and became lighter as

the weapons released. He slammed the throttle forward and jinked off right, over downtown Thai Nguyen in burner.

Flak in blankets, angry lines of tracers.

Benny lowered the nose of the aircraft and swung left. They were low, a couple of hundred feet over the rooftops, and going fast. A fuzzy-looking bubble of air appeared over the cockpits, the effect created when the Coke-bottle shape of the Thud approached supersonic speed in the humid air of North Vietnam.

"Whooo-weee," yelled the Bear. No one could harm them this low and fast. "We're in-vin-cible!"

Benny agreed. "We just went supersonic. Must be mighty noisy down there on the ground."

"Well don't stop to ask," said the Bear. "Hope we're breaking a few eardrums."

Tran Van Ngo

"Steel three has been attacked by a radar-hunter," said the lieutenant.

"Try to regain contact and get a damage report," Tran snapped.

Guided rockets, these from north of them. Speeding upward and past the flights of fighters. Up, up, until they were out of sight. Tiny white blossoms high above, where they exploded harmlessly.

09/0733L—Thai Nguyen, Route Pack Six

Bear Stewart

They heard a radio call. Swede Swendler's voice. He'd been hit over the target and was talking on the radio to his wingman.

"*Hawk lead,*" called the wingman, "*you're burning.*"

"*Aw shit,*" were the last words of Swede Swendler.

"*Hawk lead's airplane just came apart!*" yelled the excited wingman. A pause, then a leaden voice. "*He didn't get out.*"

Tran Van Ngo

More rockets crossed above from east of them, one narrowly missing the first aircraft in the next group as it was rolling on its back to begin its attack. Tran could see the aircraft shudder, try to correct itself, and torch brightly, still flying. Then, with suddenness, the aircraft came apart in the sky. It fell to earth in two separate groups of pieces.

Again and again the aircraft would appear over the hill, twisting and turning, soaring, diving, and unleashing their bombs.

More guided rockets swept through the sky.

"Black Dragon twenty-four is not responding," droned the lieutenant.

Another artillery radar destroyed. He remembered that the men of that radar had been chained to their positions, for they had been acting suspiciously nervous in the face of the attacks.

09/0734L—Thai Nguyen, Route Pack Six

Bear Stewart

"I see Tiny up at our eleven o'clock," said the Bear, squinting. A lone Thud was jinking furiously, headed back toward Thud Ridge.

"I see him," said Benny. He radioed Tiny that they were coming up on his right.

Benny had slowed somewhat, but they were still flying close to the Mach and the bubble was still there.

They slid past Tiny's wing. Tiny dropped back and flew off of their lead.

Another SAM launch, this one at Sparrow, Max Foley's flight, the last strike flight. Max called the launch, but they just continued their attack and the missiles missed. His number four was hit by flak. Foley and the rest of Sparrow flight joined protectively around number four and they started out of the target area.

Benny flew a couple miles back and to the left of Sparrow flight, trying to stay between them and the worst threats.

Tran Van Ngo

The sky grew empty and the firing diminished.

"Control reports another group of aircraft on their way across the Hong valley," said the lieutenant. His voice was quavering, and Tran could smell his fear. It smelled like fresh feces.

He spoke to calm the lieutenant, for he did not wish to shoot another of his men.

09/0734L—Red River Valley, Route Pack Six

Bear Stewart

Someone ahead called that he'd seen a MiG. The Bear looked around carefully as they ventured back over Thud Ridge and out over the valley, finally flying west toward safety.

"Wonder how the guys did on the target," he asked Benny.

"I heard one guy say part of the mill was down. I tried to see, but there was too much smoke and dust to tell much."

The mood of the strike force was strange, quiet.

They watched as the great formation from Korat, thirty-six Thuds in a single huge gaggle, approached from the west. Their combined jamming from their ECM pods caused static to buzz and hiss in the Bear's receivers. Only the Korat Weasels flew apart from the big formation.

The Korat bunch was past, and they could hear them calling flak and SAM launches. The Bear was amazed that the gomers had been able to reload missiles so quickly. One thing was damned sure. They had whittled down the defenses for them.

"It's bad back there, Bear."

"Yeah, but we did okay, made things a little easier for the strike guys." A pause. "I sure hate that about Toki and Swede."

It was obvious that the gomers had concentrated their defenses around Thai Nguyen. The receivers showed a bevy of signals back at their rear quadrant, little where they were flying.

Bear picked up a weak, distant Fansong at eight o'clock and a Firecan AAA radar at their twelve o'clock. He begrudgingly called the AAA threat. "Expect flak in a minute or two," he said. "Tracking Firecan at twelve o'clock."

The strike force had climbed to 10,000 feet, so the AAA threat was not really a big deal. Not after what they had faced back there.

"The gomers were tough today," said Benny.

"Yeah," replied the Bear. "But you know, they threw everything they had at us, and our guys still hit the target. They showed us what they've got, Benny. Now it's our turn to show them a thing or two."

11/1500L—People's Army HQ, Hanoi, DRV

Xuan Nha

"Two more Americans shot down," Xuan told General Luc.

Luc nodded. He was aging before them at the command center. He had lived there with Xuan Nha these past three days. Watching quietly, somberly, as reports of the destruction of the steel mill continued to mount.

The south buildings were down, the blast furnace that had been Ho's first great success in his industrialization and modernization program had been bombed to rubble.

Several times each day General Giap's and General Dung's offices called for status reports to be given the Lao Dong party, to Pham Van Dong's government ministers, and even to the increasingly ill and fragile Enlightened One.

A rumor had it that the Enlightened One sank deeper into his melancholy as each dark report about the steel mill was given to him. That he was acting like all was falling apart about him, and his life's work had been for naught.

Another rumor. Yesterday Colonel Huu, on Giap's staff, had presented a report that the modern refinery south of Haiphong had been heavily damaged by intense shelling from two American warships. Huu had been singled out by the Enlightened One as the culprit causing his misery. The refinery, built with the help of the Russians two years before, had been feted as one of the industrial successes of the

Democratic Republic. The colonel had been sent away by General Giap to join a unit fighting in the south as a private soldier.

Xuan decided to ask Li Binh if there was truth to that report. Their relationship had been strained during the past nights and he wondered if she would tell him even if she knew.

He was most interested, that was the proper word, *interested,* in the fact that no one had yet laid blame at his own feet. He was in control of Wisdom and all ground defenses, had given the generals hope that they could fend off the attackers. He wondered why the powerful ones had not confronted him.

He stood and walked over to Lt Quang Hanh's side at the communications desk.

"Losses?"

"Two Black Dragon battery radars," said the lieutenant. "No report yet on the status of Steel two rocket battery, east of Thai Nguyen. Wisdom lost communications with them almost an hour ago, during the last attack. It may be radio failure."

"Perhaps. Two Thunder planes down?"

"Perhaps one. It is now thought that two units may have reported the same aircraft kill. They are trying to sort it out now."

"Tell them to stop trying. Two were shot down."

"Yes, comrade Colonel." Quang Hanh wrote on the report he was preparing.

"Damage to the target?"

"Colonel Tran Van Ngo will forward that information in fifteen minutes, sir. We know that the large derrick at the center of the buildings was damaged, and that several of the adjacent workshops were destroyed. Nothing more yet."

Xuan grunted, thought about it all, then returned to the commandant's table.

"Anything new?" asked General Luc.

"Two aircraft destroyed, as we thought. My forces have suffered some losses, but not bad ones."

"The steel mill?"

"Damage to the crane and central buildings. We don't have a final report yet."

General Luc looked hopeful. "If the second blast furnace is not destroyed, the Minister of Industry says he will still be able to produce steel. He reported that to First Minister Pham Van Dong."

"Yes, comrade General," said Xuan Nha. "My forces are

doing everything possible to save what has not already been destroyed."

"Everything possible?" Luc glanced at him.

Now, thought Xuan, it will come.

But General Luc went back to reading another report, and carried the matter no farther.

He heard the sounds of chairs scraping.

Colonel-General Dung had entered the command center, and noise in the large room quickly fell to a hush as everyone stood. General Luc bowed sharply to the waist, and the others followed his lead.

"Return to your work," growled Dung. He looked fresh and prepared, as if there were no problems in the world. He wore the dark-green field uniform he preferred over the whites some of the other generals wore.

"Colonel Nha," he said, and beckoned.

Xuan Nha hurried forth, knocking over a pad and pencils as he brushed the table, and followed the general out the door.

General Dung was silent as they strode along, Xuan following in the midst of the general's entourage of aides and assistants.

They stopped at one of the smaller military intelligence offices.

"Clear that room," Dung barked, and an assistant went in and herded out three baffled men in sweat-darkened work uniforms.

"The rest of you wait," the general said quietly. He motioned for Xuan Nha to join him.

Xuan went in with him and closed the door behind them.

General Dung relaxed, leaned back, and rested his buttocks on a desktop. He tapped two cigarettes from a pack of Salems, and lit them, handing one to Xuan Nha.

They smoked quietly, creating a fog in the poorly ventilated room. Two soldiers, relaxing together.

Xuan Nha knew his time had come to face the consequences of not winning. He vowed to exit with dignity, and felt strangely serene.

"Congratulations," said Dung finally, "on shooting down so many enemy aircraft with your forces, Xuan Nha."

Xuan shrugged, as if it were a small thing. "I have done my best."

"Certainly you have. We all know that." He waved the

hand dangling the cigarette, scattering ashes. "Everyone. Giap. Van Dong. Me. We all know. We gave you an impossible task."

Xuan Nha remained quiet. He wondered if the general would do it himself, perhaps with his own side arm. That would be an honor.

"I knew," said Dung in a calculating and quiet tone, "that the steel mill would be bombed since the first day the American fighters came to destroy the railroad loading facility. It's their way. They nibble cautiously, as if they do not understand the psychology of war. One nibble, then draw back to see our reaction, then another nibble."

Dung shook his head before continuing.

"If their leaders were half as brave as their pilots and soldiers, even if they listened to them, the war would have been over almost before it began. Thankfully the Washington leaders are cautious and fearful men."

Xuan Nha smiled.

"You are a brave and intelligent man, Xuan Nha. You have an understanding of these new weapons of war that the rest of us do not. You're a man of many talents, and furthermore you are a fine patriot. You've proven all those things in your years of service."

Xuan Nha felt a wave of exhilaration.

"You could not have imagined that the Americans would persevere and continue to attack in the face of such losses. You should not feel ashamed."

Xuan bowed his head, feeling the glow of a child bringing home good marks from *école*. Not perfect marks, though.

"Just now I need such a man as you, Xuan Nha."

"I have always been your faithful servant, sir."

"Have you heard of what has happened to Colonel Huu, General Giap's staff officer?"

The colonel who was reported to have been sent to the south as a common private!

"I know him vaguely, sir," said Xuan.

"Yesterday the Enlightened One was seen to grow angry with him, to blame him for what has happened at the refinery near Haiphong. General Giap sent Huu to the south, to fight as a private soldier."

Xuan Nha nodded. "I heard that rumor."

"It is true." Dung smiled mirthlessly then. "Within reason

it is true. Huu will go south, but once there, he will help to establish a new headquarters. Three months from now, Colonel Huu will quietly be placed in charge of an elite regiment, the 320C."

Xuan Nha understood only that Huu had taken the blame, as contrived by the general staff. It was too political for Xuan to accept as right, but he understood. He did not even wonder if the rest of the story was true, whether the scapegoat was to rise from the ashes. Huu had been dishonored, and that was the worst thing imaginable for a proud soldier.

"The Enlightened One will not live much longer, Xuan Nha. He grows weaker and more foolish every day. A sick man. Control of the government is already passing to Secretary-General Le Duan, with the secret support of most of the politburo members. General Giap and Pham Van Dong will continue to be the key advisers when Ho Chi Minh is gone."

General Dung stubbed his cigarette out on the desktop, pausing and looking thoughtful.

Xuan Nha wondered what it was all about. It did not seem that Dung was going to shoot him. Had he been spared?

Dung regarded Xuan Nha. "The Enlightened One does not go easily. He is very aware of what is happening, and no one is silly enough to lie to him. So . . . until he passes, much emphasis will remain on his foolish, showplace industrialization projects. I tell you, the man is fanatical about two things, reunification and industrialization. To him both are equally important."

He drew out two more cigarettes, lit them and passed one to Xuan.

"He is shielded from the worst truths about the damage at the steel mill. When the destruction is completed by the Americans, Vo Nguyen Giap fears that he will not be able to accept it graciously, that he may resort to something foolish, like calling for negotiations with the Americans before we are ready. So . . . we need another brave man, Xuan Nha."

Xuan nodded, very slowly, letting the smoke of the cigarette curl up into his face.

"General Giap's man, Colonel Huu, was the last one. He will be publicly disgraced, harshly so, and sent on to the south."

"Harshly?"

"He will be paraded about Ba Dinh Square with placards about his neck. You've seen it done."

"To traitors."

"Yes."

"And me, comrade General?"

General Dung sighed. "Perhaps not even so gentle a public disgrace as Huu will receive, Xuan Nha. The Enlightened One must be able to take his wrath out for the loss of his precious steel mill, which he treasured far greater than the refinery. That is why I personally picked you, because of your courage and your great patriotism."

Xuan Nha tried to keep his composure. Roaring sounded in his ears. Could he beg the general? Would that change his fate, which to Xuan was certainly far worse than death?

"When?" Xuan Nha whispered.

"Not right away. I want you to go up to your Wisdom complex and take personal charge of things. Such an action might be appropriate in this time of turmoil. Perhaps when we return to the command center, you should announce that you will go up there to personally control the defenses and save the rest of the mill from destruction."

Xuan Nha was still numb.

"Then, in a week or two when the entire mill is destroyed, we will tell the Enlightened One that you were responsible for the loss of the mill. Perhaps we will be able to focus his disappointment upon you, as we did yesterday with Colonel Huu."

Xuan remembered the feeling he'd had when he had been a child happily coming to Hanoi to join his family, only to find that they detested him. He'd been an outcast, feeling blame for something he'd not done. He'd rejected them and had come to realize the Lao Dong party and the Viet Minh were his true family. He'd risked his life for them, lived for them, been accepted and called a model son. The Tiger of Dien Bien Phu.

"You will be recalled to Hanoi," continued General Dung. "Here you will be called to task before the Enlightened One, and perhaps you should even argue that your way was right. We will then strip you of your command and rank, humiliate and reeducate you, and then send you to the south to fight as a common soldier."

The general spoke positively, as if it were already decided. The buzzing grew louder in Xuan's ears.

"But not so in truth, Xuan Nha. General Giap and I will know, as will Le Duan and Pham Van Dong. No others, of course. To us you will be the greatest of heroes. You will go to the south and establish defenses for our forces. The fighters, dragon planes, and helicopters pose a great problem for us there. Then, when the Enlightened One dies, you will return to Hanoi as a hero. At that time you will replace General Luc, in command of the Army of National Defense. Do not fear. It will all be properly contrived and there will be no mistakes. You are too valuable, Xuan Nha."

"Li Binh?" Xuan breathed. "May I tell her?"

Van Tien Dung, the peasant who had risen to become a general through his wit, intelligence, and ability to inspire and manipulate subordinates, smiled graciously. "Not yet. When it happens, I will personally tell her and make certain that she understands fully. That I promise you as a fellow soldier, Xuan Nha. Until then, there should be no one except you and me to know."

CHAPTER TWENTY-THREE

Friday, March 17th—0425 Local, Takhli RTAFB, Thailand

B. J. Parker

The wing had bombed Thai Nguyen for seven of the past eight days. They'd been the first to bomb the target, and they were the unit used most persistently by higher headquarters.

Thus far sixteen aircraft had been lost bombing the Thai Nguyen steel mill. Nine strike pilots were either captured, dead, or missing. Two Weasel crews had been lost, none recovered. Of the five strike pilots rescued, two were injured. Two more aircraft class-26'ed, another badly damaged but fixable, seven more lightly damaged by flak.

At first they'd averaged two or three losses on each round-trip mission to the steel mill, but as time went on they lost fewer.

Although they'd faced the most dense concentration of sophisticated weaponry ever encountered by aircraft, they had been able to persevere. Most of the steel mill complex had been destroyed. All that remained standing was part of the new, northernmost building that housed the second blast furnace.

Was it worth it?

How the hell was a dumb-shit fighter jock colonel supposed to know?

B. J. Parker turned off his office light and walked out, toward the command post. Mack was going to lead the strike today, try to knock down the remainder of that last big building.

He found Mack worrying over maps and poststrike photos of Thai Nguyen. B. J. stared up at the lineup board.

561

"Max Foley's tail-end-Charlie again," said Mack, also looking up. "He likes it, says he sees more MiG's back there."

"That's how he got his MiG," said B. J. "I see Benny and Pudge Holden are flying together again."

"Four times over the last four days," said Mack. "They alternate leading, but the way they split their flight it doesn't matter much anyway. They're doing well at keeping the defenses busy. Yesterday they flew the afternoon go and there were no losses at all. I hope to hell we can match that today."

"So what's your pitch about this morning?"

Each time Mack led a mission he gave out one of his philosophies on flying combat, being effective, and surviving to fly another day.

"Too many of our losses at Thai Nguyen have been number two or number four. I think some of the wingmen are following right down the same chute as their lead, and when the gomers shoot at the guy in front, they're getting the guy behind him. I'm going to remind them to jink out wide and come in from odd directions to confuse the gunners."

B. J. nodded. These were things you learned from experience. Too many of the young pilots flying on the wing weren't lasting long enough to gain that benefit.

Some of the pilots were beginning to arrive in the briefing theater, taking their seats and sipping coffee from paper cups.

Bear Stewart shuffled by, cup clutched in one hand, his flight plan and lineup card in the other. He wore sunglasses, although it was still dark outside.

"Bear!" called Parker in a gruff tone.

Stewart turned and faced him coolly, sipping his coffee.

"Why the hell are you wearing sunglasses?" He'd wondered before.

That caused the Bear to fidget and look uncomfortable.

"Well?"

"They're corrected, sir. I wear corrected lenses so I can see."

"Don't you have any clear glasses?"

"Yes, sir."

"Why don't you wear them instead of sunglasses?"

"Same reason Sam Hall always wears the same cruddy boots when he flies, even though he's got two new pair. Same reason some people wear a Saint Christopher's medal and some wear the same old holey gloves when they're flying. And the same reason everyone's started growing a mustache and nobody's shaving them off. I've worn sunglasses to every mission briefing since I got here. This is my eighty-fifth mission, so I guess I'll wear 'em fifteen more times, sir."

The Bear nodded politely and went to find a seat.

Mack was grinning. "We're certainly not a superstitious group, are we?"

"I've carried the same dog tags since I started flying. You?"

"I carry a silk scarf in my flight-suit pocket. Started out bright blue, but now you can hardly tell what color it is. I can't even remember what the girl looked like who gave it to me, but I wouldn't fly combat without the scarf."

B. J. looked over where the Bear sat, slouched down with his hands laced over his chest, sunglasses hiding his eyes. "I wonder what would happen if the Bear didn't wear his sunglasses to a briefing?"

"Probably half the guys would think up reasons for not flying." Mack chuckled. "Hell, I don't know if I'd want to."

"I'm not superstitious, mind you, but me either."

Lieutenant DeWalt came in with the execution word. As all had suspected, they were returning to the Thai Nguyen steel mill.

17/0625L—Wisdom Rocket Site, DRV

Xuan Nha

Xuan Nha had acted like a man sleepwalking since coming to Wisdom. He was unable to concentrate upon the attack problems, unable to care much about the controllers who gave their instructions to the ground and air forces.

The steel mill had been all but leveled. Only a single corner of the northern walls of the building housing the second blast furnace was standing. The rest was twisted and mangled steel and ever-smaller chunks of concrete. He received the damage reports listlessly.

Following the previous day's reports, he'd realized that his time was up, and tried to mentally prepare himself for the trip to Hanoi, the confrontation, the loss of everything.

He had tried, with all his mental resources he had tried, but he could not bring himself to accept it.

The previous afternoon he'd brought Quang Hanh with him from the command-and-control center to the experimental rocket battery. Nicolaj Gregarian had also come to proudly show off the improvements his Soviet technicians had made to the system since they'd used it to shoot down the Pesky plane and the attacking radar-hunter.

Xuan had listened to the explanations of the electro-optic system, stared at the television images on the cathode-ray tube, slewed the great antenna with its attached videcon sensor, and since it was a clear day, had even used the television to watch the Thunder planes attacking the steel mill. He had been able to see the columns of smoke as the American bombs broached the few remaining tanks of fuel there.

The Thunder planes had been forty kilometers distant, and it was impossible to get the optical system to seize and track using video contrasts.

"If they were ten kilometers closer," boasted Gregarian, "there would be no trouble with it."

"And the radar remains off?" asked Xuan Nha, showing a glimmer of interest.

"All tracking may be done with the optical system. Before you fire missiles, the missile tracking beam and data-link must be activated, but otherwise there is nothing for them to detect."

"Perfect for use against the radar-hunters," Xuan said.

"My concept has been accepted by PVO Strany," said Gregarian proudly. "All future surface-to-air rocket systems will be equipped with dual tracking modes such as this."

"You will be well received when you go back home this summer," said Xuan Nha, feeling low. He was to be disgraced and this *Tay* pig would be honored. What an unjust world it was.

There were two elite teams, one Russian and the other Vietnamese People's Army, trained to man the command van of the special rocket site. Its only use was to protect the Wisdom command-and-control center. All training had been suspended at the rocket site, for Thai Nguyen had been deemed too close to Wisdom, and they did not dare to risk compromise and discovery.

The two teams, Russian and Vietnamese, alternated

shifts. The Russians worked from noon until midnight, the Vietnamese team took over until the next noon.

It galled Xuan Nha to think of these elite teams watching the battle to the south, yet carefully remaining out of the fight. They were prepared to give nothing and live their fat lives up here, pampered and isolated from the violence.

With all those thoughts in mind he started pacing, his mind churning with emotion.

Before Gregarian had departed the previous evening, to hurry off to the *Tay* sow Xuan had given him, he asked if Xuan Nha would like to accompany him for an evening meal.

Xuan ignored him and walked away, out of the oversized command van to pace the grounds of the rocket site. A short time later, Quang Hanh came out to find him, and Xuan had denied him permission to go to sleep.

"Keep me informed of what is happening," he growled. "That is why you are here, Lieutenant."

At 0100 he was still awake, prowling around in the command van, when Quang Hanh told him that Intruder aircraft were attacking the steel mill once again. He went out, watched guided rockets soaring in the distant sky, then went back inside and listened carefully to reports of the attack.

Tomorrow the summons would surely come for him to proceed to Hanoi.

Although footsore and weary, he continued to pace, once walking completely around the four-kilometer perimeter of the site, and when the sun peeked over the eastern horizon he stood staring at the glowing sky and knew what he must do.

Gregarian was away in his small sequestered villa five kilometers south, and his Russian rocket team were in the adjacent barracks he'd had built for them there. Only the Vietnamese rocket team was in place at the special site. Good.

One last kill! He would go to Hanoi to face his tormentors with the dignity of knowing that he was still the best.

The radar-hunters had attacked his rocket battalions so relentlessly the past weeks that the men of the rocket batteries were beginning to think them invincible. He would show them that they could win. That they could destroy the Americans, even the radar-hunters, and be untouched themselves. When he had done that, Xuan would go to Hanoi and dutifully face the wrath of the Enlightened One, the generals, and the people.

He strode into the double-sized command van and haughtily looked about, hands upon his hips, feeling the old satisfaction of being in control of both himself and his surroundings.

Lieutenant Hanh came to his feet, blinking sleep from his eyes.

"A warrior must remain alert at all times," Xuan growled. He wished he had promoted Quang Hanh to senior lieutenant. Perhaps there would be time before he was called.

"Where are the Americans this morning?" he demanded.

Quang Hanh sat back down to work with his radios.

Xuan motioned to the captain in the engagement commander's seat. "Move. I will take over."

He sat, tried to get the feel of it. He examined the familiar radar apparatus, then peered at the optical system. "I may need some help with that," he said to the captain.

The captain sat beside him in an instructor's seat, eager to please.

Xuan donned the headset and flipped up all the toggle switches on the communications panel.

"*Change of command,*" he announced into the microphone. "*Engagement commander is now Colonel Xuan Nha. All positions will check in and give their operational status.*"

The four rocket launcher team commanders reported, one at a time. Rockets were loaded and checked. The radar technician reported from the adjacent antenna van, which housed the electronics and supported the two massive antennas. Radar system checked. Optical system bore-sited and checked.

Quang Hanh reported over the intercom. "Thirty-six Thunder planes have crossed the Hong River and are proceeding across the valley. The anticipated target is the Thai Nguyen area. Target area commander has been alerted. Eight minutes, twelve seconds until they arrive at Thai Nguyen, comrade Colonel."

Xuan selected ENGAGEMENT RADAR WARM-UP. That would take five minutes. He should have done that when he first took the seat, he chided himself. He turned to one side and looked at the P-2 acquisition radar's auxiliary scope.

The anticipation of impending action excited him, got his juices flowing as they had not in months.

Nothing yet on the auxiliary scope. The aged P-2 radars

were cantankerous, but he thought they would likely be able to discern the attacking aircraft as they came over the ridge.

He sat back and waited.

The captain he had replaced looked uneasy. "Since we are prohibited from turning the engagement radar on, comrade Colonel, I usually just warm up the optics and the beacons."

"Today we shall shoot down some American aircraft, and we may wish to use the radar as well as optics."

The captain's jaw drooped. "Shoot them down? But—"

"That is why we are living and breathing, Captain. To fight the enemy and shoot down their airplanes. Would you prefer to be in the south, fighting our weak cousins and the Americans on the ground?"

Xuan Nha reached for the red cover, lifted it, and turned the wafer switch to FULL ALERT. He activated the siren system by pushing an adjacent button. Loud Klaxon horns sounded outside, alerting the men of impending action.

The captain looked appalled. "But, comrade Colonel. We are told not to turn *anything* on unless so ordered by Control. We are to remain covert."

"Captain, it is I who tells Wisdom what to do."

The captain nodded, very slowly. Was it fear Xuan saw there?

"Let's just sit back and wait now, until we find a suitable target."

"Aircraft are two and a half minutes away from the target," Quang Hanh relayed.

"Optical sensor is ready," said the dubious captain. "Radar is warmed and ready, in dummy load."

The rocket control officer, a senior lieutenant, was beside them now, having heard about the possibility of action. The captain motioned for him to take his position at the rocket control panel. The senior lieutenant looked eager, and Xuan Nha felt instant kinship.

"Control reports two aircraft north of the target area and two to the south, comrade Colonel." said Quang Hanh.

Xuan Nha felt alive. The radar-hunters had arrived.

He watched the acquisition scope carefully, found the targets, then took the target tracking handles and slewed the engagement antennas southward, looking closely at the television monitor.

"Here, sir," said the captain. He reached over and

selected X2 magnification, and they had a panoramic view of the distant mountains. Then he picked X5 for a closer view.

They could see two specks with wings moving smoothly in the distance, just above the mountains.

"Hello," said Xuan Nha.

"More magnification, sir?"

"Not quite yet."

The aircraft grew closer, climbing.

One of the batteries had launched rockets. They saw the rockets enter their field of view, moving upward at the radar-hunters.

The two aircraft waited, poised upside down. Then, when the first rocket seemed impossibly close, maneuvered violently toward it. The rocket could not match the maneuver and skidded past.

Xuan Nha watched closely then as the radar-hunters easily avoided the second and third rockets. He vowed they would not as easily escape the ones he launched.

"Control says that Steel two is under attack," said Quang Hanh.

The two distant aircraft reversed one more time and went swooping downward to bomb a target.

"When they turn back this way," Xuan muttered to the captain, "we shall turn on the radar and try to draw them closer. Then we shall shut down the radar and shoot them down with the optics. That way the radar-hunters cannot attack us, for they will not know where we are."

The captain nodded, getting caught up in the game, as Xuan had intended. "But if they turn south instead?"

"I feel it," said Xuan Nha, tapping his barrel chest, "in here. They will turn north. I also feel that we are about to create some American widows." His mouth curled into a grin.

The Thunder planes released their weapons, then disappeared from view for a moment. Xuan watched the first of the two reappear. Finally they saw the second one. The Thunder planes had turned north, toward Wisdom.

"More magnification," ordered Xuan Nha, and the two aircraft grew in size on the monitor. "More. Good. Now, get ready to turn on the radar. I'll want full power. We will entice them, and then kill them."

Nicolaj Gregarian

The pudgy French girl had awakened him, asking in a fearful voice what the noise was about. He'd staggered to his feet and gone to the window, peering out at the morning and listening to the distant Klaxon horns.

The horns sounded three times, paused, then sounded three times again. Over and over they sounded. *Prepare for attack!*

He scrambled into his clothing, wondering if the Americans had somehow found the site.

He needed a radio to call the rocket command van and find out what was happening. Colonel Nha had kept the utility vehicle with the VHF radio. He remembered then that one of the trucks used by the Soviet rocket team, barracked next door, had a radio.

He hurried outside, still pulling on his shirt, then ran at a trot toward the Soviet advisers' barracks.

A *kapitan* and a *starshiy leytenant* were already in the cab of the truck with the radio, warming the engine. Nicolaj scrambled up and crawled in the passenger's seat beside the *kapitan*.

"Comrade *Mayor*, what is happening?" asked the *kapitan*.

Noncommissioned and warrant officers were emerging from the barracks, yawning and looking off in the direction of the rocket site.

"Tell the men to get aboard, then put me onto the frequency with the rocket battery command van!" demanded Nicolaj, ignoring their questions. "We shall go to the site and find out what the Vietnamese are up to. I just hope the fools are doing nothing to jeopardize the site."

17/0637L—North of Thai Nguyen, Route Pack Six, North Vietnam

Bear Stewart

They came off the target hot and fast, knowing they'd hit with the CBUs.

Tracers were tracking them, moving like hoses through

the sky, but always behind them or beside them, for they were an elusive target.

They left the worst of it and turned up on a wing to watch the site being pummeled by their CBUs, dancing and glittering about the site's periphery, torching off two missiles and causing them to slither wildly about. An explosion at one side of the site. A fireball where the bomblets had hit a stack of missile boosters.

Tiny Bechler had gone down the chute off to one side, and was now raising hell on the radio because his bombs hadn't released. He'd screwed up by not having his master arm switch in the proper position.

"*Red Dog two is going back up for reattack, lead,*" called Tiny, wanting to atone for his error by going back into the maelstrom.

"*Negative!*" ordered Benny. "*We're at your nine o'clock. Join up, two.*"

"Not bright," growled the Bear.

"A dumb mistake," concurred Benny. "Situation?"

"SAMs at four and six. Lots of gun radars."

"Ah roger," breathed Benny into his mike.

They were soaring higher, waiting for Tiny to catch up.

"I'll dedicate my part of that site to Mike Murphy," said the Bear. "It's Saint Patty's day."

"We'll turn back inbound toward the target area," said Benny, "and launch a Shrike."

They were at the northern portion of rugged Thud Ridge, close to the ridge now so they would be masked from radars by the mountain.

A new SAM radar erupted onto the air, powerful and close by.

"Hold your course," said the Bear. "I've got something new. A Fansong at two o'clock, Benny." He tuned the receiver. "Looks like it may be in the Chinese buffer zone, but it's too powerful to be far. Crazy, but I think the thing is tracking us."

"We're too close to the ridge for him to be tracking," said Benny. "Maybe he just he has his antenna pointed this direction."

"Nope. He's keeping us centered, like he's slewing his antennas." The Bear continued to work with the dual beams of the radar. "We're centered in both beams."

"Either he's awfully lucky," said Benny, "or they've got something new. Neither one gives me a warm feeling."

"Hot damn. The signal just went off. Bang, like that." The Bear was puzzled, for the ACTIVITY light had illuminated on his warning panel, indicating a SAM missile guidance beam had been turned on.

Which was crazy, because there was no Fansong tracking radar signal, which meant that this was not an ordinary situation at all.

"Something's going on out there, Benny. Watch out for this one."

"Roger." Suddenly Benny soared up, away from the protection the ridge normally offered. They were well north of the target area now.

Tiny was tucked in at their right wing, close.

"Red Dog two, drop back and cross over on our port wing. I want you well clear, so you can help me look out at our two o'clock."

"Roger, Red Dog lead." Tiny dropped back out of the Bear's view.

"I just saw a missile launch," said Benny, breathing hard into the mask in anticipation. "There's a second one."

They waited for a third, but none was forthcoming.

The firings had come from a forested area several miles distant.

"SAMs at two o'clock, Red Dog lead," called Tiny.

"Ah roger, two. Keep dropping back and try to keep an eye on the site while I dodge the missiles."

"Red Dog two."

The missiles had picked up a head of steam and were charging toward them. They had soared up to 10,000 feet. Benny waited, kept the throttle pushed up, and tipped the Thud up slightly on the right wing.

The Bear watched the missiles coming, his mind racing, eyes darting back inside the cockpit periodically to see if the signal would reappear on the analysis scope. The scope was working normally with all the other radars. Why not this one?

Things moved in slow motion.

The missiles were still relatively distant when Benny sharply nosed over, selected afterburner, and shoved the throttle full forward.

The Bear was thrown against the canopy, glued there until

they had settled into a steep dive. He fumbled around to find the seat-belt straps and pulled himself snugly into the ejection seat, eyes still glued on the two SAMs. The missiles had adjusted their tracks smoothly. The maneuver had done nothing to create error in either one.

"Jesus!" yelled Benny into the mike. He normally could outfox the first missile with the dive maneuver, then yank up on the stick to evade the others.

The fuzzy bubble appeared. They were still in afterburner, and, slipping through the Mach, continued to accelerate.

Benny abruptly pulled ten degrees up, and the aircraft slid wildly through the air, stubby wings grasping for lift.

The missiles adjusted smoothly.

"Oh, shit!" yelled Benny.

The first missile was close. Benny yanked the stick toward it.

It slid by, exploding just beyond.

Benny pulled harder.

The second missile narrowly missed, exploding just as it passed them.

Benny recovered the airplane in a long arc, breathing hard into his mask, and soared upward for altitude. Heading toward the Chinese border.

The Bear realized something was amiss.

"Benny?"

Silence. He could hear the strike force talking on the radio.

"Benny!" he yelled.

"Yeah." His voice was small.

"Aren't we gonna kill the bastard?"

Silence, then a long, shuddering sigh. Benny slowly turned the aircraft back southward.

They both realized that Red Dog two had said something. Something about losing the visual he'd had on the site.

"We already dropped our bombs, Bear," said Benny, his voice strange.

"Yeah."

"Of course we got our gun, and Tiny's still got his bombs."

"Kill that bastard, Benny. I'm fuckin' fearless and he scared the shit outta me."

"*Red Dog two, I think I see him,*" called Benny then. His voice was regaining its steady tone.

"*I lost him,*" admitted Tiny.

"We're in the Chinese buffer zone," said the Bear. They were orbiting above the wooded area at 6,000 feet.

"Roger," replied Benny.

"Turn off your IFF, Benny." The Identification, Friend or Foe system could give away the fact that they were flying in the restricted zone, and that would undoubtedly piss off the brass.

"It's off."

"*What are you squawking, Red Dog two?*" Benny radioed.

"*I think my IFF is broken, lead, so I turned it off.*"

The Bear grinned to himself, muttering, "Yeah!" No one would know. Except, of course, the asshole commies down there.

They continued to circle in a wide arc as Benny pointed out a light haze of smoke he saw lingering in the trees.

"*I think that fog down in the trees,*" called Benny to Tiny, "*is from the SAM launch.*"

The Bear was peering at his equipment, wishing to hell the enemy would switch on their radar so he could use his electronics and make sure. He wanted this one, bad.

17/0641L—Wisdom Rocket Site, DRV

Xuan Nha

Using the electro-optical system they watched the aircraft circling up above, helplessly waiting for them to get outside the ten-kilometer circle. The rocket boosters would not drop off until they had pushed the rocket out eight kilometers. The rocket would not fully stabilize until ten kilometers. Only then could they guide the rockets with their data-link signal.

They waited.

"I just received a very excited call from Major Gregarian," said Quang Hanh. "He is on his way here, and asks why we are firing rockets."

"Do not answer him," said Xuan Nha disgustedly. He watched the two aircraft on the screen with narrowed eyes.

"Major Gregarian says he will be here in less than five minutes."

"He will get to see a rocket kill." Xuan smiled.

"The radar-hunters are climbing," the captain hissed. He was biting at his lip and his eyes were growing wide. "I think they are preparing to attack!"

Xuan Nha had a premonition that the captain might be about to bolt. "Stay in place," he said calmly. Keeping his movement from the captain's sight, he dropped his hand and released the leather cover that secured the Tokarev in its holster.

The video picture showed the radar-hunters were still climbing and circling, periodically rolling one way, then the other.

"What are they doing?" whispered the captain.

Xuan laughed. It was the first time he'd done that in days, and it felt good. "Why, they are searching for us. Radar-hunters hunt. That is their duty. And rocket batteries shoot them down. That is our duty."

The radar-hunters stabilized, poising themselves. He peered closer at the screen, wishing he could look into the cockpit and examine the pilots. He took a deep breath and held it.

They had seen the rocket site. He was sure of it. His mind worked vigorously, thinking of options.

"I'm bringing on the radar," said Xuan.

"Our camouflage is good," pleaded the captain. "Let us stay hidden, comrade Colonel."

"We must do something. They have seen us." He switched the radar out of dummy load and instantly boosted the power to maximum. "Prepare to launch rockets three and four."

"They're too close," agonized the captain. "They are only seven thousand meters, well inside the ten-kilometer minimum range!"

Xuan watched the command scope, saw the two distinct radar blips, smoothly moved his tracking handle controls, and manually bracketed them. The range was 6,300 meters.

The captain rose, panic in his eyes. Xuan reached down, raised the pistol, and pointed it at the captain's eye. "Sit down!"

"We can't hit them from this range!"

"We cannot sit and do nothing either, Captain. I hope to frighten them, drive them off to ten thousand meters, and then kill them."

"But comrade Colonel," he started to plead, then his eyes went to the monitor. "Look! They are attacking!" He was shrieking.

The Tokarev's blast was loud in the enclosed van. The captain's body was thrown back toward the side of the van, legs upended.

"No more distractions!" shouted Xuan, dropping the Tokarev onto the console table.

The rocket control officer cringed nearby, eyes glued to the body of the man who had been his battery commander.

Xuan reached over to the senior lieutenant's console and checked the toggle switches to number three and four launchers. They were indeed up. Green flashing lights. The batteries were warming the systems.

"Sit back down, Lieutenant," he commanded.

The rocket control officer quickly obeyed, eyes darting to the colonel, then to the video screen.

Both lights came on solid green, showing the rocket circuits were warmed, the gyros erected. "Three and four ready," said the senior lieutenant, a catch in his voice.

Lieutenant Hanh spoke. "Control asks what we are doing, comrade Colonel. Major Gregarian is speaking with them."

"Fire three and four," Xuan said to the senior lieutenant, angry that he had allowed the Russians to equip this site with only four rocket launchers.

They heard the third and fourth rockets roaring from their launchers.

"Now," said Xuan Nha, "we shall watch the cowards run. Are launchers one and two reloaded?"

The rocket officer was cringing, staring with wide eyes at the video monitor, as the first fighter continued toward them. A light began to wink and flash near its nose.

Nicolaj Gregarian

The two trucks were just passing the launchers when the rockets erupted, one passing directly over their heads with a deafening roar.

The *leytenant* driver almost turned the vehicle over. Or was it the blast from the rocket booster?

They skidded to a halt.

"Keep going!" said Nicolaj. "We've got to stop the fools."

He heard shouting from the men in the rear of the truck. Something about attacking aircraft.

Suddenly very afraid, he looked out of the cab and up at the sky.

17/0644L—North of Bac Can, Route Pack Six, North Vietnam

Benny Lewis

Although Benny knew he was in the ballpark, he was not positive where the site was located down there. With only the Gatling cannon to work with, it would be damned easy to miss. With each passing second the smoke drifted farther and his uncertainty rose.

Then the Bear whooped from the backseat. "He's turned on his radar!" he yelled over the hot mike, "and now the dumb shit's turned on his missile beam like he's going to launch!"

And about then Benny thought he saw movement down in the trees. The antenna moving as it tracked them?

"He's at your one o'clock," said the Bear. "When you've set up for your gun attack, I'm going into AZ-EL mode to put him on your heads-up display."

Benny was already jinking out left. He made a short arc, turned back in, then winged over into a forty-five-degree dive on the site.

"I've got the AZ-EL on. You oughta be able to see the radar on your combining glass!" yelled the Bear.

The electronic dot pinged around wildly. It was not very accurate at the best of times. "Not good enough," said Benny.

The Bear was working and muttering, breathing hard. The sounds were loud in Benny's earphones.

"Is that better?" the Bear asked.

The dancing dots had settled down a little. Their dispersion was still too wide, but the grouping was tight enough to reassure Benny that the motion he'd seen was indeed from the site. He could see square outlines of things not grown by nature and knew now that he was looking at camouflage nets.

A missile roared from its launcher, then a second one, both in the general direction of the two fighters. Unless this site was *really* different from the others, they were still in the six-mile dead zone, too close in for a missile to hit them.

He centered his pipper, offset a little, and lightly fingered the trigger, waiting. He finally began firing the cannon at 7,000 feet above the ground. A hundred 20mm bullets per second spewed from the six barrels. He held the trigger down, stirred the pot with the control stick, and watched the bullets impacting, then saw a missile spouting fire. He stopped shooting and pulled hard on the stick to recover.

Tiny was already diving. As Benny pulled out he rolled to watch. The missile he'd hit was still afire on the ground.

"Beautiful!" yelled the Bear. "I love it!"

Then Benny could see the site clearly as even more netting was torn aside by the wild, fire-spewing missile. Perhaps half a mile of camouflage netting, for the entire road structure between launchers was revealed, as were vans and four launchers. Two trucks moved in the site, inside the launchers and heading toward the vans. They appeared to be moving slowly, but he could tell they were speeding because of the thick plumes of dust they raised.

A smattering of automatic small-arms fire arced up at them. Was that all they had to protect the site with?

Tiny's bombs impacted, obliterating two missile launchers, several parked trucks, and a cache of equipment. A small explosion and smoke from beside a launcher.

Benny climbed.

"Where you going?" asked the Bear.

"I'm going to strafe him again. We haven't gotten him yet." The radar and vans were intact.

Tiny was recovering left, also climbing back and around for reattack.

This time Benny went in at thirty degrees and started firing 4,000 feet out. He held the hose of bullets on the antenna van, watched pieces go flying, moved the stick, then shifted, hosing the stream of tracers into the center of the control van. A very big van, twice the size of a normal one.

The gun ran out of ammunition and ceased firing. He flew directly over the vans, low and fast, and jinked off right.

"I think we were hit back there," yelled the Bear.

He checked his telelite panel. "My lights are all good. No warning or fire light."

"I couldn't see," complained the Bear. "Did you get the vans?"

"We hosed them good. Real good."

Tiny Bechler

Tiny followed Benny in on the strafe pass, watching as his leader's churning bullets tore up the antenna and vans.

Tiny picked out the trucks, now turned around and trying to escape the carnage.

He started firing at 5,000 feet, walked his bullets up, and sent a steady stream into first one, then the other truck. The first went tumbling wildly. The other spouted flames, belched a small flash of fire, and spewed smoke. He kept strafing across the site until he was too close to the ground for comfort. He stopped firing then and egressed low so they couldn't get a good shot at him. He was several miles past the site and preparing to climb when he saw something very strange.

He was flying so low he'd seen under a huge, vaulted camouflage net!

"I've got something down here, Red Dog lead. I think it's a big search radar or something, and there's a large building next to it."

Tiny was already turning to attack.

"We're getting low on petrol, two," replied Benny. *"Make one quick pass and let's get out of here."*

He came around, like he was on a gunnery range, and made a classic low-angle strafe pass. He tried to rake both the radar antenna and the building with his bullets, and easily succeeded because both were barn-sized. As far as he could tell no one was even shooting at him. That was kind of nice for a change.

Tiny climbed to rejoin Red Dog lead. He was tired, mentally exhausted and his body ached from all the g's they'd pulled. Still, he felt good about the morning's work.

Chapter Twenty-Four

Tuesday, March 21st—0655 Local, Route Pack Six,
North Vietnam

Benny Lewis

The strike force was again being sent to bomb the steel mill. The defenses were still concentrated there, but they did not seem nearly as well coordinated.

He, the Bear, and Tiny had celebrated destroying the unique SAM site, and shooting up what the Bear was convinced was the command-and-control center, but they had done so privately. The targets had been located in the Chinese buffer zone. It was a transgression punishable by court-martial.

But they knew it was worth the risk. The bombing of the mill had continued, and there had been markedly fewer losses. One or two on a bad day, none at all when things went well. That was partly due to their lopping off the head of the beast, but they also knew the strike pilots who had survived Thai Nguyen were now a much cannier group. They flew with a careful balance of boldness and caution, for they knew what it was like to spit in the devil's eye. They had learned that no defenses are impenetrable, no target impossible.

Today the strike force would fly across the valley, use Thud Ridge for a shield, then soar to delivery altitude and dive-bomb the rubble of the steel mill.

Pudge Holden and Sloppy Watson were leading Lincoln flight, and Benny and the Bear were number three. As they crossed the Red River they split the flight, taking up positions five miles forward and on either side of the strike force. Two Weasel units, separate yet able to support one another or work in unison.

579

Benny and the Bear's teamwork had become so well honed that they often communicated without words. The Bear could suck a sharp breath, and somehow Benny knew a Fansong radar was tracking and about to fire missiles. He could mutter something unintelligible, and the Bear would spit out a status report. An intake of breath, and the Bear knew to check behind them for MiG's.

If he considered a target and the Bear was reluctant, Benny didn't even think about attacking it. If the Bear was eager, he'd do his own evaluation and the Bear would trust it. They'd become an efficient, coordinated, deadly unit. The Bear said he'd willingly fly to Moscow and drop leaflets. As long as Benny was with him and they had a good Thud, he felt invincible. Benny knew the feeling.

They were at 10,000 feet, eastbound, Thud Ridge five miles in front of them, Thai Nguyen just beyond.

"We've got SAMs at ten, one, three, and five. Ignore the launch light."

"Roger, line me up with the SAM at one."

"Come right to zero-eight-five degrees. Ignore the launch light."

Hard breathing.

"Second element's out at our ten o'clock, also turning south," noted the Bear.

"Ah roger. Smoke's drifting west at about ten knots."

"East to west at ten knots."

"Lincoln four, Lincoln three," Benny called.

"Four," replied Tiny.

"We're going up to toss a Shrike. You watch out for MiG's while I'm preoccupied."

"Four."

"SAMs at nine, eleven, twelve, and three. You're lined up. Got him on your Shrike?"

"Roger," said Benny.

"SAM launch at nine o'clock. Not for us. I think they're shooting at lead."

"We got SAMs at our two o'clock, Lincoln two," confirmed Pudge Holden on the radio. *"Get ready to take it down."*

"Two!"

Benny fired his Shrike, then banked and looked for the SAM launch.

"It's at eleven o'clock low," said the Bear.

"I hoped it would be low," said Benny with a touch of comedy. "Not many flying SAM sites." He switched from the Shrike station to centerline, where they carried CBU-24's.

"Launch at three o'clock. It's valid and coming for us."

"I'm looking . . . aha, got 'em. There's booster drop-off."

"Valid launch at three o'clock, Lincoln four. Let's get the energy up," Benny radioed.

"Four."

They waited, watched, and at the appropriate last moment, broke up and right. The missiles flashed by, one by one. Benny reversed the hard bank.

"Which one you think we oughta take out?" asked the Bear.

"First one, over at eleven o'clock. He's closest to the strike force and I've got a good visual on him." He was soaring again, watching the site, mentally setting up the dive-bomb problem.

"He's tracking again, Benny."

"You don't want to take him?"

"I'm game. Valid missile launch, six o'clock."

"Damn!"

"Valid launch, twelve o'clock."

The site he was preparing to attack had launched three missiles.

"Two sites firing?" Benny was turning hard right. Six missiles were in the air coming for them.

"Lincoln four, get ready to take it down!"

"Four!" called Tiny, huffing.

"Ignore the missiles from the site in front. He's no longer tracking. I think the gomer operators chickened out and ran."

The missiles Benny watched flew in a straight line, no longer being guided.

They were soaring over downtown Thai Nguyen, and the sky was illuminated with 57mm and 85mm trying to track them.

"Jesus! Look at that flak!" yelled Benny, jinking crazily and eyeing the SAMs fired from the site they were attacking.

"The missiles from in back of us have dropped their boosters and are coming fast. You ready?"

"You call it. I don't have 'em in sight." Their energy level was high and they rolled upside down, ready to maneuver.

"Lincoln four, break," radioed the Bear.

Benny reefed the stick in, maneuvering hard left and down. They rode in a wide S-maneuver toward the ground, flak everywhere around them.

The Bear said the missiles were clear.

Benny bunted the aircraft up and then over, pulling negative g's. He eyed the site, which was where he'd planned it to be at the finish of his maneuver. Forty-five-degree dive. He brought his wings level for CBU delivery.

"Lincoln three's in hot."

"Four's on your starboard, also in hot."

"Remember the wind," muttered the Bear. "From the east at ten knots."

The aircraft bumped around a couple of times, rocked by exploding artillery rounds. Benny pickled off the CBUs, waited for a single second longer, then turned hard right.

They stayed low and fast, grew the fuzzy bubble, then went supersonic.

"We got him, Bear," he said confidently, eyes glued to the rooftops and obstructions ahead. They made a sweeping tour of Thai Nguyen, staying down at a hundred feet, popping over telephone lines and circumventing a tall radio antenna mast, climbing only when they grew closer to the safety offered by Thud Ridge.

"Lincoln four is bingo fuel," called Tiny. The wild maneuvering had used a lot of jet petroleum.

"Roger, four, let's take 'em home," replied Benny. He was also showing just enough fuel to make it safely to the tanker.

They passed over the ridge and started across the valley, flying directly to the west, climbing slowly and nursing the throttles to conserve fuel.

"You see if we really got the SAM site?" asked the Bear.

"Couldn't have missed." He'd released the CBUs dead on target.

"By the way, we got a tracking SAM at six and another at eight. Also a Firecan dead ahead. If I were you I might consider going around it, unless you like being shot."

Benny turned right and flew northwest for a few seconds, then corrected back to the west.

"You lost, Lincoln three?" asked Tiny.

"Just follow us, Lincoln four."

"I did that a bit ago and look where you took me. You musta been lost to go there," bantered Tiny. *"SAMs, guns, there was even an old guy threw his cane at us."*

They were jinking lazily, climbing through 5,000 feet, when Benny saw muzzle-flashes up ahead from a mound in the middle of a flat expanse of rice paddies.

"Watch out for flak, four," radioed Benny, *"they're shooting."*

Four bursts appeared a few hundred yards directly in front of Tiny, and he began to climb.

More bursts. The nose of Tiny's bird rotated up more.

Benny heard the Bear start to laugh. "It's like a damned circus," he cackled.

More flak bursts appeared off Tiny's left wing. He jinked right, still climbing.

When they were clear of the guns, Tiny stayed out wide and high, silent.

"I think he's sulking," said the Bear.

Benny chuckled. They crossed back over the Red River south of Yen Bai, closer to safety.

"It's damn near easy," said the Bear, and Benny knew what he meant.

Benny reflected on that for a moment, then swung his vision around the sky to look for MiG's.

As they neared the Laotian border they listened to poststrike reports. No losses, and they'd been effective. The strike force confirmed that all walls of the steel mill were down, and that there was nothing left in the complex to bomb. Pudge had knocked out a site north of the target. Benny reported destroying the SAM site just south of Thai Nguyen.

They traveled toward the air refueling tanker, quiet in their individual thoughts. The Bear spoke up then. "You still writing Liz?"

"Not since we started bombing the steel mill. Maybe I will now that we've got more time."

A long pause before the Bear spoke again. "You're not getting serious, are you?"

Benny thought about that for a moment. "She's done some favors for me. Stayed in touch with my folks, things like that. She's not as bad as I thought."

"Don't get serious, okay? I think she's a fake, just likes you because she's checked out your pedigree."

Benny didn't respond.

"Maybe it's none of my business."

"Sure glad you're here, Bear," he finally said. "This way my mother can stay back in the States and know someone's doing her worrying about who's right for me."

"Ungrateful wretch."

21/1925L—Ponderosa, Takhli RTAFB, Thailand

Bear Stewart

The end was in sight. They were flying well and he was confident that everything was under control. Whatever the North Vietnamese threw at them, they could handle. They were going to make it. He hadn't realized how uncertain he'd been. Perhaps because he'd been shot down. Perhaps because of all the friends he'd lost. All he knew now was a reasonable certainty that things were manageable.

The child in Julie's belly became even more special. He was going to be able to raise a son or a daughter, and there was so much to share. He'd never dreamed he could be so ridiculously excited about a single event. Julie would make a good mother, of that he was certain, and he was determined to be just as good as a father.

He'd sure as hell know what to tell the kid not to do, because he'd probably done about everything there was to do that was wrong. The kid would make mistakes too. Like his uncle Miles had once told him, a person who does things perfect all the time is a damn bore, and probably doesn't have an inch of fun. Maybe, the Bear thought, I can help the kid avoid the worst mistakes and learn from the others.

He hoped the kid had adventure in his life. Of course, he didn't want him having to go to war like this. Maybe there wouldn't be any more wars after this one. But if there was, he'd bet any kid of his and Julie's wouldn't know any better than to try to get into the middle of the thing out of love for his country.

So he just hoped there wouldn't be any more wars.

And as for Julie? He wrote to tell her what he thought.

Tuesday
March 21st

Dear Julie,

    God but I miss you! I receive your letters, always cheerful and happy, and I read each one over again and again, because I can hear you speaking as I read. Did I tell you that you've got the world's sexiest voice?

    Sorry I haven't written much lately, but things have been very busy. Benny and I've been flying a lot and we are giving them hell. After tomorrow, we'll only have ten missions to go before we're finished. We may get a few more tough ones, but we've proven we can take whatever they throw at us and give even better back. After the next five missions, we will get milk runs for our last five. Then the hundred mission party and we're on our way!

    Benny is the best pilot and certainly one of the finest men I've ever known. That's a real tribute, because I don't pass out compliments freely. He's a real square, and such a straight shooter that he's almost obnoxious about it, but the guy turns into an artist in the airplane. On the ground we pal around a lot, and in the air we almost know what the other guy's thinking, and you need that sort of thing if you're flying in the places and doing the things we are.

    Honey, if you ever need anything and I'm not around, call on Benny to help. That shows the kind of trust I've got in him, because you are the most dear thing in my life.

    Most of the guys here are good. Facing almost impossible odds, they just keep on going and doing their jobs, and keeping their faith in America. I don't think the people back home are aware of the great trust the pilots here place in their country, or of their belief that the folks at home support them, regardless of the fact the papers tell us that some Americans are acting differently.

    We're all doing our damndest.

    (One hour later) Benny just came in and told me

*we are both going to be stationed at Nellis Air Force
Base in Las Vegas, Nevada, when we leave here. I'll
be teaching new Wild Weasel crews on their way over
here to combat. Benny will take over a flight at the
fighter weapons school and teach gunnery tactics. I
went through Weasel training at Nellis before I came
over here, and the flying there is great!*

*I think we should buy a house. Three bedrooms,
because I'm really getting to like the idea of being a
father. Of course you'll have something to say about
that.*

*Benny also brought confirmation of our flights
from here back to the States. We'll be landing at
Travis Air Force Base (there in the Bay Area) at one
p.m., your time.*

*If I sound like I'm getting anxious to see you
again, you are right. I'll be very easy to pick out of
the crowd at Travis because I've grown a great,
bushy mustache (supposed to bring luck, and who
knows). After we get to your place, if you get out of
bed during the first twenty-four hours, it will be
because I've failed to keep your attention, and I do
not intend to let that happen in this lifetime.*

Love,

Mal

25/1955L—Hoa Lo Prison, Hanoi, North Vietnam

Glenn Phillips

On Saturday they dumped another invalid into Glenn's
room. With Pete Crawford and himself already in the small
cell, that made it awfully cramped.

This one was a burn case, a Navy lieutenant whose face
and forearms were scaling, his skin colored black and bright
red. This time there was little Glenn could do.

Crawford helped him get the flier onto a bunk.

"You okay, buddy?" Crawford asked.

"Hurts like hell, but I'll make it. Guess I look pretty
awful."

"I was born ugly. Just took you longer to get there."

They all introduced themselves, and Glenn tapped the lieutenant's name out to the captain in the adjoining cell.

"What's wrong with your arms?" the Navy lieutenant asked Crawford.

"I was a bad boy."

Crawford refused to bow to the guards when they came in. They'd beat him every time, and he'd finally do it, but he'd developed a reputation among the North Vietnamese guards as a resister and a thorn in their sides. His arms, already warped from the terrible time when he'd been tortured for trying to escape, were now permanently disabled. He couldn't straighten his elbows, and his shoulders jutted forward at awkward, uneven angles.

He continually talked about escaping. He spoke about the time that Red Williams and he had escaped, and the sense of freedom they'd savored. He hated captivity. They all despised the prison, but Crawford had a compulsion to try to get out.

"They treat you bad here, huh?" asked the lieutenant.

"Yes," said Glenn. He was the ranking man in the cell, the second-ranking man in the cell block. "But you've got to resist. Have they interrogated you yet?"

"No, sir. When I got here they just deloused me. I was in a lot of pain because the disinfectant they used hurt my burns, so I yelled a lot. They had me change into the prison uniform and just marched me here."

"Talk in a lower voice," cautioned Glenn. "They get all excited when they know we're talking to each other. Think we're inciting a rebellion or something."

Crawford scowled toward the door.

"Yes, sir," said the lieutenant to Phillips.

"Where'd you get shot down?" asked Glenn. Crawford was quiet during the questioning. Glenn was senior and doing his job.

"Over Thai Nguyen, sir. I think it was a SAM, but it could have been flak. The pilot made a right turn and we made it out a few miles. I bailed out and some soldiers captured me when I hit the ground. Didn't treat me too bad, 'cause I was burned and look like a lobster, I guess."

"What kind of airplane?"

"A-6 Intruder. I'm a Navy aviator. You'd call me a radar navigator in the Air Force."

"When they interrogate you, they'll already know your unit and your ship, but make them work to get the information. Keeps their attention from anything really classified."

"I'm supposed to give name, rank, and serial number only. That's all I'll give them, sir."

"They'll bend you and you'll talk. Just make them work for anything they get."

Crawford piped up. "The chickenfuckers can make a rock talk. They do it with ropes. Tie you up in positions you didn't know were possible."

Glenn hushed Crawford. "They may take him to another cell, because there's not enough room here. I want to get as much information as I can in case they do."

"Yes, sir," said Crawford. They were both majors, but Glenn had him on date of rank, and rank meant a lot in the prison.

"What did you see when they were bringing you here?"

"I could see out the back of the truck. Thai Nguyen's a mess. Just rubble there. The smelters are a bunch of twisted steel."

"Outstanding."

"South of Thai Nguyen I saw what looked like a power plant, all caved in on one side. I don't think it's working. Looked deserted."

Glenn nodded. "There's a thermal plant there."

"Railroad overpass on the other side of the river is down onto the highway. There were a lot of guys working on it like ants. Guys with guns were treating them pretty mean."

Crawford spoke up. "I saw the same thing down south. Slavery is alive and well here. Would've made my great-granddaddy back in Tennessee happy."

"What else?" asked Glenn, mildly irritated at Crawford's interruption. He liked the skinny Southerner, but it was sometimes hard to quell his exuberance.

"There was an air strike while we were on the road. They were hitting the steel mill again, and it was your F-105's doing the bombing. I thought the soldiers were going to come unglued they were so afraid. They wrecked the truck I was riding in trying to get out of the way, just drove off the road and into a building. Then they herded me outta there quick. We hid in the building, which was a small warehouse or something with a lot of equipment in it."

"It all ties in," said Glenn. The information the prisoners had been receiving told them the war was going badly for the North Vietnamese. They'd also noticed a dramatic change in the morale of the guards.

"They won't be able to take it much longer," said Crawford. "Our guys are starting to sting the bastards."

That was the growing consensus of the prisoners.

"No," said Glenn. "It can't last much longer."

He'd used that argument lately to dissuade Crawford from another escape attempt. Pete thought he'd found a way to get out by digging the masonry loose on the transom above the cell door.

The next day the guards returned to the cell and reduced the number of prisoners there by taking Crawford away to an isolated detention cell. The last time Glenn saw Pete Crawford he was struggling with the guards, as he always did, and calling them chickenfuckers.

The day after that the guards took the Navy lieutenant and bent him. After a while he told them his unit and ship, which they already knew, and they were satisfied. When they brought him back to the cell Glenn tried to soothe and help him, but the proud Navy lieutenant cried for a long time.

"Hurts, doesn't it?"

"Yes, sir, but it's not that. I broke. I would have told them anything they wanted me to."

A while later the lieutenant sat and Glenn gingerly tried to replace his shoulder's into their proper positions.

"I am an American fighting man." The lieutenant quoted the code of conduct. *"When questioned, I am bound to give only name, rank, service number, and date of birth."*

Glenn broke in. *"I will resist by all means available."* He recited. "And we will, Lieutenant. But the code really rests with the ending. Remember? *I will keep faith with my fellow prisoners, and I will trust in my God and the United States of America.*"

"Yes, sir."

"We won't be here much longer, not with our guys stinging them like they're doing. We know it. Even the guards know it. Just hang in there and keep your faith."

"I'll try, sir."

"The guards don't understand us and that makes them

angry. They can't understand what it's like to be a free man, like you and me. They've never been free and they probably never will be. Even in here, locked up like this, we're free men and that makes us different from them. By God's grace we were born free in a wonderful country of free men. Even if we die here, we'll die as free men. You remember that."

30/1355L—North of Hanoi, Route Pack Six, North Vietnam

Bear Stewart

They were back to bombing a two-bit target. A twenty-four-aircraft strike force was bombing a small highway overpass seven miles north of Hanoi.

Benny and the Bear were flying mission ninety-five, the last tough one, and had opted to fly as number three in the Weasel flight, call sign Kingfish, with new guys Phil Yost and Billy Dreyer leading.

Yost and Dreyer were having trouble with the Weasel mission. The best indicator was that the lieutenants disliked flying on their wing, saying they were dangerously slow and didn't act like they knew what they were doing. Benny thought they needed more experience leading Weasel flights. The Bear, not so charitable, figured they were downright incompetent.

They hadn't split the flight because Benny wanted to stay close and make sure the other Weasel crew remained out of trouble.

Kingfish flight approached Thud Ridge from the west, ingressing twenty miles out in front of the force since they weren't splitting the Weasel flight or using the new tactic.

"SAMs at twelve, two, and three," muttered the Bear. "The one at twelve is across the ridge, probably at Thai Nguyen. The one at two looks like Lead one."

"A ghost?" They had destroyed Lead one on an earlier mission.

"They must have replaced it." The radar signal was at a different frequency, and wasn't tracking as smoothly as the previous one. A different SAM battery had been installed at the same location.

Sam Hall's distinctive voice radioed an errant wingman to *get back into position!* Sam was mission commander, leading

Mallard flight, and like them was also flying his ninety-fifth mission. Before they'd gone to the airplanes, Sam had asked if they shouldn't pool their resources and throw one big hundred mission party together.

"Old Sam's gonna be his ornery self right up to the end," said Benny, as they listened to Sam chew ass again.

"Where's he gonna be stationed?" asked the Bear. He liked Sam and thought he was a good leader.

"F-4's at Davis Monthan. Tucson. He's going to be ops officer for the training unit there."

"He'll be good for 'em."

"What's happening out there? In case you've forgotten where we're flying."

"Not much. SAMs at twelve, three, and five o'clock. Powerful gun at one o'clock. They better watch out for the gun radar. I think it's smack in the target area."

Capt Phil Yost called the threats out over the radio, roughly as the Bear had said.

"He's jinking too hard," observed the Bear. "Flailing around the sky and slowing himself down, but he's still on a predictable course."

"I'll talk to him later," said Benny.

The Bear listened as the strike force encountered flak. No one was hit during the first flurries.

They had a valid SAM launch, and the Bear told Benny about it. They waited for a moment longer, for Yost to call it and take action.

"Come on, Phil," muttered Benny. "Tell us what to do."

After a couple more seconds, Benny called. *"Kingfish lead, Kingfish three has a valid SAM launch at three o'clock."*

The Bear had spotted the missiles as the first SAM's booster dropped away, splattering its liquid fire and impacting near a small village. The gomers didn't seem to care where the missile boosters landed as long as it wasn't in Hanoi or a big city. The second, then the third boosters dropped away.

Kingfish lead had not responded, but kept flying toward the ridge as if they were happy just jinking along and ignoring the world.

"Kingfish lead, three!" called Benny.

Long pause. *"Roger, three."*

"Let's prepare to evade SAMs, Kingfish flight," called Benny, now sounding concerned.

"This is Kingfish lead. We've, ah, got a SAM launch."

"No shit," fumed the Bear, watching the missiles arcing up and toward them.

Lead broke right suddenly.

"Kingfish lead, you're maneuvering too early," radioed Benny.

"Damn!" said the Bear. He continued watching. The missiles were now tracking them, not lead, who led his element away in a wild dive. The Bear confirmed that by using his analysis scope. "The missiles are tracking us," he said quietly.

"Kingfish four, prepare to take it down." Benny put the nose slightly down and pushed his throttle forward.

"Four!" came Tiny's sharp response.

They broke upward at the proper time, sliced downward to evade the last missile, then climbed to set up for a dive-bomb attack on the site.

"Kingfish four, set up for a forty-five-degree dive."

"Four!"

Kingfish lead and two were nowhere in sight.

"Here we go again," said the Bear. "We got two Fansongs up, no threats."

"Roger."

They were attacking the smoke from a site two miles north of the Red River. The Bear tried to eyeball the site, but couldn't make it out down there. "You got a good visual on the site?"

"Not very good. I think it's near that road intersection down there."

The Bear couldn't tell which intersection he was talking about. He glanced back into the cockpit. "Strong tracking gun at twelve o'clock. He's close."

"The SAM radar on the air?"

"No. He shut down soon as the missiles went by us."

They pulled several g's as Benny rolled over, then pulled hard to enter the dive-bomb. Black flak bursts appeared around the Bear's cockpit.

The aircraft lurched.

"Shit," said Benny. "The bombs just dropped away, and it wasn't me that pickled them."

Benny radioed, *"Kingfish four, three is breaking off the attack. Unless you see the site, abort your dive-bomb."*

A pause. *"Four is breaking off."*

"There was a bunch of flak just as we rolled over," said

the Bear. "I think that's what hit us." He could hear a whistling sound.

Benny pulled out high and to the right, heading toward the safety of the western mountains.

"I don't see anything. You see anything wrong out there?"

"No, but we went right through that flak." The Bear was looking out at the wings, then his eyes were drawn to the back of the canopy sill. "I got a big crack in my canopy," he said in amazement, wondering why he hadn't seen it at first glance.

"Kingfish three is off the target to the west. Come look us over, Kingfish four."

The wind made a shrill sound as it rushed over the rent in the Plexiglas.

"Hell," said Benny, "I just saw the tailpipe-overheat light flicker." He throttled back a bit.

"We just went blind," said the Bear. "The Weasel gear just blew. No power."

"Kingfish four is at your seven o'clock. I'm jettisoning my bombs, lead."

"Roger. Let's head west and you look us over, four."

"Better head about two-ninety degrees," the Bear estimated. "We've got no radar warning gear, and there weren't any threats out that way."

Benny turned right twenty degrees to a heading of two-nine-zero.

"Anyway," muttered the Bear, "we know what that area's like on the ground."

"Shit, don't say that," said Benny.

"The gomers just had to give us that shot on our last mission to pack six," grumbled the Bear. "They keep pissing me off, I'll volunteer for another hundred."

"The tailpipe-overheat light just flickered again."

"C'mon baby, you can do it," said the Bear, patting the instrument panel.

They were ten miles from the Red River, and would cross it a few miles south of Yen Bai.

The aircraft lurched violently, then recovered. "We just had a granddaddy compressor stall," said Benny, his voice steady.

"Well, stop it," the Bear admonished, trying to joke. *Hell, might as well,* he told himself.

"Tailpipe-overheat lamp is flickering more now. I don't know if we're going to make it to the Red River, Bear."

"Sure we will." The Bear tried to keep worry from his voice. "She just needs a little care and attention. You make it back home, baby, and we'll help Sergeant Tiehl give you a wax job."

The engine roared wildly, calmed, then went into a cycle of roars and calms. It was like riding a wild bronc.

"You're belching a shitload of fire and smoke, Kingfish three."

"Ro-ger." Benny's voice was jolted by a wild buck.

"You got a chunk of upper fuselage missing a few feet behind the Bear's seat, with some wire hanging out like spaghetti," called Tiny.

"We're close, Benny. Red River's just ahead," said the Bear. He'd been unable to keep a quiver from his voice. He removed his sunglasses and put them, along with his cigarettes and lighter, into his g-suit's leg pocket, zippering them securely in place.

"Yeah," said Benny. "We can glide that far. We want to make it far as we can, though."

The engine went into a sustained, loud roar.

"I've lost throttle control," radioed Benny. "It went to a hundred percent all by itself," he said to the Bear.

Benny took advantage of the situation by pulling the nose upward, and they soared higher, through 12,000 feet. They crossed the Red River, still accelerating and climbing. Out to their right, several miles away, a few bundles of white flak blossomed over Yen Bai.

Tiny Bechler followed them up in their climb, now judiciously flying out a couple hundred yards, probably in case their airplane exploded. He went off the air for a minute to call Red Crown and ask them to alert the rescue forces. Sam Hall came on the air, added encouragement, and said he'd join them soon. His flight was twenty miles back, still crossing the valley.

"I've got a good feeling about this one, Benny. If we have to punch out, it's gonna be an easy pickup." The Bear stuffed his flying map into the other g-suit pocket, then secured it with the zipper.

"Me, too. You doing okay back there?" Benny was

keeping his voice steady. The Bear was impressed; his own voice was shaky.

"No sweat."

"Solid tailpipe-overheat lamp now. This thing could come apart in the air, you know."

"Roger." The Bear remembered the guys talking about the way Tits Ringer's airplane had exploded. Such an exit would be quick, he consoled himself.

"You go ahead and punch out anytime you want."

"I'm gonna ride a little longer."

They were approaching the Black River.

"At this rate," joked the Bear, "we could make it all the way to Takhli."

The Thud heard him and showed its cantankerous self by belching and shuddering grandly. The airframe began to chatter and shake as the engine went through a series of tortured compression stalls. Then the engine quit, leaving a silence so total that the air whistling through the canopy crack was loud.

"I'm dead-sticking it," said Benny. "Trying to pick a good spot for us to punch out."

The Bear felt giddy with emotion. "Pick a good one. Maybe next to a bar down there?"

The Thud had poor gliding characteristics, and with no engine to power them they began to rapidly lose altitude.

"We're through ten thousand feet," said Benny. The engine had quit at 14,000.

They were abeam the Black River.

"Kingfish three, you are burning, starting to torch. Get out!"

"Your turn, Bear," yelled Benny. "See you on the ground."

"It's been a superb show. We done good, babe."

The Bear rotated both ejection handles back. The canopy released on only one side and hung there.

The Bear shoved upward, hard. The canopy cocked up, then was swept away by the airflow. He drew a breath, pulled himself down into the seat, and squeezed the right handle. The familiar kick in the butt and rush of wind. He tumbled, still in the seat, grabbed it, and pushed it away.

He was falling through the air near the seat, still tumbling, the world gyrating beneath him. The chute would automatically open when it sensed the proper altitude.

Screw that waiting to see if it would open! He yanked the ripcord handle free from its clamps and smoothly pulled it.

He felt a jolt, then was swinging in a great arc under the billowing chute. He reached back, found and shut off the beeper, then found the loops in the risers and pulled, reconfiguring the chute.

Hell, a few more ejections and he'd be a pro.

He disconnected one side of his mask and let it dangle free, then looked around. Lush, green, tree-covered mountainside below. Farm fields off to his left and forward. The river out there just a mile or two. He was looking and moving eastward. He laboriously guided the chute around until he was facing west and spotted a parachute in the distance. He couldn't tell if Benny was moving in his chute, but it looked like it was being steered. Good.

He looked below again, now with his bearings about him. Straight ahead was west, his favorite direction; the mountainside was below, sloping away and trees ending at the edge of a large field. Off to his left, to the south, were rows of trees. An old rubber plantation? To his right and behind were forests and a few farm fields. To his left again. A group of buildings. Dots moved about. People! Surely they could see him, with the parachute billowing above and the bright-yellow raft dangling like a beacon. He fumbled at his g-suit to find the orange survival knife with its open-hook blade.

Benny was higher, heading toward the edge of the trees near the open field.

Closer to the ground now, he could see individual trees. He reached down with the knife's hook, cut the lanyard of the suspended life raft, and watched as it fell away. He stuffed the knife back into its pouch in the g-suit and snapped it secure.

Very close to the ground now and still over trees. A last look at Benny's position, then back down. Not so lucky this time as the last. He'd be landing in trees. At the last second he tried to steer for a small clearing he saw. Was halfway there when his legs hit a limb and he banged against a tree. He was stunned with sharp pain as his chute hung up and he was jerked to a rude stop. One testicle caught in the strap. He almost clawed his way up the risers as he readjusted the crotch strap.

He was hanging suspended more than ten feet from the ground. He tried to gingerly settle back into the parachute harness, groaned at the sharp pain, then held himself up and released the chest and leg straps. He slipped through slowly, awkwardly, holding to the straps with his hands. He dangled, holding onto the harness, then dropped.

The drop was only six feet or so, but the jolt hurt. He gingerly felt himself and groused about not steering the chute toward clearing sooner. He retrieved the survival kit and looked about.

The hillside was steep. He made his way down to a relatively flat area, waddling because of the sickening ache in his balls, then slowly knelt and went through the kit.

Last time he'd had the parachute panel to carry it all in, but this time the chute was hung in the tree. He tossed aside the bullshit things, like the desalinization kit and extra knife, added the pemmican bars, signal mirror, and compass to his bulging g-suit pockets and stuffed the first-aid kit and map into his vest.

No time for more. Civilization was too close at hand.

He pushed his helmet and the survival kit under a bush, paused to rub black dirt over his face to help with the telltale smell of soap—like Grandma Bowes's people had taught him—and sucked in the biggest breath possible. He exhaled, feeling lightheaded. He pulled on his sunglasses and somehow felt better about things.

He heard the roar of jet engines. Pulling out a radio, he selected TRANS/REC.

30/1440L—Bach Mai Hospital, Hanoi DRV

Li Binh

"How are you this morning, husband?" she asked.

The apparition, swathed and swaddled in white, lay before her. They'd told her he was conscious and aware. The thing in there twitched.

She sat on the chair an orderly had put in place beside it.

He moved again, and she saw the eye flutter and try to open. There was one eye hole, a space at the nostrils, and a tiny hole at the mouth into which a tube was inserted. Other tubes ran from his groin and his arms.

"You are a hero, and General Giap himself has called attention to your brave actions at Bac Can. He spoke before the

politburo about the bravery of the Tiger of Dien Bien Phu.
Colonel-General Dung personally called me after a second
meeting, to tell me that I must bear up well myself."

A movement of the eye. It was indeed open.

"General Dung also said to tell you that he has identified
the perfidious traitor who allowed the damage to the steel mill.
Lieutenant Colonel Nguy was brought before a tribunal and
stripped of all rank and position."

The eye opened wider.

"I saw Colonel Nguy when they dragged him about Ba
Dinh Square, a placard around his neck and his hands tied
behind him. A disgraceful sight. To think that he has betrayed
your trust so totally. General Dung said they will send him to
the south as a private soldier."

Xuan spoke something unintelligible, and the croaking
sound startled her.

"General Dung said you would be interested, and to make
sure I told you about that."

The elevated hand trembled. The body with only one arm
and one eye gave a great shudder. He had tried to move and
now made a low moaning sound.

"The Russian, Gregarian, was also wounded, but not
nearly as badly as you. Just a few burns, I believe. When he
mends sufficiently, he will be returned to Russia. Many of his
men who were with him were killed, and I have heard that he
is in trouble with his people because he had guaranteed their
safety."

She heard him speak again, but could understand only the
word "Wisdom."

"The large radar there was damaged, but my nephew says
it can be repaired. I believe some of the equipment from the
control center is to be transported and set up at Phuc Yen
airfield."

He spoke low. In protest?

"You will be happy to learn that your position is being
filled by a most capable person, husband. My nephew is
working hard to rebuild your fence of steel so the Americans
will not be able to succeed again as they did at Thai Nguyen."

"Li Binh." Xuan Nha's words came in a weak hiss.

She bent down, closer to his lips, and was able to
understand some of what he said.

"We can not stop . . . We can shoot . . . but . . .

not stop them. Only you . . ." He moaned and took a breath. "Only you can . . . stop them."

The body shook again, and the eye fluttered then closed.

She thought about what he had said for a moment, then called the orderly. He edged her aside, then bent over and carefully examined him.

"Is he alive?" she asked. It did not matter to her. His continued presence would be a burden to deal with. She was the wife of a Hero of the Republic, and it would not matter if the hero was alive.

The orderly examined the patient closely, then stepped back to regard her. "He is unconscious, Madame Binh. It may be some time before he is awake again. It is like that with severe injuries, when the patient is heavily sedated. Do you wish for me to call you when he is conscious?"

She looked again, pondered, then shook her head. "I do not think so. If it looks as if he will recover, tell me."

She gathered her things and left without looking back.

30/1530L—Termite Hill, Near Black River, North Vietnam

Bear Stewart

The Bear watched from the edge of the forested mountainside. Heard nothing except the rumble of jets up above, couldn't see the slightest movement.

He was in a copse of squat trees abutting the field, a grassy expanse at least half a mile wide. Twenty yards out into the field a huge, abandoned termite mound rudely jutted ten feet upward.

He scurried out to the mound, flopped at its base, and lay still, then watched and listened for ten seconds more. He turned over and stared upward, to see another flight of Thuds arrive, this one from the west.

It was 1545. He'd been on the ground for an hour now.

More than half an hour since he'd spoken to Kingfish and Mallard flight. He'd told them he would make his way to the clearing. They'd said rescue would be arriving in an hour or so.

Benny hadn't checked in yet when he'd talked to Sam. He had switched off his emergency beeper, indicating that he was alive and functioning, but he hadn't checked in on the radio before the Bear had started down the hillside. That had concerned the Bear. Benny had landed somewhere in this general area, and the Bear had hoped to come across him.

At the base of the termite mound, the Bear laid out his treasures, like a surgeon preparing to operate: signal mirror, his .357 magnum revolver, three taped ammo pouches, two radios, two flares. Satisfied with his orderliness he hefted a radio, switched it on, and called for Mallard lead.

Sam Hall had left for the tanker to refuel, Hawk lead said. He was talking to Max Foley. The Bear flashed a two-ship element above with the signal mirror as he alternately listened and talked.

"*You in contact with Alpha yet?*" asked the Bear.

"*Roger, Bravo,*" answered Max.

"*See my flash?*"

"*Kingfish three, Bravo, this is Kingfish lead. I see your flash.*" It was Phil Yost.

The Bear knew a flutter of anger and thought if it hadn't been for Yost screwing up the SAM break, he might not be down here with his gonads swelling up the size of grapefruit. Then he realized that was silly. This was no time to be peeved. He'd have to wait until he got back to Takhli before he kicked Phil in the balls.

Hawk lead came back on. "*Bravo, switch to three-two-one point eight. Alpha says it's your button three.*"

He did, making contact once again.

"*Bravo, this—Alpha.*" Benny! The radio contact was broken up, but strong.

"*I read you, Alpha,*" he said.

"*I'm down—trees near—clearing.*" Benny wasn't far.

"*Me too, buddy. You hear or see any people?*"

"*In the chute I—some buildings.*"

"*South of us?*"

"*Roger. Maybe five—away—the south. I think I saw a—*" Static.

The Bear figured Benny was a couple miles north of his termite mound. He carefully scanned the treeline but saw nothing.

"*What's your condition, Alpha?*" asked the Bear.

"*Back hurts like—*" More crackling static.

"*Alpha, you still able to move?*" asked Max.

"Not very fast. I—hung up—" Static, but the fighters could obviously understand him.

"You just sit down there and don't move, Alpha. Won't be long until the rescue people get here," said Max Foley.

The Bear thought about that and swore. He'd gone down with two different pilots now, and both had been beat up by the ejection. He was hard on pilots.

Glenn and Benny. Two good people.

He remembered the screams and the keening sounds from the village and distractedly wondered if Glenn could be alive.

A good guy, Glenn.

"Sandies are less than half an hour out," radioed Hawk lead after a few minutes. *"You guys get ready to work with them."*

"Alpha!"

"Bravo!"

So far, so good. Better than last time, the Bear thought. There was no village around on this side of the Black River. The buildings south of them were worrisome, though. He hoped they housed only a few farmers.

By the time the Sandies arrived, Sam Hall was back, taking command, orbiting up there, and doling out confidence.

"You guys do a good job of getting outta there. I don't want to foot the whole bill for the party."

The Sandy lead pilot was an efficient one and spoke with authority. He tried to put Benny and the Bear on separate frequencies, which upset the Bear.

"Both of us together, Sandy lead," he said, adamant. He hadn't liked the separate frequencies before and didn't now. He wanted to be able to listen to his pilot, talk to him.

Sandy lead finally agreed.

The Bear felt he was getting to be an old hand at this. Sandy lead told them the Jolly Green helicopters were holding just twenty minutes away, waiting for the Sandies to declare the area clear of unfriendlies.

An A-1H Sandy buzzed closer. He heard the rattle of automatic guns. Groundfire. Not loud, but distinct. He kept listening, but heard nothing more.

The Bear cursed quietly. It had been too good to be true.

"There's a group of armed people moving in the trees south of you, Bravo."

He crawled up on the mound, holding the radio down low, and peered over cautiously. *"I don't have 'em in sight."*

"I only get glimpses, so I can't tell how many, but they're definitely armed. I saw a couple of muzzle-flashes from small arms."

"I could hear 'em, Sandy lead. Sounded like AK's."

"I'm bringing in the fighters. They'll be strafing about a mile south of you. Tell me if they get too close."

"Go to it," said the Bear, *"and don't worry about close."*

He watched the second A-1H drop down, nose toward the trees. Two 2.75-inch rockets spewed from the Sandy into the treeline.

A flight of Thuds formed a wheel, like they used on gunnery ranges, and descended in a twenty-degree dive. The Gatling guns sounded like buzz saws as each Thud strafed. He watched the treeline erupting and dancing. Trees and branches flew.

The Thuds pulled off.

"You hear anything down there, Bravo?" asked Sandy lead.

The Bear peered and listened. *"Nothing, Sandy lead."*

"Okay, I'm bringing in the Jolly Greens. You tell me if you hear anything. We'll be picking you up first."

The Bear thought he saw movement at the treeline, closer than before.

"Pick up Alpha first. He's hurting."

He turned down the radio volume, without telling Sandy lead about the green-uniformed soldier who stood 200 yards distant, peering up at the sky.

He fleetingly thought of crawling through the grass to the west, across the field. He knew he could do it without being seen by the soldiers.

Heart pounding, he settled down to wait. He couldn't forget the keening sounds Glenn had made. As he waited he unwrapped the ammunition pouches, then lined up the bullets so he could get to them quickly.

Benny Lewis

Benny couldn't hear much of the Bear's transmission because Sandy two was orbiting nearby.

When he lay very still the pain in his back was dull. When he moved it was excruciating and hardly bearable.

There was little doubt about what was wrong with him. Too often the explosive charges in a F-105 ejection seat would slam a little too hard and break the pilot's back. He had a friend who had been permanently paralyzed by one of the killer seats. Other friends had gotten compression fractures and had spent months flat on their backs. The Air Force was replacing the explosive charges with rockets, which were more gentle when they blew you out of the cockpit. They hadn't gotten to his in time.

He was right at the treeline, and wondered if that was smart. The gomers they'd seen and strafed had been moving in the trees, they'd said.

"Alpha, this is Bravo." The Bear's voice was low, and he spoke his words slowly.

"Roger."

"I got strong, tracking Firecans." The Bear's words were very distinct. *"I'm gonna try to take them out. You keep quiet about it, okay? Take care of my wingman and the kid. No use to answer."*

Sandy lead asked Bravo to repeat his transmission, but there was no response. Benny knew precisely what the Bear was talking about. He had detected big guns, very close by, and was going to slow them down. He felt an ache in his chest, then slowly and painfully stood up.

He heard a single pop.

He took the radio, leaving everything else behind, and walked out into the field. He traveled southward, toward the Bear. Gritting his teeth at the pain, falling to his knees once, and getting up. Going until he was a hundred yards out into the grassy meadow.

The grass was only three feet tall and didn't provide much concealment, but he didn't care. He saw a rock formation in the field, and crying out from the pain, went toward it. He had to rest.

"Jolly Green's five minutes out, Alpha," he heard.

"Roger, five minutes," he acknowledged, panting with exertion.

He arrived at the rocks. He looked hard for the Bear but couldn't see him.

He heard the chopper in the distance, and looked for it.

He heard two more popping sounds. Silence. Then the staccato sounds of first one, then multiple automatic weapons.

The chopper hove into view, still distant. A second chopper appeared, offset from the first but also headed his way.

"Give us smoke, Alpha," said the Jolly Green pilot.

Benny was staring southward. Saw nothing there. Looked back at the Jolly Green.

"Give us smoke, Alpha."

He got the orange smoke going. The lead chopper pilot didn't hesitate and altered course directly toward him.

Pop-pop-pop. Then more automatic weapons fire.

The radio crackled. *"Mallard, this is Bravo. I've got a bunch of bad guys cornered and I need some help. Put some bombs on my position."* Sounds of the chopper blades thwacked louder, drowning out the radio.

Jolly Green called again, his voice more urgent. *"Alpha, this will be a fast pickup. Be ready!"* The reel operator was lowering the device as the helicopter came straight for him.

Benny hobbled toward the chopper, waving the flare. He tossed it aside and reached for the pickup device. He was staring toward the south as they reeled him in, face tight with a frown.

CHAPTER TWENTY-FIVE

**Saturday, April 1st—1655 Local, O' Club, Takhli
RTAFB, Thailand**

Sam Hall

The club was filling already, the guys here to wish him well for finishing his hundred missions.

Sam had come away from the airplane wet after enduring half the one magnum of champagne poured over his head by Tiny Bechler, and another by, of all people, a grinning Bud Lutz.

"If I don't pour it on you," Bud had said, "you'd probably drink the foul stuff."

But then Bud shook his hand warmly.

There was another reporter on base, the guest of some public relations officer at the higher headquarters, but when he'd asked to see Sam, Sam shunned him. After a perfunctory debriefing he went directly to his trailer, cleaned up, and came to the bar.

Once he arrived, he felt like a has-been. When the others went out to face the guns tomorrow, he'd be completing paperwork and preparing to leave. It was a crazy, sad feeling that he hadn't anticipated.

He'd already set it up with both bars, at the NCO club and the O' Club, that he was footing the bill tonight. It would cost him at least 300 dollars, they'd told him, and he'd gulped and told them his word stood.

"How does it feel, Sam?" asked Tiny Bechler, crowded in beside him.

"I don't know. Just sort of numb, I guess." It was still sinking in.

"I've only got forty-two missions to go myself."

"You'll be finished in no time. You're doing good, Tiny. Wherever you go, you let me know. Who knows, maybe you'll show up down at Tucson one of these days. I'd be proud to fly with you anytime."

"I'd like that." Sam knew that Tiny meant it.

Colonel Mack came in and found him. Sam stared at him, then grew a wide grin.

"It feels good, Mack."

Mack pointed at the red, white, and blue 100 Mission patch on his shoulder. "Those aren't easy to earn, Sam."

Sam thought about that. He thought about the Bear calling for the fighters to bomb him, and about the Sandy pilot who had gone down to take a closer look. The Sandy driver said the soldiers had him, and it looked like they were cutting him up with machetes.

The Sandies and Thuds had bombed and strafed and dropped everything they had left on the Bear's termite mound. When Sam left the scene, other fighters were arriving.

He thought about Crawford, Toki, Swede, Phillips, and Johnny T. Polaski and all the others. He remembered Mike Murphy's last radio call. *I'll see you, babes.* Maybe not, but by God, Mike and all the others would be remembered.

"No. It's not easy," said Sam. He nodded out at the rowdy group. "I'll miss them."

Pudge Holden called out, "Let's sing Sam a hymn!"

> *Oh, he climbed up on the steeple,*
> *And pissed on all the people,*
> *But they couldn't piss on himmmm.*
> *Hymn, hymn—fuck himmmm.*

Sam bowed grandly. "Thank you, and you may consider the compliment returned."

"May you break all three legs on the way home, Sam," yelled Tiny Bechler.

"Awwww. Just two legs, please. My wife'll kill me if I break the third one."

"Smile so we can see your teeth, Sam, the lights are getting low!" yelled Sloppy Watson.

"Awwww." Sam picked up a nearby beer and poured it over Sloppy's head. Sloppy sputtered and blew and laughed.

"Give us a speech!"

"Tell us the secret of the universe, Sam."

"Speech!"

Sam Hall raised his hands, and the room quieted . . . somewhat quieted anyhow.

"Cut out the noise," someone yelled.

"I've only got one thing to say," said Sam.

They waited.

"Anyone who can't tap dance is queer!"

Everyone in the room began to tap dance wildly.

Someone started a song, and they stopped dancing. Most sang, but some just listened.

Sam Hall's great bass voice boomed. He thought about them all, the pilots and bears. The ones here and the ones who could not be. How lucky he was to have shared this time with them.

> Throw a nickel on the grass,
> and save a fighter pilot's ass,
> Throw a nickel on the grass
> and you'll be saved.

04/0750L—Reception Hall, Russian Embassy, Hanoi, DRV

Col. Feodor Dimetriev

Colonel Wu entered the large room and looked about at the new group of advisers. At least fifty of them milled around, wearing the short haircuts they got before coming to Southeast Asia and looking generally lost.

Colonel Dimetriev saw Wu and waved to get his attention.

Dimetriev nodded. "Good morning, Colonel," he said, careful to wear his social smile. "The new rank looks good on you."

Wu nodded stiffly in return.

"I would like to introduce you to Major Dmitriy Chernavin, who will be replacing Major Gregarian."

They shook hands.

"I apologize," said Chernavin, "for my Vietnamese is poor."

Dimetriev nudged Colonel Wu. "I told him how Colonel

Xuan Nha dealt with Major Gregarian's problem, and told him if he was very nice to you . . ." He laughed loudly.

Colonel Wu shook his head, showing no trace of pleasantness. "I'm afraid the major and you must deal with those problems in your own ways. I've sent both women Gregarian was keeping to retraining camps. The Englishwoman was pregnant." He shook his head again.

"Oh, we don't approve of such debauchery, Colonel," said Dimetriev, suddenly careful and on the defensive. "A full report of Gregarian's behavior has been forwarded to PVO Strany Headquarters."

"I want to talk to you about the P-50 radar, the one that was at Wisdom. As you know, it was damaged, and we are left with only the old P-1 at Phuc Yen. Totally inadequate, Colonel."

Dimetriev felt offended that Wu so quickly had completely dropped all social niceties. "Later, perhaps."

"To my men in the field there may be no later, Colonel."

Dimetriev sighed.

Colonel Wu left abruptly, seeing General Luc at the other side of the room.

Colonel Trung saw Dimetriev and came over, then watched as Wu cornered General Luc.

"Impetuous," said Dimetriev with a frown.

"His promotion was a political necessity. His aunt . . ." Trung made a helpless sign.

"Ah yes, the formidable Madame Binh."

"Colonel Nha's wife."

"Tell me, is the colonel going to live?"

Trung nodded. "I believe so. He'll be very badly crippled, but I believe he'll live." His voice betrayed the dislike he felt for Xuan Nha.

"What could be his future? He lost an arm, didn't he?"

"And one eye. But I'm sure he will be useful in some capacity or other. Perhaps we'll need more beggars," he said, showing more spite.

Dimetriev joined him in a smile. The enemies of your friends . . . "Your Colonel Wu was talking about replacing the P-50 at Wisdom."

Colonel Trung shrugged. "Wisdom is no more. We'll need new rocket sites to replace the ones the Americans have been destroying, but nothing more."

03/1715L—Air Force Regional Hospital, Travis AFB, California

Benny Lewis

The room was white and antiseptic, a precise copy of the room at the Clark hospital. Benny was flat on his back, like they said they wanted him for the next couple of months. When other decisions were made, they'd likely put him into a traction harness, they said.

It wasn't the pain or discomfort that got to him. Whenever he indicated he was hurting they drugged him, no matter how much he argued. He hated the dreamy feeling that he wasn't in command of himself, so he complained very little about pain. It wasn't the lack of attention. Doctors and nurses had hovered about him since the helicopter had landed at Udorn and he'd been put aboard the med-evac aircraft. It was the thoughts he couldn't shake away that bothered him. Private thoughts no one could share.

They had called his parents and told them he was here, even though he told the nurses he didn't want them to, not yet. But they said it was standard procedure to notify the next of kin, and that the hospital administrators hadn't wanted to get into trouble. His parents would be at his bedside in an hour or two.

He didn't argue, just lay there thinking, miserable and wishing he could change what had happened.

He'd left the Bear there to face the enemy alone. He was angry at others: the president, the craven politicians, the dope-loving peaceniks, and even the fucking Communists. He knew it was their fault, but he couldn't escape his own guilty feeling that he should have done more.

A nurse came into the room, saying that he had visitors. A Miss Richardson and a Mrs. Stewart.

He started to say no, that he wasn't ready, but the two women came in.

"Don't let him move around," the nurse cautioned. She remained, but moved into the background.

Liz came to him, bent down, and looked close, eyes misty. "Hi," she said, trying to sound cheerful.

Emotions welled inside him. He moved up in the bed, but

Liz held up her hand and shook her head, concerned and glancing at the nurse.

Julie stood at the foot of the bed. Her pregnancy was showing. What was she? Three and a half months along?

"Good to see you, Benny," Julie said.

He sighed, nodding his head. "You, too."

"You want me to go, I will," said Julie, eyes fixed on his.

"No." He most definitely did not want her to go. "I'm happy you're back."

"What did they tell you about the Bear?" he asked.

"Officially, not much. They said he's listed as missing in action. That he might come up on a POW list. The colonel they sent to tell me about it said not to give up hope."

"I see." He didn't want to tell her.

"What do you think?" Julie asked, her whiskey voice low.

He looked at her. She gazed back without blinking, and he had to look away.

"You know, don't you," said Julie.

Liz was biting her lip, holding onto his arm, as if about to break into tears.

"Leave us alone, Liz. I've got to talk to Julie privately."

Liz looked hurt. "I'll come back in a while."

He shook his head. "No. I don't think so."

Liz drew back her hand, looking angry and upset and forgetting her sadness. She glanced at Julie.

"Go ahead, Liz. I'll call you later."

Liz left, her back straight and stiff. The nurse looked at them thoughtfully and followed her out, closing the door quietly behind herself.

Benny regarded Julie again. "The Bear tried to tell me about her. I didn't listen then, but I've had time to think about it. She's so busy looking for what she calls class and breeding she can't see the individual people she shares the world with."

"Mal Bear was good with things like that," Julie said.

They didn't discuss Liz further.

"Is there really any hope he's alive, Benny?"

"Maybe," he said, then he stopped short.

"I'm going to try to take them out," the Bear had said. Benny had thought a lot about that. The Bear wouldn't have quit until it was over. He'd even called the Thuds and asked them to bomb. All of that so Benny could escape.

He was tuned to the Bear, and knew he was dead. He

hoped it was the strafing and the bombs that had finished him, the same that had taken out the soldiers. The enemy hadn't deserved to get him.

It had been the Bear and him against the SAMs, the MiG's, and the guns. He didn't know how to explain it to Julie. That a part of him was in a bomb-ravaged field in North Vietnam, and a part of the Bear was here, beginning to mend. Benny would go to his grave without anyone knowing, because there wasn't any way he could say it. But Julie had a right to know the other thing.

"I think," he finally said in the quiet of the room. He stopped and made himself stronger. "No, I know. He's dead, Julie."

"This morning I received two letters. One from Colonel Mack and another one from a man named Sam Hall. Mal Bear's friends. They said there wasn't any chance he'd survived." Julie stared at him, drew in a breath, shook her head for a few seconds, then quietly started to cry.

"He was a good warrior, maybe the best I've ever met," he said.

She stopped crying, still sniffing. "He said the same thing about you, and that he was lucky to be able to fly with you."

"We were a good team."

"He said he trusted you, and that if anything happened to him . . ." She started crying again.

That was good. The Bear deserved her tears. He would cry too, as soon as he learned how again.

Termite Hill, Route Pack Five, North Vietnam

Whenever fighter pilots from the bases in Thailand returned from missions in pack six with their bombs still aboard—because of hung bombs, bad weather, or whatever—they'd arm them up and drop them on Termite Hill.

At first the guys dropped the bombs in memory of some guy who'd been mutilated and killed on a termite mound down there. Then that was forgotten and it became one more superstition, like growing a mustache or wearing the same old cruddy pair of boots when you flew combat. It was considerably better luck to add another crater to Termite Hill than to bring your munitions home.

It was easy to find. The hillside and field had been

denuded, the mountain bombed almost level, and the surrounding area was an eerie moonscape of deep craters.

357 TFS KEY PERSONNEL ROSTER		As of: ~~25 Nov 66~~	
Cmdr:	~~Lt Col Lee, J. F.~~ (K)	MacLendon, T.F.	
Ops:	~~Lt Col Pelaski, J.T.~~ (K)	~~Hall, M.S.~~ (100)	Wayne, R.L.
A-Flt:	*~~Maj Hall, M.S.~~ (C)	*Cpt Lutz	*Maj Broughton
	**~~Capt Smith, J.A.~~ (K)	Cpt Nichols	Maj Rickman
	Capt Huffmeier, C.L. (R)	Cpt Lodge	
	~~Capt Maisey, K.R.~~ (Q)	Cpt Shively	
	~~Capt Meyer, J.C.~~ (M)		
	1/Lt Bechler, H.J.	~~Lt Radkovich~~ (K)	
B-Flt:	*~~Maj Ralston, M.A.~~ (K)	*~~Maj Rose~~ (M)	*Maj Thorsness
	**~~Capt Lewis, B.L.~~ (RW)	~~Cpt DiFazie~~ (K)	Cpt Smith
	**Capt Clark, C.R. ~~(C*)~~	Cpt Pierce	Cpt Craw
	~~Capt Raymond, T.W.~~ (M)	~~Cpt Jones~~ (M)	
	1/Lt Rodriguez, G.M.	Lt Ricard(R)	
	~~1/Lt Singleton, T.S.~~ (100)		
C-Flt:	*~~Maj Crawford, P.T.~~ (M)	*Maj Spencer	
	**~~Capt Lutz, B.T.~~ (C)	Cpt Hicks	Cpt Hoblit
	~~Capt Murphy, M.K.~~ (M)	~~Cpt Michaels~~ (M)	
	~~Capt Larkins, T.T.~~ (M)	Cpt Whitelee	
	~~1/Lt Mullens, M.W.~~ (K)	Lt Washington	Lt Martin
	~~1/Lt Silva, J.S.~~ (100)		
D-Flt:	*~~Capt Swendler, O.A.~~ (M)	Maj Bolt	
	**~~Capt Takahara, T.~~ (M)	Cpt Fowler	Cpt Gilroy
	~~Capt Maier, R.L.~~ (M)	~~Cpt Beeler~~ (M)	Cpt Wilson
	~~Capt Spalding, J.J.~~ (100)	Lt Ziegler	Cpt Johnson
	1/Lt Brown, C.C.		
	~~1/Lt Capella, R.S.~~ (RW)	~~Lt Dortmeier~~ (M)	
WW-Flt:	*~~Maj Phillips, G.P./Capt Stewart, M.S.~~ (M) (RW)		
	*~~Cpt Lewis/Cpt Steward~~ (RW)(K)		
	Cpt Holden/Cpt Watson		
	~~Cpt Persons/Cpt Hansletter~~ (M)(M)		
Atch:	Col Parker, B.J. (Wing Cmdr)		
	Maj Foley, M.T. (Wing Weapons Ofcr)		
Maint:	2/Lt Shilling, D.D./CMS Roberts, C.A.		
1st Sgt:	M/Sgt Silvester, T.S.		
Admin:	T/Sgt Hill, P.C.		
P.E.:	S/Sgt Perez, S.L.	Notes: 100 = Finished Tour	
		C = Status Change	
Flt Srgn:	Maj Roddenbush, D.L.	W = Wounded	
		R = Rescued	
*Flight Commander		P = POW	
**Ass't Flight Commander		M = MIA	
		K = KIA	

AUTHOR'S NOTE

While *Termite Hill* is a work of fiction, the novel's setting is historically accurate. The descriptions of units, airbases, cities, and locales were as described. Many of the targets were struck on the dates mentioned, using tactics and weapons described in the novel. The fighter pilot songs are presented as they were, and are, sung.

This first novel in *The Squadron* series features a Wild Weasel team. During early 1967, the handful of Weasel pilots and bears at Takhli were the most highly decorated group in the war, earning two Medals of Honor, several Air Force Crosses, dozens of Silver Stars, scores of Distinguished Flying Crosses, and far too many Purple Hearts.

The fighter pilots at Takhli were considered to be hot chargers. They liked to tell you they destroyed more targets, more MiG's, and more SAM sites than anyone else, and they did. They also paid the penalty, for there was a sixty percent probability that an F-105 pilot at Takhli would be shot down before completing his hundred mission tour.

Seemingly frivolous restrictions were imposed upon the fighter pilots flying over North Vietnam. Most of them felt that through more sensible targeting and fewer restrictions, the war could have been a short one.

The first F-4C MiG sweep, in January 1967, used the tactical ruse described. Repeated requests to attack the MiG bases were denied. Similar requests that the bombing campaign be delayed until the SAM and radar defenses could be neutralized were also denied.

The MiG's, SAMs, guns, and radar systems were deployed in the tremendous numbers depicted. Soviet technical advisers assigned to assist the VPA found them haughty and extremely difficult to work with. A surge in capability of North

Vietnamese defenses, brought about by their integration, did
occur in the spring of 1967. There was also a special SAM site,
sometimes called the training site, estimated to have electro-
optical guidance capability.

One of several successful tactics developed by the Takhli
Weasels was to "split the flight." The special SAM site was
located and destroyed using the tactic.

In early 1967, many doubted that air power could prevail
against massed sophisticated defenses. The air battle at the
Thai Nguyen steel mill was a watershed. Not only was it the
biggest escalation of the period, that effort reconfirmed General Billy Mitchell's maxim that no target can be shielded from
the determined application of air power. But after Thai
Nguyen, the surviving pilots knew it must be done smarter and
better in the future and went to work to make it possible.

Some related items of interest regarding a later conflict:
On January 16th, 1991, during the early hours of Desert
Storm, a large scale effort was waged to neutralize and destroy
Iraqi defenses. Few political restrictions were imposed and the
enemy was allowed no sanctuaries in which to hide. By the
time the bombing strikes were initiated the key radars had been
eliminated and the MiG and SAM threats had been greatly
reduced.

Wild Weasel support was provided by pilots and bears
flying F-4G Advanced Wild Weasels, and their F-16 wingmen.
F-117A's, F-15E's, and other strike aircraft were used to
supplement them by bombing known defenses.

Pilots and aircraft from the 355th Tactical Fighter Wing
were deployed to Saudi Arabia from Davis Monthan Air Force
Base, Arizona to serve magnificently in yet another conflict.
The 355th fighter pilots flew the A-10 Thunderbolt II, succes-
sor to the Thud and last of the long line of honest, heavy, and
capable war machines produced by the "locomotive works" at
Republic Aviation Corp.

ABOUT THE AUTHOR

TOM "BEAR" WILSON was a career United States Air Force officer with three thousand hours of flying time, mostly in fighters. During his five hundred hours of combat flying, he earned four Silver Star medals for gallantry and three Distinguished Flying Crosses for heroism. He also served in various roles as instructor, flight examiner, tactician, staff officer, and unit commander. After leaving the military, Wilson enjoyed diverse careers, including: private investigator, gunsmith, newspaper publisher, and manager of advanced programs for a high-tech company in Silicon Valley. Mr. Wilson resides in Northern California and has recently completed his second novel, *Lucky's Bridge*, a sequel to *Termite Hill*.